# THE SEX OF A HIPPOPOTAMUS

## A Unique History of Taxes and Accounting

# THE SEX OF A HIPPOPOTAMUS

A Unique History of Taxes and Accounting

## Jay Starkman

Edited by Mark Bixler
Book Design by www.e-bookservices.com
Hippo Cover Image by Mike Swaim
Cover Design by M.S. Design Co.


Twinset Inc.
Atlanta, GA 30329
(404) 636-1400


Copyright © 2008 by Jay Starkman
www.starkman.com

All rights reserved. No part of this book may be reproduced, stored in a retrieval system, or transmitted, in any form or by any means, electronic, mechanical, photocopying, recording, or otherwise, without the prior written permission of the copyright owner.


Printed in the United States of America
10  9  8  7  6  5  4  3  2  1

Library of Congress Control Number: 2008905869

Cataloging-in-Publication Data

Starkman, Jay,
The sex of a hippopotamus: a unique history of taxes and accounting / by Jay Starkman
p. cm.
Includes biographical references and index.
ISBN (hardcover) 0-9818063-0-9 / 978-0-9818063-0-3
1. History – Taxation
2. History – Accounting

To Leah, who has suffered ~~35~~ ~~34~~ ~~33~~ ~~32~~ tax seasons with me.
Good thing I didn't tell her about tax season before we wed.

# Contents

| | | |
|---|---|---|
| Preface & Acknowledgements | | ix |
| **Part I** | **Career Observations** | |
| One | Remember, You're an Accountant<br>Accountants as portrayed in popular culture. | 3 |
| Two | Karoshi<br>The sweathouse – Exxon – IBM-Telex anti-trust case – workpaper destruction – Lyndon Johnson's insurance policy – plant tours – discovering fraud – New York City bankruptcy – corporate gadflies – tax audits – surviving a Big Eight merger – continuing education. | 11 |
| Three | The Glamorous World of Tax Accounting<br>The "art" of taxation – preparing the witness – college instructor – investments – tax shelters – computerizing – employees – clients – adult entertainment – family time – lawyers – Las Vegas – roller coaster contest – September 11. | 38 |
| Four | Turning a Profession into an Industry<br>Ancient origins of accounting – bookkeeper to CPA – code of ethics – government commercializes the profession – the consulting challenge – battle for accounting standards – Sarbanes-Oxley – defending CPA tax practice – abusive tax shelters – The Vision – Cognitor – CPA2Biz – the library – "low competencies" – serious choices. | 65 |
| **PART II** | **History and Government** | |
| Five | Maltotier<br>Early taxation – use and abuse of Jews – Turkish capital tax – salt taxes – King Leopold – the income tax – Fessenden's law – California's racist Gold Rush – Coca-Cola and the black tax collector – sin taxes – window tax – beard tax – tax cheating – judicial tax – The Public Authority. | 105 |

| Six | Tax 'Em, My Boy, Tax 'Em | 140 |

Second Bank of the U.S. – the tariff – Civil War income tax – 1894 income tax – sixteenth amendment – tax season begins – sales tax rebellion – "temporary" income tax.

| Seven | Culture Bingo | 171 |

IRS culture – compliance difficulties – Irwin Schiff – teacher-preachers – pen pals – extensions – social security numbers – simple tax returns – e-filing – death by taxes – Samuel Swartwout – Battle of the Millionaires – Truman tax scandal – restructuring IRS.

| Eight | The Power to Destroy | 209 |

Mellon vs. Couzens – Al Capone – Roosevelt the Terrible – National Gallery of Art – Moses Annenberg – Landslide Lyndon Johnson – Martin Luther King – seditious libel – Watergate.

| Nine | The Sex of a Hippopotamus | 244 |

London Zoo – Middleton Beaman – writing tax law – the cesspool – Lyndon Johnson's KTBC – lobbyists – simplifying Georgia's income tax – charitable tax deduction – 89 million unnecessary returns – black art of revenue estimating – special tax breaks – Mr. Taxes.

| Ten | The Lawgivers | 271 |

Equity – oracle or lawmaker – Tax Court – judges – bending over backwards – a harmless error – Tax Court exam – Pennsylvania Preceptor Plan – judicial deference – What constitution? – state procedures – to pay or not to pay – Devitt Award – ethics.

## PART III  Tax Tales

| Eleven | A Prurient Interest | 317 |

Tax return publicity – Franklin Roosevelt – Henry Morgenthau – Nelson Rockefeller – Ronald Reagan – Tinseltown – athletes and entertainers – Alan Jay Lerner – Sergeant York – Joe Louis.

| Twelve | Affluenza | 342 |

Values – automobiles – retirement age – legacy tax – John Dorrance – Hetty Green – J. Howard Marshall – Howard Hughes – NYU's macaroni factory – Ted Turner – The Clintons – beyond taxes.

| Notes | | 367 |
| Index | | 435 |

# Preface and Acknowledgements

It's not easy to determine the sex of a hippopotamus. The 3,000 lb. beast lumbers through water and is apt to become hostile if a stranger should approach. It's tough to distinguish a hippo from a hippette.

At times, trying to decipher tax law can be a bit like struggling to identify the sex of a hippopotamus. You must be mightily interested in finding the answer. And I should know.

Way back in high school, as my classmates kept track of batting averages and passing yards, I clipped and saved obscure but intriguing business stories from the *Wall Street Journal*. Those stories lured me into an accounting program in college and propelled me into a career as a CPA.

I've been at it for decades now, and I'm still stumbling across stories that intrigue me.

This book is an outgrowth of my fascination, the end result of all those years of perking up at the novel and noteworthy. It's a collection of unusual tax and accounting stories told from the perspective of a practicing CPA with a passion for his craft.

Through the years, I often heard snippets or rumors about unusual tax situations. My search to nail down some of those stories led me to squint at the handwriting of Irving Berlin, pore through the papers of the Rev. Martin Luther King Jr. and thumb through 150-year-old books.

Most of the tax stories presented here have rarely, if ever, been told before. Some have only appeared in tax journals or court cases. Many come from forgotten books and newspaper clippings, or items buried in the *Congressional Record*.

Most passages in some way reflect the ancient and unchanging reality of taxation as intrusive, oppressive and essential. As E.L. Godkin explained in his April 11, 1895 editorial in *Nation*:

> The history of taxation from the earliest ages has been the history of the attempts of one class to make other classes pay the expenses, or an undue share of the expenses, of the Government. Aristocrats have always been trying to shift the taxes on to the people, and the people on to the aristocrats; the landed interests on to the commercial and the commercial on to the landed.

My research took me from Boston to Los Angeles and dozens of points in between. Many wonderful people helped me. They also shared some fascinating tales. They helped me research, gather materials, and review drafts. Without their help, this book would not have been possible, and I am very grateful to the following friends and friendly strangers:

Bennett Aaron, Miles Alexander, Joseph Bankman, Shirley Barron, Michael Berger, Sam Bettsak, Herbert Cohen, Tom Crosby, Jennifer Davis, Michael K. Deaver, Candace Ewell, Emanuel Feldman, Chris Fritz, Alan Guthartz, Martin D. Ginsburg, Sidney Goldin, Bruce Goldman, Fred D. Gray, William Grooms, David Grossberg, Selwyn Hartley, Gwen Hinze, Ward Hussey, Isabelle Jeter, Ed Koffsky, Richard Litwin, Joseph E. Lowery, Rick Malone, Monica McFadden, Rafael Medoff, Pat Meyer, Nancy Rucker Miles, Robert Myers, Karen Neloms, Thomas Netzel, Edward C. Nixon, Lee Paschak, Mary Lyn Reagan, Patti Reid, Joseph Roberts, Max Rohrlich, Barry Rosenbaum, Les Shapiro, Neil Shulman, Spence Shumway, T.Y. Steen, Eugene Steurele, Melissa Totsch, Josh Ungerman, and Michael Verner.

My very special thanks to John Milton Hendricks, librarian at the U.S. District Court in San Francisco for his invaluable research which helped me trace Judge Ogden Hoffman and the California foreign miners license tax. Col. Michael Kelley, CSA provided me with credible contemporaneous writings by Confederate leaders showing that high tariffs contributed to Southern discontent. Earl Prater, senior counsel at the IRS Office of Professional Responsibility, helped trace the history of Circular 230 by pulling old versions from the IRS building in downtown Washington despite it being closed for six months due to flooding.

My good friends Sharon Bailey, Michael Broyde, Ira Greenfest, Lew Regenstein, Chana Shapiro, and William Stromsem gave generously of time from their busy schedules to read drafts, provide editing and feedback, along with many other favors and guidance. A nationally prominent tax attorney, a friendly stranger who wishes to remain anonymous, provided hours of assistance for which no words can adequately express my appreciation.

I am deeply indebted to Mark Bixler for having accepted the assignment of editing the manuscript and making it shine. Mark, an editor for CNN, also is the accomplished author of *The Lost Boys of Sudan*. Artist Mike Swaim made the inspired hippo cover image for my idea on using Botticelli's 1485 painting, "The Birth of Venus" against a backdrop of a 1913 Form 1040. Botticelli painted "Venus" in Florence around the same time as Pacioli wrote the first book on accounting in Venice.

This book would not have been possible without the availability and help from the following libraries and depositories:

Libraries I visited:

Atlanta-Fulton Public Library System
Atlanta History Center – Kenan Research Center
Beverly Hills Public Library
Boston University – Howard Gotlieb Archival Research Center
DeKalb County Public Library
Eleventh Circuit Court of Appeals Library, especially Sara Straub
Emory University Libraries
   Robert W. Woodruff Library
   Hugh F. MacMillan Law Library
Library of Congress – Recorded Sound Reference Center
Los Angeles County Law Library
Los Angeles Public Library
The McKinley Memorial Library
Museum of Taxation, Jerusalem, Israel, especially Mira Dror
National Archives – Southeast Region
National Gallery of Art
New York Public Library
   Humanities and Social Sciences Library

Science, Industry and Business Library
Library for the Performing Arts
Richard M. Nixon Library
Franklin D. Roosevelt Presidential Library
United States Tax Court Library
United States Tax Court Records Room
University System of Georgia Libraries

Libraries I corresponded with:

Academy of the Hebrew Language, especially Ronnit Gadish
California State Library – California History Room
Gerald R. Ford Presidential Library
Herbert Hoover Presidential Library, especially Spencer Howard
House Clerk's Office of History and Preservation, especially Matt Wasniewski
London Zoological Society Library, especially Ann Sylph
National Archives – Pacific Region
Senate Historical Office
Harry S. Truman Presidential Library, especially Liz Safly
United States Capitol History Society, especially Don Kennon
University of Mississippi – AICPA Library Service

I gratefully acknowledge permission from the Michigan Association of Certified Public Accountants to reprint the Lewis Carroll parody, and to friends who let me reprint their letters.

Most important of all, I want to thank my children, Aviva, Rifka, Mendel and Natan for all their help, and my wonderful wife, Leah, for her assistance with reviewing drafts and her patience while I was "out at the library" for the past seven years.

# Part I

## Career Observations

# CHAPTER ONE

# Remember, You're An Accountant

*Nothing, it has been said, is duller than accounting.*

—Jane Mayer, *The New Yorker*

Why are accountants always portrayed as dull and boring? Because it's amusing.

An insomniac wife lies in bed, beyond the help of sleeping pills. In despair, she wakes her accountant husband. "Tell me again dear," she says hopefully, "what is it that you do?"

This image is indoctrinated into children's books. Harry Potter has just met Ron Weasley on the train to Hogwarts.

"Are all your family wizards?" he asks.

"I think Mom's got a second cousin who's an accountant," Ron replies, "but we never talk about him."

Playing a vocational guidance counselor, John Cleese offers advice. "You see, our experts describe you as an appallingly dull fellow, unimaginative, timid, lacking in initiative, spineless, easily dominated, no sense of humor, tedious company and irrepressibly drab and awful. And whereas in most professions these would be considerable drawbacks, in chartered accountancy they are a positive boon." Monty Python skits frequently picked on accountants.

Songwriters portray accounting as drudgery:

I work all day on an adding machine,
Adding the boss's dough.

—"A Lopsided Bus" from *Pipe Dream* by Rodgers and Hammerstein

Oh, ah debits all duh mornin',
An' ah credits all duh eb'nin',
Until dem ledgers be righttt.

—"I Wanna Be a Producer" from *The Producers* by Mel Brooks

Accounting as drudgery is an old tradition. The essayist and poet, Charles Lamb (1775-1834), worked as an accountant for 33 years for the East India Company. He revealed a good deal about the nature of accountancy as he mocked his vocation as one that revolved around "great dead tomes" with "fantastic flourishes" and "sums in triple columniations."

*The Adding Machine*, a 1923 play by Elmer Rice, was the first artistic use of an accounting theme. Most of the characters were named after numbers – Mr. One, Mr. Two, Mr. Three and so on. The accountant's name was Mr. Zero. He added figures six days a week for 25 years, waiting each day for the 5:30 p.m. reprieve from drudgery. Finally, an adding machine replaces him. Edward G. Robinson played Shrdlu, who Zero meets in the afterlife. Brooks Atkinson, the legendary critic for *The New York Times*, called it "the most original and brilliant play any American had written up to that time." *The Nation* praised it as "one of the major achievements in the entire field of the American Arts."

Movies took accounting to new depths when Gene Wilder starred as the timid and neurotic accountant Leo Bloom in *The Producers*. His co-star, Zero Mostel is speculated to have acquired the nickname, "Zero," either in his youth at New York's Public School 188 where he was reputed to have been a thoroughly hopeless student, or later in his career, through an act of inspiration on the part of his agent, Ivan Black. But late in life, Zero revealed that he acquired the name when he told his father he wanted to be an actor and his father said he would wind up a *gurnisht* – Yiddish for "zero." Zero had years to practice for the role of Max Bialystok tormenting Leo Bloom. His brother, Milton, was an accountant.

Will Ferrell portrayed Nazi author Franz Liebkind in the 2005 version of *The Producers*. In his next film, *Stranger Than*

*Fiction*, Ferrell was cast as a senior agent for the IRS who confides to a friend, "I was engaged to an auditor. She left me for an actuary."

Rick Moranis, the nerdy accountant in *Ghostbusters*, tried this lame pickup line on Sigourney Weaver: "I can prepare your tax return." The accountant never gets the girl.

In Brian Garfield's novel, *Death Wish*, the vigilante who hunts down and murders young hoods was a CPA. When Hollywood turned it into a movie in 1974, screenwriters made Charles Bronson's character an architect because they thought no one would believe a CPA could be macho.

The acclaimed 1932 film *I Am a Fugitive From a Chain Gang* is the true story of Robert Elliot Burns, who twice escaped from a brutal Georgia chain gang. In the chilling final line, his former girlfriend asks how he lives. As he disappears into the darkness, he whispers, "I steal." In real life, Burns became a tax accountant in Newark, N.J.

Screenwriters avoid "slide-rule accountants," as Humphrey Bogart described them to Audrey Hepburn in *Sabrina*. An accounting comedy, perhaps? Comedian Bob Newhart, a former accountant, explained, "CEO's don't like to hear a lot of laughter coming from their accounting departments. That might spell trouble."

Accountants have had at least two blockbusters featuring a macho, hero accountant. In *A Taxing Woman*, a movie that won nine Academy Awards, including Best Picture, Best Director, Best Actor, and Best Actress, a revenue agent uses her auditing skills to destroy the mob. It was so successful, they made a sequel, *A Taxing Woman's Return*. Unfortunately, few people watch Japanese films or follow the Japanese Academy Awards. Accountants got all the great lines: "So that's their secret office. I'll bet that's where they cook the books." Portraying a woman accountant surely made that line more palatable. (Groan!)

The most successful accounting comedy ever made was the 1960 blockbuster, *The Apartment*, where mousy accountant Jack Lemmon gets the girl, Shirley MacLaine. It won five U.S. Academy Awards including Best Picture.

In 2001, a 38-minute comedy about a chain-smoking, beer-guzzling accountant with an unorthodox solution to save the family farm won the Academy Award for Best Live Action Short. It was called, *The Accountant*, and I arranged for its screening at a national gathering of CPAs where the accountants gave it an 84 percent "thumbs up."

I know that Hollywood appreciates its accountants. In the credits of every modern film, you'll find a list of accountants: production accountant, post-production accountant, assistant accountant, payroll accountant and construction accountant. Twenty-four accountants are listed in the credits for *Pirates of the Caribbean: Curse of the Black Pearl* – and the sequel lists thirty-seven! Sometimes accountants are listed after the caterer, but they're there. You won't find any lawyers listed. In fact, accountants are moving up. The latest movies list "production controller" and corporate firms like "Film Auditors, Inc." Of course, a symptom that you take accounting too seriously is when you watch for the accountant credits after the movie ends, which I do.

When newspapers reported that more children were prescribed Ritalin in the affluent suburbs north of Atlanta than anywhere else on Earth, talk show host, Neal Boortz, picked this topic for his daily tirade: "I know someone will call to say that since Johnny has been on Ritalin, he's been an angel and his grades have improved. Well, Johnny might have been one of the world's greatest artists. Now, he's likely to become an accountant."

Commenting on his childhood, syndicated talk show host, Michael Savage, echoed that sentiment: "I would have been put on Ritalin. I wouldn't be here on radio today. I'd have become an accountant."

Reporting on Atlanta's "Funniest Accountant" contest, the *Atlanta Journal-Constitution* wrote, "[The] crowd consisted of fellow pencil-headed, calculator-punching numbers crunchers who chuckled at some humor that others might find lame."

*New York Times* columnist Maureen Dowd explained why George H. Bush couldn't win reelection in 1992 and why Steve Forbes' 1996 presidential bid didn't get far: "George Bush senior reminded every woman of her first husband. Steve Forbes reminded every woman of her first husband's accountant." It doesn't take much for media-types to pick on accountants.

Dreading our meeting, a client told me, "I'd rather be in Las Vegas." Who wouldn't? A doctor client said that his wife skipped the meeting we had scheduled to make a dentist appointment. A dentist client pops a pill upon entering my office. It's Tenormin, a medication that relaxes blood vessels, so blood pressure stays down. I didn't understand the significance of his tension until an advice columnist explained, "Accountants typically suffer the same fate as dentists: Their clients know they need them, but they dread the experience for the pain it brings."

Why do they dread us? Perhaps it's because accountants know their secrets, much more than their doctors, lawyers, or ministers. We see the receipts for expenditures they may not want their spouses to know about. When the tax return shows a big medical expense, we know the illness (or dental restoration). Big earned income, little investment income, and big tax bill spells "no money to pay the taxes," and we're the bearer of the bad news. Accountants know when clients are spending beyond their means. When they are excited about a new venture, they aren't thrilled to hear us pronounce that it is too risky. When our client has had a fantastic year, we're again the spoiler who announces the giant tax bill.

A doctor might endear himself by curing an illness, a lawyer by winning a case, a priest by absolving of sin. Do our clients celebrate the news that through clever planning, the giant tax bill will only be jumbo? We maintain strict confidentiality, and look after their interests, but unless we're announcing a tax refund, our message is often painful.

I know clients appreciate my work because they are grateful to find someone who will do the drudgery for them. In a 1999 survey, tax return preparation ranked as the second most loathsome task, just behind number one: washing windows. (More on window washing later.)

It's not the tax practitioner the public disdains, it's accountants. One indication is that books by tax lawyers sell far better than books by tax accountants. *Was That a Tax Lawyer Who Just Flew Over?* outsells *Confessions of a Tax Accountant* by more than two to one at Amazon.com. A book reviewer of *Internal Auditing for Management* in the *New York Times* remarked, "At first glance this volume would seem to be 'like the sex of a hippopotamus,' of possible interest only to that character with a hippopotamus skin – the internal auditor."

When the *Journal of Accountancy* asked readers why they became CPA's, among their responses were:

- No one ever asks, "How do you spell that?"
- No other profession offers April 16 as a paid holiday.
- In Scrabble, Accountant (14) is worth more than either Doctor (9) or Lawyer (12).

A survey of public perception of accountants found a general impression that they (1) work with numbers, (2) work alone in a cubicle, (3) have little public interaction, and (4) have no personality.

Another survey showed that accountants chose their profession because they liked to (1) work with numbers, (2) work alone in a cubicle, and (3) have little public interaction.

Public perception and sales statistics notwithstanding, when it comes to personality, accountants should rate higher than most other professionals. Should, but don't. An economist described members of his profession as people who like to work with numbers but lack sufficient personality to be accountants. (Actuaries also claim this distinction.) When writer Jerry Siegel and artist Joe Shuster were casting for a dull, low-profile profession for meek, mild-mannered Clark Kent, they made him – a reporter.

It's so bad that Michael Verner, president of the Georgia Society of CPAs, noted what many people see when meeting a member of his profession: "You don't look like an accountant" – as if that's supposed to be a compliment.

Accountants should be recognized for the inventive, creative, ambitious, entertaining and exciting personalities they are. (Ask my wife. Please!)

The chairman of the American Institute of Certified Public Accountants, Stuart Kessler, noted with satisfaction that a rock group in Rochester, N.Y. known as The Audit Brothers was made up of CPAs who doubled as musicians. In Bellevue, Washington, five bands of accountants with names like "Accounting Crows" and "Facial Depreciation" battled it out to raise money for accounting scholarships at Highline Community College and Central Washington University.

Accountants, and not lawyers, craft the most ingenious financial schemes. A clever accounting manipulation can go undetected for years, and when discovered, the evidence is buried so deep or destroyed with such great finesse that a bonding claim won't be paid and a jury won't convict. Al Capone might have avoided prison had he been an accountant. Capone's accountant, Leslie Adelburt Shumway, didn't go to prison.

Explaining that he could not possibly have known his company was headed for the biggest fraud bankruptcy in history, Enron's chief executive officer, Jeffrey Skilling, told a Senate committee, "I'm not an accountant." Perhaps he could have stayed out of prison had he been an accountant. Although lead partner David Duncan pleaded guilty (but only to charges of obstruction), the Supreme Court overturned the guilty verdict against his firm, Arthur Andersen, for shredding Enron papers.

Even though accountants as a whole are a pretty bright bunch, the perception persists that they are timid number freaks who yearn for a life. Harley-Davidson capitalized on that reputation – and avoided bankruptcy in the process – by reinventing itself in the mid-1980s as a company that sold the "rebel lifestyle" in addition to motorcycles.

"What we sell," an executive explained, "is the ability for a 43-year-old accountant to dress in black leather, ride through small towns, and have people be afraid of him."

Accounting aficionados recall that Walter E. Diemer, an accountant for the Fleer Chewing Gum Company in Philadelphia, tinkered in the candy lab in his spare time, and in 1928 he invented bubble gum.

Neville Chamberlain apprenticed as an auditor with the prestigious Howard Smith, Slocombe & Co., Chartered Accountants before embarking on a career in politics. He was offered a permanent position in 1890 – the British prime minister's appeasement of Germany prior to World War II might never have occurred had young Neville's father allowed him to continue in accounting.

John Grisham's novels are exciting because he has a degree in accounting, which he called "a tough degree to get." He considered becoming a tax lawyer until taking a tax course at Ole Miss. Grisham became a criminal lawyer instead.

The *Michigan Certified Public Accountant* showed that only a CPA could make the dry subject of statistical sampling into a witty essay by adopting the style of Lewis Carroll:

> "Remember," said the Wicked King, "I have placed 10 black discrepancies in this stack of 100 invoices, and you must find at least one with a sample of 20!" Alfred stepped forward and fearlessly looked at the little pile. For the lovely Princess Gwendolyn had promised that she would spread the black discrepancies throughout the pile so that no matter where Alfred took his sample he would be sure to find at least one.
>
> Alfred reached into the middle of the stack and with a single motion pulled out his sample of 20. As he peeled off one perfect invoice after

another, the Wicked King's evil snicker grew louder and louder, for not a single black discrepancy appeared! Only then did Alfred hear lovely Princess Gwendolyn's soft footsteps behind him as she entered, suppressing a small yawn. "I meant to spread those black discrepancies around," she said, "but I'm afraid I overslept. Is it all over? Oh dear."

"I put them all at the top of the pile!" the Wicked King snickered. "I knew he'd never find them there. Off with his head!"

"You shouldn't have used a block sample," the Hooded Executioner said in a kindly voice as he pushed Alfred towards the door. "You're right," Alfred was heard to murmur, "I had less than half a chance. With random sampling the odds would have been almost 87% in my favor."

Parodying Sir Walter Scott and the title of the 1942 comedy classic, *I Married a Witch* (or maybe the flop, *I Married An Angel*), a journalist penned a paean to his wife's profession, "I Married an Accountant":

> Breathes there a patent attorney
> with a soul so dead
> who never to himself has said,
> "God, this is more boring than accounting?"

He should have come to one of the accounting parties I've attended. Meetings of the semi-annual American Institute of CPAs Tax Division, for example, feature lavish receptions with entertainment. A Dixieland Jazz Band played at the meeting in New Orleans. In Dallas, tax accountants dined on Texas barbecue. At one of our Washington meetings, a tax practitioner grabbed a mike and showcased his great voice before a few hundred people by crooning Frank Sinatra songs to band accompaniment. And Elvis entertained a meeting at the Ritz-Carlton in Las Vegas. Do you think architects have as much fun?

CHAPTER TWO

# Karoshi

*To the memory of Caesar Augustus in whose reign there went forth the decree that all the world should be taxed, this book is respectfully dedicated...*
    —George S. Boutwell, First Commissioner of Internal Revenue

The Japanese call it *karoshi*. It means "death from overwork." In Japan, there are dozens of karoshi fatalities each year. Most victims work over 3,000 hours annually – that's 60 hours a week, if you factor in two weeks vacation. Japan's tax agency suffers an average of 25 karoshi deaths annually. Employees at the Finance Ministry, of which the National Taxation Agency is a branch, averaged 1,428 hours overtime in 1992, 5.4 overtime hours daily, often working all night. Their catchphrase is, "Let's go home while it's still dark."

While few American CPAs work that many hours, during tax season (busy season for auditors) we work at a rate which exceeds 3,000 annual hours for a few weeks at the beginning of the year, and as tax extension deadlines approach.

I should have realized that I was headed for a profession with grinding long work hours while still in college. At a social gathering, after asking about my major, a young woman snapped, "Stay away from me. My father's a CPA." A teenager wrote about her dad, who worked for one of the Big Eight, as the eight largest accounting firms were called, "Many times my dad has to work overtime, on Saturdays,

Sundays, and late on week nights. By working Saturdays and Sundays, I don't mean just a few hours, but usually, the complete day. Sometimes it begins to look as though he really enjoys seeing how late he can stay at the office….in future years, I will make sure the man I marry isn't a CPA!" (Years later, my own daughter went further, refusing to even date an accountant. But my son is happily married to a CPA.)

**THE BIG FOUR**

Following mergers and the demise of Arthur Andersen, the "Big Eight" became the "Big Four": PricewaterhouseCoopers, Deloitte, Ernst & Young, and KPMG. There's good reason they are called "Big." They audit more than 95 percent of public companies with market capitalizations over $750 million. KPMG, the smallest of the Big Four, has eight times the total revenue, ten times the audit revenue and five times the number of staff as Grant Thornton, the fifth largest firm. The General Accounting Office says that even a merger of the five largest second-tier auditors might not create a firm of sufficient scale to examine the biggest public companies.

Long hours are even worse at today's Big Four. One dad promised he'd work less when he made partner. "But instead, he works more," a 16-year-old girl told an interviewer. "My dad's always exhausted. He's gone when I get up, and not back when I go to sleep."

Another clue about long hours should have been evident in 1971 when I went to work for the BVD Underwear Company on the 60th floor of the Empire State Building. I had classes at New York University from 6 p.m. to 8 p.m. each night, and my supervisor had me return to work after class during the first two weeks of each month. Manhattan streets that had been teeming with people during the day were deserted and dangerous when I finally went home at midnight or 3 a.m. The long hours didn't bother me, but the attitude toward long hours still does.

**WINDOW WASHING**

Windows actually open in the art deco Empire State Building. A team of window-washers visited twice a year. They would roll up a window, step out on the window sill, latch one side of their safety belt on one of the hooks outside, step outside, latch their other safety hook, close the window, and clean it with water and a squeegee. (Is this really preferable to preparing tax returns?) In the early 1990s, the original roll-up windows were replaced with windows that pivot in, so it's no longer exciting to watch the window-washers at work.

Some accountants consider long hours a badge of honor. A colleague, Jack Hirsch, once called me at 11 p.m.
"I've been at the office since 7 a.m.," he said.
"Well, I've been here since 6 a.m."
"I'm not leaving for another two hours," he responded.
"You win, Jack," I replied. "I'm leaving as soon as we hang up."

Jack Hirsch was a very special CPA. Early in his career, he had an audit client whose president masked his true salary by charging portions to administrative, marketing, and cost of sales. Outside of SEC reports, there is no accounting pronouncement requiring disclosure of an officer's salary, but Jack insisted that the officer's full salary be disclosed in notes to the financial statements. He considered it necessary for fair presentation to shareholders. Jack won the argument, but lost the account. He was very proud that he stood up for independence and integrity. The shareholders were impressed and in succeeding years they became his clients.

> **TIME MANAGEMENT**
>
> A 1950s article explained how an accountant should manage his time: Taking the calendar week ... the total time available for all purposes is 168 hours. The accountant estimates that sleep, eating and other essentials account for 11 hours of his day or 77 hours per week ... 42 hours a week are consumed on the job. For the remaining 49 hours,
> (1) Professional Advancement. ...at least six hours....
> (2) Increase in income. ...Ten hours...devoted to strengthening relationships with clients and friends....
> (3) Recreation. ...six hours....
> (4) Individual Advancement. ..four hours...with *The New York Times* and...at least four more hours...[for] books, plays, museums and music.
> (5) Public Service and Charity. ...six hours....
> (6) Home and Family. ...thirteen hours remaining, and the wise man would also set aside all legal holidays and whatever vacation time he can command to be devoted to his wife and children.
>
> It didn't mention commuting, which in New York consumes about ten hours a week.

## The Sweathouse

I began my career in 1970, working my way through college. Accounting majors can easily find jobs. Following graduation,

I went to work for Price Waterhouse & Co., one of the Big Eight. The partner who interviewed me had just written a book, *Financial and Accounting Guide for Nonprofit Organizations*, the first such book ever written (and today in its seventh edition). He boasted that he made time to write the textbook by rising at 4 a.m. each day. I never saw him again, but worked on an assignment where he was the partner in charge. The senior and manager complained that he was a tough workaholic boss. For leisure, they told me, he flew an airplane. When did he have time for family? Or flying?

My job interview was the only time I met face-to-face with a partner during my tenure at PW. Aside from seeing them on elevators, I spoke with a partner once by telephone. PW was conducting its annual blood drive. They sent flyers to all the staff members asking them to make an appointment for donating blood. When I didn't respond to the second request, I got a call from a partner.

"You haven't yet scheduled your blood donation," he began. "When should I put your appointment down for?" I was working for a company that literally demanded blood, and I was sufficiently intimidated to make and keep that appointment.

Years later, I worked for Arthur Young & Company. They didn't demand blood, but they did demand money. They sent a memo to all staff concerning their United Way appeal: "Last year, we had 100 percent participation, and we expect 100 percent participation this year." That was followed by a phone call demanding a payroll deduction pledge.

PW had the highest staff-to-partner ratio of any of the large accounting firms. In the New York office where I worked, the ratio exceeded 30 to 1. It was a very broad and short pyramid of staff, seniors, managers and partners. As a result, managers performed tasks that other firms allowed only to partners. Seniors and staff were also given far more responsibilities than they would see at other firms.

My first PW assignment was auditing a small subsidiary of Exxon. At the time, Exxon maintained a large campus in Florham Park, N.J., near Morristown. The buildings were huge. I estimate that I had a 1/10 mile roundtrip walk to the water cooler from my cubicle. (Today, the property is the new training facility and corporate headquarters for the New York Jets.)

## Chapter Two—Karoshi

The senior met me the first day, introduced me to Exxon officials I would be working with and gave me the prior year's working papers. "If you need anything, I'll be a mile away working on an audit of Allied Chemical (today part of Honeywell)." I had taken my last final exam at NYU six days earlier. I had never done an audit before.

> ### THE VAULT
>
> In the middle of the Cold War, rumors spread of a vault somewhere on the campus that contained Exxon's most valuable records. In the event of a nuclear war, certain key personnel were to go inside the vault. The world might be destroyed, but Exxon's records would survive a nuclear holocaust with key personnel to keep the company running.
>
> On this audit, I found invoices showing compliance with the Arab boycott of Israel. The invoices were marked, "This is to certify that this material is of U.S. origin and does not contain any Israeli materials. The above vessel is not blacklisted and will not call at any Israeli port in her present voyage." I had often heard about the boycott, and this was years before Congress banned the practice after hearings which made these documents public. It was an indication of the auditor's powerful access to company records.

The hours were long and the long commute unsafe when I was so tired. One morning on the highway, I didn't see the car in front of me slow down until it was almost too late. I slammed on the brakes. Fortunately, I was driving a new car. With new brakes, new tires, and perfect alignment, I didn't swerve. I missed rear-ending the car by a few inches. Another morning, I was driving on Interstate 80 when I found myself going south on the New Jersey Turnpike. I had fallen asleep behind the wheel and had no idea how I got on the Turnpike because at the time, I-80 wasn't connected to the Turnpike. The next day, I paid attention and discovered that they had opened a new ramp connecting the Turnpike. I had taken this new exit. It was February, and I complained to the senior that I needed some sleep. "You'll sleep in July," he said.

Not true. Later that year, I got engaged, but I was working such long hours that I was unable to see my fiancée for two weeks prior to our summer wedding.

**DRESS CODE**

Price Waterhouse had an unwritten dress code. Suits only, no sport jackets, though white shirts were no longer mandatory. That was a relaxation of rules that existed not long before I started. At training class, we were told that a few years earlier, a partner would address the group, "We are now breaking for lunch. I see 30 people in this room and three hats on the rack. When we return, I expect to see three people or 30 hats." Hats had been a dress code requirement at the Big Eight until the 1960s. It was no different at the other firms. On the hottest summer days, Andersen staff were required to wear jackets outdoors, within blocks of the office or a client's office.

At training class, one staffer asked about obtaining a graduate degree. The answer: "We don't encourage it because we don't feel you will need it." Price Waterhouse had an unwritten rule: "You can attend graduate school at night, but don't ever tell us that you can't work overtime tonight because you have class."

Among the Big Eight, PW in New York was a special place for hard labor. In graduate school, students introduced themselves by the firm they worked for. Upon mentioning that I had worked for Price Waterhouse, but now worked for a private company, my classmate yelled out, "Hey fellas, this guy worked for The Sweathouse, PW." In three years attending the NYU MBA program, I met no one who was currently working for PW. Nevertheless, one brave soul I worked with attended law school at night and weekends while working for PW.

It's gotten worse. At a December 2005 PricewaterhouseCoopers seminar on SEC Accounting, one of the presenters proudly announced, "I can't imagine any PwC auditors who didn't put in 250-300 hours last January." That's an annual rate of 3,000 - 3,600 karoshi hours. Imagine what February, when it really got busy, must have been like. For us tax folks, filing extensions now provide us with a second tax season in the fall, as the September 15 and October 15 deadlines approach.

### Accountant Gets the Girl

My next assignment was the IBM-Telex anti-trust case. I immediately knew this was going to be a rough assignment. Close to midnight, my home phone rang, "Jay, I'm a senior with PW. You've been assigned to work with me. I want you in White Plains, N.Y. at 8 a.m. tomorrow."

I was half asleep, but dutifully copied directions. It wasn't a prank.

Telex Corporation, a division of Control Data Corporation, was a major supplier of IBM-compatible disk drives, tape drives and printers. They were suing IBM for monopolistic practices. To me, the case was rather straightforward. Every time IBM announced a new computer line, Telex sales dried up because their devices might not work with the new line, or IBM specifications for the new product raised fear of obsolescence for potential Telex customers. Prices for new IBM peripherals were very competitive, sometimes predatory. It would take months following introduction of new IBM computers before the market for Telex equipment stabilized. If that weren't enough, IBM would intimidate customers who strayed to competitors' products. These were effective techniques in building and preserving IBM's monopoly. The turmoil hurt Telex profits.

I already knew that Control Data Corporation made faster computers than IBM. NYU had both IBM System 360 and CDC 6600 computers on campus. As an undergraduate, I programmed both, and was surprised to observe how much faster results were processed on the CDC machine. I also learned at NYU the ruthless monopolist history of IBM, so I wasn't pleased to be working on the side of Goliath.

## IBM HISTORY

IBM traces its origins to Herman Hollerith, who invented a new tabulating method. His punched cards, called Hollerith Cards, could be quickly counted by counter-sorting machines. That allowed the U.S. Census Bureau to tally the 1890 census in just one year, rather than the projected ten years. In 1911, Hollerith sold his company to Charles Flint for $1.21 million and a ten-year consulting contract worth $20,000 annually. Flint ran a conglomerate called Computing-Tabulating-Recording Company which made a variety of business products.

Around that time, Thomas Watson was working for National Cash Register Company. NCR was founded by John Patterson, a man known for ruthless business tactics. Watson was placed in charge of driving out competitors. NCR instigated frivolous lawsuits against competitors and threatened lawsuits against competitors' customers. It used predatory pricing, bribes, and even smashed storefronts. NCR thus controlled 95 percent of the cash register business.

In 1912, Watson, Patterson and 28 other NCR executives were indicted under the Sherman Antitrust Act. They were accused of tampering with competitors' machines (to give the appearance of unreliability), buying or bribing salesmen from other companies, and seeking to establish and maintain a monopoly in the cash register business. Watson and Patterson were sentenced to pay $5,000 fines and serve a year in prison. On appeal, a retrial was ordered and the government offered a settlement allowing Watson and his colleagues to avert jail time.

Patterson fired Watson in 1914. Watson then went to work for Computing-Tabulating-Recording Company and became CEO in 1922. In 1924, he renamed the company International Business Machines. IBM adopted the techniques which the unrepentant Watson learned at NCR to build his monopoly.

IBM maintained a four-story building in White Plains, N.Y., devoted to its litigation. This was the only assignment I had while at PW where there was no budget. There was only one requirement: "Don't lose."

Every night, the accountants battled with the lawyers over who could work later. The accountants always won. We were back again before 8 a.m. and had the doors opened for the lawyers when they arrived later.

We had access to marvelous technology for 1973. Documents had been scanned into computers, and word searches could be performed. This wouldn't reach mainstream for another fifteen years. But I was working on very low tech material. Telex was required to turn over mountains of documents to IBM. They complied by giving ninth generation photocopies that were impossible to read. I had to reconstruct these spreadsheet-like financial statements submitted by Telex. I learned that one could technically comply with a demand for documentation by submitting illegible photocopies. I have on rare occasion used this method in my practice.

This assignment was only for one week, straddling a weekend. I had made a second date with a young lady for that weekend. My supervisor asked me instead to come to work.

"You want me to tell her I'm cancelling our date for tomorrow night?"

"Yes."

"I have concert tickets."

"Charge them to the job."

I kept the date and got called to personnel the next time I was downtown. I don't work for PW anymore, but I'm still married to the girl I kept my date with. In real life, the accountant *did* get the girl.

The supervisor complained that I had only worked 70 chargeable hours in six days at IBM. He had expected at least 80—a 4,000 *karoshi*-hour annual rate. That didn't count the mandatory one-hour lunch we were required to take, nor my three-hour round-trip commute. That was 94 hours in six days – nearly 16 hours a day – and he wanted 104 hours. Where was the 42-hour work week that article on time management suggested?

There was a saying among the staff at PW: "In every 24 hours, there are three perfectly good eight-hour chargeable days."

The Telex suit went to trial in Tulsa, Oklahoma, later that year. IBM initially lost, then won an appeal, and eventually settled with Telex out-of-court in 1975. As part of the settlement, both sides were required to destroy trial documents. Concurrently, there was a Justice Department antitrust lawsuit. The destruction of the Telex papers killed the separate government antitrust case against IBM because so much important evidence the government was going to rely on had been destroyed. Justice dropped its antitrust case against IBM, without going to trial.

The final chapter in the IBM-Telex case wasn't written until 25 years later. Telex had been represented by attorney Floyd Walker on a contingency fee contract. As part of its 1975 out-of-court settlement, Telex agreed to pay Walker $2,350,000 over 20 years, beginning with two $75,000 payments in 1981, and 80 quarterly payments of $27,500 thereafter. The payments stopped when Telex's successor declared bankruptcy in 1996.

Walker didn't pay self-employment tax on the payments because he argued they were attributable to legal services he provided from 1971 to 1975. In 2000, he lost his argument with the IRS when an appeals court ruled that he owed an additional $42,994 tax.

## Workpaper Destruction

In July 1973, PW assigned me to a week of workpaper destruction. The firm maintained a warehouse in Brooklyn, in a dilapidated stretch of Flatbush Avenue between the Brooklyn Academy of Music and Long Island University. Instead of a suit, I wore work clothes. People avoided sitting next to me in the bus and on the subway, a big change from when I commuted in a suit.

The warehouse was a nineteenth century high-rise building with ceiling-mounted water closets and thick black dust like a Hollywood horror film. I have no idea what I inhaled, but I would blow black gunk from my nose for hours after leaving the place. The warehouse should have been declared unsafe for human trespass.

### THE NEIGHBORHOOD

The immediate neighborhood boasted many bars and pawn shops. On Monday morning, I noticed a disabled late model car on Flatbush Avenue near the warehouse. The passenger compartment and trunk had been broken into. Tuesday, the wheels were gone and the car was left standing on milk crates. By the end of the week, it was a carcass; even the carburetor and steering wheel were gone, and the city still hadn't towed it away.

This had once been a tony district. Founded in 1883, Congregation Mount Sinai at 305 Schermerhorn Street, on the way from the subway, bore a plaque honoring the great jazz singer, Sophie Tucker ("The Last of the Red Hot Mamas") for endowing the synagogue. Located not far from Boro Hall, it had counted leading judges and politicians as members. Its prior building burned to the ground in 1948. Sophie Tucker's brother and business manager, Moe Abuza, was a member of the synagogue. She helped organize a star-studded fundraiser at the Brooklyn Academy of Music in May 1950, resulting in the plaque. The synagogue moved to a new location in 1983 and today, the building is occupied by the Hare Krishna Center.

My team was assigned to destroy workpapers created from 1950 to 1952, saving only Securities and Exchange Commission files, tax files, and permanent files. Whereas in 1973, we prepared workpapers in pencil, all these papers were written in ink. The penmanship was beautiful. There were no strikeouts on any page. Since workpapers always need corrections, there was obvious inefficiency from re-writing ink workpapers. PW was the only firm to have continued writing workpapers in ink beyond the 1920s. They finally changed to pencil in the mid-1950s under pressure to cut costs.

We destroyed the product of hundreds of thousands of hours of old work. We wondered what untold stories those auditors could have told, because we had many of our own.

Accountants stumble onto all kinds of interesting stories in their line of work, including accounts involving the most famous of the famous – people like former President Lyndon Johnson.

Lyndon Johnson died of a heart attack in January 1973. His life insurance policy had been underwritten by a PW client. "I'll bet he didn't leave it to Lady Bird [Mrs. Johnson]," the senior remarked as he decided to include this policy in his "random" audit sample. Curiosity can play a role in selecting what to audit.

This policy had a scandalous history. Johnson suffered a major heart attack in 1955 at age 47, so obtaining a jumbo $100,000 policy in 1957 took considerable influence, which he didn't lack. His former Senate secretary, Bobby Baker recounted Johnson's difficulty finding an insurer: "I've got this bad heart history, and if I died suddenly Lady Bird would need a great amount of cash to protect her radio and TV enterprises in a community-property state. The problem is, I can't find an insurance company willing to gamble on my heart."

In the fall of 1963, Bobby Baker was charged with improper financial dealings and influence peddling. During the investigation, an insurance agent revealed that in return for selling this $100,000 policy, he gave the Johnsons a $588 Magnavox stereo as a "gift" and paid a kickback in the form of $1,208 of commercial time purchased on KTBC, the Austin TV station owned by Lady Bird.

Without making new revelations, Baker wrote in his 1978 autobiography that telling the whole truth about that insurance policy would have been devastating to Johnson. Baker was sentenced to three years for tax evasion and fraud. (He served sixteen months.) Johnson would have been implicated had he not become president and pressured the Senate to drop its investigation. So, there may be more to this story that we'll never know.

A highlight of every audit was a complete tour of the facility we were auditing. If we weren't auditing a factory, we'd get a complete explanation of the manufacturing or service process. And we'd learn facts the companies did not tell consumers. Companies would volunteer that Brand X was superior to theirs. A cemetery client once showed us the vaults for people desiring above-ground burial, pointing out how building it against a hill with poor drainage made it a watery grave. How did he explain to customers the water and soil stains on the vaults?

Staff would compare tours. "Do you know how they make Gelatin?" reported one staffer. "Pig skins go up the conveyor belt at the beginning of the manufacturing line and Gelatin comes out at the other end." He seemed dismayed to learn that Gelatin came from pigs.

One of my audits was of a major drug manufacturer. Our docent explained that consumers expected a wad of cotton in a bottle of aspirin. The company could have saved $50,000 a year by eliminating that wad of cotton in each bottle, but it feared losing customers who might switch to another brand *with* cotton. So the cotton stayed – one of many interesting tidbits I picked up during my time as an auditor.

The aspirin was manufactured using an antiquated process from the 1920s. Its popularity rested on the speed at which it was absorbed through the stomach. The company could institute a new manufacturing method which would substantially reduce costs, but were reluctant to tamper with a popular product that generated so much revenue. A year earlier, they had changed the label for a roll-on deodorant from a black label to a red label. That change alone yielded 1,000 letters of complaint.

The company manufactured the plastic bottles in which their products were packaged. The petrochemicals used to make plastic bottles arrived by tank car at a rail siding at the plant. During the 1973 Arab oil embargo, when petrochemical supplies were scarce, a full tank car was stolen.

While auditing The Edison Electric Institute, the controller told stories about theft and graft at the 1964 - 1965 New York World's Fair. EEI is a trade organization of electric utilities. It sponsored an exhibit called The Tower of Light. A huge conference table was brought to the site, and a room was built around it. One morning, the table was gone. No one ever figured out how the crooks removed the table from the room when it couldn't fit through the door.

Belgium's exhibit featured a replica of a fifteenth century church for which they brought in genuine medieval silver bells to ring in the loft. The bells were stolen before the Fair opened.

Singer Sewing Machine sponsored the sports arena. In order to avoid using the expensive electricians' union, they had the scoreboard built entirely off site, then shipped to the Fair on a rail car. When the scoreboard arrived, Singer wanted unskilled workmen to transport the scoreboard to the site. The electricians union insisted the scoreboard was their domain. "It has a plug at the end of it." Four electrical workers took two days to move the scoreboard a few hundred feet.

An audit consists of testing accounting records and controls. When a mistake is found, it must be large enough to have an impact on the financial statements. At one audit, I found a $100,000 error. That was deemed immaterial. I dug deeper and found a research facility which cost $10 million to build, but was recorded on the books for $20 million. The extra $10 million was the cost of high tech equipment, which was erroneously added to the cost of the building and was being depreciated over twenty years, long past its useful life. The depreciation adjustment would have exceeded $1 million. It would have upset the client to propose an adjustment, so this too was ruled immaterial.

**Discovering Fraud**

I left Price Waterhouse and went to work for a client in the commercial finance business, best described as legal loan sharking. I got a 50 percent increase over my PW salary and the opportunity to attend graduate school. Commercial Trading Company used accounts receivable and real estate as collateral for loans to companies that banks wouldn't consider. They lent at rates substantially higher than the bank.

Commercial finance is a very tough business. A bank looks at a customer to determine the likelihood of repayment and considers collateral as insurance in case repayment doesn't occur. Banks are not geared to liquidate collateral and want to avoid a reputation of forcing customers out of business by foreclosure.

Finance companies are different. They want lots of collateral, in addition to evaluating the borrower's prospects. They prefer to have their loans repaid but are unabashed about liquidating collateral, and fast. Miss one payment and you could lose your home. This finance company did not tolerate delinquents.

If the company couldn't locate the collateral, it had other methods. I once found a letter from a Chicago attorney to the company attorney:

> We have been unable to obtain any commitments or cooperation from the debtor in the captioned matter...With your consent, I will send this claim to the collection attorney we normally use, whose motto is "They are dead, in Brazil, or I get them."

Brazil has no extradition treaty with the U.S.

Commercial Trading Company transferred about $100 million a month through 32 checking accounts. The check volume was so large that we rotated banks every week lest any one complain of overload, since the banks sent us weekly bank statements with cancelled checks.

I had a full-time employee preparing complex bank reconciliations (bank recs). It was a difficult job to fill because few wanted to do that all day, every day. Unable to hire someone for the position, I took a very promising young man who worked on client receivables into my department. Lloyd was on the verge of being fired by his supervisor because they didn't get along, but he and I got along just fine. He was very bright, and learned to prepare the bank recs. We became friends. Strangely, he maintained a nonprofit organization, The Lloyd Foundation. It would be two years before I discovered its purpose.

One month, Lloyd got backlogged. So, I asked the person who had previously prepared the bank recs for help. She brought to my attention that the prior month bank rec had been fudged. She reconciled both the current month and the prior month. Nothing was missing. It was just sloppiness. Fudging a bank rec, especially with so much money passing through the accounts, was a cardinal sin. The officers at the company had this young man on probation because of bad reviews by his prior supervisor. I had to fire him.

Several months later, we received a phone call from European-American Bank. "Your checks are ready. Please come pick them up." That was odd – we had no account at European-American Bank.

We went to the bank, and sure enough, there were checks with our company name on them. An inspection of the bank's records showed Commercial Trading Company, a *Delaware* corporation, had ordered the checks. We were Commercial Trading Company incorporated in *New York*.

Mail clerks took deposits to the bank several times daily. We suspected that whoever had established the Delaware corporation intended to collude with the mailroom to intercept our deposits. By the time we would discover the fraud, millions of dollars could be stolen.

We conducted an expensive investigation, with huge legal fees and assistance from the New York State Banking Department. Lloyd was an officer of this Delaware corporation. And clever! While it's illegal for an out-of-state corporation to do business in New York using the name of a New York corporation, opening a bank account is not an act of "doing business." Since he hadn't violated any law and hadn't intercepted funds, we had no case.

We felt that we accomplished something by scaring him with lawyers, a New York State Banking Department inspection, and threats. All the banks in New York were notified about this incident. We suspected that Lloyd didn't plan this entirely on his own, but had no idea who his accomplices were. Like identity theft, it's very hard to prevent this type of fraud, though good internal accounting control might allow quick detection. So we just made sure all employees were bonded, improved our detection methods, and prayed that this wouldn't happen again.

Some months later, the New York City Transit Authority raised the subway fare from 30 cents to 50 cents. Ads appeared the following week in the *New York Post* that The Lloyd Foundation was offering subway tokens at $3.00 for ten tokens plus 50 cents postage. The ads listed a post office box the foundation had set up to receive the money. I told the co-worker who showed me the ad that it was probably another Lloyd scam. But the co-worker thought it was quite possible that a charitable organization would want to help New Yorkers in the transition to the higher fare.

Three months later, New York Attorney General Louis Lefkowitz announced that he had just frozen the bank account of The Lloyd Foundation. His office had been inundated with complaints from people who sent checks but didn't receive tokens. Its investigation showed that The Lloyd Foundation had purchased 84,000 subway tokens at 50 cents each. Those who sent money early got tokens, but not those who ordered later. It was a classic pyramid scheme in which the early participants get paid while subsequent ones get bilked.

The newspapers later reported a $51,440 balance in the foundation's account at the Garden State Bank in Hoboken. It was brilliant to use a bank in New Jersey because New York couldn't easily gain jurisdiction over an out-of-state bank. Lloyd ordered the bank to transfer the balance to himself at a hotel in Costa Rica. Costa Rica has bank secrecy laws and no extradition treaty with the U.S. But the order arrived a few hours after the attorney general's order freezing the account. Additional funds were spread among several New York City banks, which were easier for New York to seize.

The attorney general hauled Lloyd into court but didn't accomplish much.

"I had a benefactor who is shy of publicity," Lloyd argued. "Everyone would have gotten their tokens. But since the attorney general showed up, he backed out. It's the attorney general's fault that this program failed," Lloyd argued. I believe charges were dropped.

### ROADMAP TO FRAUD

I still wonder whether the first fraud, incorporating in another state, could be used today to steal funds from a business bank account using the IRS electronic funds tax payment system (EFTPS) by manipulating bank routing numbers. That is, might IRS be used to perpetrate identity theft against a business? I wrote an article for a professional publication, exposing the fraud potential, hoping that the publicity would force IRS and banks to improve controls to prevent such a fraud. The Treasury Inspector General for Tax Administration says there's been very little fraud under EFTPS, generally limited to inside jobs manipulating routing numbers.

I also discovered a supplier fraud. As I was training a new accounts payable clerk, I noticed that we had ordered one million computer keypunch cards the prior month. We had seven full time keypunch operators, and that would be enough to keep them busy punching one card per second. Even if they could type as fast as Supergirl, the machine took three seconds to discharge a card.

Since they couldn't work that fast, our keypunch card inventory should have been quite high, but it wasn't. We had ordered 800,000 cards in the prior month, 600,000 the month before that, and 500,000 each month for the months prior. Before we engaged our current supplier, we were ordering about 100,000 a month. Something was wrong. We were missing over two million keypunch cards.

We ordered computer paper from this same supplier. I discovered that he was billing us for enough paper to keep the printer busy printing 22 pages a minute for eight hours per day. The printer could only print fifteen pages a minute. And it didn't run all day long.

In the end, we discovered that the computer department head naively trusted the supplier. When my department forwarded him the bills for approval, he signed them. I could never get him to match packing slips to the bills.

We called the supplier to demand an explanation. "I'm storing the paper for you. With prices going up, I locked you in and I've got it here for you."

"Good. Send it over."

"You want *all* of it?"

"Yes, all of it. Send it now. We'll store it."

We emptied a two-person office and filled it floor-to-ceiling with paper – so much that it took up about a quarter of the room. I then calculated that we were still short about $20,000 from this fraud. So we called back the supplier.

"Do you have more?"

Surprised, but pleased to hear that perhaps he hadn't lost a customer, he asked, "You want more? What do you need?"

"What have you got?"

"Everything. Punch cards, paper, ribbons, disks."

"Send it over."

"How much?"

"We'd like $20,000 worth of supplies."

And he sent it. It took us more than two years to use all those supplies.

**New York City Bankruptcy**

In the mid-1970s New York City went bankrupt. It didn't file for bankruptcy, but it could not afford to pay both bondholders and welfare recipients. A judge ruled that paying welfare recipients was more important. Bondholders could wait. New York State took over certain city finances, allowing the city to raise money in the capital markets while in default.

While this crisis boiled, Commercial Trading Company filed for an extension of time to file its income tax return. With the extension we enclosed a check for $10,000. Six weeks later, we got a letter from New York City that it didn't receive a payment and our extension request would be denied if we didn't immediately send a payment. I stopped payment on the original check, and sent a replacement $10,000 check.

Two weeks later, we got another letter from New York that our first $10,000 check had bounced, that it's illegal to bounce a check payable to the city, that we must replace it immediately, and by the way, what was the check for?

Around the same time, it was reported that there were 100,000 more children on the city's welfare rolls than the total number of children the Census Bureau said lived in the City. Any wonder New York City went bankrupt?

## Gadflies

While working at Commercial Trading, I was just a few blocks from RCA Corporation. I owned a few shares of RCA stock, which gave me the opportunity to attend the annual shareholder's meeting. Shareholder annual meetings are usually boring, but not this one. Some of the most famous gadflies planned to attend – people who were pestering corporate boards at that time. Newspapers reported their pointed questions and antics. Price Waterhouse published an annual list of hard questions they might ask so that its clients would be prepared.

Gadflies Evelyn Davis and John and Lewis Gilbert were there, along with some lesser inquisitors. Davis introduced a proposal to require that employee political contributions be nonpartisan. The Gilbert brothers wanted to place restrictions on the issuance of stock options. These issues are still being fought today.

I was struck by the contrasting ways in which they interacted with management. The Gilberts had apparently contacted management to keep them apprised of their resolutions and perhaps incorporate some management input. They acted gentlemanly and were treated very courteously. In contrast, Evelyn Davis was confrontational. She shouted, acted brusquely and was cut off from speaking. Though her proposals had merit, her confrontational style detracted from them.

All shareholder resolutions were soundly defeated by over 90 percent, as they always were. However, I was impressed with the difference in treatment of Davis and the Gilberts. Though they failed, management had a somewhat open door for the adversarial Gilberts. This was a very useful lesson.

## Tax Audits

Handling an IRS audit involves the same techniques crucial to haggling, while conducting yourself professionally. If you enjoy haggling over car prices, you'll like negotiating with IRS. The outcome is successful when the auditor agrees that he's seeking the fair tax liability of the taxpayer. In those instances where he acts instead like a tax collector seeking to maximize government revenues, I let him write his report, then I take up the matter with higher authority within IRS.

For example, one of my clients was navigating a messy divorce. His wife, who had no income, refused to sign a joint tax return unless he made certain financial concessions to her. Without telling me, he signed her name to the return himself. A year later, they were fighting over child custody. She applied to the IRS for a copy of the joint tax return and, upon receiving it, told the agency that the signature wasn't hers.

The IRS sent the husband a letter notifying him of its plans to conduct an audit, focusing specifically on his claimed "married filing jointly" status. He called the phone number on the IRS notice, and argued with the agent who was assigned to the audit. Making no headway, he told the agent, "I don't want you as my auditor," asked for the supervisor, and demanded of the supervisor that another agent be assigned to this audit. Then he called me.

The new agent refused to talk with me. "There's nothing you can say. She didn't sign the return. She filed her own return for the year. Therefore, the husband owes the higher taxes as married filing separately." As there was nothing I could say to this tax collector, I let him write his report. I then wrote a ten-page protest which convinced the appeals office that the agent didn't have all the facts and indeed this was a joint return, despite lack of the ex-wife's signature. I won the case without going to court by proving that the wife's habit was to file a joint return, that all her income was reported on the return, that she had no concern about unpaid taxes, and that her refusal to sign a joint return was unreasonably withheld.

I learned some unorthodox techniques from a CPA who handled an IRS audit while I worked at Commercial Trading Company. Max restricted his practice to handling IRS audits. He was committed to good tax policy and suggested in the early 1960s that the IRS translate its forms and instructions into Spanish. The agency said it lacked funds for Spanish translation, and besides, it might open floodgates for people who spoke other languages to request forms and instructions in their native tongue. For his clients, Max was a zealous advocate. His theory was that IRS would only devote a certain number of hours to an audit, and his task was to make them as unproductive as possible.

The IRS likes to begin audits by 9 a.m. Max refused to meet with agents prior to 9:30 a.m. As a very affable gentleman, he'd engage the auditor in small talk until 10:15. At 11:45, we'd break for lunch and go to a fine restaurant with slow service so that we wouldn't return until almost 1:30 p.m. At 4 p.m., the agent's workday ended and he left. Some days he would leave at 3 p.m. Today, it's against the rules to offer the agent a free soda, much less a free lunch, so this technique doesn't work. In making this rule, IRS sought to prevent the client from rewarding the agent for his cooperation. I don't believe they suspected it would make their audits more efficient.

Max taught me more practical techniques. For individuals, most audits are "office audits" that take place at the local IRS office. For businesses, audits are usually "field audits" which IRS prefers to take place at the taxpayer's place of business. The CPA should minimize the time IRS spends at the taxpayer's premises because it's disruptive to the taxpayer, and dangerous: the IRS agent may overhear something spoken in the hallway. More problematic, if a question arises, he may ask the client directly, and get a quick answer which should have been researched or presented with a better spin. So, it's preferable from the taxpayer's standpoint to have the audit performed at the CPA's office. When a question arises, the CPA can write it down and provide an answer later.

How does one get the IRS agent to the CPA's office? Transfer all the client's records to the CPA's office. Sometimes an agent insists on performing an audit at the client's premises (though he has no automatic right to this), but you usually can change his or her mind if the client doesn't have an empty chair or spare desk or counter space for a visitor. It's easy to arrange to fill every chair and desk for the auditor's visit.

On the other hand, there are times when it may be better to have the audit performed at the client's premises. *American Photographer* gave a good example, "One fashion photographer we consulted found it helpful, when an IRS auditor came to call, to have several scantily clad models running about the studio to facilitate ordinary, reasonable and clear thinking on the part of the auditor."

It really happens. A tax professor told my class that early in his career as an IRS agent, a scantily clad woman greeted him at the door to a taxpayer's residence. She told him that the taxpayer wasn't home, but invited him into the house to await his return. He declined and left. "Do you know what that woman cost me?" the taxpayer complained when he finally met with the agent.

Max also taught me never to allow an IRS auditor access to the photocopier. If he wants copies, I make them for him and make an extra copy for myself. That way I will always know what he has in his file. Years later, a colleague called me for advice. He had an IRS report assessing his client a substantial tax, but he didn't know what the auditor had copied from the client's papers to support the proposed assessment. He thought it was a required courtesy to allow the auditor free access to the photocopier. When I informed him otherwise, it was the first time anyone had ever told him a different method which would have avoided his predicament.

These techniques come in very handy when IRS is overreaching. When my client arrived at 8 a.m. to open his office, he found an IRS revenue officer waiting for him, demanding to see payroll records. Surprised by this unannounced intrusion, the client called me. (Of course, every self-respecting accountant is already in the office by 8 a.m.) I told the client to advise the waiting IRS employee that all payroll records could be inspected at my office, that he would have to call me to make an appointment, *and that all payroll records should be delivered to my office that afternoon.*

I also learned from one of the country's finest tax lawyers, Martin Ginsburg, that successful tax practice involves politics. I first met him in the mid-1970s when he was a partner at Weil, Gotshal & Manges in New York. New York State audited and assessed $250,000 additional tax against Commercial Trading Company. We took the assessment to Marty, as he is affectionately and respectfully called by people who know him. He proposed a unique strategy. The conversation went something like this:

> GINSBURG: If this goes to New York Tax Court, we will lose because the Court is a division of the Department of Revenue. They would never rule against the Commissioner in a case like this. I'm chairman of a New York State Bar committee working on making the state Tax Court independent of the revenue department.
>
> US: What are the chances of that happening?
>
> GINSBURG: Well, that depends on convincing Governor Hugh Carey to sign the legislation. Revenue Commissioner James Tulley was Carey's campaign treasurer. In order for Carey to sign, we must convince Tulley that giving up control over the Tax Court won't diminish his power. We need to delay this case from going to trial until after control of the Tax Court is transferred.

Settling this tax dispute had everything to do with politics. Eventually, Ginsburg convinced New York to settle this $250,000 case for $50,000. It would have been a difficult case for us to win in court, even with an independent Tax Court. I can only surmise that New York had limited resources and preferred to use them on easier cases that didn't involve a tax attorney with a major reputation.

Martin Ginsburg is married to an equally brilliant spouse, Supreme Court Justice Ruth Bader Ginsburg. When the TV cameras showed her walking into the Senate confirmation hearing room, one could see Marty trailing a few feet behind her.

During my employment at Commercial Trading Company, the Federal Reserve tightened the money supply to control inflation. Bank loans became scarce, and real-estate agents sought us out in greater numbers to help finance their properties. One of those properties was the Eden Roc Hotel in Miami Beach. My wife and I were planning a Florida vacation. I was introduced to Howard Garfinkle, the hotel's owner, who offered me free lodging. Heads turned when this young couple exited the limousine he sent to pick us up at the airport. We had a gorgeous tenth floor ocean view suite with meals gratis. Accountants do get respect, it turns out – even very young ones.

**Surviving a Big Eight Merger**

I left Commercial Trading Company and went back into public accounting, this time to the tax department of J.K. Lasser & Company. Lasser was one of the "Big 20" – around number 12 in size of U.S. public accounting firms. There I received wonderful professional training and had fun, too.

Accountants entering the tax business face three challenges: learning the impossibly complex tax laws, learning to handle IRS audits, and obtaining clients. Everyone approaches these differently.

In a casual conversation with a J.K. Lasser partner, I asked how to get new clients. "Attend funerals. It shows people that you care." I was stunned – because I only attend funerals to honor the dead or console the bereaved.

One of my clients, a socialite who volunteered for an international charity, kept a red diary into which she wrote all expenses she incurred for the benefit of the charity which qualified for a tax deduction. This diary read like Who's Who. "Had Lenny Bernstein and the kids over for lunch." "Took Mrs. Allende (ex-Chilean dictator's wife) to The Today Show." "Met with Ted Kennedy." She traveled the world for this charity at her own expense, which we deducted on her tax return as a contribution.

When the IRS sent her an invitation to be audited, I asked for receipts to back up entries in the diary.

"What receipts?" she said. "After entering the information in the diary, I destroy the receipts."

"In that case, let me get an itemized statement from your travel agent to support the larger expenses. I'll impress the revenue agent with who you are and together with the travel agent documents, perhaps I can convince him to accept incidental expenses like meals, lodging and local transportation without receipts."

She was indignant.

"You want to impress him with who I am? Tell him to call his boss, Bill Simon, the secretary of the treasury. He'll tell him who I am...but please ask the agent to call him during the next three weeks, as he's leaving office after that."

I was assigned to prepare the tax return for an individual who was identified to me as the Number Three person at Merrill Lynch. I contemplated the complex Schedule D for reporting all his stock transactions. Surprise. He had just three transactions, all selling Merrill Lynch stock acquired by option.

In September 1977, J.K. Lasser merged into Touche Ross & Company (today Deloitte). It was the first merger of large CPA firms. The Lasser partners voted contentiously for the merger. Different explanations were given for Lasser's agreeing to the merger: funding retirement benefits for partners, cost of liability insurance, cost of staff training, and competitive pressures.

As one of the few at Lasser who had worked for a Big Eight, I felt that Touche's corporate culture would clash badly with Lasser's entrepreneurial one. But Lasser people were excited for the prestige that they would now be working at a Big Eight firm.

Reality came quickly after the merger. J.K. Lasser partners voted for the merger. Touche Ross was also a partnership, but like all the Big Eight, was run by a management committee. Touche's management committee voted for the merger, but the partners themselves never voted. So, when Lasser partners and staff showed up at Touche Ross offices after the combination, the reception was cold. Within a few years, all the Lasser partners and staff were gone. Touche kept the Lasser clients, which is what they apparently were seeking, and discarded the personnel.

Right after the merger, I sensed that a Lasser background would taint a career at Touche Ross in New York. I had just completed my MBA degree and felt this would be a good time to move to another city. I had my eye on Atlanta.

As my new employer, Touche Ross agreed to interview me in Atlanta. Never have I had such a grueling interview. Nine people interviewed me for eight hours. Here was a firm I supposedly already worked for. They could have simply called New York and asked, "Is this guy any good?" Three weeks later, the Tuesday afternoon before Thanksgiving, Atlanta said they didn't want me.

I was still determined to move. I made an airline reservation to Atlanta for Monday morning. I then went to the Director of Taxes and asked for a week off to search for a job in Atlanta, explaining that I didn't want to remain in New York. He offered to transfer me to Newark, adding, "Our office is right across the street from the train station." Newark was one of the most dangerous cities in the U.S., so a quick sprint to the train station was apparently desirable.

I arrived in Atlanta on Monday at 11 a.m., made fifty telephone calls, arranged eleven interviews over the next three days, and left on Thursday evening with two job offers. Four weeks later, I began working for the Atlanta office of Arthur Young & Company (today, Ernst & Young) another one of the Big Eight.

Soon afterward, *The Tax Adviser* published an article I had submitted prior to leaving New York. Eleven professionals worked in Arthur Young's Atlanta tax department and all had a subscription to this magazine. I said nothing. They said nothing. It was clear that no one read the magazine.

Years later, the *Wall Street Journal* quoted me on the front page, saying that in collection matters, the IRS is more willing to bend than they once were. I have written quite a few articles for professional journals. Between researching, writing, and dealing with the editorial staff, it can take 40 hours to publish an article which few ever notice or read, but having my name on the front page of the *Wall Street Journal* attracted attention. Friends in town and out of town, even an old high school friend, called to say they had noticed.

## Continuing Education

One of my audit assignments at Arthur Young was a fast-food chain where I came across IRS correspondence assessing almost $50,000 for payroll taxes. The client showed me proof that the agency merely failed to properly record a tax deposit. It was clearly an IRS error. Five years later, it turned out that this was indeed an error, but one for which IRS refused to take responsibility. The check was drawn on the client's bank account, but the tax deposit ticket was for the account of another company. There was no way for us auditors to discover this timely and perhaps client management didn't know it either.

When it finally went to court, the judge ruled that this was an improper deposit and therefore the client was not entitled to the $50,000 it had paid. The taxpayer is responsible for problems with tax deposits. Had the judge ruled otherwise, IRS would become guarantor of such embezzlements.

I learned very few new skills at AY. I discovered that certain types of continuing professional education are useless.

In response to accounting failures in the 1970s, continuing education became a requirement for retaining CPA certification. It was predicted that this might be a problem for very bright or very advanced CPAs. Would there be sufficient stimulating programs for them?

Arthur Young provided staff with 40 hours of continuing education, often in a single 40-hour stretch. I spent a week at an out-of-town training center, with two full days on consolidated tax returns followed by three full days on partnerships. The format wasn't conducive to acquiring knowledge, and I returned to Atlanta unable to recollect anything from the 40 hours of such "intensive" study. Two graduate college courses take 40 hours of classroom instruction plus homework and testing. That's learning. After two or more days of nonstop instruction, I'd be lucky to pass a test merely asking me to name all the topics covered.

The trend of continuing professional education in accounting has been toward online courses which spoon-feed the material, so that successful completion of the "course" is assured. Live classes allow credit for merely being physically present. For an eight-hour CPE course, I was once sent two hours of preparation materials, with which I complied. In a class of twenty, only two of us had prepared. The Georgia State University instructor sounded like economics teacher Ben Stein in *Ferris Bueller's Day Off*, begging the class, "...Anyone?...Anyone?" as he answered his own questions.

The worst programs feature a state or local politician. It's usually a political campaign speech, but it still qualifies as continuing professional education. CPAs have received credit for listening to the Atlanta Olympic Committee solicit volunteers. The Georgia Board of Accountancy approved one hour of credit for completing a survey. The Georgia Society of CPAs once sponsored two days of continuing education at a Colorado ski resort, with class held in the morning, from 7 to 11. What did the accountants study at the ski resorts? They would decide as a group at the beginning of each class. The cost of hitting the ski slopes, incidentally, was tax deductible. Attending sales events sponsored by a software company, brokerage or insurance firms, or tax shelter salesmen qualify for CPE.

Mail-order courses consist of completing multiple choice trivia questions from a substantial amount of reading materials. The only way to answer correctly is to compare the questions to the reading material until answers are found. So, efficiency dictates not reading the text, but working from the questions to find the answers in the text. Using this method, an accountant can complete an hour of mail-order continuing education in less than thirty minutes. Next to the question, some vendors list the page number where the answer can be found, speeding the process even more.

Some accountants complete mail-order courses while attending an eight-hour continuing education session, getting 16 hours total credit at once. In my view, professional education would be far more effective if university classes were required, with class preparation, attendance, and exams.

I invest dozens of hours each year on education that enhances my professional ability but doesn't count as continuing-education credit. I've never received credit for learning a computer operating system, computer language or any software application on my own. I even build my own computers from parts. That knowledge allowed me to benefit from great class dynamics at the Programmer's Special Interest Group of the Atlanta PC Users Group. Among their sessions was one on "How to Write a Computer Virus." It's rather easy. There are lots of places to infect or hide malicious computer code. Learning to write a computer virus, incidentally, did qualify for continuing education credit.

A professor at New York University told my class, "If you think you'd like taxes as a career, you'd better like reading." Fortunately, I do. Every day, accountants can find hundreds of pages of new IRS rulings, regulations, and Tax Court cases, in addition to proposed tax legislation, and tax planning articles. As if that's not enough, I also study tax theory and tax history.

Among tax professionals who study more than I do, I met an Arthur Andersen tax partner who told me that he read the Internal Revenue Code, cover to cover, every six months. He always found something new and interesting.

Any wonder why Hollywood portrays accountants as dull and boring?

CHAPTER THREE

# The Glamorous World of Tax Accounting

*Who is the figure behind every great man, the individual who knows his ultimate secrets? A father confessor? Hell no. The tax expert!*

—Louis Auchincloss, *The Partners*

About a month after leaving Arthur Young, I received a phone call from a recruiter offering me a position as multistate tax accountant for a major oil company, at more than double the salary I had earned at AY. Multistate taxation is one of my areas of expertise. But I had already made up my mind to start my own accounting practice, and had I investigated the position and been hired, I might never have gone out on my own. Looking back, it seems reckless to have started on my own because I barely knew 100 people in Atlanta.

Upon embarking on a solo tax practice, a friend gave me some advice, "Two things in life are highly overrated: home cooking and having your own business." My father, a sole proprietor, was more encouraging. "Being your own boss is better than working for someone else, even if you earn less, because your time is your own." That's true. As an accountant, being my own boss allows me the freedom to work any fourteen hours of the day I prefer.

My mother-in-law didn't think I could make it on my own. She felt I was too honest. She was a New Yorker. A client who married and moved to New York called to complain that he paid far more taxes than his wife's relatives who had far more income. I explained, "All your wife's relatives have their own businesses. And they cheat. You receive a W-2, and it's very hard to underreport income from a W-2."

Can an honest accountant succeed in such an environment? Yes, he can, even in New York. But it's easier in Atlanta, where tax cheating isn't so endemic.

I quickly reached the point of needing staff and had difficulty in finding applicants qualified for my type of tax accounting. I asked a friend who owned a consulting business in electronic banking. There was no course of study for electronic banking, so perhaps he could give me clues that I might apply to accounting on where he found staff.

He answered my inquiry with a profound question, "Is your practice a science or an art?"

My practice is an art, and that's why I was having difficulty. I often deal with the cutting edge of tax law, where guidance is thin and judgment is required. I plan a client's income to minimize taxes and audit risk. I keep up with the latest developments in taxation on a daily basis, which requires hours of reading each week. I had to recruit staff who had or could develop these skills. They are quite rare.

The "art" of taxation is most evident in a complicated return. That is, complicated transactions (transactional complexity) or lots of them (transactional diversity). Those require professional care in preparation, and an investment in time. Virtually all professional tax returns today are computer-generated. When I review complex returns prepared by others at great efficiency, I often find errors, or at least issues which the preparer didn't take the time to consider. It's so easy to overpay taxes by a few thousand dollars, and the taxpayer would never have an inkling he overpaid. Even seemingly simple returns have issues, like who can or should claim a dependent exemption?

I have been engaged to review complex tax returns prepared by very competent accountants. I can always count on finding errors lurking where computer dependency is greatest. Reviewing a complex return prepared by Arthur Andersen before it was filed, I recommended changes that would reduce the tax by around

$11,000. I cited revenue rulings and court cases to support my recommendations. Andersen made modifications reducing the tax by $6,000. They considered my recommendations "aggressive," which, coming from Andersen, delighted me because some clients wonder whether I'm too conservative.

The Treasury Inspector General for Tax Administration tested five 2003 tax return preparation software packages and found that four of them prepared incorrect tax returns using facts presented in the tests. They didn't even flag some potential issues. Although individual preparers receive tax law training, they often rely on tax software to interpret the laws for them. Unfortunately, tax return preparation isn't a science that is easily programmed.

Offshore tax preparation is a new trend that is particularly worrisome to the IRS because it cannot penalize or discipline offshore preparers. Even if you believe tax return preparation is a science, there are many unresolved issues concerning quality and security. While we quickly think of India as an offshore tax preparation location, *CPA Computer Report* suggests that at least one outsource agency might be using its network in Bahrain, Jordan, Qatar, Oman, and in the Palestinian Territories, places that don't inspire confidence, especially for privacy of sensitive personal data that can be used for identity theft.

UCSF Medical Center discovered this the hard way when a disgruntled subcontractor in Pakistan threatened to post patients' confidential files on the internet unless she was paid more money. She attached two actual patient files to her threatening note. Her extortion was paid, demonstrating that the safety of offshore information can never be guaranteed, no matter how stringent the safeguards. A medical transcription firm in Ohio was the victim of a similar extortion attempt.

### Preparing the Witness

One of my early clients was a multi-city travel agency that had started an airline. Eastern Airlines was in dire financial straits and agreed to sell the company a Boeing 727 aircraft for $1.2 million, payable $60,000 a month, with $60,000 down.

The owner barely scraped together the down payment. When the delivery date arrived, he didn't have $60,000 for the first installment, so he kited his bank account. Kiting is illegal. It's accomplished by establishing accounts at separate banks and transferring funds between them. By floating checks between the banks, a company can create artificial cash balances. (A dishonest employee can hide a cash shortage by failing to record the disbursement, and only showing the deposit, in the books.) The trick is to keep up the transfers and float, or there will be a negative balance in one of the bank accounts when all the funds finally clear. The prior accountant had resigned over this, and one bank had closed their account. Kiting is detected through a simple audit technique.

A 727 is not just a plane. It's a cash cow. With each plane, the company was automatically granted a $250,000 line of credit at the gas pump, plus Eastern Airlines maintenance. So it was able to continue the $60,000 monthly payments by stretching out payments on fuel and maintenance.

They bought two more 727s, but the company couldn't generate sufficient cash to stay aloft. After three years, Eastern repossessed the planes just as the company began to generate positive cash flow. If the company could have survived another year, it might have been a success.

At the same time his business was failing, so was the owner's marriage. In preparing me for the divorce trial, the lawyer advised me not to use the word "kite." "The jury won't understand that word. Say, 'he overdrew the bank account.' Everyone overdraws his bank account at one time or another, and the jury will sympathize with what he did." That's what they mean by "preparing the witness."

At trial, the wife's lawyer challenged me, "Isn't the husband a scoundrel, having bankrupted a company, leaving unpaid debts and putting so many people out of work?"

"Why no," I replied. "He's a hero. In a recession, he created 75 high paying jobs that lasted almost three years."

Another attorney in the courtroom was so impressed with my testimony that he asked for my business card, and has been my client ever since.

This trial took place at the Cherokee County courthouse in the small town of Canton, Georgia. It was an old Southern courtroom, straight out of *To Kill a Mockingbird*, complete with a balcony formerly reserved for nonwhites. During the trial, the judge called a recess to take care of an important matter. A man in shackles was brought before the judge.

"You asked to see me."

"Yes, your honor. You sentenced me to five years, but under my plea bargain I was only supposed to receive two."

"I was unaware of any sentence arrangement. Were you coerced into the plea bargain?"

"No. I committed the crime."

"Were you adequately represented by an attorney?"

"Yes. My lawyer was OK."

"Were court procedures unfair?"

"They were fair, except that I was supposed to be sentenced to just two years."

"Well. I'm very sorry. If you admit that you committed the crime, that you were not coerced into the guilty plea, you were adequately represented by an attorney and claim nothing unfair about the court procedure, I have no basis on which to change the sentence. You'll have to take it up with the prosecutor's office. No one told me about a plea bargain."

They led away the man in chains. The divorce trial then continued, but we had a bad feeling about this judge. Months later, the husband hadn't paid alimony. "I won't pay it even if they jail me." After one week in jail, he relented and paid.

I've long told my clients that I'll send them cookies if they ever wind up in jail. In this case, though – my one opportunity to make good on the promise – it slipped my mind.

**College Instructor**

Early in my career, I took a job at Georgia State University teaching Accounting 101. It was a wonderful experience, except for one thing.

Forty-nine students registered for my class. Every seat in the room was taken. Over the next two weeks, 20 students dropped my class. I asked the department head whether I might be causing students to drop at a high rate. I had never seen this in my years at NYU.

"No," he assured me, "this is quite normal at GSU."

At the end of the quarter, just 22 students remained. Twenty-seven had dropped, and I was still assured that this was normal for Accounting 101 at Georgia State. I was almost left with only twenty;

one student wanted to drop, but upon my assurances she was running a "B," she stayed. I helped another student with commuting to avoid another drop.

The department provided a course outline that designated the textbook chapters to cover each week. The tests were multiple choice, prepared by the department, and graded by machine. The grade curves were set by the department, too. The lowest passing grade was a 40, which constituted a "D." An 80 or above earned the student an "A." Under this system, I was allowed to fail just one student, who never attended class.

I've given many lectures to accountants through the years. The most memorable was a speech I gave at Georgia Tech to 20 visiting Chinese accountants. It was a 2½ hour session to explain the United States tax system. I researched Chinese taxation so that I could compare the two tax systems. I only had about an hour to speak. The remaining time was taken by the translator and questions. These visitors taught me the meaning of respect for a teacher. That respect continued into the hallway, where the students stood aside to let me walk ahead of them. They held the door for me, insisting that I be the first to enter the elevator, and the first to step off the elevator. I didn't care for the honors, but was very impressed by their cultural esteem for a teacher.

**Investors and Investments**

Accountants have much valuable information in their records that others want.

Dun & Bradstreet, a company that gathers financial information for its subscribers, frequently asks for financial reports about my clients. I advise clients that they should consider information submitted to D&B as public as posting their financial statements on the internet. D&B generally requests information at the request of a customer who is considering extending credit to the company in question. But there can be other reasons for a request, including lawsuits. I tell D&B that my client will be happy to submit the information directly to the customer, but they don't take too kindly to that.

"We will say you refused," they threaten.

"No," I reply. "That would be a lie. Tell them I said my client will submit information directly to them."

A Justice Department investigation resulted in a subpoena of my workpapers. Investigators were after records that might provide evidence of money laundering by investors in one of my client's business ventures. I had photocopies in my files of more than a dozen $5,000 cashier checks. My client was not involved with the suspects, and he had no objection to my turning over the files, but I arranged with prosecutors to go before a magistrate as a formality to obtain a court order demanding that I release the records.

That was the end of it, until about four years later. An assistant U.S. attorney appeared at my office to return the workpapers. He told me that my records were the clincher in securing a conviction. Years later, I saw the name of the financial adviser who had found these investors (he was not involved in the money laundering) on the list of passengers who died on TWA Flight 800 when its fuel tank exploded after it took off from New York on a trip to Paris.

When brokerage firms package an investment vehicle, they ask only, "Can it sell?" They assign quotas to their brokers, rewarding those who push products to clients, and firing those who refuse. There's a lot of truth to the saying, "Your broker is not your friend. Your dog is your friend. Your dog never brought you anything that smells bad."

Tax deferred annuities smell bad. In theory, the person with the annuity should be in a lower income tax bracket on withdrawal day than when he bought the annuity and profits from tax-deferred interest compounding. In truth, annuities pay high sales commissions, and early withdrawal is subject to redemption and tax penalties. The annuitant may not be in a lower income tax bracket at withdrawal time. If not withdrawn before death, his heirs won't be in a lower tax bracket when they must cash out over five years. There's also the risk that the annuity company may go bankrupt. While the sales department can be difficult to deal with (just try to get a copy of the terms *before* handing over cash), the redemption department is impossible, especially after death.

A banker complained to my client, "In ten years of selling annuities, this is the first time anyone has asked me for a prospectus." My clients don't buy tax deferred annuities.

In the 1980s when startup discount airline People Express needed operating funds, it mortgaged its airplanes in a public offering. The old 727s they possessed were worth a little over $2 million apiece in a horse trade. The airline got an appraisal that the planes were worth $6 million each, and parlayed this to the public as "equipment certificate" secured bonds. The offering materials made no mention concerning what People Express had paid for the jets.

Those who knew nothing about airplanes, including all the brokers who hawked the bonds, didn't realize that at the maturity date, these $2 million planes they were financing for $6 million each would be due for a "D check." A "D check" is a complete overhaul, down to the rivets, meaning investors would have a nearly worthless jalopy of a plane. They didn't have to wait that long. People Express went bankrupt about two years later. Investment analysts reported that the lucky investors were those holding the equipment bonds because they would fetch about 25 cents on the dollar.

**Tax Shelters**

What's a tax shelter?

It is preferential tax rates, like long term capital gains; a deduction for personal expenses, like home mortgage interest; a timing deferral, like an IRA; a tax exemption, like municipal bonds; or a tax credit, like child care. An abusive tax shelter is one not contemplated by law, which could not survive scrutiny by IRS, like deducting residence expenses by claiming a bogus home-based business. In between, is aggressive tax planning.

In the early 1980s accountants and lawyers could supplement their income with substantial commissions by referring clients to tax shelters. This took several forms, including cross-referrals. For example, one could become the accountant for a real estate tax shelter by referring investors to that shelter's promoter. This violated the spirit, though not the letter, of published professional ethical standards.

Another very common practice was accepting commissions for referring clients. This did violate professional ethics in effect at the time. The bigger the abusiveness of the shelter, the bigger the commissions.

I received many offering materials for abusive tax shelters, and had an arrangement with the IRS. They came to my office to pick up the materials, took them downtown to photocopy, and returned them to me. IRS would then obtain the list of investors and notify them before they filed their income tax returns not to attempt any deductions or credits associated with this tax-abusive investment.

One such abusive tax shelter was Barrister Associates, which sold "lease rights" to publish books by unknown authors. An investor would pay $50,000 cash and sign a $575,000 non-recourse note for property that was given a fair market value of $625,000. The taxpayer claimed an immediate $50,000 tax credit on his tax return, and amortized the $625,000 fair market value. So not only did the government pay his initial $50,000, but he also benefited from phantom depreciation on the $625,000. The publishing venture would have to be wildly successful for this to have been a reasonable business venture, because the first $575,000 would go to pay the remaining nonrecourse note. Its sole selling point was the abusive tax benefits.

Barrister's offering materials stated that the main principal had been recently cited by the Securities and Exchange Commission for securities violations in connection with selling coal tax shelters, a discredited abusive tax shelter in the 1970s. He had paid a $100,000 settlement, without admitting any wrongdoing. That should have been a red flag to anyone contemplating an investment. Did no one read the offering memorandum?

Barrister offered me a five percent commission. "Why so little?" I complained. I knew the going rate was at least eight percent.

"Because I get 9½ percent, which I must split with the accountants," the salesman replied.

He called back the next day. "Can you produce volume? If you can produce volume, I can pay you nine percent."

He said that all accountants want commissions before dealing with him, so he was prepared to meet my demand, and admitted that he received an extra four percent designated as travel allowance for which he incurred no expenses. I pressed for confirmation of this offer in writing, which was provided, signed by the president of the shelter. He also offered me a free trip to New York, ostensibly to meet the promoters, and Broadway show tickets.

Barrister scheduled a continuing education seminar on tax shelter investing sponsored by the Georgia Society of CPAs. The Society was unaware that it was lending its name to an abusive tax shelter promoter. Attendees paid a fee to receive eight hours of continuing education credit for listening to an abusive tax shelter promoter.

The IRS assessed Barrister's officers millions of dollars in penalties for promoting abusive tax shelters. There were about 125 Barrister partnerships with over 5,200 sales of limited partnership interests during 1981, 1982, and 1983. At $50,000 apiece, that represented over $250 million dollars in revenues for Barrister Associates

Like all abusive tax shelters, the deductions and credits were disallowed by IRS. In addition, each investor faced another $100,000 or more in penalties and interest. Twenty-five years later, the courts were still dealing with Barrister investors challenging the IRS assessments against them.

The practice of harvesting CPA clients continues today, in a more sophisticated form. CPAs are the number one referral source for stockbrokers, insurance salesmen, and a host of other financial service companies. At seminars, CPAs are asked, "Who are your best clients?" The answer, "The client who pays you to do nothing." That's easily arranged. Major brokerage firms have established "CPA Alliance" programs with various incentives to compensate CPAs who send over their clients. They will pay up to 50 percent of the commissions they charge clients referred by the CPA. Some CPAs take the Series 7 securities exam so that they can sell investments directly to clients and keep all the commission.

Recently, I received an offer from a mortgage broker to split commissions for referring clients. "How much?" I asked.

"Twenty-five percent to start," he said. "Sixty-five percent after you gain experience."

"Twenty-five to 65 percent of what?" I asked.

"The loan origination fee and the interest kickback from the bank," he said.

I could have made a fortune off all my clients who refinanced their home mortgages.

Each scheme is different, but my clients are always the target. The barrage is constant: direct mail, phone solicitations, advertising in some prestigious journals, and multi-level marketing arrangements with other CPAs.

I consider it unethical to refer a client in return for any consideration. But many CPAs now seek to distance themselves from hourly fees to profit from more lucrative pursuits.

The line between an abusive tax shelter, a permitted tax shelter, and aggressive tax planning, can be very gray. In the 1990s, there was a little-known dispute over how to treat forgiven debt of an insolvent S corporation. An aggressive tax plan was to claim a full deduction for the loss on repossessed assets, while not recognizing income on the forgiveness of indebtedness. The result was a huge tax deduction without spending any cash, instead of a net zero (because the loss was offset by the income).

At my client's request, I took the aggressive approach on a 1992 tax return claiming a $27 million deduction. He had income from other sources that would enable him to utilize this deduction. I was fairly certain that this deduction would be overturned by the courts, though my client would not be the test case. I disclosed the aggressive position in the tax return so that if IRS prevailed, my client would owe taxes plus interest, but no penalties. My client was willing to pay interest to the IRS against the small possibility that the plan might work, as it was cheaper than bank financing. In 2001, to my surprise, the U.S. Supreme Court upheld the windfall deduction. Congress quickly changed the law to close this loophole.

Some shelters are politically abusive of the taxpaying public though not tax abusive. Just prior to the 1996 Atlanta Olympics, a proposal for City Plaza circulated among potential investors. The City of Atlanta owned 3.2 acres adjacent to City Hall, valued (or perhaps undervalued) at $4.5 million. It would rent the property to a developer for 50 years, in return for 30 percent of the cash flow. There would be three tiers of investors. The first was the developer and his family who received the sweetheart deal where his initial cash outlay was soon refunded while he still retained the major equity stake and control over the project. Second tier investors (many friends and family) would provide the equity cash and reap a high return with low risk. Finally, came the "low income housing tax credit" investors who merely received the discounted value of a tax benefit because part of the property would be rented to tenants with low income.

The City of Atlanta and Fulton County agreed to a ten-year real estate tax abatement, valued at over $2 million. Atlanta would issue $12.3 million of tax-exempt bonds to build the "mixed use" project at 3.75 percent interest. Georgia would pay $1.6 million to lease the unfinished building for "Olympic security" for 12 weeks. The project would be eligible for $1.4 million in low-income housing credits, which would be sold to third tier investors for $800,000.

The 40 second tier investors at $50,000 apiece (total $2 million), would receive a preferred return of 12 percent plus 50 percent of the remaining cash flow. The developer would get the balance. Confused? Basically, the city, county and state (along with federal tax credits) provided the land and most of the financing for a prime investment. The politically connected developer and his friends profited.

**Computerizing**

In 1979, I bought a Vector Graphic computer. It had a 4MHz Z-80 processor, with 64K memory and dual 630K floppy drives. It was a very powerful machine for its day, and with a 45 character per second daisy-wheel printer, a bargain at $10,000. I soon added a 5MB hard disk (cost $4,000) and networking. The original IBM-PC introduced in 1981 had no hard disk and only 160K floppies. VG cost the same as IBM, and it was faster. That the IBM-PC succeeded in trouncing the competition is attributable to what economists call "informational cascade" and "conformity preference" to do what everyone else does. IBM computers soon dominated the market and programmers wrote software that ran exclusively on IBMs.

Most small CPA firms kept bookkeepers on staff who would visit small clients each month to "write-up" the monthly cash receipts and disbursements journals, as well as reconcile the bank statement. The PC decimated the CPA firm bookkeeping department. It gave the client the ability to maintain his own accounting records. Small CPA firms lost a major steady source of revenue. I never did "write-up," preferring to train someone at the client's office to perform the chore, or I farmed it out to an independent bookkeeper.

As an early adopter, the computer gave me a distinct recruiting advantage. In the early 1980s everyone wanted to become computer literate. I offered to train professional and administrative staff to become proficient. That advantage helped me recruit staff.

**Employees**

On certain days, an accounting clerk whom I supervised at Commercial Trading Company was especially difficult to work with. I finally sat down with her to reach some understanding. Her live-in boyfriend worked a night shift, so she didn't often see him. In his absence, she vented her frustrations about him against me.

Years later, I had a secretary who also acted upset with me for little reason. I took her to lunch and told her this story. Then I asked if she was venting her frustration at me because of her boyfriend's absences (whom she didn't live with). She blushed, smiled, and admitted it was true.

I can hardly believe this happened to me twice. But in both cases, they never directed boyfriend frustrations toward me again.

I hired a secretary who could type 70 words a minute. She was exceptional, but she called in sick on one of her first days.

A few days later, she called to say that she'd be late because she had lost her contact lenses. It took her a full day to purchase replacement contacts. I called an optometrist to inquire whether it should take a full day to buy contacts. "No, unless she needs astigmatic lenses." The next day, she returned with new contacts.

"Why did it take a full day to get contacts?"

"I need astigmatic lenses, which opticians don't stock."

The following week, she passed out at her desk. A staffer took her to a doctor, and a friend took her home. She was out sick the next day.

The following Monday, she didn't come to work. Calls to her home went unanswered. She lived alone and I had no phone number for calling a relative in Atlanta. Worried, by afternoon I called the police, but they refused to help until she was missing for at least 24 hours. The next morning, she explained that her car ran out of gas. A friend came to help. While driving with the friend, they were cut off in traffic and the friend's car fell into a ditch. She hit her head and was taken to the hospital, but wasn't released until evening.

At least she was all right.

The next week, she again failed to come to work. I knew it wouldn't help to call the police. Late that afternoon, she called, sobbing.

"My father died last night of a heart attack. I'm on the road headed home to New Orleans. I'll need a few days. So sorry I'm missing work again."

Offering my condolences, "Don't rush back. Take the time you need with your mother. We'll manage."

The next day, her half brother called.

"Where is she?" he asked.

"She's in New Orleans. Her father died."

"Jay, if her father died, don't you think I'd know about it?"

When hiring, I always check references, especially prior employers. This secretary asked me not to call her current employer. Instead, I called her previous employer and he gave a glowing report, which comported with her performance, except for her absences. Now, I called her immediate prior employer.

"We don't give references."

"Look, she's missed a lot of work. Had many absences. Now she's out claiming that her father died."

That gained me a sympathetic ear. "Her father died on us too."

I reviewed with him the list of her absences. She had given the same excuses to the prior employer. Her brother alerted her to the fact that I knew. She didn't return.

Clients' staff are just as interesting.

One bookkeeper boasted that she could forge signatures, and indeed had forged signatures on checks so that bills could be paid in her boss's absence. She challenged me, "See if you can find the forged check in this month's bank statement." I picked one. "No." I picked another. "No, no." Finally, she showed me the forged check. The signature looked perfect.

As is my duty, I reported the incident to my client. It turned out that this bookkeeper had previously spent time in prison for forging checks. She hadn't stolen anything in the years she had worked for him, and he was aware of her record. The client was quite upset, but retained her with an admonishment.

She was very resourceful. The client ran a medical clinic. Once, she bought at auction a pharmacy's inventory, most of which could be used by the clinic. One item for which they had no use was condoms. (This was before AIDS.) Two years after the auction, and who knows how long in storage prior to that, this bookkeeper found a customer for the old condoms: an Emory University fraternity.

One client had a dyslexic bookkeeper, who did a wonderful job – except for the times when she posted the debits as credits and the credits as debits.

Another bookkeeper did terrific work – until she developed a drug habit. Regardless of whether you believe that drug use should be treated as criminal activity or a social problem, you don't want addicts working for you. The books became a disaster. Payables and receivables were posted to the wrong accounts. Payroll and sales taxes were improperly paid, and untimely filed.

I'm very cautious about talking with clients on cellphones or cordless phones. Often, I ask a client to switch to a corded phone to continue a conversation. Non-corded phones can be tapped. Just ask former House Speaker Newt Gingrich, whose illegally scanned and recorded cellphone conversation caused a national scandal. Or one of my client's bookkeepers. One of his favorite activities is driving around with a radio frequency scanner, eavesdropping on cellphone conversations. "It gets racy on Saturday night," he tells me.

**Clients**

One of my early clients was one of only two in my career who consistently, year-in year-out made money in the stock market. About six months after becoming my client, he asked, "How's business?"
"Very good."
"It's improved since I became your client, hasn't it?"
"Yes, as a matter of fact, it has."
"I'm lucky. I bring luck to everyone who has contact with me. I'm so lucky that after meeting me, prostitutes get married. Can you get any luckier than that?"
Most income tax increases are enacted by Democrats. Have taxpayers made the connection? I called a client upon completing his return to break the bad news that he owed a lot, but first, I wanted to know if he had voted for Bill Clinton.
"Of course."
"Well, Clinton raised tax rates last year. As a result of increased rates, you owe an additional $60,000."
"[Expletive]!"
An accountant becomes a friend and trusted adviser to his clients. I often learn far more intimate information about clients than I care to.
I've dealt with tax issues surrounding out-of-wedlock children, pre-nuptial agreements, pre-cohabitation agreements with mistresses (and I know from seeing the bills that I can't afford one), messy divorces, and trouble with the law. Some of it is quite embarrassing, and I try to know as little as necessary.
One divorce agreement devoted a page and a half to the division of Atlanta Falcons season tickets, including a provision that covered what would happen in "the unlikely event that the Falcons get to the playoffs...." It was almost as long as the section dealing with their children. Soon after, the Falcons made it to the playoffs.

Clients bring me their children's tax return information. One young adult had a W-2 from The Goldrush, an "adult" night club. Dared I ask the parents what to write on the return for "occupation"? "Waitress," replied her mother, which was likely true because dancers get 1099s not W-2s. I wonder whether the mother knew what The Goldrush was. I didn't tell her. A doctor once offered to introduce me to "Miss Nude World," when she was in his office for treatment and I was working on his books. "She'll be performing at The Goldrush this evening," he mentioned.

One of my areas of expertise is independent contractor issues. Working this specialty, I learned more than I ever wanted to know about the exotic dance club business. A colleague in Connecticut told me that a mutual friend in Orlando had an unusual independent contractor issue that would interest me. My Orlando friend is a highly regarded tax accountant, and I was happy to have an excuse to call to say, "hello."

The unusual issue was his exotic dance club clients. The clubs paid the girls nothing. Indeed, girls paid rent to the clubs for the right to dance there. IRS was proposing employment tax assessments against the clubs for the estimated tips the women earned.

Appreciating this interesting situation, but rather surprised, I asked, "You're the CPA for exotic dance clubs?"

"They're great clients, Jay. I'll introduce you, and show you how to do it. You'd do great for them."

"I should be the CPA for exotic dance clubs?"

"Jay, they use all the best accountants and lawyers. The most respected professionals work for them."

Whenever there's a scandal concerning these clubs, the accountant is often implicated. I could just see my name in the newspapers. (And, how would I explain the "facility tour" to my wife?) I declined his offer.

Exotic dance clubs became a leading battlefield for independent contractor issues. Most court cases involved variations of the facts presented by my Orlando friend.

One of the first major court cases involved 303 West 42nd Street Enterprises, Inc., otherwise known as "Show World." It was an "adult" emporium across the street from New York's Port Authority Bus Terminal, offering perversions that didn't involve customer bodily contact. The case gave a behind the scenes tour of the facility, including price list, of this shadowy world, before Mayor Rudolph Giuliani replaced it with a comedy club.

The New York District Court found a way to rule against Show World that constituted a rare major victory for IRS against the exotic dance industry. Other circuits ruled in favor of the industry. Eventually, my Orlando friend reported that the IRS had dropped its case against his client. On appeal, Show World won the right to a retrial, but the retrial ruled against them too. Hey, it's New York.

Accountants should only accept clients where client needs and practice goals match. A few years ago, someone claiming to represent a motorcycle gang called The Pagans asked me to be their CPA. "We're just like Hells Angels, only they get more publicity." They had been referred to me because I do taxes for nonprofit organizations.

I declined, but referred them to a friend of mine who works with a lot of churches. He was thrilled for the referral, but told me they never called him.

Shortly thereafter, The Pagans began a publicity campaign. They had a rumble with Hells Angels at the Hellraiser Ball on Long Island in February 2002. Four people were shot, one Pagan fatally, and at least eight others injured. Police recovered knives, baseball bats, brass knuckles, handguns, shotguns, a Tech-9 machine pistol, and an Uzi automatic machine gun.

I had made a wise decision refusing that engagement.

Often, I receive "Thank you" notes and occasional gifts from clients in gratitude for having done fine work for them. The accolades are both heartwarming and amusing. I've been called "an accountant's accountant." Some older colleagues refer to me as their mentor. And I've been complimented for "thinking outside the box."

I also have my detractors. Once I advised a lawyer that he was making a procedural mistake in dealing with an abusive IRS agent. "You are a very skilled person," the lawyer emailed back. "However, you are NOT an attorney with more than 30 years experience in this area, as I am."

Occasionally, I receive a letter of a different nature, such as the following from a client whose tax return I completed by working on July 4th. I thought I was providing an extra service by hand delivering it to his home that same day:

My Dear Mr. British-toady Starkman,
As you obviously do not recall, on the 2nd of July, 1776, the Continental Congress adopted the Declaration of Independence which was proudly signed on the 4th of the month. I am sure you must remember, even if only vaguely, the five-years war which followed the Declaration and led to the founding of our glorious, if imperfect, democratically organized country.
Can you recall the events of the decade prior to 1776? High handed and corrupt English bureaucrats, the drafting of colonials into the British Army, and most importantly, the imposition of peremptory taxes (taxation without representation!) that led directly to the outbreak of fighting at Lexington and Concord in April 1775? So what is a major celebratory event of every July 4th? The freedom from unjust taxes! Only an England-lover, a monarchist, a lover of red coated uniforms, an umbrella carrier, a teetotaler, a Masterpiece Theater watcher would ever forget or, worse yet, pervert this day by delivering a person's government income tax returns on this very day when there are 364 other days of the year for such a delivery!!!!
One cannot be indifferent to this unpatriotic slur. A noble cause defiled! I intend to ask the Justice Department to immediately investigate. I shall organize the far right-wing, and wave after wave of protesters will march upon your office. Bill Buckley and Rush Limbaugh will excoriate you in print and over the airwaves. However, most importantly, I intend to take up lessons in fencing post-haste and challenge you to a duel at the earliest convenience. Delivering tax returns on the 4th of July, indeed!

Harumph-ph,
BJR

Never again did I sign, mail or deliver a tax return on July 4th.
Another time, a client wouldn't return my phone calls, so I mailed him a two sentence note. I received the following reply:

Dear Jay:
I don't know. I just don't know. It's not that I have ignored your query. Quite the contrary. It has moved in and possessed my mind like a troupe of gypsies arriving in a new community. The phrase dominates my thoughts and repetitiously pounds my memory like the "nevermore" to that unfortunate gentleman. Although I have always been an admirer of Poe's works, only now can I begin to understand his possession.
Saturday, as I was driving home from work, I found myself three exits beyond my home when I momentarily recaptured my thoughts from their possession by your question. And then, on Sunday, as I was driving to

work, again possessed by this demon; I almost ran down a Harley-Davidson and its occupant, who was doing 90 at the time. I was able to swerve at the last minute, and with screeching tires, I was able to avoid eliminating a priceless art treasure (he had beautiful tattoos on both arms).

If he had been mounted astride a Yamaha or a Honda, I might not have gone to so much effort, but a Harley-Davidson! One cannot destroy a Harley-Davidson lightly, I am sure you would agree. It is very fortunate that I have cat-like reflexes. Of course, I was very happy that I did not have my dog along....[three more paragraphs about his dog named, Magnolia...]

My mind has been so engrossed in this dilemma at times, that I have studied it so hard that I fell asleep and my wife had to awaken me. She has also told me that I have skipped meals and even missed my mother's funeral on Tuesday.

I know that I will never again be able to concentrate on anything else until I have found the answer to this question. I will keep searching and will notify you of the answer as soon as I have found it.

Sincerely,
STH

Was this two-page letter his response to my two-sentence note asking why he hadn't yet paid my bill? Three weeks later, his check arrived.

**Family Time**

One great benefit of having your own CPA practice is that your children can visit you at work whenever they please. You're always there.

After his first day at high school, my son stopped by my office. His math homework consisted of a set of word problems in his textbook. The teacher wanted him to copy the problems on paper and write his answer. Requiring a high school student to copy a page of problems as math homework is an absurd waste of time.

It was 1989, and I had just bought a scanner and image-to-text conversion software. Few people had this technology at the time. I scanned the textbook and had my son type his answers into the word processor. We printed it on a daisy-wheel printer, which was indistinguishable from a typewriter.

The next day, he handed in his assignment. As I instructed, he explained to an astonished math teacher that he had difficulty copying longhand and found it easier to type the pages from the math book. This teacher never gave a copying assignment to any class again.

**Lawyers**

CPAs often work with attorneys and so gain insight into the real world of lawyers.

In many states, before a tax dispute can be heard in court, it must first be appealed at an administrative hearing. This is the situation in Georgia, where the administrative law judge almost never rules against the government. It's very unfair.

In one case, my client made a determined effort to present winning arguments. The state's lawyer confidently came to the tax hearing unprepared. He soon realized that what he thought was an open and shut case was far more complex than he had expected. It wasn't yet 11:30 a.m. when his turn came to cross-examine the witness. Realizing he was unprepared, he pleaded with the magistrate:

"I'll be honest with you. I haven't eaten anything since last night. It's getting close to the noon hour. Could we break for lunch?"

The judge granted his request.

Old joke: How can you tell when a lawyer is lying? His lips move.

Lawyers talk truthfully to their CPAs. One lawyer was especially cheerful on a Friday afternoon. He had just won a criminal case.

"Was he really not guilty?" I asked.

"Jay, we're all guilty of something."

Another lawyer gave "preparing defense for a capital murder case" as his reason for needing an extension to file Form 1040.

"Is he falsely accused?" I asked.

"How the hell should I know? He says he didn't do it."

Is it any surprise they write all those lawyer jokes?

In 2002, I was a member of a group that would receive $150 each from a class action lawsuit against St. Paul and MetLife automobile insurance. It was a nuisance lawsuit, a very easy case to win because another class action suit had found less reputable insurers liable for "diminution in value" for automobile repairs. The $5.6 million settlement would allow the lawyers to draw "reasonable attorneys' fees and reimbursable expenses." The fees amounted to $1.64 million, which I considered unreasonable.

I wrote a two-page objection complaining that it amounted to what economists call "opportunistic rent" from a captive settlement pool, with no indication of how the fee was determined. I challenged the court to discourage nuisance lawsuits by reducing the legal fee so that it did not exceed a reasonable hourly rate plus out-of-pocket costs.

One month later, I received a package from the class action lawyer containing a 51-page "Memorandum of Law...In Opposition to the Objection of Jay Starkman." It was a rebuttal to my two-page complaint, arguing that $1.64 million was indeed a reasonable fee. There was no mention of hours spent on the case. I guess they could afford to spend an extra week or two researching and writing a paper supporting a windfall fee. And, of course, they were awarded that ransom.

**Las Vegas**

I had a three-day meeting in Phoenix beginning on a Monday morning. The flight cost $1,100. The American Institute of CPAs was paying the bill, but I couldn't burden them with such a charge. A $400 fare was available if I would take red-eye flights, changing planes in Las Vegas, but such arduous travel would ruin my brain's ability to function. I could also get a $400 airfare if I stayed over a Saturday night. So I asked my travel agent to book me a Saturday evening flight from Atlanta to Las Vegas, continuing to Phoenix the next afternoon. That qualified for the reduced airfare, gave me a chance to see the Hoover Dam, 50 miles south of Las Vegas, and I could return to Atlanta from Phoenix at 4 p.m., rather than on the red-eye.

My travel agent cautioned, "I don't know if I can get a room for you for one night on Saturday night in Las Vegas."

"I don't need a room. Las Vegas is alive all night long, especially on Saturday night. I hear it's quite beautiful to see. I'll tour the hotels at night, see the Hoover Dam in the morning, and sleep when I get to Phoenix on Sunday."

Two days before my trip, I had a meeting with a wealthy client. I mentioned that I was going to be in Las Vegas that weekend.

"Where are you staying?"

"I've no reservation anywhere."

"I think I can get you a complimentary room."

He called my office an hour later and left a message that he had reserved me a room at Caesar's Palace.

I arrived in Las Vegas, picked up my rental car, and drove to Caesar's Palace. It was 12:30 a.m., and the traffic on Tropicana Avenue was gridlocked like Manhattan during rush hour. I went to the check-in counter.

"I think I have a reservation for tonight?"

"You think? When did you make your reservation? We've been completely booked for weeks."

"A friend said he made a reservation for me on Thursday."

"Let's see. Oh yes, Mr. Starkman. Here are your keys. Go through the casino to the elevators for Centurion Towers. Your room is on the fourth floor."

A guard was standing at the elevators. This was my first visit to Las Vegas, so I assumed that they posted 24-hour guards at all the entrances to guest rooms, but these were special rooms.

On the fourth floor, all the rooms had single doors. Mine had double doors. Wow! A complimentary four room suite with a dining room and servants' entrance. The living room had a wet bar, baby grand piano, and 35 inch television. The bedroom had a four poster bed, 25-inch television and Jacuzzi.

Impressive, but I wasn't there to enjoy the room. I dropped my bags and headed out to tour the Strip.

It was 40 degrees outside. I was wearing a heavy jacket and sweater. People were walking around outside in short sleeves, obviously intoxicated.

I passed some hawkers handing out flyers. Assuming it was tourist information, I accepted one. Before I could look at it, three others approached and put flyers in my hand. Prostitution is legal in Nevada, and the flyers were nude pictures of prostitutes with phone numbers.

Before dropping them in the nearest waste basket, I noticed one ad for a male prostitute which read, "New Merchandise. Just turned 18." No wonder they call it Sin City.

The first thing that struck me upon entering a casino was all the people playing slot machines. It looks like a mindless, boring activity: Take a 20-ounce container filled with coins, place one coin into a slot, pull a lever, watch the rotating display fail to match up. Repeat the process. Where did they get all these automatons?

I took two courses in behavioral accounting – how to use financial incentives and results to motivate people, even to do boring work. The best example they gave was Bingo. Slot machines are a much better example. At least Bingo is a group activity.

A line of people were waiting at the customer service desk to fill out a form for a "free pull" for a $10,000 slot machine prize. Match three red-white-blue sevens to win. I watched a woman match the three sevens. She screamed with delight. But the machine attendant denied her winning because she matched blue-white-red sevens, the wrong order.

At the MGM Grand craps table was a tuxedoed 60-ish man with a 50-ish woman bedecked in jewelry. I know nothing about craps. He had a large pile of chips on the board. I have no idea how much money that represented, but I recognized the pile of hundred dollar bills also on the board with the chips and imagine that he ran out of chips and that this was a very big bet.

He would drink a slug of whiskey, pick up the dice and hold it before his girlfriend. She would blow on them. As he shook the dice in his hand, she yelled, "Go Joey! Go Joey!" I don't know what the results of the roll represented, but he picked up the dice again and repeated the ritual.

He drank another slug. She blew on the dice and yelled, "Go Joey! Go Joey!" Again, he rolled something. Then he picked up the dice to roll a third time. Same ritual.

Drink a slug. Blow on the dice. Yell, "Go Joey! Go Joey!" This time he had apparently lost. The house claimed his chips and pile of hundred dollar bills from the table. She gave a small sigh. He showed no emotion. The loss of a small fortune, and it meant nothing to him.

I returned to my room after 4 a.m. The guard at the elevator didn't believe that I belonged in this section with the high rollers and made me show room keys before letting me pass. Once in my room, I hoped to get three hours sleep before heading out to the Hoover Dam. I turned off the light and lay down on the bed. Then it occurred to me that if this room was as fancy as it appeared, I should have a mirror above my bed. I turned on the light and looked up. Yep, mirror on the ceiling. I realized it was 7 a.m. in Atlanta, so I called my wife to tell her I was in a penthouse and unfortunately, it's a memory she would not experience with me. I turned off the light and got some sleep.

Many tax stories are associated with Las Vegas. Perhaps the most unusual concerns *Searchlight Nevada*, a novel about prostitution. In order to authenticate the story and develop characters for his book, the author visited numerous Nevada brothels, acting as a customer, paying prostitutes in cash or credit card, and keeping a detailed journal of the visits. Sometimes he met women outside the brothels because the rooms were bugged. The Tax Court allowed deductions for writing his book, but his visits with prostitutes were "so personal in nature as to preclude their deductibility."

**Roller Coaster Contest**

Tax season is an annual burden that runs in full swing from mid-January until April 15. It's a stressful time with 60-80 hour work weeks, and little time for recreation. Attending an entertainment event during this time is a luxury generally forgone.

As April 15 approaches, I awaken in the middle of the night remembering all the work that awaits me. I dream about 1040s. I long ago stopped going to work on April 16 because I could never accomplish anything. Sometimes, it takes until mid-May to recover from tax season burn-out and get any new work out the door.

CPAs survive tax season by finding activities to relieve stress and divert attention from tax season. It's important to make time for exercise. Some arrange for chair massages in their offices, or dessert parties. Distractions, like following wars in the Persian Gulf, both of which happened during tax season, help alleviate the time burden.

One memorable diversion was the 1998 roller coaster marathon at Six Flags Over Georgia. I kept a diary of the event as an amusing distraction from the grind of tax season, and sent email updates to friends.

It began on March 12 when a local radio station sponsored a roller coaster contest at Six Flags Over Georgia. Initially, 24 contestants rode The Great American Scream Machine continuously. The survivor would win a $16,000 Jeep Wrangler. They rode for 12 hours a day, one lap every 2½ minutes with a short break every hour.

The TV news interviewed two of the 17 remaining contestants on Day Four. "I'm staying until I win my Jeep." The guy next to him said, "I've got a job, so I can only stay a few weeks."

On Day Five, it was 41 degrees and raining, all day. Day Six was 47 degrees and raining. Rain continued the whole week. This 12-hour-a-day roller coaster ride proceeded in the rain and cold, unless there was thunder and lightening (due to the risk of electrocution).

I pondered that this would eventually make national news, that a long term medical study should be conducted in conjunction with this experiment, and how glad I was to be preparing 1040s instead of riding the roller coaster.

A week went by without any mention in the news regarding the roller coaster contest. So, on March 26, Day 14, I called Six Flags public relations. They were glad to fill me in. Ten people were still riding The Scream Machine. These folks got a five to fifteen minute break every hour, and 45 minutes for lunch and dinner. Otherwise, they rode from 8 a.m. to 10 p.m. every day.

"But that's 14 hours a day. It was reported that they were riding 12 hours a day."

"They *were* riding 12 hours a day. We decided to make the contest harder so that some would drop out."

"The park is open on weekends. What do you do for the ride on weekends?"

"We have a second track. Guests ride on the second track, and on those seats on the first track that are not occupied by contestants."

"So, if I come out this weekend, I can ride with the contestants and see what they look like?"

"Yes. I hope you'll come out this weekend."

"I'd love to, but I'm a CPA, and I can't spare the time this time of year. I'll have to wait until after April 15."

"Then come after April 15. I have no doubt that they will still be riding that roller coaster."

"What exactly do you do on a roller coaster for 12 or 14 hours a day?" my daughter asked me in an email. "Think? Sleep?"

On April 16, with tax season finally over and still no contest word in the news, I called the amusement park again. It was Day 34. The public relations office told me that three contestants were still on the roller coaster, still riding all day long. No one imagined that it would last this long. Officials thought it would last just seven to fourteen days.

A representative of the Guinness Book of World Records had been there and certified the contest. The prior U.S. record of 11 days and world record of 23 days had been broken.

They got to three contestants by tightening the rules again. They now rode 17 hours a day, from 8 a.m. until 1 a.m. That change occurred on Day 22. Then they moved from The Scream Machine to The Georgia Cyclone, a much rougher roller coaster ride.

Seven of the original 24 contestants had jobs. Only one of the remaining contestants had a job, from which he'd taken a leave of absence. Several were disqualified when they got hurt, the officials discovered a medical emergency or undisclosed risk. They slept outside in sleeping bags on the coaster platform. They did not stop for Easter.

Two weeks later, on Day 48, they finally made the front page of the *Atlanta Journal-Constitution*. Radio station 96 Rock had offered them $1,000 each to go away. They couldn't listen to radios or read books to kill the boredom. Nor could they take aspirin to relieve the aches and pains from being knocked around in a metal box 17 hours a day. Friends and family could visit only on the weekends, and had to buy a ticket to get in. The contestants missed weddings and other family events.

Finally, on May 11, it was over. Each of the three contestants received a 1998 Jeep Wrangler. They rode 12,456 laps – about 25,000 miles – in 60 days.

"If we continued and let one person win," the radio station said, "we would still be here next year."

These contestants should have learned to prepare income tax returns. In 60 days of tax season, working 12 to 14 hours per day, anyone experienced in preparing 1040s can earn $16,000, about $22 per hour. And they would still owe income tax on their prize Jeep. I know – only an accountant would think in those terms.

**September 11**

On Tuesday September 11, 2001, my wife was in Manhattan. She was supposed to fly back to Atlanta that evening. Following the terrorist attacks, air travel was halted for days, and she was stranded in New York.

Wednesday evening, air travel remained halted. Amtrak was unreachable by phone or internet. Greyhound bus service from Manhattan was closed because the Port Authority Bus Terminal and Lincoln Tunnel were closed. So, I decided that the only way to get my wife back to Atlanta was to drive up to New York and drive her back.

But first, I had a business tax return due on September 15. With two hours sleep, I left Atlanta at 2 a.m. on September 14, making a stop in suburban Atlanta to deliver the return. As I stuffed the tax return envelope into the door slot, a police car pulled up, blocking the driveway. "Hello, officer. I'm the CPA for this business, and I'm delivering a tax return at 2 a.m." Incredibly, he believed me. Maybe I do look like an accountant.

I picked up my wife in New York, turned around, and drove back to Atlanta. The 1,800-mile round-trip took 37 hours, including stops for naps. The Brooklyn-Queens Expressway was covered with sheets of letter-size paper and what appeared to be snow slush. It was ashes from the World Trade Center, and smoke could still be seen rising from Ground Zero across the East River. One comfort, driving through Baltimore and Washington was a breeze at 2 a.m. New York airports were still closed on Friday, and half the flights to Atlanta were still cancelled on Sunday.

Despite all that I've said about an accountant's long hours, it's done out of devotion and enjoyment of the profession. I have control over my work hours. A CPA friend in Phoenix took a vacation to Japan from March 31 to April 9. "I simply told my clients that they had to bring me their tax information by March 1, or they would have to go on extension."

Inspired by this, my wife and I planned a road trip to celebrate our 30th wedding anniversary. We took a six-week vacation beginning in August and told clients who for 20 years had dragged me out until the extended October 15 deadline for filing Form 1040, that they had to bring me their materials by July 1 or make other arrangements to prepare their returns. Only one client failed to make the deadline (and he came back to me the following year). We drove from Atlanta to Mt. Rushmore, to Seattle, to the Grand Canyon and saw everything in between. We covered 8,000 memorable miles in a few days less than the roller coaster marathon.

CHAPTER FOUR

# Turning a Profession into an Industry

*If investors were to view the auditor as an advocate for the corporate client, the value of the audit function itself might well be lost.*
 —*United States v. Arthur Young & Co.*, 465 U.S. 805 (1984)

*I'm motivated by money....I'm just about making money. That's why I'm here.*
 —Arthur Andersen partner, *Final Accounting* (2003)

Accounting scandals occur with regularity, dating at least to the South Sea Bubble of 1720, when investors in the South Sea Company in England took a beating after the much-hyped company failed to live up to expectations. In the scandals of this era, Arthur Andersen was merely the most aggressive accounting firm. This chapter is not a story about Andersen. KPMG might also have been put out of business for its excesses but for the government's fear of leaving too few firms capable of performing multinational audits. This chapter discusses the commercialization of the accounting profession.

John Cook, a professor at Georgia State University, traces accountants' current problems to a shift from thinking of their endeavors as a profession to viewing them as an industry. "In a profession, the emphasis was on service to their clients and to the public. In an industry, the emphasis is on profit for themselves and for their clients."

## Bookkeeper to Technician

Some trace the practice of keeping accounting records to the ancient Sumerians, and modern bookkeeping to Luca Pacioli's *Summa de Arithmetica, Geometria, Proportioni et Proportionalita*, the first accounting book, printed in Venice in 1494 ("Everything About Arithmetic, Geometry and Proportion"). It included 36 short chapters on bookkeeping, *Particularis de Computis et Scripturis* ("Of Reckonings and Writings"). Long hours were already an occupational hazard, as the book cautioned a person not go to sleep at night until the debits equaled the credits. The first use of double-entry bookkeeping, however, pre-dates Pacioli.

Ancient bookkeeping suffered from a primitive numeric system. Alphabetic characters doubled as numbers. There isn't a Roman numeral for zero. But don't pity the Roman bookkeeper calculating, XCIV - LXVIII = XXVI. The abacus was well suited for such tasks, and it made possible Roman numeral multiplication and division. The Roman abacus was so popular that European bookkeepers didn't adopt Arabic numerals until the second half of the fifteenth century.

Early audits were designed as an inspection to determine the honest discharge of fiscal responsibility. The town treasurer, the tax collector, or one entrusted with the finances of a private enterprise were subjected to audits. Early accounting had no concept of determining profitability, net equity, or financial condition. Financial statements weren't invented until the nineteenth century. Roman numerals perpetuated narrative accounting, as receipts and expenditures could not efficiently be represented in tabular columns.

Since most people were illiterate, an audit involved "hearing the accounts." Hence the word "audit" originally meant "to hear." Or, in ancient Israel, "to see" following the "inspection" aspect of auditing. In modern Hebrew, an accountant is called, *ro'eh cheshbon* ("he who sees the accounting"). It comes from Biblical references to internal accounting control and auditing of Temple receipts and disbursements:

> Whenever they brought the chest to the king's officers under supervision of the Levites, and they would see (Hebrew: *ro'eh*) that it contained much money, the king's scribe would arrive with an official of the high priest, and they would empty the chest. They then carried it back to its place. By doing this daily, they collected much money.
>
> —Chronicles II, 24:11 (elaborating Kings II, 12:11)

> They did not make an accounting (Hebrew: *cheshbon*) with the men... because they were honest.
>
> —Kings II, 12:16

The internal controls in the first verse are the oversight of the money chest by the king's officials under Levite supervision, and counting money by two opposing parties, the king's representative and the high priest's representative. The Bible relates that for 23 years prior to instituting these controls, the priests handled collections and never seemed to collect much money. By negative implication, the second verse refers to the fact that many transactions were audited.

The occupation of auditing is quite old.

> If you suspect my husbandry or falsehood,
> Call me before the exactest auditors,
> And set me on the proof.
>
> —William Shakespeare, *Timon of Athens*, Act II, Scene II

> Here lyeth part of Richard Bowle, who faithfully served diverse great lords as auditor on earth, but also prepared himself to give up his account to the Lord in heaven....He died on 16th December 1626, and of his age, 77.
>
> —old mural slab in Buckinghamshire, England

Financial reporting evolved from "venture accounting." Lacking inventory methods, each batch of inventory was considered a "venture." After the inventory was sold, the venture was closed and profits were determined. East India Company syndicates used this method in the seventeenth century. Each voyage was capitalized as a venture, and upon completion of the voyage, investors divided the profits. Venture accounting avoided issues like balance sheets, depreciation, and accounting periods. Lloyds of London still operates on the venture principle.

In the nineteenth century, bookkeeping expanded into accountancy. Tremendous social and industrial changes were taking place, including frequent financial crises and bankruptcies. Bankruptcy statutes were enacted. These required delivery of records and books of account to an official, specifically, a "balance sheet" and a sworn statement of the assignee's receipts and disbursements, before concluding the case. Bankruptcy work became the impetus for the development of professional accountancy.

Accountancy came of age with the Industrial Revolution and rise of the corporation. The factory system required development of cost accounting so that raw material costs, wages, and profits could be determined, allowing prices to be set intelligently, as well as searching out waste and unprofitable products, and increasing unit productivity. This far exceeded the skills of bookkeepers. Railroad companies adopted internal auditing as an essential means for controlling their far-flung operations, followed by chain stores, public utilities, and other enterprises with widely scattered activities, usually after some act of fraud had been discovered. Accounting became lucrative with passage of the income tax, which required even small businesses to determine profits upon which taxes were owed.

Under the Companies Acts, enacted from 1844 to 1856, Britain created statutory audit requirements for incorporating and maintaining a joint stock company. This generated demand for accountants. It also required a board of directors to oversee management. An audit of the records and financial statements would allow shareholders to determine whether directors were properly discharging their responsibility. This is the origin for direct election of directors and auditors by shareholders. Both are supposed to represent shareholder interests.

As the demand for professional accountancy services increased, amateurs, incompetents and greedy elements proclaimed themselves to be accountants, hoping to serve bankrupts or creditors or perform audits. To differentiate themselves, skilled and experienced accountants banded together to form professional associations and educate the public on distinguishing between qualified and unqualified accountants.

Scotland established societies of professional accountants beginning in 1854; England in 1870. The Institute of Chartered Accountants of England and Wales was organized in 1880. The American Association of Public Accountants, the direct predecessor of the American Institute of Certified Public Accountants, was formed in 1887. (The American Bar Association is slightly older, organized in 1878.)

In Britain, accountants petitioned the crown for royal charters. Thus Commonwealth accountants are known as chartered accountants. In the U.S., the professional designation became certified public accountant. It means that the accountant has a license (certification) from the state to practice accountancy, and that his services are offered to the public with an obligation to the public interest.

The first CPA certificate was issued to Frank Broaker, president of the American Association of Public Accountants. In 1893, a client whom he had charged $3 per hour thought his work was worth only $1 per hour. Broaker sued and won. To minimize this problem for the future, he used his political clout to have accountancy recognized as a profession. His contacts with the New York legislature led to enactment in 1896 of the first CPA statute.

The financial scandals that presaged the Great Depression resulted in the Securities Act of 1933 and the Securities and Exchange Act of 1934. These mandated auditing for public companies and entrenched certified public accountancy. Thus, all companies issuing stock to the public require financial statements which are audited by independent accountants.

Becoming a CPA today requires a five-year college degree, passing a four-part fourteen-hour competency test, and (in most states) internship with a practicing CPA. Internship was a formidable entry barrier for minorities because no one would hire them. It wasn't until 1921 that John W. Cromwell Jr. became the first black CPA. Unable to secure employment with a CPA firm, he ultimately obtained his CPA license in New Hampshire, which did not require work experience. The first black female CPA was Mary Thelma Washington, who obtained her license in Illinois in 1943. She interned for Arthur J. Wilson, the country's second black CPA. Only 56 blacks became CPAs from 1921 until 1959. America had 100,000 CPAs in 1969, but only 150 were black.

**Code of Ethics**

With licensing that began late in the nineteenth century, accountancy was quickly recognized as a sterling profession, the third after law and medicine. This was an incredible achievement for a brand new profession. A June 1932 *Fortune* article praised CPAs: "One mistake and a C.P.A.'s career is ended....They are by nature skeptical, cool, cautious, and conservative; to them understatement is a golden virtue and overstatement almost equivalent of fraud."

What makes a profession? John L. Carey, an officer at the American Institute of Certified Public Accountants from 1925 until 1969, listed:

1. a body of specialized knowledge,
2. a formal educational process,
3. standards governing admission,
4. a code of ethics,
5. a recognized status indicated by a license or special designation,
6. a public interest in the work that the practitioners perform, and
7. recognition by them of a social obligation.

Certified public accountancy has all these characteristics.

Carey wrote extensively on professional ethics. He explained that a code of professional ethics announces to the public that in return for their faith and trust, members of the profession accept the obligation to behave in a way that will be beneficial to the public. What cannot be reduced to a written ethical rule is that a professional will exercise no less care in dealing with the affairs of his clients than he would in dealing with his own. That is what distinguishes a profession from a business.

Who would engage a professional who was known to put personal gain ahead of service to his client? Who would trust a professional whose main interest was making money? The CPA must have the confidence, not just of his clients, but also of those who rely on his reports. Since countless third parties who may rely on a CPA's report cannot know him personally, it is essential that they have confidence in CPAs generally. Confidence in the CPA franchise was built through the Code of Professional Ethics.

The 1950s through 1970s were a golden age for CPAs. The profession grew both in stature and fortune, assisted by ethics rules that promoted professionalism and restricted competition.

The 1962 rules restricted advertising to announcing a change of address, opening a new office, or adding partners and supervisors. The prohibition extended to indicating special skills, like "tax expert" or "management consultant" in directories, on letterhead, business cards, anywhere, even if a particular practice was restricted to special services. The objective was to promote the profession as a whole, rather than individual CPAs.

Help-wanted ads could not show the CPA firm name in bold type or capitals. Listing a CPA firm name among the credits in a theatre program or having a license plate with the letters "CPA" were prohibited. Merely appearing on a television program was ruled a violation.

Somehow, announcing Price Waterhouse as the tabulator for the annual Academy Awards on national television wasn't advertising. PW began that engagement in 1934, and it was first televised in 1953. The Academy Awards "advertisement" gave PW greater public name recognition than any other large accounting firm, until the Arthur Andersen debacle.

Soliciting clients was strictly proscribed. CPA firm marketing departments were euphemistically called "professional development." Offering to prepare income tax returns for church members who contributed to a fundraiser was considered solicitation and encroachment upon the practice of another accountant. You couldn't even solicit staff of another CPA to come work for you. A CPA was expected to obtain new clients and staff by word of mouth, referrals, reputation, participating in outside organizations, and writing articles.

The profession theorized that independence in mental attitude of an incumbent auditor could be impaired if, during an audit engagement, the auditor became aware that his client was being solicited by a competitor. Restricting competition strengthened independence, the theory went, by prohibiting encroachment, competitive bidding, advertising, solicitation, and acceptance of commissions.

CPAs could not participate in "incompatible occupations," especially those which might feed clients to his accounting profession or violate the advertising prohibition. So a CPA couldn't sell insurance, securities, or real estate. Such a business would advertise, and refer tax and accounting business to the CPA firm. The designation, "Member of the AICPA" was restricted to those partnerships where all the members were CPAs and members of the American Institute of Certified Public Accountants.

The ethics rules were revised in 1973 and made more rational, but they remained very anti-competitive. The changes allowed members to be listed as contributors to charitable, civic, cultural, or educational organizations. Vanity license plates bearing the letters "CPA" were permissible. In recognition that not all rules could be written, the 1973 Code began by quoting Marcus Aurelius, "A man should BE upright, not be KEPT upright."

This golden age ended as a result of government interference and a change in attitude among some CPAs who wanted to treat their calling as a business, rather than a profession.

## Government Commercializes the Profession

In the 1970s and 1980s, Justice Department actions and court decisions took aim at anti-competitive rules of the American Institute of CPAs and American Bar Association, which had similar rules. A series of Supreme Court decisions struck down ethics bans on solicitation and advertising as violations of free speech and restraint of trade.

Under threat of action by the Justice Department, the AICPA in 1972 entered into a consent decree striking its proscription against competitive bidding.

A 1975 Supreme Court decision rejected the claim of a special status for the "learned professions." "In arguing that learned professions are not 'trade or commerce' the County Bar seeks a total exclusion from antitrust regulation....We cannot find support for the proposition that Congress intended any such sweeping exclusion." Two years later, the Supreme Court ruled that it violated the First Amendment for professional associations or government agencies to totally prohibit the advertising of professional services. This jettisoned the traditional distinction between professional services and commerce. Thereafter, very little kept Congress and federal agencies from regulating or applying antitrust statutes to professionals.

AICPA's counsel, Kaye, Scholer, Fierman, Hays & Handler, advised that a ban on direct uninvited solicitation was no longer permissible. Accountants might have argued that the anti-competitive rules were important to maintain auditor independence. However, counsel felt there was no practical way to prove the validity of this theory. And even if they could, any ban on solicitation might only apply to audit engagements. So the encroachment, solicitation and advertising proscriptions were reduced to prohibiting advertising that was false, misleading or deceptive.

Under pressure from the Justice Department, the AICPA in 1981 withdrew its rules prohibiting self-designation as an expert or specialist. Then the Federal Trade Commission took aim at the AICPA ethics code, resulting in a sweeping July 26, 1990 consent decree.

Prior to the decree, contingent fees in tax services were restricted to appealing an IRS assessment. An ethics interpretation explained: "A properly prepared return results in a proper tax liability, and there is no basis for computing a saving. To make a fee contingent upon the amount of taxes saved presumes a tax liability has been established which an accountant is attempting to reduce, whereas all persons concerned with the preparation of a tax return should attempt to determine only the correct tax liability." The proscription would now only apply to the preparation of an original and most amended tax returns.

The decree also allowed members to pay or accept "any disclosed referral fee," and permitted all forms of advertising and solicitation. It required that AICPA drop the rule prohibiting a member from practicing under a trade name or fictitious name, provided it was not misleading.

In 1994, commercial considerations caused AICPA to liberalize the use of the "Members of AICPA" designation when not all its owners were members of the institute. That allowed firms to admit non-CPA consultants as partners. This eliminated a 1962 rule that allowed consultants who were not accountants to participate in firm profits as "principals," but not as partners.

Thus, from 1972 until 1994, the AICPA Code of Professional Ethics eviscerated the rules proscribing encroachment, competitive bidding, advertising, solicitation, commissions, and ownership. The Supreme Court, Justice Department, and Federal Trade Commission forced ethics changes whose thrust was that professional accounting services was a commodity. This is what pioneers of the profession strived to avoid, and they had prognosticated what would happen next.

**The Consulting Challenge**

What should a CPA practice? That serious debate began in the 1920s. Some were aggressive and believed that CPAs should do all things which a client may seem to require. They were opposed by those who took as their motto, *Sutor ne supre crepidam judicaret* (Let the cobbler stick to his last). Arthur Andersen, founder of the firm which bore his name, was aggressive. George May, legendary senior partner of Price Waterhouse & Co. from 1911 to 1940, was opposed.

Prior to the 1980s, the Big Eight traditionally focused on audit, accounting, and tax. Thanks to consulting, they have grown so large that the Big Four today each rank among the top ten largest unincorporated businesses in the country. The top partner is now called CEO, highlighting the business rather than professional aspect of the firm. The shift to consulting has rendered the profession leaderless because no one credible voice can speak responsibly for the divergent interests of consultant, product salesman, and professional CPA – roles that carry conflicting obligations to clients, the bottom line and the public.

CPAs pressured themselves to look at their firms as businesses. They were advising their clients to maximize revenues. Why not follow their own advice? The profession's decline resulted from the seductive profits of providing consulting services to audit clients. As *trusted* professionals, CPAs already had their foot in the clients' doors. It was access they were *trusted* not to abuse. Ultimately, CPA firms decided to undertake consulting services as a "business" while simultaneously carrying on an accounting practice as a "profession."

CPA firms created consulting sales forces, enlisting partners to assist them. Partners started knocking on doors like any other salesman. "Are you my auditor or a salesperson?" became a famous complaint. One of today's fastest-growing CPA firms attributes its growth to a policy of firing partners in the lowest three percentile of year-to-year revenue increases.

The *Wall Street Journal* told of an audit partner in the Buffalo office of Ernst & Young who started in 1973, the same year I started at Price Waterhouse. E&Y gave him a $3 million quota to sell consulting services to his audit clients. "I couldn't do it if I knew my clients didn't really need it," he told the *Journal*. First, they cut his salary. Then they fired him. Many others suffered his fate, and had I stayed with a Big Eight firm, so would I.

As CPAs were called on to perform more consulting engagements, they discovered that audits could be used as a "feeder" for consulting engagements. In the 1970s, consulting services became more lucrative than auditing. AICPA's 1972 consent decree with the Justice Department permitted bidding wars among CPAs. This turned audits into loss leaders in order to secure access to consulting engagements. Consulting revenues would readily offset audit losses.

By 1999, large public accounting firms earned $2.69 in non-audit fees for every dollar of audit fees. As consulting revenues dwarfed audit revenues, all the major CPA firms dropped "Certified Public

Accountants" from their titles, becoming instead, "Accountants and Consultants." What was once considered status – to call a firm "Certified Public Accountants" – was now shunned in favor of showcasing a multidisciplinary professional service organization.

> This morning, as I walked through Logan Airport, I could not help but notice the many advertisements for the big accounting firms. They seem to always extol their IT talents, corporate finance capabilities, and financial planning tools. But rarely do I see an advertisement that conveys to the public and their clients their passion for living up to their public mandate of keeping the sanctity of the numbers inviolate—never a mention of the public interest.
>
> —SEC Chairman Arthur Levitt

AICPA leadership dismissed the consulting threat. Reminiscing on his 1980 to 1995 presidency at AICPA, Philip B. Chenok still refused to acknowledge this failure in his memoir published in 2000:

> But the idea that large consulting fees somehow threatened the independence of the audit has never made much sense to me....no empirical evidence had ever been found to demonstrate that the provision of [consulting] undercut the independence, quality, or objectivity of audits. In fact, providing management consulting services often helps auditors understand their client's business better, and therefore improves their ability to conduct a thorough audit. Besides, the threat of litigation, combined with the loss of the firm's reputation, was more than enough of a safeguard....

CPAs have always engaged in consulting services, but prior to 1950, it was casual and unplanned, usually an outgrowth of auditing and tax work. Bankruptcy engagements from which the profession developed are consulting services. A public interest is served because it enables the court to adjudicate and discharge a debtor. Tax consulting furthers compliance with the public interest in the functioning of our nation's tax laws.

Initially, consultations involved accounting, information and control systems, inventories, credit policies, cost accounting systems, and computerizing financial departments. Trouble began when CPAs started offering consulting unrelated to professional accounting, like actuarial services, operations research, asset valuation, investment banking, risk management, merger and acquisition advice and computer system design and implementation. These projects serve no public interest.

Plenty of scandals emerged to show the downside of this new focus by accounting firms.

Ernst & Young was distracted with "janitorial inspections" of HealthSouth's toilets as the company overstated earnings by some $2.5 billion using fake invoices and fictitious assets. Arthur Andersen erected "stovepipe operations" so that auditing was segregated from consulting. Each fire (service) had its own chimney (staff), so the smoke never co-mingled. That, they rationalized, allowed them to perform internal auditing for Enron, a service forbidden to the independent auditor.

It was once assumed that CPA partners would be competent to evaluate and supervise all consulting engagements. John Carey, the AICPA officer from 1925 to 1969, worried that the proliferation of services might obscure the identity of CPAs as masters of a specific body of knowledge. He was right. Consultancy by CPA firms eventually developed into operations supervised and staffed entirely by non-CPAs.

CPAs once agonized over whether consulting services impair independence. The answer was given that when the CPA confines his consulting service to giving advice, and does not participate in decision-making, his independence is not impaired. Doubters contended that a CPA cannot avoid participating in a management decision because he must sit in on the discussions that lead to the final decision.

Most CPAs insisted that they could be trusted to determine when consulting services would impair independence and avoid such conflicts. Others wondered whether consulting engagements might be more a business than a profession. This internal discord made it impossible to resolve the conflict between consulting and independence in a code of professional conduct.

The 1973 ethics rules contained a naive soliloquy on auditing and consulting:

> The more important question is whether a CPA would deliberately compromise his integrity by expressing an unqualified opinion on financial statements which were prepared in such a way as to cover up a poor business decision by the client and on which the CPA has rendered advice. The basic character traits of the CPA as well as the

risks arising from such a compromise of integrity, including liability to third parties, disciplinary action and loss of right to practice, should preclude such action.

In the late 1970s, I was in the office of a partner leading the campaign for a new audit engagement when he told the prospective client, "They said they would do it for $25,000? We'll do it for $20,000! No, I don't have to confirm that with anyone." The firm estimated the engagement should cost $40,000, but initially bid $30,000. Now, they offered to do it for $20,000, which was below staffing costs. In the end, the engagement went to another Big firm that bid even less. Such cutthroat pricing can only be sustained when the audit becomes a device to get a foot in the door for other profitable products and services.

Consulting held the promise of increasing revenues by replacing the hourly billing method. A few firms required audit staff to show eight chargeable hours per day, no matter what. The result was inflated hours charged to clients, a practice known as "time cramming." Beginning in the 1980s, one suggestion for increasing revenues was called "value billing." When you had a particularly successful result for a client, you would add a line to your invoice with a "bonus" for your good work.

### The Battle for Accounting Standards

The politics of setting accounting standards began with the Crash of 1929 and the accounting scandals it revealed. There was only one authoritative accounting pronouncement at the time, the *Federal Reserve Bulletin* of 1917, which the American Institute of Accountants had written (and revised in 1929). Congress created the Securities and Exchange Commission in 1933 and granted it authority to set accounting principles.

The accounting profession consisted of two rival organizations: the American Institute of Accountants and the American Society of Certified Public Accountants. To speak with one voice, the rivals set aside their differences and in 1936, the society merged into the institute, which was under the leadership of Robert Montgomery.

The combined organization quickly issued a report, "Examination of Financial Statements by Independent Public Accountants," designed to impress the SEC. It contained the first use of the term, "generally accepted accounting principles" (GAAP). The efforts were rewarded. In April 1938, the SEC delegated its authority to set accounting standards to the American Institute of Accountants.

Under pressure to develop accounting standards, the American Institute of Accountants formed a "Committee on Accounting Procedure" in 1938. It was initially headed by Price Waterhouse's George May, and it consisted of respected partners from the largest CPA firms and other giants of the profession. This committee issued 51 Accounting Research Bulletins. These were authoritative – but not binding – accounting principles. They emphasized theory rather than specific issues. It was succeeded in 1959 by the Accounting Principles Board. APB pronouncements beginning in 1964 were binding, and any deviations had to be disclosed and justified. The institute also issued auditing standards.

The right of the AICPA to "unfettered expression of its views" on setting accounting principles was affirmed by the courts in 1959. Three public utilities obtained an injunction restraining the institute from prescribing an accounting method for income taxes. The injunction was overturned by the district court and the appeals court. It was a serious challenge, but the profession's fine reputation won it judicial support and great deference.

When the investment tax credit (ITC) was introduced in 1962, the APB ruled in favor of conservatism: ITC should be amortized over the life of the asset to which it applies. The SEC overruled, saying it would accept immediate full income recognition, allowing public companies to report higher income, and the Big Eight agreed. APB relented, admitting that its 1962 conclusions "have not attained the degree of acceptability which it believes necessary to make the Opinion effective." When ITC was re-enacted in 1971, Congress for the first time, included an accounting statute. It allowed companies to use immediate income recognition.

The political interference had a purpose. ITC was intended to boost the economy. It would be a double boost to refund a percentage of the purchase price of assets *and* also let this show up as increased profits. The inability of APB to survive this political humiliation contributed to its demise. AICPA organized two study groups in 1971. The Wheat Commission, headed by former Securities and Exchange Commissioner Francis M. Wheat, would study how accounting principles should be established. The Trueblood Committee, headed by Robert M. Trueblood, an AICPA past president, would study the objectives of financial statements.

They studied the mission of the accounting profession and recommended an independent new entity with strong links to AICPA for issuing accounting pronouncements. So, in 1973, AICPA delegated authority to set accounting standards to a newly formed Financial Accounting Standards Board (FASB), an independent organization funded by AICPA and other organizations, and the SEC concurred.

Audit firms had participated meaningfully in setting accounting standards under the AICPA. This forced them to justify before their peers the accounting standards established by the institute as well as their firms' positions on accounting treatment of items not yet dealt with by the APB. A CPA firm's reputation depended upon its tough stance on interpreting accounting standards. Clients viewed this as evidence that their auditors were honest and trustworthy and would keep them out of trouble. This era ended with the FASB.

FASB moved accounting standards from "principles-based" to "rules-based." This replaced an accountant's discretion and judgment with volumes of detailed rules.

Accounting standards, almost unknown before World War II, have come to overwhelm the accountant's work. Complaints about the complexity of standards are beginning to rival complaints about tax complexity, as financial statements have become incomprehensible. Many accountants now call for returning to a "principles-based" system as a means to simplify and restore comprehension to financial statements.

FASB has been a mixed success as independent auditors transformed themselves into rule checkers. If FASB's intricate and complex rules were satisfied, then the statements were fair. This diminished the need for independent judgment about fairness and alerting the public to aggressive financial statements by rejecting or qualifying them. Aggressive clients would successfully argue with their auditors, "Show me where it says that I can't do this."

An auditor's report certifies that financial statements are "presented fairly...in conformity with generally accepted accounting principles." Some auditors feel that merely following the letter of FASB pronouncements (and lobbying for client-favored rules changes) results in proper financial statements, even if they are misleading. My friend, Jack Hirsch, went beyond GAAP when a specific situation required an officer's full salary be disclosed for a fair presentation.

Accountants have forgotten the lesson of *Continental Vending*. This 1969 case was the first time CPAs were subject to a criminal trial on charges they certified financial statements they knew were false. Their defense was that they followed the rules, which was true, but the statements presented an unfair picture. The jury found them guilty because "presented fairly" and "in conformity with GAAP" are two separate burdens that auditors incur.

Following a rash of notorious bankruptcies and frauds at Penn Central, National Student Marketing, Equity Funding, and Stirling Homex, Congress investigated the accounting profession in 1976. Senator William Proxmire (D-WI), Senator Lee Metcalf (D-MT) and Rep. John Moss (D-CA) led the charge. Their work resulted in a 1,760-page report calling for government takeover of accounting and audit rulemaking. The Metcalf Report charged that the Big Eight exerted tremendous influence on the Financial Accounting Standards Board and the Accounting Principles Board. It argued that the Big Eight served their corporate clients by advocating lax standards. The report suggested that public companies rotate auditing firms every few years, and it called for the Federal Trade Commission and Justice Department to investigate the Big Eight to determine if their size and market share violated antitrust laws. While this contributed to FTC and Justice forcing ethics changes, the profession had sufficient political clout to fend off legislation.

In 1993 and 1994, the Financial Accounting Standards Board proposed that stock options should be expensed. While industry groups and their auditors argued that stock options had no value, the truth is that other stockholders' share values are diluted when options are exercised. SEC Chairman Arthur Levitt supported FASB, but AICPA, Congress, and the Clinton administration opposed. Sen. Joseph Lieberman (D-CT) persuaded the Senate to pass a May 1994 nonbinding resolution, on a vote of 88 to 9, to oppose the FASB stock option proposal. He soon introduced legislation that would require the SEC to vote on every statement issued by FASB. That could have destroyed the accounting rulemaking agency. FASB withdrew its proposal. The failure to force expensing of stock options contributed to the stock market bubble and the corporate scandals that followed.

After a ten-year brawl, FASB finally ruled in December 2004 that companies must deduct the value of stock options from earnings beginning in 2005. That prompted unsuccessful threats from Sen. Mike Enzi (R-WY), the Senate's only CPA, to introduce opposing legislation, as he declared, "I don't know what the rush is." The FASB stock option pronouncement was quickly followed by three interpretations which prompted the SEC to issue a pronouncement complaining that industry and their auditors had better take seriously stock option expensing.

## Sarbanes-Oxley

It took decades for the CPA profession to deconstruct itself. It was foreseen, but no steps were taken to avert disaster. Off-balance-sheet financing was a common feature of the 2001 audit failures and 2007-2008 credit crisis. It was foreseen in 1983 by Enron's auditor:

> Of central importance to accounting standard-setters should be an evaluation of the impact that off-balance-sheet financing arrangements may have on the credibility of financial data. One can prophesy that at some point the credibility will become so impaired that a clamor will arise for an overall reconsideration of the accounting framework. Some may be comfortable in concluding that liabilities belong in the footnotes, but that belief is open to question — a question that cannot be avoided indefinitely.
>
> —Arthur R. Wyatt, Managing Director for Accounting Principles, Arthur Andersen Worldwide Organization (and later, 61st member of the Accounting Hall of Fame)

The audit failures were not merely the result of accommodating auditors. Accountants lobbied for and protected accounting loopholes their clients favored when the FASB set accounting standards. As a member of the FASB in the mid-1980s, Arthur Wyatt reminisced:

> My time at the FASB was more frustrating than satisfying. Too many people with interests in the work of the Board were less concerned with the mission of the Board and more concerned with achieving their own private agendas...too many outsiders with perceived political power prevented us from making the progress we could have made.

While the Accounting Research Committee and Accounting Principles Board gave much guidance in the form of broad accounting theory principles, the FASB and SEC generally rely on narrow rules. Theoretical principles require the accountant to assume responsibility and justify his method of reporting. It fosters conservatism. In rules-based accounting, the rule-makers can be lobbied to bless a particular method. The result has been an explosion of lengthy accounting rules, some of questionable soundness, and a reversal of conservative positions long ago assumed by the profession. For example, recent shifts to fair market value accounting, the annual valuation of goodwill, and capitalizing tax loss carryovers as assets are clear reversals of accounting pronouncements from the 1960s which rejected these methods.

Answering critics, the FASB said that it considered the trade-off between relevance (fair value) more important than reliability (historical cost). Were that truly the case, we would abandon the age-old requirement to depreciate real estate. For assets lacking an active market, fair market value is often calculated by mathematical model, imagination, or make-believe. FASB adopted a method which, in normal times, permitted companies to program earnings, without fulfilling a central accounting concept – realization. Fair value accounting for illiquid securities became contentious in the 2007-2008 credit crisis.

Questionable assets like deferred tax are recorded while weird financing liabilities are not. When companies get into trouble and announce "big bath" write-offs, they invariably reduce deferred tax assets and fair value assets. Ostensibly intended to clean up the balance sheet, the "big bath" often overstates write-offs, so that future earnings can be overstated through reduced expenses.

When Enron needed an additional $100 million of earnings to achieve budget targets, it simply recorded an increase in the fair value of its offshore oil and gas exploration company, thanks to FASB fair value accounting pronouncements. Though it paid no income taxes, Enron participated in abusive tax shelters because an FASB pronouncement allowed the tax losses it generated to be recorded as assets for reducing deferred tax expense, thus increasing current book income.

Wall Street's favorite game is projecting financial results. Companies that show smooth, steady earnings growth are favored by Wall Street. It's partly a game, "playing with the numbers," like recognizing revenue too soon, or delaying it. Arthur Levitt explained "earnings management," a widespread pernicious practice:

> There are estimates like sales returns, loan losses and warranty costs which allow you to stash away unreported income in "cookie jars" during good times and reach into them when needed in bad times. Then there's materiality. Is a 6% error "material"? So, you

intentionally record errors within the defined percentage ceiling, and excuse the fib by arguing that the effect on the bottom line is too small to matter. Why do they work so hard to create these errors? It might pick up the last penny of a consensus estimate.

In addition to the protected audit and unprotected tax franchises, the AICPA fought hard to win the right to regulate the CPA profession. It accomplished this through enforcement of its Code of Professional Ethics, writing and grading the Uniform CPA Examination which all 50 states use, and the most important power – the writing of accounting and auditing standards.

In response to accounting scandals, Congress passed the Sarbanes-Oxley Act of 2002 (SOX). As SOX wended its way through Congress following Enron, the CPA lobbyists were confident that it stood no chance of passage. Then came the Worldcom bankruptcy. Congress wanted to pass something quickly, and SOX was the best proposal sitting on the shelf. Accounting lobbyists hit a brick wall as AICPA couldn't find a sponsor for any of its seven amendment proposals. "They have fought this thing tooth and nail from the beginning," scoffed Senator Paul Sarbanes (D-MD). "They never said, 'There are some changes that have to be made to what we do.' All we heard were objections."

SOX created the Public Company Accounting Oversight Board (PCAOB). It has the power to set auditing, independence, ethical and quality control standards for auditors of public company reports filed with the SEC. SEC must approve PCAOB pronouncements. It can also discipline public company auditors who fail those standards.

This low-point in the profession was captured in a song, "Sarbanes-Oxley Blues."

> Board of directors resigning
> My auditor's front page news
> My CFO's calling in from Rio
> I got the Sarbanes-Oxley Blues

Today, auditors delight in the higher fees from audits and internal accounting control reviews mandated by SOX. PCAOB has a governing board, which SOX says cannot include more than two CPAs. The result is that the two PCAOB accountants are also lawyers, so in essence a group of lawyers oversees the accounting profession.

PCAOB's first pronouncement required the audit report of a publicly traded company to refer to "the standards of the Public Company Accounting Oversight Board" rather than standards established by the AICPA. That showed who was now in charge. Concerned that non-public companies might request a PCAOB-standard audit instead of an AICPA-standard audit, AICPA responded with an auditing interpretation suggesting nonpublic companies seeking a PCAOB audit be issued an audit report with language that mentions AICPA standards as well.

In an effort to close gaps in generally accepted accounting principles, the SEC issued Staff Accounting Bulletins 101 and 104 in 1999 and 2003, two lengthy pronouncements titled, "Revenue Recognition." They are the broadest accounting pronouncement the SEC has ever issued, with considerable principles-based concepts challenging the profession to meet higher expectations.

Nor has the Federal Trade Commission lost its desire to regulate accountants. The Gramm Leach Bliley Act of 1999 requires "financial institutions" to send annual privacy notices to clients. FTC has jurisdiction and it ruled that CPAs and attorneys were subject to this burdensome nonsense. The New York State Bar Association and the American Bar Association fought the FTC in court and won complete exemption for attorneys. AICPA succeeded in convincing Congress to pass legislation exempting CPAs from the annual privacy notice rules on the grounds that an enforceable ethics code guaranteed privacy, but otherwise FTC could continue to be treat CPAs as "financial institutions."

**Defending CPA Tax Practice**

At first, few lawyers considered income tax a profitable vocation. That changed after World War I. Excess-profits tax and high income tax rates generated controversies that made tax practice highly lucrative, and accountants handled most of it. Lawyers took notice. Controversy began brewing in 1920. Suddenly the bar began to argue that "income tax is law, and therefore should be interpreted by lawyers."

By 1932, the American Bar Association's Special Committee on Unauthorized Practice of the Law considered whether tax practice by public accountants encroached upon the field of law. In 1933, the

ABA asked the Board of Tax Appeals to exclude CPAs from practice. Senator Robert Wagner (D-NY), a former New York Supreme Court justice, introduced legislation in 1935 to exclude non-attorneys from representing others before any government department or agency involving construction of law. That would have prevented CPAs from representing taxpayers before the Bureau of Internal Revenue. It didn't pass.

By 1936, the bar association sought to restrict tax practice by accountants to marshalling the contents of financial records and making mathematical computations. Questions involving statutes, regulations, and settlement agreements would be restricted to lawyers. The Chicago bar won a ruling that only a lawyer may represent another in a worker's compensation claim and brandished the court's dictum:

> These prerequisites (the character and fitness requirements for a lawyer) are not for the purpose of creating a monopoly in the legal profession, not for its protection, but are for the better security of the people against incompetency and dishonesty.

Emboldened, the bar took aim at Treasury regulations that allowed tax practice by non-attorneys. ABA published a statement in 1938 that it considered giving tax advice, determining tax law issues when preparing a tax return, protesting tax assessments, and representing taxpayers at Internal Revenue appeals hearings, to be unauthorized practice.

With the World War II conversion of the income tax to a mass tax, local bar associations began threatening accountants in state courts. In 1943, the Lowell (Massachusetts) Bar Association successfully obtained an injunction against two non-certified accountants, forbidding them from continuing to prepare tax returns on grounds that it was the practice of law. The defendants prepared only simple individual tax returns, charging a maximum of $3.75 for both federal and state returns. The final order barred them only from the "unauthorized practice" of representing clients before IRS. This left open the question of complex returns. So the ABA proposed that preparing tax returns for income over $5,000 should be construed as practice of law.

Bernard Bercu, a New York CPA, wrote an opinion that city taxes accrued in 1935 - 1937 were deductible when paid in 1943, and correctly cited a Treasury ruling to support his opinion. The company's regular accountant, who was also a lawyer, had told the client it was not deductible. Upset at being upstaged, the New York County Lawyers Association brought suit for contempt and to enjoin Bercu from giving tax advice.

The New York court ruled that when one must resort to an outside consultant because his regular tax return preparer cannot resolve a tax question, that consultant must be a lawyer. It barred Bercu from giving tax advice except in the course of preparing an income tax return and fined him $50. "We must either admit frankly that taxation is a hybrid of law and accounting and...permit accountants to practice tax law, or...while allowing the accountant jurisdiction of incidental questions of law which may arise in connection with auditing books or preparing tax returns, deny him the right as a consultant to give legal advice," the court ruled.

This 1949 decision made it illegal for any New York accountant to give tax advice to a client whose income tax returns he had not prepared, or for whom he had not rendered any other accounting services. Ironically, the court acknowledged that the Treasury ruling Bercu cited had been written by a Treasury unit "staffed principally by accountants."

Congressman Gregory McMahon (R-NY), a certified public accountant, commented:

> It is unfortunate that the Tax Code is called a code. It is strewn throughout its sections with references to sound accounting principle. The entire basis of the law rests on sound accounting principles — income, capital gains, depreciation. There would be no code if reliance were not upon sound accounting principles. The executive branch of the Government recognizes this to be a fact when it insists that the Treasury Department is the one that should be represented by counsel before the Tax Court; not the Attorney General.

The Ramsey County (Minnesota) Bar Association obtained an injunction in 1944 against two accountants permanently barring them from preparing income tax returns, except "for individuals, whose entire income is derived solely and only from the source known as salaries or wages, but for no other person, whether an individual, partnership, or corporation." The order went on to define wages and salaries.

The Minnesota bar wanted a court decision, not a mere injunction. So it hired a private investigator who pretended to be a taxpayer and asked accountant Clifford Conway for tax advice. The investigator asked whether money spent on building improvements was deductible and whether a produce loss from frost and flood was deductible. Digging down to the Anglo-Saxon Statute of Westminster enacted in 1275, the Minnesota Supreme Court ruled that a "layman, whether he is or is not an accountant, may not hold himself out to the public as a tax consultant or a tax expert, or describe himself by any similar phrase which implies that he has a knowledge of tax law...When an accountant or other layman who is employed to prepare an income tax return is faced with difficult or doubtful questions...it is his duty to leave the determination of such questions to a lawyer." The Minnesota Supreme Court ordered Conway to cease the unauthorized practice of law.

In 1953, the Rhode Island Supreme Court barred a non-CPA from preparing income tax returns for anyone except non-itemizing wage-earners whose income was less than $5,000. The next year, the California Supreme Court ruled that an accountant named Reuben Agran had crossed the line and given legal advice. Suddenly accountants risked sanctions for giving tax advice.

An insurance company tried weaseling out of paying a malpractice claim in 1962 by denying coverage because "the insured CPA committed a criminal act in engaging in unauthorized practice of law and therefore was not covered under the professional liability policy." The Louisiana District Court ruled that the insurance company should have known that CPAs are engaged in the practice of giving tax advice, and if it had not intended to include such practice under the professional liability coverage, it should have excluded tax advice from coverage.

The controversy was diffused when Harvard's Dean Erwin Griswold made this the subject of his address to the Association of the Bar of the City of New York. "The two fields clearly overlap...with no clear line between them," he said. Later in 1955, he addressed the tax section of the ABA in the same tone. This led to cooperation between the ABA and AICPA. The Supreme Court pointed to a solution when it ruled that a non-lawyer patent office practitioner could not be accused of unauthorized practice for something expressly permitted by federal statute. That laid the framework for finally resolving the controversy, and in 1965, Congress passed legislation saying that:

> An individual who is duly qualified to practice as a certified public accountant in a State may represent a person before the Internal Revenue Service of the Treasury Department on filing with that agency a written declaration that he is currently qualified as provided by this subsection and is authorized to represent the particular person in whose behalf he acts.
>
> —5 U.S.C. 500(c), P.L. 89-332

Or did this truly end the controversy?

In 1991, the South Carolina Bar Association's Unauthorized Practice of Law Committee proposed anachronistic definitions of tax practice. It wanted to bar CPAs from giving tax advice, appearing before the State Appeals Office or preparing estate tax returns. The South Carolina Association of Certified Public Accountants, the AICPA, and the Big Six, submitted a 55-page brief petitioning the South Carolina Supreme Court to reject the bar's proposed rules.

The court recognized the unique status of CPAs in a ruling it issued on September 21, 1992. "We hold that CPAs do not engage in the unauthorized practice of law when they render professional assistance, including compensated representation before agencies and the Probate Court that is within their professional expertise and qualifications." Rather than rule on whether this constituted the practice of law, the court simply said that CPAs could do it.

The battleground shifted to Texas, where Arthur Andersen and Deloitte & Touche were investigated for the unauthorized practice of law. This was not the old feud over preparing tax returns or giving tax advice. Rather, the big firms had lawyers on their staff who were drafting legal documents and representing clients in tax litigation. It was part of their strategy to build a multidisciplinary consulting practice.

The accounting firms admitted that what they were doing was "undeniably the practice of law, but it is practice authorized by federal statute." They openly challenged the bar's ethical rules and model code that prohibit lawyers from practicing law in an accounting firm. The Texas State Bar Committee on Unauthorized Practice of Law backed away from a fight with two of the biggest unincorporated business in the country. It terminated the investigation and dismissed the complaint.

## Abusive Tax Shelters

Tax practice is a professional accounting and consulting service involving compliance with tax laws, and research and planning to minimize tax liability. It is quite profitable, courtesy of complexity and frequent tax law changes. A senior Arthur Andersen tax partner told me in 1993, "My partners want a new tax law every two years. Enough time to learn the new rules, and justify increased fees for additional work to clients." It can be even more profitable if the practitioner can wink.

During an investigation into IRS corruption in the mid-1920s, Senator James Couzens uncovered collusive and unethical accountants who filed questionable refund claims prepared for a contingency fee. The American Institute of Accountants had an absolute prohibition against contingent fees.

A.C. Ernst, managing partner of Ernst & Ernst CPAs in Cleveland was not an AIA member. His firm also advertised, another AIA taboo. He obtained the Gulf Oil Company engagement by preparing a $3,775,515.51 tax refund claim. It hinged upon application of an absurdly low five percent discount rate applied to lease values, thereby generating enormous depletion tax deductions, and a contentious Senate hearing:

> **Couzens:** Can you explain to me how it is possible to give a larger credit for [depletion] than the earnings of the company show?
>
> **Ernst:** I think this would be more clear if it would be of any advantage to you gentlemen, to refer to the Government regulations on this subject. They are quite exhaustive and quite clear and were made in 1919.

It was later revealed that the Ernst & Ernst partnership returns for 1918 to 1920 listed seven partners, of whom only four worked for the firm. The other three were wives of the partners. This split their income before joint tax returns were permitted and saved "in excess of $400,000 for the three years." There were other irregularities including backdated documents, leading the revenue agent to write in his 1923 report, "The examiner has never before investigated a case in which there was such obvious subterfuge employed to evade tax liability." The case was investigated by the Treasury's Committee on Enrollment and Disbarment.

Of Seidman & Seidman's aggressive tax planning, the report noted, "Frank E. Seidman is very clever; he even hoodwinks his own clients by leading them to believe that they are justified in following his advice."

Fortunately, the CPA profession had a most ethical face in Price Waterhouse's George May. Appearing before the committee, he pointed out that none of his firm's clients were included in the extensive investigation. He shared, in general terms, the abusive practices being peddled by tax practitioners and specifically what abusive proposals were being marketed to his clients, as well as "fixer" tax consultants being suggested by Internal Revenue personnel during an audit.

Senators listened to his theory about the five percent discount rates. He said they originated with practices of Michigan and Minnesota tax assessments, which applied four and five percent valuation rates in overvaluing (and overtaxing) mines. "[I]t was very difficult to resist the argument of the taxpayer that he is entitled to at least as high a valuation for depletion as he is for the purpose of tax on capital. That, to my mind, started off depletion valuations on a high level."

George May was so ethical and circumspect in avoiding any conflict of interest that he refused to socialize with clients or join the many clubs that invited his membership. He refused to join boards or attend dinners with important clients. He wanted to avoid any scintilla of lacking independence with his audit clients. He saved the profession's reputation.

In the early 1980s, Ernst & Whinney hatched a scheme to turn tax advice into a "product" which could be sold to many clients. They would claim investment tax credit on items clearly ineligible for the credit. E&W described concrete block walls as "knock-out panels." A section of a roof was called "equipment support." Fixed walls were "movable partitions – gypsum." Doors were "movable partitions – wood." The deceptive terminology was a subterfuge, but instead of selling hourly tax advice, E&W could sell a pre-packaged tax shelter at a huge markup. This became the first court case where the IRS shut down an abusive tax shelter that a major accounting firm had developed and marketed. Consequences from losing this case were insignificant to deter future abuse.

The 1991 FTC consent decree requiring AICPA to allow its members to charge contingent fees for tax advice invited the abusive tax shelter as a "professional product." Firms required that the client sign a legal agreement guaranteeing confidentiality, making it harder for IRS to detect and allowing the CPA firm to sell it as a fresh idea to other "customers." Some firms registered U.S. patents for their schemes. It was a race to the bottom for big firms as they sought to boost their bottom line. Competitive pressures, lack of ethics restrictions and low morals created the atmosphere which bred abusive tax shelters. It would cost the government tens of billions of dollars in lost tax revenues.

BDO Seidman, the sixth largest CPA firm after the demise of Arthur Andersen, promoted growth through selling tax shelters. "One word sums up the Tax strategy," BDO head Denis Field told his partners, "Money!" He headlined emails with "Tax $ell$!!!" and stressed that a $1 million tax shelter fee generated as much profit as $5 million of hourly billings for traditional accounting work. BDO set a "wolf pack" on the prowl for revenues. Deloitte & Touche informally called its tax shelter sales group, "Predator." KPMG paid a $456 million fine to the Justice Department for creating and selling abusive tax shelters. PricewaterhouseCoopers reached an agreement with IRS to pay an undisclosed large fine regarding corporate tax shelters. Prosecutors accused Ernst & Young's VIPER unit of generating nearly $125 million in fees through the sale of four tax shelters. About 1,200 investors in just one product had to pay over $3.7 billion in back taxes, interest, and penalties.

The American Jobs Creation Act of 2004 finally put teeth into the fight against abusive tax shelters. It added requirements to disclose abusive transactions with onerous sanctions for noncompliance and increased the regulation of those admitted to practice before the Treasury.

**The Vision**

"The AICPA has a public responsibility different from any other association. It is a self-regulator and its role in the standard-setting process is critical," cautioned Barry Melancon upon becoming AICPA president in 1995.

In 1998, AICPA introduced "The Vision." The organization never clearly came out and said what "The Vision" was, but made it seem critical that CPAs change in order to survive. Change to what? The ulterior motive was to address a concern that people who wanted to be consultants should not have to learn auditing to become CPAs. AICPA Chairman Robert Elliot explained, "[We must] think carefully about either the breadth of the CPA license or who will qualify as institute members. We have to change one, or we are destined to become the Institute of People Licensed to Do Audits."

Members were asked to look beyond traditional CPA services. In a computer and internet age, historical reporting of financial results could theoretically be completed in a day. The challenge was to bring new competencies to CPAs so they could prosper in this new era.

The Vision divided potential CPA services into growth areas, the "High-Opportunity Competencies" and non-growth areas or "Low-Opportunity Competencies." The "high" list was long: analytical skills, business advisory skills, business knowledge, capacity for work, comprehension of client's business processes, communication skills, efficiency, intellectual capability, learning and rejuvenation, marketing and selling, model building, people development, relationship management, responsiveness and timeliness, technology, and verification.

The "low" list had the protected franchise and traditional services: accounting and auditing standards, administrative capability, and managing audit risk.

In a nutshell, products and consulting were "high" and accounting was "low." Tax services were not mentioned among either competency. This wasn't an oversight. In 1999, the AICPA disbanded 20 of the 22 Tax Division committees. The motivation was cost-cutting, but low placement in The Vision's pantheon left the tax committees exposed to decimating cuts. Vigorous protest by the Tax Executive Committee compromised on replacing the most important committees with "Technical Resource Panels" where six to eight volunteers would perform the work formerly done by fifteen.

AICPA created new consulting membership divisions and specialty certification for Personal Financial Specialist/Planner (PFS/PFP, organized in 1991), Certified Information Technology Professional (CITP/IT, organized in 1992), and Accredited Business Valuation Consultant and Forensic Litigation Services (ABV/FLS, organized in 1993). Fewer than two percent of the membership have undertaken these specialty designations, and AICPA Council continues to fund millions of dollars in deficits generated by these specialties. There is no accredited tax specialty.

It was quite natural for CPAs to specialize in personal financial planning. But some PFP practitioners expanded into selling insurance and brokerage services. It is no longer an ethics violation to accept a commission for these services, though the CPA's advice may be tainted by the commission incentive for steering clients in a particular direction.

Soon AICPA expanded into "information integrity." It started promoting a service called WebTrust, which sought to evaluate an internet site's practices and controls. The organization spent $1.5 million advertising WebTrust, but it failed as other companies developed online-integrity systems that proved more popular.

AICPA was a primary force behind the development and promotion of XBRL, a system of software data tags for use in financial reporting. Of the original 19 member xbrl.org steering committee, seven were current or former Big Four consultants, two were AICPA consulting division employees, and one was from Microsoft. None were traditional CPA practitioners. The Big Four advertised a new consulting service — converting clients to use XBRL. PricewaterhouseCoopers published a 56-page book hawking its XBRL expertise. AICPA issued a pronouncement to assist consultants with wording for reports on XBRL consulting engagements. The Federal Reserve awarded $39 million of contracts in 2003 to modernize bank reports using XBRL.

R. Corey Booth, SEC director of information technology painted a somber picture, admitting that the SEC received just 22 XBRL filings from nine companies in 2005, most of which were involved in promoting XBRL. He also admitted that there was no investor demand for XBRL information, and that it was difficult to rendering XBRL documents in human readable format. Despite this, in 2006, SEC Commissioner Christopher Cox committed his agency to spend $54 million toward bringing XBRL to financial reporting. By 2008, just four dozen public companies were voluntarily using XBRL, and the SEC was moving toward making its use mandatory. Australia, China, India, Japan, and the United Kingdom require mandatory XBRL reporting.

The Vision proposed a new professional designation, initially called "Cognitor." Cognitors would be super consultants, not necessarily CPAs, qualified to administer a host of diversified financial and professional services. AICPA would spawn a new separate organization with the proviso that members of the AICPA would have easy access to becoming Cognitors during the first five years of the new organization's existence. However, membership approval was required because AICPA bylaws prohibit it from organizing another professional organization. Bylaw amendments require a two-thirds majority vote. The entire September 2001 issue of the *Journal of Accountancy* was devoted to the upcoming vote. AICPA's November 2001 *CPA Letter* boasted that over 60 percent of members "reacted positively" to Cognitor when surveyed by an independent research organization it had hired.

The New York, Illinois, Texas, Massachusetts, New Jersey, and Vermont CPA societies all went on the record opposing the project and advised members to vote against it. In a late 2001 vote, Cognitor was defeated by 62.7 percent, almost the inverse of the two-thirds consent required for approval. AICPA had wasted $4.7 million developing and marketing the proposal.

The Vision, with its emphasis on consulting services, came to a crashing halt with passage of the Sarbanes-Oxley Act of 2002, which banned auditors from providing consulting services to audit clients as an ethical conflict of interest. One critic summed it up, "The Vision Project exemplifies how a profession can attempt to change without substantial advances in its underlying knowledge base, but instead with a repositioning of claims to knowledge." Undeterred, there are calls for developing the Cognitor II business consultant.

## CPA2Biz

The AICPA determined that its antiquated publication and distribution system needed an internet outlet and a means to leverage the vast market its 335,000 members offered. So in 1999, the board transferred the marketing and distribution of all AICPA products to a new for-profit company, CPA2Biz Inc., including the very profitable continuing education books, courses, and accounting software, generating $60 million in revenues. It was a commercial web portal affiliated with AICPA, designed and modeled on dot-com businesses just before the bubble burst.

The original concept was that CPAs would earn commissions by helping CPA2Biz sell products and services to clients, including insurance, financial planning, mortgages, and perhaps computers, office furniture, and equipment, too. The AICPA was commercializing the CPA profession. Brett Prager, chief executive officer of CPA2Biz, boasted:

> Market studies demonstrate that CPAs are the most trusted advisers to small businesses. Most importantly, this trust translates into meaningful influence with the small business owner. The average small business owner is highly influenced by his or her accountant in virtually all business decisions. So far, no one has cracked the code to the small business market, which represents roughly 50 percent of the U.S. Gross Domestic Product. But with more than 400,000 CPAs working within or on behalf of small business, we believe the CPA — with the support of the cpa2biz portal — has the ability to crack that code. Microsoft and Thomson recognize the potential for growth in this area.

Microsoft and Thomson Publishing each invested $25 million in cash. Microsoft wanted the site to market bCentral and its small business accounting software, a product so weak at the time that CPA2Biz begged Microsoft not to release it. Thomson received an exclusive contract to administer the electronic version of the CPA exam. The Board allowed several top AICPA managers to buy shares at a bargain. Barry Melancon paid just $100,000 for a one percent ownership. Had the planned initial public offering (possibly $10 a share) been achieved, his stake might have been worth $12 million.

A *Journal of Business Ethics* article criticized this spin-off as violating widely recognized public policy standards. AICPA received inadequate compensation for transferring non-profit assets to a for-profit entity. Providing equity interests to management raised conflict-of-interest issues and allowed management to enrich themselves at the expense of the organization's membership. The ethics of encouraging CPAs to earn commissions from distributing products and services to clients was problematic, especially when promoted by AICPA. CPA2Biz continues to distract AICPA from its core mission and causes governance issues.

The New York State Society of CPAs sent a four-page questionnaire to AICPA Chair Kathy Eddy for consideration at the May 2002 AICPA board meeting, "the sort of questions we feel a member of the governing body of a nonprofit organization should ask its management...we have been troubled with the air of secrecy surrounding CPA2Biz." The questions were never answered. BDO Seidman sued AICPA charging that its special arrangement with CPA2Biz raised competitive issues with members. They reached a secret settlement in 2004.

After the dot-com bubble burst, and following much condemnation from members who likened the sweetheart stock purchase to Enron, it was reported in 2002 that Melancon would contribute his CPA2Biz stock "to an AICPA charity that funds education." The contribution was valued at over $5 million. It doesn't appear in any IRS tax filings for the AICPA Education Foundation. The other AICPA managers apparently kept their shares.

As losses mounted, AICPA bailed out CPA2Biz, eventually winding up with enough ownership to turn it into a subsidiary and require consolidation of their financial statements. CPA2Biz claims to have turned profitable, but many AICPA employees work on CPA2Biz projects for which AICPA receives no reimbursement, such as creating website content, and AICPA promotes CPA2Biz offerings for free. Any expense borne by AICPA is profit to CPA2Biz. No one has ever acknowledged whether CPA2Biz pays for the many pages of advertising it prints each month in AICPA's *Journal of Accountancy* and *The Tax Adviser*.

**The Library**

Founding a library was one of the institute's earliest objectives. Plans were first mentioned in the December 15, 1892 board minutes. Four years later the minutes of October 13, 1896, recorded a resolution to "consider the feasibility of establishing Headquarters downtown for the purpose of acquiring a library and for general purposes."

John Carey wrote with pride about the establishment of the library in 1917. The institute had just 1,000 members when George May raised $150,000 as an endowment. It soon became the most complete accountancy library in the world. Carey noted its "immense value to members and others, throughout the U.S. and abroad, in supplying references to practicing CPAs, to students preparing for the examinations, to thesis-writing candidates for advanced degrees, and to many accounting professors in their research activities....There can be little doubt that even when the institute's popularity was at its lowest ebb in some quarters a few years later, the library's service was a significant influence in holding the membership together."

The library grew to house 31,000 books and journals, 890 periodical titles, 84,000 pamphlets, 120,700 annual reports on microfiche and more on CD-ROM as well as every CCH Federal Tax Service since 1918. The collection included 168 rare books. It had nine professional librarians and seven support staff. In 1994, staff answered 30,615 telephone research requests, 253 letter requests, loaned 13,965 items (most by mail), responded by letter to 7,092 research requests and had 10,639 walk-in visitors to its 10,000 sq. ft. midtown Manhattan facility.

A major achievement of the AICPA library was publication of the annual *Accountant Index*. The first volume, published in 1921, referenced "the known English literature on the subject of accounting in print" from 1912 through 1920. The last *Accountant Index* was published by AICPA in 1991. AICPA sold *Accountant Index* to UMI (formerly, University Microfilms, now part of ProQuest).

AICPA moved the library to Jersey City, N.J. in 1995 and reduced its size to 7,000 sq. ft. With space-saving mobile carriage shelving already used in Manhattan, the collection couldn't be squeezed into a smaller space. So a substantial amount of materials were warehoused 100 miles away. Walk-in traffic declined dramatically, as few traveled to New Jersey. Soon the reading room was closed.

Citing cost savings and under-utilization, AICPA dismantled its library in July 2001 and shipped 36 trailer truckloads of books to the University of Mississippi, including two of its four rare folio editions by Pacioli, the Italian friar of the late 1400s who wrote the first book on accounting. AICPA pledged to pay Ole Miss $585,000 over five years. In return, Ole Miss pledged to provide library services to AICPA members. The pledge agreement has a ten-year term, but there's no penalty for terminating; not even to return the books. Hopefully, goodwill will maintain a relationship between AICPA and Ole Miss for a long time. Abdicating leadership in the acquisition and dissemination of accounting literature was a natural consequence of labeling accounting and auditing a "low-opportunity competency." It leaves a void in the "body of specialized knowledge" that makes certified public accountancy a profession.

The library budget was $1 million annually, about $3 per member, 0.6 percent of the institute's budget. By comparison, the AICPA Member Innovation Advisory Panel, meeting in New York just a month after the library was dismantled, was told that the XBRL project might cost $1 million, but this was "about our members becoming 'Premier Information Professionals'...turning the CPA Vision statement into reality."

AICPA management also wanted to cease publishing *The Tax Adviser*, a scholarly journal with a monthly circulation of 25,000. The Tax Executive Committee was aghast and organized a task force that saved it.

**Erosion of "Low Competencies"**

As AICPA pursued The Vision, Cognitor and other distractions, the Association of Certified Fraud Examiners pursued fraud detection. ACFE was founded in 1988 by Joseph Wells, a CPA and former FBI agent who specializes in white collar crime.

In 20 years, ACFE has grown to 45,000 members. Half have passed their examinations. The rest are associate members. As an infant profession, ACFE does not have much of an education requirement. One doesn't have to be an accountant or have a college degree. Its code of ethics contains just 265 words. One can obtain the title of Certified Fraud Examiner by taking a test for $250, and there is a "Money-Back Pass Guarantee" if you buy an $800 preparation course and fail admission.

CPAs number over 8,000 in ACFE's membership, outnumbering the 6,100 combined members in AICPA's Personal Financial Planning, Accredited Business Valuation, and Certified Information Technology Professional sections. ACFE has snatched fraud — the oldest auditing credential — and has gone global, with members in 125 countries. Half of ACFE's CPA members have not bothered joining AICPA. This is what AICPA's Vision calls a "low opportunity competency."

AICPA formed an alliance with the ACFE, jointly establishing the Institute for Fraud Prevention and joint educational presentations. Never before had AICPA lent its credibility to an organization which competed in auditing. If traditional auditors lacked fraud training, AICPA leadership might better have promoted forensic accounting, a specialized CPA skill.

H&R Block also saw opportunities in low competencies. From 1998 to 2005, it acquired 35 accounting firms, including McGladrey & Pullen in 1999, the seventh largest CPA firm. American Express bought the Chicago firm, Checkers Simon & Rosner, in 1997, and the New York CPA firm, Goldstein Golub & Kessler, in 1998. That allowed these public corporations to offer audit services. In 2005, H&R Block's RSM McGladrey Business Services subsidiary paid

American Express $220 million to acquire its CPA division. Block's CPA division now boasts $1.2 billion in revenue, making it twice the size of otherwise fifth place Grant Thornton.

During the 2003 tax season, Block's TV advertising began targeting CPA clients. One ad promoted its service of reviewing prior year returns: "H&R Block reviewed my return for last year, and they found over $2,000 in tax savings that my CPA missed." Another TV ad demonstrated how to select someone to prepare your tax return. It featured a drab and confusing line of offices in a darkened side street, some with neon lights saying "CPA" and "Prestige CPA," with a shining beacon down the street that turns out to be the H&R Block office, where the picture gets brighter and more colorful. The photography and images gave the impression of CPAs as being shoddy and unprofessional.

Brainstorming about how to respond to these ads, someone at AICPA suggested an opposing ad with the message, "H&R Block did my tax return, and next thing you know, the manager was using my credit card and stole my identity." It was based on a widely reported criminal case of an H&R Block manager who pleaded guilty to using her position to commit identity theft by stealing personal information of 27 H&R Block customers. "We had to get subpoenas," a postal inspector spokesman complained over lack of willing cooperation from H&R Block with the investigation. A polite letter from AICPA President Barry Melancon to H&R Block succeeded in Block's discontinuing only the first ad.

**Serious Choices**

Fisher College in Columbus, Ohio, has an "Accounting Hall of Fame." All the members, which include George May, Robert Montgomery, and John Carey, have demonstrated honest and unselfish professionalism. This devotion still exists among CPAs.

Saul Braverman, a Beverly Hills CPA, would implore members at AICPA Tax Division meetings to leave client advocacy behind when promoting public policy. He was repeating Dean Erwin Griswold's advice to the bar, "Lawyers should sell their services but not their souls." He was telling us what Treasury General Counsel Randolph Paul told a prior generation, that tax professionals should share with policymakers their...

peculiar knowledge of what is wrong with tax law and tax policy, and what may be done to remedy existing defects, and...what may be done to adapt tax law and fiscal policy to the economic demands of an imponderable future...

Many of these specially qualified persons will feel inhibitions because they have clients to whom they owe responsibilities. They will properly feel that they may not mix into their work for these clients their own personal notions of tax and fiscal policy....The country most sorely needs the contribution they are so well qualified to make to the serious problems the government faces at home because of its obligation to take a leading part in international affairs....[Experience] teaches them what will work in practice, as distinguished from what looks good on paper.

At its 1987 centennial anniversary, Michael Cook, chairman of both Deloitte Haskins & Sells and AICPA (and later, 62nd member of the Accounting Hall of Fame), recognized that the AICPA was at a crossroad:

> The next few years are critical — serious choices must be made that will affect the very essence of our professional lives. Is AICPA to be regarded as a professional "club," with initial entry requirements and yearly dues, whose principal emphasis is on serving the needs of its members? Or will it be a serious, self-regulatory body, intent on monitoring and demonstrating the quality of our professional services and responding to the needs of the public on an equal footing with the needs of our members?

In the ensuing twenty years, AICPA made many questionable choices. Barry Melancon became a lightning rod for discontent. A derisive nine-stanza parody song, "Ballad to Barry," (to the tune of "The Beverly Hillbillies" — Barry came from Louisiana) was anonymously written and circulated.

> Ole BM went to work, Lawd his job wuz great,
> Got a half-a-mil, which was jus to compensate...
> PFP, ElderCare, and WebTrust hit the floor,
> His Vision fer de future changed CPA to Cognitor...
> Bozos we were! Idiots too! Uninformed and Old-Fashioned!
>
> Stocks went up, techs were hot, He had to make his play,
> How could he mint money off The Trusted CPA?
> A portal for the masses, cheap stock for the Boss,
> Enron-type accounting and 37 million lost.
> Insider dealing! Conflict of Interest! Breach of fiduciary duty!

*Business Week* named him one of the worst managers of 2002. A follow-up article further castigated his leadership, but noted that the board was also responsible for AICPA problems to such an extent that Melancon's departure would not solve AICPA's problems. It noted the profession's loss of standards setting and self-regulation, that AICPA lost millions promoting Cognitor which membership overwhelmingly rejected, over $80 million in losses from CPA2Biz, and AICPA membership for the very first time was dropping.

The board felt differently. Melancon fulfilled 120 performance goals that board members had established, and they paid him a nearly $1 million salary in 2002. That was a 22 percent increase in 2002, which followed a 32 percent increase in 2001.

A 1990 study on governance and structure suggested that a Presidential Review Committee be appointed at least one year before the end of the president's term. It would evaluate the institute's needs and the incumbent's performance, strengths and weaknesses in meeting those requirements. Yet in February 2004, seventeen months before its expiration, the AICPA board extended Melancon's contract for another five years, until July 2010.

The 1990 study explained that AICPA would not move its president's office to Washington, D.C. to avoid a situation where "both members and outsider observers...perceive the Institute as a trade association rather than a professional organization." A professional organization accrues benefits and credibility by advocating the public interest. A trade association balances member and public interest.

No study was released when the AICPA Governing Council voted on October 25, 2005 to relocate "approximately 400 job functions" from Jersey City and New York City to Durham, North Carolina. The AICPA press release extolled the labor cost savings worth "approximately $10-11 million dollars per year over a 15-year period." It didn't mention the $49 million up-front relocation cost. North Carolina Governor Michael Easley issued a press release saying that AICPA had "become the 29th Job Development Investment Grant recipient...equivalent to 70 percent of the state personal income withholding taxes derived from the creation of new jobs," worth a maximum of $6.98 million over ten years. No one mentioned the non-financial factors for deciding upon relocation, particularly the intellectual capital that would be lost upon relocating an intellectual enterprise. Only ten percent of the AICPA staff accepted transfer — with substantial salary reductions.

Thirty years ago, the American Medical Association boasted that 75 percent of U.S. physicians were members. Today it represents less than 30 percent. The AMA concluded that one reason for declining membership was a misalignment between membership, governance, and representation. The AMA once wielded immense power but entered a period of weak leadership and bad decisions. Today, a weakened AMA has resulted in a splintered voice of medicine. Outside forces, especially government, employers, and managed care organizations, have gained an upper hand. It can be argued that the quality of health care has suffered as a result.

From 1980 to 1995, AICPA membership almost doubled from 161,000 to 325,000. Membership peaked in 2001 at 337,000. By 2005, it declined to 327,000, the same as it was in 1996. Is AICPA headed down the AMA path? AICPA membership is slowly recovering, reaching 334,000 members in 2007, but I wonder if younger accountants aren't joining at the same rate as did members of my generation.

The cover of the January 2004 *Journal of Accountancy* featured a picture of money growing on a tree being irrigated by a professionally dressed man holding a watering can with the caption, "Grow a Bigger, Better Investment Practice." It contained articles, "Working With a Solicitor to Get New Business," "Facilitate Your Way to New Business," "Making Money with Basic Accounting Software." The December 2004 *Tax Adviser* featured an ad for the latest AICPA-published book, *Introducing Tax Clients to Additional Services*. It hit bottom when the April 2006 *Journal of Accountancy* advised on "Getting Started With Direct Mail and Telemarketing."

> The leaders at the Big Four that I've dealt with over the last five years cause me concern for the accounting profession. They're more business-development types and not that focused on building the accounting and auditing profession.
>
> —Charles Bowsher CPA, former Comptroller General of the U.S. and 57th member of the Accounting Hall of Fame, 2003

# Part II

History and Government

# CHAPTER FIVE

# Maltotier

*The art of taxation consists in so plucking the goose as to obtain the largest amount of feathers with the least amount of squawking.*
—Jean-Baptiste Colbert, finance minister to Louis XIV

*Voilà le maltotier, si cruel et si barbare...si dénaturé.*
—song about Colbert's "evil tax collectors, so cruel and so barbaric...so corrupt."

Moses collected a tax in the wilderness, though Biblical commentators reason that it wasn't really a tax. Rather, God loved his people and just wanted them counted. Since it was unseemly to count heads, Moses collected a half shekel from every man and counted the money. Indeed, God loved his people so much that He had Moses count them three times during the first year after they left Egypt. Moses collected over 300,000 shekels each time, almost one million in total. According to the Hammurabi Code, a year's wage for a working man was between six and eight shekels. So this was a substantial levy.

Joseph had to travel with Mary to Bethlehem to pay the census tax decreed by Caesar Augustus. Many people traveled to Bethlehem to pay the tax, so when they arrived, the inn was full and they stayed in the manger. Taxation was the reason Jesus wound up being born in a manger.

The earliest tax professionals were tax collectors. Even then, nobody liked them.

> Two men went up to the Temple to pray, one a Pharisee, and the other a tax collector. The Pharisee stood there and said this prayer to himself: "I thank you, God, that I am not grasping, unjust, adulterous like the rest of mankind, particularly that I am not like this tax collector...."
> —Luke 9:9-14

To avoid the bad reputation associated with collecting taxes, rulers sought to insulate themselves from revenue raising. "Go to Joseph and do what he tells you," Pharaoh tells his subjects [Gen. 31:55]. Priests were exempt from Joseph's levies [Gen. 47:22]. (Why is Joseph remembered as a successful and popular tax collector?)

A ruler would sell the right to collect taxes within a district, thus freeing the government from the evils of tax collection. This practice was called "tax farming." It was usually sold to the highest bidder and compared to a farmer planting seeds. The "tax farmer" who purchased this right decided how vigorously to extract, extort, or "harvest" taxes from which he would recover his investment and make a profit.

## Use and Abuse of Jews

In the Middle Ages, Jews were barred from the artisan guilds and from owning land. Their communities' major income source was money-lending and finance. The situation of Jews was precarious. They could remain in a country only while they had protection of the king and while the king was powerful enough to protect them. Protection came at a heavy price in taxes and services.

England taxed Jews on goods, chattels, debts, gifts, and through licenses, fines, and ransoms. Payment was enforced through imprisonment, property confiscation, seizing of women and children, gouging out eyes, extracting teeth and other cruelties. In preparation for the third crusade, Henry II assessed £60,000 against the Jews. This was one-fourth of their movable property. Before embarking on the crusade, the marauding hordes massacred the Jews of York and other communities. Jews were not allowed to emigrate because they were a valuable source of income to the crown. By 1290, they were impoverished and degraded, and King Edward I expelled England's

16,000 Jews. Most went to France, whose 100,000 Jews met with expulsion in 1306. They were allowed to take with them not much more than the clothes they wore.

In Spain, the king knew that Jews depended on him for protection from hostile masses. Distrusting the noblemen and rich townsmen, he enlisted Jews to collect his taxes. Tax farming was a major source of wealth for the Jewish financiers in pre-sixteenth century Spain. The Jewish community felt pride in the status of the few of their number who served in the king's court, where the Spanish tax collection system was mostly, if not entirely, administered by Jews. This did not endear them to the Christian population, who felt exploited. It resulted in Spanish pogroms, and the hatred of the crowds was used by the Inquisition to pressure the king to expel the Jews.

The king wanted Jews to remain unmolested so their services to the Crown would continue undisturbed. But following the conquest of the Moorish city of Granada and unification of Castile and Aragon, Ferdinand and Isabella knew that Torquemada and the Inquisition represented an intense and widespread opposition that might assume a revolutionary character. So on March 31, 1492, they issued an order expelling the Jews, to take effect on August 2, 1492, the day Columbus sailed for the New World, coincidentally *Tisha B'Av*, the saddest day on the Jewish calendar. Jewish converts to Christianity assumed the tax collection function. These *conversos* and their offspring were called *marranos*, "pigs."

In the sixteenth century, Polish nobility used the hostility of the local population toward Jews to make money in two ways. They sold to certain cities and towns, such as Warsaw, the privilege of keeping Jews out. They made even more by appointing local Jewish councils as tax collectors to milk their own Jewish communities for protection money.

This enterprise was expanded in the seventeenth century. The Ukraine and Little Russia, with their Greek Orthodox Cossacks, were under the jurisdiction of the Polish nobles who were Catholic. The nobles would lease their estates, both land and businesses, as well as tax collection, to Jews. They expected the Jews to extract taxes from the peasants who worked the fields and factories. The nobles' objective was to turn the rebellious Cossacks into profitable serfs. Polish Jesuits hoped to convert these Greek heretics to Catholicism. The Jews were middlemen in their plans. Among the hated levies were taxes on every marriage, christening, and mass for the dead. Adding to the enmity, the Polish noblemen gave Jewish tax farmers the keys to the Greek churches. That prevented tax evasion because the clergyman had to request the keys to perform a marriage, baptism or mass.

The Cossacks hated the Polish nobility and clergy, but they hated Jews more. They revolted in 1648. Over the next ten years, the frightful Chmielnicki massacres murdered 100,000 Jews, many under brutal torture. Chmielnicki broke the Ukraine away from Polish domination and placed it under the Russian czar.

The Germans appointed Jewish councils to run the ghettos during World War II. They subjected inmates to bizarre taxes. Wages, rent, water, electricity, prescriptions (at 40 percent, if medicine was available), ration cards, burial plots, and requests for information on the whereabouts of missing persons were taxed. Newcomers paid a registration fee for the privilege of moving into the ghetto and to receive mail. Jews spared relocation because they already resided in the slum that became the ghetto paid a tax to finance the moving expenses of newcomers. Those aged 12 to 60 paid a handling fee to register for forced labor duty. An exemption could also be purchased. There was a head tax per inmate and an extraordinary tribute to be paid by wealthy newcomers.

Around 1942, most ghetto taxes were abolished because all the Jews' money had been plundered. Thereafter, ghettos were financed with profits of various enterprises where inmates slaved for a daily bowl of cabbage soup and a weekly loaf of bread. Germany wasn't the only oppressor with such guileful taxation.

Turkey began forcefully removing all Jews and other "non-Turks" from Eastern Thrace in 1934, including the historic Jewish communities of Edirne and the Straits zone. That same year, an anti-Jewish campaign orchestrated by the Turkish press forced 8,000 - 10,000 Thracian Jews to seek refuge in Istanbul. In 1935, Turkey forced Jews, Greeks and Armenians to abandon traditional surnames and adopt new ones. A 1938 law compelled all to speak only Turkish. Greeks and Jews were fired from their jobs for speaking a non-Turkish language. After Turkey signed a Treaty of Friendship with Germany in June 1941, it conscripted all Jewish, Greek, and Armenian males between 18 and 45 to forced labor camps. Harsh conditions and high mortality rates were reported. In an attempt to channel discontent, Ankara blamed Jewish and Christian businessmen for the severe economic crisis of 1939 - 1941, aided by a vitriolic anti-Jewish, anti-minority campaign in the press.

On November 11, 1942, Turkey enacted the *Varlik Vergisi*, a tax on assets. Five employees at the Ministry of Finance secretly decided what each person earned, what he was worth, and the amount of tax he should pay. There was no published tax rate and the assessors had no data whatsoever for thousands of people. They used resourceful imagination and guesswork.

Muslims were taxed on earnings at low rates, non-Muslims on earnings and wealth at rates exceeding 100 percent. This is in accordance with a commandment in the Koran to tax nonbelievers into subjugation. Donmes (apostate in Turkish) were assessed two to ten times the Muslim rate. These are descendants of followers of the false messiah, Shabbetai Tzvi, who converted to Islam in 1666. International law stipulates that foreign residents may not be taxed more heavily than citizens. So, foreigners were taxed at Muslim rates, except Jewish subjects of the Axis states were taxed as Donmes.

The assessments were issued on December 17. The tax was due and payable in cash within 15 days (January 1, 1943) in the amount that the ministry assessed in secret deliberations, from which there was no appeal. A 15-day extension was available for a two percent penalty. Thereafter, a delinquent taxpayer was sent to a forced labor camp in Askale ("Turkish Siberia") and his property confiscated, together with that of his next of kin. As tax assessments far exceeded their net worth, 1,400 non-Muslims and Donmes were deported to labor camps, including delinquents who were aged, sick or infirm. Twenty-one prisoners died. They were released in December 1943, a week before Turkish President Ismet Inönü met with Churchill and Roosevelt in Cairo.

Non-Muslims constituted less than one percent of the population, but were assessed 93 percent of the tax. A number of governors refused to collect taxes from Muslims. They had to be convinced to collect at least a token levy to give the facade of a uniform fiscal measure.

Total assessments in Istanbul Province alone totaled almost 50 percent of the currency in circulation. Actual revenues exceeded the original estimates. The resulting confiscations and fire sales depressed the Turkish economy for years after World War II, but the tax accomplished its secret goal of impoverishing minority businesses out of existence so that Muslims could control the economy.

The reputation for religious tolerance that the Turkish Republic had built since its establishment was shattered. During the first year after the State of Israel came into existence, one quarter of Turkey's Jews emigrated to Israel. Greeks and Armenians left Turkey *en masse* during the 1950s and 1960s.

**Salt Taxes**

Historians argue over the causes of the French Revolution in 1789, but taxation is generally in the top five. Taxation in pre-revolutionary France was one of the most regressive, intrusive, and oppressive in history – so hated that the new republic considered replacing the tax word, *impôt*, with *contributions publiques*.

The tax bureaucracy employed 200,000, about two or three percent of the population. They were derisively called, *maltotiers* (evil taxers) or *gabelleurs* (after the most hated levy). The equivalent today would be six million IRS employees, not the mere 100,000 it actually employs.

France had a tradition to exempt nobility and clergy from taxation. It was argued that the knight's sword and the clergyman's prayers provided substitute service to the state. There was also a practical reason to exempt nobles. Collectors were usually peasants. They were no match for nobles who carried weapons and dominated local judicial and economic institutions.

To finance the Hundred Years' War, France imposed an income tax in 1355. Rates were set at four percent on the rich, five percent on the middle class, and ten percent on the poor. After all, at four percent, a rich man would pay more tax than a poor man at ten percent.

Around that time France also introduced the salt tax, *la gabelle*. Prior to refrigeration, salt was a commodity essential to man's survival. Salt preserved meat and fish and cured animal hides. It was considered a poor man's currency. The word, "salary" derives from "salt." (It was in such short supply in the Confederate States that death compensation to a soldier's bereaved family included a 25-pound bag of salt.) Thomas Hart Benton observed, "[p]eople hate the salt tax because they are obliged to have salt, and cannot evade the tax: governments love the tax for the same reason—because people are obliged to pay it."

The gabelle wasn't so much a tax as a franchise. The king bought 5200 pound lots of salt for three or four shillings and six pence. He would resell it to his subjects in small quantities grossing £256 (3,328 livres in French currency).

So that the high price of salt wouldn't discourage consumption, each family was obligated to purchase a certain quota, based on the number of family members and wealth. According to one account, every person over age eight had to buy seven kilograms annually. Resale was prohibited. A first offense was punishable with a 300 - 500 livre fine (which if not paid would be raised to a second offense). Second offense was branding with a red fleur-de-lis on the cheek or shoulder. Third offenders were sent to the slave galleys. Just for reselling a little salt.

The gabelle steadily increased until the revolution, and was imposed at six different rates according to province. Six provinces were exempt from the gabelle. This encouraged smuggling. A first smuggling offense brought three to nine years in the galleys. A second offense, the gallows or a torture death on the wheel. Fishermen and seacoast residents were prohibited from using salt water, subject to the same penalties as smugglers. About 3,000 Frenchmen were imprisoned or executed each year for gabelle crimes.

Only 40 percent of these tax receipts reached the King's treasury. Each collector took his cut, and self-interest motivated them to forcibly extract more than the poor could afford. In addition to transportation, between 20 and 30 thousand men were employed in enforcement of this one tax. The low yield made the gabelle very inefficient.

In addition to taxes, France exacted forced loans. And the monarchy bankrupted with regularity, in 1602, 1643, 1648, 1721, and 1789, thus keeping the principal and relieving itself of the burden of paying interest.

Ferme Général was a syndicate of investors that submitted the high bid and won the tax collection contract for "indirect" taxes on tobacco, salt, wine and other commodities, subject to renewal every six years. Ferme was very intrusive, oppressive, and hated. The 40 members of the syndicate became targets of the French Revolution. Thirty-two eventually went to the guillotine.

One Fermier who lost his head was the great scientist Antoine-Laurent Lavoisier. He inherited a large fortune from his parents and invested it in the Ferme, which promised a 20 percent annual return. He served as a director before it was abolished. In 1794, during the Reign of Terror, he was subject to a trial lasting a few hours, then guillotined.

America might not have won its War of Independence without financial and naval support from France, particularly at the Battle of Yorktown in late 1781. At a cost of a billion livres, France financed its participation primarily with loans, which bankrupted the treasury. Servicing this heavy debt became an unsustainable burden, so Louis XVI raised taxes again after 1786. This became one of the triggers for the 1789 French Revolution.

"No taxation without representation" was a great slogan, but taxation wasn't the reason for the Boston Tea Party. Taxes was way down the list – number 17 of 27 grievances in the Declaration of Independence. Tea had been taxed since 1768. So what caused the Boston Tea Party in December 1773? In May 1773, the financially strapped East India Company appealed to the British government for aid and was granted a monopoly on all tea exported to the colonies. The company began selling tea directly to the American public without any middlemen.

Eliminating middlemen made tea with tax cost less than it had before, less than it cost in England, even less than tea smugglers. In protest, Boston merchants (and smugglers) dumped 342 chests of British tea into Boston Harbor and blamed the tea tax as justification. The harsh British retaliation, including passing a series of Coercive Acts and closing the port of Boston to commerce until the tea was paid for enraged the colonists and made the "Tea Party" a major reference point in the American Revolution.

France wasn't the only place where salt was heavily taxed. England imposed a salt tax for 150 years until repealed in 1822. The United States imposed it twice. Anticipating a war with France, Congress passed several levies, including a 1797 temporary tariff on salt, to cease as soon as the war was over. Salt cost 24 cents per bushel, of which 12 cents was a tax that had been levied since 1790. The new 1797 levy raised the tax to 20 cents (30 cents if imported on ships not of U.S. registry). In an early form of subsidy, curers and exporters of fish were paid a bounty (rebate) by the Treasury to offset the salt tax paid by them, but weak controls resulted in these industries receiving double the intended cash.

The quasi-war never happened, but the salt tax raised $500,000 annually and remained until March 1807, when President Thomas Jefferson forced its repeal. It was reinstituted in 1813, again as a temporary measure to terminate one year after the end of war. Congress also legislated that 56 pounds would constitute a bushel of salt, when the true weight of a bushel of salt was 84 pounds. That artificially inflated the tax to 30 cents per true bushel. The War of 1812 ended in 1815, but not the salt tax.

The existence of a federal tax on imported salt helped finance construction of the Erie Canal, which began in 1817. Because domestic salt was exempt from the tariff, New York easily imposed a state levy of 12.5 cents per bushel on domestic upstate salt to pay for the canal.

Under the direction of President Andrew Jackson, Congress reduced the tax in 1830 to 10 cents per 56-pound bushel, but some bounties remained into the 1850s. The U.S. salt episode proved the difficulty of repealing a temporary tax, the greater difficulty of repealing a tax benefit, and that a high protective tariff does not assure increases in competitive domestic production.

The British had a predilection for unfairly taxing their colonies. The East India Company had a private army which helped capture the Indian subcontinent in the mid-1700s. The Regulating Act of 1773 and Pitt's India Act of 1784 granted the East India Company colonial rule. The company plundered India, bringing in one-fifth of its worldwide revenues. Salt levies, begun around 1780, were the most onerous, accounting for more than half its revenue from India.

Modeled after the French gabelle, the British claimed a monopoly on salt production and distribution. Tax collection was farmed out to salt agents, and the price soared. Many people died for lack of salt because they could not afford it. Illicit production and smuggling were punished with severe penalties.

On March 12, 1930, a 61-year-old Mahatma Gandhi began a 241-mile walk lasting 25 days, from Sabarmati Ashram to Dandi on the west coast of India, a frail man in poor health marching against a mighty empire. He started with 78 marchers and ended with thousands. There, in defiance of the Salt Act, he walked into the ocean and picked up a small lump of natural salt. Others followed suit, and within a week, the jails were full. Less than a year later, Britain reduced the tax. Thus was born "nonviolent political struggle." Its first use was to protest against taxes.

## King Leopold II

Before the invention of plastic, elephant tusk ivory was shaped into implement handles, piano and organ keys, chess pieces, jewelry, even false teeth. Bringing ivory out of the jungle required an army of workers to build roads and porters to carry it.

The Dunlop Company invented the inflatable rubber tire in 1890, allowing a gentle bicycle ride without springs. This was soon adapted to the newly invented automobile. More uses for rubber soon appeared: hoses, tubing, gaskets, electrical insulation, and waterproof garments. Prior to cultivation of rubber tree plantations, vines in the Congo were a major source of wild rubber. But gathering rubber in the jungle was unpleasant and dangerous work that could not be supervised.

Belgium was formed in 1830 as a neutral country with a limited monarchy, like England. King Leopold II ascended the throne in 1865 at age 30. He became immensely rich by taxing the Congo, a country as large as all of Europe, excluding Russia, with an estimated population of 20 million. In 1885, with the help of the famous explorer, Henry Morton Stanley ("Dr. Livingstone, I presume?"), he established the Congo Free State, not as a Belgian colony but as his personal possession, to loot its ivory and rubber riches. How did this ruler of a small new country with no great army, navy or colonial experience manage to snare the Congo from the great powers?

In 1881, Leopold created "The Society for Studies in the Upper Congo," which sounded harmless and academic. Under its guise, he sent Stanley to establish stations along the Congo River and make treaties with native chiefs to establish his sovereignty in the region. An international conference attended by 15 nations was held in Berlin in 1884-85. It declared the Congo Basin neutral territory, open to all nations, with no tariffs. Believing he was a sincere philanthropist who would spend his own fortune bettering the Congo, and coming from neutral Belgium, they appointed Leopold guardian of the international orphan.

Slave trading was a big problem in the Congo. Leopold hosted an International Congress on the Slave Trade in 1889-90. There followed an International Conference on Customs Tariffs in 1890, which granted Leopold the right to set a 10 percent tax on imports to the Congo. Tariffs meant border controls and sovereignty. Leopold quickly violated the intent of the agreement by taxing all commerce, including real estate, river vessels, servants, and exports of ivory and rubber. His Congo administration dismissed all English employees and replaced them with Belgians.

The U.S. participated in all three conferences. The 1884 Berlin Conference was promoted by U.S. minister to Belgium, John A. Kasson, and assisted by former minister General Henry S. Sanford, as well as explorer Stanley, who was an American. The U.S. was the first nation to sign the treaty handing Congo to Leopold, but President Chester Arthur did not submit it to the Senate for ratification. His successor, Grover Cleveland, annulled the treaty because of strong American sentiment against foreign entanglements. The U.S. minister to Belgium, Edwin Holland Terrell, represented the U.S. at the 1889-90 Brussels Conferences. President Benjamin Harrison submitted the Act of Brussels to the Senate, which ratified it. Leopold decorated Terrell for his services.

Under the guise of suppressing slavery, Leopold sent soldiers to the Congo. He established stock companies, traded on the Antwerp exchange, to exploit ivory and rubber, giving each a Congo "tax farming" district and giving collectors financial incentives for maximizing the extraction of ivory and rubber. These companies had interlocking directorates and straw men who held a 50 percent interest for the king. Companies were taxed 50 percent of their profits for the privilege of assessing and collecting taxes in the Congo, and the high fees they charged brought huge revenues to Belgium. Rubber and ivory poured through the Belgian port city of Antwerp.

Leopold decreed that all Congo land and products were his, including the natives and their property. Agents of the king conscripted natives into forced labor by murdering entire villages that refused to work, or taking their women and children as hostages. Brutal whipping was a lighter punishment as natives were shot, hanged, sexually mutilated, or starved for the crime of not meeting their tax quotas. Between the mass murders and fleeing tribes, the Congo lost much of its population, but Leopold got a steadily increasing supply of ivory and rubber. "The Congo State is the most unique government on earth, a commercial monopoly farmed by an autocrat," wrote a critic.

Bullets were strictly controlled and counted. A bullet could only be used to kill a native. Some claim that millions were murdered. To prove the proper use of bullets, Leopold decreed that the victim's right hand be cut off and produced. As bullets were misspent for hunting, or missed their human target, agents would hack off the right hands of living people. Firsthand accounts from missionaries with photographs of the masses of surviving natives with missing right hands eventually convinced the outside world that the Congo had to be wrested from ruthless Leopold.

Despite the weight of evidence proving that Leopold was a monster, there were sufficient big lies about his Congo humanitarianism to confuse the gullible. Leopold created The Congo Press Bureau, a very effective propaganda machine, which denied all charges. A 391-page book, published in 1905, dismissed critics with alternative explanations about native-on-native violence and praised Leopold's accomplishments, with pretty Theresienstadt-like pictures.

It was estimated that by 1906 Leopold's income from the Congo was $5 million annually. When the Belgian Parliament finally bought him out in 1908, Leopold and his descendants had made hundreds of millions of francs from 23 years of plundering the Congo. To this day, there are occasional attempts at reforming history's verdict, but the financial records prove his financial plunder beyond doubt.

Congo tax revenues paid for grand public works like the Triumphal Arch in the Parc du Cinquantenaire in Brussels, Antwerp's exquisite Central Station "Railway Cathedral," and the palatial Royal Museum for Central Africa in Trevuren, all built at a cost of severed hands. The turmoil in the Congo that continues to this day is King Leopold's legacy.

**The Income Tax**

Economists consider a 1797 levy by the Dutch Batavian Republic (Indonesia) as the first income tax. Prussia introduced income taxation in 1808. Britain imposed a temporary income tax in 1799 to help fund the Napoleonic War. Except for a short gap in 1802, it remained in place until after the Battle of Waterloo in 1815. Repeal in 1816 was accompanied by the greatest cheering and loudest exultation ever heard in Parliament, with celebrations and ringing of church bells. Upon motion of Parliament, the chancellor of the exchequer made a huge bonfire where all the income tax records were burned. "There was more celebration and more joy over abolition of the first income tax than there was over defeat of Napoleon at Waterloo," an historian told the House Ways and Means Committee. The early income tax was so hated because measuring income was subjective and somewhat arbitrary prior to development of modern accounting.

Britain reintroduced the income tax in 1842 to reduce import duties. Although intended as a temporary tax, it has remained in place ever since.

The concept of an income tax and its limitations is ancient. Plato wrote in *The Republic*, "when there is an income tax, the just man will pay more and the unjust less on the same amount of income." Jewish communities in Italy imposed an income tax on ghetto residents to pay their burden to the state, over 100 years before its adoption by Great Britain. It was a tax on *parnasa* (Hebrew: income), including rents, interest on money lending, and store receipts. However, these taxes are best described as "faculty" rather than "income" taxes because they directed an individual to pay taxes according to his faculty, or ability, based on assumptions as to his well-being. Measuring income prior to the nineteenth century was mathematically haphazard and unverifiable.

Hebrew books with voluminous tax laws and regulations were published on the Italian ghetto income tax. The seventeenth century rabbis urged moral and strict righteousness in paying the Jewish income tax and threatened excommunication for tax evasion. "Any man...should not seek ways to lighten his tax burden in any manner whatsoever....Nor should he find loopholes." The rabbinic prohibition against loopholes is the exact opposite of American doctrine which permits tax avoidance (but not evasion). The tax was needed to pay protection money to the Italian nobility for the right to remain in the ghetto relatively unmolested.

Catholic Church Catechism 2240, issued in 1992, made paying taxes a moral obligation, based on Romans 13:7, "If you owe taxes, pay taxes." The American Institute of Certified Public Accountants added compliance with tax obligations to its ethics rules in 1999. Treasury made this a requirement for practice before IRS in 1958.

The income tax is one of the most flexible and useful taxes. The redeeming value is its ability to raise large amounts of revenue. It can also be used as a weapon against inflation or to redistribute wealth. Adjusting rates and the taxable base at the high end influence savings and investment. Those same adjustments at the low end influence consumption. It has been overused to effect social and economic policies, another proof of its utility. No other single tax serves so many functions. As the most intrusive of taxes, it is heavily criticized:

> The tax has no Passover; the destroying angel visits every door, allows of the validity of no mark of blood on the lintel and side-posts, to induce him to pause in his destructive course; for the destroyer comes, with ferocious swoop, into our houses, to smite us and our first-born; no door is exempt from his dire visitations.
>
> —Col. John Grey, London, 1810

A Yale professor testified before Congress that Americans "need to get over their traditional feeling that taxes are a plague." The next day, the *Wall Street Journal* admonished the professor for comparing taxes to a plague. "If he had said that Americans think of taxes as a necessary evil, yes; as an abomination, yes; but a plague? No. Most Americans [know that] even the Biblical plagues finally came to an end."

**Fessenden's Law**

Is tax appeal an administrative or a judicial matter? It's only in modern times that taxpayers were allowed to address their grievances in a court of law. Through most of history, the only redress taxpayers had was an appeal to the tax collector himself. The cry of "no taxation without representation" was merely a slogan. The American colonists knew that having some minuscule representation in Parliament would not bring any relief from British taxation. Taxation after independence was sometimes just as unfair and onerous as the British levies.

The Whiskey Tax Rebellion protested a 1791 tax on moonshine. The tax ranged from 5 to 30 cents per gallon, depending on what it was distilled from and its proof. A gallon of moonshine without the tax sold for around 25 cents locally and 50 cents east of the mountains. The entire Allegheny region refused to comply, claiming they could not shift the tax to customers through higher prices. (Some said this was a tax on "poor man's currency" because moonshine barter was used in lieu of cash. Others said that they only opposed the intrusive collectors who snooped in barns, closets and cellars to catch evaders.) Opposition by southwestern Pennsylvania farmers turned violent. President Washington called on the state militia and put down the rebellion in 1794. He proved the federal government's ability to enforce its own laws. Henceforth, tax grievances would have to be settled through appeal. But what form would that appeal take?

Tax appeal falls under the doctrine of sovereign immunity. So access to courts can be blocked by statute. Several sections of the Internal Revenue Code, rewritten many times, codify a requirement that appeal must first be sought with the commissioner.

Section 7421 contains the oldest passage in today's Internal Revenue Code. It is a remnant of this doctrine, virtually unchanged from its original wording as passed in 1867: "…no suit for the purpose of restraining the assessment or collection of any tax shall be maintained in any court." This says that courts cannot intervene to prevent assessment or collection. It's commonly called The Anti-Injunction Act. The only modification since 1867 is that relief is sometimes available in Tax Court prior to paying the tax. Otherwise, a tax must be paid prior to seeking redress in court.

The Supreme Court decided in 1875 that tax collection trumps fairness. "[T]he payment of taxes has to be enforced by summary and stringent means against a reluctant and often adverse sentiment….a court should not thus interfere, as it would in any transaction between individuals [because] it has no power to apportion the tax or to make a new assessment." (The Tax Court *has* this power, a reason for sometimes avoiding that forum.) In a spurious explanation, the justices declared that should any court be able to restrain assessment or collection, "the very existence of the government might be placed in the power of a hostile judiciary." This may be the only time the court has worried about its own excesses.

Section 7421 was authored by Senator William Pitt Fessenden (R-ME). He was Finance Committee chairman from 1861 to 1867, with an absence to serve as treasury secretary from 1864 to 1865. His nickname was "Mr. Lincoln's Prime Minister." He was so revered that when he died in office in 1869, the Senate and House devoted half a day to eulogizing him, recorded in sixteen triple column pages of the *Congressional Globe*. Horace Greeley's *New York Tribune* wrote, "A just History of the war or the Union will give him a place beside the great Generals who have won the Union victories." A street in the northwest corner of Washington is named after him.

Fessenden believed taxation was an administrative matter. When presented with a clear case of abuse by tax collectors, the mild-mannered senator responded, "[T]his awful hard case is...now under the consideration of the Secretary, who has the power to relieve from this suffering, if on the whole, on examination, he thinks it best to do so." He then introduced Section 7421 as an amendment, which was accepted on a voice vote without any discussion.

Why was Fessenden so revered that Congress would pass a law on his word alone? As chairman of the Senate Finance Committee (before there was an Appropriations Committee), it fell upon him to navigate passage of tax laws and spending authorizations during the Civil War, on a scale which the nation had never before experienced. He championed passage of an income tax.

When Treasury Secretary Salmon Chase resigned in June 1864, public debt stood at $1.74 billion, only $817 million of which was loans, with more than $100 million coming due in October. Inflation was high. Gold dollars were trading between $2.25 and $2.85 in greenbacks, the Union's paper currency. (The back was printed in green ink instead of the usual black, making it harder to counterfeit.) Government credit was low; its bonds were selling at a substantial discount, and prospects for selling new issues were hopeless. A bond yielding six percent in gold coin meant sixteen percent interest in greenbacks with gold at 270 ($2.70 greenbacks). Lincoln needed a new treasury secretary who could instill badly needed confidence in the Union's finances. Though Fessenden was in poor health, under great pressure from Lincoln, he reluctantly accepted the position.

Fessenden ceased increasing the currency in circulation, thereby taming inflation. He couldn't raise the funds through banks, so he instituted the sale of Treasury debt directly to the public in denominations of $50 to $5,000. This was the first time Treasury sold debt directly to the public. Sherman's September 2, 1864 victory in Atlanta, his capture of Savannah in December, and Lincoln's November re-election instilled confidence that induced people to buy bonds, thus saving the Union from bankruptcy.

Fessenden's son (who lost a leg in the War; another son was killed) wrote a biography about his father, which noted the poor state of Union finances when his father became treasury secretary: "The armies of Grant and Sherman were stopped before Richmond and Atlanta for want of money." This statement is not corroborated by Civil War historians nor U.S. Grant's *Memoirs*. W.T. Sherman, in his *Memoirs* specifically states in August 1864 and again in September that his supplies were "ample." But Sherman relied on the advice of Prussian military theorist Carl von Clausewitz, supplying his army by seizing provisions from households and communities in his march to Savannah.

The Union also had a savior in the form of patriotic banker, Jay Cooke, who in the Civil War performed the role that Robert Morris had performed during the Revolutionary War. He successfully sold $500 million of bonds in 1862-1863, and following Lincoln's re-election and more Union battlefield victories, sold $600 million more in early 1865. Gold dollars fell to $1.98 in greenbacks.

Having saved the Union's finances, Fessenden returned to the Senate in March 1865. He chaired the Joint Committee on Reconstruction that drafted the Fourteenth Amendment, which guarantees rights of citizenship, including due process and equal protection by the states. He was the first and the most prominent undecided of seven Republican senators who voted against the removal of President Andrew Johnson after the House impeached him. It is believed that his influence convinced other Republicans to vote against removal. The other six senators failed to win re-election on account of their unpopular vote. Fessenden died in office before his term expired. John F. Kennedy picked the wrong hero when he chose Senator Edmund G. Ross as Andrew Johnson's savior for *Profiles in Courage*.

Why did this remarkable man foster a harsh "pay first, squawk later" tax policy? Perhaps the answer lies in the observation of his 1962 biographer: "The law was the law, and to subvert it with ideas of mercy, mitigating circumstances, and what-have-you, was to Fessenden's mind little short of sacrilege." There's also another reason. Treasury had little collection and enforcement mechanism in the nineteenth century, so pay first was the best way at that time to protect government revenue.

## California's Racist Gold Rush

In October 1876, three senators and three House members traveled to San Francisco under a congressional mandate to investigate Chinese immigration. They produced a 1,290-page document featuring dozens of interviews, including four Anti-Coolie Club leaders, but not one Chinese person. Among its conclusions, "[T]here is not sufficient brain capacity in the Chinese race to furnish motive powers for self-government. Upon the point of morals, there is no Aryan or European race which is not far superior to the Chinese as a class." The report detailed how California failed to discourage Chinese immigration through taxation.

The first California legislature enacted the Foreign Miners License Tax in April 1850, five months prior to becoming a state. It began as a $20 monthly levy on foreign miners who did not desire (or were prohibited by law) to become citizens. The purpose of this tax was foremost to reduce the number of Chinese and Latinos immigrating to or remaining in California, and secondly to exclude foreigners and reduce economic competition to whites mining for gold. The tax later varied from $3 to $8 per month, and the reduction from $20 substantially increased revenue.

At $20 a month, the tax raised just $34,150 in 1850. No one could afford $20, so evasion was a necessity. But when reduced to $4, it raised $185,759.35 in 1856 because miners could afford to pay it. (Proof again that more revenue may often be obtained with lower tax rates.)

The 20-year revenue from this tax was $5.1 million, averaging about 15 percent of the annual California budget, with over $2 million going each to the state and counties, and $1 million to the collectors. Chinese groups claim they paid over 90 percent of the total and though there is little substantive evidence supporting that claim, it appears true. Though applicable to all foreigners, the 1877 Congressional study revealed that in practice the tax was only collected from the Chinese. Besides, most Latinos fled south, making the Chinese by far the main target of this and other discriminatory taxes.

Enforcement was abusive and often violent. There were few months in which the ordinary miner earned enough to support himself at the high prices that prevailed in California during the gold rush. This was especially hard on the Chinese, who were relegated to gleaning uneconomic mines. Ruffians pretended to be state tax collectors, resulting in people paying the "tax" more than once. With no jails or prisons in California's wild mountain regions, frontier justice consisted of banishment, whipping, or execution. An October 12, 1852, resolution of miners in Sonora ordered foreigners out of mines. Frenchmen were forcibly driven from their mining claims. Americans assisting foreigners were threatened with confiscation of their mines, to be sold at auction on one hour's notice.

The California Supreme Court ruled the Foreign Miners License Tax constitutional in December 1850. Emboldened in its efforts to stop Chinese immigration, California in 1855 imposed a tax of $50 per person not eligible to become a U.S. citizen, payable by the owner of the ship that attempted to land them. In 1858, California prohibited ship captains from landing any person "of the Chinese or Mongolian races," subjecting them to a fine of $400 - $600 for each offense or three to twelve months imprisonment. It also made anyone employing or entering into partnership with a foreigner, liable for the foreign miners tax.

The legislature broadened the Foreign Miners License Tax in 1861 to read, "All foreigners not eligible to become citizens of the United States, residing in any mining district in this State, shall be considered miners," subject to the tax. It was pure racist legislation designed to rid areas of California of non-whites. The authorities soon arrested a Chinese washer-man, Ah Pong, for refusing to pay the tax, and jailed him for refusing forced labor on public roads to pay his tax debt. This time, the court ruled that it must first be established that the foreigner was engaged in mining. It could not be presumed that a foreigner by his mere presence was subject to the tax.

California reacted with the "Chinese Police Tax" in order "to protect Free White Labor against competition with Chinese Coolie Labor, and to discourage the immigration of the Chinese into the State of California." It was a $2.50 monthly levy on every "male and female of the Mongolian race" over age 18 who did not pay the foreign miners tax, except those engaged in the production and manufacture of sugar, rice, coffee and tea. Employers of Chinese were held liable for the unpaid tax of their employees.

The state passed two more racist bills in 1870. The first sought "the prevention of the coming to our shores of Chinese or Japanese prostitutes." It passed without any serious opposition. The second was titled, "An Act to prevent the importation of Chinese criminals, and to prevent the establishment of coolie slavery." By these acts, Oriental women were banned because they were deemed prostitutes, and men because they were deemed criminals.

Finally, Federal District Court Judge Ogden Hoffman struck down the Foreign Miners License Tax in 1871 because it violated the newly ratified Fourteenth Amendment of 1868 and the Civil Rights Act of 1870. This ended a dark episode in California history.

Undaunted, California's congressional delegation introduced and succeeded in having Congress pass the infamous Chinese Exclusion Act of 1882. It defined "Chinese laborers" as "both skilled and unskilled laborers *and Chinese employed in mining.*" [Italics added.]

**Coca-Cola and the Black Tax Collector**

The telephone excise tax was originally enacted in 1898 as a tax on a luxury item to help finance the Spanish-American War. Initially, it affected only the few and wealthy who had telephones. The tax was repealed, then reinstated to fund World War I. It was again repealed, then reinstated to fund World War II. A major campaign targeting the telephone excise tax as a "Spanish-American War" relic passed Congress in 2000, but President Clinton vetoed it. Cellphone and flat-rate services led to five circuit courts ruling the tax invalid as applied to long-distance charges that do not vary by both time and distance. IRS finally admitted defeat in 2006 and announced that it would cease enforcing that portion of the tax and issue refunds. The excise tax on local telephone service awaits repeal by Congress.

Another Spanish-American War revenue measure was a stamp tax on "proprietary medicines in general, or which are advertised...as remedies or specifics for any ailment, or as having any special claim to merit...." Coca-Cola's 1892 articles of incorporation state that the purpose of the corporation was to manufacture and sell a "medicinal article known as Coca-Cola." The company trumpeted "the tonic properties of the wonderful coca plant, and the famous cola nut." It advertised the product as curative of headache and nervous exhaustion. The company distributed clocks advertising Coca-Cola as "The Ideal Brain Tonic, Delicious Beverage, Specific for Headache, Relieves Exhaustion." Cocaine was a frequent ingredient in patent medicines of the day.

The medicinal ingredients and advertising led the collector of Internal Revenue for the District of Georgia to consider Coca-Cola, not a beverage, but a drug subject to tax. He sought to collect a $1.75 per gallon tax on the syrup, a very steep 1.4 cents per eight ounce glass of the diluted product, which sold for five cents. From July 1, 1898 to August 5, 1899, Coca-Cola paid $10,858.76 in tax, then sued Henry Rucker, Georgia's collector, for a refund. The tax would indicate that Coca-Cola sold less than 500 gallons of syrup per month, while company history boasts annual sales of 281,000 gallons at the end of the nineteenth century.

On the witness stand, Coca-Cola President Asa Candler was asked, "There is cocaine in it?" "A very small portion....a very small trace of it," admitted Candler, as he insisted that it was not medicine. The cocaine was a byproduct of coca leaf extract, an ingredient the company at that time considered essential to retain its trademark name, Coca-Cola.

The judge instructed the jury that the "only real question is whether, notwithstanding its use as a beverage,...the company holds it out to the public [as] medicinal in character. The act very clearly, in the opinion of the court, makes those preparations subject to tax that are held out by advertising matter...as medicinal in character, whether they are really so in themselves or not." With less than 15 minutes deliberation, the Atlanta jury gave Coca-Cola its refund. One researcher suggests Coca-Cola prevailed by arguing that, unlike medicine, carbonated sugar water is unhealthy.

The collector twice appealed the Coca-Cola ruling, but was denied. He argued jury nullification because the jury ignored the facts and the judge's instructions. The very short deliberation would not have allowed time to review even the eight-page Coca-Cola brochure included in the evidence, which clearly touted the beverage's medicinal qualities. Coca-Cola's connection with cocaine is preserved in excise tax history.

The town of Waleska, Georgia was so alarmed about the presence of cocaine that around 1912, it passed an ordinance making it illegal to sell Coca-Cola. Coca extract continued as a Coca-Cola ingredient until 1935. No one knows whether the ordinance was ever repealed, so it might still be illegal to enjoy a Coke in Waleska.

Perhaps the real reason Coca-Cola won is that Henry Rucker, collector of revenue for the District of Georgia, was black. The jurors were white. Internal Revenue had between 64 and 185 collectors at any one time between 1862 and 1953 (65 in 1902). Rucker was the only black man ever to hold the position of collector of revenue.

Rucker was born a slave in 1852. When the Civil War started, he was owned by Dr. William King of Athens, Georgia, the father-in-law of legendary *Atlanta Constitution* managing editor Henry W. Grady. In describing his lineage, the *Atlanta Journal* noted that his mother *belonged* to Rev. Richard Golden...and his father *belonged* to Captain Clayton." [Italics added.]

In an effort to solicit black votes for the Republican Party, President William McKinley appointed 70 blacks to federal posts throughout the country. That could be unhealthy in the old South. Isaiah H. Loftin, the black postmaster of Hogansville, Georgia, lasted four months. He quit after surviving three gunshot wounds and the burning of the building he owned and used as a post office. Of the would-be assassins, the *Atlanta Constitution* wrote unsympathetically, "[I]t was not their fault that the bullets aimed at him did not reach a vital spot."

Rucker was familiar with the Atlanta Internal Revenue collector's office, having worked there from 1880-1885 and 1889-1893. He was active in Republican politics, a delegate to the 1880 Republican National Convention at age 28, and succeeded in carrying the entire Georgia delegation for McKinley after a bitter fight at the 1896 Republican Convention. In July 1897, McKinley rewarded him with the plum federal patronage job in the state at a salary of $4,500.

Immediately upon hearing of his nomination, the Georgia congressional delegation went to McKinley to "protest against the appointment of a negro" and complain about "the barber," a reference to a Decatur Street barber shop he opened in the 1880s. Racist cartoons were printed on the front page of Atlanta newspapers denouncing his appointment. One showed a mob of blacks with job applications in hand descending on a "Rucker Barber" storefront. The *Atlanta Constitution* featured most stories about his appointment on the inside pages, together with racist cartoons like one titled "The Forthcoming Triumph of Barber Rucker" and editorialized, "The appointment of a colored man as revenue collector of Georgia furnishes no just cause for complaint on behalf of those who [voted for] Mr. McKinley." The *Constitution's* front page was reserved for more important Southern headlines, like "Thrilling Story of the Hanging. How Dr. Ryder Was Lynched by Fifteen Men."

Rucker was a prosperous and successful businessman, proven by the fact that he was able to post a $75,000 bond for the position of collector plus an extra $15,000 bond for custodianship of the customs house. He owned the barber shop, but he obviously didn't work at the chairs. His appointment had the support of Mayor Charles Collier, most of the city and county officers and many outstanding businessmen. One Atlanta society woman was so incensed at these endorsements that she threatened to rent her fashionable house at 409 Peachtree Street to Rucker. The *Atlanta Journal*, tepid in its approach to the appointment, asserted that what was made to appear as endorsements were merely testimonies to his good character. It called his barber shop, "a place exclusively for the better class of negroes." The Georgia Republican Executive Committee adopted a resolution, "Resolved. That we condemn the discrimination against whites."

As Georgia collector of revenue, he had over 100 men working under him. Just six white revenue employees resigned rather than work for a black man, a big disappointment to hate-mongers who predicted mass resignations. Apprehension that he would replace whites proved unfounded, as only about ten percent of employees were black. He hired the best qualified and earned a sterling reputation. He was invited to march in the 1901 presidential inaugural parade in Washington as an "Aide with rank of Colonel" and thereafter was often referred to as Colonel Rucker. Of necessity, the *Savannah Tribune* had to quote the *Washington Bee* in order to praise a black man in 1904, "Mr. Rucker is a man of spotless integrity and unimpeachable character, and has been, and is now, a faithful, upright and efficient officer."

Serving under three presidents, Rucker discharged his duties with honesty and efficiency, while enduring 13 years of racist protests against his holding office. A campaign was mounted after William Howard Taft became president in 1909. Replacing Rucker became an issue in the 1910 Georgia congressional election. The urgency came from the 1909 corporation income tax. Returns were due on March 15, 1910 and taxes were payable between June 15 and July 10. When the work of the Bureau of Internal Revenue only dealt with customs and excises, few had to deal with the collector. But the corporation income tax would bring the collector in contact with the leading businessmen in Georgia. That couldn't be tolerated. So, in September 1910, President Taft replaced Rucker with a white man.

## Sin Taxes

The first U.S. attempt at using taxation for non-revenue purposes was the 1914 Harrison Narcotic Act. As amended in 1919, Congress imposed a $300 per pound tax on the manufacture of opium for smoking, an annual occupation tax of $24 on narcotics importers and manufacturer, $12 on wholesalers, $6 on retailers, and $3 on physicians, dentists and veterinarians administering narcotics, and a one-cent-per-ounce stamp tax on the sale or importation of opium, coca leaves, heroin, and the like. A $2,000 fine and five-year prison sentence awaited anyone violating the law or filling prescriptions without using forms supplied by Internal Revenue. From 1919 through 1928, the U.S. Treasury collected $1 million annually from the opium tax. There was a separate tax on marijuana.

The federal narcotic drug laws were significantly overhauled in 1930. The changes exempted importation of de-cocainized coca leaves "to make available an increased quantity of certain extracts derived from coca leaves which enter into the manufacture of a certain beverage widely used in the U.S. and foreign countries." The Internal Revenue Code of 1939 provided for taxes on opium and marijuana, and continued the exemption for Coca-Cola's coca leaves. These excise taxes were repealed in 1970 after the Supreme Court overturned the conviction of hallucinogenic drug enthusiast, Dr. Timothy F. Leary, ruling it violated the Fifth Amendment privilege against self-incrimination.

Jonathan Swift was the first to propose taxing sex, in his classic, *Gulliver's Travels*: "The highest tax was upon men who are the greatest favourites of the other sex, and the assessments according to the number and natures of the favours they have received; for which they are allowed to be their own vouchers." Today, Texas imposes a $5 per customer admission fee on "sexually oriented businesses" (SOB tax). It's expected to raise $60 million annually. Police in Lubbock arrested eight Chippendale dancers in February 2007 just as they were about to perform before 1,100 women because the club hadn't complied with SOB.

Arizona tried some unusual short-lived experiments with taxation. It enacted a license tax and a luxury sales tax on hemp and marijuana vendors in 1983: $10 per ounce on cannabis, or $500 for three cannabis plants and $500 for each additional cannabis plant. This was supplemented in 1995 by a law requiring marijuana growers to obtain a license for $100. The intent was to give the state another weapon against hemp and marijuana. After a justice of the peace interpretation that payment of the marijuana tax protected dealers from further prosecution, more than 80 marijuana dealer licenses were sold in four months. Embarrassed by the *New York Times* headline, "Meet Arizona's Happiest Taxpayers," it quickly repealed these taxes, but not before collecting a total of $327,008 during the thirteen years it was in effect. Twenty-three states have laws taxing marijuana, which are collected when one is caught in possession of the illegal substance.

In an effort to promote cleaner alternative fuels, Arizona offered in 2000 to pay one-third of the cost of any vehicle which had the ability to burn both gasoline and propane. On a $45,000 Chevrolet Tahoe, the state offered $7,000 to cover the SUV's propane-conversion gear, waived $2,400 of sales tax, and exempted the vehicle from ever having to pay the $600 annual registration fee. Vehicles that only burned alternative fuels had higher incentives, as much as a $15,000 savings on a $21,000 natural gas Honda Civic. Until its emergency repeal, the program cost Arizona nearly $600 million, ten percent of the state's $6 billion annual budget, instead of the $3 - $10 million the legislature had estimated. All this occurred without any requirement to use alternative fuel or keep the vehicle in Arizona.

In Tennessee, crime really pays. The state imposes a $12 tax on all bail bonds, plus another $12 tax for an appeal bond. You must pay the tax to get out of jail. There is also a litigation tax — $29.50 upon conviction in criminal cases, and lesser taxes for bringing a civil suit (or losing a civil suit initiated by the city, county or state). Challenge that parking ticket and you'll owe a tax, even if you win. Tennessee raises close to $2 million annually from the bail bond tax alone.

**Window Tax**

In order to deal with a financial crisis resulting from inflation due to conflicts in Ireland and the Continent, Scotland imposed a tax on windows beginning in 1696. This resulted in bricking-in and camouflaging as many windows as possible to avoid the tax, without shutting residents in smothering darkness. People painted windows in place of real ones. The Scots were promised that this drastic tax was an emergency measure and would be repealed when the emergency ended, but it lasted 155 years. Though derided as a tax on light and air, it was actually a crude, simple method for estimating real estate values to be taxed.

Other countries experimented with taxes on windows (and doors), including the U.S. A 1798 property tax signed into law by President John Adams valued homes by, among other attributes, "the number and dimensions of their windows." It was a direct tax upon dwelling houses, land, and slaves; a national property tax, apportioned among the states on the basis of population with graduated rates from 2/10 of one percent to a full one percent of value. There was fierce opposition in Bucks and Northampton Counties north of Philadelphia, where assessors caught measuring windows were doused with hot water. Taxpayers won "The Hot Water War." The tax was not implemented.

When local authorities realized that they could not enforce this direct tax, they arrested some protesters. Fifty-year-old John Fries led about 140 armed men to the jail and forced their release. No one was killed or injured, but Fries was tried for treason, convicted and sentenced to be hanged — an incredible charge and punishment for resisting a tax. Chief Justice William Rehnquist commented in 1992, "Had he committed a similar act in our day, he probably would have been charged with obstruction of justice." President Adams pardoned Fries, and thereby helped shape constitutional law on treason.

The Fries Rebellion ranks with Shay's Rebellion in 1786 and the Whiskey Rebellion in 1794 as violent tax protests in the young republic. Its most enduring legacy is Fries' unfair trial presided over by Supreme Court Justice Samuel Chase, while assisting the local court. The injustice to Fries became the first of three articles of impeachment against Chase in 1805. Chase narrowly escaped conviction and removal by the Senate, resulting in our tradition that judges should not be impeached for the content of their rulings from the bench. This forms the cornerstone that makes our judiciary an independent and equal branch of government, courtesy of a window tax.

## Beard Tax

As part of his efforts to modernize Russia, Peter the Great was determined to have a shaven society. The beard had become unfashionable in Europe, but it was still considered an attribute of manhood in Russia. In 1705, he issued a fiat that the army and all citizens, from nobles to serfs, should shave their beards. After allowing some time for people to get used to the idea, those who chose to retain their beards had to pay a tax of one hundred rubles. Priests and serfs could retain theirs upon payment of one copeck every time they passed through the city gate.

The receipt for payment was a small copper token called the *borodováia*, or "the bearded," which bore the image of a nose, mouth, and moustache with a long bushy beard. Those who refused to pay the tax, or could not produce this receipt upon entry into a town, were thrown into prison.

Peter's beard tax was not only daring, but successful; an early example of how taxation could be used to change social behavior. That success was partly attributed to his reputation for ruthlessness. He executed almost every Strelitz (Moscow militia) in 1698 and murdered his own son in 1718. Discontent with the beard edict was widespread, but men thought it wiser to pay the tax or cut off their beards than risk ruthless Peter cutting off their heads.

**Tax Cheating**

In many countries, taxes are negotiable. In India, one of the best jobs is auditor for the Revenue Department. The job pays very little, but the tips are great. In Israel, a revenue agent who accepts bribes to "fix" a tax assessment is called a *macher*, a deal-maker. In Indonesia, you can get a receipt for your bribe so that you can be reimbursed by your company. The worldwide practice of bribery prompted *New York Times* columnist Thomas Friedman to praise the U.S. "Do you know what a luxury it is to be able to start a business or get a license without having to pay off some official?"

Prior to World War II, many governments required businesses to maintain bound journals and ledgers with numbered pages. Each page bore an official government seal, sometimes requiring affixing of revenue stamps. This was a system based on French and Spanish laws, practiced from Mexico to Poland to Iran. Iran still used this system under the Shah and required that only Farsi language be used. Any erasures or alterations were penalized and resulted in arbitrary tax assessments. Journal entries had to be made daily, in chronological order, and the ledger posted shortly thereafter. Errors could be corrected only by an adjusting entry. Enterprising businessmen kept two sets of books.

Some Arab countries levy *zakat*, a religious tax. In Saudi Arabia, the Department of Zakat and Income Tax levies a 2½ percent zakat on the net worth of Saudis. Non-Saudis are subject to 20 percent income tax, based on audited financial statements prepared by a recognized public accountant. Failure to submit audited statements results in an assessment under the "arbitrary profit method," which is negotiable. Zakat is voluntary in Egypt, but there is an income tax. In the recent past, there was also a 2½ percent *jihad* tax, their term for a war levy.

Prior to Margaret Thatcher's tax reforms, British taxes were so high that people refused to work for cash, preferring barter or leisure. A March 8, 1978 *New York Times* article, "Tax me, I'm British," described the absurd results of the British system, where rates reached 83 percent on earned income and 98 percent on investment income. Tax-free perks made the system tolerable. The tax-free company car was credited with keeping British Leyland Motor operating. Inland Revenue recently published documents showing that Winston Churchill cancelled a 1931 lecture tour of the United States after advisers warned him that the earnings would raise his average tax rate to about 60 percent.

British taxes went back up under Tony Blair's Labor Government. The Rolling Stones scrapped four British concerts in August 1998, reportedly claiming it would cost them $20 million in taxes and make their entire European tour a money-loser. Perhaps the real reason was that they simply hated taxes. The *Daily Mail* reported that the Stones created trusts in Holland to receive their royalty income and became British tax expatriates. The result was that from 1986 until 2006, they paid just £3.9 million in taxes on £242 million of income, about 1.6 percent.

The Beatles complained about confiscatory British taxes in their 1966 song, "Tax Man." Cole Porter wrote a song, "No Wonder Taxes Are High," for his 1958 musical, *Aladdin*. Porter also included lyrics, "you're next year's taxes," in his 1934 list song, "You're the Top" from *Anything Goes*.

Compared with most industrialized countries, the U.S. is a tax haven. A tax lawyer specializing in taxation of foreigners told how he explains to his European clients that they don't have to go to great lengths to hide income because the U.S. rates are so much lower than Europe. However, for his South American clients, he begins by explaining what taxes are.

Tax cheating is a national pastime in Italy. Italian lawyers declare less income than Italian writers. Restaurant owners less than schoolteachers. Jewelry store owners less than the yearly rent on a small apartment. Tax audits show 90 percent of hotels cheat on taxes. Italy assigns each business and vocation a minimum income. Proprietors must file forms proving that they earned less. Still, tax litigation drags out for as long as 15 years, and a tax amnesty is declared about every ten years. So, if caught, tax cheats wait for the next amnesty to be declared to settle their cases. Prime minister and billionaire media mogul Silvio Berlusconi had been charged with bribing tax police, false bookkeeping and tax evasion. He was acquitted (and the statute of limitations expired) on some charges while guilty verdicts were overturned on appeal.

Tax cheating is also pandemic in New York. Large numbers of well-known established restaurants kept expanding, while reporting little or no profit year after year. When New York sent auditors, 96 percent of the restaurants were shown to be skimming cash. Some reported no cash sales at all.

In 1987, New York City began to subpoena records from car garages. Officials found that ten percent of the cars were registered outside New York state. There are many advantages to registering a car out-of-state. The sales tax was 8¼ percent in the city — among the highest in the nation. But the main reason for registering a car out-of-state is that New York City auto insurance costs about three times more than it does elsewhere.

To find out where the owners lived, investigators checked income tax records, telephone directories and building directories near where the cars were usually parked. They sent notices asking car owners to explain why they had out-of-state license plates yet lived in the city. Penalties for those caught were assessment of 8¼ percent sales tax, annual registration fees, and insurance problems. Interest and penalties were added to all assessments. If residents registered their cars outside New York, might they be filing income tax as non-residents? They sent auditors to work on that, too.

## The Judicial Tax

Alexander Hamilton, in *The Federalist Papers*, explained the function of the judicial branch. "The executive...holds the sword...The legislature...commands the purse...The judiciary...has no influence over either the sword or the purse...and must ultimately depend upon the aid of the executive arm even for the efficacy of its judgments...." Only, the courts don't agree.

In 1987, unelected tenured District Court Judge Russell Clark ordered Kansas City, Missouri, property taxes raised from $2.05 to $4.00 per $100 of assessed valuation and ordered a 1½ percent surcharge on state income taxes on city workers and residents. That the Missouri constitution barred a rate higher than $3.25 without a two-thirds super majority of voters was no barrier to Judge Clark. He wanted to fund his school desegregation order and was frustrated that voters had rejected, on four separate occasions in 1986 and 1987, property tax rate increases and a bond proposal needed to fund his order. Judge Clark also decided that the city must spend $461 million initially. He rejected cheaper alternatives.

The judicial tax imposed on Kansas City was upheld by the Eighth Circuit Court of Appeals and by a 5-4 decision by the U.S. Supreme Court. The state was required to pay 75 percent and the city 25 percent of the cost. Congress made loud noises and held hearings, but took no action.

The plan was astonishing for its extravagance. Judge Clark increased salaries for educational faculty and staff. He ordered the city to build 17 schools with air-conditioned classrooms, a planetarium, greenhouses and terrariums with animals, a 100-acre model farm with a petting zoo and air-conditioned meeting room for 104 people, a Model United Nations wired for language translation, broadcast-capable radio and television studios with an editing and animation lab, a temperature-controlled art gallery, movie-editing and screening rooms, a 3,500-square-foot dust-free diesel mechanics room, a 25-acre wildland area, Olympic-sized swimming pools with six diving boards, a padded wrestling room, a classical Greek theater, a gymnastic center stocked with professional equipment and an eight-lane indoor track.

This spending blitz included hiring philosophy teachers for seventh graders, private violin lessons, and a world-class Russian fencing coach, who took his high school athletes to matches in Europe and Africa. One school boasted 900 computers for its 1,000 students.

During more than 15 years of court administration, this experiment cost $2 billion. It was a colossal failure. The schools became even more segregated, with 80 percent minorities. In May 2000, the Kansas City School District became the first big-city school district ever to lose its accreditation. Its schools flunked every one of Missouri's 11 academic performance standards.

To the very end, Judge Clark refused to acknowledge his failure, insisting that his desegregation plan was on track and merely needed more time. Finally, in June 1995, the U.S. Supreme Court told Clark that his unproven theory of "desegregative attractiveness" had to end. The only real change was the make-up of the Supreme Court. Conservative Clarence Thomas had replaced liberal Thurgood Marshall. So, the 5-4 decision of 1987 upholding the judicial tax swung to a 1995 decision 5-4 against it. The Clinton administration unsuccessfully argued for continuation of court supervision.

*Missouri v. Jenkins* remains the clearest example of a court that seizes power by raising revenue to accomplish its own agenda. Judge Clark never had to answer or apologize for his failure, nor did the Supreme Court, which validated his actions. The judicial tax is clearly taxation without representation that disregards over 200 years of constitutional history and fundamental tenets of democracy.

**The Public Authority**

Robert Moses was New York's "Master Builder." The Long Island Expressway, Harlem River Drive, Major Deegan Expressway, Van Wyck Expressway, Cross-Bronx Expressway, Brooklyn-Queens Expressway, Grand Central Parkway, Belt Parkway, Triborough Bridge, Verrazano Bridge, Throgs Neck Bridge, Henry Hudson Bridge, Whitestone Bridge, Jones Beach, Shea Stadium, Lincoln Center, the United Nations headquarters, the 1939 World's Fair, the 1964 World's Fair – he built them all, and much more. State parks and play areas from Niagara Falls to Montauk Point, and massive housing developments. He built 35 highways, 12 bridges, and two hydroelectric dams.

The Public Authority was first created in Elizabethan England. It's called "Authority" because Parliament's enabling legislation began with the words, "Authority is hereby given." (Had it been invented in the U.S., it probably would have been called a "Whereas.")

Originally, authorities in the United States were created to construct and operate a single public project, issue bonds to pay for that project, which when retired would eliminate the tolls or fees, turn the project over to the city and go out of existence. The Port of New York and New Jersey Authority was established in 1921 as the first to have a perpetual existence.

A public authority is a corporation created and backed by the government. It can issue tax-exempt municipal bonds to raise capital at low interest. Some possess the power of eminent domain (seizure of private property) and even their own police force. Some are self-perpetuating, because the existence of bonds creates a legally enforceable mandate to continue the authority's operation. So the person who heads the public authority wields great power from the financing capital and toll or service revenues generated by the authority.

The Triborough Authority is a 1933 creation of the New York State legislature upon request of New York City. Robert Moses was its first chairman, and he remained chairman because he also controlled the majority of appointments to its governing board. The single-project formula was originally planned for the Triborough Bridge. The mayor, legislature, and the press reminded citizens that bridge tolls would be removed once the bonds had been paid. But Moses had other plans for those revenues.

He wanted to use the profits to borrow money at low tax-exempt rates in perpetuity. His authority had an annual profit of $4.5 million, which at four percent and some cushion, could float $81 million of bonds in 1933. That extra fortune could be used to build more toll bridges, earning more profit, enabling the issuance of more bonds. Moses only required that he be allowed to hold on to the money, not pay off the bonds and turn over paid up projects to the city.

He convinced the New York legislature to grant the Triborough Bridge Authority the power to make contracts, refinance bonds which had not yet matured and use the proceeds for any corporate purpose. The legislature had no idea that Moses had tricked them. The Constitution prohibits states from passing laws which impair the obligation of contracts (Article I, Section 10). This rendered the 40-year life span limit on the authority meaningless. He could issue 40-year bonds and refinance them in the 39th year, or sooner, with new 40-year bonds. The U.S. Constitution's provision on contracts granted his authority a perpetual existence. It would never have to turn its bridges over to the city.

Moses made Triborough an autonomous and sovereign governmental power, an independent fourth branch of government, unaccountable to the electorate, and exempt from checks and balances. It has its own flag, great seal, and license plates; its own uniformed officers, some of whom bear arms; a fleet of yachts, automobiles and trucks. It owns Randall's Island, its private domain (jointly with the City Parks Department, which Moses also headed). Most important, toll booth collections provide it with revenue.

The revenues and power of his authority were used to build massive projects of beauty and efficiency, while molding New York into his vision. With the power of eminent domain, he could build most anything, almost anywhere.

New York City's first four bridges — Brooklyn, Williamsburg, Queensborough, and Manhattan — are toll-free. But New York City's highways lead directly into Triborough toll crossings, not to the free crossings. Like razors that manufacturers give away for free, making their profit on the sale of blades, Robert Moses' free highways feed vehicles to his toll projects. His bridges and tunnels still charge tolls on projects that were paid for long ago. These tolls — user fees far exceeding the cost of operations — are a form of government taxation, no different from gasoline tax.

Robert Moses combined political acumen with eminent domain power, revenue sources, construction skills, ambition, and a great sense of public service to promote projects that politicians could not. His political cunning rendered his enemies ineffective. When Stuyesant Town, Cross Bronx Expressway, and Lincoln Center displaced tens of thousands of city residents, politicians could blame Robert Moses for the dislocations while reveling in the glorious results.

Though Triborough was his private empire, Moses was assiduously honest. Billions of public dollars passed through his hands. When he died in 1981 at age 92, he left an estate worth under $50,000.

His masterful work remains controversial. Through eminent domain, he displaced up to one million people. The Cross Bronx Expressway makes it easy (when not gridlocked) to transverse the Bronx, but contributed greatly to its urban decay. Although it would have defaced lower Manhattan's skyline, he had planned to build a Brooklyn-Battery Bridge because of his preference for bridges — visible monuments rather than invisible underground tunnels. In one of the few successful oppositions to Moses, Mayor LaGuardia forced him to stick with the original plan for the Brooklyn-Battery Tunnel instead of defacing lower Manhattan's skyline.

He refused to include mass transit in his plans because it was unprofitable. It cost $500 million to build the Long Island Expressway in 1955. Urban planners unsuccessfully begged Moses to spend an additional $20 million to acquire right-of-way and lay a heavier foundation down the center of the highway for future railroad tracks. He refused to consider an extra $2 million for right-of-way acquisitions on the $30 million construction cost of the Van Wyck Expressway in the late 1940s to allow a subway to reach Kennedy Airport. On his parkways, he built the bridge overpasses 11 feet above the road, guaranteeing that buses, which need 12 feet of clearance, could never use the roads he had built.

The Port of New York and New Jersey Authority lacked the independent autocracy of Robert Moses. It lost money until 1931, when it was given control of the Holland Tunnel, which had opened in 1927. Among its assets were two money-losing bridges connecting Staten Island to New Jersey. Those bridges could become profitable if there was a bridge connection from Staten Island to Brooklyn.

Only Triborough Authority had the right to build that connection, and Robert Moses used that to full advantage. The Port Authority would pay for construction of the Verrazano Narrows Bridge. Triborough would lease and operate it, maintain it, and have absolute control, including the right to buy it. Robert Moses built his greatest bridge with the Port Authority's money. That allowed him to use Triborough's cash to build the Throgs Neck Bridge. Each toll bridge increased Triborough's net income and power.

The Port Authority was also tapped to fulfill the desires of powerful business and political interests. In the late 1950s, the chairman of Chase Manhattan Bank, David Rockefeller, sought to revitalize lower Manhattan's financial district. He built One Chase Plaza and conceived of a World Trade Center. After his brother, Nelson, was elected governor, a plan was hatched to have the Port Authority build it. As a bi-state authority, the approval of New Jersey's governor was required. His price was that Port Authority would take over the bankrupt Hudson and Manhattan Railroad commuter line, which they renamed, PATH (Port Authority Trans-Hudson), and build a major container port in Elizabeth, N.J.

Eminent domain proceedings cleared the 16-acre site. To keep the World Trade Center from becoming a vacant financial disaster, the majority of initial tenants were government agencies. Political attempts to require the Port Authority to contribute more to public transit beyond PATH were overturned by the Supreme Court because of bond covenants, relying on that constitutional limitation prohibiting states from impairing contracts.

Without Moses, there would be no Jones Beach or Flushing Meadow Park (formerly the city dump). New York would not have the great highways, bridges and tunnels, and United Nations headquarters that help it retain its premier position among the world's cities. It is alas too late to change the layout of New York from the world that Moses built, and traffic gridlock is worse for his adamant refusal to accommodate mass transit. During his reign, money flowed freely, without accountability, fed by the tax revenues of bridge and tunnel tolls that he controlled.

After Robert Moses resigned in 1968, the Triborough Bridge and Tunnel Authority became part of New York's Metropolitan Transportation Authority. Tolls were raised exponentially, and the extra revenue now subsidizes the city's public transportation. The model he created has been duplicated throughout the U.S. as an indirect means of raising taxes to fund projects.

Robert Moses, the master builder, never learned to drive a car.

CHAPTER SIX

# Tax 'Em, My Boy, Tax 'Em

*Tax 'em, my boy, tax 'em.*
   —Felix Frankfurter to William O. Douglas

Taxation with representation doesn't assure good tax policy. Our present tax system is the result of many battles. The practice of using the tax law to benefit special interests originated with salt tax bounties paid to fishermen in the eighteenth century. Senator Nelson Aldrich used tariffs to turn taxation into a graft machine in the nineteenth century. The twentieth century income tax introduced politicians to previously unimaginable powers — advancing social goals, punishing enemies, rewarding friends, and sophisticated means for political and personal self-enrichment.

Andrew Jackson became one of our greatest presidents because he triumphed in crises involving the Second Bank of the United States and the Nullification Movement. He succeeded despite fierce opposition from the Senate's Great Triumvirate: Henry Clay, Daniel Webster and John C. Calhoun. It would have been easier for Jackson to simply compromise, but the old general instead chose to defeat them in political battles. Both crises involved taxes.

### The Monster Bank

In the early 1800s, the Second Bank of the United States was part of the tax-collection machinery that today belongs to the Internal

Revenue Service. Monies owed to the federal government — including tariffs and other taxes — had to be deposited with the bank in a currency or state bank note that it approved of. It was a publicly traded, private bank and doubled as our nation's central bank. It was like a combined IRS, Federal Reserve Bank and regular bank.

President Andrew Jackson was politically opposed to a central bank, and he believed that this bank was corrupt. So in 1832, he vetoed Congress' legislation to re-charter the bank, which was to expire in 1836. As a result, the bank threw its support behind Henry Clay, who ran against Jackson in the 1832 presidential election.

Jackson won re-election and claimed that his victory was a mandate from the people to abolish the bank before its charter lapsed. Unable to get Congress to revoke the charter, Jackson tried to rescind the bank's authorization to collect taxes and withdraw the $10 million that the U.S. had on deposit, sprinkling it among smaller regional banks that constituted his base of supporters, which became known as "pet banks." Without this deposit base, the Second Bank of the United States would go bust.

Jackson sought support from his cabinet in a March 19, 1833 memo. Attorney General Roger B. Taney wrote a response dated April 3 expressing "strong doubts whether the bank continued to be a safe depository for the public money" and arguing that the government could "dismiss it at once," in which event Taney preferred distributing the revenue among "judiciously selected" state institutions.

Seven weeks after Taney's letter, on May 20, Treasury Secretary Louis McLane delivered a 91-page manuscript opining that the bank should not be re-chartered without reorganization. McLane admonished that only the Treasury secretary, not the president, had the power to remove deposits, to be exercised according to his sense of duty. He felt no adequate reason existed for removal because the bank was solvent and state banks were unsafe.

Jackson decided to replace his treasury secretary. He named Secretary of State Edward Livingston as ambassador to France, fulfilling Livingston's desire for that position. On June 1, Jackson promoted McLane to secretary of state and appointed William J. Duane as his new treasury secretary.

The president sent two communications to Duane on June 26 notifying him to discontinue using the bank by September 15 "at the furthest." Taking note of McLane's contrary opinion on who held power to remove deposits, Jackson concluded he took "upon himself the responsibility."

The bank was a formidable adversary. It began demonstrating its capacity for trouble by denying credit to Boston merchants, who needed a million dollars to pay duties on cargoes out on the wharves. This was accomplished by discontinuing discounts and demanding return of bank balances held in state banks. The bank held this power under its tax-depository authority and used it to cripple commerce in Boston. It was intended as a show of force should Jackson proceed with his plan.

Jackson held a cabinet meeting at which he presented the strongest evidence he had of the bank's moral unfitness: secret loans to congressmen, payoffs to newspaper editors, and $60,000 spent on anti-Jackson propaganda. Within his own administration, Treasury Chief Clerk Asbury Dickins was allowed to settle a debt to the Bank of the United States for 50 cents on the dollar and Postmaster General William T. Barry received generous extensions on a loan.

Taney and Levi Woodbury (Navy) supported him, but McLane, Duane and Lewis Cass (War) opposed. Barry was absent. So on September 14, Jackson suggested that Duane retire, which he refused. Five days later, Jackson fired Duane and appointed Taney as treasury secretary. Taney gave immediate official notice that government deposits would not be made in the bank after September 30, 1833.

Daniel Webster had "borrowed" $32,000 from the bank. In July 1832, as this crisis began, he demanded of bank president Nicholas Biddle, a $10,000 loan that should not be recorded on the bank's records. The great orator sent a letter to Biddle on December 21, 1833, "I believe my retainer has not been renewed or *refreshed* as usual. If it be wished that my relation to the Bank should be continued it may be well to send me the usual retainers."

Henry Clay owed the bank $1,000, and he "referred" others to the bank for extraordinary favors. Georgia's John Forsyth was the first senator to stand up for Jackson. He owed the bank $20,000 which he could not pay, and offered to deed his property in that amount.

The bank retaliated by tightening credit throughout the land, creating a recession. It hoped that the ensuing suffering would bring a storm of protest, threatening a panic or actually creating one. The protest and blame would fall on Jackson and ruin him. After all,

McLane's 91-page manuscript had warned this might happen. The administration would be forced to reverse course.

Taney predicted that if virtue were to prevail and vice overthrown, no other president besides Andrew Jackson would have the courage to carry to the death a fight with the bank. Indeed, Jackson claimed he received one or two anonymous letters a day threatening assassination if he failed to restore deposits. Pro-bank forces, led by Henry Clay, censured Jackson for refusing to turn over bank documents that he had shared with his cabinet, using a theory we today call "executive privilege." This remains the only time the Senate has ever censured a president.

The Jackson administration steered the nation past the shoals of panic and freed it from a corrupt financial institution. In effect, Andrew Jackson put the tax collection agency, the IRS of its time, out of business. It wasn't until 1862, that a new tax collection agency named, Bureau of Internal Revenue, was created.

Jackson rewarded Taney for his support in the Bank War by appointing him chief justice of the Supreme Court to succeed John Marshall. While Marshall ruled in favor of the bank on two occasions (his famous aphorism, "The power to tax involves the power to destroy" dealt with a ruling in favor of the bank), Taney's appointment would lessen the possibility of a judicial reprieve for the bank. Taney served the court with distinction from 1936 until 1864, marred by the 1857 decision in *Dred Scott*. Vice President Martin Van Buren succeeded Jackson as president and that assured a veto of any legislative resurrection.

If not for Jackson, the bank might still be here today. Probably, it would have undergone reform so that it wouldn't become like Japan's *Okurasho*, the Ministry of Finance. No institution in Japan has more power, nor is there any comparable government entity with such concentrated powers in any industrialized democracy. The destruction rather than reform of the bank denied the United States a central bank just as it was becoming rapidly industrialized. Had it survived, it might today be the tax collection agency, more feared than IRS.

All that is left of the Second Bank of the United States is a magnificent Greek revival temple where a beautiful portrait gallery collection of government-owned art work is on display. Be sure to see it when you visit Philadelphia. The bank's president, Nicholas Biddle, was an admirer of Greek architecture, and the 1824 temple was constructed to his whim. Biddle's Greek revival country manor in Andalusia is also a tourist attraction.

**The Tariff**

In its first 150 years, the United States' main revenue sources were import tariffs, excise taxes and the sale of public lands.

Tariffs were every bit as politically controversial as income tax is today. Should we have free trade? Should tariffs be used for raising revenue? Should tariffs be used to protect U.S. industry? The industrialized Northern states favored protective tariffs. The agrarian South opposed this because it added to the cost of goods. Complex tariff schedules taxed luxury goods at high rates as a crude method to build some progressivity into this levy. Many goods entered free of tariff. Widespread abuses generated graft, political patronage and protected monopolies.

The only president to write a book on taxes was William McKinley who wrote a 300-page tome, *The Tariff*. He named Henry Clay as the founder of the protective tariff system. The Tariff of 1824 was framed under Clay's direction, as he declared, "The sole object of the tariff is to tax the produce of foreign industry with a view to promoting American industry."

The 1828 "Tariff of Abominations" marked the origin of serious divisions between North and South and the doctrine of "nullification." Following unsatisfactory tariff reductions in 1832, South Carolina passed the Ordinance of Nullification, a law declaring that the new tariff was unconstitutional and void. Legislators proclaimed that if any attempt was made to enforce the tariff in their state, "South Carolina will no longer consider herself a member of the Federal Union." South Carolina Senator John Calhoun built a political base on free trade and nullification. The nullification issue was diffused by Henry Clay who, during two weeks in February 1833, secured quick passage of gradual reduction of duties, while still preserving intact the protective system. This tax compromise was the second of his three "Great Compromises" for which he is remembered.

Senator Thomas Hart Benton, whose family owned 20 slaves in his youth, observed that South Carolina's objection was not to the high tariff. Rather, protectionism fostered high domestic wages, something inimical to the employment of cheap or enslaved labor. President Andrew Jackson was prepared to collect tariffs in South Carolina through the Force Act, which Congress passed in February 1833, together with tariff reductions. The nullification movement was quickly abandoned.

Clay's 1833 Compromise Tariff Act brought tariffs down to 20 percent over a 10-year period. This compromise shifted the government toward tariff for revenue rather than protection. But it led to a flood of foreign goods, which created a trade imbalance. McKinley wrote that the imbalance was settled by sending the $640 million in wealth from the California gold rush to Europe. Republicans adopted a protective tariff as a party plank at their 1860 convention. Most Republicans felt that they could not carry Pennsylvania without this plank.

Some Southerners today hold strong beliefs that tariffs were a major cause of the Civil War. A few contemporaneous attacks on the tariff in Southern manifestoes and speeches of Confederate leaders support that belief. They recalled the Tariff of Abominations and the Nullification Movement, which ultimately contributed to secession and eventually war. Southern propaganda figured it as a "cause" in their quest for securing foreign aid from a sympathetic audience in Europe, which hated the tariff. But the documentary evidence does not fully support the claim that tariffs were a major, compelling cause of the war, on the scale of issues such as states rights and slavery.

Georgia's Robert Augustus Toombs was a U.S. congressman (1845-1853), U.S. senator (1853-1861), a signatory to Georgia's Ordinance of Secession, and the Confederacy's first secretary of state. He railed against the Morrill Tariff of 1861, the first strongly protective tariff since 1832. It had passed the Republican-controlled House on May 10, 1860. But Republicans didn't control the Senate, and it couldn't pass — until after the Southern members withdrew following secession. When the Republicans found themselves in control of the Senate in February 1861, they passed the Morrill Tariff on a straight party vote. All 25 Republicans voted "yes." All 14 Democrats voted "nay." President Buchanan, a Democrat whose entire term (1857-1861) was plagued by an operating deficit, which the tariff would cure, signed it into law on March 2, 1861, within 48 hours of the close of his administration.

South Carolina's Robert Barnwell Rhett was known as the "Father of Secession" because he began promoting secession in 1826. He never accepted Henry Clay's Great Compromise of 1833, which reduced tariffs, despite acceptance by his mentor, John Calhoun who voted for it. Rhett was an owner-editor of the Charleston *Mercury*, a U.S. congressman (1837-1849), U.S. senator (1850-1852), a signatory to South Carolina's Ordinance of Secession and chairman of the committee which wrote the constitution of the Confederate States. The Civil War began at Fort Sumter, a tariff collection point in Charleston harbor, near Rhett's home base.

Most Southern congressmen, including the entire South Carolina delegation, had voted for the Tariff of 1857, and the Congress of the Confederacy re-enacted it. Had the South written a Declaration of Independence, it likely would have included taxation way down on the list. The Confederate constitution was a carbon copy of the Union constitution, with a few modifications. It omitted "general welfare," prohibited protective import tariffs and bounties (subsidies and grants), and permitted export tariffs. For spending, most appropriations required a two-thirds vote of Congress. Had the South not seceded, the protectionist Morrill Tariff could not have passed, and that "cause" would have been somewhat moot.

Political parties diverged on the tariff in the 1876 election. Republicans unanimously resolved, "That the revenue necessary for current expenditure and obligations of the public debt, must be largely derived from duties upon importation, which, so far as possible, should be adjusted to promote the interests of American labor and advance the prosperity of the whole country." Democrats voted 651 to 83 to "denounce the present tariff...It has impoverished many industries to subsidize a few...It promotes fraud, festers smuggling...We demand that all custom-house taxation shall be only for revenue." The nation gave no mandate to either camp. It sent a Democratic majority to the House, a Republican majority to the Senate, and Republican Rutherford B. Hayes to the White House.

The 1890 tariff was called, "The McKinley Tariff" (and William McKinley eventually became known as "The Tariff President"). It included an $11 million bounty to the Sugar Trust, a provision added by Senator Nelson Aldrich (R-RI). Graft from the Sugar Trust and other special interests would make Aldrich one of the richest men in Congress. The American Protective Tariff League lobbied for high tariffs. To this day, tariff bills contain dozens of clauses that benefit and enrich special interests, which a bewildered public cannot detect.

### BARACK OBAMA, TARIFF ENVIRONMENTALIST

Senator Barack Obama (D-IL) was a member of the Senate Environmental and Public Works Committee and he is a staunch environmentalist. That didn't prevent him from introducing 15 bills on May 25-26, 2006 proposing the suspension of tariffs on a host of hazardous chemicals that the Environmental Protection Agency labels as environmental toxins that cause cancer and birth defects. His proposals were enacted as part of two tax laws in 2006 with the common names of the compounds changed to their chemical formulas which made it hard to trace back to Obama's original bills. The beneficiaries were Nufarm Ltd., an Australian chemical company, and Astellas Pharma Inc., a Japanese drug company. This cost the U.S. Treasury $12 million. Why would an environmentalist champion the cheap importation of dangerous environmental toxins? The *Boston Globe* suggested that Obama had longstanding cozy relationships with lobbyists and political action committees.

Obama's changes were among nearly 200 tariff suspensions and reductions proposed by various members of Congress that were passed in the Pension Protection Act. Congress passed another 382 tariff provisions in the Tax Relief and Health Care Act of 2006. It should have been called the Tariff Reduction Act because tariffs occupied over 200 of the 540-page law, while other taxes were 110 pages and health provisions took 68 pages.

McKinley explained why he favored a protective tariff: "The American workingman was from two to four times better paid for the same labor than his European competitor, while against his Asiatic or Australasian competitor there was scarcely any comparison possible, so great were the advantages in favor of the laborers of the United States." Rep. Thomas B. Reed (R-ME) asked, "Where is the best market in the world? Where have the people the most money to spend? Right here in the U.S. of A. after 27 years of protectionist rule. And you are asked to give up such a market for the markets of the world?"

Protectionists charged that "free-trade tariffs have always ended in panics and long periods of financial distress." Whether high tariffs fostered economic growth during the late nineteenth century remains controversial, but they surely fostered high domestic prices.

> I had made a tour of the hardware shops of Mexico City, and as we had suspected, we found American cutlery selling for much less there than it sold for in the United States; some articles costing 50 percent less. This fact seemed to prove to the friends of tariff reduction that the tariff wall enabled manufacturers to charge the American consumer any price he chose, and then dump the surplus on the foreign market, and still make money on a 25 to 50 per cent reduction.
>
> —Mary Baird (Mrs. William Jennings) Bryan

In 1903, Senator Augustus Bacon (D-GA) introduced a resolution calling upon the Secretary of Commerce and Labor to report to the Senate on the practice of American trusts selling their products abroad at lower prices than domestic consumers were charged. He attacked the unnecessary $7.84 per ton protective steel tariff for an industry that easily competed abroad without protection.

> He backed it up with masses of facts — how "our" sewing machines sell abroad for fifteen dollars and here for twenty-five dollars; how "our" borax, a Rockefeller product, costs seven and a half cents a pound here and only two and a half cents abroad; how "our" nails, a Rockefeller-Morgan product, sell here for four dollars and fifty cents a keg and abroad for three dollars and ten cents; how the foreigner gets one dollar as much of "our" window glass as we get for two dollars; how [Carnegie Steel president, Charles] Schwab, in a letter to [Carnegie Steel chairman, Henry] Frick on May 15, 1899, had said that, while steel rails sold here at twenty-eight dollars a ton, he could deliver them in England for sixteen dollars a ton and make four dollars a ton profit; how the beef trust sold meat from twenty-five to fifty per cent dearer in Buffalo than just across the Canadian line; how the harvester trust sold its reapers cheaper on the continent of Europe than to an Illinois farmer coming to its main factory at Chicago; how on every article in common use among the American people of city, town and country, "the interests" were boldly robbing the people.

Bacon's efforts were stymied by Senator Aldrich, father-in-law to John D. Rockefeller, Jr. But even the *Wall Street Journal* chimed in, publishing a calculation showing that steel rails cost no more than $12.50 per ton to manufacture.

Following enactment of the 1913 income tax, Democrats reduced tariffs in the Underwood Tariff of 1914. Republicans regained control in the 1920s and pushed tariffs to all-time highs, culminating in the Smoot-Hawley Tariff of 1930. The Great Depression convinced all major countries to lower tariffs to stimulate their economies through foreign trade. Following World War II, with our factories intact and Europe's in ruins, America became the world's major exporter. Tariff reductions helped us export, while war-destroyed foreign competitors posed little threat.

Ways and Means Chairman Wilbur Mills recounted that Europe adopted the value-added tax as a trade barrier in return for lowering tariffs:

> We didn't say anything, publicly, at least, about the fact that the European Common Market adopted such a system. They did it to offset the concessions, which they had given, in a trade agreement to us in the way of reduction of duties...the Value Added-Tax did make it more difficult for us to export into the European Common Market.

Chrysler Corporation's legendary chairman, Lee Iacocca, explained to a July 22, 1981 gathering at the National Press Club the pernicious effect of the value-added tax refunds a foreign manufacturer receives upon exporting:

> [A] Japanese car that sells for $8,000 in Japan sells for $600 less in this country solely on the basis of a Japanese tax policy that provides them an export incentive. And we allow it to happen in the name of free trade.

For the past three decades, trade treaties have passed under "fast-track" procedure, whereby a newly negotiated trade treaty is swiftly submitted to the Senate, which can only vote yes or no. Amendments are not allowed. The stated logic is that no nation will negotiate trade deals with us if a draft treaty is subject to Senate amendments. In essence, Congress has abdicated its historic role in setting tariffs and subscribed to free trade.

Former California Governor Edmund G. Brown Jr. in 1992 described problems with the free trade fetish. It creates a race to the bottom as domestic manufacturing jobs depart for cheaper labor markets abroad, resulting in lower average weekly paychecks for our workers. He predicted that competition from subsidized lower-cost American agriculture would drive hundreds of thousands of Mexicans from their farms, crossing illegally into America in search of work.

U.S. sovereignty has been diminished. We are now under the jurisdiction of foreign-dominated tariff dispute panels that deliberate in secret. They ruled in 1991 and 1994 that the U.S. Marine Mammal Protection Act of 1972, which restricted imports of tuna caught using a technique that killed large numbers of dolphins, constituted an illegal trade barrier. (Pressure from conservation groups has prevented the U.S. from conforming to the panel's ruling.) In 1992, the panel found state alcohol taxes and regulations inconsistent with General Agreement on Tariff and Trade, and that GATT trumped state and local law. Recently, the World Trade Organization overturned our method for deciding whether other nations were dumping merchandise in the U.S. It also ruled that America could not ban internet gambling, even under a "public morality" exemption, unless it outlawed all domestic internet and telephone betting, including state betting laws not under federal jurisdiction.

Free-traders in the nineteenth century believed that our prosperity depended upon foreign trade. We must buy from them in order to sell to them. Today's justifications add peace and international understanding. Nations will not lift up sword against trading partners. Resources, they contend, are best allocated by free markets, which in the long run guarantee economic growth for everyone and raises living standards, despite the temporary dislocations. There can be no doubt that free trade has enlarged the world economic pie, but the dislocations are many, including a dangerous trade deficit, and loss of jobs, factories, and entire industries in the United States.

Both protective tariffs and free trade have alternately been credited with prosperity and blamed for depressions. Both can transfer wealth from the public to narrow private interests. In Aldrich's era, this was accomplished with high tariffs that profited monopolist trusts. Today, it's done with low tariffs that benefit multinational corporations.

Today's most pernicious use of tariffs forces other countries to pass laws favored by certain U.S. political interests. For example, as part of their bargain to secure a U.S. free trade pact, Singapore, Chile, Morocco, Costa Rica, El Salvador, Guatemala, Honduras, Nicaragua, Dominican Republic, Australia, Bahrain, Oman, Peru,

Colombia and Jordan were required to enact copyright laws which mirror the Digital Millennium Copyright Act of 1998.

Protective tariffs still exist for sugar and other favored interests. Non-tariff barriers, such as quotas and regulations, restrict a trade free-for-all. Treaties today subject our policies toward tariff and non-tariff barriers to review by the World Trade Organization, rather than U.S. courts or Congress. Unlike tariff laws which Congress can rather easily modify with a new law, treaties are set in stone.

Tariffs once financed most of the federal budget. Today, they make up barely one percent of our revenues. The income tax has enabled the U.S. to supplant the tariff. Low tariffs could be a major source of revenue replacing the income tax for most individuals. Like low sales taxes, it would not harm international trade and could easily be justified as an offset to the trade disadvantage caused by the value-added tax.

**The Civil War Income Tax**

When the United States enacted an income tax in 1861 to finance the Civil War, there was no Second Bank of the United States to collect it. The difficulty in starting administration of such a new and complex tax delayed implementation until 1862.

The 1862 income tax was three percent on incomes above $600, plus a two percent surtax on incomes above $10,000. Rent paid for a residence was deductible. Arguments over tax complexity began before the bill passed. The *Congressional Globe* includes a senator's complaint about ambiguity:

> The bill levies a tax upon incomes. I desire to know whether he means the gross income or the net income? I presume he means the net income; but the expression is "income."

The reply didn't help:

> I think we had better not put that word in....[It] would cause trouble. Suppose a person owned a dozen stores on one of the wharves in Boston, from which he got $10,000 a year rent. I mean to tax $9,000 of that amount by this bill. If I put in the word "net" income, he would try to have all the repairs, and so on, deducted, and would make them amount to as much as the income....I thought of putting this word "net" in; but I could see so many ways of evading it that I thought it

better to let the Secretary of the Treasury prescribe his rules, and let the bill cover all incomes.

Former Massachusetts Governor George S. Boutwell became the first internal revenue commissioner. He and three Treasury clerks created the blank forms and bookkeeping needed to organize the new income tax. The law failed to provide for a cashier to collect the tax. Boutwell appointed Marshall Conant, a Bridgewater, Mass. school principal, to the post. He accounted for $37 million collected from September 1, 1862 until March 3, 1863, "without any other security than his own good name, and all for a compensation of about eight hundred dollars."

Letters inquiring how the tax should be applied poured into Boutwell's office. He and his staff met evenings to issue rulings. Boutwell was elected to the U.S. House of Representatives and resigned his tax post on March 3, 1863 to take his seat. He served one of the shortest terms as commissioner. As a member of the House, he was one of the managers in the impeachment of President Andrew Johnson and one of the 15 members of the Joint Committee on Reconstruction that drafted the Fourteenth Amendment, which guarantees rights of citizenship, including due process and equal protection by the states.

Toward the end of the Civil War, the top bracket reached 10 percent for income over $5,000. The income tax was an issue in the 1864 presidential election. A Democratic campaign song featured the lyrics, "Oh! we want no more high rates, no more galling income tax." Ten percent was considered too high.

Following retirement of the $2.3 billion Civil War debt, there was a prolonged and bitter attempt to abolish the income tax. It was finally repealed in 1872, mainly because the revenue was not needed. It wasn't until 1880 that the Supreme Court upheld the constitutionality of the Civil War income tax.

The author and journalist Fletcher Knebel quipped, "Our forefathers made one mistake. What they should have fought for was representation without taxation." The Confederacy tried "representation without taxation." It was a major reason it lost the Civil War. Instead of imposing new taxes, the South initially financed the war through borrowing and printing un-backed paper money. This caused roaring inflation, which wiped out savings and devastated the economy. An export tariff raised only $39,000 in five years due to the Union blockade and uncooperative state tax collectors.

The South was fiscally ill-prepared for the Civil War. Its industrial base was tiny. Wealth was mostly invested in land and slaves, which could be subjected to property tax. The commercial and professional classes could be taxed on income. But there was no mechanism to do either and no gold-backed currency to pay with.

One of the first emergencies facing the Confederacy involved printing paper currency and bonds. Treasury Secretary Christopher G. Memminger reported to the Confederate Congress on March 14, 1862, "We had become so entirely dependent upon the North that but a single bank-note engraver could be found in the Confederate States, and none of the material necessary for a bank-note was manufactured amongst us." His biographer added, "In none of the Southern cities could engravers on steel or stone be found." Lithographs were substituted for steel engravings.

The few paper mills in the South manufactured only newsprint and wrapping paper. Bank note paper had to be smuggled from the North or abroad, through an embargo and blockade. Engravers were imported from abroad to print Treasury papers on improvised appliances and machinery. The first Confederate notes were of poor quality and appearance, having been engraved upon old and inferior stones formerly used for common placards and paper smuggled from Baltimore. They looked like carnival script. It took almost two years for the South to develop a Bureau of Engraving and Printing.

Belatedly, in April 1863, the South imposed comprehensive taxes: property, occupation, and graduated income taxes with a top rate of 15 percent. The most detested of these levies was a 10 percent tithe on crops, payable in-kind or in Confederate currency. These tax measures failed to raise substantial revenues because they couldn't be administered.

Georgia Governor Joseph E. Brown explained why tithing was so hated:

> [S]helled corn are thrown together in heaps and left to must and spoil...[H]ay in bales is [stored] without cover and permitted to take rain as it falls and is soon rotten. Potatoes and other like productions, collected in places remote from the army, are almost an entire loss. Much of the meat...will be thrown together in heaps before it is well cured, and will be tainted and spoiled....[In many counties], the storehouses are so far from railroad transportation that it is worth nearly half the tax in kind to haul it to the road, when...there is not...a

sufficient supply of provisions to sustain the lives of the people....[The people] are not willing to pay a tax in kind which is very burdensome to them to deliver, and which, after all their toil, they often have the mortification to see wasted without benefit to the government or any one else.

One general was very grateful for those heaps, as he prepared to march from Atlanta to Savannah with limited supply lines. "I knew that within that time we would reach a country well stocked with corn, which had been gathered and stored in cribs, seemingly for our use, by Governor Brown's militia," wrote General William T. Sherman in his memoirs.

Since the Confederacy had been conceived on a platform of states rights, there was a popular clamor against taxation. Unlike the North, which instituted a Bureau of Internal Revenue, the South left tax collection to the individual states. Only South Carolina, Mississippi, and Texas cooperated. The Atlanta *Daily Intelligencer* ran a notice from the tax collector on August 28, 1863 belatedly reminding people to file their income tax returns by July 1, 1863. The November 11, 1863 Charleston *Mercury* charged that the income tax was an unconstitutional unapportioned direct tax because no census had been taken. Jefferson Davis retorted that since the war precluded the taking of any census, the apportionment provision could be dispensed with. Besides, there was no Confederate Supreme Court where this could be challenged.

The top income tax rate was raised to 25 percent in 1864, with an even higher rate for joint-stock companies. A 30 percent sales tax was imposed. Yet total Confederate tax receipts over four years were less than $27 million.

At the end of the war, the Confederacy owed floating debt estimated at $400-$700 million, plus many months of soldiers' pay, obligations for materials, rentals, services, and interest on the public debt. About $1.5 billion of worthless Confederate paper money had been printed. Poor fiscal policy was the greatest single weakness of the Confederacy. The inability to responsibly enact and administer taxes destroyed the economic and social structure of the South. Lack of adequate tax revenues was one reason that the South lost the war, despite the many other great sacrifices of its soldiers and the general population.

The most unusual Civil War levy occurred when Union General Robert Granger required Nashville "public women" (prostitutes) to furnish surgeon's certificates of health and procure a license. Confederates derided it as "Yankee taxation." It raised $400 in its first month.

The Civil War introduced not just income tax and greenbacks, but the "deadline." In Civil War POW prisons, the deadline was a dirt or wooden marker representing a line prisoners couldn't cross within the stockade, or they would be shot from the guard tower. By the 1920s, newspapers began using the term as the time by which the copyreader had to complete editing his story. Later, it came to be known as the time by which a tax return must be filed. Just like those POWs, a bad fate awaits all taxpayers who mess with the "deadline."

**The 1894 Income Tax**

William Jennings Bryan is famous for his "Cross of Gold" speech, given upon accepting the Democratic Party's 1896 presidential nomination, but it pales in comparison to his magnificent 1894 extemporaneous debate on the House floor in favor of reinstating the income tax. With a $4,000 exemption, the tax would affect only 85,000 out of a population of 65 million. It was clearly intended to be a tax on the wealthy, with a flat rate of just two percent.

The opposition branded income tax as a plot by communists, socialists and anarchists. Magazine articles with titles like "The Communism of a Discriminating Income Tax" fueled emotions.

William Bourke Cockran (D-NY), the Democrats' best orator in the House, argued against:

> You have not attempted to tax the people, but you have attempted to tax the incomes of 85,000 of them. You have undertaken to set aside a class on which alone this tax is to fall, and to degrade the balance of the people to a plane of inferior importance....He who is relieved from taxation, who is exempt from his share in one single burden of government, forfeits to that extent the grounds upon which his right to control the Government is based.

Bryan (D-NE), just 34 years old, retorted eloquently:

> Why, sir, the gentleman from New York [Mr. Cockran] said that the poor are opposed to this tax because they do not want to be deprived of participation in it, and that taxation instead of being a sign of servitude is a badge of freedom. If taxation is a badge of freedom, let me

assure my friend that the poor people of this country are covered all over with the insignia of freemen. [Applause.]

Regarding a charge in the newspaper that the rich would flee the U.S. on account of the income tax, Bryan enumerated the income taxes in Europe: England, 2 percent; Prussia, 4 percent; Switzerland, 8 percent; Italy, 12 percent; Austria, 20 percent.

> Whither will they fly? [Applause.]....If "some of our best people" prefer to leave the country rather than pay a tax of 2 per cent, God pity the worst. [Laughter.] If we have people who value free government so little that they prefer to live under monarchical institutions, even without an income tax, rather than live under the stars and stripes and pay a 2 per cent tax, we can better afford to lose them and their fortunes than risk the contaminating influence of their presence. [Applause.]....if we are to lose some of our "best people" by the imposition of an income tax, let them depart, and they as leave without regret the land of their birth, let them go with the poet's curse ringing in their ears....[Loud and long-continued applause.]

### THE MAN WITHOUT A COUNTRY

Bryan ended with a stirring recital of "My Native Land" from Sir Walter Scott's *The Lay of the Last Minstrel*, popularized in Edward Everett Hale's 1863 patriotic short story, *The Man Without a Country*. It told of an army officer who was "sick of service" and in a fit of frenzy cried out, "Damn the United States! I wish I may never hear of the United States again!" He was sentenced to "never hear the name of the United States again" and kept a prisoner-guest on U.S. warships at sea. He soon repented but continued to suffer this sentence until his death 56 years later. Bryan got "loud and long-continued applause" because everyone present recognized this perfect analogy of the curse awaiting those who would flee the country.

The bill passed and became law without President Grover Cleveland's signature. It was quickly challenged. There were five days of hearings before eight justices of the Supreme Court in March 1895. Seriously ill, Justice Howell E. Jackson took no part in the proceedings. The court decided 6-2 that taxing income from land was an unconstitutional direct tax. The justices split 4-4 on whether to hold the entire act unconstitutional or merely sever the offending provisions.

The Constitution required that direct taxes be assessed uniformly in proportion to state population. The court said that income from real property was a direct tax which must be assessed in proportion to state population, and the tax on municipal bond interest infringed on state and local taxing powers. It equated a tax on rental income to a tax on real property. However, it ruled that taxes on wages, professions and trades were constitutional.

After three days of rehearing in May 1895, the Supreme Court, with Justice Jackson participating, voted 5-4 that taxing income from personal property (rents, bonds, stocks, and investments) was unconstitutional, and the entire statute was void. But Justice Jackson voted to uphold the tax. This should have resulted in a 5-4 decision in favor, except that someone who voted for the government on the first hearing changed his mind after the second hearing. The Court never reveals the votes of individual justices in evenly split decisions. Which justice changed his vote and his reason may not be the mystery some claim it is. William McKinley had been chairman of the House Ways and Means Committee and successfully ran for president in 1896. He identified Justice David Brewer as the turncoat.

Years later, in 1909, Brewer broke the Supreme Court's supposed neutrality on political issues when he attacked the proposed Sixteenth Amendment. It suggests that his 1895 Supreme Court vote was based on conservative ideology, rather than law. Or, it could be that Brewer was swayed by his uncle, Justice Stephen J. Field. Yes, an uncle-nephew team sat on the Supreme Court from 1889 until 1897. Field was its most outspoken conservative on this issue. He wrote a concurring opinion in the 4-4 decision, strenuously protesting that the 1894 tax should be unconstitutional.

Chief Justice Charles Evans Hughes wrote in 1936, "There can be no objection to a conscientious judge changing his vote, but the decision of such an important question by a majority of one after one judge had changed his vote aroused a criticism of the court which has never been entirely stilled."

To comply with the apportionment rule for a direct income tax would require the government to apply a different tax rate to every state so that the aggregate amount paid by each state was in proportion to its population rather than the value of the rents within its borders. Poorer, less densely populated states would pay a higher rate than wealthier, densely populated states. Thus, a Massachusetts resident might pay 2.8 percent on his income and a Minnesota resident, 32.9 percent. Such a complex computation, requiring a different income tax rate based on state of residency, would be inequitable and impossible to administer.

The case and its rehearing occupy 341 pages in the official Supreme Court reporter. It's alleged that Attorney General Richard Olney was distracted from preparing for the case because he was more interested in prosecuting noted socialist Eugene V. Debs, whose American Railway Workers Union had challenged the Interstate Commerce Act, a more pressing issue to the administration than the income tax which President Cleveland didn't sign. The Debs case was argued just 12 days after the first income tax case. It propelled Debs' attorney, Clarence Darrow, to national prominence.

The history of the Continental Congress and the later Constitutional Convention indicates the direct tax clause was intended solely to resolve representation issues, as it begins with "Representation and direct Taxes..." in discussing, "...excluding Indians not taxed, three-fifths of all other Persons." The "three-fifths compromise" was unrelated to any dispute over tax matters. The other mention, "No capitation, or other direct, tax..." was meant to prevent the northern majority from unfairly taxing slaves. Both clauses were intended to resolve the difficulty of maintaining slavery.

Turn of the century Columbia University tax professor and historian, Edwin Seligman, concluded that "direct taxes" was a very vague term, which certainly meant a tax on land or a poll tax, perhaps even a tax on buildings, personal property and slaves: "no one knew exactly what was meant by a direct tax, because no two people agreed." At the Constitutional Convention, Rufus King of Massachusetts asked for the precise definition of "direct taxation." "No one answered," wrote James Madison. Of the 1895 decision, Seligman called it "beyond all doubt erroneous [and] deplorable."

The only prior decision on direct taxes was in 1796, when the Supreme Court (then comprised of four justices) ruled unanimously that an unapportioned excise tax on carriages was a constitutional indirect tax. Of the four justices, three had been delegates to the Constitutional Convention, and the fourth had been a delegate at his state convention that ratified the Constitution. The case was argued by Treasury Secretary Alexander Hamilton, one of the authors of the Constitution and the Federalist Papers. No group could have been closer to understanding this issue. Properly applying the precedent of this 1796 case should have resulted in a ruling upholding the 1894 tax.

Hardly noticed, the 1894 tax included a provision taxing gifts and inheritances as income. This codified an 1862 ruling by Internal Revenue Commissioner George Boutwell, that gifts and inheritances were taxable income.

**The Sixteenth Amendment**

This issue remained dormant until President Theodore Roosevelt proposed an income tax and an inheritance tax in 1906. It was known how to write an income tax law that would survive a Supreme Court challenge. Had Roosevelt run for a third term in 1908, we likely would have had an income tax a few years earlier, and without a constitutional amendment.

In 1909, the House passed an income tax. It appeared that the Senate would concur and an income tax would be enacted. The corrupt Senate boss, Finance Committee Chairman Nelson Aldrich (R-RI), played a key role in its defeat. He spent his entire career in elected office and turned public service into such a lucrative racket that he amassed a $16 million fortune through graft. He lived in a 99-room chateau and sailed a 200-foot yacht equipped with eight staterooms and a crew of 27. His daughter, Abby, married John D. Rockefeller Jr., and he was Nelson A. Rockefeller's grandfather. He was the subject of explosive muckraker exposes such as Lincoln Steffens' 1905 "Rhode Island: A State for Sale," and David Graham Phillips' 1906 "The Treason of the Senate: Aldrich, The Head of It All."

Steffans told how Aldrich gained control of the Rhode Island Electric Railway, though he had no experience running such a business, and how it was financed by his buddies from the Sugar Trust, whom he protected with tariffs on imported sugar. Phillips exposed the campaign contributions and loot payments that constituted his sources of power. The *Providence Journal* was secretly owned by Aldrich, and he had significant holdings in the *New York Sun*.

Aldrich even had a partnership with King Leopold II. When Leopold's atrocities in the Congo became public, he sought refuge by selling the rubber, mining, and railroad rights to a syndicate headed by Wall Street magnate Thomas F. Ryan. (Ryan and Aldrich already had major holdings in Continental Rubber Company.) It was reported that the sale was for the promise of annual payments of just $69,000 to members of Leopold's family and $45,000 for maintenance of museums and palaces in Belgium. However, Leopold secretly owned half of the new syndicate. Aldrich became an owner and organizer of the Congo syndicate, worked to neutralize Leopold's American critics, and manipulated rubber tariffs for his own benefit.

Suffrage in Rhode Island was restricted and apportionment of representatives was skewed. Voter bribery was the rule and just a few thousand votes determined the state legislature. A few thousand dollars of voter bribes allowed Aldrich to easily control the state Senate that elected him. When confronted with scandal, his motto was, "Admit nothing. Explain nothing." He became a poster child for advocates of the Seventeenth Amendment calling for direct election of senators.

Aldrich and President William Howard Taft concocted a compromise to defeat the income tax. They would immediately pass a one percent "excise" tax on corporate income over $5,000 (excluding dividend income from other corporations), and sponsor a constitutional amendment to allow an income tax without apportionment among the states so that individual income could be taxed. (To this day, several states call their corporate income tax an excise tax.)

So confident were congressional leaders that the income tax amendment would never be ratified, they wasted no time for serious consideration by any committee. Only four hours were allotted for discussion of the amendment in the House, and even less in the Senate. The compromise passed unanimously in the Senate and by a vote of 318 to 14 in the House. Income tax opponents were certain that the income tax was dead. After all, the Constitution had not been amended in 40 years. Over one thousand constitutional amendments had been introduced in Congress during the first 100 years of the republic, and only 15 had been adopted. Of those, 10 were the Bill of Rights. The Eleventh and Twelfth amendments were adopted in 1789 and 1804, and three resulted from the Civil War. Even if the amendment was adopted, there would be another fight in Congress to prevent passage of an income tax law. The income tax was dead.

But the plan went awry. After 1909, the U.S. underwent a major political transformation. Democrats and Roosevelt Republicans won state elections. Woodrow Wilson won the 1912 presidential election. Democrats controlled both houses of Congress, and by February 25, 1913, the required 36 states had ratified the income tax as the Sixteenth Amendment. It was just 3½ years after the Taft-Aldrich Compromise conspired to relegate income tax to the dust bin. The Seventeenth Amendment was ratified just six weeks later. Nelson Aldrich had already retired in 1911.

> **WAS THE SIXTEENTH AMENDMENT NECESSARY?**
>
> The main change made by the income tax amendment was to remove the apportionment requirement for taxing income from any source. Had the Supreme Court revisited its 1895 twisted-logic-and-vote-switching 5-4 decision with new justices, it might well have ruled that an income tax which excluded rents was constitutional. So lack of the Sixteenth Amendment was probably not an impediment to the income tax.
>
> Constitutional issues the Sixteenth Amendment didn't address were eventually resolved. Initially, the Supreme Court ruled it was still unconstitutional to subject presidents, judges and state employees to the new income tax. But by 1939, these exemptions were gone. The Supreme Court revisited and overturned its prior rulings, without a constitutional amendment.
>
> Similarly, there's no longer any constitutional prohibition against taxing municipal bond interest income. However, a legislative exemption has been in effect since the earliest days of the income tax because of the 1895 Supreme Court ruling that such a tax was unconstitutional.
>
> For these reasons, this author believes that the Sixteenth Amendment was unnecessary. Salary income was undoubtedly taxable. An income tax exempting real and personal property would have met the requirements of the Supreme Court's 1895 *Pollock* decision, and later court rulings would eventually have upheld income taxation of other income too.

Immediately following his inauguration, Wilson called Congress into special session. Tariff reductions were soon enacted, followed later that year by an income tax to replace the lost tariff revenue. It was supposed to be a flat four percent tax, but a proposal by Ways and Means members Dorsey W. Shackleford (D-MO) and John Nance Garner (D-TX) turned it into a graduated tax of one to seven percent. Garner argued for "capacity-to-pay" and won despite opposition from the Ways and Means chairman.

Rep. Ira Copley (R-IL) proposed a top rate of 68 percent and when defeated, he retorted, "within twenty years, the country would see such a law." He was wrong. Just five years later, it reached 77 percent to finance World War I. Garner justified the high rate, telling House Speaker "Champ" Clark (D-MO), "we have got to confiscate wealth."

The constitutionality of the 1913 income tax law was quickly challenged, and upheld. Even without the Sixteenth Amendment, the Supreme Court unanimously upheld the 1909 corporate excise tax. In so doing, the court signaled that the constitution did not forbid the income tax – only the particular way it was done in 1894. Randolph Paul explained, "The reasoning of the justice may seem thin, but the job of distinguishing embarrassing precedents is perhaps the hardest work of our highest court."

To this day, the constitutionality of the Sixteenth Amendment is still challenged by tax protesters. A frustrated Tax Court, in addition to ruling in favor of IRS, adds up to a $25,000 penalty against anyone raising that frivolous argument in court.

**Tax Season Begins**

The 1909 corporation excise tax required returns to be filed on a December 31 calendar-year basis. Prior to passage, 12 accounting firms jointly advised Congress and the attorney general that many corporations were on fiscal years, rather than calendar years, making it impossible for such companies to file a true return of profits as of December 31. Their argument was rejected.

When the 1913 income tax passed, it corrected this problem, allowing returns to be filed for natural fiscal years. However, the 1909 law caused many corporations to switch to a calendar year. This forced accountants to concentrate most of their work in the first three months of the year. Robert H. Montgomery, president of the American Association of Public Accountants later wrote, "It was a blow from which we have not fully recovered....This congestion has made the practice of public accounting far more hazardous than it should be. It is difficult and expensive to carry a competent staff throughout the year." This phenomenon became known as "tax season."

The 1913 Tax Act was enacted on October 3, and took effect on November 1, retroactive to March 1, four days after the Sixteenth

Amendment was ratified. It taxed high income individuals (over $3,000 single and $4,000 married). Treasury was inundated with thousands of letters and telegrams suggesting regulations. The new regulations included withholding "at the source" for interest paid by banks and corporations and for salaries and wages over $3,000. Only 357,588 individual returns were filed that first year, together with 316,908 corporate returns.

The first Form 1040 was three pages plus one page of instructions. Its design is attributed to Nina Wilcox Putnam, and got its number in 1914 in the ordinary sequence of numbers used by the Bureau of Internal Revenue. Ms. Putnam went on to write other horror classics. She co-wrote the 1924 stage version of *Dracula*, and the screenplay for the 1932 Boris Karloff classic, *The Mummy*.

A tamer explanation is that Treasury began 1913 income tax forms with number 1000 (withholding on interest coupons). The numbers worked up to 1019a, skipped to 1030 (financial institutions) through 1035 (corporations), then skipped to 1040 (individuals) and 1041 (fiduciary). Form 1040 had similarities to the 1862 Form 24 developed by George Boutwell for the Civil War income tax. (The preceding form was numbered, Form 23½.) But the Putnam story sounds so much fancier.

## The Sales Tax Rebellion of 1932

John Nance Garner served thirty years in the House, his last two as speaker, followed by eight years as Franklin Roosevelt's vice-president. He was the second most powerful politician in the United States during the Great Depression and arguably, the most powerful vice president in U.S. history. He died in 1967 at the age of 99. He brought us the progressive income tax in 1913, prevented repeal of the estate tax in 1921, and figures prominently in why we have no national sales tax.

To fill a desperate need for revenue in 1932, Speaker Garner nebulously agreed with Herbert Hoover's Treasury Secretary Ogden Mills, and Ways and Means Chairman Charles Crisp, to support a 2.25 percent national sales tax on everything except food and cheaper clothing. Almost every national political leader from the president to the leaders of both houses of Congress supported the sales tax. So did financier and economist Bernard Baruch and newspaper magnate

William Randolph Hearst. To disguise the nature of the tax, it would be called a "manufacturer's tax."

Led by Fiorello LaGuardia (R-NY), who later became mayor of New York City, and Robert Doughton (D-NC) who later became chairman of Ways and Means, members rebelled against their House leaders. The tax was opposed by the American Federation of Labor, four farm groups, retailers and wholesalers. Mass meetings were held throughout the country to protest the tax. It was overwhelmingly defeated.

The general feeling was that sales tax was the domain of the states, and the federal government should not enact a sales tax since that would compete with the states' ability to raise revenue.

To cover the revenue shortfall, The Revenue Act of 1932 boosted income tax and estate tax rates. In a lame duck session in December 1932, Hoover asked Congress to again enact the sales tax, and Garner promised to allow the bill to reach the House floor. Thereupon, President-elect Roosevelt announced that he opposed a federal sales tax. From his experience as New York's governor, Roosevelt decided it was best that federal and state governments not levy new taxes on the same source and that a general sales tax should be the exclusive domain of the states.

The sales tax rebellion contributed to Garner's defeat as a presidential candidate in 1932. He became Franklin Roosevelt's running mate instead. In the vice-president's role as president of the Senate, Garner pushed Federal Deposit Insurance, over Roosevelt's objection. Had Roosevelt decided not to run for a third term in 1940, Garner might have succeeded him as president.

Publisher Frank Gannett headed the Committee for Constitutional Government, which failed in a 1936 attempt to pass an amendment through Congress to limit income tax to 25 percent of income, except in wartime. Undaunted, the backers then tried to get two-thirds of the states to call for a constitutional convention where ratification by three-quarters of the states could pass a tax-limitation amendment. They slowly got 22 states to approve — 10 short of the two-thirds necessary — but seven states subsequently rescinded their approval. Their effort died in the early 1950s.

The top rate was 25 percent from 1925 until 1931, so that's probably the source of their proposed rate. Treasury Secretary Andrew Mellon proposed the 25 percent rate shortly after taking office in 1921, but was unable to immediately repeal the high World

War I rates due to successful opposition led by John Nance Garner. The life of this forgotten star of American politics is remembered at The John Nance Garner Museum in his home town of Uvalde, Texas about eighty miles west of San Antonio.

Stranger yet is the recent outpouring of support for a 2003 proposal by Congressman John Linder (R-GA) for "The FairTax," which claims that a 23 percent sales tax could replace income and payroll taxes. The President's Advisory Panel on Federal Tax Reform reported that it would require a sales tax rate of 34 - 49 percent (plus the state rate; higher still if some transactions were exempted or there was substantial tax evasion). The tax burden on middle income taxpayers would increase by 29 - 36 percent, and there would still be a need for a tax enforcement agency like IRS.

Linder and syndicated talk show host Neal Boortz wrote *The FairTax Book: Saying Goodbye to the Income Tax and the IRS*. It became the first tax book to hit the bestseller list, helped by Boortz, who for months hawked the book five days a week on his radio show. Mass rallies were held promoting the Fair(sales)Tax to replace the income tax. How sentiments do change, as just 70 years earlier, there were demonstrations against a national sales tax.

**The Temporary Income Tax**

New York tax lawyer Randolph Evernghim Paul is the architect of our modern federal income tax. He served in many government posts, and founded the law firm, Paul, Weiss, Rifkind, Wharton, and Garrison, still today a major law firm. Among his many works are *The Law of Federal Income Taxation* with Jacob Mertens in 1934 (a multi-volume treatise still updated by Thomson Publishing) and in 1954 his best-known book, *Taxation in the United States*, a lucid history, part of which he created and recites in the first person. His 1947 book, *Taxation for Prosperity* argued for high progressive income taxation in the postwar era and, together with his continuing active participation in tax policy, exerted a strong influence against Truman and Eisenhower reducing income taxes to pre-World War II levels.

Following Pearl Harbor, Paul accepted the position of Treasury general counsel to help enact revenue-raising measures that would be required for World War II. He shared Roosevelt's dislike for a national sales tax and rejected Republican calls in 1942 for its enactment to finance the war. Together with Treasury Secretary Henry Morgenthau, he convinced Congress that sales tax was regressive and that the rate would have to be quite high if food and other necessities were exempt.

Up until that time, the income tax only affected the elite. The exemptions were generous, thus sparing the majority of the population from its reach. Paul proposed expanding the income tax to reach down into the masses through a draconian decrease in the personal exemption. That made most everyone subject to income tax. In order to minimize the pain of paying a high income tax, he proposed withholding at source — or rather, *overwithholding*, so that people would be motivated to file an income tax return to obtain a refund of the overpayment. He also introduced the idea that income tax was not just for raising revenue, but for controlling inflation — a precursor to using the income tax for social purposes too.

In the 1942 Revenue Act, Congress included a "Temporary Income Tax on Individuals," promoted as a "Victory Tax." It introduced withholding tax on the masses in order to help fund World War II. The law said that withholding would end upon the "date on which hostilities in the present war between the United States and Germany, Japan and Italy cease." Later, the 1943 Current Tax Payment Act increased the withholding rates and removed the "temporary" title, as well as the expiration provision. The withholding tax helped convert the income tax from a tax on the upper-class to a tax on the masses. Without withholding, the lower classes would not have funds to pay the tax bill when it came due the following year.

The reason for removing "temporary" was the permanent move to withholding, a "pay-as-you-go income tax plan." The conversion would be difficult, as 1943 would require people to pay two years' taxes at once: the 1942 taxes, and the pay-as-you-go 1943 taxes. Beardsley Ruml, Treasurer of R.H. Macy & Company and chairman of the Federal Reserve Bank of New York proposed that 1942 taxes be forgiven, and correctly pointed out that the new withholding tax would produce more revenue than the forgiven 1942 taxes. Congress refused to embrace a full forgiveness for the wealthy but recognized that it could not collect two years' taxes at oppressively high war tax rates. A compromise was reached whereby 75 percent of the lower of 1942 or 1943 taxes would be forgiven (100 percent if $50 or less). The unforgiven tax was payable in two installments, half on March 15, 1944 and half on March 15, 1945.

To win public acceptance of the war emergency income tax, a 1942 Walt Disney propaganda cartoon, *The New Spirit*, promoted timely filing and payment of federal income taxes, demonstrated by Donald Duck's patriotic filing of his tax return. Disney produced a sequel, *The Spirit of '43* with Donald Duck again promoting acceptance of higher taxes as a patriotic duty, with the slogans: "Taxes to bury the Axis." "Spend for the Axis or save for taxes?" "Taxes will keep democracy on the march."

At Treasury Secretary Henry Morganthau's request, Irving Berlin wrote a flag-waving propaganda song, "I Paid My Income Tax Today," which was announced at the end of January 1942. It complimented "Any Bonds Today," Berlin's 1941 patriotic song popularized by the Andrew Sisters. Treasury sent copies of the recording to radio stations throughout the country for broadcast. Naturally, the song didn't become a hit. Today, it's one the rarest of Berlin's sheet music with equally rare Decca and Victor 78 RPM recordings.

Berlin had difficulty writing the lyrics. The Decca version begins:

> I paid my income tax today.
> I'm only one of millions more
> Whose income never was taxed before.
> A tax I'm very glad to pay.

Holographs for the song at the Library of Congress show the third line originally read, "Who've never paid a tax before," which is too taunting to be patriotic. "A tax I'm very glad to pay," was crossed out in his draft, then reinserted.

Berlin began writing the music on December 19, and completed these lyrics on December 26, 1941, just 19 days after Pearl Harbor. It alludes to a tax on the masses, but in 1941, income was still an elite tax. The Roosevelt administration had to have spawned the idea of a mass tax before December 7 because it was a major policy equal to implementing social security in 1935. Surely they didn't hatch the idea after Pearl Harbor and first thing call their friend Irving Berlin to request a song be written.

A major problem with taxing the masses is that they lack money when payment comes due, having spent their earnings. Early in 1941, Morgenthau considered selling "tax anticipation certificates" for this purpose. New Jersey Bell Telephone Company president, Chester Barnard, proposed in October 1941 a new payroll deduction for "personal emergencies" — a forced savings plan by another name. These two ideas combined into a November 5 proposal to Ways and Means Chairman Doughton and Senate Finance Committee Chairman Walter George (D-GA) to initiate withholding on salaries and wages under the guise of wartime preparedness. Withholding would reduce the deficit and cool inflation.

Pearl Harbor provided the emergency that Roosevelt would exploit to press for withholding. Congress preferred a federal sales tax for funding the war, an idea Roosevelt had always opposed. Morgenthau suggested lowering the personal exemption so that the income tax would penetrate to the lowest income groups, selling this idea as a compromise and enforcing collection through withholding. Calling it "temporary" made it acceptable as a wartime emergency. Thus in May 1942 was born the mass tax via withholding.

The Bureau of Internal Revenue hired 11,000 new employees just to administer the withholding tax. The administrative cost to affected employers was much higher. In 1940, the bureau's 22,000 employees processed 19 million tax returns, collecting $5 billion. By 1951, 57,000 employees were processing 82 million returns, collecting $40 billion. Today the IRS has 100,000 employees and processes 226 million tax returns, collecting $2 trillion. The cost of collection is around one-half cent per dollar, making it the most efficient tax collection agency in the world.

After World War II, President Harry Truman refused to reduce the high World War II income taxes or remove participation of the masses in the income tax. The excuses included inflation fears and funding the Korean War.

President Eisenhower made recodification of the Internal Revenue Code the centerpiece of his tax policy. The World War II policy subjecting lower-income individuals to income tax was a major feature of the revised code. Eisenhower echoed nineteenth century philosophy when he threatened to veto any act that removed the masses from income tax, declaring:

> When the time comes to cut income taxes still more, let's cut them. But I do not believe that the way to do it is to excuse millions of taxpayers from paying any income tax at all...every real American is proud to carry his share of any burden...I simply do not believe for one second that anyone privileged to live in this country wants someone else to pay his fair and just share of the cost of his Government.

## Chapter Six—Tax 'Em, My Boy, Tax 'Em

The 1947 personal exemption of $600 wasn't raised until 1969, when it became $625. The personal exemption was $3,000 in 1913, just a little less than it is today. Tax rates didn't decline until John Kennedy reduced the maximum 91 percent rate to 77 percent. Richard Nixon made income from personal services subject to a maximum 50 percent rate. Ronald Reagan finally brought rates down to peacetime levels, a maximum 28 percent, but retained its mass tax feature. His successors tinkered with higher rates.

So, Franklin Roosevelt's "temporary" withholding tax on the masses is still upon us. He would have gone farther had Congress not stopped him. Robert Jackson reported that soon after Germany invaded Poland in September 1939, Roosevelt drafted a "weird plan for excess profits taxation" on corporations. He would allow a six percent return on capital and tax the excess at 99.9 percent. The administration waited until the right time to float this trial balloon, which came in September 1941 when Treasury Secretary Morgenthau "startled the House Banking and Currency Committee, as well as his own assistants [by testifying] that 'in times like this' a corporation earning six percent on its invested capital ought to be satisfied," subjecting the excess to 100 percent tax.

On April 27, 1942, Roosevelt fantastically proposed a 100 percent individual tax rate to finance World War II, declaring, "[I]n time of this grave national danger, when all excess income should go to win the war, no American citizen ought to have a net income, after he has paid his taxes, of more than $25,000." Treasury said this top rate would only affect 11,000 taxpayers. Ways and Means pronounced it dead-on-arrival. Undeterred, Roosevelt issued Executive Order 9250 on October 3, 1942 under authority of an amendment to the Price Control Act passed on October 2:

> In order to correct gross inequities and to provide for greater equality in contributing to the war effort, the Director is authorized to take the necessary action, and to issue the appropriate regulations, so that, insofar as practicable no salary shall be authorized...to the extent that it exceeds $25,000 after the payment of taxes...

Congress stepped in and overturned this EO when it passed the Public Debt Act of 1943. Still, the top World War II rate reached 94 percent, not too far shy of Roosevelt's 100 percent.

170  History and Government

| C | U | L | T | U | R | E |
|---|---|---|---|---|---|---|
| I use "Decision Points" in my audits. | I use creative audit techniques. | Testing "Internal Controls" has led me to adjustments. | I can verify the truthfulness of oral testimony. | Effective performance on examinations is rewarded. | I use summonses to get third-party records. | I have access to the MSSP electronic bulletin board. |
| A | B | C | D | E | F | G |
| Customer service means treating everyone in a "fair" manner. | Fraud referrals help an examiner get promoted. | The IRS is changing for the better. | The IRS rewards "Risk taking" by examiners. | Management keeps asking me to do the impossible. | TCMP audits should concentrate on unreported income. | A three-year comparison of tax returns helps determine audit potential. |
| H | I | J | K | L | M | N |
| I feel job satisfaction when I find unreported income. | I know what my priorities are. | If appropriate, I would not hesitate to assert the fraud penalty. | Omitted income can usually be detected from books and records. | My manager could audit as effectively as I do. | I have used MSSP Market audit techniques guides. | An examiner should not ask for assistance during an audit. |
| O | P | Q | R | S | T | U |
| I can explain internal controls. | Taxpayers seem to live better than I do. | I effectively use a cash T. | Voluntary compliance levels are at an all time high. | Personal pride in our work helps achieve "Quality". | I routinely use a personal living expense (PLE) computation. | I audit "the taxpayer" vs. "the return." |
| V | W | X | Y | Z | AA | AB |
| I contribute to the IRS strategic objectives. | Planning and scheduling properly lead to success. | Courts require IRS to prove the specific source of unreported income. | I know how to deal with taxpayer procrastination. | I am proud to work for the IRS. | IRS organizational goals are important to me. | I have issued an inadequate records notice. |
| AC | AD | AE | AF | AG | AH | AI |
| I know what "Economic Reality" means. | Corporate examination work is the best career path to a Grade 13. | I know the impact of a peer quality audit on a taxpayer's future compliance. | Most taxpayers deposit unreported receipts in their bank accounts. | I could estimate my personal living expense and be within $2,000 of the actual annual cost. | I can identify most of the computer external sources of information available in PSP. | Disclosure laws prevent examiners from contacting customers of the taxpayer. |
| AJ | AK | AL | AM | AN | AO | AP |
| Indirect method cases are almost always conceded by Appeals. | I am always looking for non-compliant market segments. | Our yield per hour will fall if we spend more time examining income. | Taxpayers can skim $20,000 and we'll never find it! | Taxpayers have the right to refuse to talk to an examiner once a Power of Attorney is appointed. | Taxpayers and POA's treat me with respect. | Finding unreported income is worth the time and effort. |
| AQ | AR | AS | AT | AU | AV | AW |

** By signing a box you are saying, "This statement represents something I either "DO" or "BELIEVE"."

CHAPTER SEVEN

# Culture Bingo

*Now, eh, f-f-forget the surtax and subtract the total from Schedule G, page 3 from line 24 and add line 1g, eh, plus line 15, less s-s-s-s-six percent of of whichever, or or whichever is greater.*

—Porky Pig reads instructions while preparing his tax return, *Cracked Quack*, Friz Freleng (1951)

Everyone picks on the Internal Revenue Service. Luntz Research, a Republican polling firm, asked 800 registered voters nationwide which federal government agency they disliked the most. The landslide winner: the IRS, America's Favorite Enemy Number One.

The Town of Brookhaven, New York acquired a 42-acre site in Holtsville which it leased to IRS beginning in 1972. The Holtsville Fire District challenged exemption of the IRS facility from a property tax which funded fire protection. Reasoning that the Internal Revenue Service does not enhance the health, education, safety, or welfare of the residents of Holtsville, the Suffolk County Supreme Court revoked the IRS tax exemption.

What kind of person collects taxes? IRS Commissioner Donald Alexander (1973-1977) rationalized becoming the nation's top tax collector by noting that Matthew was a tax collector before he became a saint.

Despite frequent calls to abolish the IRS, it won't ever happen. George S. Boutwell (1862-1863), the first internal revenue commissioner, wrote in his 1902 autobiography, "In the year 1901 it may be assumed that the Internal Revenue Office will exist while the Government shall exist, although it came into being as a [Civil] war measure and as a temporary policy." Yet only one president has ever entered the IRS building: John F. Kennedy. The event was so significant that IRS placed a plaque in the National Office commemorating the event.

**They've Got Culture**

Some people believe that the IRS slogan is, "We're not happy until you're not happy."

It's been my experience that most IRS employees at all echelons are highly professional, anxious to help, and truly believe in giving "customer service" however elusive the goal. Although IRS is the largest paper shuffling organization in the world, when I call, I still get a live American person fairly quickly. With its emphasis on customer service, I have been greeted with, "Thank you for calling IRS. My name is Matt. How can I help you?" Really! It's a refreshing way to begin a conversation with a feared agency.

You may be surprised to learn that there exists an "IRS Rules of Conduct" and a revenue procedure stating IRS policy to act fairly toward taxpayers. And generally, they do. In addition, IRS employees are governed by Standards of Ethical Conduct for Employees of the Executive Branch. The IRS Mission Statement aims to "Provide America's taxpayers top quality service by helping them understand and meet their tax responsibilities and by applying the tax law with integrity and fairness to all."

When Larry Gibbs (1986-1989) became commissioner, he instituted the policy that taxpayers were "customers" of IRS. When the IRS views taxpayers as customers, there is a presumption and attitude that the level of service must rise to satisfy customer needs. Tax collectors of old viewed their primary function as collecting (or extracting) taxes. The IRS realizes that helping taxpayers with self-assessment (backed by enforcement) is the way we raise revenue. Implementing this ideal meant changing IRS culture, but that wasn't easy.

Major management problems existed at the service centers in the 1980s, particularly in Philadelphia. Clerks discarded tax returns with checks in wastepaper baskets and in burn barrels. Refund checks were allegedly back-dated to avoid payment of interest. Checks filed with tax returns were reported to have been held for five weeks before the IRS cashed them. The agency then billed taxpayers for late payment interest.

The IRS insisted that it had a strong policy against evaluating its agents based on the amount of taxes they collect. That was discredited when in 1987, a memorandum signed by the Chief of Field Branch II in Philadelphia described monthly statistics of the group's collection actions as "a sorry report." It warned, "The revenue officers that are performing above a satisfactory level will be rewarded, and the ones that are not will be documented, with corrective action taken....You will be evaluated on your accomplishments or lack of accomplishments. Need I say more?" (Evaluating agents on the amount of taxes they collect is now prohibited by a 1998 statute.)

In the early 1990s, IRS began "economic reality" audits for ordinary examinations. They included questions more appropriate for a fraud audit. For example:

> What cash did you have on hand in 1993 usually, personally or for business, not in a bank — at your home, safe deposit box, hidden somewhere, etc.?
>
> Do you own any large assets (over $10,000) besides auto and real estate? What is it, where is it kept? Is it paid for — if not, what is the payment?

The low point in "economic reality" came when it was discovered in 1995 that an IRS training course featured a game called "Culture Bingo." Instead of numbers, the "Bingo cards" featured anti-taxpayer propaganda like, "Taxpayers seem to live better than I do," "Fraud referrals help an examiner get promoted," and "Taxpayers can skim $20,000 and we'll never find it!" Course participants circulated around the classroom to find other participants who believed or performed the characteristics in the boxes. Instead of "Bingo!" winners who completed a row, column or diagonal would yell, "I'VE GOT CULTURE!"

Problems continued. Beginning in 1993, the IRS privatized processing of tax receipts by asking taxpayers to send payments to post office lockboxes. Lockbox collections are processed by commercial banks. In 2001, some 77,000 tax receipts valued at over $1.3 billion were lost or destroyed at a Pittsburgh lockbox operated by Mellon

Bank. Another contractor lost 30,000 estimated tax payments from 13 states when they fell into San Francisco Bay following a September 11, 2005 traffic accident on the San Mateo Bridge. There have also been instances of employees stealing and cashing checks sent to lockbox banks. A 2003 General Accounting Office report questioned whether any cost efficiencies result from using lockboxes.

Congress has authorized the IRS to privatize collection of delinquent tax accounts. Collection agencies can earn a 25 percent bounty. It's a modern form of "tax farming." Commissioner Mark Everson (2002-2007) admitted at a congressional hearing that the IRS could collect the tax for less, but increasing the IRS budget counts against the 10-year revenue projection, while hiring outside contractors does not. One of the companies hired by the IRS had a partner who was convicted in a 2002 bribery scheme for obtaining a collection contract with San Antonio. The company also settled a lawsuit in 2004 in which it was alleged the firm offered illegal gifts, bribes and rigged bids to win government collection contracts.

Federal experience with private collectors isn't good. One of the many Grant administration scandals concerned an experiment with privatizing tax collection. Under Congressional authorization, Treasury Secretary George Boutwell hired John Sanborn in 1872. Sanborn could keep 50 percent of the tax he collected. He was supposed to collect from delinquents, beginning with the dangerous task of confronting 39 distillers and liquor retailers, but he padded his list with the names of almost all the nation's railroads. A congressional investigation concluded that most of the $427,000 that Sanborn collected would have wound up at Treasury absent his efforts. Their report asserted that "any system of farming the collection of any portion of the revenue of the Government is fundamentally wrong," and concluded that only the Internal Revenue Bureau should collect taxes. George Boutwell in his two-volume autobiography, didn't mention the Sanborn scandal.

States have had poor experiences with private collections. New Jersey's 12-year experiment came to a scandalous halt in 2005 after an investigation reported systematic acceptance of gifts, meals and entertainment from its private collection contractor. The contractor also overbilled the state for its services. For New Jersey graft, this was small, about $65,000 in gifts and $1 million in overbilling over five years. The State of Virginia took a 17 percent commission for collecting city debts, with 73 percent success. The City of Richmond thought it could benefit from privatizing. The company it hired charged 30 percent and collected just 36 percent of what it tried to recover.

## Compliance Difficulties

The IRS has a difficult and delicate task requiring it to maintain the goodwill of presidents, congressmen, and most taxpayers. That's in addition to dealing with those unable to pay, tax protesters unwilling to pay, aggressive tax planning, and abusive tax shelters. Consider the hate mail.

A widow sent an envelope containing the gray ashes of her husband's cremated remains. The enclosed note read, "You took everything else. Why don't you take him, too!" Another pasted a lock of hair to his return and wrote beneath it, "You have scalped me." Returns have been fastened with Band-Aids, sewing needles, nails, and chewing gum. Forms have been smeared with blood, excrement and urine.

I suppose that in a post-9/11 environment, the IRS wouldn't accept such shenanigans anymore. They'd have you arrested for sending biohazards, and charge you with costs for evacuating the building.

Some people staple their return in the right hand corner, or down the whole right side. Forms arranged in the wrong order, or facing the wrong way require extra processing. A drop of glue will prevent the automatic envelope opener from extracting the papers. Just sending the IRS a letter of appreciation can gum up their normal processing.

There's no law requiring payment of individual income taxes by check. You can visit the IRS and pay your tax in person with cash. Be sure to get a receipt. The IRS employee accepting your return will require two assistants to verify the cash payment. Depositing cash isn't a normal procedure for the IRS. Enclosing a one dollar bill in partial payment when filing your return poses processing difficulties.

Of course, doing any of these will irk the IRS, increase scrutiny of your return, and may result in some undesired correspondence. Chuckle, but don't try them. E-filing has taken some of the "fun" out of filing tax returns.

Training the public to comply with the income tax took decades. Compliance with the Civil War income taxes in both the North and the South was uneven. The problems included concealment of and failure to report income as well as fraudulent claims. Commenting on the 1909 corporation income tax, the February 1911 *Journal of Accountancy* noted, "Ever since the law was passed, it has been an open secret in business circles that corporation managers of all kinds have taken a keen interest in practical accounting, and have eagerly cast about for methods guaranteed to render profits temporarily intangible and invisible." This to hide from a one percent income tax.

The notion that "Corporations don't pay taxes. People do," began circulating. This slogan against imposition of corporate income tax because it's always passed on to individuals — consumers or owners or workers — has been repeated so often that many believe it means more than it says. Economists call this a tautology. Even if it were true that only individuals bear tax burdens, it still may be best to collect taxes from corporations either directly or indirectly when they are efficient collecting organizations. After all, we depend upon business to collect sales and withholding taxes, and a properly constructed "corporate tax" could be nothing more than a way to "withhold" tax from individual owners. Meanwhile, corporations undertake many devices to avoid the taxes that they supposedly don't pay.

Compliance was a major problem after passage of the 1913 income tax. In 1916, *The New Republic* conjectured that there was only 50 percent compliance. There was no way to be sure. Aside from anecdotal evidence known to that generation, they reasoned that the 65 collectors of internal revenue were sparsely scattered throughout the country and had few assistants. So while it might be possible to enforce an income tax in cities, in the countryside compliance might be nonexistent. (Virginia's 1909 state income tax collected less than $100,000 and was repealed after some agents sent to rural areas were never heard from again.) The 1913 Act mandated withholding on interest, dividends, and high wages to create a roster of taxpayers liable for income tax. Once on that list, the taxpayer would have to explain the financial misfortune that might cause him to be dropped.

Income tax was a class tax on the rich. During the 1930s just five percent of American paid it, and it accounted for less than 20 percent of federal revenues. The non-rich paid consumption taxes in the form of tariffs and excises.

World War II transformed the class tax into a mass tax. Yet even with a low exemption and standard deduction, only half of all families were liable for income tax after the war ended. As late as 1947, farmers still paid little or no income tax even when their incomes were high because they kept no books and had never been expected to do much paperwork.

Over the years, the personal exemption and standard deduction have not kept pace with inflation, so that today, 70 percent of the population is subject to income tax. Income tax on the lower middle class is inefficient. Some argue for the need to keep these people accustomed to paying income tax because once they drop out of the system, they may not be found again. So today, almost everyone is on the IRS tax list.

Treasury polices those admitted to represent taxpayers through the IRS Office of Professional Responsibility. Les Shapiro, who headed the predecessor IRS Director of Practice, traced the genesis of this office to the Horse Act of 1884. After Congress enacted legislation providing for restitution for the value of horses lost during the Civil War, claims made on the Treasury Department for lost horses exceeded horses actually lost. Congress subsequently enacted legislation giving Treasury authority to discipline any attorney or agent engaged in misconduct in representing a claimant. This was the origin of the enrolled agent, a profession which preceded the first CPA law by twelve years.

Grievances against the tax system are sometimes used to justify cheating. A Russian proverb rationalizes, "Where all are stealing, none is a thief." There's a French proverb, "No one can steal from the state." J.P. Morgan put an American twist on tax evasion when in 1937 he said, "Congress should know how to levy taxes, and if it doesn't know how to collect them, then a man is a fool to pay the taxes." These are dangerously wrong ideas, largely rejected by society.

Before she died in 2007, Leona Helmsley was ranked 369th richest person in the world by *Forbes*, worth an estimated $2.5 billion. For evading $1.2 million in taxes, she was sentenced to four years in prison. A housekeeper testified that she heard her say, "We don't pay taxes. Only the little people pay taxes." Helmsley served 21 months and was reviled as the "Queen of Mean."

American prosperity and power, indeed the strength of our democracy, stem from our ability to manage fiscal policy and collect taxes. I advise clients who complain about their tax burden that it's taxes which create the conditions for them to earn their comfortable incomes. Taxes are low in Nevada, but people prefer to live in highly taxed California. It's not just the weather and scenery. California has the infrastructure that allows them to earn more. Our triumph in the Cold War resulted from our ability to collect taxes to fund a military buildup, and the Soviet's inability to do the same. The South might have won had it been able to collect taxes needed to finance the Civil War.

> [The] power to tax is the one great power on which the whole national fabric is based. It is as necessary to the existence and prosperity of a nation as the air he breathes to the natural man. It is not only the power to destroy, but it is also the power to keep alive.
> —*Nicol v. Ames*, 173 US 509 (1899)

## Irwin Schiff

There's a whole industry of tax protesters: people who refuse to pay income tax. Some make a good living convincing others not to pay.

Irwin Schiff had a 30-year career as the top weasel of tax protesters. He authored several books including, *The Biggest Con: How the Government Fleeces You* (1976), *The Tax Rebel's Guide to the Constitution: How Anyone Can Stop Paying Income Taxes* (1982), and *The Federal Mafia: How It Illegally Imposes and Unlawfully Collects Income Taxes* (1990). Other credits included a 1977 *Washington Star* interview on "Social Security, The World's Biggest Chain Letter," and a 1978 appearance on Tom Snyder's NBC talk show, *The Tomorrow Show*. More recently, he was interviewed on ABC's *20/20* and Fox News' *Hannity & Colmes*.

His attacks on the system were protected by the First Amendment — until he went further and took his own advice. For 1974 and 1975 he sent IRS a Form 1040, altered to read, "U.S. Individual Income Confession." Neither form contained any income data, but were accompanied by pages and pages of tax protest statements.

NBC invited an IRS public affairs official to appear on *The Tomorrow Show* with Schiff. The IRS declined, but videotaped the broadcast. At his trial, this tape was introduced as evidence over Schiff's objections. Schiff was sentenced to six months imprisonment, six months of probation, and a $10,000 fine.

Never before had a case involving a defendant's appearance on a television talk show been allowed as evidence in a criminal case. And there was ample evidence of intent, without the tape, to support a jury conviction. The tape showed Snyder telling Schiff, "you're going to wind up in Leavenworth one day." The appeals court ruled in 1979 that statement (and others on the tape) unfairly prejudiced the jury and ordered a new trial.

In this early phase of his career, Schiff was convicted twice and served two terms in jail, totaling four years, for his tax crimes. His book, *How Anyone Can Stop Paying Income Taxes*, sold very well. After the IRS levied against his royalties in 1983, publisher Simon & Schuster paid $197,000 to the IRS toward Schiff's 1976 to 1978 taxes.

The Tax Court complained about his frequent lawsuits, "Petitioner has had so many bites at the apple with respect to these frivolous claims that there is nothing left but the core," as it imposed a $25,000 frivolous penalty on his 1992 complaint against the income tax.

Irwin Schiff maintained a website, www.paynoincometax.com. He advertised a $50,000 finder's fee to anyone who provided proof of a law requiring Americans to pay income taxes, but never paid that reward. He demanded to be shown plain language that said one is "liable" for paying income taxes. He had a technical point. The Internal Revenue Code begins, "There is hereby imposed," when discussing who the income tax is "imposed" on. The word, "liable," is reserved in the Code when discussing who is "liable" for imprisonment. Occasionally, Schiff got sued by those stupid enough to follow his advice. They discovered the hard way that paying taxes isn't voluntary.

Many believed his rant that payment of taxes is "purely voluntary." At least 3,100 clients attached Schiff's frivolous two-page explanation to their returns from 1999 to 2001. The IRS handily spotted them. Still, they tied up the equivalent of seven IRS agents in Nevada full time for two years, stopping attempted evasion of over $56 million in income taxes. Dozens of his clients went to prison and many filed for bankruptcy.

Between 1997 and 2002, Schiff sold over $4 million of tax protester products to the gullible. He concealed his income by using offshore bank accounts, conducting financial transactions through secret banking services and offshore debit cards, opening bank accounts using multiple tax identification numbers, and hiding assets through use of nominees. In June 2004, a court held Schiff liable for over $2 million in 1979 to 1985 taxes, interest and penalties. Following a five-week trial, a jury later found him guilty of 1999 to 2001 criminal tax violations.

Schiff pleaded for leniency, claiming he had recently been diagnosed as suffering from a "chronic and severe delusional disorder" which resulted in his irrational and incorrect beliefs regarding the federal income tax. His girlfriend, Cynthia Neun, confided to an online "friend" who inquired about this insanity plea, "We are sick about having to use this defense. It's ridiculous."

The judge called him a flimflam man. Stating that Schiff was unable to be rehabilitated, in February 2006 he sentenced the 78-year-old to 12 years in prison, plus an additional year for contempt, and ordered him to pay over $4.2 million in restitution. Neun, 52, was sentenced to 68 months in prison and ordered to pay $1.1 million in restitution. Another accomplice, Lawrence Cohen, was sentenced to 33 months.

By statute, the IRS may no longer label anyone as an "illegal tax protester." It may only use terms like "non-filer" or "frivolous," and when appropriate, "potentially dangerous." Still, it's very hard to beat an IRS charge of this nature, and in any event, it's ruinously expensive. Bay Shore, N.Y. accountant Paul Petrino was charged with underreporting taxes by $506,763 on returns he prepared for 36 clients, using a common tax protester argument that salaries are not taxable. He faced a maximum potential sentence of three years imprisonment and $250,000 in fines for each return. His first trial in February 2006 ended in a hung jury. His second trial three months later ended in acquittal. He hired an excellent lawyer, Robert Fink, who picked pliable juries. Fink has authored several books, including, *How To Defend Yourself Against The IRS* and *You Can Protect Yourself From The IRS*.

Actor Wesley Snipes was acquitted in January 2008 of fraud, conspiracy and six counts of failing to pay taxes on more than $58 million of income for the years 1999 through 2004. Still, the jury found him guilty of failing to file returns or pay taxes from 1999 through 2001. Snipes was sentenced to the maximum—three years, a $5 million fine, and he still had to pay all the back taxes, interest and penalties.

His co-defendants were well-known tax protesters Eddie Ray Kahn, who served prison time for prior tax crimes, and Douglas P. Rosile, a disbarred CPA. One of Snipes' trial attorneys was Robert G. Bernhoft, who had been an active member of the U.S. Taxpayers Party and had been barred by court order since 1999 from selling a program under which he said people could legally stop paying income taxes. While spewing familiar and discredited tax protester arguments and paperwork, Snipes successfully proved to the jury that he relied on the advice of Kahn and Rosile when he quit paying taxes in 1998 and filed amended returns seeking millions in refunds from earlier years. Kahn and Rosile were convicted of fraud and conspiracy charges. They were sentenced to 10 years and 4½ years, respectively. The jury recognized them as the criminals and Snipes as their victim.

**An Unholy Mess**

A few people can successfully intimidate the IRS. Congressman Omar Burleson (D-TX) sat on the tax-writing House Ways and Means Committee. Burleson was also a member of the board of trustees of Abilene Christian College, which is affiliated with the Churches of Christ.

Back in 1968, the parsonage (housing) allowance for ministers employed by religious schools was subject to social security tax (FICA). Schools had to withhold and match the FICA tax even though housing allowances are not subject to the income tax. Abilene didn't pay the required FICA, and the IRS proposed an assessment against the college for 1964 to 1967 for around $75,000. The college appealed to Burleson.

Six IRS conferees met with Burleson on May 6, 1970. He made them an irresistible offer. Rescind the assessment, or he would introduce a legislative fix the next morning. The IRS decided "that a favorable response should be given to Congressman Burleson [and] that a revenue ruling be published....It was also agreed that any change in social security [from FICA to SE (self-employment tax)] should be done prospectively...."

So the IRS issued two rulings without any explanation of its reasoning, subjecting all teacher-preachers to self-employment tax on their parsonage and relieving religious schools from withholding and matching FICA. It was issued solely for political reasons – the IRS did not want to make an enemy of Ways and Means member Burleson.

To this day, there is no statutory authority or judicial precedent for imposing 15.3 percent self-employment tax on teacher-preachers, rather than 7.65 percent FICA. In its haste, the IRS failed to obtain the required consent from the Social Security Administration for the FICA/SE switching aspect of the ruling. It is the Social Security Administration's domain to define whether income is subject to FICA or SE tax. Yet, every teacher-preacher now pays Omar Burleson's SE tax.

The parsonage allowance remains controversial and sacrosanct, despite some televangelists who live in multimillion dollar mansions tax-free. The original Treasury proposals which became the Tax Reform Act of 1986 included a provision "to repeal the current exclusions for...housing allowances for ministers...." It didn't survive the proposal stage.

Burleson wasn't the only one who forced IRS favors. Lyndon Johnson's protégé, Bobby Baker, related how his boss secured delegates at the 1960 Democratic Convention:

> We finally made a deal with [Congressman Bill] Green who had been harassed for years by the Internal Revenue Service: he could choose Lyndon Johnson's Secretary of the Treasury if he would switch Pennsylvania to the Johnson banner....Albert Greenfield, a wealthy Pennsylvanian with tax problems...asked to trade away a possible $10 million in potential tax revenues for a political endorsement....I never followed up on the details, but I do know that the IRS dropped its case — and that Greenfield delivered a handful of votes for LBJ from among the Pennsylvania delegates...

It's not just congressmen who wield influence with IRS. Carolyn Agger was a leading Washington tax lawyer and wife of Supreme Court Justice Abe Fortas. After receiving an erroneous IRS notice regarding her own income tax, she complained directly to IRS Commissioner Sheldon Cohen (1964-1969). Personally attending to the matter, Cohen wrote back on September 16, 1965, "Dear Carolyn," acknowledged the error, and added, "After all we may need Abe's vote one day."

## Pen Pals

I spend a few hours each week replying to IRS correspondence. Years ago, it was much easier. Accountants would make the acquaintance of a friendly someone at the IRS. Whenever a minor problem arose, we would call that IRS contact and on the strength of our relationship with them, could get penalties abated and problems resolved, without the formality of a power of attorney or correspondence.

In the early 1980s, a General Accounting Office report correctly noted that penalties were often improperly abated under this system. Furthermore, any letter from a taxpayer or his representative complaining about a dunning notice would temporarily stop the IRS computer from sending notices. Under pressure of budget deficits, the administration and Congress directed IRS to assess all penalties. The IRS continued to send notices while investigating correspondence that the assessments were wrong. There was an abrupt end to informal dealings with accountants which had worked very smoothly, but lost too much revenue.

The IRS claims that 75 percent of its notices are correct and get paid without complaint. My statistics show the opposite. Many accountants won't challenge an IRS notice under $100-$200, which helps the IRS statistics. Not on my watch. I challenge every incorrect IRS notice, no matter how trivial. A 1998 Congressional study found that the IRS is sustained for just 30 percent of their assessments when challenged.

In 1981, I had a $43 ($30 tax plus $13 interest and penalties) IRS error involving a lost refund check. The IRS spent five years looking into this $43 matter, and I became telephone- and pen-pals with the assigned employee. She told me that she developed a three-inch file to finally get this straightened out. She retired after settling my case.

The most trivial IRS notice I ever dealt with was my own account, and I reported it to the media. "Atlanta CPA Jay Starkman received a notice from the Internal Revenue Service that he owed $0.03," wrote the *Atlanta Journal-Constitution*. WAGA-TV devoted a full two minutes of evening news broadcast time to my story. I kept the high ground for the interview by insisting that the solution to the problem was for people to call their congressmen and demand more money for the IRS to buy new computers.

Television is such a powerful medium. I was featured for four days on an afternoon Atlanta TV broadcast about tax return preparation. Six months later – *six months later* – I got a call from someone in Helen, Georgia, about 85 miles north of Atlanta, who wanted to hire me. She remembered me from the TV program.

I once got a frantic call from a client's bookkeeper. An IRS revenue officer called and announced that he was coming right over to collect a $14.45 balance, and threatened to padlock the business if he didn't get it. I called and asked the agent if he really intended to make a special trip to personally collect a check for $14.45, and whether he had made the padlock threat. "I always tell the people what I'm going to do way in advance so when I come out with my locks and chains, there won't be any surprises," he replied.

I convinced the IRS officer that he didn't want to do that because the business that owed the tax had actually moved. I then contacted IRS Atlanta District Director Paul Williams, whom I had met on several occasions, to complain that I shouldn't have to drop everything over an "urgent" $14.45. I also hinted that I could have had the media present when the agent came for that $14.45 check.

The director was outraged. "If he's making a special trip to collect $14.45, what ELSE is he doing?" He said that he would personally resolve the matter and that I should call him if I ever felt that IRS was attempting any sort of retribution against me or my clients for reporting this incident.

No retribution ensued. Nor was I concerned because I knew how to contact IRS leadership in Washington who, like the district director, wouldn't tolerate such behavior by the collection division. I suggested to the director that the problem likely wasn't a wayward agent, but rather the lack of training or supervision. That allowed me to make my point against such aggressive IRS tactics rather strongly, while allowing IRS a face-saving explanation.

A client who had prepared his own 1980 income tax return received an IRS notice for over $3,000, without any explanation. Repeated letters to IRS went unanswered, until I finally received a phone call in September 1984 telling me that the return contained an error in calculating self-employment tax. The IRS was correct, except by then the statute of limitations had expired. An IRS assessment must state the reason for assessing the tax, which we had not received during the statutory period. IRS had mailed the balance due notices to the taxpayer, but mailed the reason to an old address. The law requires that all notices be mailed to the taxpayer's "last known address."

The IRS refused to admit its error. We went to district court and won. My client was an attorney, so his legal costs were nominal. IRS sent a lawyer from Washington to represent the government at the pretrial hearing and later at the trial, incurring transportation and overnight hotel charges both times. At the trial, IRS sent two agents to testify, taking half a day work from each of them. Following the trial, I asked the government attorney why a compromise settlement wasn't offered. "I recommended that a settlement be offered, but my superiors decided better to prosecute." The agency spent more on prosecuting that weak case than the tax at stake.

The most perplexing notice I received was not from IRS, but from the Department of Labor, both of which audit qualified retirement plans. I got a "no change" letter from the IRS. Without telling me that Department of Labor was going to do another audit, the client decided he could handle this one himself. He contacted me after the Labor Department sent him a four-page letter detailing violations and advising that there would be a 20 percent penalty in addition to restitution he would have to make to the plan for bad investments. It ended with, "We hope this letter will be helpful to you in the execution of your fiduciary duties...."

I suspected that the Department of Labor wasn't sure what to do to resolve its audit findings, and I was right. "It's complicated and new. We're still trying to feel our way through," admitted the auditor. I suggested a solution which he agreed to. It took 20 hours to go through 10 years of workpapers for two plans. The net result was a $2,000 realignment in the allocation of plan assets between participants and three small checks had to be issued to terminated employees. There was no restitution and no penalty.

**The Extension Ritual**

IRS receives an avalanche of tax returns close to the deadline. Income tax returns were originally due on March 1, with no extensions. At the request of the American Institute of Accountants, IRS began granting extensions in 1918. From 1919 until 1954, the deadline was March 15. To ease the burden for IRS, Congress extended the deadline to April 15 beginning in 1955.

Today, IRS grants an automatic six-month extension upon request. In the past, an acceptable reason had to be given. The IRS often accepted the excuse, "additional time is needed," but not always. I never used that excuse. There was always a good reason. An accountant with a national firm once wrote that his client's tax records were stolen. That was true, but the records related to a different tax year. The IRS once ruled that the death of your CPA would be accepted as a reasonable excuse for failure to file timely.

Proposals have been floated to extend the filing deadline until April 30 or May 15. H&R Block has been the most vocal opponent because that would dramatically increase its labor cost. Other tax preparers are largely opposed because it would extend the *karoshi* grind by a few weeks.

## Social Security Numbers

Randolph Paul described in 1947 "unfounded" fears about uses of social security numbers:

> The *New York Sun* printed a fearsome story headed "New Deal Will Tag Workers." In a picture next to the story was a regimented victim of social security, stripped to the waist and wearing a metal tag on a chain around his neck. A Western newspaper began substituting social security numbers for by-lines over reporters' stories. The editor signed himself 525-10-9454.

Social security numbers on tax returns were optional prior to 1962. Then Congress made it mandatory "to make possible a greatly expanded use of automatic data processing equipment and to also fully utilize the information documents presently coming into the Internal Revenue Service." Following this legislation, the legend at the bottom of social security cards was revised, adding "and tax purposes" to read, "FOR SOCIAL SECURITY AND TAX PURPOSES — NOT FOR IDENTIFICATION." The legend was dropped in 1972 as social security numbers gained acceptance as a "tag."

The Social Security Administration insists that social security numbers are unique, that a number is never issued to more than one individual. But when told that an IRS southeast regional director and credit reporting agencies have confirmed to me that duplicate numbers are shared by unrelated individuals, they admit that there are some duplicates, however rare. When they become aware of two individuals who share the same number, they take action to split the earnings and issue a new number to one of the individuals.

**Simple Tax Returns**

Most people have simple finances and don't itemize. With so much information on its computer databases, IRS could automatically prepare tax returns for them, send the completed returns to taxpayers for review, revision, and signature in order to get their refunds. Many countries using withholding have return-free income tax systems. Legislative proposals to do the same here have been made occasionally during the past 20 years.

The main reason this isn't implemented is that it would take months for the IRS to calculate and send refunds. People run to a tax preparer in January to get a quick refund, much faster than the IRS can calculate. Employers needn't file W-2s with the Social Security Administration until February 28 (March 31 if filed electronically) and a 30-day extension is available. The IRS doesn't have complete W-2 information before May.

Electronic filing is fueled by the refund anticipation loan, where the tax preparer makes a good commission by arranging an "instant loan" at exorbitant interest rates against the anticipated tax refund the preparer has calculated. Most of my clients owe taxes on April 15, so the quick refund incentive is lacking.

Before such loans, return preparers would write the client a check for an "Instant (reduced) Refund" and keep the IRS refund for themselves. Since 1977, in order to protect the public from unscrupulous preparers, tax preparers are not allowed to cash refund checks. So preparers contract with third parties to advance a loan on the funds and receive a commission for the referral. Thus, the refund anticipation loan was invented as a marketing device by commercial tax preparers. The heavily promoted loans rely on electronic filing to speed cash flow to the preparer.

The engine behind the H&R Block revolution is the earned income credit (EIC), introduced in the Tax Reform Act of 1976. EIC induces masses of working poor to file a return in order to claim a large refund. Besides high-margin refund anticipation loans and e-filing, Block invented "Peace of Mind" protection. For an additional fee, Block covers any interest or penalties resulting from an audit of tax returns they prepared, as well as additional taxes assessed up to a specified amount. "Express IRA" is another new product. Thus Block earns fees from tax return preparation, loans to people expecting refunds, e-filing, audit protection, and IRA fees.

Ask the man-in-the-street, "Who is expert in income tax preparation?" Thirty years ago, the answer would have been CPAs. Today, they answer H&R Block, the company that prepares 15 percent of income tax returns, mostly low- and middle-income. Block advertises, "*Solicita tu ITIN aqui.*" This is a disguised appeal to illegal immigrants for help in obtaining an individual taxpayer identification number (ITIN). Eleven million ITINs have been issued since the IRS introduced them in 1996. (Citizens and legal residents use social security numbers and are ineligible for an ITIN.) Our tax law allows ITIN filers to claim deductions for dependents who live in Mexico and Canada, reducing their taxable income by $3,400 per child. About 80 percent file income tax returns claiming refunds. ITINs can also be used for opening a bank account, credit card account, even obtaining a home mortgage.

Since 1990, dozens of lawsuits have been filed against H&R Block and its refund-anticipation loan provider, Beneficial National Bank, alleging that plaintiffs were cheated out of an estimated $2 billion. Beneficial charged interest in the range of 100 to 800 percent. Block received 15 percent of the loan for cashing the check, in addition to splitting an undisclosed amount of the interest. These helped Block earn a pretax margin of 60 percent, mostly from low-income customers.

The New York City Department of Consumer Affairs cited Block in 2002 for charging $197 to prepare and file a tax return, giving the client a $500 loan in anticipation of a refund. The loan fee worked out to 522 percent interest a year. H&R Block settled claims in Texas for $43.5 million, stemming from its failure to disclose fees on high-interest loans marketed to customers. In a dispute over its additional charge for "audit protection," H&R Block agreed in 2003 to pay 42 states attorneys general $2.3 million plus an additional $1 million toward a consumer fund. "Express IRAs" have come under litigation for annual fees that allegedly exceed income earned by these H&R Block initiated retirement accounts.

During the 2007 tax filing season, injunctions were filed against five corporations that operated more than 165 Jackson Hewitt franchises in Chicago, Atlanta, Detroit and Raleigh-Durham, N.C. They alleged filing fraudulent returns claiming bogus deductions and earned income credits totaling over $70 million in phony claims. "I am deeply disturbed by the allegation that a major franchisee of the nation's second-largest tax-preparation firm is intentionally preparing improper tax returns with inflated refunds," said IRS Commissioner Mark W. Everson about the firm which prepared nearly three percent of income tax returns. IRS dropped its audit of the corporate franchisor Jackson Hewitt after receiving a "voluntary compliance payment of $1.5 million," according to a September 20, 2007 SEC filing.

**e-Filing**

A major reason the IRS promotes electronic filing of tax returns is that it supposedly reduces return processing cost to the agency by around $2 per return. The IRS claims that electronic processing costs 29 cents, but the General Accountability Office says it "cannot independently verify this estimate." A 2005 IRS Oversight Board report on e-filing included among its goals, "Substantially reduce IRS electronic filing per return processing costs." While paper returns are labor-intensive with high variable costs, e-filed returns are capital-intensive with high fixed costs for computer hardware, software, and maintenance. Intuitively, we believe that e-filing is cheaper, but after 20 years IRS still cannot reliably quantify the savings.

Taxpayers may pay around $20, to file electronically. Isn't that worthwhile so the IRS can save $2 and commercial tax preparers can earn a bigger profit? It's a financial drain on the nation's poorest taxpayers and inefficient extra work for low volume return preparers. Presently, you can't beat a postage stamp for cost efficiency at the taxpayer's end. But making others bear the cost, however inefficient overall, appears not to be a concern in setting IRS policy.

The IRS savings are so small for several reasons. Most electronic returns are simple returns that are among the least costly paper returns to process. It requires a large investment in technology to process electronic returns, and there are competency and fraud issues. A refund is promised within three weeks, which is long before the Social Security Administration sends W-2 data to IRS to match against tax returns. So IRS must often accept on good faith that an e-filed return claiming a refund is not fraudulent. To minimize fraud, a system must be maintained for admitting those authorized to transmit returns electronically, which includes fingerprinting many preparers.

When e-file fraud strikes, there are many little people to chase, or one big transmitter who has disappeared. The IRS acknowledges that e-file fraud is a big concern, concentrated among EIC filers. As a result, a low-income taxpayer is as likely to get audited as a high-income taxpayer. Using the tax code to distribute welfare is costly.

Prisoners have discovered that filing fraudulent returns claiming EIC means easy money. In 2004, the IRS identified 18,000 false prisoner returns claiming $68 million in refunds. The IRS was able to stop the issuance of 78 percent of these refunds. The IRS doesn't bother prosecuting prisoners already serving long sentences. As a result, blank tax forms are now contraband in some prisons. A prisoner caught with a blank tax form is subject to discipline.

Prior to 1943, tax returns had to be notarized. The Revenue Act of 1942 substituted an oath declaration, under penalties of perjury, for the notarization requirement. E-filing required the IRS to create alternative signature methods, which are still evolving. The main reason signatures are required under penalties of perjury, a former IRS chief compliance officer once told me, is so the Criminal Investigation Division can obtain an average of four convictions annually for tax evasion. Most criminal convictions involve fraud or tax schemes, not perjury. Must we physically sign millions of returns just for the sake of sending four people to prison for perjury? In civil cases, the Tax Court has held that an income tax return lacking a signature "was no return at all."

One of the strongest benefits to e-filing is that the IRS gains instant access to filed returns for determining audit potential. With paper returns, it can take up to six months to complete that review. Speaking before the Tax Executives Institute, IRS Deputy Commissioner Bruce Ungar told the 2006 gathering that e-filing provides "a rich and fertile field" of data. The president's fiscal 2009 budget said the same, "Electronic filing provides efficiency because the IRS is better able to make use of its computer infrastructure to target returns with audit potential." It would be difficult to sell this feature to the public.

**The Cause of Death Was Taxes**

Dealing with IRS Collections can be one of the most difficult and frustrating assignments facing a tax practitioner. In 1990, I called Collections to offer a compromise. My client would obtain money from a relative to pay the tax, provided that the IRS would forgive the interest and penalties. Otherwise, he would file for bankruptcy and owe nothing. The revenue officer refused saying, "Go ahead. File for bankruptcy." He did, and IRS got nothing.

When compromise and installment negotiations with the IRS fail, taxpayers facing liens, levies, and seizures have few options. Banks advise customers to purchase traveler's checks for levy protection. I've had several clients discharge taxes in bankruptcy. Two of my clients have fled the country. Bankruptcy and fleeing the country work. Death doesn't.

Bankruptcy works because the bankruptcy court, unlike other courts, doesn't shower IRS with preferential treatment. The purpose of bankruptcy proceedings is to discharge debtors from accumulated financial obligations. Finding that "peace of mind is invaluable," the bankruptcy court awarded debtors $1,000 for the "trauma" they experienced in receiving a "Notice of Intent to Levy" from the Service.

IRS Collections can be flexible. It's a relief to work with a revenue officer who is fair and willing to bend IRS procedures. The Internal Revenue Manual provides that no lien can be placed on a taxpayer if it might impair the taxpayer's ability to pay. A client who was an officer of a publicly traded company avoided an IRS lien because it might have been a reportable event with the Securities and Exchange Commission, resulting in his being fired.

The 1998 IRS Restructuring Act demanded greater flexibility from the revenue service. In 1999, this helped me settle a $110,000 liability for just $9,000. It was a *pro bono* case for a low-income taxpayer, a multi-year liability, mostly self-employment tax, and half the assessment was interest and penalties.

However, a year later, the IRS misapplied his current year estimated tax payments to the old $110,000 liability. Then the IRS threatened to void the settlement if the taxpayer didn't immediately pay the current tax a second time, something he could not afford. This necessitated a court filing, and *pro bono* assistance from Miller & Chevalier, a major Washington tax law firm. We were able to hold the IRS at bay until I could get the case accepted by the newly created IRS Taxpayer Advocate Service, which corrected the situation.

Outside of the Mafia, the IRS is unlike any other creditor when you fall behind. Following some perfunctory legal procedures, the delinquent taxpayer finds himself in financial purgatory. Some people can't take the strain. Houston revenue agent, Jennifer Long told CBS-TV's *Face the Nation* that she knew of at least five suicides attributable to troubles with the IRS. There are many more she didn't know about.

After a friend committed suicide, his family told me that taxes were a contributing factor. The IRS had been hounding him for money. He never mentioned a word to me. I related this to an attorney who specializes in IRS collection matters. It wasn't news to her. She had three clients who committed suicide over IRS debts. Given these anecdotes, I suspect IRS troubles might be a leading cause of suicide.

A letter threatening suicide is usually a desperate call for help. Not at the IRS, where suicide threats are treated as harassment against IRS personnel rather than a taxpayer in extreme emotional and financial distress. Treasury has published a directive, The Employee Protection System Records, "to enhance the security and safety of Internal Revenue Service employees....The records contained in this system of records will include reports by Internal Revenue Service employees of incidents of threats of harm to, or harassment of, employees by individual taxpayers, *threats of suicide made by a taxpayer in response to a contact by an Internal Revenue Service employee...*" (italics added). So a letter to IRS threatening to commit suicide is considered harassment against the IRS employee, not a threat of self-harm.

A few IRS-induced suicide cases have been documented.

In the late 1960s, attorney Robert Cleveland began a 15-year dispute with the IRS, involving multiple trials and appeals. He was unable to pay his legal bills or the $250,000 IRS assessment. Starting in 1991, the IRS confiscated his social security income. The agency levied on money he obtained in a settlement for one of his law clients, causing the client to wait years to receive his settlement and causing Cleveland to be disbarred in Illinois. He suffered severe depression. His therapist wrote the IRS to say that Cleveland was suicidal.

In 1996, Cleveland retained tax attorney Michael Rotman for advice in resolving the dispute. Rotman advised Cleveland to file ten years of delinquent tax returns. Since the financial records had been lost, Rotman allegedly told Cleveland to estimate his income and expenses for the relevant years.

His estimates did not agree with IRS figures, so the agency decided to audit him again. Concerned over Cleveland's suicidal depression, his therapist succeeded in postponing the audit for a year. Shortly before the delayed audit was scheduled to take place, Cleveland took his own life on January 26, 1998.

Cleveland's estate sued Rotman for malpractice, because his advice triggered the proposed IRS audit, which in turn triggered Cleveland's suicide. The district court dismissed the case for failure to state a claim for which relief can be granted under Federal Rules of Civil Practice. The appeals court affirmed, saying, "Suicide is generally not a likely result of bad tax advice, especially when that advice concerns the relatively routine matter of filing tax returns."

Bruce Barron committed suicide in 1996 at age 47 over a $330,000 tax debt. He and two friends started a waste-disposal partnership in 1984, which failed in 1986. The IRS disallowed the deductions and credits taken over several years, billing him $233,268 with penalties and interest in 1991. Broke, he made an offer-in-compromise for $25,000, which the IRS refused. His death came when the IRS levied on his vacation home.

The revenue service then went after his widow, Shirley Barron, and the life insurance proceeds. She countered with a $1 million wrongful death lawsuit against IRS. The agency assigned an army of 22 lawyers to the case. Discovery proceedings showed that the agent who refused the $25,000 compromise offer had written instructions from her superiors to accept a $30,000 offer. However, she never told the taxpayer. "He could have come up with an additional $5,000," said his CPA, Rick Maloney. Only the intervention of IRS Commissioner Charles Rossotti (1997-2002), who was following the bad publicity in the media, brought a 1998 out-of-court settlement. Mrs. Barron agreed to drop her lawsuit and IRS agreed to drop its now-over-$400,000 assessment and pay $44,000 toward her legal fees.

It's not just IRS. Many New York counties exercise their right under the state's Uniform Delinquent Tax Act which allows municipalities to keep all the equity on property foreclosed for unpaid taxes. Judith Orlando committed suicide in May 2004 on account of $20,367 of unpaid taxes when Suffolk County foreclosed. A county auction with a starting bid of $125,000 was withdrawn after her death. Under New York law, the county would keep the full proceeds of the sale, not just the $20,367 it was owed.

Not even death will stop an out-of-control revenue officer.

Ehsanolla Motaghed worked at the U.S. embassy in Tehran and came to the U.S. after the Ayatollah expelled him. He ran a successful optical lens importing business, but ran afoul the IRS, owing $157,000 in unpaid 1985, 1986 and 1987 taxes. He was also indicted for offering a cash bribe to an IRS agent. His lawyer explained, "He was told he owed the IRS money, and the agent said he had to pay, and so he gave the agent $4,000." He died in Omaha on June 9, 1990 from Lou Gehrig's disease. A death certificate was insufficient for the IRS to write-off the debt. It demanded an exhumation to be sure he was dead. Fortunately for the departed, Nebraska only allows exhumation for the purpose of performing an autopsy.

His lawyer accused the U.S. Attorney's Office of "watching too many Alfred Hitchcock movies." *Newsday* ran the story under the headline, "Eternal Revenue Service." One columnist quipped, "This sure gives a whole new meaning to the terms *late taxpayer* and *stiff penalties.*"

## Samuel Swartwout

Historians vilify Samuel Swartwout, collector for the Port of New York. He sailed to England in August 1838 with the amazing sum of $1,225,705.69 stolen from tax collections over the previous eight years — more than five percent of the entire treasury of the U.S. To this day, it's the largest single official theft in American history. Only, it's not true – or at least it wasn't that large.

Swartwout first appeared on the national stage as a courier of the famous cipher letter in Aaron Burr's "western conspiracy." His attorney, Francis Scott Key, was able to have the case transferred to the U.S. Supreme Court to decide whether a writ of habeas corpus was improperly denied, as well as the issue of treason. He was acquitted. The *New York Times* listed this February 1807 case as one of the most important early decisions by the Supreme Court.

Swartwout was one of 140 witnesses at the August 1807 trial of Aaron Burr, where he met and became fast friends with Andrew Jackson. He worked (unsuccessfully) to swing the New York vote to Andrew Jackson in his first run for the presidency in 1824. When Jackson became president in 1829, he rewarded Swartwout with the most lucrative position he could appoint, collector for the Port of

New York, through which passed two-thirds of all imports into the U.S. and $15 million in annual tariff revenue. The annual salary was $6,400 (when the average workingman earned $500), plus $500 - $1,500 a year from charging New York merchants for storing their imports in government warehouses. The New York customs house gave Swartwout control over more federal patronage jobs than anywhere else outside of Washington, with employment rising from 199 to 407 during his nine-year tenure. Swartwout was a power within New York City's corrupt Tammany political machine.

Martin Van Buren, who succeeded Jackson as president, distrusted Swartwout from the start. As president, Van Buren appointed Jesse Hoyt to succeed Swartwout when his term expired on March 29, 1838. Swartwout admitted that he retained $210,096.40 of the federal government's money after leaving office to reimburse merchants who might win court suits against him for excess duties he might have charged. That was also his predecessor's practice at the customs house.

Seeking to raise capital for a business venture, Swartwout departed for England in August 1838, without settling the retained federal funds before he left. He gave a power of attorney to a trusted friend, Henry Ogden, who had served as his cashier in the collector's office.

Shortly after he departed, a $1,225,705.69 shortage was discovered by Collector Hoyt. Swartwout was accused of embezzlement, and on November 12, 1838, the government levied against all his assets while he was out of the country. Ogden signed over all of Swartwout's properties to the government: 435 acres in Bergen County, N.J., 333 acres in the Meadowlands between Hoboken and Newark, N.J., 10 acres in Manhattan, his New York City residence, and all his other assets, including properties in New Jersey, Maryland, Virginia, and Illinois.

A congressional investigation resulted in a 261-page report, only 99 pages of which dealt with Swartwout. Among its conclusions was that there were no defalcations prior to 1837.

Swartwout remained in exile until August 3, 1841, when he returned during the administration of President John Tyler. He was not arrested. Tyler initiated his own investigation into corruption at the New York customs house. It concluded that Swartwout's defalcation amounted to only $400,000 and that any other missing funds were pocketed by his successors.

Besides the levies, the $1,225,705.69 was never recovered. The issue was so mired in politics and the books so thoroughly cooked that it must be doubted how anyone could ascribe a defalcation to the penny of accuracy. One must ask why anyone would embezzle over $1 million and wait five months to make a getaway. The government never won a judgment against Swartwout or any of his sureties. He lived in penury both in Europe and for the remainder of his life in the U.S. Swartwout would testify that took just $1,000 for his England trip, and after paying for his family's transportation, was left with $500. His defalcation was the subject of two Supreme Court cases, one relieving his surety company of liability; the other, that his Hoboken properties could be seized without due process of law. A May 1845 government lawsuit against his surety company seeking $150,000 against an alleged defalcation of $435,052.21, resulted in a jury verdict requiring the government to pay the surety $20,545.59. Finally, Collector Hoyt, who "discovered" Swartwout's defalcation, defaulted on about $200,000 when his own term expired.

**The Battle of the Millionaires**

The Bureau of Internal Revenue was established in 1862 to administer the Civil War income tax. While public attention focused on taxpayer compliance, the bureau was evolving into an agency known for graft, bribery, intimidation, widespread corruption and secret deal-making. Three major investigations and reforms have made IRS a professional and honest agency. These investigations started in 1924, 1951, and 1997.

The first investigation started as a result of the efforts of James Couzens, the financial genius behind Ford Motor Company. At the time of his resignation in 1915 as vice-president and treasurer, he owned 11 percent of the company, making him the largest shareholder after Henry Ford.

He went on to a career in politics, becoming Detroit's police commissioner, where he fought corruption, then as mayor where he installed the municipal streetcars. He was appointed to the Senate in 1922 to complete the two years remaining in Republican Truman Newberry's term after Newberry resigned amid a campaign-finance scandal. As a result of evidence that Henry Ford, the Democratic

Senate candidate in the 1918 election, turned over to the Justice Department, Newberry was convicted of violating the Corrupt Practices Act. That conviction was eventually overturned by the U.S. Supreme Court.

Senator Couzens risked his reputation and his fortune fighting to clean up the Bureau of Internal Revenue. The opening shot came on February 21, 1924. After accusing the bureau of graft, Couzens introduced a resolution calling for the creation of a select committee to investigate.

It quickly became a clash between Couzens, the financial and political maverick, and the banking and industrial titan, Treasury Secretary Andrew Mellon. Only someone like Couzens, the wealthiest multimillionaire ever in Congress up to that time, could stand up to Mellon, who was one of the four richest men in America. It was called, "The Battle of the Millionaires."

Mellon rebuffed Couzens, telling him to mind his own business and let "Alexander Hamilton's successor" handle such complicated matters as taxation. Couzens responded by convincing the Senate to pass his resolution to investigate the bureau, which was under the jurisdiction of the treasury secretary. Since its formation in 1862, there had never been an investigation of the bureau. Under administration pressure, the Senate initially denied Couzens chairmanship of the investigating committee and loaded it with friends of Mellon, giving the chairmanship to James Watson (R-IN).

The Senate intentionally omitted funding for a counsel from the resolution. So Couzens hired Francis J. Heney, the famous "terror of graft" prosecutor, and paid him from his own pocket. Heney had mixed success fighting municipal corruption in San Francisco. In the process, he was shot through the head in the courtroom. In critical condition, he was heard to say in the ambulance, "I'll get them yet!" He suffered loss of hearing in one ear, and the city refused to pay him for three strenuous years of service from 1906 - 1909. He was fearless and un-bribable.

The bureau's files on all the corporations which Mellon owned were subpoenaed. President Coolidge protested that if wealthy Senator Couzens were permitted to pay for legal counsel for an investigating committee, the Constitution would be subverted, or worse, Andrew Mellon ("the greatest treasury secretary since Alexander Hamilton") might be forced to resign.

Couzens' committee found a revenue agency that was lopsidedly pro-business, especially toward mega-business. And corrupt. From 1921 to 1923, 796 officials were dismissed for tax fraud. In 1925, five Bronx deputy collectors were accused of blackmailing taxpayers by threatening to bring charges of filing fraudulent returns.

The committee report showed incompetence and favoritism, especially abuse of the depletion allowance. Depletion lets a business write-off the cost of mineral assets, just as depreciation permits the cost of real and personal property to be expensed over time. During World War I, the oil industry introduced geological experts who bemoaned that our scant supply of oil would be exhausted in 10 years. Congress responded with generous depletion provisions to stimulate production and protect the prospector or wildcatter. Industry interpreted the law liberally.

Businesses took advantage of this favorable climate to amend prior year tax returns and correct "erroneous" calculations of depletion, claiming huge refunds. From 1922 to 1926, Treasury paid over one billion dollars in refunds, plus six percent interest, to the nation's leading corporations. Mellon was the founder and principal owner of Gulf Oil Company, which received $4,590,385. Standard Oil of California received $3,378,000, and Sinclair Consolidated Oil Corporation got $5,000,000.

The companies receiving the refunds calculated depletion on the capitalized value of oil leases, discounted at five percent in the case of Gulf Oil. The average oil investor never expected less than a 15 percent discount, sometimes reaching 40 percent. A low discount percentage made the underlying property appear more valuable, thus increasing cost depletion. A 1918 law increased the propensity for mischief by allowing property to be valued at March 1, 1913, rather than the actual purchase date, and under certain circumstances, at the date of discovery of oil or gas (which gave a much higher valuation), and this deduction was split "equitably" between lessor and lessee. When Gulf Oil discovered that Treasury would accept an absurdly low five percent valuation with these loose rules, it applied for big refunds. The committee's report noted that "the allowances to Gulf Oil Corporation are so excessive as to constitute gross discrimination against even the oil industry."

The Couzens' report cited improper depreciation on World War I production facilities, resulting in refunds of $15,589,614 to Aluminum

Corporation of America (a Mellon company), $55,063,312 to United States Steel, $22,103,942 to Bethlehem Steel, and $15,369,123 to E.I. DuPont. The refunds were not illegal, but Couzens exposed that the process was corrupt. Historian Matthew Josephson summarized the situation:

> ...mobs of corporation accountants and lawyers, all demonstrating how oddly "stupid" they had been in other times, what whimsical errors of overpayments of taxes had been made, the sum of which they drew up and had duly honored by the treasurer.

The Mellon refunds were granted in great haste because Andrew Mellon wanted the cases of all outside interests with which he might be connected closed prior to March 4, 1921, the day he would take office. Gulf Oil's amended returns were filed on February 19, 1921, the valuation reports made by the taxpayer were accepted as filed, and the refunds were approved on February 28, 1921. Ordinarily, such large refunds required one to two years for processing. These revelations tarnished Mellon's reputation. He was accused of abusing his high office through his control of the bureau for personal gain.

Couzens' efforts established that Congress should have a say in formulating tax policy. His investigations resulted in formation of the Joint Committee on Taxation in 1926 to oversee tax laws and their administration. In 1928, the Joint Committee's authority was extended to review all refunds over $75,000 and publish an annual report for Congress with the names of all individuals and entities, together with the amount of refund that the committee reviewed. In addition, President Hoover issued an executive order in 1929 that refunds over $20,000 would be publicized. The Joint Committee refund review threshold today is $2 million, and 1,163 refund cases were examined in 2004, but without publicity.

History books refer to the scandal of 1924 as Teapot Dome, rarely mentioning the Couzens revelations. Teapot Dome was a scandal involving Harding administration officials over secret leasing of Navy oil reserves in Wyoming for $400,000 in graft. Both scandals broke at the same time, but the IRS scandal dominated newspaper front pages and involved much more money.

Andrew Mellon didn't benefit just from tax favors resulting from his high office. He had difficulty drawing the line between public servant and private businessman. As treasury secretary, he helped Gulf Oil investigate obtaining a franchise to drill for oil in the British protectorate, Kuwait. He completed the deal while serving as U.S. ambassador to Great Britain. It became Gulf Oil's principal source of crude oil.

**The Truman Tax Scandal.**

In 1950, the Internal Revenue Service was still known as the Bureau of Internal Revenue. Revelation of another tax scandal began when Senator John R. Williams' (R-DL) 1948 tax payment was swindled by a cashier in the Wilmington collector's office, along with about 500 other taxpayers. The amount swindled totaled $30,000 over seven years. The cashier had Democratic party connections, and Williams was shocked that he could force no swift action against the cashier.

Cecil R. King (D-CA) headed the investigation into the IRS scandals by a subcommittee of Ways and Means. It continued under the chairmanship of Robert Kean (R-NJ) after Republicans took control of Congress in 1953. The two-year investigation uncovered large pockets of incompetence, political pressure, and corruption.

For a full year, from mid-1951 until mid-1952 the newspapers featured almost daily front page stories about scandals in the Bureau of Internal Revenue. There were allegations of conflict of interest, bribery, favors, shakedowns, negligence, extortion, false statements, falsifying tax records, failing to prosecute fraud cases, and fixing tax cases to please local politicians.

The scandals caused Commissioner George J. Schoeneman (1947-1951) to suddenly resign on June 27, 1951 "for reasons of health." Assistant Commissioner Daniel A. Bolich resigned three months later, giving the same reason, and was later sentenced to five years in prison for tax fraud, but was acquitted at his third trial.

Below the national office leadership were 64 regional collectors of internal revenue. The positions were presidential political appointments, and senators were deeply involved in getting their nominees approved. That made key bureau officials beholden to their respective patrons. Nine of the 64 collectors were dismissed or forced to resign in a little over a year. About 166 lesser employees were discharged or asked to retire in 1951 alone. Four of the collectors and over a dozen other employees were indicted on charges of fraud, bribery or other corruption.

Commissioner Joseph Nunan Jr. (1944-1947) earned a $10,000 government salary. Upon becoming commissioner, outside earnings from his New York law practice skyrocketed. After leaving office, he became one of the most successful tax practitioners in the country.

By law, a former federal employee could not prosecute a claim against the government within two years after leaving office if the claim covered the years he worked for the government. Treasury regulations went even further, prohibiting a former employee from representing a taxpayer in any case if he worked on that case for the government, regardless of how long he had been out of government service. However, Nunan received special permission to handle 102 tax cases before the bureau. His law firm partner, John Wenchel, former bureau chief counsel while Nunan was commissioner, obtained 86 waivers.

Among the people and firms receiving Nunan waivers were Indianapolis Brewing and Lawrence Burdin, its former general manager. A $636,000 tax claim against the company was settled in 1949 for $4,500. A $436,000 tax lien against Burdin was settled for $100,000. Nunan denied ever representing the company. Those were small savings compared to the $38 million income tax claim against New Yorker William Rhodes Davis. He was represented by President Truman's good friend and Democratic national chairman, William M. Boyle, Jr. The claim was settled for $850,000 upon recommendation by then Commissioner Nunan and Chief Counsel Charles Oliphant — just three cents on the dollar.

Unfortunately, Nunan didn't report all his outside income during the years he was commissioner. In his defense, he explained that the $160,000 unexplained cash had been removed from his bank accounts before the 1933 bank holiday and placed in a "tin box." The "little tin box" was a bogus defense used by Tammany crooks. Nunan explained that his wife had inherited the money from her father and her Tammany boss uncle. Nunan was convicted in 1954 of evading $91,086 in income taxes from 1946 to 1950 and sentenced to five years, of which he served two.

Though President Truman was not implicated, his operatives were. His appointments secretary and political lieutenant, Matthew

Connelly, was indicted for having accepted, while serving in the White House, cash, clothing, and a $3,600 oil royalty for his part in a tax-fixing case involving a St. Louis wholesale shoe dealer. He served six months in prison.

Assistant Attorney General Theron Lamar Caudle, who headed the Tax Division of the Justice Department, was fired. He had received a $5,000 commission upon the sale of a $30,000 Lockheed Lodestar from an agent of suspects he was trying for tax evasion. He and Oliphant accepted a paid vacation in Florida from a manufacturer they were investigating. Caudle began a prison term at the same time as Connelly, and was pardoned by President Lyndon Johnson in 1965. Oliphant resigned in December 1951 amid allegations that he was involved in a $500,000 shakedown attempt.

Judge Welburn Mayock, general counsel to the Democratic National Committee, received an envelope with $65,000 from William Lasdon in September 1948. Mayock earmarked $30,000 for a desperately needed contribution to Truman's 1948 campaign to pay for radio air time, kept $17,500 for himself, and split $17,500 between the two men who introduced him to Lasdon.

In return, Mayock helped Lasdon obtain a favorable ruling from revenue officials that a proposed $6 million sale of assets to his private foundation would be treated as long-term capital gain. The bureau had refused to issue the ruling. Indeed, Oliphant pressed an employee to change his strongly written memo recommending an adverse ruling. As Lasdon was in a 90 percent tax bracket, allowing the 25 percent capital gain cost the Treasury close to $4 million, bought for just $65,000.

Denis W. Delaney, collector for Massachusetts, was tried and sentenced to two years in prison and fined $10,500 for bribery and tax fixing.

Monroe Dowling, collector for Manhattan, was dismissed in March 1952 on charges of irregularities on his own income tax return. He had been in office only seven months since replacing the previous Manhattan collector, James Johnson, who was dismissed for "administrative inefficiency." Eight deputy tax collectors from the Manhattan district had already been convicted of crimes involving bribery and favors. The head of the New Jersey, New York and Puerto Rico Alcohol Tax Unit resigned amid accusations of having profited from side deals with liquor companies.

Joseph Marcelle, collector for Brooklyn, resigned after being charged with failure to report $32,834 of income in 1948. His salary as collector was $10,000, but he kept his private law practice at the same time, earning a gross income of $135,776. He invested $5,000 as part-owner of a vending machine company and received a $175,000 return over three years.

Ernest Schino, chief field deputy for San Francisco, got taxpayers out of tax trouble after they bought worthless shares in his dummy mining corporation. The San Francisco office maintained an Internal Revenue employee welfare fund which collected $10,400 from 1944 to 1948 from brewers, bookies, brothels, and others with potential income tax issues.

James Smyth, collector for San Francisco, together with two assistants, was indicted for backdating his own and other peoples' tax returns. There had been unfavorable reports in 1935, 1941, and 1945 on his drinking and failure to file personal income tax returns for 1939 - 1943. Despite knowledge of these shortcomings, in 1945 Franklin Roosevelt appointed Smyth, who was his northern California presidential campaign manager, on Senator Sheridan Downey's (D-CA) recommendation. Tax collections in San Francisco doubled in the three months following Smyth's replacement.

James P. Finnegan, collector for St. Louis, who had ties to Harry Truman, was convicted on two charges of bribery, sentenced to two years in prison and fined $10,000. He had collaborated with an insurance agent to sell policies to firms with tax delinquencies and other schemes to fix tax cases.

Frank Scofield, collector for Austin, resigned by request of the bureau for "the best interest of the revenue service."

Corruption existed among staff too. New York auditor Robert Selden earned less than $4,000 a year. Yet he invested $41,600 in the stock market over a three-year period. He had $23,000 of insurance on furs, jewelry and a collection of Chinese art objects. He couldn't explain satisfactorily how his assets jumped from $474 in 1935 to $23,700 some ten years later. His net worth jumped by $13,500 in 1946 alone, a year in which he invested $11,000 cash through a broker.

Adrian Ash was assigned to audit the $20 million refund claimed by Universal Pictures Company. Universal housed him at the Beverly Wilshire Hotel while he was working on the case. They paid the airfare so that his wife and son could join him from New York. Ash's final report recommended granting the $20 million refund. Upon review, his superiors reversed his recommendations, allowing only a $5 million refund.

Ash was suspended on March 7, 1952 after the bureau learned that for the five years 1946 to 1950, he spent and had on hand $36,700 more than he and his wife earned. It wasn't just Universal. He explained how he got it: won $5,800 gambling, $7,500 borrowed from a friend, $10,500 gifts from family, $1,250 sale of property, $1,400 income tax refunds, $3,000 gifts for his son upon graduation, etc. He couldn't explain where $3,500 came from. There was no documentation to support the $7,500 loan from the "friend," a former vice-president in charge of sales for Duplex Fabrics, a company whose 1942 tax return he had audited. The property gain came from 110 shares of Dumont stock which the assistant treasurer of Gimbel Brothers bought him in 1945 while he was auditing Gimbel's 1943 return.

The corruption extended to Congress. Senator Styles Bridges (R-NH) and William Maloney, former special assistant to the attorney general, pressured the bureau to settle a $5,227,000 assessment against Hyman Harvey Klein, a Baltimore wholesale liquor distributor, for $1 million. From 1944 to 1947, Klein made $5 million on a $1,000 investment in Cuban and Panamanian distributing companies. He contended that the profits represented capital gains and paid only $1.2 million in tax. Publicity from Congressman King's investigation prevented settlement. Klein was sentenced to prison for tax evasion in 1955.

Pressure was building on the president to respond to the inefficiency and corruption. Belatedly, he did. On January 2, 1952, President Truman submitted to Congress, his "Reorganization Plan No. 1" to fix the Bureau of Internal Revenue. After some squabbling by senators who didn't want to lose influence over powerful patronage appointments, it was approved on March 13 and swiftly put into effect.

Bureau officials were placed under the civil service system, and senators were taken completely out of the appointment process, except for confirmation of the commissioner and chief counsel. The 64 collectors of internal revenue were replaced by 25 district commissioners. District commissioners were forbidden to have outside employment or business interests, a big change from the 20 of 64 collectors who had outside interests. For enforcement, a permanent Office of Investigation was established to prevent corruption within Internal Revenue.

The plan succeeded because President Truman genuinely wanted the bureau fixed. His successor, Dwight Eisenhower, not only supported the reorganization, but made the scandal a 1952 campaign issue against the Democrats, insisting that the only hope for greater honesty was in a Republican victory. Truman's reorganization and Eisenhower's support effectively cleaned house at the Bureau of Internal Revenue, and it has been a professionally run organization ever since.

The King subcommittee report recommended improvements in administrative and civil procedures, such as stricter regulation of federal tax practice. Circular 230, which governs who may practice before the Treasury Department, was revised to restrict federal tax practice to certified public accountants and attorneys to keep so-called "tax experts" and influence peddlers from negotiating with revenue officials. Licensed practitioners were less likely to bribe and corrupt tax officials. In 1958, enrolled agents were admitted to practice upon passing an examination.

These year-long headlines on the front pages of the *New York Times* ran concurrently with one of the biggest stories of 1952, the recapture of notorious bank robber and prison escape artist, Willie Sutton in Brooklyn. Asked why he robbed banks, Sutton famously replied, "Because that's where the money is." He should have become a tax auditor instead. After 1951, he didn't rob any banks and tax auditors stopped shaking down taxpayers. As a tax auditor, Sutton would have faced much less jail time.

**Restructuring IRS**

In the mid-1990s, in response to widespread problems and discontent, Congress formed a National Commission to Restructure the IRS. It eventually resulted in the IRS Restructuring Act of 1998. Testimony taken by the commission appeared mostly as IRS bashing.

The commission learned about IRS rigidity in non-disclosure. A paid IRS informant, who was supplying information on an organized crime tax case, reported that a murder was being planned, and provided enough information to prevent the crime. The special agent was shocked, but wondered whether this information could be legally shared with local law-enforcement agencies under tax confidentiality laws. He asked his supervisor for guidance. The supervisor referred the question to the IRS National Office. The National Office assigned it to a disclosure specialist. The specialist studied his reference materials but could find no clear precedent. He referred the question to counsel for a legal opinion. Counsel studied the matter but could offer no immediate opinion.

After a time someone asked whether this was a hypothetical question or a live case. The specialist called the special agent for more information. The response was yes, it had been a live case, but there was no longer any need for an answer, for neither the question nor the victim was now "live." The murder had been committed while the National Office was considering whether authority existed to tell anyone about it.

An Alaska tax consultant told of a taxpayer in a rather barren area of Alaska who received an IRS notice. After a phone discussion, the IRS told him to visit his local IRS office. The taxpayer complained that would require him to travel three days on his snowmobile, flag down a passing train and then ride for another two days to get to the Anchorage IRS office. The Seattle IRS agent, obviously untrained about the Anchorage district he administered, called him a liar.

IRS Commissioner Larry Gibbs told the commission how computer-generated notices from the IRS got lost. A quality improvement study determined that the root cause was excess glue. The contractor who recommended the amount of glue to seal envelopes had miscalculated. The excess glue caused the batched envelopes to stick together. Several envelopes were all mailed to the taxpayer whose name appeared on the top envelope. When that taxpayer received all of the envelopes, he opened the one addressed to him and discarded the rest, all addressed to taxpayers who would never receive them.

Through a Freedom of Information Act request, *Tax Analysts* discovered that regional counsel was improperly flying first class on business trips. The deputy chief counsel had no authority to authorize first class travel and she was ordered to repay the government about $55 for a combined business and personal trip. She demurred. After lawyers spent about 30 hours trying to justify not paying, the amount was reduced to $45.

Among the reforms in the IRS Restructuring Act of 1998 was a five-year term for the IRS commissioner. Previously, the commissioner would tender his resignation upon election of a new president, or he would leave as a career choice. The average tenure for an IRS commissioner was about two years. As it took nine months to learn the job and order reforms, then another nine months to have them carried out, obstinate bureaucrats wouldn't heed orders to change because there would be a new commissioner before there would be discipline for failing to carry out the reforms.

The act also created an IRS Oversight Board. This proposal met with stiff Treasury opposition. It wasn't until a week after the American Institute of CPAs met with the Joint Committee on Taxation and presented the reasons it had to be an outside board, a meeting which I attended, that Treasury relented and agreed to this proposal. However, the Clinton administration showed its continued contempt for this proposal by failing to nominate any candidates for the board until four months after the deadline set by Congress.

The law calls for nine board members, including the treasury secretary, IRS commissioner, and a Treasury Workers Union member. That leaves six "private" members. President Clinton chose people whose qualifications were wanting for a tax organization that collects over $2 trillion a year. He established the IRS Oversight Board as a weak, rubber-stamp organization.

The initial private members included the owner of Kolbe Cattle Co. in Iowa, who was nominated by Senate Finance Committee Chairman Charles Grassley (R-IA). Chairing the board was a former partner from McKinsey, a major consulting firm. Other board members included a retired partner with Andersen Consulting, a prestigious Washington lawyer experienced in federal budget practices, and a vice president for Enterprise Rent-A-Car with four years experience as director of revenue in Missouri and Illinois. A long vacancy was finally filled with a former Yale classmate of President George W. Bush, an indication that diffidence toward the board continues. A 2006 nominee was "an anthropologist and classical archaeologist." No tax practitioner served on the board until 2007 when Paul Cherecwich, a retired tax attorney was appointed.

Board members appear to be appointed for political patronage, and many are unsuitable. They lack understanding of the IRS' business which renders them incapable of making critical comments or participating in open discussion. This was evident at a meeting in Atlanta of the Commissioner's Advisory Group in the late 1980s. The presentations were similar to those now made to the Oversight Board. One presentation explained how Form 8109, which accompanied payroll tax deposits, had reduced deposit errors by 98 percent. The presentation took half an hour, after which an advisory group member who was Virginia's revenue commissioner asked, "What's a Form 8109?" Every paymaster and tax practitioner in the country was familiar with Form 8109. Seated to my right was the IRS Director of Taxpayer Services, who whispered to me, "And these folks are supposed to advise the commissioner what to do?"

CHAPTER EIGHT

# The Power to Destroy

*The power to tax involves the power to destroy.*
   —*McCulloch v. Maryland*, 17 U.S. 327 (1819)

*Power is one thing, its wise exercise is another.*
   —Boris I. Bittker, *Federal Taxation of Incomes, Estates and Gifts* (1981)

The IRS is an agency of the executive branch. That makes it subject to the dictates of the president, the secretary of the treasury and other powerful bosses. Treasury Secretary Andrew Mellon was the first member of the executive branch to abuse the IRS, setting it against Senator James Couzens in 1925. President Franklin Roosevelt used it against Andrew Mellon in 1934. President John Kennedy used it to revoke the tax exempt status of "extremist organizations" (all of which were fundamentalist conservatives that had been criticizing the president) and, among others, audited Richard Nixon and Robert H. Finch, one of Nixon's campaign managers. President Richard Nixon used the IRS against his "enemies."

## The Second Battle of the Millionaires

Senator James Couzens' attack on the powerful interests who controlled the Bureau of Internal Revenue and benefited from its cozy attitude toward business came at a price. Treasury Secretary Andrew Mellon's use of the bureau to attack a political enemy – James Couzens – remains among the most egregious abuses of revenue-service power.

As a senator appointed to fill the two-year unexpired term of Truman Newberry, the administration hoped that Couzens would lose the 1924 election, thus ending his investigation. With Couzens' re-election, the administration sought other means to end the investigation.

On March 7, 1925, at the height of Couzens' investigation into the Bureau of Internal Revenue, Commissioner David Blair went to the Senate and summoned the senator off the floor. There, in the presence of legislators, lobbyists, and reporters, Blair personally handed him a letter demanding that Couzens sign a waiver of the statute of limitations so the bureau could continue an investigation of his 1919 income taxes. Historian David Burnham called this incident an attempt "to bully the senator into abandoning his investigation of the agency and the corrupt deals it was cutting."

Included with the letter was a memorandum from William Boyce Thompson to Treasury Secretary Andrew Mellon detailing charges that Couzens had grossly understated the profit from his sale of Ford stock in 1919. Henry Ford had bought back shares from all non-family shareholders, paying Couzens $29.3 million.

Treasury Secretary Andrew Mellon was believed to be personally responsible for the retaliation against Couzens. The Thompson memo is the only written connection between Mellon and the campaign against Couzens.

William Boyce Thompson was a fundraiser and large contributor to the Republican campaign fund and had been chairman of the Republican Party Ways and Means Committee in 1920. Among the revelations of the Couzens Committee was that the bureau had allowed Thompson to claim questionable losses of $597,480 for 1918. Thompson, who headed the New York tax consulting firm of Thompson and Black, had enmity for Couzens.

Couzens refused to sign the waiver. So on March 13, just two days before the five-year statute of limitations expired, the Bureau of Internal Revenue made a jeopardy assessment for $11 million. If Internal Revenue believes that the assessment or collection of an income tax deficiency will be jeopardized by delay, the law allows the agency to make an immediate assessment and demand payment – when the statute of limitations is about to expire, for example.

As a jeopardy assessment, Couzens had to deposit a bond for $20 million to stay collection activity before he could challenge the assessment in court.

In its 140-page opinion issued on May 5, 1928, the Board of Tax Appeals included a detailed history of the Ford Motor Company. It's 140 pages, not because there's information necessary for the decision. Rather, it seems to glorify Couzens' contribution for the company's success as equal to that of Henry Ford.

Ford incorporated in 1903. Couzens invested $2,400 of borrowed money and was among the original shareholders. He was vice president and treasurer of Ford until his resignation in 1915. Of the 20,000 shares outstanding, Couzens owned 11 percent. John and Horace Dodge each owned five percent. Company bylaws gave current shareholders a right of first refusal before Ford stock could be sold to outsiders.

The Dodge brothers made their fortune supplying Ford with parts to build cars. They eventually decided to stop supplying Ford so that they could build their own cars. For capital, they depended on receiving a dividend from Ford. Henry Ford did not want to pay dividends, especially not to finance a rival start-up automobile manufacturer. Nor would he buy their stock, and no one would buy the Dodge's Ford stock given that Henry paid no dividends and the stock had transfer restrictions. Thus, they were denied the millions of dollars they were counting on to finance their new venture.

The Dodges sued, seeking to force Ford Motor Company to pay dividends. They won, and Ford was ordered to pay a $19 million special dividend to shareholders. Henry was furious. As a 58.5 percent owner, he would receive almost $12 million, subject to heavy income tax, to provide capital to his competitors, and he might be required to continue paying future dividends.

So Henry Ford, to drum up publicity, tendered his resignation. He gave an interview to the *Los Angeles Examiner* on March 5, 1919, announcing that he planned to start a new company, Henry Ford and Son Incorporated, in California to compete against Ford Motor Company. The story received wide circulation.

While publicly announcing threats of resignation and competition, Henry and Edsel Ford hired an investment banker to purchase the remaining 41.5 percent for them as undisclosed principals.

One major issue was how much income tax the sellers would owe on the transaction. That was complicated. In 1919, there was no preferential tax treatment for capital gains. The gain would be taxed as ordinary income at 73 percent. However, the law provided that the fair market value at March 1, 1913, the effective date of the income tax, would be considered the basis of Ford shares, thus exempt from tax. This raised a big question of what Ford was worth on March 1, 1913.

Ford secured a private ruling from the revenue bureau on what the tax agency considered the fair market value of Ford as of March 1, 1913. Four agents calculated a value of $2,055.79 per share. Their superior overruled the calculation and set the value at $9,489.34, based on 10 times the average of 1912 and 1913 earnings.

Commissioner Daniel C. Roper wrote an opinion on May 19, 1919 stating that the bureau "is disposed to regard $9,489.34 as a fair valuation of the stock on March 1, 1913 and one which should be used in computing any profits made by the sale." After receiving this opinion, all the shareholders agreed to sell their stock to Henry and Edsel Ford.

Couzens sold his shares for $13,444.43 per share, a total of $29.3 million. He also received a $2.3 million settlement in the Ford-Dodge dividend lawsuit. Couzens filed his 1919 income tax return reporting an $8.6 million profit on the sale of Ford Motor Company, the difference between the selling price of $29.3 million and the March 13, 1913 value of $20.7 million computed at $9,489.34 per share.

Previously, none of these details were publicly known. However, rumors concerning the conflicting fair market valuations and the prices Ford paid to take full control of his company were pretty close.

On February 11, 1922, Senator James E. Watson (R-IN) sent a letter to the home of the new Internal Revenue Commissioner, David H. Blair, "because I want you to get this letter." It asserted that the valuation was artificially set so that three-quarters of the sale price would be exempt from tax. The letter pointed out that in 1913, Ford sold about 170,000 passenger cars and didn't manufacture tractors or trucks, whereas in 1919, Ford sold tractors, trucks and nearly 800,000 cars. Its repair business alone earned more profit in 1919 than car sales in 1913. That begged a question of how the value of the stock had risen by only $4,000 per share between 1913 and 1919 when Ford grew so spectacularly. It was a troublesome question.

The Board of Tax Appeals detailed the impressive success of Ford Motor Company until 1913, particularly the extraordinary Model T. The case described in great detail Ford's innovations in assembly line manufacturing, its pioneering of the dealership distribution system, and aggressive annual price reductions. Though it boasted features of cars that cost $2,000, the Model T sold for just $850 in 1908, $550 in 1913, and $290 in 1924. (Sounds like today's personal computer pricing.) With a 100-inch wheelbase, it was the size of today's compact car. Its four-cylinder engine generated 20 horsepower. The 10-gallon gas tank gave it a 170-mile range. A "magneto" flywheel allowed the car to power spark plugs without a battery. It had a useful life of five years, after which it was junk. Look for the three-pedal "planetary" gear transmission next time you visit a car museum.

The tribunal ruled that Ford shares at March 1, 1913 were worth $10,000 each. "We have not arrived at this value by application of any mathematical formula, because we believe that there is no authoritative formula available." The tribunal concluded that in 1919, Couzens had "sold for less than what a careful study would have shown to be the full value of their stock."

This is the only case known to this author where a tax tribunal ruled a taxpayer was entitled to more than he asked for. Why did the court rule that the value was $10,000, rather than $9,489.34 per share? One can only surmise that the judges knew this was a political persecution instigated by Andrew Mellon, though they dared not say so. Mellon was still treasury secretary when this decision was handed down in 1928. By ruling that the value was $10,000 per share, the board humiliated Mellon, saying that Couzens had overpaid his taxes and was owed a $1 million refund for the trouble he had been put through.

The Revenue Act of 1921 granted preferential tax treatment to capital gains, setting the rate at 25 percent. Henry Ford was offered $1 billion for his company in 1925. Couzens' 11 percent of Ford Motor Company would have been worth $110 million, he would have kept much more of it after taxes, and been spared a 1925 jeopardy assessment. The original shareholders sold out too soon.

## Al Capone

It's generally known that Al Capone went to prison for income tax evasion because the authorities couldn't convict him of his more heinous crimes. The St. Valentine's Day massacre of 1929 won him control of Chicago's underworld. This gave 30-year-old Capone control of Chicago's illegal liquor trade, gambling, and prostitution. He headed a vicious, murderous gang with gross revenues estimated at over $100 million annually.

The year 1927 brought a watershed Supreme Court decision. Fighting charges of income tax evasion, bootlegger Manley Sullivan challenged the contention that through income taxation, the U.S. government would cut itself in on the gains of his illicit business, or require him to violate his Fifth Amendment right against self-incrimination by requiring him to file an income tax return. Confusion arose because the Revenue Act of 1913 taxed income from various sources, including "any lawful business carried on for gain or profit." In 1916, Congress deleted the qualifying word "lawful" from the statute without giving any reason for the change.

The Treasury Department relied on this unexplained change when prosecuting bootleggers for failing to report income from the unlawful sale of liquor. The Supreme Court told Sullivan that illegal income was taxable and required filing a return. A Fifth Amendment objection could be protected by reporting the income but not disclosing its source. This decision opened a new avenue for prosecuting criminals.

Following the *Sullivan* decision, Vice President Charles G. Dawes, a former Chicago banker, asked President Calvin Coolidge to begin investigating Al Capone's income tax affairs. On October 18, 1928, Coolidge authorized the case.

President Herbert Hoover continued the campaign, enlisting Treasury Secretary Andrew Mellon to investigate and prosecute Capone. A special intelligence unit of the Bureau of Internal Revenue carried out the assignment. Revenue undercover agent, Pat O'Rourke, infiltrated Capone's organization. He was financed by "The Secret Six," a committee of prominent, then-anonymous public-spirited Chicagoans, who reportedly raised $1 million to rid Chicago of crime and corruption. Over the next two years, O'Rourke provided information to a five-man revenue investigative team, headed by Elmer Irey and Frank Wilson. By the summer of 1930, they still had found no evidence to document Capone's income.

It's said that one hot August night, working well after midnight, Wilson bumped into a file cabinet which snapped shut and automatically locked. Lacking a key, and needing a place to store a batch of documents, he sought to temporarily place them in an old file cabinet in the hallway until he could get a key the next morning. In the old file cabinet was a package he hadn't seen before.

The package contained three black ledgers dated 1924-26, seized four years earlier during a police raid. The second ledger had columns headed BIRD CAGE, 21, CRAPS, FARO, ROULETTE, HORSE BETS. The books showed a net profit of over $500,000 in one 18-month period.

"Every few pages a balance had been taken and divided among 'A' (for Al Capone, Wilson surmised), 'R' (Ralph Capone, his brother), 'J' (Jake Guzik, Capone's treasurer), etc." From a $36,687 balance on December 2, 1924, A and J received $5,720.22.

The ledgers were checked against handwriting records from automobile registrations, courts, banks, and other sources. A bank deposit slip was found with handwriting of a bookkeeper, Leslie Adelburt Shumway, matching the ledgers.

They found Shumway four months later in February 1931 working as a cashier at a Miami racetrack. Needing Shumway's cooperation, Wilson made him an offer he couldn't refuse. If he continued pretending ignorance about Capone's operations, Wilson would hand him a subpoena in a very public way. Capone was known for assassinating anyone posing a risk to the organization. Or Shumway could cooperate with the bureau without a subpoena.

With Shumway's grand jury testimony and other evidence, Capone was indicted for failing to file income tax returns and failing to pay income taxes for 1924 through 1929.

Agent O'Rourke called Wilson's team five days before the trial began, "They got the jury list, chief. The boys are out talking with jurors with a wad of dough in one hand and a gun in the other."

Worried that Capone might escape justice, Judge James Wilkerson ordered that the regular panel of jurists available to the other judges replace those on the list that Capone's thugs had been working on for two weeks. The trial began on October 6, 1931. Eleven days later, Capone was found guilty. He was sentenced to 11 years in prison, fined $50,000, and assessed $30,000 court costs (another version says $8,692.29 prosecution costs). At the time, it was a record penalty for tax evasion.

The jury found Capone guilty of tax evasion for 1925, 1926 and 1927, and for failing to file returns for 1928 and 1929. The government felt it was a weird verdict. How could he be guilty of failure to file 1928 and 1929 returns and not guilty for paying no taxes those years?

Capone served two years in the Atlanta penitentiary and was then transferred to Alcatraz, a small island in San Francisco Bay, until January 6, 1939. He was finally released from Terminal Island, a federal prison in California, on November 16, 1939, partially paralyzed with syphilis. He retired to his small Palm Island estate in Biscayne Bay near Miami and died on January 25, 1947 at age 48.

Eliot Ness, a Treasury detective, wrote the 1957 runaway bestseller, *The Untouchables*, exaggerating his crusade against Capone. It was made into a television series, a 1987 movie, followed by yet another television series. The truth is that Eliot Ness, brother-in-law of the Prohibition Bureau chief in Chicago, was a minor figure. His two years in Chicago resulted in just one indictment against Capone — conspiracy to violate the Prohibition laws — which wasn't used in the prosecution that sent him to prison. Ness was a courageous law enforcer who got the headlines, but accountants with the Bureau of Internal Revenue were the real heroes in the Capone case. Though, no one makes movies about macho accountants — except the Japanese.

The successful prosecution of Al Capone is celebrated to this day. It marked the first use of a witness protection program and introduced the term "Public Enemy," and specifically "Public Enemy Number One" as applied to Alphonse Capone.

By prosecuting Al Capone, Calvin Coolidge and Herbert Hoover established a precedent for presidents to use IRS for purposes unrelated to taxation. The non-revenue abuses for the tax agency are many: harass political rivals and enemies, implement policies, enforce moral or political ideology, and protect friends from audits.

Why are so many people who should be found guilty of other crimes, convicted and sent to prison on charges of tax evasion? Because the jury instructions make a tax conviction easy:

> For you to find the Defendant guilty of this crime, you must be convinced that the government has proved each of the following beyond a reasonable doubt:
>
> One: A substantial income tax was due from Defendant,
>
> Two: The Defendant attempted to evade or defeat this tax, and

Three: In attempting to evade or defeat such tax, Defendant acted willfully.

[Fourth: Defendant did not have a good-faith belief that he was complying with the provisions of the (Internal Revenue Code section). A belief may be in good faith even if it is unreasonable.]

The key finding is "willfulness," which is very hard to defend. In very few circuits is the fourth instruction given, and without it, the defendant is toast. This raises two important questions: Is it necessary to punish tax evasion with a stiff prison sentence? Should there be a higher standard than "willful" for finding criminal tax evasion? A "responsible person" who "willfully" fails to deposit employment taxes only faces a civil charge.

R&B legend Ronald Isley had engaged in "pervasive, long-term pathological" evasion of federal taxes. Despite suffering from the effects of a stroke and kidney cancer, the judge refused probation for the 65-year-old and sentenced him in September 2006 to three years and one month in a Bureau of Prisons hospital facility. (He could have been sentenced to 26 years.) He was ordered to pay $3.1 million in back taxes, despite bankruptcy and IRS seizure of his valuables. Was financial purgatory insufficient without prison?

The Capone technique is still used. Authorities suspected that Tucson (Arizona) Superior Court Judge William Scholl was accepting bribes, but they couldn't prove it. Scholl was a compulsive gambler. He erroneously assumed that gambling wins and losses could be netted. In any year when losses exceeded wins, he reported nothing on his income tax return. The law requires that all gambling wins (not just those reflected on Form W-2G) be reported as income and the losses deducted as itemized deductions. Though there was no tax deficiency or assessed penalty, he had signed a return that was incorrect as to a material matter because it didn't disclose his gross winnings. That's perjury. A jury found him guilty of filing false tax returns for 1990, 1991, 1992 and 1994. He was sentenced to six months home arrest and five years probation. He resigned from the bench, and the Arizona Supreme Court suspended his law license for six months.

Under this standard, millions of taxpayers commit perjury each year — all those "instant" lottery winners, for example — especially if they claim the standard deduction because all winnings are taxable income, and all losses are only deductible if they itemize.

## Roosevelt the Terrible

Franklin Roosevelt was ruthless with his enemies, and generous with his friends, as his treatment of Andrew Mellon, Moses Annenberg and Lyndon Johnson demonstrate. He used the revenue agency to persecute anti-Semitic Catholic priest Charles E. Coughlin, Rep. Hamilton Fish and many others.

Huey Long was a "political racketeer" who ruled Louisiana through a large organization of corrupt politicians, goons, and graft. From 1930 to 1932, he concurrently held office as both governor and senator. Elmer Irey began investigating Long during the Hoover administration. The investigation of Roosevelt supporter and fellow Democrat Long was shelved following the 1932 election. It was revived in 1934 when Long began opposing passage of the New Deal. Treasury Secretary Henry Morgenthau assigned over 50 agents, headed by Irey. The tactics and goal would be similar to that employed with Capone: an income tax conviction, first against the Long machine, then Long himself. Irey's name was entered into the "Sonuvabitch Book," a real book Long actually kept. It guaranteed political death in Louisiana and severe danger in Washington.

> **A TAX ON LYING**
>
> Upset at allegations of his corruption printed by Louisian's major newspapers, Huey Long had the legislature pass a law in 1934 assessing a two percent tax on the gross receipts of every Louisiana newspaper having a circulation above 20,000 copies per week. Long called it "a tax on lying." The tax applied to just 13 out of 163 newspapers in the state, of which "twelve were active in their opposition to the dominant political group in the State, which group controlled the Legislature and at whose dictates the Legislature passed this law," noted the U.S. Supreme Court. In a 1936 ruling, it said the tax was an unconstitutional abridgement on freedom of the press, adding, "The power to tax the press is the power to destroy it."

Irey obtained an April 1935 tax conviction against Louisiana state Rep. Joseph Fisher, a Long associate who had let contracts for Long's massive road-building projects. On September 8, 1935, at age 42, Huey Long was assassinated in the Baton Rouge capitol building. A month later, Irey couldn't get a conviction against Long's tax collector

Abraham Shushan, the government's strongest case. With Long out of the picture, the government decided to dismiss indictments against the other Long leaders. (That lasted until 1939 when further scandals brought new indictments and imprisonment of Long's political heirs.) No one ever located Long's "deduct box." It held over $1 million from salary deductions of state employees, donations from corporations doing business with the state, and contributions from various backers. It was intended as the campaign chest for his 1936 presidential bid.

Father Charles Coughlin was an acrimonious Roosevelt critic and a rabid Jew-hater with a national radio audience. Working with Huey Long, he delivered a surprising Senate defeat to Roosevelt's attempt to bring the U.S. under jurisdiction of the World Court in 1934. Coughlin blamed the Jews for starting World War II and incited Americans to believe their soldiers were dying to protect the big interests of "the international Jews." He was investigated by the Justice Department, FBI, and Bureau of Internal Revenue.

Many have speculated over the reasons and methods that finally silenced Coughlin. Columnist Drew Pearson said that Treasury had a very good case of income tax evasion against Coughlin. In addition to questionable finances of various Coughlin enterprises, the BIR discovered a $50,000 or $68,000 payment from Father Coughlin to Dr. Bernard Gariepy for what Pearson called, "alienation of affections" of Mrs. Gariepy by the radio priest. Gariepy claimed it was nontaxable because of the purpose for which he had received it and was convicted of tax evasion. It would have been impolitic for Treasury to publicly shut down Coughlin because the treasury secretary was Jewish. In April 1942, Roosevelt ordered another tax investigation to stop this powerful anti-war critic. The following month, a deal was struck with the Catholic hierarchy to silence Coughlin in return for ending the investigation.

Hamilton Fish was the Republican congressman from Duchess County, New York, Roosevelt's home district, and his constant critic. When Roosevelt railed against tax cheaters, Fish tried to expose Roosevelt's aggressive personal tax planning. He was a pro-German appeaser who met with Nazi leaders in August 1939 and vacationed at the castle of Hitler's foreign minister, Joachim von Ribbentrop. Roosevelt considered invoking the Logan Act of 1799 which bars citizens from interfering in relations between the United States and foreign governments. As no one had ever been indicted for violating the Logan Act, in 1942, Roosevelt ordered a tax investigation headed by Elmer Irey which revealed misdeeds, but insufficient evidence for an indictment.

Peter Bergson headed the Emergency Committee to Save the Jewish People of Europe. In a race against death, it ran full-page newspaper ads, held rallies featuring celebrities, lobbied on Capitol Hill, and sponsored an October 1943 march on the White House by 400 rabbis. Bergson's group was the only American Jewish organization actively working to save European Jewry from the Holocaust. He was opposed by most of the major Jewish organizations and the Roosevelt administration.

The FBI sent a team of accountants to review the books for seven weeks, from 9 a.m. until 4:30 p.m. Bergson told an interviewer that upon completion, "one of them came in...in order make clear his feelings, he took out some money and he said this is our contribution, but it has to be anonymous." The Bureau of Internal Revenue also swooped down. Half a dozen agents poured over the books for two or three weeks in an effort to revoke the organization's tax-exempt status. When they left, "All of them, without exception pitched in and gave a contribution," said Bergson.

## The National Gallery of Art

The most scandalous Roosevelt tax inquisition was the 1934 persecution of millionaire capitalist Andrew W. Mellon, the Republican treasury secretary from 1921 to 1932. Self-indulgent and taken by his own importance, it was said that three presidents served under him. He enjoyed being billed as "the greatest secretary of the treasury since Alexander Hamilton." With Roosevelt's approval, the famous financier and industrialist faced prosecution by the agency he formerly headed.

Mellon was 65 when he became treasury secretary. He served three successive presidents: Warren Harding, Calvin Coolidge, and Herbert Hoover. Before serving in government, he had a long career as a highly successful investment banker with huge holdings in Pittsburgh giants Alcoa, the Mellon National Bank and Gulf Oil. He was one of the richest men in America, in the same league with Andrew Carnegie, John D. Rockefeller and Henry Ford. As a financier his only peer was J.P. Morgan.

He earned a $15,000 annual salary at Treasury while paying $20,000 a year for an apartment in Washington. He was also one of the nation's foremost art collectors and a great philanthropist.

As the worldwide depression took hold in the 1930s, Stalin tried filling the communist state's coffers by selling off Russia's art treasures. A spectacular art collection was taken from the Hermitage Museum in Leningrad (now St. Petersburg, a city built by beard-tax czar, Peter the Great and named after his patron saint).

From 1930 to 1931, Andrew Mellon bought about 25 Hermitage masterpieces for almost $7 million. These purchases represented one-third of all 1931 U.S. imports from the Soviet Union. He saw no inconsistency in publicly opposing trade with the Soviet Union while privately buying the plundered artworks. His buying spree only came to light when he was accused of tax evasion in 1934.

These paintings formed the core for the creation of the National Gallery of Art of the Smithsonian Institution, courtesy of Mellon's generosity — and a tax controversy.

In May 1933, Congressman Louis T. McFadden (R-PA) charged on the floor of the House (where he had protection against slander) that Mellon cheated on his 1931 tax return. McFadden demanded a Justice Department investigation. Five months later, Mellon was subject to a three-week audit which found no errors or omissions but raised issues concerning complex transactions and aggressive tax planning.

"Investigate Mellon, I order it," went the telephone call from Treasury Secretary Henry Morgenthau. Elmer Irey had worked under Mellon and liked him. Morgenthau ignored Irey's belief that Mellon was innocent. He ordered Irey, Treasury's best criminal investigator, to head the effort.

Without any demand by Treasury for additional taxes or an appeal hearing as provided by law, the attorney general announced on March 11, 1934 that he was seeking a criminal indictment against the former treasury secretary on charges of tax evasion. Two months later, a federal grand jury in Mellon's hometown of Pittsburgh refused to indict its most distinguished citizen. So Treasury moved the case to the Board of Tax Appeals to prosecute as a civil rather than a criminal case.

The government proposed $1,319,080.90 in additional taxes for income Mellon earned in 1931. Suddenly the man who had gone after Couzens ten years earlier found himself on the receiving end of a tax assessment. Unlike Couzens, however, Mellon also was hit with a 50 percent fraud penalty that added an additional $659,540. The asserted deficiency was later increased to $3,089,261.24.

Discrediting Mellon was important to the New Deal administration. In a 1926 speech, Franklin Roosevelt had called Mellon, "the master mind among the malefactors of great wealth." Vice President Garner once said on the House floor that he wanted to "look into Uncle Andy's books." In private practice years before, Attorney General Homer S. Cummings had waged two unsuccessful private anti-trust lawsuits against Mellon's Aluminum Company. Treasury Secretary Morgenthau wrote in his diary, "I consider that Mr. Mellon is not on trial but democracy and the privileged rich and I want to see who will win."

Mellon's tax trial began in February 1935, with the final argument in June 1936. Among the seven complex issues decided was the profit on a stock sale to Bethlehem Steel. Mellon had assigned a 1913 value of $500 per share to minimize his taxable gain upon sale, while the revenue service argued the value was $158. This issue was identical to that which had confronted Couzens with his Ford shares. In addition, there were purported sham transactions transferring assets to his children, while recognizing tax-sheltering losses.

For years, Mellon denied that he had ever bought paintings from the Hermitage Museum. It was presumed that he deducted the purchase price from his tax return in 1931 on the grounds that they had been donated to a charitable foundation he established. Mellon's Democratic critics faulted him for spending lavishly on art during the Depression and cited him for conflicts of interest, which drove him to resign from the Treasury in early 1932. President Hoover appointed him to serve as U.S. ambassador to Great Britain for a year. As ambassador, he brought artworks into the U.S. by diplomatic pouch.

From the tax trial we learn that Mellon didn't originally deduct the paintings. He had no need. In 1931, deductions for charitable contributions were limited to 15 percent of income. Mellon's cash contributions exceeded that. However, when he was accused of understating his income, the deductions for a contribution of paintings became valuable offsets to income. So, Mellon countered the government's assessment by claiming a $3,247,695 deduction for five paintings contributed during 1931 to the A.W. Mellon Educational and Charitable Trust. That's what he paid the Soviets for Raphael's "Alba Madonna," Botticelli's "Adoration of the Magi," Titian's "Venus with a Mirror," Van Eyck's "Annunciation," and Perugino's "Crucifixion."

Ultimately, Mellon's tax deduction for the paintings was upheld because, unlike others which adorned his apartment, these five were stored at Washington's Corcoran Gallery of Art. Meanwhile, the Roosevelt administration launched new tax investigations into his finances. The inquiries were called off around Christmas 1936, when Mellon officially informed President Franklin Roosevelt that he was donating his $25 million art collection to what is today the National Gallery of Art.

Mellon died on August 26, 1937. Four months later, the Board of Tax Appeals upheld most of Mellon's positions and dismissed all fraud penalties. It ruled that he owed $485,809. The case exposed his aggressive tax positions, and some abuse of his office as treasury secretary, but his honor was upheld.

Assistant General Counsel Robert Jackson of the Bureau of Internal Revenue (later a Supreme Court justice) rose to fame as prosecutor in the case. As a matter of trial strategy, Jackson preferred treating the matter as a civil case, that no fraud penalty be assessed because fraud charges required the government to prove its case. The sham losses on transferring stock to his children was a common technique tolerated at treasury, and the case would be tried before the Board of Tax Appeals, all of whose judges were appointed during Mellon's reign as Treasury secretary. Despite his pleas, the Justice Department opposed his recommendations. Jackson believed that President Roosevelt personally ordered proceeding with fraud charges. Had it initially been treated as a civil case, he later learned, Mellon would have paid the tax.

The National Gallery of Art in Washington, D.C., an affiliate of the Smithsonian Institution, was established by act of Congress, March 24, 1937. It opened on March 17, 1941. Today, the gallery's paintings exceed 1,200 works.

Andrew Mellon donated $15 million for construction of the building, as well as his collection of American portraits, major works by Van Dyck, Rembrandt, and Vermeer, including most of the paintings the Soviets sold him and 46 works in painting and sculpture purchased in a single transaction in 1936. In total, he donated 121 paintings and 21 works of sculpture. Mellon had Congress stipulate that any works added to the gallery must "be of a similar high standard of quality."

A persistent but untrue rumor contends that there was a "deal" with Roosevelt to stop hounding Mellon in exchange for his art collection and building the National Gallery. Mellon's aide, David Edward Finley, and his son, Paul Mellon, both present credible evidence that Mellon envisioned creating The National Gallery in 1927 and acted consistently throughout the early 1930s with building an art collection of excellence for a gift to the nation. Logically, it would be absurd to exchange $40 million in art and building to avoid a proposed $3 million IRS assessment.

Yet, on November 14, 1934, the eve of his civil tax trial, the *Wall Street Journal* published Mellon's denial: "I have engaged no architect, have caused no plans to be drawn, and have made no commitments to build or endow a gallery at Washington, Pittsburgh, or elsewhere."

When you visit the National Gallery of Art, recall the tax dispute between the Roosevelt administration and the banker and collector Andrew Mellon, who served as treasury secretary and ambassador to Great Britain. Be sure to see the five masterpieces from his 1931 tax controversy. Many of the Hermitage paintings acquired in the 1930s were originally bought for Catherine the Great and Tsar Alexander I. On the National Gallery website, search for works contributed by Andrew Mellon and his Hermitage collection. In the Gallery, the plaques next to Mellon's original paintings are identified as "Andrew W. Mellon Collection, 1937.1.xx."

Pay tribute to Andrew Mellon that he did not allow himself to become embittered and made this gift to the nation, despite abuse by the Roosevelt administration.

### Moses Annenberg

Moses Annenberg ran the *Daily Racing Form* and the *Morning Telegraph* in Chicago, allegedly paying money to Capone to keep out rival racetrack papers. He used his monopoly profits to buy the *Philadelphia Inquirer* in 1936. Annenberg attacked the New Deal. The *Inquirer* became a major factor in the 1938 defeat of Pennsylvania's

New Deal Democratic Governor George Earle. During that election campaign, Annenberg's group made threats against Interior Secretary Harold Ickes who went to Philadelphia to campaign for Earle.

In retaliation, Roosevelt ordered a tax fraud investigation of Annenberg. Treasury Secretary Morgenthau assigned 35 agents, led by Elmer Irey, who reviewed the records of 5,000 gambling establishments attempting to prove that Annenberg earned $6 million annually, the highest individual income in the country. Annenberg desperately wanted to settle, but Roosevelt wasn't interested. He considered Annenberg a threat to his New Deal.

Joseph Hafner was his head bookkeeper, earning (would you believe?) just $175 a week overseeing the books of a multi-million dollar enterprise composed of 84 companies. Annenberg was charged with criminal income tax evasion for underreporting his 1932 - 1936 tax by over $3.35 million. (Hafner was also indicted for tax evasion.) The books were messy and coded as he commingled personal and business expenses. The government claimed that he concealed income and deducted as business expenses his daughter's gala wedding at New York's Hotel Pierre and a South American cruise with his mistress.

Annenberg set aside a small room in his Chicago office for the revenue service to review his records. One morning, 19 metal boxes marked, "Private Records," shipped from Annenberg's Long Island home, intended for his lawyers down the hall, were accidentally delivered to revenue's small room. They clearly explained the codes used in the bookkeeping records to conceal income. There were cancelled checks, cash books, bank statements, correspondence, and ledgers which Annenberg had denied existed. These proved the government's case.

Under threat that his son, Walter, would be indicted too, Annenberg agreed to plead guilty to a single count, expecting three years probation. Judge Wilkerson (same who presided over the Capone trial) helped secure the plea without any advance agreement on a likely punishment. He privately told the prosecutor, "Don't let them stampede you into anything on this income tax case. Tell the attorney general I respect him as a very reputable law enforcing officer. If he wants to tell me privately, or through you, of a recommendation, I will do my best to follow his recommendation. I'm all for you, my boy."

Wilkerson sentenced Moe Annenberg in 1940 to three years in prison and ordered him to pay $8 million in back taxes and penalties. It was the biggest award Treasury had ever secured. Moses Annenberg was released for treatment of a brain tumor after serving two years. He died seven weeks later on July 20, 1942.

Walter Annenberg inherited his father's three newspapers and turned them into a media empire. He created *TV Guide*, *Seventeen* magazine, acquired six radio and six television stations, and sold his empire to Rupert Murdoch in 1988 for $3 billion. He served as U.S. ambassador to Great Britain for 5½ years beginning in 1969 and gave billions to charity. He died in 2002 with an estimated net worth of $4 billion. The Annenberg Foundation is part of his legacy.

**Landslide Lyndon**

A July 1942 income tax audit of Texas contractor, Brown & Root, Inc. disclosed hundreds of thousands of dollars in bonuses and attorney fees that were really illegal campaign contributions to Congressman Lyndon Baines Johnson's failed 1941 senatorial campaign.

Johnson had a political godfather in Herman Brown, owner of Texas engineering and construction contractor Brown & Root. Brown also delivered to Johnson, "support" from all his company's subcontractors. As a freshman congressman, Johnson brought them major government contracts to build the Mansfield (originally Marshall Ford) Dam, a massive project near Austin, and the Corpus Christi Naval Air Station, which made millions of dollars in profits. In return, they financed his campaigns with as much money as he desired. Johnson was thus freed from campaign fundraising. His 1941 Senate campaign cost $30,000 according to his official report. *Life* magazine estimated the cost at $250,000, while others say $500,000.

The Corrupt Practices Act limited an individual's campaign contributions to $5,000 per candidate. Brown & Root circumvented these limits by disguising the contributions as "legal fees" paid to their lawyers or "bonuses" paid to company vice presidents. The company deducted the payments as business expenses. The recipients laundered checks through their bank accounts, kept part for taxes, and contributed the balance to the Johnson campaign.

Johnson was first elected to the House in 1937, and was relatively unknown in Texas when he ran in the 11-week special election campaign for the Senate in 1941 for the remaining term of the deceased Morris Sheppard. Johnson offset this handicap by having President Roosevelt appear with him at Texas rallies. Roosevelt was deeply indebted to Johnson, who had single-handedly killed fellow Texan John Nance Garner's presidential aspirations in 1940. Garner had been the main credible support for the anti-third term tradition that might have damaged Roosevelt's campaign.

In seeking an unprecedented third term, Roosevelt felt a unanimous party draft was needed to break the two-term precedent. His vice president, "Cactus Jack" Garner, opposed a third term, opposed the New Deal with the resulting budget deficits, denounced the court-packing plan and sought the presidential nomination for himself. In July 1939, Roosevelt loyalist and labor leader, John L. Lewis, called the vice-president "a labor-baiting, whiskey-drinking, poker-playing evil old man." The charges were true (except perhaps the "evil" appellation), and 71-year-old Garner felt compelled to neutralize the insult.

Garner demanded that all 23 members of the Texas congressional delegation pass a resolution saying that Lewis' statement was untrue. Only one Texan, Lyndon Johnson, heeding calls from Roosevelt to quash the resolution, refused to sign. Johnson explained that everyone knew Garner bitterly opposed labor and was a heavy drinker. During Prohibition, Garner had a room in the Capitol he called, "The Board of Education," where congressmen sworn to uphold the Constitution would gather most evenings to drink liquor and thus "strike a blow for liberty." (They provided their bootlegger with space in the Cannon House Office Building.) Johnson wouldn't even sign a watered down resolution that merely called Lewis' attack "unwarranted and unjustified." The resolution died and Johnson was endeared to Roosevelt.

As the 1940 Democratic National Convention in Chicago neared, it was proposed that the Texas delegation split their vote in favor of Garner. Johnson and others rejected this proposal and wanted the Texas delegation to condemn the "Stop Roosevelt" movement. Roosevelt himself proposed a compromise that the Texas delegation could vote for Garner as a first-round favorite-son candidate, and in return, Garner supporters would insist that the state convention praise the administration record and repudiate any "Stop Roosevelt" movement. The compromise passed, and junior Congressman Johnson was named vice chairman of the Texas delegation that went to Chicago.

Johnson was a rising star and hero among Democrats. He single-handedly raised $100,000 for the Democratic Congressional Campaign Committee, turning it into a major national fundraising machine for congressional candidates (thanks to Brown and Root donations). Through liaison with the White House and government departments, Johnson furnished candidates with information from high levels of government. He also relayed information from candidates back to the White House. This was unheard of in 1940, when congressional races were local events without much help from the national party.

With Brown's money and Roosevelt's appearances, Johnson should have won his Senate seat in 1941, but it was stolen by his opponent, who won through ballot box stuffing by just 1,311 votes out of 349,869 cast.

When the revenue service audited Brown & Root's 1941 income tax return, it discovered a major tax fraud and circumvention of the Corrupt Practices Act by many individuals. Even more threatening, the Corrupt Practices Act limited the permissible expenditure by a candidate to $25,000. The manner in which the Johnson campaign had concealed this was too blatant.

Johnson met with Revenue Commissioner Guy Helvering, then with Treasury Secretary Henry Morgenthau, asking the investigation be dropped, to no avail. Finally on January 13, 1944, at 11:50 a.m., Johnson met with Roosevelt. At 4:30 that afternoon, Elmer Irey was ordered to tell his six agents who had been working this case for 18 months, convinced they had a sure fraud case, to quickly wrap up the investigation.

The agents proposed tax deficiencies of $1,099,944 plus a $549,972 fraud penalty, to which interest would be added. Without any publicity or trial, Internal Revenue compromised with Brown & Root and settled the case for just $372,000.

Irey didn't mention this incident in his 1955 memoir about tax cases he handled, possibly because Johnson was then the powerful Senate majority leader. Historian Paul Johnson commented that Roosevelt "used his executive authority, unlawfully and unconstitutionally to save Johnson from going to jail for criminal tax fraud."

Without Franklin Roosevelt's intervention, violation of the Federal Corrupt Practices Act would have destroyed Lyndon Johnson's political career, just as it destroyed many other political careers. There had been more expensive campaigns. William Vare spent $800,000 in the 1926 Pennsylvania Republican primary, defeating incumbent Senator George Wharton Pepper, who spent nearly $2 million. Senator Frank Smith spent $460,000 defeating incumbent Senator William Brown McKinley, who spent over $500,000 in the 1926 Illinois Republican primary. Both Vare and Smith were denied their seats in the Senate due to charges of "fraud and corruption" in their campaigns. Truman Newberry (R-MI) was put on trial and resigned his Senate seat in 1921 for spending $100,000, bringing James Couzens to the Senate as his successor.

Johnson applied the lessons he learned in 1941. He won the 1948 Texas Senate Democratic primary election by just 87 votes, out of almost a million cast, curiously traced to 203 suspicious votes in the Duval County Precinct 13 ballot box, earning him the derisive nickname, "Landslide Lyndon."

A federal district court judge ordered Johnson's name be left off the general election ballot pending an inquiry into possible primary election fraud. Relief would have to be sought from the appeals court or the Supreme Court, both of which were in recess. Johnson had only a week to get his name back on the ballot.

In a genius procedural initiative, Johnson's attorney, Abe Fortas, convinced Supreme Court Justice Hugo Black to vacate the order. Under an old law, Black served as senior justice for the fifth circuit. He accepted Fortas' argument that he could act alone and that the lack of time before the election demanded this extraordinary action.

The Senate voted to investigate the contested primary, but dropped the probe after discovering that most of the ballots in "The Land of Parr" were destroyed by "some illiterate Mexican janitors who must have thought they were trash ready to be burned." Quite simply, Johnson became a senator through fraud, with the help of Abe Fortas, whom he would eventually reward with a Supreme Court seat.

George Parr, "The Duke of Duval," was the Democratic Party boss who engineered Johnson's 1948 victory. He spent nine months in prison during 1936 for income tax evasion, but received a pardon from President Truman in 1946, influenced by Congressman Lyndon Johnson, allowing him to re-enter politics. In 1957, Parr was sentenced to ten years in prison for stealing $200,000 of tax funds from the Benavides Independent School District, but that conviction was overturned by the Supreme Court in 1960 on a technicality. He was represented before the high court by Johnson's lawyer, Abe Fortas. In 1975, the Fifth Circuit Court upheld his conviction for income tax evasion for failing to report $276,000 in extortion received between 1966 and 1969. He was fined $14,000 and sentenced to five years. A week later, the 74-year-old committed suicide rather than face prison again.

Today Kellogg, Brown & Root, is a subsidiary of Halliburton Company. The controversy surrounding Halliburton's no-bid contracts in Iraq evolved directly from lessons Lyndon Johnson taught them on the *quid pro quo* between campaign contributions and government contracts.

## Martin Luther King's Tax Perjury Trial

Martin Luther King rose to fame as a civil rights leader in Montgomery, Alabama. After Rosa Parks was arrested for refusing to give up her seat, King led the successful bus boycott of 1955 – 1956, which ended segregated seating on the city buses.

Alabama sought retribution by deploying its tax agency upon him. When he announced in December 1959 that he was moving to Atlanta, the state arranged for a hasty audit of his 1956, 1957, and 1958 income tax returns. It is unheard of for a state tax agency to initiate a tax audit for an individual at King's income level. States piggyback their income tax off the federal return and rely largely on federal enforcement.

Under pressure from supervisors, tax auditor Lloyd Hale disputed gifts King received, reclassifying them as income. For example, a $500 gift that he received after his home was firebombed in January 1956 and $1,500 to cover hospital costs from a September 1958 stabbing in Harlem were ruled "income." Hale also disputed speaking honorariums for the benefit of the movement and expense reimbursements as unreported income.

Alabama assessed $1,722.23 in back taxes and interest for the three years. They threatened King with a lien on his bank accounts if he failed to pay. Picking his fights carefully, King paid the tax on January 27, 1960. The following week, he moved to Atlanta.

## Chapter Eight—The Power to Destroy

King wasn't in Atlanta a month when Georgia sheriffs came to arrest him on February 17, 1960 for an Alabama warrant charging that he had falsified his 1956 and 1958 Alabama state income tax returns.

There was no chance that Georgia Governor Ernest Vandiver would fail to honor Alabama's extradition request. When King announced his intention to move to Atlanta, Vandiver remarked, "We'll watch his actions very carefully. We intend to preserve peace and good order in the state." At a press conference the day following the arrest, the governor told reporters that it was customary "to return criminals to another state unless there are unusual circumstances."

That wasn't all. The Alabama Department of Revenue sent King a letter on February 16 that said it had made a mistake in calculating his deficiency. The correct amount was $1,667.83. Rather than cash his $1,722.23 check and issue King a $54.40 refund, they demanded that he send them another check for $1,667.83 and "the department will return your check in the amount of $1,722.23." The two outstanding tax checks and a $2,000 bail bond placed a financial burden on King.

King had reported income of $9,150 in 1956 and $25,248 in 1958. Alabama claimed his income for those years was $16,162 and $45,421. Income tax evasion is not a felony under Alabama law, but swearing to a fraudulent return constitutes perjury, which is a felony punishable by one to five years in prison. King reported $18,132 as 1957 income, but didn't sign the return, so Alabama couldn't charge him for that year. The state claimed his 1957 income was $25,718.

In denying the charges, King said, "I have no pretense to absolute goodness, but if I have one virtue — just one — it's honesty."

His defense had a major weakness. Frequently, men devoted to a cause do not maintain good accounting records, sloppily commingling personal funds with their movement. King often received a $1,000 or $1,500 honorarium for making a speech. He cashed some checks to use for expenses, and set aside the rest for the movement. The prosecution wanted to make this appear as a crime. The CPA hired to assist in his defense wrote to King's attorneys, "it must be borne in mind that certain monies were paid to the Rev. King in cash, and further, that he drew checks to cash, the proceeds of which he used for sundry purposes, including that of redeposits."

Though he paid Alabama back taxes, and though he was charged with tax fraud, King didn't even have copies of the tax returns in question. On February 24, he addressed a letter to the Bureau of Internal Revenue (though it had changed its name to Internal Revenue Service almost eight years earlier), "I would like to have a copy of my 1956 and 1957 State and Federal Income Tax Returns." The IRS sent him all 11 pages of the two returns on March 17 with a note saying, "you will have to contact the State Department of Revenue... for copies of your State returns."

This was a very grave situation for King. He lacked funds to pay for his legal defense. He would be tried by an all-white jury in Alabama, an insurmountable hurdle for a black man. The mere charges stained his reputation, as there were people willing to believe he had stolen money. And he faced prison time, up to five years for each return found fraudulent. If convicted, Alabama might signal to the world that while leading thousands in the bus boycott, King was dishonest in his financial dealings. Of this episode, Coretta Scott King wrote:

> The implication was that Martin had received money from [the Montgomery Improvement Association and Southern Christian Leadership Conference] that was unaccounted for....Though the accusation was utterly false, it caused Martin more suffering than any other event in his life up to that point...despite all the bravery he had shown before under personal abuse and character assaults, despite the courage he was to show in the future, this attack on his personal honesty hurt him most.

The trial began on Monday, May 23, 1960. Alabama tried him only on the 1956 charges, preferring to hold the 1958 charges for a second trial. The amount of underpaid tax for 1956 was $318.81. Though King had twice paid the tax four months earlier, Alabama still hadn't cashed either check.

About 1,400 exhibits were introduced into evidence. The Alabama prosecutor complained that, although the federal government usually prosecuted tax cases, "I would not expect the Federal Government to prosecute this defendant for any violation." An IRS agent from Atlanta sat in on the trial taking notes, raising speculation of possible federal income tax charges against King. Georgia sent a senior revenue auditor to testify regarding King's Atlanta bank records. King's attorney objected so frequently during the trial that he didn't sit down between objections.

William R. Ming of Chicago, an expert in defending tax cases, and five other black attorneys provided excellent legal defense. The Committee to Defend Martin Luther King was organized with the goal of raising $200,000. Each lawyer charged King between $100 and $300 per day in court, plus expenses, and $10 - $25 per hour for research. Donations were probably tight, as later correspondence between the attorneys indicates they would halve their fees.

They hired Jesse B. Blayton, a black CPA in Atlanta and one of just 60 black CPAs in the U.S. at the time. As the star witness for the defense, he reconstructed and accounted for King's entire $9,150 income for the jury. Blayton rang up a bill for $4,610.18 in three months, expecting the committee to cover it, but there was no money to pay him.

The defense proved that documents introduced at the trial and dated in January were actually prepared after King was indicted in February. Under questioning, the state's star witness, tax auditor Lloyd Hale, admitted there was no evidence of fraud. Still, the defense was expecting a conviction simply because that was the nature of the bigoted Southern courtroom. Their strategy was to create and preserve a record of the proceedings that could be overturned on appeal.

The six-day trial ended on Saturday, May 28. After just three hours and 43 minutes of deliberation, to everyone's surprise, the all-white male jury returned a "not guilty" verdict. A Southern white jury tradition was shattered. Fred Gray, one of King's defense lawyers wrote, "No one would have predicted that an all-white jury in Montgomery, Alabama, the Cradle of the Confederacy, in May 1960, in the middle of all of the sit-ins and all of the racial tension that was going on, would exonerate Martin Luther King, Jr. But it really happened."

King returned to the Ebenezer Baptist Church on Sunday, the day following his acquittal, and told his congregation, "Something happened to that jury; it said no matter how much they must suppress me they must tell the truth."

The prosecutor waited until July 18 to finally announce that he was dropping the 1958 charges. On August 3, the Department of Revenue returned King's first check for $1,772.23, with a letter which ended, "We appreciate your cooperation." King is the only person ever charged in Alabama with perjury in filing state income tax returns.

Martin Luther King's political persecution continued. The FBI began an intensive campaign to neutralize him as an effective civil rights leader starting with approval given on October 10, 1963 by Attorney General Robert Kennedy to wiretap him. Federal agents scrutinized his tax returns, monitored his financial affairs, sought any secret foreign bank account, and tried especially hard to find evidence that he was a communist. This harassment continued until his assassination in April 1968.

The Committee to Defend Martin Luther King was not organized as a tax-exempt charity, and it would have been difficult to obtain the required IRS approval. In 1963, the IRS disallowed tax deductions claimed by contributors. The agency audited King's Southern Christian Leadership Conference in 1968.

At one point, the IRS began an investigation of the Ebenezer Baptist Church, seeking to revoke its tax exempt status. Louis Regenstein Jr., one of the senior partners with a major Atlanta law firm, Kilpatrick, Cody, Rodgers, McClatchey & Regenstein undertook the defense *pro bono* and IRS retreated. No one recalls the year, but the church was likely a victim of Richard Nixon's "Special Services Staff," whose specialty was revoking the tax exempt status of civil rights groups.

**Seditious Libel**

The *New York Times* was instrumental in publicizing awareness of Martin Luther King's plight, raising money, and staining Alabama's reputation. Libel suits were filed.

Montgomery Public Affairs Commissioner Lester B. Sullivan filed a lawsuit on April 19, 1960 against the *Times* and four Alabama black clerics – Ralph D. Abernathy, Solomon S. Seay Sr., Fred L. Shuttlesworth and Joseph E. Lowery – on account of a full page advertisement the newspaper ran on March 29 soliciting funds for King's legal defense. The third and sixth of ten paragraphs read:

> In Montgomery, Alabama, after students sang "My Country 'Tis of Thee" on the State Capitol steps, their leaders were expelled from school, and truckloads of police armed with shotguns and tear-gas ringed the Alabama State College Campus. When the entire student body protested to state authorities by refusing to re-register, their dining hall was padlocked in an attempt to starve them into submission.

> Again and again the Southern violators have answered Dr. King's peaceful protests with intimidation and violence. They have bombed his home almost killing his wife and child. They have assaulted his person. They have arrested him seven times — for "speeding," "loitering" and similar "offenses." And now they have charged him with "perjury" — a felony under which they could imprison him for ten years....

The advertisement cost $4,800 and was signed by 64 celebrities, including Eleanor Roosevelt, religious and union leaders, and many stars of stage and screen. Twenty southern civil rights leaders were listed as having signed the ad, including the four Alabama clerics.

Sullivan contended that the word, "police" referred to him as the Montgomery commissioner who supervised the Police Department. The accusation that police "ringed" the campus, "padlocked" the dining hall, and "they" arrested Dr. King, could all be imputed to him, thus subjecting him to ridicule.

The advertisement was also inaccurate. Students sang the national anthem, not "My Country, 'Tis of Thee," and nine students were expelled for demanding service at a lunch counter in the Montgomery County Courthouse on another day. Not the entire student body, but most of it protested the expulsion. The campus dining hall was never padlocked. Nor did police "ring" the campus, and they were not called to the campus regarding the State Capitol steps demonstration. King had been arrested four times, not seven. Though King's home had been bombed twice, the ad didn't make clear that police weren't implicated. Police had nothing to do with King's perjury indictment. And, prior to being served with a lawsuit, the four clerics were unaware of the ad, let alone that their names had been listed in it.

The trial ran for three days. Though Sullivan conceded in his testimony that his reputation had not suffered, the jury awarded a judgment of $500,000 against the defendants. The *New York Times* buried this November 4, 1960 story on page 67. Abernathy's car and land he owned were seized and sold for $4,750 in partial settlement.

Concurrent with King's acquittal, Alabama Governor John Patterson sued for $1 million in damages. Lawsuits were also filed by Montgomery Mayor Earl James, City Commissioner Frank Parks, and former commissioner Clyde Sellers, for $500,000 each. So the ad to raise funds for King's tax perjury trial defense had the *Times* facing $3 million in damages.

These were not the only lawsuits. The *Times* wrote articles on April 12 and 13, 1960 about racial conditions in Birmingham, triggering another lawsuit that sought $3,150,000 in damages. *Times* reporter Harrison Salisbury, who wrote the series, was under indictment on 42 charges of criminal libel and faced $1.5 million in damages. It was clearly a strategy by the segregationist South to intimidate northern news media not to report on the civil rights movement.

The case went to the U.S. Supreme Court. In a 1963 landmark decision, it unanimously ruled, "A State cannot under the First and Fourteenth Amendments award damages to a public official for defamatory falsehood relating to his official conduct unless he proves 'actual malice' — that the statement was made with knowledge of its falsity or with reckless disregard of whether it was true or false."

*New York Times v. Sullivan* transformed American libel law. It demonstrates that everyone's freedom was enhanced through this victory for the Civil Rights Movement. It began with a tax audit.

**Watergate**

The break-in at the Watergate office of Democratic National Committee Chairman Lawrence O'Brien Jr., occurred in the early hours on Saturday, June 17, 1972. Watergate is a hotel/office complex near the Kennedy Center in Washington, DC. No one is sure why five political burglars were there. The conventional theory is that the burglars were attempting to repair a telephone bug they had installed three weeks before, as well as ransack and photograph files. They worked under the direction of G. Gordon Liddy, a White House operative who was general counsel at Nixon's Committee to Re-Elect the President ("CREEP").

The Watergate scandal culminated in Richard Nixon's resignation as president. Few people are aware that Watergate began as an IRS audit of Lawrence O'Brien, which was ordered by President Nixon, and ended in IRS audits of Richard Nixon and G. Gordon Liddy, with big assessments.

Not since Franklin Roosevelt had any president used the Internal Revenue Service as a weapon against his enemies as much as Nixon. He had the IRS organize a group called the Special Services Staff to investigate civil rights and antiwar activists. It reviewed the tax status of 8,000 individuals and 3,000 groups, including the Ford

Foundation, Head Start, and 50 branches of the National Urban League. An IRS activity called the Information Gathering and Retrieval System collected news clippings, gossip and other data about prominent people for possible use in future tax investigations. "Operation Leprechaun," had an IRS task force investigate and assemble information about the sex and drinking habits of 30 Florida political figures. It was called Leprechaun because green ink was used to write the headings on most of its files. None of this had anything to do with tax administration.

An income tax return contains a wealth of private information — sources of income and spending habits. The first page of Form 1040 contains information useful for identity theft. The remaining pages detail much about a person's personal life. The White House obtained copies of tax returns of Republicans whose political loyalties they doubted, Democratic candidates and their contributors, as well as "enemies."

The Nixon White House maintained an "Enemies List" of people it didn't like. Enemies were regularly referred to IRS with pressure to audit them. The White House planted Roger Barth, its own spy, as an assistant to the IRS commissioner. He delivered confidential reports directly from the commissioner's office to the White House to alert the staff to sensitive investigations that the IRS was conducting.

A confidential IRS report listing names of prominent people undergoing tax investigations was leaked by the White House to columnist Jack Anderson. He printed the list in his newspaper column.

IRS Commissioner Randolph Thrower refused White House pressure to appoint G. Gordon Liddy and John Caulfield to head the alcohol, tobacco and firearms division of the IRS because he thought they were too inexperienced. So, Nixon ordered Thrower removed and Thrower submitted his resignation. He served as Nixon's first IRS commissioner from April 1969 until January 1971, and was succeeded by Johnnie Walters.

In late 1970, Lawrence O'Brien was appointed Democratic National Committee chairman. Soon after, Nixon launched "Operation O'Brien." The IRS audited his 1969 and 1970 income tax returns in 1971-1972. A January 1971 memo from Nixon to Chief of Staff H.R. Haldeman said the "time has come to make O'Brien accountable" – the first recorded indication that the president was after him.

"During 1971, I found myself focused upon by the Internal

Revenue Service. There were audits and repeat audits....As later revealed, I was being scrutinized under direct orders of the White House," recalled O'Brien.

His consulting firm had received a $190,000 payment from Hughes Tool Company in 1970. IRS audits of Hughes' businesses in late 1971 and early 1972 revealed a pattern of kickbacks. Roger Barth alerted John Ehrlichman, then the executive director of the Domestic Council of the White House, that O'Brien's name was on a Hughes Tool Company Sensitive Case Report because of consulting payments. This interested Ehrlichman because it might prove a connection between O'Brien's finances and Hughes kickbacks. In early July 1972, Barth obtained O'Brien's 1969 and 1970 income tax returns together with those for his partner, and their consulting firm.

Ehrlichman told Treasury Secretary George Shultz that O'Brien should be interviewed by the IRS. It was then IRS policy that candidates and other leading political figures would not be audited or questioned during an election year unless the statute of limitations was about to expire or there was some other compelling consideration. Despite this policy, Shultz and IRS Commissioner Walters bent to White House pressure, and O'Brien was interviewed on August 17, just eleven weeks before the 1972 election.

Eventually, Johnnie Walters flatly refused White House pressure to audit the people on Nixon's "enemies list" and like his predecessor, Randolph Thrower, also resigned. His successor, Donald Alexander, announced his firm stand on evenhanded tax administration, and the pressure finally came to an end. The integrity of the IRS and taxpayer respect for our revenue system was shaken, but not irreparably damaged by Watergate thanks to the integrity of these commissioners.

At the height of the Watergate scandal, Nixon suggested that the IRS audit all members of Congress. He sent an "eyes only" memorandum to Haldeman on March 12, 1973, "What I have in mind is that the IRS run audits of all top members of the White House staff, all members of the Cabinet, and all members of Congress. It could be said, if any questions are raised, that this is what we are doing because of letters we have received indicating that people in government do not get IRS checks because of their special position."

Article 2.1 of the Impeachment Articles of the House Judiciary Committee summarized Nixon's tax abuses:

He has, acting personally and through his subordinates, endeavored to obtain from the IRS, in violation of the constitutional rights of citizens, confidential information contained in income tax returns, for purposes not authorized by law, and to cause income tax audits or other income tax investigations to be initiated or conducted in a discriminatory manner.

Nixon's 1974 resignation didn't mark the end of Watergate's tax story.

Prior to 1969, Presidential papers came to be donated to the National Archives via a tax deduction. Truman, Eisenhower, Kennedy, Johnson and Nixon all contributed presidential and pre-presidential papers to the National Archives to gain an extraordinarily large charitable contribution tax deduction.

Nixon delivered 828 boxes of papers from his vice-presidential years to the National Archives on March 27, 1969 for "courtesy storage." This meant they still belonged to the donor until a formal legal transfer was signed. Courtesy storage is not considered a completed gift to the National Archives.

Noted Lincoln scholar Ralph G. Newman of Chicago, who had appraised the Johnson papers, was hired to appraise the Nixon papers. He appraised the 828 boxes in December 1969 and advised Nixon's tax attorney, Frank DeMarco, that 300 more boxes would be required to reach the desired $500,000 deduction. Newman then arranged for an additional 348 boxes to be included in the gift, for a total of 1,176 boxes, which he gave an appraised value of $576,000.

A major tax law was passed on December 30, 1969 under Richard Nixon's signature. It included a provision making donation of personal papers after July 25, 1969 ineligible for a charitable deduction.

DeMarco missed the deadline for a proper tax deduction. To hide this failure, DeMarco and White House attorney Edward Morgan prepared a deed on April 10, 1970 transferring legal title to the National Archives, backdated to March 27, 1969. DeMarco falsely notarized it as of April 21, 1969. The tax deduction was lost forever because April 10, 1970 was the actual date for the completed gift of Nixon's pre-presidential papers.

The tax-motivated gift of the papers was mentioned in a deposition of a White House official, taken in the civil suit brought by the Democratic National Committee against CREEP, which arose out of the 1972 Watergate break-in. If not for Watergate, this tax deduction story would never have come to light.

In 1974, both the IRS and the Joint Committee on Taxation examined President Nixon's income tax returns for 1969 through 1972. The IRS found an underpayment of $432,787 and the JCT found an underpayment of $444,022. Including interest and a five percent negligence penalty, Nixon owed $305,376 for the open years of 1970 through 1972. An underpayment of $171,055 for 1969 was beyond the statute of limitations, but Nixon pledged to pay that additional assessment too. It has never been ascertained whether he honored his pledge.

(*Money* holds an annual tax preparer competition to see who gets closest to the "correct" tax on hypothetical facts. Note that the Joint Committee and IRS, who write the tax laws and regulations, reached different results in calculating Nixon's "correct" tax.)

Newman and Morgan served jail time for their role in defrauding the IRS. Charges against DeMarco, who prepared the fraudulent papers, were dismissed on a technicality. Among other Watergate conspirators, Haldeman served 18 months in prison and Liddy served 4½ years. President Gerald Ford's pardon precluded any criminal investigation of Richard Nixon's possible role.

The Richard Nixon Library in Yorba Linda, California put a spin on the tax audit:

> By March 27, 1969, Nixon donated papers to the National Archives, claiming tax deductions of $576,000. In December 1969, Congress passes a law retroactive to July 25, 1969 repealing this provision in the tax code.
>
> The Joint Committee Staff was highly partisan. [Chairman Wilbur] Mills was a Democrat. Not one Joint Committee staffer (25 total) was a Republican. There was a 1,000 page report.
>
> Unbeknownst to the President, a staff assistant had back-dated the form which confirmed the gift which had been delivered three months before the July 25 deadline. Later, nonpartisan tax experts pointed out that since the papers had been physically delivered, no deed was necessary.

It's a bad "spin." The Joint Committee staff were appointed by House and Senate committees controlled by Democrats, but that doesn't give truth to the statement that "[n]ot one...was a Republican." JCT staff are known for nonpartisanship, and part of their mission is to review tax refunds. That made them ideal for reviewing Nixon's returns. The fact that they arrived at a similar figure as the IRS, whose commissioner and chief counsel were appointed by

Nixon himself, should confirm the fairness of their review.

A dishonest adviser could rightly assume in 1970 that the risk of audit of the president's 1969 tax return was negligible. The risk of the president's anger if he were told that the deadline was missed and it couldn't be fixed was real.

Nixon knew that he was getting a huge tax refund, and that he was paying negligible taxes on his $200,000 presidential salary. I doubt he knew of the subterfuge involving the presidential papers deduction at the time it happened. The president's brother, Edward, confirmed to me that Richard Nixon didn't pay close attention to his personal finances.

Nixon was one of those busy individuals who relied on advisers to handle the details of complex transactions. He had no reason to knowingly allow the July 25, 1969 effective date to stand when he signed the 1969 tax law on December 30, 1969, as a fraud was being perpetrated. The effective date was arbitrarily set as the date the proposal was introduced in the House. Upon Nixon's demand, the effective date would certainly have been delayed, or as is often done in tax legislation, an exception could have been written into the proposal to embrace transactions in an advanced state of completion but not yet consummated. The backdating of a notarized deed perpetrated by his advisers would have been too crass for a president when a legal method was easily at hand.

Nixon wasn't the only one trapped by this change in the law. Hubert Humphrey donated the papers from his years as Lyndon Johnson's vice-president to the Minnesota Historical Society. Humphrey placed restrictions on access to the papers, which made it a "gift of future interest," not deductible until the restrictions lapsed, and no longer deductible after July 25, 1969. The IRS disallowed his deduction too. The "incomplete gift" reason was similar for both Humphrey and Nixon.

For his role in Watergate, Judge John Sirica sentenced G. Gordon Liddy to 20 years in prison, a $40,000 fine, plus an extra year and a half in the notorious D.C. dungeon-jail for refusing to talk. By not allowing potential jurors to be individually questioned, Sirica seated a man who could barely speak or understand English. In order to avoid personal embarrassment, Sirica ordered the official record of this incident sealed. Despite serious errors at his trial and the fact that his sentence might be considered excessive given a first offense and a burglary where nothing was taken except photographs, his appeal was denied. President Carter commuted his sentence in 1977, but the $40,000 fine remained.

Liddy also had to deal with the IRS regarding payments from CREEP. He received a $2,500-a-month salary and reported gross income of $31,000 on his 1972 income tax return. He received other funds to organize the Watergate break-in. Following the break-in, he destroyed all the records in his possession, including financial records.

The IRS claimed that Liddy received $374,300 from various persons and from CREEP and that since only $197,500 was disbursed on behalf of CREEP, the balance of $176,800 was taxable income. The Service also assessed a 50 percent fraud penalty for a total assessment of $155,300 plus interest.

A petition to the Tax Court, affirmed by the Fourth Circuit Court of Appeals, found that Liddy claimed $386,000 of receipts against which he could credibly explain $340,370 of expenses. However, he was liable for taxes on the remaining $45,630 that he couldn't explain. The courts rejected the fraud penalty because Liddy had plausible reasons for destroying his records and the IRS could not prove intent by Liddy to conceal or mislead that would warrant the fraud penalty.

So according to a Tax Court case, the Watergate break-in cost about $386,000.

Following Nixon's problems, all presidential candidates, and many candidates for lower office, routinely release their income tax returns for public scrutiny. While candidates publicize their returns, confidentiality of tax return information for everyone else has improved to minimize the risk of future abuse.

Would Article 2.1 of Richard Nixon's impeachment articles have applied even more so to Franklin Roosevelt? Through the Watergate investigation and impeachment proceedings, we learned about Nixon's tax abuses. Our extensive knowledge about Roosevelt's tax agency abuses comes only from public and biographical records, as there never was an inquest into his widespread abuses.

Conrad Black wrote of FDR, "To use the government's legal apparatus to terrorize opponents and whitewash supporters while putting on the airs of pristine political virtue is abusive and hypocritical."

Presidential abuse of IRS continues. An independent counsel investigation into a multi-year tax fraud by Secretary of Housing and

Urban Development, Henry Cisneros, was thwarted by the Clinton administration. Joseph Farah's Western Journalism Center was audited after appearing on a Clinton Whitewater "damage" control list. The White House attorney referred to the organization by its proper name, The Western Center for Journalism, which it never used, except in filings with the IRS.

# CHAPTER NINE

# The Sex of a Hippopotamus

*The longer I'm in Washington the more I realize that most people in this town tend to act with the calm forethought of a beheaded chicken.*

—Herman Wouk, *Inside, Outside*

In May 1850, the London Zoo acquired Europe's first hippopotamus. A hippo spends most of its time in the water and is very dangerous to approach. As a result, gender can be difficult to determine. Tougher still is determining the gender of a young hippo calf because it has ambiguous plumbing. Inquiring about gender wasn't appropriate in Victorian England. The London *Times* ran a lengthy article describing how the ten-month-old animal was captured and brought to the zoo, its dimensions, diet – every detail except the animal's male gender.

Four years later, the zoo procured a female hippo. The couple produced one offspring that survived infancy. Born on November 5, 1872 the zoo named the calf, "Guy Fawkes," after the man executed that day in 1605 in a failed plot to blow up Parliament. It was more than a year before the zoo discovered its error and renamed the offspring, "Miss Fawkes."

Tax professionals can relate to zookeepers struggling to determine a hippo's gender. One of them was Middleton Beaman, who was the chief legislative draftsman for the House of Representatives from

1919 until 1949. He had a passion for drafting well-written legislation. He complained bitterly about complex tax provisions that members of Congress were writing, as he chided members of the tax committees that the sex of a hippopotamus was a matter of interest only to another hippopotamus.

According to Beaman, the main objective of bill drafting is "to phrase the bill that when it comes before a court it will be interpreted just as it was intended by the drafters." A poorly worded statute would make predicting the interpretation courts would give to a complex new statute just as difficult as determining the gender of a hippo.

### MORE HIPPOS

"That was one of his favorite sayings," confirmed Ward Hussey in a telephone conversation with the author. Hussey was hired by Middleton Beaman in 1946 and was House legislative counsel from 1972 until his retirement in 1989. Thomas Henry Huxley, the nineteenth century zoologist and evolutionist, is reputed to have coined the phrase, "The sex of a hippopotamus *is* a matter of interest to another hippopotamus," meaning it is important in preserving the species.

Some say Guy Fawkes was renamed, "Miss Guy." There was a petition to change her name to Cleopatra after the London Zoo acquired a male hippo from the Amsterdam Zoo named, Anthony.

A few law schools have departments that teach bill drafting. Columbia University was first in 1911. As a professor in Columbia's Legislative Drafting Department, Beaman would mock poorly worded statutes:

> A recent Act creates a Commission to administer it, consisting of five commissioners "one of whom shall be designated by the Governor as Chairman, not more than three of which shall belong to the same political party." I have heard politicians called some hard names, but I never before heard one called a "which."

Establishing a staff function to assist Congress with legislative drafting was controversial. Senator Augustus Bacon (D-GA) declared in 1913 that the time had not come, nor was likely to come, when the Senate would need a schoolmaster to teach it how to draft a bill. So from 1916 to 1918, Beaman volunteered his services. And what did Congress give him? The legislation no one wanted to draft — taxes!

He did a little work on the Revenue Act of 1916, gave much more input into the Revenue Act of 1917, and did substantial drafting for the Revenue Act of 1918.

Beaman's work was praised on the House floor. In debating the war profits and excess profits tax section of the 1918 Revenue Act, Congress marveled that the British law occupied nearly a hundred pages, while Beaman's U.S. incarnation took a little over three pages. During consideration of the 1918 Revenue Act, John Nance Garner, a member of Ways and Means, won approval for the appointment of an Office of Legislative Counsel – on the stated condition that Beaman be appointed head of the House branch.

Upon Beaman's retirement, the House paid tribute in the *Congressional Record*, crediting his many months of drafting the Social Security Act with saving it from challenge before the Supreme Court. "I have marveled at his capacity for work. I have sat in conference committee with him early and late, and there never was a word of complaint because the hour of the meeting was too early or the hour of adjournment too late...A gentleman and a patriot always, he has set a good example for the rest of us to follow," said Earl Michener (R-MI) whose 30 years in the House from 1919 to 1950 paralleled Beaman's.

### HOW A TAX BILL BECOMES LAW

Congress passes tax laws. The IRS administers tax laws. Courts are the final arbiter for interpreting tax laws.

A tax bill begins as a proposal introduced by a member of the House of Representatives, and according to House rules, is assigned to the Ways and Means Committee for deliberation. Hundreds of tax bills are proposed annually, and most die at the Ways and Means doorsteps. Following approval of a tax bill by Ways and Means, it is voted on by the full House.

Upon House passage, it is sent to the Senate Finance Committee. The Senate may concur, make changes, or add amendments to the House bill. Following approval of a tax bill by the Finance Committee, it is voted on by the full Senate.

After Senate passage, the bill goes to a House-Senate conference committee to reconcile any differences. It then returns to the House and Senate where it is again voted on. Upon approval by both Houses, the bill is sent to the president.

The president has ten days to sign the bill into law, or veto it. If he vetoes the bill, it is returned to Congress, where a two-thirds majority in each house can override a veto. A veto override of a tax bill is extremely rare. If the president fails to sign or veto the bill within ten days, it becomes law if Congress is in session, or it dies (a "pocket veto") if Congress is not in session.

An army of staff assistants helps Congress draft legislation, especially the Joint Committee on Taxation, which makes tax studies used for policy decisions, and the Office of Legislative Counsel which assists with legal drafting.

Tax laws are complex because they deal with a complex world. For example:

The term "alcohol" includes methanol and ethanol but does not include alcohol produced from petroleum, natural gas, or coal (including peat). Such term does not include alcohol with a proof of less than 190 (determined without regard to any added denaturants).

—Internal Revenue Code, Sec. 4081(c)(3)(A)

This provision is understood by ethanol refiners. The rest of us rely on journalists, like Paul Gigot who translated it into plain English: "Ethanol is made by mixing corn with your tax dollars."

Congress lowered the corporate income tax rate for favored businesses by three percent phased in starting in 2005. The provision is so complex, it's almost impossible to administer. For example, the movie industry qualifies for this reduction, excluding sexually explicit films. Does Congress expect the IRS to interpret obscenity laws?

The legislative counsel's office knows how to write unambiguous statutes. But sometimes, staff is ordered to leave the statute ambiguous. The reasons range from gaining votes, creating an opportunity to insert a colloquy, or leaving well-heeled campaign contributors an opening to out-gun IRS in court.

### WHAT'S A COLLOQUY?

Few tax professionals have heard of colloquies. When you can't get a tax bill modified to your liking, and can't get the committee report to state how the bill should be interpreted to your liking, a statement entered into the *Congressional Record* by the chairman of Ways and Means or Senate Finance (and preferably both) backing up your client's interpretation of a new law may be respected by IRS or the courts.

> Dozens of colloquies are entered into the *Record* with every tax bill, but no tax service reports them, so only the authors and their clients know where the discussion is buried. It's one more reason that the tax-writing chairmen are among the highest campaign contribution recipients in Congress.

In 1993, for example, Congress enacted a $1 million cap on deductible compensation for officers of publicly held companies. Lobbyists convinced tax writers to limit the compensation cap to the CEO and four highest compensated officers and include an exception for "performance based compensation." This ambiguity rendered the provision non-controversial. While Congress boasted that it had solved the problem of runaway compensation, members actually gutted the essence of the statute. IRS regulations conveniently provide that merely "maintaining the status quo or limiting economic losses" fulfills the standard. The IRS issued its first ruling — in 2008 — when it announced that payments made upon death, disability or termination would fail the performance standard. (Applause!) In 15 years, this provision has never been the subject of a court proceeding and despite inflation, there have been no calls to raise the cap. If Congress were serious about limiting the deductibility of public company salaries, Congress would have defined "performance," or put a solid period after "$1,000,000."

**The Cesspool**

In the late 1860s Congress removed appropriations from the jurisdiction of the tax committees. Though most people feel they are parts of the same equation, tax and spend are two very separate government functions.

Finding real spending cuts is easy. The Congressional Budget Office publishes an annual brick thick book, *Budget Options* with more than 200 suggestions on saving over one trillion dollars through spending cuts.

I was once a guest for two hours on a national radio program explaining the need for tax simplification. We had 12 callers, and every one asked for a flat tax. It's an uphill battle to explain that a flat tax sounds great, but after folks learn the details, no one would want it. Complexity stems not from the rate of taxation, but from defining what is taxed.

In 1984, the Treasury Department held hearings in six major cities to gather ideas about tax reform. I testified at the Atlanta hearing. The hearing was into its second hour when I arrived. The three top Treasury officials looked half asleep. This was the third city they were visiting, and from what I read in the tax press, they had heard nothing useful in the prior two.

I began my speech, "A former legislative aide would chide members of Congress that the sex of a hippopotamus...." As soon as I said "sex" the TV lights and cameras turned on. I made every local news program, as well as the newspapers the next day. The *Atlanta Constitution* called me "the biggest attention getter at the hearing."

I was noticed, but only momentarily. Years later, I had dinner at the Blair House in Washington with one of the Treasury officials at that hearing. I complained that it appeared to be merely a dog and pony show because no suggestions that might have been meaningful were ever followed up on. He admitted that his orders were just to make the rounds and allow people to vent. It was a publicity stunt.

Did he recall my speech? No, but he remembered the woman who spoke after me and called the tax code, "a harbor and cesspool of favoritism." I remembered her too, and she also made the news. Most everyone can agree with her assessment. But was it fair that Peggy June Griffin traveled 400 miles from Evansville, Tennessee to attend a bogus hearing?

That dinner was for an ABA-AICPA joint conference on tax complexity, at which I was a moderator. I learned two lessons working on this conference. First, proof of the adage, "If you want to get something done, ask a busy person." They really know how to manage time, and won't commit to something they can't complete. When they accept a project, it will be finished timely and well. Second, I learned the sources of complexity, the power of contacts, and why tax simplification won't happen.

My session was "The Role of Congressional Staff and Taxpayer Representatives in Tax Complexity." One of my panelists was the current chief of staff of the Joint Committee on Taxation, Congress' tax writing arm. I had a morning meeting with a tax lawyer at a major Washington firm to discuss our session.

"Jay, I hope you don't mind, but we're likely to be interrupted because of a new tax bill in the final stages of passage."

Just then a staffer popped in. "Big Beer says they cannot live with that provision we discussed."

"Call and tell our congressional contact that Big Beer's pension plan, which has 120,000 participants, will be hurt by this provision and it needs to be modified."

Another staffer entered. "Have you gotten those colloquies ready?" asked the partner. "We need to submit them right away if we are to have any chance of getting them entered into the record."

Finally, we talked.

"Why is our session fourth for the day?" he asked. "It should be first."

"It's fourth because the chief of Joint Committee can't make it earlier that morning."

The conference was going to be in January. This was July. He picked up the phone and dialed a number.

"Hi." He didn't introduce himself to the person who answered. "Would you please look at his calendar and tell me what he has scheduled for the morning of January 11?" A pause, followed by, "No, it's all right. I'll let you know."

He hung up and looked at me. "He has a dentist appointment." Now I understood how such easy access to people in power is one reason that top congressional staffers work for a pittance – so they can earn a thousand dollars an hour when they move to private practice.

I asked why tax simplification was so elusive. He explained that despite their public support for simplification, professional groups oppose it. As an example, he recalled a talk he gave to an estate planning group where participants complained about complexity.

As a high ranking government tax official at the time, he thought out loud to the group that since the estate tax raised only $4 billion a year (and budget deficits weren't a problem back then), why not recommend that the estate tax be repealed?

His idea was greeted with a howl of dissent. "No, no! We don't need it *that* simple."

"Why doesn't Congress ignore the lobbyists and contributors and just do right by simplifying the tax law?" I asked.

"Because they wouldn't get re-elected. If you were in Congress, you'd do the same."

"No," I protested. "I'd do what is right."

He paused to reflect a moment. "I believe you. You'd do the right thing. And when you lost the next election, you'd go back to being a CPA. However, most of these guys in Congress have no other vocation. If they lose an election, they're unemployed."

Lyndon Johnson knew that. When he became president in 1963, his family assets were estimated at $20 million, including a radio and television station, land, a cattle empire, and a large portfolio of stocks and bonds. How did the son of an impoverished father, whose income during most of his adult life came from a government salary, become one of the richest men ever to occupy the Oval Office?

In 1941, he gave John Russell Kingsbery, son of an Austin Republican a coveted appointment to the U.S. Naval Academy at Annapolis. It would keep young Kingsbery out of an anticipated war. In return, Johnson applied to purchase from E.G. Kingsbery, the father, radio station KTBC because, should he lose an election, he would be out of politics, and "I have no means of making a living. I want to get into business." FCC approved the sale the following year and Johnson paid Kingsbery a mere $17,500 for the station, registering Lady Bird as the new licensee.

"It was no accident that Austin, Texas, was for years the only city of its size with only one television station. Johnson had friends in high places," wrote his protégé, Bobby Baker. Those "friends" were at the Federal Communications Commission. Upon his election to the Senate in 1948, Johnson became a member of the Commerce Committee, which oversees the FCC. Indeed, Austin didn't get a second TV station until 1965, when a UHF license was granted to KHFI-TV, whose president was John Russell Kingsbery.

Lyndon Johnson left no fingerprints on his masterful arm twisting, amply illustrated by Louisiana Senator Mary Landrieu, describing a tactic used against the Finance Committee chairman, Louisiana Senator Russell Long:

> When LBJ had a provision he wanted to pass in regards to agricultural aid to India, Russell said, "I can't help you, I can't help you, I am against it." Well, LBJ's top aide, Bill Moyers, called back in a little while and said, "Why don't you come by the White House this evening, just a quiet dinner." And Russell said, "I'm glad to go by the White House, the president is my friend, but I do not want to talk about agricultural aid to India." And Bill said, "Well, that's a deal." So they were sitting in the family room after dinner, just the three of

them in their rocking chairs, and after a couple of hours Russell got up to go home, and the president said, "Now one more thing," and Russell's eyes shot through him. And LBJ said to him, "You know that fifth circuit judge from Louisiana you recommended. Well, we've got a candidate from Texas who's pretty good, too." And nothing else was said. You know Texas and Louisiana share the fifth circuit. Well the next morning Russell told his staff, "Call Bill Moyers, tell him we have an understanding."

Johnson's colleague, House Speaker Sam Rayburn (D-TX) once said, "I have been unable to save much money in my life. I have been in politics, and in politics an honest man does not get rich." Rayburn served over 48 years in the House, one of the longest tenures in history. At his death in 1961, his savings totaled $15,000.

## The Lobbyist

In our complex society, lobbyists are a necessity. They are often the only source for useful information the government needs to write legislation or regulations. The lobbyist seeks to obtain a benefit, or avoid a detriment, for a client. The same can be accomplished by securing a detriment, or blocking a benefit, for a competitor. Non-partisan public interest groups are lobbyists, too. Sometimes, it's a private practitioner attempting to solve his client's tax problem by legislation. Or it can be a citizen petitioning Congress on his own.

The target of the lobbyist needn't be Congress. Often, a favorable regulation, ruling, interpretation, action or inaction from an executive agency is equally effective, and much faster and easier to obtain. All it takes is help from an elected or appointed official. Contact with staff can be just as useful as contact with an official. That's because officials rely on staff.

When legislation is needed, officials provide the broad framework of proposed legislation and assign staff to fill in the details. Or staff may initiate the proposal. Staff can insert a provision that no one will realize is present. If it's controversial, no one need admit authoring it.

Justice Antonin Scalia commented, "The Congressional Record or committee reports are used to make words appear to come from Congress's mouth which were spoken or written by others (individual members of Congress, congressional aides, or even enterprising lobbyists)."

Contacts must be nurtured. Former members of Congress, the administration, and their staff have excellent contacts. Many public interest groups have clout through force of their vocal or voting membership. Unfortunately, the most influential are those who purchase their contacts through campaign contributions or less wholesome means. Sometimes Congress extracts contributions with a "milker bill," harmful legislation with no intention of passage, designed to milk payments from affected taxpayers, as illustrated by the following fictitious narrative from a law journal:

> Representative Sam, in need of campaign contributions, has a bill introduced which excites some constituency to urge Sam to work hard for its defeat (easily achieved), pouring funds into his campaign coffers and "forever" endearing Sam to his constituency for his effectiveness.

The ultimate "milker bill" is the pending estate tax repeal which is effective for 2010, after which the pre-2001 law returns. If an estate is worth $100 million, and potentially subject to a nearly $50 million estate tax, it can be well worth $1 million in campaign contributions to have private conversations and influence with lawmakers on what to do with the estate tax. Insurance companies have even more at stake. Both Democrats and Republicans benefit from this cliffhanger law. A Ralph Nader group reported on 18 super-wealthy families with net worth in the billions who are pumping millions into campaigns and political committees to influence permanent repeal of the estate tax.

"Set-up Your Own Charity" is another scheme for raising money. Four years after he was elected to Congress in 1984, House Majority Leader Tom DeLay established the DeLay Foundation Inc., a charity to help abused and neglected children. DeLay's political campaign staff ran the charity and raised over $2.15 million in its 2004 fiscal year by soliciting major corporations and arranging golf tournaments at exotic overseas retreats where business leaders and members of Congress could spend time together. Lobbyist Jack Abramoff had his clients contribute to the golfing ventures. Two of DeLay's aides were convicted in the 2006 Abramoff scandal, and DeLay resigned his seat in Congress after he was indicted on criminal charges of conspiring to violate campaign finance laws.

Contributions to politician-affiliated charities are not subject to campaign finance limits. So checks for $25,000 or $100,000 can flow freely. Though charities are prohibited from providing excessive economic gain to insiders who control it, it's very hard to prove "private benefit" by politicians using nonprofit entities as conduits for political influence. House Speaker Newt Gingrich was reprimanded and assessed an extraordinarily large $300,000 fine in 1997 by the House Ethics Committee, but his Progress and Freedom Foundation escaped IRS sanctions.

Congress rejects any inference that it can be bought. David S. Barry was Senator Nelson Aldrich's protégé, and he served as Senate sergeant-at-arms when Republicans controlled the Senate from 1919 to 1933. He wrote an article in the February 1933 issue of Al Smith's *New Outlook* magazine, "Over the Hill to Demagoguery," which began:

> Contrary perhaps to the popular belief, there are not many crooks in Congress, that is, out-and-out grafters or those who are willing to be such. There are not many Senators or Representatives who sell their vote for money, and it is pretty well known who those few are; but there are many demagogues of the kind that will vote for legislation solely because they think that it will help their political and social fortunes.

For this libel, outraged senators denounced and fired him less than one month prior to his retirement, as the Democrats would take control of Congress in March. It was an ignoble end to an otherwise distinguished 49-year career in Washington.

Without money, one can still be heard in such a crowd by representing a constituency, or having personal influence with government officials. It's not that hard to be heard, provided your arguments don't clash with monied interests. Just find a constituency that will allow you to speak in its name.

This game is not lost on bureaucrats. In 1948, Senator Forrest C. Donnell (R-MO) remarked in frustration at a witness before the Judiciary Committee:

> [I]n various committees of the Senate at numerous times gentlemen appear with the very best motives and sincerest intentions, and assure us they represent 6,000,000 people, or 3,000,000, or 40,000 people, or any number of people and it frequently simmers down to the fact that a board consisting of about 11 persons or maybe 20, or maybe a hundred has passed upon it, and is undertaking to act for the 3,000,000 or 40,000 or whatever the number may be.

Congress gets tons of form letters and postcards from organized writing campaigns, requiring nothing more from the sender than affixing postage. E-mail and form letters count very little, though members of Congress do keep a tally. However, a "kitchen-table" letter (i.e., written at your kitchen table) can have a much stronger impact than a hundred form letters.

In October 1986, I wrote to Congressman J.J. Pickle (D-TX), chairman of the House IRS Oversight Committee, suggesting public inspection of tax returns of public charities because even board members of national charities had no access to financial information of the charities they served on. That suggestion was enacted in 1987 legislation. It mandated public inspection of tax returns at the charities' office. Today, this disclosure provision permits posting all charitable tax returns to the internet.

Congressmen don't read voluminous bills which cross their desks, nor follow the minute changes inserted as the bill wends its way through revisions. They don't have time. Senate Finance Committee member Daniel Patrick Moynihan (D-NY) admitted as much to Chairman William Roth (R-DE):

> Mr. Chairman, last night, by a vote of 83 to 14, something like that, we passed a bankruptcy bill which had a large tax section. Mr. Chairman, I attest that I did not read a line of it, have not the slightest idea of what was in it, do not know where it came from. Now, I know that will not be the case with you, sir..... You have gone over it carefully. But I do not think many of the other of the 84 had. That is beginning to be a problem.

This is not a recent phenomenon. The House accepted the 1936 Tax Act with little debate. Three-quarters of the members were absent during most of the time the bill was debated, "and it is doubtful whether more than a handful of those who remained on the floor understood the complicated 236-page measure," wrote Randolph Paul.

It is commonly agreed that tax laws would be simpler if legislators were required to prepare their own income tax returns. I believe tax laws would be simpler if legislators were merely required to read the bills before they could vote on them. A congressman's recent call for three days to read these thousand page bills before they vote was disregarded.

At a December 4, 2001 Washington conference on tax complexity, staff of Congress' tax writing committees were jovial about the success of the complex higher education tax incentives (13 at this writing). They rationalized the complexity:

> [We never] received a single letter or communication from any constituent saying he had too many choices for these education tax incentives..., "Would you please simplify it so we have less choices?" Not a single communication.
>
> —Russ Sullivan, chief tax counsel, Senate Finance Committee
>
> Nobody complains about a multitude of opportunities in the tax code.
>
> —Bob Winters, special counsel, House Ways and Means Committee
>
> [P]eople have suggested that using computer software really masks for individuals the complexity of the individual tax system.
>
> —Mary Schmitt, deputy chief of staff, Joint Committee on Taxation

Not really. Computer software cannot yet decide among all the choices in claiming credits vs. deductions, the multi-year timing, elections, or on whose tax return an incentive should be claimed when there is a choice.

Lobbyists promote tax complexity to benefit their clients. As part of a comprehensive 1986 tax reform, Congress disallowed deductions for personal interest expense. Home mortgage interest remained deductible. Lobbyists convinced Congress that interest on recreational vehicles and boats should qualify as a second home if they had eating and sleeping facilities and a toilet.

A prime example of lobbying power was seen in 1985, when the Treasury Department proposed taxing veterans' disability benefits. A small army of veteran groups met with the assistant secretary for tax policy. They were led by Chad Colley, national commander of the Disabled American Veterans, who had lost both legs and one arm in Vietnam. Assistant Secretary Ronald Pearlman explained that Treasury based the proposal on fairness because some veterans had high paying jobs while getting tax-free disability benefits. But the veterans were not in a negotiating mood.

They convinced a powerful senator to introduce a resolution not to tax veterans' disability benefits. Then they scheduled a second meeting, this time with the secretary of the Treasury. They showed him a full-page ad they were planning to run in *The New York Times*, *The Washington Post*, and *USA Today*. It had a huge picture of Commander Colley in a wheelchair, his missing appendages painfully evident. The copy read, "WHAT'S SO SPECIAL ABOUT DISABLED VETERANS? That's what a top Treasury official said to Chad Colley..." The treasury secretary dropped the issue.

Gentlemen's agreements often determine which laws are enacted. A CPA told me she had been the White House appointment secretary during Lyndon Johnson's administration. The Senate minority leader, Everett Dirksen (R-IL), would have secret early morning meetings with Johnson. They would map out how Democrats and Republicans would spar over certain issues for public consumption, playing to their respective constituencies, and agreed on how they would finally be resolved. The whip system worked much better back then, and congressmen would usually vote as their leadership dictated.

Lobbying is more brazen at the state level. In 1998, the legislature re-wrote the law on how multistate corporations should apportion their income to Georgia. A lengthy new provision allowed airlines to figure Georgia taxes based on revenue earned while flying over the state. For Atlanta-based Delta Air Lines this meant that payroll and property (including maintenance facilities) would no longer be factors in calculating Georgia income tax. This dramatically reduced the airline's Georgia income tax. Upon inquiry, the Ways and Means Committee told me the legislation originated with the Department of Revenue. The Department of Revenue said the legislation was "dictated" to them by lawyers for Delta Air Lines. State Senator Terrell Starr was chairman of the Senate Finance Committee. He represented Clayton County, home of Delta Air Lines.

Atlanta-based Coca-Cola was able to convince a new chairman of the Ways and Means Committee to pass a law doubling the sales factor in the Georgia apportionment formula, a change that would cut its taxes. The former chairman had always objected because it was a big revenue-loser for the state.

**My Life As A Lobbyist**

I've had success as a tax lobbyist. From 1981 through 1986, Georgia's income tax law differed significantly from the federal laws. With the major changes Congress made in 1986, failure to conform would make 1987 and subsequent year tax return preparation a nightmare. I was invited to testify before the Georgia House Ways and Means Committee on behalf of the Georgia Society of CPAs.

I explained how difficult it would be to prepare a Georgia tax return because of the many differences from the federal return. The legislators asked me how much it would cost to prepare the Georgia portion of an income tax return without conformity.

Seeking to impress them, I said, "If Georgia doesn't conform, I have some clients with so many Georgia tax differences that it would cost $200 just to prepare the Georgia portion."

"Mr. Starkman," asked a lawmaker, "how much extra will tax return preparation cost the average Georgia taxpayer if we fail to conform?"

"About $50," I replied.

Unbeknownst to me, a reporter was present. The next day, the newspaper reported, "Atlanta CPA, Jay Starkman, testified that it would cost the average Georgia taxpayer about $50 more for tax preparation if Georgia fails to conform. However, Starkman said he would charge his clients $200."

(Did I neglect to mention that for $200, I would guarantee that the return showed a refund?)

Following my presentation, I walked up to Ways and Means Chairman Tom Crosby and suggested that the Georgia Society of CPAs might help with drafting tax conformity legislation and making revenue estimates. He accepted my offer, saying, "Get me a revenue estimate."

My committee was aghast. "How are we going to make a revenue estimate?" I suggested that we take the federal revenue estimates for the 1986 Tax Act and apply income statistics supplied by the Georgia Department of Revenue to calculate the impact of conforming Georgia's tax law to federal tax law. A week later, using this method, we had an estimate: "Georgia will have between $170 million and $220 million extra revenue in 1987 if it does not conform to federal law."

Crosby accepted our estimate and asked that we calculate the revenue impact under different scenarios: full conformity, increasing the standard deduction, simplification of itemized deductions, changes to Georgia's rate structure, and preferential taxation of capital gains.

What I didn't learn until later was that Georgia had paid $30,000 to Peat Marwick's Economic Policy Group to make a revenue estimate, and theirs came in smack in the middle of ours. That gave us credibility.

That tax season, my committee was on call serving as staff to the Georgia House Ways and Means Committee. We often got just two hours' notice to drop everything and come downtown.

Ways and Means Committee members asked questions about the conformity bill.

Q: "What is the highest Georgia corporate income tax rate?"

A: "It's a flat 6 percent. It's been a flat 6 percent for 30 years."

This is such a basic question that one who must ask it should not be a member of Ways and Means.

A very straightforward conformity bill was crafted to be revenue neutral. With $200 million in tax reductions to play with, the legislature made Georgia's the nation's simplest — even allowing a deduction for state income tax. Only Georgia's antiquated 1937 rate structure was left unchanged.

I watched legislators over the next 20 years complicate it: three dozen tax credits, exclusions for retirees, and check off contributions to favored charities. It takes five pages to claim a $150 driver education credit. After the 2001 Tax Act, Georgia decided it would not conform to certain federal practices, like "bonus depreciation." So, Georgia again has nonconformity and complexity.

Tom Crosby authorized Georgia House Resolution 534 to honor me and other members of the Georgia Society of CPAs. The Georgia Society of CPAs gave me its Distinguished Member Award. Crosby received no recognition for his noble success. Without him, there would have been no true tax simplification in Georgia.

Crosby represented rural Waycross, Georgia. He knew that there were poor rural counties where timber undervaluation resulted in $400 of additional property tax per family because Georgia property tax values forests as raw land. The value of the standing timber was disregarded. As a matter of equity, he felt that timber companies should pay tax on the value of timberland, not on a fictitious raw land equivalent.

He sponsored legislation to tax timber for property tax purposes at fair market value, not as raw land. That brought out a lobbying onslaught by landowners, national lumber and paper companies, and even Georgia Power Company which owns much rural timberland.

The lobbyists mischaracterized his proposal, and ran a major ad campaign against it, defeating the bill. Their next target was Tom Crosby. He had won seven consecutive elections, and ran unopposed after his fourth victory. Now, the timber interests introduced a candidate with timber connections, and Crosby was defeated.

Tom Crosby did the right thing and lost re-election. Georgia has a part-time legislature that is in session just 40 days a year. The pay stinks, even for part-time work, but that attracts a citizen legislature, rather than professional politicians. So, when he lost the election, he went back to being a pecan farmer. He never ran for public office again. Georgia lost a great, honest and underappreciated legislator.

I was asked to explain the provisions of the new law to 1,000 CPAs who would be attending the Society's Tax Forums in Savannah and Atlanta. I was to share podium time with Senate Majority Leader Roy Barnes, who was to speak on the political background.

Upon meeting Barnes in Savannah he asked, "Jay, can you keep your remarks short to give me more time. I have a lot I need to explain." Of the 35 minutes devoted to our session, I used less than 15 minutes, and referred the audience to my written materials in the handout. Roy Barnes then gave a 20 minute political speech. You'd think he was running for state-wide office.

When we got to Atlanta, he made the same request. I didn't make the same mistake. I took almost 20 minutes to cover my material.

A dozen years later, Roy Barnes was elected governor of Georgia.

**The Charitable Deduction**

Passage of the Revenue Act of 1917 to finance World War I was influenced by one of the earliest successful tax lobbying efforts. The top tax rate was about to be raised to 77 percent.

Senator Henry Hollis (D-NH) introduced an amendment on June 16 for a charitable deduction. He offered telegrams from millionaires Jacob H. Schiff and Felix M. Warburg of New York urging passage. Both telegrams cited support of Jewish charities for the amendment. Senator Albert Cummins (R-IA) also announced his support for the bill. Hollis and Cummins were not members of the Finance Committee, nor was either senator from New York.

The following day, it was suggested that the Red Cross would have difficulty raising $100 million for the war effort if a charitable deduction was not allowed. Renowned lawyer and Jewish philanthropist Samuel Untermyer wrote Senate Finance Committee Chairman F.M. Simmons (D-NC) that the high income tax rates would reduce charitable contributions:

> Men of large incomes, however generously inclined, will hesitate to make gifts...when by so doing they...are penalized anywhere from 25 to 50 percent upon the amount they thus contribute, (dependent on their incomes,) for the privilege of having thus contributed from their private means to a worthy cause that is largely governmental in character.

The Red Cross fundraising campaign was essential for the relief facilities needed by the U.S. Army. New York was assigned to raise $40 million. The *New York Times* listed some 300 of the wealthiest and most prominent New Yorkers serving on the fundraising teams, which held a kickoff campaign dinner at the Waldorf-Astoria on Monday, June 18. It included Daniel and Harry Guggenheim, Charles Hayden, John D. Rockefeller Jr., J.P. Morgan, Jacob and Mortimer Schiff, Mrs. Thomas A. Edison, and George Merck. On Thursday, there was another Red Cross dinner at the New York Ritz-Carlton, attended by Theodore Roosevelt, Governor Whitman, and Mayor Mitchel.

The movement that began in New York City quickly spread across the entire country. Timing introduction of the measure around the Red Cross fundraising campaign was clever, and it couldn't but help that President Woodrow Wilson was honorary president of the American Red Cross.

The Finance Committee did not include the charity deduction in its bill. Senator Hollis proposed it as an amendment on the Senate floor, up to 20 percent of income. Finance Chairman Simmons accepted the proposal with a 15 percent income limitation. The proposal survived the House-Senate conference, and that's how the charity deduction became the fifth deduction, after business expenses, interest, taxes, and losses.

The tax lobbying campaign succeeded because it framed the charity tax deduction as essential for raising $100 million for the Red Cross war fund. In the background, it was led and directed by rich philanthropists. As a bonus, the 1916 estate tax law was amended to allow an unlimited charity deduction in computing estate tax.

Prior law made charities exempt from paying income tax as early as 1894. Now contributors would be able to deduct the contributions, too. Exemption from income tax and deductibility of contributions are a double benefit for charities.

The U.S. is unique in allowing a broad deduction for charitable contributions. Few other countries allow a charitable deduction against income tax. Yet, there has never been a study conclusively proving that the tax deduction for charitable contributions raises for charity more than it costs in government revenue. There are only anecdotes. In particular, there's no evidence of a correlation between the charitable deduction and giving by lower income individuals. There was a charity deduction for non-itemizers in the early 1980s. It was a revenue loss for the government and was repealed before it could be determined whether it resulted in a significant increase in donations.

Total U.S. giving exceeds $280 billion annually, about 1.85 percent of gross domestic product, the highest percentage in the world. This is the best anecdotal evidence that the tax deduction is pivotal to the uniquely American broad base of privately funded charitable institutions. In few other countries will you find many privately funded nonprofit universities, hospitals or museums.

Criticism that U.S. foreign aid as a percentage of gross domestic product should be larger fails to consider at least $34 billion in private charity to overseas causes. When added to $10 billion U.S. government foreign aid, the U.S. is the premier benefactor in terms of GDP. Let no one accuse the U.S. of not being sufficiently generous.

**Tax Simplification**

The primary and historic function of the tax code is to raise revenue. Today we also use it to administer means-tested benefit programs like the earned income tax credit, economic incentives in the form of business tax credits, and social programs by monitoring nonprofit groups. These non-revenue functions divert limited resources, forcing IRS to audit low-income taxpayers as often than those with high incomes. The added complexity generates disrespect for the tax system, particularly when the law is poorly understood or enforcement is lax.

Simplifying the income tax law is rather easy. Convert it from a mass tax back into a class tax, as it was prior to the 1940s. About 130 million individual income tax returns are filed annually and raise almost $800 billion of income tax. Roughly 89 million tax filers in low tax brackets pay $72 billion in tax. That's everyone making $35,000 or less if single and $60,000 or less if married. The other 41 million returns raise $725 billion.

The U.S. doesn't need a complex system to collect the $72 billion raised from the 68 percent of tax returns filed by people with relatively modest incomes. In the past, low and middle-income taxpayers were subject to consumption taxes (in the form of tariffs) rather than income tax.

A taxpayer population only one-third the present size would allow IRS to work much more effectively. Its computer modernization program would become more manageable. And the Internal Revenue Code could be vastly simplified because it wouldn't be concerned with fairness for moderate income taxpayers no longer subject to income tax.

It won't happen, unless we get another president like Andrew Jackson. Congress doesn't want to lose influence over the finances of 68 percent of the public. Tax preparers will complain that the present system works and that the masses should not be deprived of participation in the income tax. (Shades of William Jennings Bryan!) Charities will fear lower contributions due to loss of deductibility. Realtors will warn of a collapse in real estate values as interest and real estate tax deductions disappear. States would loathe adjusting their regressive income tax schedules to accommodate those who would no longer file federal returns but continue to file state returns. Advocates of social programs administered through the income tax (e.g., earned income tax credit, child credit, education programs and retirement provisions) would be opposed. There is no constituency that would champion repeal of this mass tax.

Texas Congressman George H.W. Bush introduced a proposal in 1970 for "A Committee for Simplification of Federal Taxation." A California CPA had saved this and sent it to me in 1990, when I chaired the AICPA Tax Simplification Committee. Somewhere in those 20 years, George Bush, having become president, lost interest in simplifying taxes. My committee couldn't interest anyone in his administration in the president's former idea. A more important lesson: be careful what you write because someone has saved it. (However, President George W. Bush established a Tax Reform Commission fulfilling his father's suggestion without outside prodding.)

Among the ideas I pondered as chairman of the Tax Simplification Committee was publicizing tax complexity and proving there was a constituency for simplification. I suggested a protest demonstration by CPAs outside the Capitol. "The only way you'll get a turnout at that demonstration is if you bring McKenna's Wagon," I was told. McKenna's Wagon was a meals-on-wheels for the homeless.

Taking a cue from the 2005 anti-government action film, *V for Vendetta*, about 60 protesters from around the country, all costumed in Guy Fawkes masks and capes, staged a 2006 anti-tax protest outside the White House. They were led by tax protester Bob Shulz, who "hasn't filed a tax return in several years." It was a clever publicity stunt, but largely ignored by the media.

Some media outlets have great influence. Responding to a reader's complaint about tax complexity, Ann Landers suggested in her April 8, 1990 column, "Every accountant who is fed up with this totally incomprehensible gobbledygook should tear this column out of the paper, scribble across it 'I agree' and send it to the American Institute of Certified Public Accountants. The address is...." This generated over 10,000 letters to AICPA in two weeks. "Do you know what 10,000 letters looks like?" an AICPA manager complained. "We can't get our mail. We had to hire temporaries to open and sort the mail."

I came away disappointed, but with the realization that the primary roadblock to tax simplification is neither the political climate nor the Washington bureaucracy. Professionals are not angry about tax complexity, and politicians are not worried about the degeneration of the tax system to make simplification a priority.

The best ally in tax simplification is the IRS, because complexity inhibits its mission. The IRS once approached my committee to ask for our assistance with regulation projects. Ken Kempson, special assistant to the deputy chief counsel, met with us on November 9, 1989. He indicated that the agency wanted regulations that were fair and true to congressional intent. Revenue neutrality would be secondary to regulation simplification. He offered us close contact and meetings with responsible IRS personnel so that we could learn the agency's reasoning for existing regulations and exchange ideas. His department had written a "Report of Treasury-IRS Regulation Simplification Task Force."

IRS had extended the golden scepter to AICPA. Unfortunately,

I couldn't raise the volunteers willing to work with IRS. The chairman of one AICPA committee complained, "Why should we do IRS' work of writing regulations?" Those 25 AICPA committees were excited at the opportunity to submit proposals suggesting changes in the law, but couldn't see the value in working with Treasury to simplify the tax law.

IRS took one of my committee's proposals and simplified it even more. We proposed that the complex and confusing method of determining when payroll tax deposits were due should be changed to require that a payroll tax deposit be made three business days after the payroll date. Treasury modified our proposal to the method in use today, setting a simple three-day rule, but fixing the deposit due dates as Monday and Wednesday. Regulatory simplification can be as effective as legislation.

## The Black Art of Revenue Estimating

Every tax proposal must be accompanied by projected revenue gains or losses. Revenue estimating starts with old IRS income statistics. They are "massaged" with information from the U.S. Census Bureau and other statistical data. The assumptions, and guesswork behind the estimates, are rarely disclosed to avoid arguments over their veracity.

How accurate are revenue estimates? The 1986 Tax Act required taxpayers to enter a social security number for each dependent age five or older. Intended to make divorced parents very careful about who claimed the exemption, it was considered a minor revenue raiser. Seven million dependents disappeared in 1987, a drop of more than nine percent. IRS began auditing those with large exemption changes between 1986 and 1987 and averaged over $2,000 per assessment. This small revenue raiser in the 1986 Act budget estimate turned out to be one of the biggest — worth about $3 billion a year.

Congress took notice. Subsequent tax laws lowered the threshold requiring social security numbers for dependents by age two, then age one, and finally, at birth. That's why today you apply for a social security number at the hospital right after you name your baby.

When the Georgia income tax reform bill was completed in 1987, my Georgia Society of CPAs committee was invited to review a follow-up study of the revenue estimates prepared by

Peat Marwick's Economic Policy Group. They made a slightly lower revenue estimate than we did. However, they omitted the disallowance of bank reserves for bad debts, one of the biggest revenue raisers in the federal 1986 tax reform. Georgia paid them $100,000 for the understated revenue estimate.

In 2000, Treasury made an "official" estimate that abusive corporate tax shelters were costing the government $10 billion annually. The estimate originated with an anecdotal conjecture by Stanford University law professor Joseph Bankman. After former Joint Committee Chief of Staff Ken Kies joined PricewaterhouseCoopers, he became a defender of corporate shelters and tried to discredit Bankman:

> Bankman's claim represents a mere conjecture by a non-economist. It is not supported by any analysis of actual revenue or economic data. My concern is that the Bankman "guesstimate" has now been repeated by the media so often and for so long that it has now assumed the patina of authoritative analysis. The latest example is an April 17 Business Week article...that states, "Treasury reckons it loses at least $10 billion a year from corporate shelters."

At the time, no one had any idea how much revenue the government was losing. I spoke with Professor Bankman shortly after this controversy arose. His estimate, he admitted, depended on how one defined "abusive" and it was an educated guess. At first, I was skeptical, but as revelations of abuse increased, I felt that his guess was probably understated.

Even revenue estimators can't keep their estimates straight. A proposal imposing new reporting on credit card receipts was scored in the fiscal 2008 budget as raising $10.7 billion over ten years. The same proposal in the 2007 budget was projected to raise just $225 million.

**Special Tax Breaks**

The fast food industry is subsidized. It benefits from the earned income credit, which is effectively a $2 per hour subsidy on the minimum wage. It receives work opportunity credits of up to $2,400 per worker for hiring the disadvantaged. Developing new menus earns research tax credits.

Some tax breaks are simple graft, not unlike Sen. Nelson Aldrich's perverse relationship with the Sugar Trust. Today's graft is more sophisticated. Washington lobbyist Jack Abramoff's currency consisted of campaign contributions, gifts, trips and "favors." The tax code provides opportunities for return payments to which no one admits authorship and no one asks.

Some benefits are tailor-made. The Tax Reform Act of 1986 included this clause: "In the case of any pre-1987 open year, neither the United States nor the Virgin Islands shall impose an income tax on non-Virgin Island source income derived from transactions described in clause (ii) by one or more corporations which were formed in Delaware on or about March 6, 1981...." Two investigative reporters for the *Philadelphia Inquirer* translated the section: "A man named William M. Lansdale, a pal of Ronald Reagan and California's then-Governor George Deukmejian, wouldn't have to pay Uncle Sam about $4.5 million on some investments."

In 2004, Congress turned professional sports into a tax shelter by allowing a complete tax write-off of the purchase price over 15 years. (Does a sports franchise depreciate in value?) Congress cited as reasons the need to "minimize disputes [with IRS]" and the fact that "[amortization] should apply to all types of businesses regardless of the nature of their assets." What campaign contributions justified a $382 million loss to the Treasury Department over ten years?

Congress was even more generous with NASCAR by allowing depreciation of "any motorsport entertainment complex" over a mere seven years using accelerated depreciation, instead of 39 years with straight line depreciation. Our lawmakers also wrote an unprecedented admonishment that IRS should abandon pending cases where it had challenged aggressive tax returns which depreciated auto racing facilities over seven years. The aggressors had made a wild interpretation of an old tax law that allows seven-year depreciation for amusement park rides by arguing that auto racing qualified as an amusement park.

In effect, Congress made the law retroactive. Why? Normal practice is for Congress to write, "Nothing in this Act shall be construed to create any inference with respect to the proper tax treatment prior to [2005]."

How many jobs were created by these professional sports and NASCAR provisions that they were germane to a law titled, "American Jobs Creation Act"? This is on top of the tax-exempt bonds used to finance stadiums given for free to sports franchises. That started in 1957, when Los Angeles lured the Brooklyn Dodgers to the West

Coast with 300 acres and $4 million to build a new stadium. The following year, the New York Giants baseball team fared even better, with the $32 million Candlestick Park that San Francisco built so they would move west. Senate Finance Committee member Daniel Patrick Moynihan (D-NY) opposed federal tax breaks for stadiums. He sought to draw attention to the waste with a 1997 proposal to deny tax-exempt financing for stadiums, though he knew it had no chance of passage. Today, government spending on sports facilities exceeds $2 billion annually, though no independent economic study has shown any significant positive impact from these expenditures.

When Atlanta Mayor Bill Campbell was first elected in 1994, I knew his chief of staff. Budget problems soon surfaced, and I sent him an article from a professional tax publication showing that Atlanta had one of the lowest hospitality taxes in the country. I naively suggested that the city might increase the hotel and rental car tax to close the deficit. He sent me a thank-you note saying the information would be very useful. Atlanta no longer has the lowest hospitality taxes, but the tax increase was earmarked to fund construction of Phillips Arena. Budget deficits could be closed but for a tax and spend mentality.

Though George W. Bush took a hatchet to federal taxes, it was through raising Texas taxes that he rose to prominence. Around 1990, he sold two-thirds of his holdings in the money-losing Harken Energy Corporation for nearly $850,000 and bought an 11.8 percent interest in the Texas Rangers for a sweetheart bargain price of $606,000. Others paid $86 million for the remaining 88.2 percent. The new owners wanted a new stadium. They got it, thanks to more than $200 million in public subsidies paid for through an increase in sales tax, state tax exemptions and other financial incentives. Bush's political connections made this easier to achieve. The team was sold in 1998 for $250 million, and Bush netted $14.9 million. Without the sales tax increase that paid for his stadium, George W. Bush might not have had the money or public exposure to win the Texas governorship, and might not have become president.

Democrats decry a "culture of corruption" but stop shy of calling for a full investigation of the effects of campaign contribution shakedowns. An independent investigation on the scale of the IRS investigations of the 1920s and 1950s would jolt the foundations of how political power is wielded and result in many resignations and criminal prosecutions.

## Mr. Taxes

I previously mentioned that I knew a CPA who read the Internal Revenue Code cover-to-cover twice a year. Rep. Wilbur Mills (D-AR) had it memorized. "The reach of his familiarity with the bleak terrain of federal tax law is beyond the perception of anybody else in Washington; during committee sessions, in fact, he is wont to recite without falter whole sections of the tax code," noted *Life*. *Newsweek* called him, "Mr. Taxes." The *New York Times*, "Pied Piper of Taxes" and "Steering Wheel of the House." *The New Republic* referred to him as "The Most Powerful Man in Congress." He held no personal business interests that might have benefited from his legislative activities; he didn't even itemize his tax deductions.

Mills was elected to the House in 1938, at the age of 29, and won appointment to Ways and Means in 1943. At age 50, he became the youngest chairman of the House Ways and Means Committee in history, and served the longest consecutive term as chairman. Under Mills, the committee turned all-powerful.

The 25 members of Mills' Ways and Means Committee (compared to 41 today) all came from safe districts, which minimized turnover and encouraged integrity. No public record of committee meetings was maintained, so lobbyists were in the dark and members could vote their conscience. As the "Committee on Committees," Ways and Means controlled committee assignments for the whole House. Any House member desiring a seat on a particular committee or tax legislation had to befriend Chairman Wilbur. Presidents couldn't pass tax legislation without the OK from Wilbur Mills. When President Kennedy sought legislation, one of the quid pro quos was that he personally appear in Arkansas at the 1962 dedication of the Greers Ferry Dam, about 70 miles northeast of Little Rock.

The Senate Finance Committee had 16 members (compared with 20 today). There were no subcommittees. In that era, if the chairman of the Ways and Means Committee and the chairman of the Finance Committee and their staff at the Joint Committee on Taxation concurred with a Treasury proposal, it was virtually an accomplished fact.

Mills ran for President in 1972, but withdrew after doing poorly in the early primaries. Democratic candidate George McGovern announced that he would name Mills as treasury secretary if he became president.

During the late 1960s, Mills began to drink heavily and became addicted to prescription drugs, used for pain from a chronic back problem. Police stopped a drunken Wilbur Mills at 2 a.m. on October 9, 1974 for speeding with headlights off. His face was bloody from a scuffle. An Argentine stripper, Fanne Fox, leaped from his car and jumped into the nearby Potomac River Tidal Basin. Blaming a drinking problem, the married chairman relinquished the chairmanship and though he won re-election in 1974 by a good margin, didn't seek re-election in 1976. Men in higher positions had survived worse scandals, but reformers anxious to dilute the power of Ways and Means targeted Mills for removal. With Mills' departure, Congress stripped Ways and Means of its Committee on Committees jurisdiction to make House committee assignments and added members. This made it much less able to resist political bargaining and diminished its power to forge good tax policy.

The chairmen of the congressional tax-writing committees are especially targeted by enemies. Ways and Means Chairman Dan Rostenkowski lost re-election in 1994, and Senate Finance Committee Chairman Robert Packwood resigned in 1995, both amid scandal. But never did the loss of any chairman have such ramifications as when Wilbur Mills was deposed.

"Wilbur Mills, where are you?" began a 1979 *New York Times* article complaining how the lack of leadership left Ways and Means unable to resolve conflicting tax issues. Mills was committed to delivering rational tax policy and spending cuts to pay for tax reduction. He explained his simple tax philosophy to an interviewer: "The function of taxation is to raise revenue...I do not go along with economists who think of taxation primarily as a means for... manipulating the economy."

CHAPTER TEN

# The Lawgivers

*Nay, whoever hath an absolute authority to interpret any written or spoken law, it is he who is truly the Lawgiver to all intents and purposes, and not the person who first wrote or spoke them.*

—Sermon by Bishop Hoadly before King George I (1717)

*It is emphatically the province and duty of the judicial department to say what the law is.*

—*Marbury v. Madison*, 5 US 137, 177 (1803)

As shown in prior chapters, taxation generates a culture. At the IRS that culture has in the past been quite corrupt. Presidents have used the agency to cultivate friends and abuse enemies. Congress has refined the tax code into a vehicle that generates campaign contributions.

Our courts have a culture of believing they are fair toward taxpayers. "The court bends over backwards with the taxpayer," Tax Court Chief Judge Howard A. Dawson Jr. told *Business Week* in a 1984 interview. Not true, especially in regard to "Bend Over Backwards" Dawson, whose name appears frequently in this chapter.

Tax Court has some rules that are unfriendly to taxpayers, and it denies taxpayers access to affordable counsel. When Congress passes laws to create a friendlier judicial forum for taxpayers, like shifting burden of proof to the IRS and awarding litigation fees to taxpayers, courts resist implementing them. It's a little known scandal that is almost never mentioned in the press. Tax Court Judge Herbert Chabot spoke frankly in a 1989 dissent.

> "Equity" and "equitable" are appealing words. They conjure up visions of "doing right", of "mercy", and of Solomon-like wisdom. Certainly, none of us wants this Court to be perceived as "inequitable". However, this connotation of "equity" and "equitable", and awareness of the antonym, should not be allowed to affect the nature and work of the Court or our decision-making process.

Tax Court judges insist that Congress has denied them equity authority. That's debatable because the court has clearly applied principles of equity. True, equity authority is limited to keep judges from doing favors for taxpayers they feel sorry for. The question is "How limited?" The judge's dissent quoted above dealt with a case where the Tax Court claimed equity power so that it could rule in favor of the government.

Just what percentage of cases are won by taxpayers? One academic study asserts that the IRS should win 60 percent of cases because the taxpayer makes claims that are clearly unallowable. This category includes unallowable deductions (e.g., claiming pets as dependents), as well as those lacking evidence (e.g., no receipts to prove deductions) and those involving tax protester arguments (e.g., the income tax is unconstitutional). Of the remaining 40 percent, an unbiased court might theoretically rule in favor of taxpayers half the time, granting victory in 20 percent of all cases. Taxpayers aren't likely to be right that often because IRS settles most of its weaker cases, taking only the stronger ones to trial.

The taxpayer wins outright or in a split decision in almost 15 percent of cases, according to the Taxpayer Advocate Service (the "consumer advocate" office within IRS) and studies by academics. A review of 945 "most litigated issues" for June 2006 to May 2007 shows that the taxpayer won outright just 8 percent of the time. It is often difficult to determine whether a taxpayer actually won much worthwhile in a split decision of multiple issues. The tax may be upheld, but the court abates penalties, so it's counted as a split. A decision that a taxpayer may deduct 10-20 percent of what he claimed is a split.

A group I worked with undertook to study all small case decisions (under $50,000, where the taxpayer elects this procedure) by the Tax Court from January 2001 to December 2002. There were about 400 cases in all, and counting splits, we also found that the taxpayer won almost 15 percent. But the outright wins were only 6 percent, and the splits often saved taxpayers relatively small amounts. (The results were not published.) Still, the splits are important because, as a tax professor told me, they "demonstrate that the judges will make adjustments where they are warranted....it's not a slam dunk for the IRS."

Despite the discouraging taxpayer odds, lawyers whom I admire and respect feel that the Tax Court is a fair forum. Martin Ginsburg wrote, "just as often, it seemed to me, TC decided one for the taxpayer that might more reasonably have gone for IRS."

In my view, taxpayers should win *a little* more often. It would be outstanding if taxpayers could really win 15 percent of the cases. That would not require going against statutes. Rather, when the statute is ambiguous, deference shouldn't automatically be given to the IRS interpretation. "Tax statutes are *penal* in nature," declared the Oklahoma Supreme Court (emphasis in original). "Where there is reasonable doubt about the taxing act's meaning, all ambiguity must be resolved in favor of the taxpayer." That's an unusual ruling because it indicates a pro-taxpayer attitude.

This chapter was the most difficult to write because the topic of court bias is highly controversial. Accusations range from "[bias] so insidious as to be indiscernible to both the judges themselves as well as to the public," to calling this a canard. It's such a hot-button topic that a nationally prominent tax lawyer gave me hours of assistance and requested anonymity. How can one illustrate major failings in our judicial system without sounding like a protester? The system is not corrupt. Rather, it has some cultural failings. Our judges have a strong sense of duty and often serve at great financial sacrifice. They could earn much more in private practice. Their service in tax litigation keeps funds flowing reliably to our government, and their decisions are overwhelmingly correct. But when they err, it's usually against the taxpayer.

### TAX TRIBUNALS

Taxpayers have access to four different trial courts in which to litigate a federal tax matter: Tax Court, district courts, Court of Federal Claims, and bankruptcy courts. With limited exceptions, taxpayers have an automatic right to appeal the trial court decision, generally to a circuit court of appeals.

A taxpayer has 90 days to appeal an IRS deficiency notice to Tax Court, without having to first pay the tax. The IRS is barred from assessing or collecting the tax while the case is pending. Suing without paying makes Tax Court the most popular litigation option. District court and claims court are alternative forums, but the tax must first be paid. Each court has different procedures, discovery and appeal rights. Jury trials are available in district court. Bankruptcy courts can adjudicate certain tax matters as part of a bankruptcy filing.

The Supreme Court accepts few tax cases, leaving the lower court decision as final.

## Oracle or Lawmaker

Tax guru James Eustice distinguished between two types of tax judges:

> ...the "strict constructionists," who follow the "letter" of the statute, and those that bend or twist the literal legal rules a bit to make the answer come out "right" (or at least how they think the answer should come out) and are said to follow the "spirit" of the statute. This leads to a fierce philosophical debate as to whether judges "make" the law or merely interpret it. The short answer is that they do both;

Faced with an ambiguous statute, a strict constructionist judge acts as an oracle to explain what Congress intended as the law's hidden meaning, thus interpreting the law. The result is sometimes very harsh. A taxpayer will be lucky for his case to instead be assigned to a judge who will bend and twist things to create an equitable result.

### JUDGE LEARNED HAND AND DEAN ERWIN GRISWOLD

Billings Learned Hand (1872-1961) was one of the stellar jurists in American history. His unusual name came from the tradition of his mother's family of using family surnames as given names. Her father and brother were both named Billings Peck Learned. His father was Samuel Hand. He dropped his given first name, Billings, after receiving his law degree from Harvard in 1896. Judge Learned Hand compared his fortuitousness in being a judge with the name, Learned, to an army officer with the name, Colonel Courageous Stanton.

He became a judge in the U.S. District Court for New York in 1909. Promoted to the Second Circuit Court of Appeals in 1924, he served there until his retirement in 1951 at age 79. Hand was the nation's most eligible candidate for a Supreme Court appointment, but he was overlooked. William Howard Taft, the former president, served as Supreme Court Chief Justice from 1921 to 1930 and opposed Hand because he had supported Theodore Roosevelt's Bull Moose Party, which contributed to Taft losing his 1912 re-election bid. Franklin Roosevelt was unsure Hand would support the New Deal, and once convinced, Hand was too old under Roosevelt's failed court-packing scheme.

Harvard Law School's Dean Erwin N. Griswold (1904 – 1994) is among the record-holders for arguing the most cases before the U.S. Supreme Court. Following graduation from Harvard Law School *summa cum laude* in 1928, he went to work as a staff lawyer for the solicitor general (the Justice Department office which directs all U.S. litigation in the Supreme Court and oversees appellate litigation). He became the office's expert at arguing tax cases before the Supreme Court, principally because no one else in the office wanted to handle tax cases.

A former student recalled a day in Dean Griswold's federal taxation class when another student admitted that he was not prepared: "Anyone who ever had an experience with Dean Griswold can testify that on some of his better days, his countenance was somewhat like that of a pit bull with indigestion. This was not one of his better days." He announced, "Very well, Mr. Smith. Read the case now. We'll wait for you." And everyone sat in silence and waited. No one came unprepared to that class again.

The most celebrated aphorism about income tax avoidance, which has become a common law of U.S. tax policy, was written by Judge Learned Hand:

> Any one may so arrange his affairs that his taxes shall be as low as possible; he is not bound to choose that pattern which will best pay the Treasury; there is not even a patriotic duty to increase one's taxes.

He agonized over the difficulty in deciding tax cases fairly:

> [T]he words of such an act as the Income Tax, for example, merely dance before my eyes in a meaningless procession: cross-reference to cross-reference, exception upon exception — couched in abstract terms that offer no handle to seize hold of — leave in my mind only a confused sense of some vitally important but successfully concealed (purpose), which it is my duty to extract, but which is within my power, if at all, only after the most inordinate expenditure of time.

Dean Griswold had a more direct philosophy:

The *first* matter to consider in *any* tax case is: What are the exact words of the statute? There is no use in thinking great thoughts about a tax problem unless the thoughts are firmly based on the controlling statute.

He advised against basing tax arguments on equity or novel theories. Griswold might be considered a "strict constructionist," while Hand pursued "the spirit of the statute." Their concerns might have been purely academic because tax cases almost lost the right to have a full hearing in court.

By 1918, the Supreme Court had ruled that there is no constitutional right for access to the courts in tax cases. Fifth Amendment protection only requires a fair and adequate administrative remedy. In the 1920s, the IRS unsuccessfully argued that the Court of Claims had no jurisdiction to review tax assessments.

Codification of the 1939 Internal Revenue Code was headed by Treasury Undersecretary Roswell Magill, University of California law professor Roger Traynor (later, California Supreme Court Chief Justice), and University of Michigan law professor Hessel Yntema. Randolph Paul was their consultant, and he commented, "At one point I found the group working strenuously on a plan which would give complete fact-finding jurisdiction to the Treasury. Yntema was especially fond of the plan." Traynor wrote a 1938 article proposing that review by the Board of Tax Appeals be restricted to the grounds, documents, and facts outlined in the taxpayer's protest and issues listed in the commissioner's findings of fact. A taxpayer could not raise new issues in court. Their misguided effort failed.

What could not be accomplished by Magill, Traynor and Yntema through congressional legislation was partially achieved through judicial legislation. To rid itself and the lower courts of the need to hear tax cases, the Supreme Court in 1943 issued the *Dobson* ruling. Tax Court decisions were to be final and immune from review unless a clear-cut mistake interpreting the law was identified, rather than mere legal error. This is one of the Supreme Court's most dismal tax decisions. Neither the government nor taxpayers had supported this entirely new principle. William A. Sutherland, chairman of the American Bar Association Section on Taxation, complained, "I know no lawyers who even claim to know where the principle of judicial review set forth in the *Dobson* decision originated."

The *Dobson* decision was written by Robert H. Jackson, the most tax-experienced justice ever to sit on the Supreme Court. Though he never graduated law school, he became a prominent trial attorney and was appointed general counsel of the Bureau of Internal Revenue in 1934. He rose to prominence by winning the 1937 judgment against Andrew Mellon. President Roosevelt promoted him to head the Justice Department's Tax Division, then to attorney general and then appointed him to the Supreme Court in 1941 — a meteoric rise in seven years. He helped write the Revenue Act of 1936, a major depression-era tax revision. He won decisions before the Supreme Court upholding the Social Security Act and Unemployment Insurance Act. In 150 years of American history, these were the first Supreme Court cases interpreting the general welfare clause of the Constitution.

When it came to taxes, he was still in the bureau's general counsel mindset. Otherwise, Jackson was a great civil libertarian, as demonstrated by his dissenting opinion in *Korematsu v. U.S.*, where the majority upheld the internment of Japanese-Americans during World War II. He took a one-year leave of absence from the court to serve as chief of counsel for the United States at the International War Crimes Tribunal at Nuremberg. He was a great orator. His four-hour opening address and his closing remarks at the Nuremberg trial are a triumph in prosaic speechmaking. ("The terror of Torquemada pales before the Nazi Inquisition.") *Dobson*, an eloquently written and reasoned opinion in the Jackson style, demonstrated that he had developed little patience for tax cases.

*Dobson* led to some absurd results. John Kelley Co. and Talbot Mills deducted certain payments as interest expense. Their facts were similar, and IRS treated them as nondeductible dividends. The cases were heard at about the same time by different Tax Court judges. One judge ruled that Kelley had paid interest. Another judged ruled that Talbot had paid dividends. Upon appeal, the Seventh Circuit Court reversed Kelly and the First Circuit Court affirmed Talbot, consistently treating both as nondeductible dividends. Citing *Dobson*, the Supreme Court in 1946 reinstated the inconsistent Tax Court decisions. Jackson was in Nuremberg, so he did not participate in this case.

At the urging of the American Bar Association, Congress overturned *Dobson* in 1948. It amended the Internal Revenue Code to provide that Tax Court decisions could be appealed "in the same manner and to the same extent as decisions of the district courts in civil actions tried without a jury." But that period from 1943 to 1948 had taxpayers avoiding Tax Court because its decisions were virtually impossible to appeal.

Undoubtedly the Supreme Court regrets the *Dobson* amendment, as levity peppers its distaste for tax cases:

> [W]hen asked why he sings along with the chief justice at the Court's annual Christmas party, Justice Souter replied, "I have to. Otherwise I get all the tax cases." ...[I]n the middle of a lofty legal discussion about a boring tax case, [Justice] Marshall leaned over to [Justice] Powell and said "You can have my vote on this for a future draft pick." ...Justice Brennan's normal reaction to a certiorari request in a tax case: "This is a tax case. Deny." ...Justice Powell describing cases "you wish the Chief Justice had assigned to some other Justice: [A deadly dull case,] a tax case..." ...Justice Blackmun, "If one's in the doghouse with the Chief [Justice], he gets the crud. He gets the tax cases...."

Harry Blackmun must have been in the doghouse a lot. He authored more tax decisions than any other justice in history. Thurgood Marshall was the runner-up. One theory is that Chief Justices Warren Burger and William Rehnquist refused to assign the liberal Marshall more important tasks in constitutional law, so they loaded him with federal income tax cases. Of his 14 opinions on substantive tax law, Marshall ruled 13 against the taxpayer.

Even their clerks dread tax cases. Chief Justice William Rehnquist let his clerks vote on case assignments. A clerk who voted carelessly "could get stuck with a lot of tax cases," said a former Rehnquist clerk.

"Dissent without opinion" became a trademark for Justice William O. Douglas as he protested against tax disputes he felt should be resolved by legislation or regulation. He would generally vote in favor of the taxpayer, often as a lone dissenter, without giving any reason. Erwin Griswold surmised that "Douglas, like many others, finds no intellectual interest or challenge in tax cases — or, to put it more directly, he dislikes tax cases and does not regard them as worthy of his careful attention." Douglas revealed a more primordial attitude in a 1961 book review he wrote for the New York *Herald Tribune*:

> Our tax system was not designed by noble men only to be subverted by base people. It represents a series of victories by special interest groups, each motivated by selfish ends. Ability to pay is the slogan that philosophers and politicians use to justify the progressive income tax.... However one looks at the concept of ability to pay, it is distorted and unreal in its application. Should not artists, poets, and authors need incentives as well as businessmen?

This repeated a theme he expressed in a Supreme Court tax decision earlier that same year:

> In an early income tax case, Mr. Justice Holmes said "Men must turn square corners when they deal with the Government." The revenue laws have become so complicated and intricate that I think the Government in moving against the citizen should also turn square corners.

This was his protest that ambiguities should be resolved in favor of the taxpayer, rather than litigated. Some have speculated that this attitude caused him to refuse, as a justice, to support the tax system created by Congress.

Supreme Court justices have written many autobiographies and books about the court. Although tax cases constitute about ten percent of the Supreme Court docket, very rarely do the justices mention taxes in their books. Rarely do lists of landmark cases mention a tax case; not even the only Supreme Court case overturned by a constitutional amendment — the decision that the 1894 income tax was unconstitutional, which led to the Sixteenth Amendment.

Why should the Supreme Court and appeals courts non-grudgingly give deference to tax cases? Because after a limited period of courtroom access, a taxpayer's income and property become subject to levy and seizure, which by law cannot be restrained. As has been shown, some taxpayers commit suicide when IRS enforcement turns overbearing or abusive. And because our Constitution vests the judicial power in only "one supreme Court." Otherwise, it might have given us the French model, where the *Cour de Cassation* (the supreme appeals court) consists of 85 judges and 40 assistant judges, divided into sections (called "chambers") that each deal with a specialized type of "normal" litigation.

But tax cases in France are not heard in the Cour de Cassation. Tax cases are relegated to local administrative courts, with final appeal to the *Conseil d'Etat* (Council of State), an alternate judicial system unaffiliated with the Cour de Cassation. The Conseil d'Etat follows *droit administratif* (administrative law) which defines laws between citizens and the state and is different from those of one citizen toward another. Though it's considered a bulwark of French democracy and it's a fixture in Louisiana, *droit administratif* is inconsistent with due process of law or the law of the land, because it assumes that the ordinary courts have no jurisdiction to administer it. If the U.S. practiced *droit administratif,* it might explain why one does not fare as well against the government as he might in a dispute with another citizen.

**The Tax Court**

Until 1924, an assessment by the Bureau of Internal Revenue had to be paid in full before it could be contested in court. Then Congress established the Board of Tax Appeals, where a taxpayer could contest a deficiency prior to paying.

It was renamed "United States Tax Court" in 1942, but remained an "independent agency in the executive branch." It became a real court in 1969, when Congress classified it as a judicial entity under Article I of the Constitution, but it remains subject to jurisdiction of the House Ways and Means Committee and Senate Finance Committee — the tax-writing committees — rather than the judiciary committees.

Tax Court issues three types of opinions: regular opinions (disputes involving law), memorandum opinions (disputes of fact deemed of little value in terms of precedent), and summary opinions (small case procedure, under an election of the taxpayer, non-appealable, with relaxed rules of evidence and procedure). Until 2001, the court kept summary opinions secret from the public, but the IRS had every one. It was a private law in that IRS knew how the Tax Court would rule in a given situation, but the taxpayer didn't. Public criticism led to their release and publication beginning in 2001.

Tax Court judges are nominated by the president and confirmed by the Senate to fill nineteen seats. The Tax Court chief judge appoints "special trial judges" (similar to magistrates in district court) to hear routine and minor cases.

The chief Tax Court judge assigned a special trial judge to a 1987 tax case implicating 3,000 taxpayers and $1.5 billion in tax deficiencies. This was one of the longest and most complex trials in the Tax

Court's history — lasting 14 weeks, with 9,000 pages of transcripts and more than 3,000 exhibits. The very same day that the special trial judge ruled against the taxpayers, Chief Judge Samuel Sterrett (who did not hear the case) adopted the 44-page decision (rubber-stamped, alleged the taxpayers), and it became the Tax Court's ruling. The taxpayers appealed the propriety of assigning such a major case to a special trial judge.

The Justice Department argued that the Tax Court was so empowered as a component of the executive branch. Tax Court judges loathed this approach as demeaning because they had fought hard battles to wrest their court from its origins as an executive agency. So they asked 86-year-old Erwin Griswold to help with their 1990 appeal to the Supreme Court of this case challenging their authority to appoint special judges.

Griswold argued in an amicus brief submitted to the Supreme Court that the Tax Court is a "court of law," thus vested with the right to appoint "inferior officers." The majority cited Griswold's amicus in its ruling, indicating that he won this case in the Supreme Court without even stepping up to the podium.

That wasn't the only special trial judge controversy.

In 1983, the Tax Court began concealing special trial judge reports. It became the only court in the United States where an appeal excluded the original finding of facts, so that no one had access to the findings of the judge who heard the trial. This was especially onerous in cases where the regular Tax Court judge overruled the opinion of the special trial judge working under him.

Three taxpayers had their case assigned to Special Trial Judge D. Irvin Couvillion who held a five-week trial in 1994 and prepared his report in 1999. In accordance with court procedure, Couvillion's report was reviewed by Judge Dawson. Dawson issued the Tax Court's 606-page decision holding the taxpayers liable for millions of dollars in underpaid taxes and millions of dollars in fraud penalties. However, the taxpayers believed that Couvillion had ruled in their favor and that Dawson had overruled him. The Supreme Court found the integrity of the Tax Court wanting and ordered the release of Couvillion's report.

It turned out that the Couvillion report was indeed changed in secret deliberations, and the Tax Court had misrepresented its actions. The Tax Court was forced to hold a retrial which was merely a review of the record, and in a new 457-page opinion, Tax Court Judge Harry A. Haines ruled against the taxpayers. He found that Judge Couvillion's recitation of the facts was incomplete, incorrect, or "manifestly unreasonable." Upon yet another appeal, the Eleventh Circuit Court in 2008 ordered the Tax Court to vacate Judge Haines' opinion and approve and adopt Judge Couvillion's opinion.

The House Ways and Means Oversight Committee began an investigation. In response to a request for cases, the Tax Court told the committee that it could only locate 117 of 923 reports requested. In five of the 117 cases, the special trial judge's opinion was reversed in secret, granting victory to the IRS. One of the five dealt with the failure of the IRS to send the proper notice to the taxpayer's last known address. (This is the same issue my client won in district court, discussed on page 184.) Dallas attorney, Josh Ungerman, told me that he left the courtroom confident he had won his case before Special Trial Judge Stanley A. Goldberg. A few weeks later, he received the decision showing he had lost. He didn't learn until years later that Judge Goldberg had indeed ruled in his favor, but that Judge Dawson had changed the trial judge's opinion to rule in favor of the IRS.

One wonders what embarrassments were hidden in those 806 lost reports. As a result of the Supreme Court decision the Tax Court revised its rules and now it releases the trial judge's report.

**Tax Court Judges**

Who becomes a Tax Court judge? The job attracts highly qualified, and many overqualified lawyers. Of the 102 judges who have sat on the Tax Court in its first 83 years, I was only able to identify two who were promoted to higher office. President Hoover promoted Benjamin H. Littleton to the Court of Claims in 1929, and in 1981 President Reagan promoted Cynthia Holcomb Hall to district court and in 1984 to the Ninth Circuit Court of Appeals. Otherwise, it's mostly a dead-end position.

J. Edgar Murdock was one of the Tax Court's first judges. President Coolidge appointed him in 1926, just after it became independent from the Treasury Department, when it was still known as the Board of Tax Appeals.

Murdock had a gift for making his point in few words. A court case usually begins with a headnote, which describes in a few sentences what the case is about. Murdock holds the record for the shortest Tax Court headnote ever written: "Fraud — Proof woefully inadequate."

He spoke that way from the bench too. Nearing the close of one trial, a taxpayer exclaimed, "As God is my Judge, I do not owe this tax!" According to legend, Judge Murdock replied, "He's not. I am. You do."

He could be acerbic. In denying a deduction for graduate school education, he wrote, "its cost is not a deductible expense of this petitioner any more than would be the cost of fattening himself if he were too thin physically instead of intellectually." An appeals court overruled him.

Murdock served on the Tax Court until his retirement in 1961, and was recalled until 1968 to assist when the court was overloaded. He served 42 years, including nine years as chief judge.

Theodore Tannenwald Jr. was the Tax Court's most brilliant jurist. He graduated *summa cum laude* in political science and mathematics from Brown University in 1936, and received the Fay Diploma from Harvard Law School in 1939, which to this day is awarded to the graduate with the highest three-year average in his class.

He joined the then-small New York law firm of Weil, Gotshal & Manges as its sole tax associate, and became a full partner in 1947. He served in the Roosevelt and Truman administrations, and as foreign aid adviser to Presidents Kennedy and Johnson.

In 1958, Tannenwald hired Martin Ginsburg, thus doubling the size of Weil, Gotshal's tax department. Ginsburg wrote that until President Johnson appointed Tannenwald judge on the United States Tax Court in 1965, "I enjoyed the best one-on-one professional education any young lawyer might hope for." To accept a position as Tax Court judge, Tannenwald must have had a keen sense of public service, because he was so overqualified. He would truly "bend over backwards" for the taxpayer, making him exceptional and atypical.

I spent a day as a spectator in Judge Tannenwald's courtroom in May 1978. I was struck by his fatherly approach. He carefully explained the law and described to the taxpayer what he, as judge, would have to consider in rendering a decision. He would counsel the taxpayer to negotiate a compromise with IRS when the consequences of an adverse decision would be severe.

One case that morning concerned a taxpayer who didn't show up. The government attorney requested a default judgment. Upon inquiry, Judge Tannenwald was told that the taxpayer had been incarcerated in Tennessee and that he was once on the FBI's Ten Most Wanted list. He was brought to Atlanta to attend the Tax Court hearing that morning, but had escaped from the Atlanta Federal Penitentiary in the past 24 hours. In deference to fairness, the judge ordered that a notice be sent to the taxpayer at the Atlanta Federal Penitentiary, his "last known address," advising him to appear at the next visit of the Tax Court to Atlanta. If he failed to appear, Judge Tannenwald agreed to grant the government a default judgment.

Tannenwald's Solomonic wisdom and fairness were evident in his rulings. Both his former clerk, Howard E. Abrams, and his former partner, Martin D. Ginsburg, gave the same example. A poor Mexican family had won the $3 million grand prize in the Mexican National Lottery. The IRS sought a $1.62 million cut, as the ticket was bought in the name of Alfonso Diaz, a U.S. citizen. Diaz argued he had bought the winning tickets for his uncle, Jose Diaz, a Mexican citizen, who was not subject to U.S. taxation. Most of the testimony was given in Spanish through an interpreter, and it would have been simplest and consistent with the Tax Court's general anti-taxpayer skepticism to rule in favor of IRS. Tannenwald created a detailed record of the testimony and concluded:

> This case epitomizes the ultimate task of a trier of the facts — the distillation of truth from falsehood which is the daily grist of judicial life. He must be careful to avoid making the courtroom a haven for the skillful liar or a quagmire in which the honest litigant is swallowed up. Truth...often has an exclusive quality which makes the search for it fraught with difficulty. That this is so is clearly illustrated by the situation herein. Many of the objective facts are as consistent with a finding that the lottery tickets belonged to petitioner as they are with a finding that they belonged to his uncle, Jose; indeed, some of these facts support the former conclusion, for which respondent strenuously contends....
>
> [T]he story unfolded principally through the testimony of petitioner, Jose, and other members of the family, all of whom ultimately benefited from that wealth and concededly had an interest in the outcome of this case. But the fact of the matter is that, despite some confusion, there was a consistent thread to their testimony which supports the conclusion that petitioner's uncle owned the winning tickets. Beyond this, the testimony of petitioner's 86-year-old grandmother, who was also Jose's mother, was most convincing. Obviously closer than most

to her Maker and face-to-face with her priest in the courtroom, she completely corroborated the essential elements of the testimony of petitioner and his uncle (her son) — testimony which she had not heard because witnesses were excluded from the courtroom.

Diaz won a second lottery when Tannenwald was assigned as judge for his case, and ruled in his favor.

Tannenwald opinions were always well reasoned, and rarely overturned on appeal. A Tax Court librarian told me that Judge Tannenwald often visited the library to do his own research. Ginsburg told how appellate judges facing a complex tax issue sighed relief when presented with an appeal of a Tannenwald decision because they could simply affirm it. He served a stint as chief judge, and following retirement, often worked as a senior judge to help alleviate a heavy workload; a stellar judge who went to great lengths to render a fair decision.

**Bending Over Backwards**

About 90 percent of Tax Court cases are settled without going to trial, largely because IRS offers settlements to taxpayers whose cases have merit. Cases that go to trial face hurdles in the form of unfriendly court rules and procedures.

The "presumption of correctness" that graces an IRS assessment is a judicial doctrine, not a statute. It first appears in an 1882 Supreme Court discussion, presented as dictum (a comment which is not required to reach the decision but which may state a related legal principle) taken from a Wisconsin District Court jury instruction:

> When, therefore, an assessment has been made by [the Commissioner of Internal Revenue], it is to be presumed, until such presumption is overcome by proof to the contrary, that it was made upon sufficient evidence, and it is not necessary that the evidence upon which the commissioner acted should be laid before the jury. In other words, the jury (has) a right to presume until the contrary appears that when the commissioner made the assessment in question he had before him proofs which were sufficient to satisfy a just and fair-minded person that such assessment ought to be made;

Congress challenged this anti-taxpayer rule when, in 1998, it placed the "burden of proof" upon the IRS, provided that the taxpayer introduced credible evidence, maintained tax records and cooperated with the agency. The statute is upbeat: "If...a taxpayer introduces credible evidence with respect to any factual issue...the Secretary shall have the burden of proof." The court browbeats by interpreting this new law: "the Commissioner's determinations are presumed correct, and the taxpayer bears the burden of proving that those determinations are erroneous....however...the burden of proof may, under certain circumstances be shifted to the Commissioner if the taxpayer introduces credible evidence with respect to any factual issue."

Cases that actually shift the burden of proof to the IRS under this statute are almost nonexistent. Should the taxpayer fail to assert his right to shift the burden to the IRS, the Tax Court gruffly notes, "[Taxpayer] does not contend that [IRS] bears the burden of proof." (How should a taxpayer who appears without an attorney know that he waives this right if he fails to formally assert it?) When an appeals court ruled that IRS bore the burden of proof and remanded a case to Tax Court to explain its 2002 conclusion that the commissioner had met that burden, the Tax Court reversed itself in favor of the taxpayer, admitting that IRS had indeed not sustained its burden of proof.

The most difficult cases involve statutes which give no hint one way or the other on a point in question — the "sex of a hippopotamus" moment — where there is no legislative history or administrative pronouncement on the issue being litigated. These require the courts to act as oracle and declare legislative intent. In these cases, judges usually defer to the government. This prejudice was declared in a 1935 Supreme Court ruling that "taxes are the life-blood of government and their prompt and certain availability an imperious need." The manner in which Tax Court interprets ambiguous statutes lends a sense of unfairness to its rulings. For example:

One can deduct interest on up to a $1 million home mortgage, plus interest on up to $100,000 of home equity loans. Suppose someone borrows $1.1 million to buy a home? The Tax Court ruled the extra $100,000 was used to acquire the residence, not a home equity loan, so it disallowed interest on that last $100,000. The court could have ruled for simplicity by allowing up to $1.1 million of total loans including no more than $100,000 of home equity loans. In my view, the statute supports both interpretations.

Marshall Hugo Martin made Individual Retirement Account transfers between brokers the simple way. He obtained a check in person from one broker and delivered it directly to a second broker on the same day. He did this three times in 1987 and twice in 1988. He sought telephone advice from the IRS as to whether this was proper, and was assured that it was a permissible trustee-to-trustee transfer, but erroneous IRS telephone advice isn't binding. Upon receiving the brokerage information reports, the IRS said these were not direct inter-broker transfers and taxed him on "rollover" distributions in excess of the allowable one per year. Judge Dawson sided with the IRS. Martin should have asked the first broker to mail or courier the checks to the second broker. Instead, he acted as his own courier. On these narrow facts, where he didn't cash the checks, the statute would not have been diluted by classifying this as a mere conduit for trustee-to-trustee transfer, achieving an equitable result.

The Tax Court even refused to accommodate a religious objection. It dismissed Betty Ann Ferguson's petition after she refused to swear or affirm before testifying. Her objection was rooted in two Biblical passages, Matthew 5:33-37 and James 5:12. She offered the *Stanton* statement, set forth by the Louisiana Supreme Court, as an alternative:

> I [Betty Ann Ferguson] do hereby declare that the facts I am about to give are, to the best of my knowledge and belief, accurate, correct, and complete.

On appeal, the Fifth Circuit Court upheld her religious right to use the *Stanton* statement and remanded the case to Tax Court for further proceedings.

David Zarin was an engineer, and tax lore's most famous compulsive gambler. He moved to Atlantic City in 1978 and set up shop at the Resorts International craps table. By December 1979, Zarin had lost $2.5 million, which he paid in full. The casino extended him credit. By April 1980, he lost another $3.5 million — on credit. The casino eventually settled for $500,000. Enter the IRS, which assessed Zarin tax on $3 million "cancellation of debt" income. The Tax Court agreed.

Here was a man with heavy losses from a game of chance weighed heavily in favor of the house. The house would never allow him to cash those $3.5 million of chips to spend outside the casino. It was money he never held or had access to. Yet legal commentators fretted that there was no "right" answer in the case.

Tannenwald participated in the Zarin decision. He dissented from the court majority and would have ruled in favor of the taxpayer. Fortunately, the appeals court sided with Tannenwald and overturned the Tax Court's unfair ruling.

In a 2002 sex discrimination and harassment district court suit against her former employer, the court awarded Chicago police officer Cynthia Spina $300,000 in compensatory damages for pain, suffering, and humiliation plus $950,000 for attorney fees. The IRS concluded that she had received $1,250,000 income, but denied her a deduction for the $950,000 attorney fees due to alternative minimum tax. So the federal and Illinois income tax was $399,000 — $99,000 more than she received. (Cynthia Spina earned $50,000 a year.) And her attorney, Monica McFadden paid income tax on the $950,000, minus expenses. The IRS collected a double-tax.

In a similar case, a circuit court admitted that this outcome "smacks of injustice" but stuck to a mechanical application of the statute. Unfortunately, in another similar case, our Supreme Court ruled *unanimously* that a litigant's income includes the attorney fees. The court acknowledged the very real problem where a litigant could lose for winning, based on tax rules. Not a single justice dissented.

Learned Hand once wrote, "A tax may be so 'arbitrary and capricious,' its 'inequality' so 'gross and patent,' that it will not stand...." Zarin and Spina were trapped by courts that wouldn't protect them. Judges cannot claim to "bend over backwards" when they interpret ambiguous statutes against taxpayers for an unfair result.

**A Harmless Error**

The Tax Court cannot be relied upon to protect the taxpayer from IRS misconduct.

An abusive tax shelter case had been ongoing in Tax Court for more than 20 years. About 1,800 taxpayers were involved in the scheme, which ran from 1968 until 1981. To minimize the number and cost of trials, about 1,300 investors who wouldn't settle signed "piggyback agreements" to be bound by the decision of a test case trial involving a few taxpayers.

In 1989, the Tax Court held a one-month trial in Honolulu for the test case. As an abusive tax shelter, it was logical for the court to conclude that the taxpayers were liable for all assessed deficiencies, negligence, and tax-motivated transaction penalties.

Crucial to the government's case was the testimony of John Thompson, an investor who testified that he believed the tax shelter was a sham. Thompson had not fully paid for his "investment," and the promoter had threatened to sue him. Having it declared a sham would bolster his position against the shelter promoter.

Unknown to any of the 1,300 investors, IRS attorneys Kenneth McWade and William Sims had entered into a secret settlement agreement with Thompson and another test case petitioner, John Cravens. McWade agreed to reduce Thompson's and Cravens' tax deficiencies, provided they remained test case petitioners. McWade also convinced Cravens to appear *pro se* (without an attorney) at trial. The Thompson and Craven cases were settled, and the conditions of settlement were not revealed to the Tax Court or any taxpayer representative.

The Tax Court's judgments against all the investors also applied to Thompson and Cravens. In order to honor their secret settlement, the IRS revealed the deception to the Tax Court and moved to set aside the Thompson and Cravens judgments.

When the 1,300 investors learned of the deception, they moved to have the judgments dismissed. The Tax Court held a hearing and concluded that there was merely a "harmless error." Nonetheless, the Tax Court modified the judgment, relieving the taxpayers of increased interest and penalties for negligence and imposing costs and attorney fees on IRS.

In 2003, the appeals court determined that the Tax Court had committed a clear error of judgment. It found that McWade and Sims defrauded both the taxpayers and the Tax Court because the original trial "was a charade fraught with concealed motives, hidden payments, and false testimony." It remanded the case to Tax Court with instructions to settle the cases on terms equivalent to those provided to Thompson. In subsequent proceedings, the Tax Court ordered the government to pay hundreds of thousands of dollars for taxpayer legal fees, and offer reduced settlements on the tax assessments.

As punishment, the IRS suspended McWade and Sims for two weeks without pay. Sims accepted the censure and was transferred to San Francisco. McWade retired and kept the $1,000 bonus paid him for winning the original Tax Court case. The appeals court noted that this was little punishment for such misconduct, and wouldn't dissuade future abuses. But personnel punishment was an IRS matter, outside the court's jurisdiction.

## The Tax Court Exam

When the Board of Tax Appeals was formed in 1924, the income tax was only 11 years old and accountants dominated tax practice. Both attorneys and CPAs were admitted to practice before the Board of Tax Appeals. In his most famous movies, Spencer Tracy played a lawyer, but when he went before the Board in 1937, he hired a CPA to represent him.

Concerned that a "Board" renamed in 1942 as "Tax Court" would exclude accountants and restrict practice to attorneys, Rep. John Dingell Sr. (D-MI) inserted a provision in the 1942 Act, "No qualified person shall be denied admission to practice before [the Tax Court] because of his failure to be a member of any profession or calling." This provision is still law, virtually unchanged since 1942.

The judges, all lawyers, had other ideas. Following passage of the Dingell amendment, with Judge Murdock as chief judge, the Tax Court announced that since it could not bar any individual from practice, it would require non-attorneys to pass an exam for admission to practice, though CPAs who were already admitted did not have to take the test. In effect, the Tax Court took a position in an ongoing struggle between accountants and lawyers that tax practice constituted the practice of law.

Similar tribunals, like the Board of Patent Appeals and Interferences, require attorneys, scientists, and engineers to pass the same examination demonstrating proficiency to practice before it. Like the Tax Court, adverse patent decisions may be appealed to the Court of Appeals. Unlike Tax Court, no preference to practice is given attorneys.

About 7,300 CPAs were admitted to practice before the Tax Court from 1926 until 1943. Out of 26,000 CPAs in the U.S., some 28 percent were admitted to practice. The new Tax Court exam seems to have been purposely designed not to test for qualification to practice, but to discourage and deny admission to non-attorneys. Attorneys, even those who knew nothing about tax law, were automatically "qualified." It took hold with little protest because "during the period from 1942 to 1945 people in that age category were properly engaged in military service for their country and were in no position to become certified public accountants. They came back to find that they were operating under a different state of facts....the examinations are of such difficulty that it would not at all be surprising that many members of the bar would find difficulty in passing those examinations."

The exam often tests knowledge that is of questionable practical value. For example, "Taxpayer owned at death 'Project Notes' issued pursuant to Section 5(e) of the Housing Act of 1937. Are the fair market values of such notes includable in the gross estate of Taxpayer?" This is based on an obscure court case involving a situation which no tax practitioner is ever likely to experience. It has no practical value.

The 1994 exam had a straightforward question, "Explain the circumstances under which and the extent to which the Tax Court may award costs (including attorney fees) to a petitioner." The question had dubious practical value because the Tax Court granted just 21 awards in 1994. Grading was even more dubious. This author prepared a motion for litigation and administrative costs just five days prior to taking the 1994 exam, won a rare award in 1995, but received only eight out of a possible 20 points for his answer.

The 2000 exam asked a question regarding an unresolved issue under a new law. It was based on a case that was pending in Tax Court. Even the exam grader couldn't have known the correct answer when the grades were released in March 2001 because the case wasn't decided until May 2001.

Courts refuse to protect applicants from this Tax Court tyranny. In 1946, an applicant who twice failed the exam could not sue to compel admission because he had not exhausted his available remedies by taking the exam again. A Dallas CPA, Sidney Goldin, took the exam in 1994. Though he achieved higher grades than passing candidates who took the 1990 and 1992 exams, the court said he did not pass. The passing score was arbitrarily set each year after the exams were graded. (This author also failed the 1994 exam with higher grades than 1990 and 1992 passing candidates.) He hired a major law firm to grade his exam and proved that the Tax Court had made grading errors, but the court still wouldn't admit him, so he sued. After four years and $50,000, the district and appeals courts ruled that "re-examination provides an adequate means of exposing grading errors." This was an appalling insensitivity to grading irregularities.

To file a Tax Court petition when his accountant cannot docket the case, a taxpayer's choices are either to hire a lawyer (which can cost several thousand dollars — more money than a small case is worth), file *pro se*, apply for tax clinic help, or give up. An accountant already familiar with the situation can handle certain cases most efficiently, but court rules exclude him. Of small cases docketed in Tax Court (under $50,000, where the taxpayer elects "small case" procedure), the Taxpayer Advocate writes that 93 percent of represented cases settle, but only 83 percent of *pro se* cases settle. The IRS staffers who handle settlement negotiations work in the same office that accountants deal with in normal tax practice. The accountant who did the tax planning, prepared the return, and protested the assessment can negotiate with the IRS lawyers on behalf of his client, but he cannot address the judge in Tax Court.

A baffled taxpayer wrote in his petition, "What chance has a pro se litigant got entering Tax Court for the first time?" Restricting practice before the Tax Court to attorneys hurts taxpayers. In 1947, 85 percent of Tax Court litigants had legal representation. Until recently, up to 85 percent of taxpayers appeared *pro se*. At a May 2002 meeting with the American Institute of CPAs and National Association of Enrolled Agents, Tax Court Chief Judge Thomas B. Wells said he preferred that taxpayers appear *pro se* to being represented by a non-attorney.

The need for greater access to representation is recognized by the Tax Court, which champions law school tax clinics to assist otherwise *pro se* taxpayers. Tax Court admits students enrolled in tax clinic programs, under the supervision of an attorney who is a member of the Tax Court bar, but not practicing CPAs or enrolled agents. The Taxpayer Advocate's annual report shows the percentage of people representing themselves has declined to roughly the 70 percent range. This can be attributed to the success of tax clinics. Seeking further reduction in *pro se* cases, the Tax Court successfully lobbied Congress in 2006 to allow it to allocate part of a nominal (up to $30) periodic attorney registration fee "to provide services to pro se taxpayers."

The Tax Court has failed to exploit a potential remedy Congress gave it by awarding attorney fees. District courts, bankruptcy courts, and appeals courts have indulged in granting fees to *pro se* taxpayers, if only to compensate them for their time, where the IRS position was unreasonable and the taxpayer substantially prevailed. They interpret the statute for its punitive and deterrent effect against IRS overreaching. The Tax Court's narrow-minded position is that "Congress intended [attorney awards] as a fee shifting statute... However, petitioners did not pay or incur fees for legal services."

### PERSONAL EXPERIENCES

I once faced an IRS appeals officer who admitted that my case had merits but felt that existing rulings allowed him to take the position against my client. I suggested that he consider a compromise based on hazards of litigation because my client might take this case to court. He looked me in the eye and said flatly, "It would cost your client at least $5,000 to take this to court, so I don't believe he would do it." He was right. Thereafter, I studied how to go beyond IRS Appeals, so that this wouldn't happen again.

In a *pro bono* case I handled, five grandchildren lived with their mother in their grandparents' home. The daughter had never married and was unemployed. The grandparents properly claimed their grandchildren as dependents. The IRS sent the grandmother a letter saying "Based on information we received from welfare agencies, it appears you weren't the custodial parent of this dependent, who has received welfare." Even with disallowance of five dependents, there was no taxable income. However, the IRS assessed an earned income credit decrease of $953, plus interest.

The IRS agent demanded cancelled checks and other proof that the grandmother provided more than half the support of her grandchildren. "What checks?" I protested. "They pay their bills with cash, including visiting the utility company payment window. The grandfather is illiterate and signs his name with an 'X.'" I filed a Tax Court petition, which brought the matter to intelligent life at the IRS Appeals Office, where the assessment was immediately abated.

In another situation, someone who failed to file an income tax return received an IRS notice assessing $48,430 taxes, penalties and interest on $93,000 of taxable income. IRS hadn't made the slightest attempt at an accurate computation. There were mechanical errors in the assessment, all in favor of the IRS. It required a Tax Court petition, but after corrections to IRS computations, the case settled for under $14,000.

I attended a Tax Court session in early 2006 where I met a low income petitioner who showed me his papers. He hadn't a prayer, especially before this judge who was granting every IRS motion to dismiss when Hispanic surnamed taxpayers failed to appear in court. (This was no Judge Tannenwald!) His case dealt with gambling winnings which he improperly netted against losses. The law requires that winnings be reported as income. Losses may only be claimed as itemized deductions. I saw that the IRS had made a reasonable calculation of his tax liability after substituting itemized deductions for the standard deduction. He was very grateful when I pointed this out, and promptly settled with the IRS for about $600 before his case was called. The law professor representing tax clinic cases was an acquaintance of mine and he was overburdened with cases. He told me that this individual had applied for assistance, but they rejected his case because it hadn't a prayer. True, but this guy just needed some hand-holding.

These examples illustrate how my Tax Court knowledge permitted me to settle cases where clients would otherwise be at the mercy of the IRS because they couldn't afford lawyer representation. A CPA who plans the transaction, prepares the tax return, and handles the IRS appeal, can bring many cases to court at reasonable cost, assured in the knowledge that he has a 90 percent probability of settling. If only Tax Court would open its doors to CPAs and enrolled agents so they could assist taxpayers to the next level of appeal.

## The Pennsylvania Preceptor Plan

The exclusion of CPAs from Tax Court practice has its origin in a legal establishment tradition for exclusion. The American Bar Association first issued Canons of Professional Ethics in 1908. These rules included non-ethical concerns such as restricting competition and racism, designed to keep out minorities.

In 1912, the ABA inadvertently approved membership for three New York lawyers whom it did not know were black. Under pressure not to rescind their admission, the ABA instead determined not to allow another such "mistake" and passed a resolution declaring "the settled practice of the Association has been to elect only white men as members." A racial identification question was added to the membership application. It only required five ABA councilmen to veto an application, and with a large Southern contingent, blacks were excluded for many years.

When Woodrow Wilson nominated Louis Brandeis, a Jew, to the Supreme Court in 1916, the Bar opposed him on grounds of ethics and character. Seven former ABA presidents, and nationally prominent men such as former President William Howard Taft, former Senator Elihu Root (R-NY), and former Connecticut Governor Simeon Eben Baldwin opposed his appointment. "Character" was a term of art among lawyers which referred exclusively to those whose religion, national origin, or politics threatened the professional status quo.

Prominent Philadelphia attorney Henry Drinker, chairman of the ABA's Committee on Professional Ethics, unabashedly declared before the ABA in 1929:

> I happen to be Chairman of the Committee on Grievances of the Law Association of Philadelphia. I was on that committee for three years, and in that way I came in contact...with the type of lawyer that this Association wants to keep from studying law, if it can... [O]f the men who came before us who had been guilty of professional abuses, an extraordinarily large proportion were Russian Jew boys....

Drinker used his position and influence to establish the "Pennsylvania Preceptor Plan." Implemented in 1928, prospective lawyers faced a character investigation when starting law school and when applying for admission to the state bar. They were required to find a lawyer with five years experience to act as a preceptor who would monitor their conduct through law school and a six-month clerkship. The definition of unworthy character was elastic and subjective. It included "dull," "conceited," and "lacking a proper sense of right and wrong." Under this screening mechanism, not a single black was admitted to practice in Pennsylvania between 1933 and 1943, and Jewish applicants declined by more than 20 percent.

The Tax Court still practices the preceptor concept. In addition to passing an examination, non-attorneys seeking admission must list on their application, two sponsors *who are members of the Tax Court bar*. Upon passing the exam, these sponsors will be required to send letters regarding their acquaintance with the applicant and their opinion of his or her moral character, repute, and qualifications directly to the admissions clerk. There is no such preceptor requirement for attorneys applying for practice before the court. One of the most common questions I get from Tax Court exam candidates is, "Where can I find two sponsors?"

## Judicial Deference

Congress never legislated that the courts should resolve tax ambiguities in favor of the government. But in those many situations of first impression, where the tax law is ambiguous, the court grants deference to the government interpretation of the law.

Every law enacted by Congress and every regulation issued by a government agency assumes an aura of legitimacy. Courts have set a high burden upon the citizen to prove that a law is unconstitutional or that a regulation fails to follow the intent of Congress.

The Supreme Court has ruled that courts must grant "deference" to a government agency's interpretation of the law because there is a "presumption that Congress, when it left ambiguity in a statute meant for implementation by an agency, understood that the ambiguity would be resolved, first and foremost, by the agency, and desired the agency (rather than the courts) to possess whatever degree of discretion the ambiguity allows."

Laws and executive orders govern the issuance of regulations. The Administrative Procedure Act (APA) requires public hearings. The Regulatory Flexibility Act (RFA) requires studies prior to finalizing regulations. The Internal Revenue Code requires that tax regulations be submitted to the Small Business Administration for comments. Executive orders issued by Presidents Bill Clinton and George W. Bush set additional safeguards on regulatory rulemaking. At a 1996 law symposium, one presenter complained about "less than rigorous judicial enforcement" of RFA, resulting in "a limited, if any, impact on rulemaking choices."

Despite Congressional estimates showing billions in revenue from certain tax provisions, every new Treasury regulation includes boilerplate language that executive orders, APA, and RFA simply do not apply. No one has ever taken Treasury to court for failure to follow these rules, but other agencies have been sued. Courtroom and administrative attempts to enforce RFA against non-complying agencies have at best resulted in remanding the regulation back to the agency for further analysis.

RFA allows an exception to preparing a regulatory flexibility analysis when the head of the agency certifies that the new rule will not have a significant economic impact on a substantial number of small businesses. Courts have ruled that an agency's failure to comply with RFA is not subject to judicial review, so long as the agency has properly determined that these rules do not apply.

The Small Business Administration has resources to comment on just a handful of regulations that the IRS sends its way. However, the SBA has warned Treasury that a "mere statement that there will be no effect without substantiation is not sufficient. Therefore, the agency should conduct an analysis demonstrating that it has considered the potential effects of the regulation on small entities." The law requires that such SBA comments be discussed in the preamble to regulations. So, Treasury Decisions finalizing proposed regulations simply enhance their disclaimers by certifying that a regulation "will not have a significant economic impact" and that any burden "is minimal." It's probably sufficient to satisfy the courts.

**What Constitution?**

The Constitution requires that all duties, imposts and excises be uniform throughout the U.S. A district court ruled that the 1980 Crude Oil Windfall Profits Tax Act was a clear violation because it exempted oil produced in Alaska while taxing oil produced in Texas and elsewhere. About $30 billion in refunds – and billions more in lost future revenues – were at stake if the district court ruling finding the tax unconstitutional was upheld. The deficit-plagued Reagan administration could ill afford a defeat.

In one of its cleverest decisions, the Supreme Court declared the term "exempt Alaskan oil" really meant oil produced in certain arctic and sub-arctic regions. The exemption applies to all states with oil producing territory above the 49th parallel. It's irrelevant that only Alaska is above the 49th parallel.

The Constitution requires that "all bills for raising revenue shall originate in the House." But the courts don't enforce it. The origination clause traces from the Magna Carta of 1215. Among its 65 provisions, it required the king to obtain the advice and consent of the nobility before raising their taxes. Later interpretation asserted that a tax increase required the consent of the people, so only the House of Commons was permitted to originate revenue bills. Echoes of "no taxation without representation" led to the House origination clause in the U.S. Constitution.

When Senator Henry Clay proposed the second of his "Great Compromises," the Tariff Reduction Act of 1833, he attempted to have it passed first by the Senate. This was essential legislation to avoid a confrontation over the high tariff, between South Carolina's attempt at nullification and Andrew Jackson's intention to use the Force Act. He was rebuked by Senator Daniel Webster:

> It was purely a question of privilege...and the decision belonged alone to the other House. The Senate, by the constitution, could not originate bills for raising revenue. It was of no consequence whether the rate of duty were increased or decreased; if it was a money bill, it belonged to the House to originate it...the constitutional provision was taken from the practice of the British Parliament, whose usages were well-known to the framers of the constitution, with the modification that the Senate might alter and amend money bills, which was denied by the House of Commons to the Lords. This subject belongs exclusively to the House of Representatives. The attempt to evade the question, by contending that the present bill was intended for protection and not for revenue, afforded no relief for it was protection by means of revenue. It was not less a money bill from its object being protection.

So the 1833 tariff was passed by the House on February 25, then by the Senate on March 1, and was signed by President Jackson on March 2. Subsequently, the origination clause was allowed to deteriorate, so that today, it is largely meaningless.

The 1909 corporate income tax originated in the Senate when a House inheritance tax provision was replaced with a Senate corporate income tax. The Supreme Court upheld the amendment.

The Tax Equity and Fiscal Responsibility Act of 1982 (TEFRA) was the biggest tax increase in our history up to that time. It originated in the House as a 21-page minor tax *reduction* proposal. When it reached the Senate, all the provisions were removed. Only the bill number "H.R. 4961" was retained, and 679 pages of Senate tax *increases* were substituted. H.R. 4961 went to a joint House-Senate conference to work out the "differences" between the 21-page House tax reduction and 679-page Senate tax increase, which had not a single provision in common.

The Conference Committee made major new additions to the Senate bill. The bill then went back to the House and Senate for a vote.

This second vote was the first and only time House members would have a say on H.R. 4961. In an unusual move, Chairman Dan Rostenkowski bypassed his own Ways and Means Committee and put the conference bill to a vote of the full House. He justified bypassing his committee:

> While this may seem a somewhat extraordinary procedure for House consideration of a major revenue bill, the severe economic distress and volatile political environment at this moment, in the judgment of the Committee, dictate we travel this route.

I called my congressman's office the morning they were going to vote to voice my concern. His legislative assistant was also concerned. "We just got the bill this morning. It's very hard to read because there are so many pages with handwritten cross-outs and inserts. We're not sure what's in it, but there isn't any time. They are allocating four hours for debate: two hours for Democrats and two hours for Republicans. Then they will vote."

Seventeen members of the House of Representatives filed a lawsuit challenging TEFRA. They argued that it violated the Constitution, which requires that all revenue measures originate in the House. Since the 21-page tax decrease they voted on had nothing in common with the 679-page Senate increase bill, they were deprived of a first vote on anything resembling the massive bill. Government attorneys argued that the House ratified the Senate changes. They even debated it for four hours on the House floor. The district court skirted the issue by ruling that members of the House had no standing to bring a lawsuit that TEFRA violated the origination clause.

Individuals sued to have TEFRA declared unconstitutional. But TEFRA turned into an art what came to be known as "cats and dogs" revenue provisions: a phase-out here, a limitation there, more information reporting, and higher penalties. It was hard to point to an actual tax increase. That left suing for excise tax refunds. One taxpayer sued over the three percent increase in the airline ticket tax, demanding a refund of $1.94. Another based his refund claim on a $3.11 increase in his telephone excise tax. The courts upheld TEFRA. The Ninth Circuit Court said that despite the far-reaching and extensive amendments, they were germane to the subject matter that originated in the House. The Fifth Circuit Court declared that the Constitution's term, "raising revenue" is ambiguous. It does not mean "increasing revenue," but "relating to revenue." When TEFRA originated in the House as a "relating to revenue" tax decrease, the Senate was empowered to turn it into a tax increase. The Supreme Court denied review. It is unlikely there will ever be a court ruling finding violation of the origination clause.

The Constitution prohibits *ex post facto* laws. It only applies to criminal cases. So that's not an impediment for our courts when tax revenue is involved. The 1864 Civil War income tax increase was an emergency war measure, which retroactively applied to 1863 income. The Supreme Court upheld it, ruling:

The right of Congress to have imposed this tax by a new statute, although the measure of it was governed by the income of the past year, cannot be doubted; much less can it be doubted that it could impose such a tax on the income of the current year, though part of that year had elapsed when the statute was passed. The joint resolution of July 4th, 1864, imposed a tax of 5 per cent upon all income of the previous year, although one tax on it had already been paid, and no one doubted the validity of the tax or attempted to resist it.

The 1913 Tax Act was enacted on October 3, and took effect on November 1, retroactive to March 1, four days after the Sixteenth Amendment was ratified. The Supreme Court dismissed the challenge:

[T]his limited retroactivity is assailed as repugnant to the due process clause of the Fifth Amendment, and as inconsistent with the Sixteenth Amendment itself. But the date of the retroactivity did not extend beyond the time when the Amendment was operative, and there can be no dispute that there was power by virtue of the Amendment during that period to levy the tax, without apportionment.

Even death won't stop a retroactive tax increase. Ruth S. Dinsmore died on April 14, 1993, when the maximum federal estate tax rate was 50 percent. On August 20, 1993, President Clinton signed the Omnibus Budget Reconciliation Act which increased the highest rates to 53 and 55 percent, retroactive to January 1, 1993. The result was a $175,137 estate tax increase. The district court dismissed the case for failing to specify proper grounds in its claim for refund. Claiming that the retroactive tax increase was "unconstitutional and invalid" was so vague and ambiguous that the IRS could not reasonably be required to know, let alone defend such a claim. Alternatively, the court ruled that the retroactive increase in the tax rate was not unconstitutional, and did not violate the apportionment clause, due process clause of the Fifth Amendment, or the takings clause under the Fifth Amendment, and did not contravene the prohibition against ex post facto laws.

Ellen Clayton Garwood died in March 1993. With a gross estate of $28,108,968.72, the additional tax was $1,320,190. The appeals court rejected the argument that the retroactive increase was an ex post facto law because that prohibition only applies to criminal enactments, and NationsBank avoided any possibility of criminal sanctions by paying the tax. Judge S. Jay Plager dissented, "there are times when the gap between law and justice is too stark to be ignored. This is one of them....I believe it should be unconstitutional...." An appeal to the U.S. Supreme Court was denied.

### MANIFEST INJUSTICE

New Jersey has a reputation as a notoriously difficult state for a taxpayer to prevail in a dispute with the Division of Taxation. The state enacted a law on July 1, 2002 increasing the estate tax retroactive to January 1, 2002. Cynthia Oberhand died on March 28, 2002 and her estate was assessed an additional $25,915.49 estate tax as a result of the retroactive law. The state Tax Court held that the retroactive law was constitutional. Yet, in a big surprise, it ruled in favor of the estate. The court applied the equity principle of "manifest injustice" to prevent application of a tax law which did not exist at her death. The appeals court reversed in favor of the state, saying "the doctrine of manifest injustice has no place in the judicial evaluation of retroactive tax laws." The New Jersey Supreme Court sided with the taxpayer, agreeing with the Tax Court that retroactive application was manifest injustice.

Nor is science a defense. The Tariff Act of 1883 taxed imported vegetables. Botanically, tomato is a fruit, a form of berry. The Commerce Department sought to tax imported tomatoes as vegetables. John Nix, a New York tomato importer, challenged the tariff. The Supreme Court agreed that tomatoes contain seeds, which technically, vegetables do not — but it chose revenue over botany and ruled that the tomato is a vegetable because it is eaten like a vegetable (in salads or cooked) rather than plain or raw like a fruit.

When revenue is concerned, federal courts waive uniformity and origination requirements, the ex post facto prohibition, and science. Congress in 2004 passed a law assessing a penalty of up to $200,000 for failure to report certain tax shelter activities. Once imposed, the penalty can only be rescinded by grace from IRS and no judicial appeal is permitted, **even if the taxpayer wins the underlying case in court.** It's a certainty that the courts will not consider this a constitutionally prohibited "bill of attainder" because it's a civil, rather than criminal, penalty.

## State Procedures

In some states, tax administration can be unjust because even the requirement for a fair and adequate administrative remedy is withheld. Beginning in the 1970s, many states enacted "administrative proceedings" which abolished appeal within the revenue department in favor of a formal hearing before an administrative law judge (ALJ). In some states, it's almost a corrupt form of *droit administratif*. In theory, the courts to which an ALJ decision may be appealed have a voice in overturning rulings that are wrong, but few taxpayers or their representatives have any idea how difficult obtaining a favorable ALJ ruling can be. Unless represented by a very skilled lawyer at great expense, there will be an insufficient record to permit a meaningful appeal to a court. This results in taxation by fiat of the revenue department.

A freestanding minor medical emergency center had a radiologist visit for just 15 minutes every day to read X-rays. The Georgia Department of Labor decided the radiologist was an employee because the center restricted his hours — he could only visit to read X-rays during working hours, 8 a.m. to 10 p.m. This was upheld by the ALJ and affirmed by the superior court. Another Georgia case involved a Michigan resident who established trusts for her grandchildren, none of whom resided in Georgia. An ALJ decided that the nonresident beneficiaries were taxable in Georgia because the investment adviser, the accounting firm and bank accounts were in Georgia, and the adviser established a Georgia-based investment partnership for these trusts to pool their investments. This violated a basic principle of multistate taxation that income from investments is taxed to the recipient in his state of residence. With unfair appeal rules, the superior court simply affirmed the ALJ's decision without a hearing and the appeals court refused to review the tax case.

A Texas ALJ ruled that merely hiring a Texas law firm to defend against a Texas lawsuit can subject an out-of-state business to Texas taxation. As in many other states, Texas tax ALJs are usually former audit supervisors and tax department prosecutors. But even genuine state courts demonstrate taxpayer injustice.

Shell Oil Company sued St. Charles Parish (a Louisiana county) for a refund of excessive interest and penalties. Upon filing the lawsuit, the parish added 10 percent to the assessment to cover the expected litigation costs, as permitted under Louisiana law. An appeals court agreed that the interest and penalty were excessive and ruled for Shell, but upheld the additional 10 percent assessment to cover the Parish's litigation costs — even though the parish lost. Ouch! Who can afford to appeal an assessment when threatened with a 10 percent penalty just for bringing a lawsuit to assert one's rights, in addition to the costs of bringing the lawsuit? (Shell lost on appeal to the Louisiana Supreme Court, so Shell was liable for tax, interest, penalty and the extra 10 percent.)

Michael D. Hamilton's Baton Rouge residence, which he inherited from his father and lived in all his life, was foreclosed on in 1995 over $27.09 in unpaid taxes. A unanimous Louisiana Supreme Court ruled in 2006 that the Louisiana constitution and the due process provision of the U.S. Constitution's Fourteenth Amendment permitted the tax sale. Such was the bestial result of a court interpreting the law so mechanically that a man's home was seized over a $27.09 delinquent tax.

How should a town notify the owner of a vacant building about a pending foreclosure sale for nonpayment of property taxes? In Great Neck, N.Y., a certified letter was sent to a vacant residence. The postman left a notice to claim and sign for it at the post office. When owner Alan Guthartz went to the post office, he discovered that the letter had been returned to the sender after 15 days, and there was no record of who sent it. He didn't learn of his problem until after Great Neck sold the property for the $7,568.98 outstanding tax liability. The new owner resold it for close to $2 million. In effect, a very valuable property was confiscated from Guthartz.

Upholding the foreclosure, New York's highest court ruled that the village and the new owner both complied with the law by sending certified mail. It dismissed as "factually inapposite to the matter before us," a 2006 U.S. Supreme Court decision that when a certified mail notice is returned unclaimed, the state must take additional reasonable steps to attempt to provide actual notice to the owner before selling property. "Had they simply sent the notice by regular mail, or tacked the notice to the door, I'd have known about it," moaned Guthartz.

Both the Baton Rouge and Great Neck cases were appealed to an unsympathetic U.S. Supreme Court which swiftly denied granting them hearings. The unjust state court decisions were thus sustained. Inequity in tax cases seemed not to concern the Supreme Court.

## To Pay or Not to Pay

Is there a tax that judges won't support? A class of taxpayers judges will protect? Yes.

In February 1863, Chief Justice Roger Taney wrote Treasury Secretary Salmon Chase protesting application of the Civil War federal income tax to federal judges because the Constitution prohibits diminishing a judge's salary. Though he thought the levy was unconstitutional, Taney conceded that "all of the judges of the courts of the United States have an interest in the question, and could not therefore with propriety undertake to hear and decide it." It was a plea that Chase reverse his position. But Chase had not issued the ruling. Revenue Commissioner George S. Boutwell wrote the Treasury decision that judges be taxed.

It wasn't that judges grudgingly paid the income tax. They had no choice. Boutwell issued a ruling on December 1, 1862 ordering, "Whenever a person in the employ of the government receives an amount exceeding the rate of 50 dollars per month, the tax of three per cent should be deducted from such excess."

Taney died in October 1864 and Lincoln appointed Chase to succeed him as chief justice. George Boutwell was appointed treasury secretary in 1869 and asked Attorney General Ebenezer Rockwood Hoar for a ruling on Taney's protest. Hoar ruled that the tax on judges' and presidents' compensation was invalid. The Civil War income tax on the compensation of the president and the judges was immediately discontinued, and the amounts previously collected were all refunded, part through administrative channels and part through lawsuits.

This is the only instance known to this author where the attorney general, rather than Treasury or Internal Revenue, has issued a revenue ruling. Did Chief Justice Chase have a change of heart and ask Boutwell for a ruling? Why did Boutwell defer to Hoar, rather than issue the ruling himself?

Boutwell had criticized Joseph J. Lewis, his successor at Internal Revenue, for issuing rulings which contradicted prior bureau rulings. I suspect that Boutwell deferred to Hoar for an opinion Treasury was vested to issue, with some prodding from Chase. By having Ebenezer Hoar rule, Boutwell avoided contradicting his own 1862 ruling as revenue commissioner.

Boutwell and Hoar were old friends. When Boutwell was governor of Massachusetts, Hoar was an associate justice on the Massachusetts Supreme Court. Indeed, Boutwell suggested Judge Hoar to President Grant for attorney general. (Hoar was a cousin of General William Sherman.) When Hoar issued his ruling on October 23, 1869, he was expecting that President Grant would nominate him to the U.S. Supreme Court. So he was ruling on his own future compensation. Hoar was nominated on December 15, but the Senate would not confirm him. He resigned on June 15, 1870, having served just 15 months as attorney general.

Abraham Lincoln really was "Honest Abe." He knew it was important to lead by example — or perhaps it was due to Boutwell's withholding tax. He paid $1,279.15, representing a five percent income tax on his 1863 income. The Revenue Act of 1862 imposed an income tax on "salaries of officers...of the United States, including senators, representatives, and delegates in Congress...." It said nothing specific about the president's salary, nor judges. Congress raised the tax in mid-1864 to five percent retroactive to the prior year. So with just three percent withholding, he had to pay a cash balance for 1863.

Lincoln probably knew from Taney's protest that he, too, could claim exemption, but I suppose he felt duty-bound to participate in the income tax he helped enact. In 1872, three years after Hoar's ruling, Lincoln's administrator filed a refund claim for $1,250 tax paid on his $25,000 presidential salary. Former IRS historian, Shelly Davis, notes that the National Archives has a letter from Internal Revenue to Lincoln's estate saying that the president had overpaid his income tax. So the refund was probably granted, or there would be a record of some public squabbling. A copy of the refund claim is on display at the Museum of Taxation in Jerusalem, Israel.

After passage of the Sixteenth Amendment and the 1913 Tax Act, judges again argued that the Constitution forbade taxation of their salaries. During World War I, Congress specifically challenged this view by defining income in the 1918 Tax Act as "including in the case of the President of the United States, the judges of the Supreme and inferior courts of the United States and all other officers and employees, whether elected or appointed." The committee reports noted that "compensation of these officials under [pre-1918] law is not subject to income tax." Federal judges sued and their judicial colleagues granted continued exemption with approval from the Supreme Court. By the same logic, the president's salary was also exempt. Justices Oliver Wendell Holmes and Louis Brandeis dissented:

> The exemption of salaries from diminution is intended to secure the independence of the judges, on the ground, as it was put by Hamilton in the Federalist (No. 79) that "a power over a man's subsistence amounts to a power over his will." That is a very good reason for preventing attempts to deal with a judge's salary as such, but seems to me no reason for exonerating him from the ordinary duties of a citizen, which he shares with all others. To require a man to pay the taxes that all other men have to pay cannot possibly be made an instrument to attack his independence as a judge. I see nothing in the purpose of this clause of the Constitution to indicate that the judges were to be a privileged class, free from bearing their share of the cost of the institutions upon which their well-being if not their life depends.
>
> [Besides], the Sixteenth Amendment justifies the tax, whatever would have been the law before it was applied. By that amendment Congress is given power to "collect taxes on incomes from whatever source derived." It is true that it goes on "without apportionment among the several States, and without regard to any census or enumeration," .... I do not see how judges can claim an abatement of their income tax on the ground that an item in their gross income is salary, when the power is given expressly to tax incomes from whatever source derived.

The technicality allowing judges to hold others liable for taxes while exempting themselves could not have inspired respect from ordinary citizens. Their contempt for tax on themselves was for petty amounts. District court judges earned $6,000, plus a $1,000 allowance for a stenographer. They had to pay for their own law clerks out of the $6,000, giving rise to a tax deduction. On a $6,000 salary, a married judge was liable for only about $240 income tax in 1918 at high World War I rates, and $28 in the mid-1920s.

One of the first actions by Herbert Hoover upon becoming president was to request a ruling from the Treasury Department as to the taxability of his presidential salary. The letter he received from the Internal Revenue general counsel described court rulings where judges exempted themselves from income tax, and concluded, "The line of reasoning indicated above applies equally to the salary of the President, which salary is not to be increased or diminished during his term of office."

Hoover did not release any of his personal financial papers to the Herbert Hoover Presidential Library. So we don't know whether he took this advice, but it seems odd that a president should ask when the revenue service would gladly accept his tax payment. Perhaps Hoover wanted a legal opinion so that he could change the law.

At President Hoover's request, Congress passed legislation making presidents and federal judges taking office after June 6, 1932 subject to income tax. Judges in office prior to June 1932 remained exempt. Bowing to extensive criticism of their position both by American legal scholars and English-speaking courts abroad, the Supreme Court in 1939 upheld this tax on judges and presidents.

Governors and state employees also claimed exemption from income tax. Even employees of the Port of New York Authority claimed exemption. The Supreme Court ruled in 1938 that Port Authority employees were not exempt, and it was feared that this ruling might extend to all state workers.

At President Franklin Roosevelt's request, Congress in April 1939 enacted legislation prospectively taxing officers and employees of states and localities, as well as federal judges who took office prior to June 6, 1932. Thus ended the exemption for certain judges and state employees. The reciprocal exemption of federal officers and employees from state income taxation also ended.

Whether presidents actually claimed exemption of their government salary from income taxation is debatable. A 1932 *New York Times* letter writer claimed, "the taxes paid by Presidents Wilson, Harding and Coolidge were remitted either to them or to their estates."

Calvin Coolidge appears not to have claimed exemption. He became president on August 3, 1923 following the heart attack death of Warren G. Harding. As result of publicity in effect in 1924-25, we know that his income tax was $6,643.01 in 1923 and $14,091.86 in 1924. That calculates to taxable income of $56,242 in 1923 and $90,854 in 1924, an increase of almost $35,000.

Coolidge had government salary of $38,000 in 1923 ($7,000 as vice-president plus $31,000 as president) and $75,000 in 1924, an increase of $37,000. It's close enough to the net $35,000 increase in taxable income from 1923 to 1924 to conclude that he probably paid income tax on his presidential salary. (This analysis also indicates he had income from other sources of about $17,000 per year.)

In the depths of the Great Depression, Congress passed the Economy Act of 1932 reducing salaries of all government workers. It reduced the salaries of the vice president and House speaker by 15 percent, senators and representatives by 10 percent, congressional staff by 8⅓ percent, and mandated cuts to almost everyone else in government service — except the president and certain judges because the Constitution prohibits a diminution in their compensation.

Tucked into the Economy Act was a provision allowing the president and judges to voluntarily remit part of their compensation back to the Treasury. To his credit, President Hoover contributed 20 percent of his salary back to the government, starting August 1, 1932, until the end of his term in March 1933.

I have found no biographies or autobiographies which mention that the presidential salaries of Woodrow Wilson, Warren Harding, Calvin Coolidge and Herbert Hoover, as well as salaries of all federal judges, were exempt from income tax. Shelly Davis says that the IRS still possesses those early presidential returns. So the nation might one day learn to what extent they participated in the income tax on their presidential salaries, provided we can also trace refund claims.

Taxation of judges' salaries is still litigated. In 1983, Congress subjected judges to social security tax. The Supreme Court declared that unconstitutional in a 2001 case. Justices Clarence Thomas and Antonin Scalia concurred, adding that income tax on judges should also be unconstitutional.

**The Devitt Award**

Edward J. Devitt was a one-term Republican congressman from Minnesota, where he was a booster for Minneapolis-based West Publishing Co. Six years after his 1948 loss to Eugene McCarthy, he was appointed U.S. District Court judge in Minnesota, where he served for 38 years, most as chief judge. He also wrote books on jury instructions for West. He was a tough judge who kept control of his courtroom. Thirteen years after his death, one criminal attorney recalled, "Judge Devitt...was my all time favorite judge and a wonderful guy, and if you could practice in front of him, you could practice in front of anybody."

## JUDGE DEVITT AND JUDGE DAWSON

A jury found Loren Barta guilty of failing to report $54,000 and $44,000 of income in 1983 and 1984. His defense attorney argued that Barta suffered from "a personality disorder called detail phobia." He had an aversion to numbers. Judge Devitt would not allow him to call Dr. John Cronin to testify about his alleged detail phobia, and sentenced Barta to prison. Barta appealed that he was denied a fair trial. The Eighth Circuit refused to rule on whether Dr. Cronin's testimony should have been permitted; rather it said, "trial judges have considerable discretion to admit or exclude expert testimony" as it held in favor of Judge Devitt's discretion.

A more lenient Judge Dawson allowed Stanley Grosshandler to bring a hypnotist to Tax Court. Under hypnosis, he said that he prepared his 1964 return in his home and gave it to a conductor on the railroad to be mailed in Chicago. Dawson said that the testimony was inadequate and incredible. He decided that IRS records showing that no return had been filed were more credible. Thus the Tax Court fulfilled one of its main goals in letting the taxpayer feel he has had a fair hearing even when ruling against him.

Norbert Stelten had the misfortune of professionally meeting both Judge Dawson and Judge Devitt. Appearing *pro se*, Stelten expressed fear that complying with Dawson's order to produce documents would violate his Fifth Amendment privilege against self-incrimination. Ruling that he failed to show reasonable cause to apprehend such danger, Dawson imposed sanctions against Stelten. Subsequently, the government dragged Stelten before Judge Devitt, again *pro se*, where a jury convicted him of tax evasion, and he was sentenced to prison.

West Publishing Co. has a near monopoly in legal publishing. It was a privately held business run by a father-son team, Dwight and Vance Opperman. Dwight Opperman is a highly respected member of the bar. He is affiliated with a long list of legal organizations and served as vice president of the American Judicature Society, an organization devoted to promoting the independence, integrity, and understanding of the judicial system.

Opperman became Devitt's patron when he initiated the annual Edward J. Devitt Distinguished Service to Justice Award in 1982. The Devitt Award has become the most prestigious honor awarded to federal judges throughout the country. It pays $15,000 to an outstanding federal judge. The Devitt selection committee consists of three sitting federal judges: a Supreme Court justice, a circuit court judge, and a district court judge. Whereas other judicial award deliberations take place over the phone or at bar association meetings, the Devitt Committee deliberates in person, sometimes at posh resorts with their spouses, at the sponsor's expense, with another free expense paid trip to the awards ceremony. The award is funded annually by a single sponsor, rather than from an endowment.

Even if Opperman and his company sponsored the Devitt Award for the most noble reasons, the judiciary, lamentably, allowed them to become its patron at the same time that West litigated cases before the courts. Judge Devitt may have been the most deserving judge in America to have an award named after him. Still, it seemed peculiar that the award for judicial excellence sponsored by West was named after the chief judge in its home district.

Devitt's District Court of Minnesota heard a 1985 case brought by West Publishing against Mead Data Central. Mead had begun listing court cases (which are always in the public domain) on its Lexis-Nexis dial-up computer database. The database listed case citations which referred to page numbers in West's law books. The Minnesota District Court held that referring to those page numbers infringed on West's copyright. The decision was affirmed by the Eighth Circuit Appeals Court. Mead then agreed to pay a license fee to West.

For decades, West had been the sole publisher of statutes for some two dozen states. West held the contract with Texas from 1941 until 1985. When publisher Bancroft-Whitney Company was the successful bidder in 1985, West used copyright claims to block it from using West's arrangement — numbers and titles of state statutes — in an electronic version of Texas laws. Texas sued for an injunction. The state argued that the law belonged to the people, not a private company. Without access to those parts over which West claimed copyright, the law would be inaccessible. Federal district and appeals courts both dismissed the case for lack of an "actual controversy." It was never disclosed to Texas that just four months earlier, Judge John Minor Wisdom, one of the appeals court judges, had received $15,000 from West as co-winner of the Devitt Award. Texas appealed, unaware that Justices Byron White, William Brennan and Sandra Day O'Connor had enjoyed lavish trips at West expense to California, Hawaii and Florida. The Supreme Court denied review.

West was winning cases presided over by judges who were on the Award Committee or who had won the award. A firestorm of criticism followed a 1995 *Minneapolis Star Tribune* exposé on the Devitt Award. It revealed a decade of West-sponsored travel during which time "five cases involving West came before the Supreme Court. Each suit had been decided in West's favor by a lower court; in each instance, the justices declined to review the previous ruling. And none who vacationed at West's expense saw fit to abstain from deciding whether to hear the cases."

The judiciary establishment denounced the *Star Tribune* for "character assassination." Nonetheless, later that year, the American Judicature Society assumed responsibility for administering the award. The Oppermans sold West Publishing in 1996 to Thomson Corporation for $3.4 billion.

After the sale, Matthew Bender & Co. sued in New York District Court. The case was scheduled before Judge Loretta A. Preska. Matthew Bender's counsel had her disclose some connections to West Publishing, and, under vigorous protest she was forced to recuse herself. Her replacement, Judge John S. Martin Jr., ruled in favor of Matthew Bender. On similar facts, he overturned the Mead decision. The Second Circuit Court of Appeals upheld, ruling that West's pagination lacked "even minimal creativity" required for copyright protection and challenged the Eighth Circuit ruling for citing no authority for protecting pagination.

This was a major victory for the public and the electronic age. One wonders whether, absent the Devitt Award, this victory might have been won 12 years earlier.

Today, the Dwight D. Opperman Foundation funds the Devitt Award which is administered by the American Judicature Society. The AJS grants several other awards annually. It seems that only one other judicial award pays cash: The Dwight D. Opperman Award for Judicial Excellence pays $5,000.

How significant an ethical matter is a $15,000 cash gift? Justice Abe Fortas' 1968 nomination for chief justice was filibustered over his "sense of propriety" for accepting a $15,000 "honorarium." Senator Robert Griffin (R-MI) accused Fortas of violating Canon 32 of the Code of Judicial Ethics, "A judge should not accept any presents or favors from litigants, or from lawyers practicing before him or from others whose interests are likely to be submitted to him for judgment." Later revelations of additional monetary ethical lapses led to Fortas' resignation from the Supreme Court in May 1969.

By law, a judge must disqualify himself when his impartiality might reasonably be questioned, or he has served in governmental employment where he participated as counsel, adviser or material witness or expressed an opinion concerning the merits of the particular case. But as Justice Robert Jackson observed, "each Justice is the keeper of his own conscience." Justice David Brewer saw no conflict trying a case in 1893 argued by his son-in-law. (He ruled against his relative.)

Justice Ruth Bader Ginsburg was general counsel of the American Civil Liberties Union and served on its National Board of Directors, but doesn't recuse herself from ACLU cases.

Justice Antonin Scalia was severely criticized following his 2004 duck-hunting trip with Vice President Richard Cheney, just one week before participating in a case involving the vice president. Ethics rules forbid a lawyer from talking with a judge about a case in the absence of the opposing party. Arguing the "rather clear" Code of Judicial Ethics, Scalia wrote a 21-page opinion explaining "there is no basis for recusal." The *Georgetown Journal of Legal Ethics* commented, "his opinion is both disappointing and disingenuous."

Joel Gerber was Deputy Chief Counsel for Litigation and Acting Chief Counsel of the IRS before his appointment to the Tax Court in 1984. James and Marialice Nobles had invested in a tax shelter for which Gerber's office had responsibility while he was at IRS. Judge Gerber was assigned to their case. He refused to recuse himself, claiming no knowledge of or involvement in their case while at the IRS. And then he ruled against them.

Tax Court Rules of Practice contain no recusal provision. When the appeals court heard the *Nobles* case, it ruled that "the term 'judge' for purposes of this statute means judges of the courts of appeals, district courts, Court of International Trade, and any court created by Act of Congress, the judges of which are entitled to hold office during good behavior." Since Tax Court judges serve only a 15 year term (even though always re-appointed), they do not fall within this definition.

The appeals court blamed "a significant oversight" by Congress. Congress provided for mandatory recusal in other specialized courts. "It may make sense to extend similar rules to the Tax Court. That judgment should rest with Congress or the Tax Court, rather than this court." So, in any other court except Tax Court, Judge Gerber would have been required to recuse himself. Erwin Griswold in 1990 successfully argued that Tax Court is a "Court of Law" with rights of other courts, but here in 1997, they won the right to refuse ethical responsibilities of other courts.

Justice Louis Brandeis refused to accept honorary degrees, fearing that the bestowing universities might one day be a party to a suit before the court. California's legendary Judge Ogden Hoffman was the longest serving federal judge in the U.S. when he declined a dinner in 1891 in honor of his fortieth year of service because "it would not be in good taste...while occupying a judicial position." Before a Code of Judicial Ethics was created in 1923, Brandeis and Hoffman exemplified that a judge should avoid situations which might create a perception that he has been influenced.

The Tax Court responds to very loud criticism, lost battles, scandal, or where tactics dictate. In response to a Supreme Court decision, it now releases special trial judge opinions. Sidney Goldin's failed lawsuit to compel his admission to practice resulted in Tax Court setting a passing grade of 70 percent, where previously the passing grade was set arbitrarily. It also repealed its three-time limit on taking the exam. Sometimes Congress steps in, as it did in 1928, when it required the Board of Tax Appeals to change its rule and make IRS bear the burden of proof in fraud cases. Sometimes the Tax Court just digs in, waiting for the storm to pass, as it still has no recusal rule.

Taxpayers continue to face hurdles. The good news is that tax litigation is getting friendlier, as a result of new laws and appeals court rulings requiring the Tax Court to enforce placing burden of proof on the IRS and awarding attorney fees to taxpayers. Even Texas in 2007 transferred administrative law judges out of the jurisdiction of the revenue department and into an independent agency. Perhaps, one day all tax tribunals will have a culture that requires the government to turn square corners when dealing with taxpayers. The best judges do just that.

# Part III

Tax Tales

# CHAPTER ELEVEN

# A Prurient Interest

*Having already seen many of her videos, your editors admit to being more excited by the thought of Madonna's naked tax return than by Madonna herself.*

—Shop Talk, *Journal of Taxation* (September 1999)

Income tax return information was once a public record. The Civil War income tax contained no provision either permitting or requiring publicity. Nevertheless, income tax lists were printed, resulting in the widespread publication of personal incomes. Lacking modern methods for determining persons subject to the income tax, publication of lists was considered a primary means for detecting non-filers as neighbors might snitch on anyone understating income.

Tabulating machines hadn't yet been invented. Information had to be hand-matched. Income tax return lists were kept by name and address. Once a person's name was put on the tax rolls, it stayed there until he proved that his income had fallen below the filing threshold.

Only a minority of citizens — the high earners — were subject to income tax, and therefore, publicity. To save space, newspapers only published names with reported incomes over $10,000. Those were the ones of major interest to the general public. William B. Astor topped the list with incomes of $854,000, $1,300,000, and $1,079,000 in 1863, 1864, and 1865, respectively. Cornelius Vanderbilt was a distant second at half the earnings of Astor.

A delightful 1865 song about publicity of tax lists demonstrated the potential for mischief. In the song, a man had borrowed every valuable he could from friends, sold them for cash, then handed the money to the income tax clerk, claiming it was taxes on his falsely inflated income.

> While eagerly scanning the paper, next day,
> To his great delight, did appear
> His name, with his income in figures set down
> At full twenty thousand per year.
> The plan was successful.. he married the girl:
> And, though he was not worth a pin,
> His wits got a wife who had plenty for both:
> And That's where the laugh comes in!

Congress banned publication of tax lists in 1870, but inspection by individuals at the local collector's office was allowed to continue.

Repeal of the Civil War income tax in 1872 brought an end to publicity — until the 1909 corporation income tax. Far more onerous than this mere one percent tax was the public inspection of the income tax return itself. That would make the business' financial affairs a public record, even for privately held corporations. The art of tax planning was born as accountants advised corporations on taking depreciation and changing from the corporate form to non-taxable partnerships or associations.

Before any disclosure took place, protests led to the 1910 repeal of corporate return public inspection. Thereafter, the law provided that income tax records would be considered public records and open for inspection only upon order of the president. J. Edgar Hoover would rely on this directive for his FBI to snoop through Internal Revenue income tax records starting in 1931.

Publicity was resurrected in 1924, and 1923 return information was soon released. The name, address and amount of tax paid again became a public record. Reading about your neighbor's income, and that of celebrities, turned into a national pastime.

Most inspection requests came from women. A young woman wanted to know how much her fiancé made. A woman separated from her husband sought to determine how much alimony to claim. Others simply wanted to know how much their husbands earned. "I'm finally going to know how much my husband makes," a woman told the *New York Times*. "For years I have suspected that he made much more money than [he] has ever told me about, and I have felt that I was entitled to a whole lot more than I have been getting." There was a lively trade in the purchase and sale of lists.

Celebrities' 1923 finances were published in the newspapers. Chewing gum magnate William Wrigley, Chicago retailer Marshall Field, and John D. Rockefeller all had their finances publicly aired. Treasury Secretary Andrew Mellon paid $1,173,987 in taxes. Multimillionaire Thomas A. Edison, a leading shareholder in General Electric, the many Edison utility companies, various manufacturing companies and U.K. holding companies, paid only $9,787. Hollywood stars and moguls were listed: Douglas Fairbanks Sr. paid $225,769, Gloria Swanson $38,800, D.W. Griffith $26,167, Harold Lloyd $22,662, and Louis B. Mayer $10,221.

The law allowed publicity, meaning inspection. It did not condone publication of the findings in newspapers. Lawsuits were filed against the Baltimore *Daily Post*, the New York *Herald Tribune*, and other newspapers. The cases swiftly wound up at the Supreme Court, which ruled in favor of the newspapers.

Some New York businessmen paid income tax on mythical income. They feared that reporting losses or low income would alarm creditors. Chicago tax receipts set a record. The Chicago collector thought that thousands who had previously evaded the tax were paying out of fear from publicity.

Armed with this public information, arguments over proposed income tax reduction bills started to focus on the amount of taxes specific millionaires would save. Treasury Secretary Andrew Mellon and President Calvin Coolidge opposed the publicity provisions. The Treasury Department eventually announced that the cost of compiling publicity records far exceeded any extra revenue. No numbers in support of that assertion were provided. Publicity was repealed in 1926.

It was again resurrected in 1934 in a broader way that required taxpayers to submit a pink slip, Form 1094, with their Form 1040 income tax return. Form 1094 listed the taxpayer's name, address, gross income, total deductions, net income, credits and taxes, and was intended to be public information. A taxpayer failing to file a pink slip would be fined $5, and the bureau would prepare the form for the public record. Corporations would be required to submit a yellow slip open to public inspection, listing the salaries it paid to officers.

The public condemned this as a shopping list for kidnappers, thieves, stockbrokers, charity solicitors, etc. Congress reconsidered and repealed pink slip publicity in March 1935, shortly before it took effect. The yellow slip rule was implemented, but was repealed in 1936. While blocked from the general public, income tax returns remained open to inspection by every federal agency and available for sharing with all state tax agencies. In order to minimize government costs for complying with the latter, starting with the 1935 returns, taxpayers were required to file a duplicate return on green paper. That return would be sent on request to the taxpayer's state tax agency.

Thus, Congress granted virtually every federal and state agency access to tax returns. Moreover, anyone could still inquire of his local IRS office whether his neighbor had filed an income tax return.

Tax publicity remained a sensitive issue. Richard Nixon signed Executive Order 11697 on January 17, 1973, granting the Department of Agriculture access to income tax records "of persons having farm operations...for statistical purposes only," going back to the year 1967. Treasury regulations were published in the Federal Register the following day. No one took notice until the *New York Times* printed a tiny story on February 11. Then protests rang out.

The stated intention was to help the Agriculture Department develop better lists of farmers and livestock producers for its sample surveys. However, the accompanying regulation allowed access to "any other data on such returns or make returns available for inspection and taking of such data as the Secretary of Agriculture may designate." Farmers denounced it. The uproar resulted in a new executive order, issued on March 27, restricting the Agriculture Department's access to the name, address, taxpayer identification number, type of farm activity, and some measure of the size of the farming operations, such as gross income from farming, but precluding disclosure of non-farm income. As Watergate revelations over tax abuses unfolded, both executive orders were revoked on March 24, 1974.

Watergate and similar revelations of inspection abuse for political and other non-tax purposes threatened public confidence in the privacy of tax returns. Congress responded with a 1976 law making tax returns and return information confidential — not subject to disclosure except in those limited situations where an agency's need for information exceeded the citizen's right to privacy. The IRS seized upon these new laws as an opportunity for secrecy in its operations and an excuse for failing to properly archive our nation's tax history. Its relationship with the National Archives and Records Administration remains contentious and adversarial.

That privacy lasted until 1998, when Congress buried a single paragraph into a 920-page appropriations bill granting the Agriculture Department access to tax returns for census purposes. It now requests more than 2.5 million tax return extracts a year. The department hired a contractor who, in February 2006, inappropriately released to eight financial institutions, the social security and taxpayer ID numbers for 350,000 farmers and land owners participating in the $9.5 billion tobacco buyout program. Following September 11, 2001, Congress again opened inspection of income tax returns to a wide range of bureaucrats upon the mere assertion of need for a terrorist investigation.

A perfidious attempt was made to open the IRS record vault to anyone authorized by the chairman of the House or Senate Committee on Appropriations. The single sentence provision was buried deep inside a 3,000-page budget bill that the conference committee inserted in the Surface Transportation Act of 2004 and not noticed until after the House had approved it. This stealth provision wasn't appended to the Internal Revenue Code, so it would only be known to those claiming snooping authority. It provoked such an outcry, that the Senate and House passed concurrent resolutions deleting it. Democrats seeking political points forced Republicans to reveal the author. A 19-year veteran staffer who worked for Rep. Ernest J. Istook Jr. (R-OK) took blame, pronouncing himself "dumbfounded" by the commotion.

Legislatures still experiment with publicity, particularly with "lists of shame." The Treasury Department publishes a quarterly list in the *Federal Register* of wealthy individuals who renounce citizenship for tax reasons. No explanation was given for enacting this 1996 provision. At least 18 states post on the internet names of delinquent taxpayers and the amounts owed. Many famous names appear on Georgia's list, together with one of my clients who fled the country because he couldn't pay his taxes.

**Tax Planning Under The New Deal**

Fortunately for Franklin Roosevelt, there was no call for publicity of presidential candidates' tax returns when he ran for office. He might have looked very bad against Herbert Hoover.

Franklin Roosevelt took advantage of the exemption on state salaries. He did not report his $25,000 annual salary as New York governor from 1929 to 1932, all the while slashing the state budget and hiking taxes. Despite being crippled by polio, every year he deducted losses from operating two farms while holding a full time job as governor or president. One farm was his estate in Hyde Park, New York, just a mile down the street from the Vanderbilt Mansion, the other his "cotton plantation" in Warm Springs, Georgia, where he went for polio rehabilitation. His 1929 return showed a $3,184.08 loss on Warm Springs (including a $3,526.17 expense for hired help on just $2,183.34 in farm sales). In 1937, he deducted losses of $914 for Hyde Park and $1,942 for Warm Springs.

Beginning in 1921, Roosevelt received a $25,000 annual salary from Fidelity & Deposit Company while simultaneously practicing law. Fidelity was the nation's fourth largest surety bonding insurance company. His biographer, Ted Morgan, asked, "Why did [they] hire a novice like Roosevelt as vice president of the important New York office? Because...getting the business depended on whom you knew...Roosevelt knew everyone in New York politics." He appears to have had a problem collecting his $25,000 salary in 1927 and 1928, but after he won the governorship, his 1929 income tax return shows that Fidelity & Deposit paid him $50,000 in back salary.

While President Coolidge may have voluntarily paid income tax and President Hoover contributed 20 percent of his presidential salary back to the Treasury, Roosevelt became the first president required by law to pay income tax. After he increased income tax rates in 1934 and filed his return, Roosevelt got the idea that he should be exempt from the new higher rate. He filed an amended 1934 income tax return claiming a $915.01 refund because his "compensation was diminished during the term for which he was elected (March 4, 1933 to January 20, 1937) in violation of Section 1, Article 2 of the Constitution." The refund was based on his tax at 1932 tax rates. Thereafter, he filed 1935 and 1936 returns based on 1932 tax rates, until re-election. He sent his 1937 return directly to Commissioner

Guy Helvering with a letter explaining that he should be taxed until January 20, 1937 at 1932 rates and thereafter at 1937 rates. "I am wholly unable to figure out the amount of the tax...As this is a problem in higher mathematics, may I ask that the bureau let me know the amount of the balance due?"

With unabashed chutzpah, Roosevelt sent a message to Congress on June 1, 1937 citing a Treasury study he had ordered. It revealed tax avoidance and evasion "so widespread and so amazing both in their boldness and their ingenuity" and that prompt action was "imperative." "The decency of American morals is involved," he declared. The study violated privacy and accused individuals of avoiding taxes by devices which were legitimate under laws of the time:

> Mr. Charles E. Merrill and Mr. Edwin C. Lynch of Merrill-Lynch & Company, 40 Wall Street, New York, have 23 personal holding corporations and 40 trust funds...these corporations constantly engage in transactions with each other which produce no real change in the individual stockholder's holdings but which do affect his tax liability. Mr. William Randolph Hearst was interested in 1933 in some 96 companies scattered all over the United States, some of which seem to be personal holding companies...

Public hearings were held before a Joint Congressional Committee on Tax Evasion and Avoidance from June 17 to July 28, 1937, describing schemes and mentioning names. Congressional action was swift. The Tax Loophole Revenue Act of 1937 passed the House 173-0, and the Senate passed it with no recorded vote in just two minutes.

As he signed it into law, President Roosevelt declared it would repel the attack upon the "foundations of society." The reforms included penalty taxes for corporations used as personal holding companies, unreasonable accumulations of income, and disallowance of losses from sales between family members.

While this legislation was pending, Treasury Secretary Henry Morgenthau learned of an ongoing investigation of his own tax returns, as well as the returns of his father, his wife, and Franklin and Eleanor Roosevelt. He spent the better part of July 6-8, 1937 taking behind-the-scenes charge against potential damage.

Morgenthau discussed the situation with Ways and Means Committee Chairman Robert Doughton on July 6. He next called

Elmer Irey (Al Capone's nemesis), who reported that he was leading the investigation under orders of Undersecretary of Treasury Roswell Magill and Treasury Tax Legislative Counsel Thomas Tarleau. Then he called Commissioner Guy Helvering, and ordered him to come to his office at 3 p.m., together with Irey. He called back Irey and ordered him to deliver the tax returns to the commissioner, effectively killing the investigation.

At his 3 p.m. meeting with Helvering, Irey, and Magill, Morgenthau learned that returns for 1933, 1934, 1935, and 1936 were being investigated and that Rep. Hamilton Fish (R-NY) would present damaging evidence at a public hearing later that week. Fish represented Roosevelt's home district of Hyde Park and probably learned of Roosevelt's aggressive tax posture through a leak at Internal Revenue or the New York State Income Tax Division. He wanted to expose the hypocrisy of the New Dealers by publicizing the tax loopholes *they* were claiming.

Morgenthau called back Doughton on July 8 to announce that the president was mad, "pretty hot." After more phone calls and discussions, he called Doughton again and asked to appear at the hearing Doughton was holding at Fish's request. He spent the rest of the afternoon calling leaders of both parties, including members of the Ways and Means Committee, to rally support. He obtained their promise that they would not hear anything Fish had to say regarding the president.

The committee held its hearing on July 9 with Morgenthau in attendance. The first order of business was that there be no discussion of President Roosevelt's taxes or finances. Joint returns weren't allowed prior to 1948, so Fish presented evidence of a contract Eleanor Roosevelt made with Selby Arch Preserver Shoe Company for a series of radio talks. For each broadcast, she received $1, and Selby sent $3,000 to American Friends Service Committee and a $1,000 "commission" to Miles Lasker. Lasker sent $400 of his commission to Nancy Cook, a friend of Mrs. Roosevelt.

At the hearing, Assistant Attorney General Robert Jackson claimed to have given an opinion in 1934 (when he was Internal Revenue General Counsel) that the proceeds of Eleanor's radio broadcasts were not taxable to her. He told the committee, "Mrs. Roosevelt declined to work for money and was only willing to serve for charity's sake. It was and is my opinion that such benefit broadcasts do not result in taxable income." He told the committee that the opinion was informal and oral, and not rendered in writing.

This testimony contradicted the transcribed telephone conversation between Morgenthau and Helvering three days earlier. "I want to let you know officially that we have found the letter — we have a copy of it that we sent Mrs. Roosevelt in '34...And it said that the General Counsel of Internal Revenue passed on it." He went on to tell Helvering that Luther Cannon had written the ruling and Robert Jackson sent it. "And [Jackson] said that Cannon and he both hold that [based on] Mrs. Roosevelt's contract as they saw it in '34, that she has no Federal tax to pay...And he still holds that position." A doubtful Helvering asked, "we still stand on that ruling?" To which Morgenthau replied, "Well, I should think so but that's up to you... I'll see you at 3 and you have Irey with you, please."

The American Friends Service Committee acknowledged that it had received approximately $100,000 from Mrs. Roosevelt's radio talks. The White House had no comment. Robert Jackson saved Roosevelt from embarrassment. A grateful administration soon promoted him to attorney general, and later to the Supreme Court.

Eleanor Roosevelt's arrangement was "assignment of income," and whether by agreement or understanding, it has always been the tax law in this land that income must be reported by the person who rendered the service. A corresponding charitable deduction was available, limited to 15 percent of income in the 1930s. There are ways to arrange performance of nontaxable services for a charity, but specifying that payments be made to others doesn't work. Otherwise, we might each designate a few hours rendered to our employers for charity and those wages would escape taxation.

Fish alleged that Henry Morgenthau's father used "foreign holding corporations in order to evade or avoid taxes...and family trusts...." Treasury Secretary Morgenthau also created family trusts to transfer back and forth stocks at a loss, which they deducted on their tax returns, just like Charles Merrill, Edwin Lynch, and Andrew Mellon. Fish challenged the committee to subpoena their 1929 and 1930 tax returns, which would expose these transactions. Morgenthau graciously offered to furnish the committee all the returns, "and after the committee has examined them, if there is the slightest thought in their minds that those returns are in any way not honestly made, I would be glad if the committee would ask me any questions and I will be more than pleased to answer them." Of course, the committee did not accept his offer.

After the hearing, Fish held a press conference trying to reveal the story he wasn't allowed to tell the committee, but a pro-Roosevelt press wouldn't report his revelations. His accusations are preserved in the *Congressional Record* concerning the president's claiming farm losses on his tax return and that the hand-picked names Treasury had submitted to the Joint Congressional Committee on Tax Evasion were all Republican contributors or Roosevelt opponents. Today, we have access to Franklin Roosevelt's income tax returns, and they confirm all of Hamilton Fish's accusations that he was a tax hypocrite who persecuted others for doing what he did himself.

The Roosevelt administration equated legal tax avoidance, the simple effort of a taxpayer to pay the minimum required by law, with law-breaking tax evasion. The Bureau of Internal Revenue unsuccessfully attempted to make the combination of failure to file a return and failure to pay tax — two tax return misdemeanors — into a felony with jail time, rather than 5 - 25 percent penalties.

Hitler also developed a chummy relationship with the tax man. But he didn't pay taxes at all. By the time he took power, he owed 405,494 reichsmarks, mostly from book royalties on *Mein Kampf*. Teachers had annual salaries of 4,800 marks, so this was a huge debt. The infamous 1933 Enabling Act which gave him dictatorial powers resolved his tax problems. The Munich tax office declared him free of tax obligations from 1934 forward. Ludwig Mirre, head of the Munich tax office wrote Hitler asking permission to absolve his pre-1933 tax debts. An aide wrote back, "Herr Hitler accepts your proposal." A month later, Mirre was promoted to head the German tax office with a 41 percent pay increase.

**Rich As Rockefeller**

When Gerald Ford nominated Nelson Rockefeller in 1974 to become vice president, Congress demanded to know the entire extent of the Rockefeller family fortune, including his brothers. Estimates of the fortune ranged from $5 billion to $60 billion. The submitted documents showed the entire family worth a little over $1.3 billion. It was still a huge fortune, but not larger than it was estimated their grandfather, John D. Rockefeller had amassed, which was the largest personal fortune in history, nearly two percent of the American economy in the early 1920s. Great and successful as the Rockefeller brothers were, it does not seem they were able to grow their inheritance, or perhaps they weren't interested in doing so.

The Rockefeller fortune examined by Congress in 1974 did not include the value of charitable foundations uncovered in a 1963 investigation by Senator Wright Patman (D-TX). Patman cited the economic power concentrated in a complex of seven Rockefeller family foundations which helped the family control major oil companies. Gifting corporate stock to a charitable foundation generates a current income tax deduction, avoids estate tax, and by requiring the governing body to consist of family members, allows the foundation to be used as a device for passing control of corporate stock from generation to generation without paying estate tax.

Rockefeller incurred $550,159.78 of expenses in connection with the investigation and congressional hearings leading to his confirmation. He claimed a $63,275 tax deduction, an amount equal to his vice presidential salary. The Tax Court ruled it nondeductible, because it wasn't an "ordinary and necessary expense." This case provided additional disclosures that his 1975 gross income was almost $4.5 million, charitable contributions were over $1.3 million, and taxable income was just $609,131.

## Reagan's 1976 Presidential Bid

Personal experience is one of the reasons given for Ronald Reagan's tax slashing in the 1980s. He claimed that he reached the 94 percent bracket during his top Hollywood years. Reagan believed that high taxes stifled hard work and hurt economic output. As president, he slashed the top tax rate to 28 percent.

When Ronald Reagan made his first bid for the presidency in 1976, he refused to publicize his tax returns. In an attempt to embarrass Reagan, Gerald Ford released his own 1975 return showing that he paid $94,568.93 tax on $251,991.24 of gross income, an average 38 percent rate; 42 percent with state tax. This was the first time that tax returns were publicized by a presidential candidate, and it has become a post-Watergate tradition ever since.

Reagan was a major threat to Ford. He had 476 delegates against the incumbent's 333 going into the May 18, 1976 Michigan and

Maryland primaries. Ford was fearful that he could be hurt by a mere narrow win in his home state of Michigan. So, the timing was just right to break the Reagan tax story.

California had a big deficit in 1970, when Governor Reagan made big cuts in state spending and blamed falling revenues on tax avoiders. Shortly before the Michigan primary, it was revealed that although his 1970 income was $73,000, Reagan paid no state income tax and just "several hundred dollars" in federal income tax. Reagan claimed that "business reverses" were the cause, but it was revealed that two tax avoidance shelters, Yearling Row Ranch and the Reagan Cattle Co., made his taxes negligible. It was also clear that someone at the IRS or the California Franchise Tax Board had leaked his return information.

Ford did well in Michigan on May 18, and he won in Maryland, too. Reagan was favored to win five of the six primaries the following week, but he won only three. There was no polling on whether the income tax revelations hurt Reagan, but someone considered it advantageous for Ford. Less than a month before the August Republican National Convention, Jack Anderson reminded everyone in his syndicated newspaper column under the title, "Ronnie's taxes: what's the whole story?"

Ford was only slightly ahead when the convention began. His nomination was in doubt as there were over 150 uncommitted delegates and he lacked the 1,140 votes needed. Ford won the nomination with 1,187 votes, against Reagan's 1,070, making this the closest convention of the twentieth century. It might not have switched 70 delegate votes needed to have made Reagan the Republican candidate facing Jimmy Carter in 1976, but without the tax revelations, the convention vote may have been even closer.

Reagan's tax shelters and Nixon's pre-presidential papers charitable deduction created scandals for the taxes they avoided. Jimmy Carter's 1976 taxes were sheltered by investment tax credits from his peanut farm, which reduced an $11,675 tax to zero. Embarrassed, Carter made a $6,000 donation to the federal government "[b]ecause of my strong feeling that a person should pay some tax on his income...approximately 15 percent of our net taxable income."

Years later in 2004, Arnold Schwarzenegger refused to publicize his tax returns when he successfully ran for governor of California. "There's a balance here between what is a prurient interest versus why this data is thought to be important to disclose," announced his spokesman. Really? Someone who completely exposes himself in movies condemns financial disclosure as prurient! There's no substitute for disclosure to dispel notions of crookedness, hypocrisy, and to gain insight into the individual.

**Tinseltown**

Celebrities don't always appreciate attention from the public. Supreme Court Justice Clarence Thomas complained, "I can't go to the hardware store anymore without somebody recognizing me, or thinking they recognize me, gawking at me. I have already lost that anonymity. I don't wish that on anybody." And it's not just when they are out in public. A colleague reported that a famous film star was his client. When she visited, many of his co-workers found an excuse to stick their heads into his office to catch a glimpse of the beautiful actress. Buried in tax disputes are some details of their lives we would otherwise know nothing about. And absent celebrity status, we wouldn't be interested.

At first, Hollywood didn't take income tax seriously. Criminal investigations in 1928 snared Charlie Chaplin for $1,174,627, silent screen star Marion Davies for $750,000, and some 200 other celebrities for millions more.

Since then, Hollywood's expertise in the art of make-believe has no longer been confined to making entertainment. "The accounting department is the most creative part of Tinseltown," read the headnote of a February 1996 article in *The CPA Journal* entitled, "Hollywood Profits: Gone with the Wind?" It described how films gross over $100 million in revenues but fail to show a profit. The early motion picture industry concocted tax avoidance ideas, not just film scripts.

Film legend Charles Laughton hired himself out to his wholly owned corporation for a small salary. Metro-Goldwyn-Mayer, Paramount, and Twentieth Century Pictures paid his 1934 and 1935 compensation to his corporation. Not to be denied his earnings, the actor borrowed heavily from his corporation, depleting it of cash. Since the corporate income tax rate was substantially lower than the individual rate, the tax savings were huge. IRS was unsuccessful in convincing the court to disregard the corporate entity, treat the transaction as a sham, and tax the corporation's earnings directly to Laughton.

Laughton's "personal service contract," became a target of Roosevelt's tax shelter crusade. This device was buried by a 1937 law subjecting such income to double-tax — once at the regular corporation rate, and to the extent not distributed as a dividend, taxed again at the highest individual income tax rate. It's a penalty tax to be avoided.

For some tax advisers, 70 years has not been long enough to learn about this tainted income. It still surfaces occasionally among sports stars, though the IRS generally disregards the corporation and taxes the service income directly to the individual, which minimizes the penalty tax. Washington Bullets star Charles Johnson tried this device and lost in 1982. It trapped Minnesota North Stars hockey stars Gary Sargent and Steve Chistoff in 1989 (but they won on appeal in a rare reversal of a Tax Court Judge Tannenwald decision), and Houston Rockets star Allen Leavell in 1995. I saw it marketed among the Atlanta Hawks in the early 1990s. Willie Nelson, as part of his tax woes, faced personal service contract issues in his IRS assessment.

Another tax scheme invented by the motion picture industry in the 1940s converted ordinary income, taxed at 91 percent, into long term capital gain, taxed at just 25 percent. A corporation was organized for each picture produced. Prior to release, the corporation would be liquidated ("collapsed"), transferring the film to the shareholders. The shareholders reported income on the fair market value of the film as long-term capital gain, rather than ordinary income. This method was adapted to the building-construction trade and even to the infrequent sale of inventory.

Congress banned the practice with a penalty tax on "collapsible corporations." While the Gettysburg Address was 268 words, split into ten sentences, collapsible corporations had a single sentence that was 456 words. So that the reader wouldn't recover too quickly, the next subsection had a 306-word sentence. (Recall, I once met an accountant who made a hobby of reading the code cover to cover twice a year! And Wilbur Mills memorized these sentences.) Tax law changes in 1986 made the collapsible corporation device unworkable. This law was finally repealed in 2003. (If it sounds complicated, pity the jury foreman who requested clarification about the "combustible corporation" on which he was deliberating.)

As clients, celebrities are often tragic heros. They can earn seven figures for a few years, and one would think that fortune should last a lifetime. Unfortunately, there's a coterie of white collar criminals chasing them, plus an assortment of poor relations, and most celebrities are poor money managers. For these reasons, malpractice insurance costs more for an accountant with celebrity or professional athlete clients.

The cons are ongoing. In January 2004, the Securities and Exchange Commission shut down an investment firm that counted 20 NFL players and some NBA players among its clients. Investors were guaranteed a ten percent monthly return on their investment for the first ten months, followed by five percent monthly thereafter. It was a Ponzi scheme, where abnormally high returns to investors came from money collected from subsequent investors rather than from income leading to eventual collapse of the scheme and investor losses. The *Wall Street Journal* wrote, "Fraud is a real risk for NFL players. The Players Association conducted a survey showing that between 1999 and 2002, 78 players were defrauded of about $42 million."

While vacationing in California in November 1934, Irving Berlin was approached by RKO Pictures to write the musical score for *Top Hat* starring Fred Astaire and Ginger Rogers. He received $75,000 for six songs. The studio signed him to another contract in March 1935 to write the score for the next Astaire and Rogers film, *Follow the Fleet*. He received another $75,000 for seven songs. He would also receive ten percent of the gross profit exceeding $1,250,000 for each film, same as Astaire.

### IRVING BERLIN'S SONGBOOK

"No Strings (I'm Fancy Free)" and "Isn't This a Lovely Day" were written expressly for *Top Hat*. He wrote another ten songs for *Top Hat* that were not used in that movie. The other songs Berlin sold RKO came from his inventory. "Top Hat" and "Cheek to Cheek" had been written for an unproduced play, *More Cheers*. "The Piccolino" came from his *Music Box Review of 1922*. Of the seven songs in *Follow the Fleet*, only "I Would Rather Lead a Band" and "Face the Music and Dance" were written expressly for that movie. One song was lifted from *More Cheers*, and the other four songs were recycled from his old Broadway shows. It's all detailed in a Tax Court decision.

Berlin stayed at the Beverly Wilshire Hotel in Los Angeles. His suite included an office with a piano, and was staffed by a secretary. His 1935 income tax return reported the $150,000 as capital gains, offset by $25,415 of expenses and $38,534 of capital losses. IRS reclassified the capital gain as ordinary income. The Tax Court agreed that Berlin owed an additional $11,093 of income tax. Maybe that's why he crossed out, "A tax I'm very glad to pay," in one version of "I Paid My Income Tax Today" which he wrote two years after this 1939 decision.

Will Rogers was denied a casualty deduction for termite damage and dry rot severe enough to require razing his house because it happened over too long a period of time. A Tax Court case tells us that Jose Ferrer earned just $30,000 for his Oscar winning performance in the fabulous 1950 classic, *Cyrano de Bergerac*.

Little known facts about Jack Benny's radio history and his jump from NBC to CBS are detailed in a 1955 Tax Court case. Benny began in radio in 1932. He was sponsored by the biggest advertisers: General Motors, General Tire, General Foods, and Canada Dry Ginger Ale. Back then, advertisers were exclusive for a given show, with just two commercial announcements of one minute each. His 1944 NBC contract with American Tobacco Company required him to provide for his 30-minute weekly AM radio show: actors, male vocalist, announcer, orchestra leader, 17 musicians, all script, materials, and sound effects. Benny was paid $22,000 per week from which he had to pay all these expenses. The advertiser provided an annual allowance of $200,000 for publicity and celebrity guests. Benny anticipated he would net $10,000 per week, but high expenses resulted in his netting considerably less, and he became dissatisfied with the contract. A new 1947 contract guaranteed him $10,000 per show. In 1948, CBS offered over $2 million to get The Jack Benny Show on its radio network, and the court allowed Benny to treat the payment as capital gain.

A 1957 Tax Court case tells a similar story for Groucho Marx and his show, "You Bet Your Life." Groucho's career hit bottom and he was unemployed in the summer of 1947. The Marx Brothers had disbanded after several flops. Groucho appeared alone in one unsuccessful movie, and couldn't find a job in radio. He became quizmaster of "You Bet Your Life" in the fall of 1947 for about $3,600 per week because Gary Moore was unavailable. The show began on ABC, where it was only moderately successful. It switched to CBS in 1949 and became one of the most popular programs on radio. The contract with advertiser DeSoto-Plymouth automobiles required Groucho and his partner to provide ten musicians plus an orchestra leader, a commercial announcer, and other expenses including paying the cash prizes to contestants from their own pocket. NBC bought the show in 1950 for $2.5 million, moved it to television and paid the show expenses with a $5,000 weekly salary to Groucho. The court allowed Groucho to treat a $750,000 portion of the NBC buy-out as capital gain.

Musician and entertainer Walter V. Liberace experienced a slump in popularity in the late 1950s. His income fell from $50,000 per week to just $6,000. So, he reintroduced his "glamour and elegance" image. This consisted of elegant costumes, unusual musical instruments and stage settings. (Actually, they were garish.) His annual earnings climbed back over $1 million. He moved out of his Sherman Oaks home in 1959 because it lacked privacy. It had become a tourist attraction because, among other things, it contained a piano-shaped swimming pool.

He incorporated his business, which had six employees, with two men supervising the design and maintenance of his elaborate wardrobe. The corporation acquired a three-story, 28-room, 20,000 sq. ft. Hollywood Hills mansion with a circular staircase for just $95,000. It then spent $250,000 for exquisite antique-style furnishings acquired from Liberace, who had a sideline business as proprietor of an antique shop in Los Angeles. The house had landscaped grounds, a cabana and swimming pool, gymnasium, projection room, seven pianos, several violins, an organ, and his trademark candelabras. The home was used for press publicity and partially restyled every two or three years to maintain continued public interest.

The corporation deducted over $50,000 annually for depreciation and maintenance, in addition to property taxes and interest. Liberace leased these premises from his corporation for just $300 per month. The IRS assessed over $66,000 against the corporation and $60,000 against Liberace for 1962 - 1964. The agency claimed that 84 percent of the costs did not constitute an ordinary and necessary business expense and assigned dividend income to Liberace. The Tax Court allowed a deduction for 50 percent. So, he still owed about $75,000 in tax.

Willie Nelson had the misfortune of investing in abusive tax shelters in the late 1970s, on which Price Waterhouse advised he would receive $10 in tax deductions for each $1 invested. The IRS hit him with a $16.7 million tax bill in 1990. The Service sold his ranch and auctioned his belongings in partial payment, collecting $3.6 million. Nelson made a double album, "The IRS Tapes: Who'll Buy My Memories?" which raised over $1 million for the IRS. His lawyer joked that his period of indentured servitude might include, "The IRS Presents Willie Nelson." He eventually reached a settlement in 1993 whereby he paid IRS a total of $9 million, $5.4 million of it over five years. His $45 million lawsuit against Price Waterhouse was settled in 1994 for an undisclosed sum. Nelson could have escaped the taxes by filing for bankruptcy, but he refused to do so.

Fellow celebrity country music balladeer, Conway Twitty, failed in his 1971 restaurant venture, Twitty Burger Inc. He repaid (and deducted) some $100,000 to about 75 investors. As he was under no obligation to do so, the IRS disallowed this deduction. In what must surely rank as its friendliest decision ever, the Tax Court allowed the deduction, saying they were made to protect his business reputation. The judge was so smitten with Twitty's good intentions that he included a five-stanza "Ode to Conway Twitty" in his opinion, which ended:

> Had Conway not repaid the investors
> His career would have been under cloud
> Under the unique facts of this case
> Held: The deductions are allowed.

Not to be outdone, the IRS Chief Counsel's official Action on Decision ended with a four-stanza "Witty Twitty Ditty" doggerel:

> He repaid his friends
> Why did he act
> Was it business or friendship
> Which is fact?
>
> Business, the court held
> It's deductible, they feel
> We disagree with the answer
> But let's not appeal.

There's something about certain celebrities that brings out the friendly troubadour in judges. When baseball commissioner Bud Selig owned the Milwaukee Brewers, he was treated to a delightful victory opinion which included a history of baseball, with irrelevant and entertaining quotes about the game. It ended with a recital of the complete last stanza of "Casey at the Bat." "...But there is no joy in Mudville — mighty Casey has Struck Out." The judges concluded, "There should be joy somewhere in Milwaukee — the district court's judgment is affirmed."

Basketball star Dennis Rodman paid $200,000 in an out-of-court settlement for kicking TV cameraman Eugene Amos Jr. Part of the agreement was that the settlement be kept confidential. Amos treated the settlement as a tax-free payment on account of injury. The IRS insisted the entire amount was taxable. The Tax Court held that 40 percent was taxable. In the process, the court printed the confidential settlement agreement in its decision.

It's not just the IRS. State income taxes also cause grief.

Rodman's former girlfriend, Madonna, sued her former financial advisers in 1999, believing that they caused her to lose money in state income taxes. She filed and paid tax as a California resident. New York claimed she had spent more than 183 days in their state in 1992 and conferred New York residency upon her together with a $2 million tax bill. Tax news writers were hoping for more publicity. "Having already seen many of her videos, your editors admit to being more excited by the thought of Madonna's naked tax return than by Madonna herself."

Connecticut resident Martha Stewart suffered the same fate when she failed to prove that she spent fewer than 184 days in New York in 1992. She eventually paid New York more than $221,000 in taxes, penalties and interest.

Chicago Cubs slugger Sammy Sosa paid a total of $65,316 in state income taxes to California, New York, Pennsylvania, Colorado and Missouri in 1998. Illinois charged him an extra $38,169, which he paid under protest, claiming Illinois was taxing income already taxed by other states. The Illinois Department of Revenue agreed that it was double taxation but insisted that the other states were at fault. Only Illinois, they said, had the right to tax Sosa's estimated $10 million annual paycheck, and Illinois courts agreed. Illinois added a box to its individual income tax form, "Check if you were a member of a professional athletic team" in order to flag other athletes for scrutiny.

Nonresident state income tax compliance is a major problem for athletes and entertainers.

Concert pianist, David Bar-Illan complained, "I have to cope with foreign and out-of-state taxes as if I were a multinational corporation...I file tax returns in almost every state in which I appear...And because I must file a return even if I play only one concert in any given state, my accountant's fee can be 10 or 20 times the amount of the tax due." No state income tax is one reason entertainers love to perform in Las Vegas.

A state income tax targeting athletes has become known as a "jock tax." The California Franchise Tax Board employs one person whose sole job is monitoring arriving and departing pro athletes so they can be taxed. Louisiana has a special law assessing a $500 to $2,500 penalty on nonresident athletes (including professional golfers) who fail to file a timely return using its "Nonresident Professional Athlete" income tax form, in addition to a five percent negligence penalty and a late payment penalty of up to 50 percent, plus interest.

The jock tax ensnared Yankee star, Derek Jeter, one of baseball's highest-paid players. Claiming residency in Florida (which has no income tax), he filed nonresident New York returns for 2001-2003. He earned $14 million in 2003 (excluding signing bonus). Unfortunately, he bought an apartment in Manhattan's Trump World Tower for a reported $13 million in 2001, so New York claimed he was taxable as a resident even though he might have spent less than 184 days in the state. The combined New York state and city income tax rate was 12.15 percent.

Still, IRS grabs more headlines, especially when celebrities are involved.

In the middle of the first round of Sugar Ray Robinson's September 23, 1957 middleweight championship prizefight at Yankee Stadium, the IRS served Robinson's promoters with a $514,310.72 levy for unpaid taxes. Robinson lost the 15-round split decision, losing his crown to Carmen Basilio. His $527,485.52 share of the proceeds, including motion picture rights, was paid to the IRS. The agency eventually released $107,000 for Robinson to pay expenses incurred in connection with that fight. He went to Tax Court and secured a split decision. He still owed the tax, but the IRS had to recalculate it using a different accounting method, which resulted in some savings for Robinson.

Entertainer Sammy Davis Jr. owed the IRS nearly $2 million in taxes plus an equal amount in interest and penalties for an abusive coal tax shelter he invested in during the late 1970s.

Judy Garland was hounded by the IRS for back taxes. Lorna Luft wrote that the IRS attached her mother's salary, and revenue officers would come knocking on the door in the middle of the night. A biographer noted that when Garland died on the night of June 21-22, 1969 at age 47, she owed $4 million to the IRS and other creditors.

Sometimes, a celebrity causes someone else grief which winds up in Tax Court. Gerald and Kathleen Chamales had the misfortune of buying a $2,849,000 home next door to O.J. Simpson in the Brentwood Park section of Los Angeles just a few days before Nicole Brown Simpson and Ronald Goldman were murdered at a condominium in West Los Angeles. The Brentwood neighborhood began crawling with media personnel and equipment and celebrity-enthralled sightseers ("looky-loos"). They blocked streets, trespassed on neighboring residential property, and flew overhead in helicopters while attempting to get close to the Simpson home. To no avail, police erected barricades at various Brentwood Park intersections to restrict traffic. Their real-estate agent estimated that the Chamales' home had decreased in value by 20 to 30 percent. The Tax Court denied their claim for a $751,427 casualty loss because there was no physical damage to their property and the situation was considered temporary. However, the judge wouldn't allow a negligence penalty because a CPA had prepared their return.

**Alan Jay Lerner**

Broadway lyricist Alan Jay Lerner who wrote *Brigadoon*, *My Fair Lady*, *Camelot* and *Gigi*, died broke. He owed the IRS more than $1.4 million for taxes for 1977 through 1981, and the interest kept mounting. He had married eight times and divorced slightly less. The seven divorce settlements were a cause of his poor financial condition.

He was born into wealth. His father was one of the founders of the Lerner Stores chain of women's apparel. The street where he lived was Park Avenue.

Lerner divorced his fourth wife, Micheline, in 1965. She took him to court so often for falling behind in alimony that the *New York Post* ran a 1979 headline, "4th Ex-Wife Sues for Sixth Time." The *New York Times* couldn't resist writing, "The dispute had come up in court so many times that everyone connected with it had grown accustomed to the pace."

Judges didn't believe he could not afford alimony. Justice Felice Shea ruled that Lerner's poverty plea was "unsubstantiated" and awarded Micheline alimony of $50,000 annually. Justice Hortense W. Gabel accused him of conduct "outrageously contumacious of the judicial process." She appointed Micheline as receiver and sequestrator of all assets belonging to him in New York.

His tax debts resulted from improper deductions, tax shelters, foreign transactions, and personal holding company issues. The *New York Post* reported on July 9, 1984 that Lerner was threatening to sue his accountants for his tax problems. "I am a playwright and lyricist and not familiar with business affairs and taxes," Lerner complained to the *Post*. His executor told me that Lerner didn't carry out that threat. It wasn't his nature.

Composer Charles Strouse who wrote *Bye Bye Birdie*, *Annie* and in 1983 collaborated with Lerner on his final show *Dance a Little Closer*, reminisced, "Alan told me I was foolish to pay all my taxes, that I should keep my money on the Isle of Wight and send my lawyer there to bring back cash in a suitcase when I needed it." Lerner didn't like the IRS, but better tax advice could have minimized his problems.

At his death on June 14, 1986, the IRS had a lien on his property, including song royalties. The very day he died, a New York court ruled in a case involving who had priority over Lerner's principal New York asset, $135,000 in royalties that Micheline Lerner had collected in the receivership account. The case involved wife number 4, wife number 5, wife number 7, publisher Viking Penguin, and the IRS. Lerner had asserted no claim against the funds but prior to his death, urged the court to award the money to Micheline rather than the IRS. The court gave first crack to Viking for $75,000. The IRS got the rest.

Tax collection efforts don't stop at death. This case dragged on in Lerner's estate longer than the 17-year locust. His estate didn't settle with the IRS until 2003. The government compromised and accepted

$730,000 for his 1977 - 1981 obligations. The statute of limitations had remained open all those years under agreements between IRS and the estate. His executor told me that IRS was very professional, if not compassionate, in its handling of this collection matter.

**Sergeant York**

Sergeant Alvin York was the greatest American hero of World War I. He received a dozen medals, including the Medal of Honor, France's Croix de Guerre, and Italy's Croce di Guerra, for single-handedly wiping out a German machine gun battalion at Argonne Forest, killing 25 Germans and capturing 132 in the process. He sold the motion picture and book rights to his life story to pioneer movie producer Jesse Lasky in 1940 for $50,000 plus two percent of the movie's gross receipts.

*Sergeant York* was the top grossing film of 1942. York received $134,000 royalties in 1942. Though there are no firm totals, his contract probably earned him a little over $200,000. Lasky made over $1 million from the movie. Gary Cooper was paid $150,000 and won the 1942 Academy Award for Best Actor for his portrayal of York. (Ronald Reagan tested four scenes with 17 takes, and might have been cast if Warner couldn't get Cooper released from his contract with Samuel Goldwyn.)

York reported his income as capital gains, used most of the proceeds to build a bible school, and invested some funds in a failed wildcat oil venture on his Appalachian land. Then the IRS asserted that York's movie royalties were taxable as ordinary income and assessed an additional $85,442 tax. With the high ordinary income tax rates of World War II plus interest and waning movie royalties, he would never be able to pay this debt. The IRS thereby made a distinction between book and movie royalties by allowing Presidents Truman and Eisenhower to treat the sale of their book memoirs as capital gains, while York's movie royalties were ordinary income.

Finally, in 1961, under pressure from House Speaker Sam Rayburn and Tennessee Rep. Joe Evins, the IRS settled York's $172,723 tax claim for $25,000, an amount raised through contributions from 10,000 grateful Americans in just six weeks. York's monthly income was $177.45, and he was bedridden from a 1954 stroke. The IRS issued a statement saying that the $25,000 "appears to be in excess of the sum collectible from a forced sale of all the taxpayer's assets, and it gives adequate consideration to his earning capacity and future prospects." York died three years later.

While a case is pending in Tax Court, the IRS must suspend collection activity, so the agency never hounded Alvin York. Around the time the agency settled, it issued a revenue ruling allowing capital gains treatment for the sale of memoirs in exchange for movie royalties. This removed the distinction between book and movie royalties. After everything that had transpired, York never learned that the IRS owed him a refund and an apology.

**Joe Louis**

The great boxer, Joe Louis earned over $4.6 million during his career. He died in 1981 owing the IRS more than $2 million. He was very generous and charitable, lived a flamboyant lifestyle, and managed his finances rather poorly. "He has been a soft touch for any glib tongue with a proposition to sell and has sunk cash in everything from a chicken shack to a dude ranch," wrote *Ebony*.

His tax problems began when the IRS assessed him $81,000 in unpaid tax following his 1941 fights with Billy Conn and Louis Nova, which earned him $350,000. Louis claimed his accountant advised him not to pay because he felt he could strike a deal to pay less. His career was on hold while he served in the army during World War II. By 1946, his IRS debt had ballooned to $196,000, but his accountant erroneously advised him that a $194,000 business loss would offset the tax. His divorce agreement provided that he pay 25 percent of his gross income to his ex-wife, but his advisers neglected to write into the agreement that it was alimony, which made it nondeductible. The IRS asserted nondeductible personal expenses and personal holding company tax issues. Combined with over 90 percent income tax rates plus interest and penalties, it's easy to see how he wound up in financial purgatory. *U.S. News & World Report* estimated that Louis would have had to earn an average of at least $310,000 a year for 20 more years to pay this debt (including accumulating interest) and to keep up with current income taxes.

Attempting to pay his tax bill kept him in the ring until he could no longer box. He turned to professional wrestling where his ribs were crushed and his heart damaged. For relief from the severe pain, he turned to alcohol and drugs. At some point around 1961, the statute of limitations on collections expired. Thereafter, the IRS taxed him only on his current income, which in 1961 was just $10,000. In the 1970s, he became a celebrity greeter at Caesar's Palace in Las Vegas. Billy Conn, his also broke former rival, became a celebrity greeter at the Stardust.

Louis bemoaned IRS financial purgatory in his autobiography, which is filled with references to this misery.

> ...these tax guys hang onto you. Always calling you up. Showing up where they don't belong. Getting on your nerves.
>
> I signed an agreement with them to pay them $20,000 yearly on back taxes. I must have been earning about $33,000 and when I paid $12,000 tax on the $33,000, plus the $20,000, I'd only have $1,000 left. You know, something like that can depress a man. Well, there would be no way I could honor that $20,000 a year and still be Joe Louis so I just tried my best to give them what I could.

# CHAPTER TWELVE

# Affluenza

*It's very expensive to be me.*

—Anna Nicole Smith

Affluenza is the unhappy condition of overload, debt, anxiety and waste resulting from the dogged pursuit of more. CPAs witness affluenza in action. From these observations, I've confirmed two postulates: Once financial comfort is reached, wealth has little correlation to happiness, and a person's house is more a reflection of his wealth than his needs.

A client described his penthouse suite at the Westin hotel: "It's nice. The shower overlooks downtown. But I much prefer the penthouse at the Hyatt."

Another client with a penthouse apartment in Manhattan couldn't decide which expensive house in South Florida he liked better. So, he bought both. His tax organizer listed a helicopter trip.

"I went to Miami Airport. Some people take a cab. I took a helicopter."

"Which business trip was that?"

"My plantation in Colombia."

"Your lawyer says you don't have a plantation in Colombia."

"That's right! Scratch the helicopter fare."

> **THE DEL**
>
> San Diego's luxurious Hotel del Coronado, built in 1888, is the greatest surviving gilded age beachfront hotel. It has a grand history. Frank Baum wrote many of his *Wizard of Oz* sequels while staying there, and he designed some small chandeliers that still adorn the banquet hall. Prince Edward met Wallis Spencer Simpson at The Del, where she rented a cottage. Many movies, including *Some Like It Hot*, were filmed on site. It has one haunted room and a waiting list to spend a night in it. A small card is prominently displayed in each room: "This room is equipped with the Edison Electric Light. Do not attempt to light with a match. Simply turn key on the wall by the door. The use of electricity for lighting is in no way harmful to health, nor does it affect soundness of sleep." There's a free museum gallery in the hotel.
>   Adjacent to the original wooden structure, The Del has a modern brick high-rise. Some attendees at the AICPA Tax Division meeting insisted on rooms in the new building. In the original building, one could open a window, hear the surf from the adjacent Pacific Ocean and enjoy the cool December ocean breeze. But these affluenza-afflicted folks required the "new building" with sealed windows and air conditioning.

CPAs observe the effects of affluenza on children who grow up to cheat their parents out of the family business, "borrow" money to start a business which hasn't a prayer, and extort or steal money from parents. Invariably, the children are living beyond their means. Elderly parents are defenseless against the verbal or physical abuse or shunning which accompanies a refusal to surrender wealth.

I overheard a client's teenage son late one afternoon saying to his father, "Let's surprise Mom. We'll stop by the dealer showroom on the way home and buy me a new car." Another teenager tells a friend that when he makes his fortune, "I'm going to get myself some cheap immigrant help."

Early in my career, I prepared tax returns for a substantial estate, saved during a lifetime of frugal living. It took the two sons just six months to lose the inheritance on an ill-conceived expansion of their father's business. I've seen this repeated several times, where a large inheritance was quickly and foolishly squandered.

Saving money can be difficult regardless of income. Usually, it's the wife who asks how to modify spending in order to save. Responding to that question, I once volunteered to a client with a seven-figure income, "Well, remember that trip you and your husband took to Australia last year? You bought first class tickets for $12,000. Coach tickets can be bought for under $1,000 each." Insulted, she retorted, "You expect me to sit (gasp!) in the back of the plane, all the way to Australia? Jay, it's an 18-hour flight." It was as if I had suggested steerage class.

**Automobile**

A tour of the NBC Studios in Burbank, California includes a visit to Tonight Show host Jay Leno's reserved parking space. He owns 100 vehicles, a lesser number of motorcycles, drives a different one to work each day, and employs a crew with a 17,000 sq. ft. "Big Dog Garage" to maintain them.

I once prepared a *pro bono* tax return for a single mother earning minimum wage. She was about to lose her job because it was moving to a new location not served by public transportation. The $2,000 earned income tax credit refund enabled her to buy a used car so she could keep her job. Leno could never be more thrilled with a car acquisition than she.

In 1985, a client asked my advice on what he could afford to spend for a luxury foreign car. He didn't want a "flimsy" American car. He wasn't sure whether he could find anything for the $10,000 I told him he could afford. He called me a week later. "You'll be proud of me. I followed your advice and found a 10-year-old Mercedes with 100,000 miles for just $10,000." At the time, he could have bought a fine new American car for that money.

Another client called asking advice on financing the purchase of a replacement Jaguar.

"Why are you replacing your Jag? Didn't you just buy it?"

"It's almost three years old. Jaguar has replaced the transmission three times and the engine twice. The warranty expires soon. This car would be unaffordable without a manufacturer's warranty."

The maintenance manager at a Rolls Royce dealership told me that anyone who can appreciate a burled walnut dashboard, matching leather seats, and lamb's wool carpets will be happy with a Rolls Royce. However, anyone expecting a mechanically superior car will be disappointed. His dealership sold 75 Rolls Royces annually and employed three full time mechanics to service them.

Advertising helps. Volkswagen achieved wild success in the U.S. thanks to Doyle Dane Bernbach's innovative ad campaign. Eighty percent of the ad poster featured a picture of an ugly Volkswagen. The caption below read simply, "Lemon" with some fine print. It really was a lemon. The Volkswagen Beetle was underpowered and would slow down on navigating a slight hill or in a headwind. Valve jobs were a frequent repair. Despite the many problems, owners still thought they had made a "good buy." Car ads aren't just to entice new buyers. They serve the dual purpose of convincing owners they made a wise decision.

Years ago, while visiting Israel, my wife's cousin picked us up in his BMW 318, which he bought for $21,000, slightly more than it sold for in the U.S. (A Mercedes cost $50,000, and they are quite common in Israel.) I noticed an Oldsmobile Delta 88 and pointed it out to her cousin. "That's a $70,000 car," he replied. I felt so proud when I got back to the states and started driving my $70,000 car again. Abroad, American is the ultimate luxury car.

Speaking before the National Press Club on November 17, 1988, after having relinquished his seat on the General Motors board, billionaire H. Ross Perot was asked "if you drive one of those GM cars?" He replied:

> Absolutely. Drive one every day. Drive an '84 Oldsmobile...Everybody always says, "Gee, why don't you get a new car?" I believe in using the things you buy. This is my opinion. I buy something, use it forever.... it's a good car and it's fun to drive....So, I am still driving General Motors cars and will continue to drive General Motors cars and would like to always be able to go down and buy an American car and write the check, and *know* that I had bought the finest car in the world. [emphasis his]

## Retirement at Age 65

Financial planners have put folks on an affluenza treadmill with dire projections of what they need for retirement. One of my clients feels he must have $8 million in savings before he can afford to retire. Another happily retired with social security, $200,000 in savings and a paid-for residence. It's tragic when clients with years of very high income approach retirement with nothing in savings.

Retirement is a recent invention. Moses never retired. Frank Lloyd Wright did his best work after age 65. Given man's violent history and the lack of sanitation and modern medicine, people had short life spans. Prior to the twentieth century, no able-bodied aged person "retired." Most aged people who could no longer work became destitute.

German Chancellor Otto von Bismarck created the first national government social insurance system to assist German industrial workers and thus make them less susceptible to socialism. His Sickness Insurance Law was passed in 1883, followed by accident insurance in 1884, and old age and disability insurance in 1889. Given that average life expectancy was about 45, he set age 70 for eligibility for the government pension. In 1889, it was rightly assumed that 70-year-olds were dead or disabled. Bismarck was 74 in 1889, and lived to be 83. Around 1915, the Reichstag lowered the retirement age to 65.

> **RETIREMENT AGE**
>
> Some believe that Bismarck set the retirement age for pensions at age 65. Robert Myers, for many years chief actuary at the Social Security Administration, thoroughly researched the question, going back to the original German documents. He reported in several journals that Bismarck established 70 as retirement.

When Franklin Roosevelt's social security system was adopted in 1936, the 65-age requirement was selected based on systems in other countries, coordination with corporate pensions, and because it was a good, round compromise figure. Our social security system consists of several benefits. The legal name of the major component is "Old Age, Survivors, and Disability Insurance" and it originates from the 1889 belief that old age meant disability.

Vacations are also a recent invention, which began with the age of railroads. Prior to railroads, people didn't travel very far from their birthplace. But that's another story.

**The Legacy Tax**

"Squander it! Be not only generous but a spendthrift. That is the way to beat the federal taxes imposed on gratuitous shifting of interests in property." So advises a major estate tax treatise.

The Romans and ancient continental Europe taxed the transmission or receipt of wealth by inheritance. It was introduced to the American colonies and modeled after Great Britain's probate and estate duties. From 1797 to 1802, Congress imposed a "legacy tax" of two percent on bequests excepting those to parents, spouses, or lineal descendants. Beginning with Pennsylvania in 1826, states began enacting inheritance taxes. Congress imposed an inheritance tax from 1898 to 1902 to pay for the Spanish-American War.

Our present federal estate tax was enacted in 1916. Whereas prior estate taxes were used to raise revenues, the 1916 tax was also intended to redistribute wealth. Wealth redistribution is a powerful argument in favor of the estate tax. The tax could be avoided by gifts, so a gift tax was enacted in 1924. The gift tax was briefly repealed from 1926 to 1932.

President Coolidge proposed repeal of the estate tax in 1925. Though Republicans held a 64-seat majority in the House, it failed because of adroit opposition from John Nance Garner, who argued, "The estate tax is essentially a tax upon wealth. It operates on wealth and ability to pay regardless of geography or state lines. It is a question of exercising the right to levy a tax for the transfer of property." Opponents frame the issue as a "death tax," but like the gift tax, it's really a tax on transfers of wealth.

Andrew Carnegie argued that heirs do not earn their wealth through their own efforts, so there was no injustice in depriving them of their inheritance. President Theodore Roosevelt supported the estate tax in an April 1906 speech. Congressman Fiorello LaGuardia in 1932 referred to an increase in the estate tax as "not only to raise needed revenue [but] to establish social legislation which will eventually prevent the concentration of wealth of The Nation into the hands of a few families." Bill Gates and Warren Buffett support the estate tax. Like Carnegie, they gifted the bulk of their fortunes to charity.

As tax policy, the estate and gift tax is one of the most progressive features of our tax laws, falling entirely on the rich. It encourages charitable donations, life insurance sales, and redistribution of wealth. If repeal advocates ever succeed, expect the estate tax to return in a few years. A five-year repeal, followed by re-enactment, would be great for the estate tax planning industry. Tax planning for repeal, followed by more tax planning for reenactment. Count the professional fees!

An estate is taxed in the state where the decedent was domiciled at the time of his death. Unlike residence, domicile is one's permanent home, the place a person intends to return to despite absences. A domicile, once acquired, remains unchanged until a new domicile is acquired. Affirmative actions are needed to renounce an old domicile and acquire a new one. States frequently fight over the estates of individuals who through poor tax planning may have more than one domicile.

The first major multistate estate tax dispute involved the robber baron steel industrialist, Henry Clay Frick. He died in 1919 claiming Pennsylvania domicile, while living in New York and maintaining a residence in Massachusetts. His estate was estimated at $150 million, and the total federal and state estate taxes came to $10 million. In an act of comity, New York courts ceded the right to tax the estate to Pennsylvania. This would not ever happen again.

**Soup and Taxes**

Dr. John Dorrance was a chemist. He owned the Campbell Soup Company and invented condensed soup. By eliminating water from canned soup, he lowered costs for packaging, shipping and storage. That allowed Campbell Soup to sell a ten-ounce can for a dime, compared to over thirty cents charged by competitors. Dorrance also pioneered mass advertising and promotion.

Until 1925, Dorrance lived in Cinnaminson, N.J. He then moved to a 137-acre estate in Randor, Pennsylvania, a suburb of Philadelphia. Campbell Soup Company was based in Camden, N.J. Dorrance always declared that his home was in New Jersey, including in his will. At his death in September 1930, he was worth $115 million. His executors probated his will in New Jersey. New Jersey law allowed the accumulation of income to pay estate taxes so his children wouldn't have to sell Campbell stock to pay estate tax.

Both New Jersey and Pennsylvania courts held that John Dorrance died domiciled in its borders. Each insisted that it alone was entitled to collect estate tax. Pennsylvania claimed that he was domiciled in Randor at his death. New Jersey insisted that he never abandoned his Cinnaminson domicile, proven by the fact that he kept the house constantly in perfect repair and had made improvements looking toward his eventual return, and had died at the Cinnaminson house.

Dorrance was the first victim of a tax trap known as "multiple domiciles."

The New Jersey estate tax was $14.4 million; the Pennsylvania estate tax, $15.6 million. Pennsylvania also assessed an additional $1.1 million for personal property taxes for the years that the state felt that he had been a Pennsylvania resident.

Adding insult, New Jersey refused to allow a deduction for the taxes paid to Pennsylvania because "Pennsylvania made an erroneous assessment." New Jersey statute permitted only deductions of valid taxes paid to other states. Appeals wended through the courts until 1936. The U.S. Supreme Court twice refused to break the deadlock. As a result, New Jersey and Pennsylvania both taxed Dorrance's estate. Despite the tax burden, Campbell Soup Company remained privately held until 1953.

His great grandson, John Dorrance III, with an estimated net worth of over $2 billion, moved to Ireland and renounced U.S. citizenship in the early 1990s. He thus avoids U.S. income and estate taxes. He's not alone. Exxon heiress, Cecil Furstenberg, adopted Austrian citizenship, renounced U.S. citizenship, and resides in Paris and Monte Carlo. Kenneth Dart, heir to the Dart Container family's $1 billion fortune, became a citizen of Belize.

**The Woman Who Loved Money**

Hetty Green was the shrewdest and richest woman in America, and an eccentric miser. Three biographies have been written about her, and a song, too. She was heir to a family fortune made in the nineteenth century Massachusetts whaling industry. In 1896, the *New York World* estimated her fortune at $60 million. Though her annual income was at least $3 million, she lived at cheap boarding houses, and spent only a few hundred dollars a year. William Jennings Bryan used her as part of his winning arguments for passage of the 1894 income tax: "That woman, under [the tariff], does not pay as much toward the support of the Federal Government as a laboring man whose income of $500 is spent upon his family."

Luckily, the 1894 income tax was ruled unconstitutional. "Mrs. Green, I understand, does not intend to comply with the law unless the courts compel her to do so," Acting Collector Alexander McKinney of the First Internal Revenue District told the *New York Times*.

In order to avoid New York City tax on $1.5 million of personal property, she swore to the tax commissioners that she resided in Bellows Falls, Vermont and she was able to prove it in court because her estranged and penniless husband resided there. It was a common practice called, "swearing off a tax," but it wasn't easy. Theodore Roosevelt was successful, but financier Jay Gould failed to prove that he was a resident of Lakewood, N.J.

Amusing legends about her miserliness abound. Once, she spent an entire night looking for a two-cent stamp she had dropped. She owned few clothes, and would instruct the washerwoman to wash just the bottom of her skirt (which became soiled from contact with floors, streets, and sidewalks) so that it might last longer and cost less to launder. Fearing assassination by lawyers, she paid $50 for a New York City permit to carry a pistol. When her New York bank asked a $100 fee to transfer $1 million of Reading Railroad shares, she took a satchel with the certificates on a $4 roundtrip train ride to Philadelphia to deliver them to the transfer agent herself.

The *New York Tribune* reported, "Mrs. Green wore what once had been a black dress, which must have been of practically indestructible material. It turned brown, then green, and still she wore it; and carried an umbrella and handbag of about the same era as her dress." This outfit was quite a sight in the financial district, and it earned her the nickname, "the Witch of Wall Street." (Her agent who collected rent on her Chicago properties was named W.B. Frankenstein. Really!)

Hetty sued and was sued frequently, often by her own lawyers, who had to sue to collect their fee. Stories about her miserliness resulted in frequent newspaper headlines and made her a celebrity. People flocked to court to catch a glimpse of her. All that recognition caused another patient to identify her when she feigned poverty in order to obtain free charity medical care, for which she was then compelled to pay $600.

At age 14, her son Ned injured his left knee. She treated the wound herself and relied on free clinics to avoid a medical bill. His leg eventually turned gangrenous and had to be amputated above the knee.

Hetty had no grandchildren. Her daughter, Sylvia was six feet tall, not pretty, and reportedly had "no trace of a personality." She didn't wed until 1909 at age 38 when she married Matthew Astor Wilks, the 63-year-old great-grandson of John Jacob Astor. The upcoming engagement prompted Hetty to take a spacious suite at the Plaza Hotel, for $15 a day. That lasted about a month before she moved back to a $19 Hoboken, N.J. flat on Bloomfield Street ahead of tax collectors where she assumed the name, Mrs. Dewey, after her shaggy dog, Dewey. It left collectors guessing where to find her and the proper state in which to tax her. Hoboken imposed a $2 annual dog license, which she also refused to pay, so she had to keep ahead of the dog catcher too. She adored Dewey. Though she subsisted on oatmeal (heated on a radiator), graham crackers (purchased in bulk), and raw onions, she always fed Dewey tenderloin steaks and rice pudding.

Just two months before a federal estate tax was enacted in 1916, Hetty died at the age of 82, worth an estimated $100 million. (Woodrow Wilson's vice president, Thomas R. Marshall, suggested her untaxed death was the impetus for Democrats to pass an estate tax.) She left her estate, which included an interest in Chemical National Bank (today part of JPMorgan Chase), several railroads, and real estate, to Ned and Sylvia. Her will was probated in Vermont which imposed about $50,000 estate tax. New Jersey claimed her estate was worth $150 million and unsuccessfully sought to collect $5.5 million of inheritance taxes based on her Hoboken residence. New York wanted $6 million, but its courts ruled that Hetty was a resident of Vermont, and even the $38 million of her estate that was tied to New York business could not be taxed.

Ned lived in Texas, was president of the Texas Midland Railroad, and tried to run for governor in 1898, backed by a surprising $1 million campaign pledge from mother. He tried again in 1906. Texans wanted to nominate him as McKinley's vice president in 1900 (given to Theodore Roosevelt instead).

Following a 1910 interview in Paris where he expressed a desire to find a wife, Ned received 5,000 written marriage proposals. But he claimed that women were only interested in his money. This six-foot-four, 300 pound eccentric, who lavished millions on racing cars, yachts, planes, coins, stamps, politics and pornography, didn't marry until age 48, a year after his mother died. His 47-year-old bride, his "housekeeper" for 15 years, was a former prostitute. They built a 61-room stone and marble mansion costing $4 million near Dartmouth, Massachusetts.

Ned died in 1936 at Lake Placid, New York "where he was temporarily sojourning for reasons of health." He was 67. His wife and his sister were his only heirs and next of kin. He lived part of his adult life in Texas, and spent some years in Florida following an operation and illness under advice of a physician. Ned had moved from state to state, had multiple residences, and made conflicting statements on his intended domicile. At the time of his death, he claimed domicile in Texas, but Florida, New York, and Massachusetts each claimed Ned was domiciled in their state.

| The estate tax claims were: | |
|---|---|
| United States | $17,520,987 |
| Texas | 4,685,057 |
| Florida | 4,663,857 |
| New York | 5,910,301 |
| Massachusetts | 4,947,008 |
| Total | $37,727,210 |

Unfortunately, his net estate was worth only $36,137,335. And New York made an additional claim for $920,827 of unpaid individual income taxes. That the heirs might receive nothing was of no concern to the states or the courts. But the estate was insufficient to satisfy all the competing tax claims. So, the states looked to the U.S. Supreme Court to resolve their dispute.

The Supreme Court appointed a special master who concluded that Massachusetts was Ned's domicile. The court did not intervene for the benefit of the estate, or the heirs, or even because of the conflicting claims. Rather, it intervened because of the bizarre fact that the states' claims on the estate exceeded its assets.

In accordance with his mother's wishes, Ned's will left nothing to his widow, everything to his sister. The will was written in 1908 and never revised. His widow signed a prenuptial agreement before they married in exchange for life income of $18,000 a year. She settled an estate dispute with Sylvia for an additional lump sum of $500,000.

Sylvia was worth $95 million when she died in 1951 at age 80, leaving no husband or children. The top estate tax rate was 77 percent, plus inheritance levies for New York and Canada. She left her estate to 63 charities, reserving some $2 million for other purposes on which $1.3 million estate tax was paid. Included was a $10,000 bequest to Robert Moses, in appreciation for his public work, which he promptly endorsed over to charity.

Hetty Green's wealth ranks among the greatest American fortunes of the Gilded Age. The $2 million inheritance she received as a young woman grew to $100 million by averaging a modest 7 percent annual return during her 60-year stewardship. It was an age of no income tax and low inflation – and she spent very little. Yet, her fortune eventually disappeared without a trace through estate taxes and contributions to too many charities. Her only legacy is Hetty Green Hall at Wellesley College, paid for by Ned and Sylvia with a $500,000 contribution (paid over five years) in the early 1920s.

## The Billionaire Without Character

When the Supreme Court heard the 2006 case of Anna Nicole Smith, it was not for the purpose of resolving an inheritance dispute between her and her late husband's son. The former stripper and Playboy Playmate of the Year was 26 when in 1994 she married 89-year-old billionaire oil tycoon J. Howard Marshall II. They did not live together, and he died 14 months later without providing for her in his will. Pierce Marshall, the tycoon's son, who was 29 years her senior, referred to Smith in private notes as "Miss Cleavage." Following a five-month trial, a Texas probate court jury determined that she was entitled to nothing. (The estate was represented by Rusty Hardin, who would later become lead Arthur Andersen attorney in the Enron trial.) A federal bankruptcy court later awarded her $470 million, reduced to $88.5 million by a federal district court, and to zero by a federal appeals court, which ruled that only state courts have jurisdiction over probate matters.

The salacious background that made headlines had no bearing on the U.S. Supreme Court's reasons for granting a rare hearing. Federal courts had a longstanding policy to defer to state courts in probate matters. Here was an opportunity to expand the scope of federal judicial authority. The case attracted eight amicus briefs against Smith and four in her favor. Those opposed included the State of Texas and the National College of Probate Judges, who feared losing power. In favor included the U.S. Solicitor General, which wanted to keep probate claims, especially tax matters, in federal court. The Supreme Court ruled unanimously for expansion, that probate needn't be restricted to state courts, and remanded the case back to lower courts for further proceedings. (Both Pierce and Anna Nicole died shortly after the Supreme Court decision.)

This wasn't the only case that Marshall's estate had to deal with as a result of his relationship with Smith. Fourteen months before their wedding, they visited a famous New York jeweler. While Marshall "relaxed" in his wheelchair for an hour, Smith picked out nearly $2 million in merchandise. That wasn't all he spent.

J. Howard Marshall II was born in 1905. He graduated from Yale Law School in 1931 *magna cum laude*, and became assistant dean. In 1933, he served as assistant solicitor to Department of Interior Secretary Harold Ickes, where he helped write oil and gas legislation and regulations. He became president of Ashland Oil and Refining Co. in 1944. He married Eleanor Pierce in 1931, with whom he had two sons, and divorced her in December 1960. In 1961, he married Bettye Bohannon, who was diagnosed with early signs of Alzheimer's in 1982.

Around November 1982, 77-year-old Marshall met 42-year-old Jewell Dianne ("Lady") Walker at a "gentlemen's club," where she and her daughter, Cerece, worked as strippers. At the time, Walker was living with a boyfriend while still married to her fourth husband. He began lavishing her with gifts to tune of about $2 million annually. Among the gifts was a 1987 Rolls Royce convertible valued at $175,000. In 1990, when he was 85, she convinced Marshall to purchase an insurance policy on his life naming her as beneficiary. The face value of the policy is not disclosed in the record, but the annual premium was $416,024. In addition, during the first 7½ years, he paid her $6,032,173 in cash.

Marshall had his lawyers write a "Personal Services Agreement" in September 1990, where "Walker agrees to act as Marshall's companion and escort at such times and such places as he reasonably requires." Her compensation was set at $25,000 per month but "Marshall may, in addition, pay additional amounts as Marshall and Walker shall from time to time agree." It also provided for "jewelry, furs and other accoutrements to permit her to carry out her responsibilities in the manner required by this contract."

So smitten was he that in an undated letter handwritten on his personal stationery, apparently in 1991, Marshall wrote to his son:

Dear Pierce

This package relates to a wonderful lady — indeed her nick name is "Lady." Without her I don't quite know how I would have survived these last nine years. She is intelligent, gracious and beautiful as her picture will attest. I am sure you will understand where others might not. I would marry her tomorrow if there was any honorable way. If I predecease you, as a father who loves you, I charge you to take care of her in any way she may need — financially and in all ways. I know I can trust you.

Dad

Lady Walker died suddenly on July 9, 1991 at the age of 51, the result of anesthesia complications from facelift surgery. Marshall's wife, Bettye, died later that same year. Then Marshall learned that his relationship with Walker had been a complete lie. She lived with two other lovers throughout their relationship, whom she kept hidden from Marshall. Money obtained from Marshall paid one lover's child support. Outraged, he sued her estate seeking the return of gifts he had given her over nine years.

This lawsuit came to the attention of Marshall's tax attorney, who realized that gift tax returns had never been filed. So, he filed late returns, reporting about $6 million in gifts. The IRS decided to audit and determined that he had made additional unreported gifts of over $14 million. The agency assessed nearly $17 million additional gift and generation-skipping transfer tax, before penalties and interest. They soon added another $5 million in unreported gifts to Anna Nicole.

Marshall died on August 4, 1995. The estate tried to introduce into evidence a report by Dr. Charles Gaitz, an expert in geriatric psychiatry. He had examined Marshall in 1992 and concluded that all the gifts Marshall gave to Walker from 1983 to 1991 resulted from undue influence she exercised over him and therefore were not gifts in the eyes of the tax law. The estate also argued that Marshall's premarital transactions involving Smith were not taxable gifts, but rather an investment in her image and persona. He was promoting her film career, through which he intended to generate a profit.

The lawsuit with Lady Walker's estate was settled in 1997, with Walker's children retaining many of the assets, including a 1990 Rolls Royce Corniche Convertible and 1991 Rolls Royce Silver Spur. (It was said that she used Rolls Royces as accessories to match her outfits.) The Walker tax issues with the IRS were settled for a fraction of what the tax agency was seeking. The Tax Court's case file for Anna Nicole Smith gift tax issues contains a tentative settlement, also for a fraction of the original assessment, pending resolution of Anna Nicole's claims against the estate.

Marshall disguised gifts as legitimate business operations by forming corporations which "employed" Lady Walker, enabling him to claim the gifts as tax deductions. (This is a common ploy to pass tax deductible money to mistresses. It also enables men to hide mistress support from their spouses.) The district court, ruling in the Anna Nicole case remarked that the "IRS may want to take a closer look at the summaries written on J. Howard's personal account, and passed on to his accountant, for illegitimate tax deductions."

"The amount and value of gifts from Marshall to Walker are simply mind-boggling," noted a 1997 IRS trial memorandum. The district court added in its 2002 decision that Marshall "taught [Anna Nicole] to spend money at a breathtaking pace that most Americans cannot fathom." It concluded, "this court is not impressed with the character of a man who had the finest private school and legal education and who consciously avoided the very taxes that millions of American families comply with every year. It is in the collection of these taxes that the government must rely on the good faith and honesty of our citizens to fund our nation's needs in time of peace and war. The fact that J. Howard could not see fit to comply with these laws, despite the great advantages that he was afforded by American society, speaks poorly of his character."

Forbes once listed Marshall as the wealthiest man in Texas and one of the 400 wealthiest men in America. He could have left a legacy of funding great charitable works. Instead, he will be remembered as the foolish octogenarian playboy who wasted millions chasing strippers.

Sometimes, the younger woman winds up in Tax Court over gift issues. Sebastian Kresge was founder of S.S. Kresge Company, which became K-Mart and merged into Sears Holdings. Today, he is best remembered for the millions he left to fund the S.S. Kresge Foundation and its charitable works. He was worth about $475 million in 1924, when he divorced his wife of 27 years, with whom he had five children, giving her $10 million in settlement, and married Doris Mercer a 31-year-old chorus girl and opera singer. Between 1923 and 1924, Mercer received $750,000 of S.S. Kresge Company stock from the 56-year-old founder in contemplation of divorcing his first wife, after which he promised to marry her.

They had a scandalous divorce in 1928, with front-page headlines and a multi-million dollar settlement. Mercer later married a cousin of the Shah of Iran and became Princess Farid-es-Sultaneh. She divorced him in 1936, but kept her princess title. A 1947 tax case valued the stock she received from Kresge in contemplation of divorcing his first wife. The appeals court reasoned that she had "purchased" the shares with an ante-nuptial contract (when she "sold" herself) and could use the $10.66 per share basis on the date she received the stock, rather than $0.159, which would have been the basis had it been a "gift."

**The Reclusive Philanthropist**

Billionaire Howard Hughes died on April 5, 1976 on an airplane carrying him from Acapulco, Mexico to Houston, Texas to seek medical treatment. He was an only child, left no undivorced wives, had no children, and no will.

California and Texas both claimed that Hughes was domiciled in their state at the time of his death. The combined federal, California and Texas estate taxes would be 101 percent of the estate. The heirs contended that he was domiciled in Nevada, which imposed no estate tax at that time. However, with no tax to collect, Nevada had no incentive for entering the fray.

Under California or Nevada laws, the estate would go to the closest relative, his 85-year-old aunt, who had not seen him in 39 years. However, in Texas, half the estate would go to maternal relatives and half to paternal relatives through first cousins once removed.

Hughes was born in Texas in 1905, but left as a teenager. He spent two days there in 1938, a few hours in 1948 to deliver an airplane, and stopped there in 1956 for a plane refueling on a trip from Florida to California without leaving the plane. During his lifetime, he often referred to Texas as his residence, perhaps because Texas had no income tax.

By contrast, he had spent 40 years in California, made his fortune there in movies, aviation and electronics, and had owned a residence there. He moved to Las Vegas in 1966 and took up residence at the

Desert Inn Hotel, one of several Las Vegas casinos he bought. He left the U.S. in 1970. For the last six years of his life, Hughes was a nomad, moving between hotels in the Bahamas, England, Canada, Nicaragua, and Mexico.

Living in hotels and moving between places would complicate proving that he had established a new domicile after leaving California. Hughes was certainly not a Texas domiciliary. However, a Houston probate court jury declared Howard Hughes a Texan, and therefore his estate should pay Texas taxes.

William Rice Lummis, son of Hughes' aunt, was appointed temporary administrator of the estate, together with other administrators in several states where Hughes had assets. The administrators argued that at the time of his death, Hughes was domiciled in Nevada. That would minimize the state estate taxes and minimize the number of heirs. After a newly discovered Texas branch of Hughes' extended family surfaced, Lummis worked out a complex agreement among the relatives on how to split the remainder of the estate, regardless of which state domicile was ultimately determined. This remarkable agreement allowed the estate to concentrate its attention on the fake wills, squabbles with Hughes' corporate managements, and state tax issues.

The administrators valued the estate at $168 million. The IRS countered with $460 million. California decided the estate was worth $1.1 billion. Through skillful negotiation, Lummis settled with the taxing authorities valuing the estate at $362 million, with $316 million in taxes going to IRS, Texas and California.

Delaying the estate tax for the years necessary to negotiate a settlement with IRS and the states, allowed Lummis to resuscitate some of Hughes' moribund businesses and turn them profitable. This allowed him and 21 other relatives to share $500 million, mostly post-mortem appreciation in value, after settling the tax bills.

Hughes' most valuable asset, Hughes Aircraft, was not part of his estate. It had been gifted to the Howard Hughes Medical Institute (HHMI) in 1953 as a colossal tax dodge. HHMI was incorporated for the purpose of engaging "primarily" (rather than "exclusively," as required by law to qualify for tax-exempt status) in promoting medical research. The IRS refused to recognize HHMI as an exempt organization until 1957 when it bowed to lobbying by the Hughes organization.

Hughes Tool Company donated to HHMI all its patents, trademarks, and goodwill. That generated a $2 million charitable tax deduction. As an added bonus, HHMI was able to record the patents, trademarks, and goodwill at a new $15 million fair market value. HHMI then "subleased" these inflated assets to Hughes Aircraft. The higher value generated by the sublease was passed on to government contracts, boosting the cost of future military hardware that the United States purchased from Hughes Aircraft.

Foundations were a common scheme for private enterprise to save taxes under the guise of charity, while the original owner retained control. The law changed in 1969 to restrict abuses using private foundations. When the IRS issued final regulations in 1971 to implement the new law, language was added that allowed "medical research organizations" to escape being classified as "private foundations," the result of lobbying by the Hughes organization. Otherwise HHMI would be a private foundation required to disburse substantial amounts for charitable purposes annually and risk penalties for "self-dealing."

As a result, HHMI funded relatively little medical research during Hughes' lifetime; only about $1 million per year. This allowed Hughes to control its assets, while avoiding income tax on the profits (except on "unrelated business income").

Following Hughes' death, HHMI sold Hughes Aircraft to General Motors Corp. for $5.2 billion in 1985, transforming the tax shelter into one of the world's great philanthropic institutions. Thus did the reclusive billionaire turn philanthropist.

### NYU's Macaroni Factory

Before 1951, there were many loopholes involving privately owned businesses under the guise of charity. At hearings in 1942, Treasury General Counsel Randolph Paul told the Ways and Means Committee about hotels operated by colleges, an orphans' home that operated a waterworks, electric power and gas company, and a charitable corporation that operated a bathing beach. They not only deprived the government of tax revenue, but also obliged privately owned businesses to compete at a disadvantage with businesses exempt from tax. The abuses expanded so that colleges were producing automobile parts, chinaware, food products, operating theatres, oil wells, and cotton gins.

The most famous of these was New York University Law School's macaroni factory. When Henry Mueller died in 1946, his heirs sold the company to the NYU School of Law for $3.5 million, financed with a loan. NYU reincorporated C.F. Mueller Co. as a tax-exempt charity on the theory that the destination, not the source, of income determined charitable status. The appeals court agreed with NYU that it indeed had a tax-exempt macaroni company. (NYU sold C.F. Mueller Co. in 1976 to Foremost-McKesson, Inc. for $115 million in cash.)

Congress changed the law so that beginning in 1951, such enterprises would be subject to an "unrelated business income tax" — unrelated to the charitable enterprise — subject to tax rates paid by corporations.

NYU was also the beneficiary of Knapp Shoe Manufacturing, which devised a novel approach for reducing its taxes. Rather than nondeductible "dividends" from the captive company, the school would receive "charitable contributions." Contributions are partially tax deductible by corporations and reduce taxable income. The appeals court ruled in 1970 that the payments to NYU were nondeductible dividends.

**Ted Turner**

Most children who inherit wealth lack their parents' abilities to earn similar wealth themselves. Ted Turner is an exception. He took his father's large billboard company and turned it into a huge media empire.

Concurrent with his resignation from AOL Time Warner, Turner announced on January 31, 2003 that he was changing his residence. Despite working for AOL in New York, Turner had continued to call his penthouse atop the CNN Center in Atlanta his official home, and paid Georgia income taxes. His spokesman explained that he felt a moral obligation to Georgia as founder of Turner Broadcasting and CNN, even though his accountants had urged him for years to list Florida, which has no individual state income tax, as his residence. He spent twice as much time in Florida, at his 25,000-acre Avalon Plantation outside Tallahassee, than Atlanta. Avalon is the family home where he spends Christmas, New Year's and Thanksgiving, and it's where he married Jane Fonda.

However, prior to January 31, 2003, Georgia was probably a cheaper tax state than Florida for billionaire Ted Turner. In April 2001, he owned 153 million shares of AOL, worth about $7.5 billion, at which time he began selling a substantial number of shares. Georgia imposed a 6 percent income tax. Florida imposed a 0.1 percent intangible tax. So, when his AOL shares were worth $7.5 billion, Turner would have had to pay an annual $7.5 million in Florida intangible tax, equivalent to Georgia income tax on $125 million annual income. While his annual investment income was less than $125 million, Georgia residency offered lower taxes than Florida. (His salary was taxable in New York and other states where he performed services, for which Georgia allowed a credit.)

After he switched residency to Florida, he sold $50 million of stock in February 2003, $5 million in March 2003, and 60 million shares (more than half his stake in AOL) for $790 million in April 2003, leaving him with 45 million shares. Had he not switched to Florida residency prior to selling $845 million in AOL shares, he would have owed $50 million in Georgia income tax, plus more as he sold additional shares. So, it probably saved taxes for him to continue as a Georgia tax resident prior to February 2003, and saved more by becoming a Florida resident afterwards.

Ted Turner pledged a stunning $1 billion to the United Nations in September 1997. The contribution had some interesting tax aspects. Direct contributions are not tax deductible because the U.N. is not a qualified charity. He organized the United Nations Foundation as a public charity, rather than a private foundation which required soliciting outside contributions and grants. Unlike a private foundation, a public charity is allowed to campaign on public issues, like pressuring the United States to pay its back dues to the U.N. He could fund contributions with appreciated stock in AOL Time Warner and avoid capital gain taxes on the appreciation. With a public charity, he could deduct stock contributions up to 30 percent of his income, rather than the 20 percent allowed to a private foundation. His gift was so generous, that he might never fully utilize the entire charitable deduction that would be available to him.

Ted Turner is generous with his time as well as money. I met him in 1985 when the Jewish National Fund named him the recipient of its "Tree of Life" award. The award is given annually in several cities to raise money by honoring a non-Jewish business leader. Turner gladly provided a list of his friends and associates that JNF could invite to the affair, at $175 per person, together with any other assistance required to make the event a success. It was very well attended. Just before the night of the dinner, Turner announced a takeover bid for CBS. He complained that he preferred speaking "off the cuff," and he was quite upset that on account of the proposed acquisition, his lawyers (wisely, because he had a few drinks) insisted he deliver a written speech.

## The Clintons

One of the saddest aspects of tax preparation is witnessing the low rate of charitable giving. A tax return with $500,000 income and $50,000 home mortgage interest often shows just $500 of charitable contributions. Others become addicted to charitable giving. I've never seen anyone harmed by giving ten percent. But when it rises above that, and it comes from income rather than accumulated wealth, financial problems ensue.

Some think the super wealthy are charity tightwads, citing 2006 figures compiled by *Slate*. Microsoft mogul Paul Allen, net worth $16 billion, gave away $53 million, one-third of one percent of his fortune. Software magnate Larry Ellison, net worth $20 billion, gave away $100 million, half of one percent. Pierre Omidyar, founder of eBay, net worth $7.7 billion, gave away $67 million, less than one percent. Nike tycoon Philip Knight, net worth $7.9 billion, gave away $105 million, little more than one percent. That's in a year when the stock market rose by 16 percent. Industrialist Andrew Carnegie, the richest man in his generation, gave away close to 90 percent of his fortune. In our generation, Bill Gates has pledged over 99 percent of his fortune to charity, beating Carnegie's record.

Bill and Hillary Clinton's tax returns tell the story of a very charitable-minded couple. They were generous before they achieved national office and wealth. This is probably their most underappreciated and underacknowledged attribute. (Of course there was the time when they gave bags of used clothes to charity, claiming up to $2,300 in annual tax deductions and supposedly valuing Bill's used underpants at $1 each, and $3 per used undershirt.) Today, Bill Clinton devotes more than half of his time to charity. His latest book, *Giving*, is a testament to this couple's dedication to charitable causes. But their tax returns also tell of dubious income sources.

The Arkansas governor appears to be the most underpaid position in America. His salary was just $35,000 in 1991. She was paid $110,000 at The Rose Law Firm, rather low for a partner in a prestigious firm, especially someone listed among the 100 most influential lawyers in America. She earned an additional $65,000 from director fees. And they earned $5,500 apiece in honoraria. It would appear that Bill Clinton was able to afford serving as governor because of his wife's earnings. Or, perhaps his wife's earnings were the result of his being governor. Fortunately, Arkansas provided a few perks: a $51,000 "mansion fund" and a $19,000 "public relations fund" which appear improperly omitted from income on their tax returns, at least to the extent not spent on official business.

The Clintons' outside financial ventures included the commodities trading and Whitewater scandals. On April 11, 1994, they paid nearly $15,000 to cover back taxes and interest on a $6,498 short-term capital gain attributable to Hillary's fantastic commodities trades in 1980. Though the statute of limitations had expired, they took responsibility and paid back-taxes and interest that they were legally not required to pay.

In the seven years after leaving the presidency, Bill and Hillary had gross income of over $110 million from which they made over $10 million in charitable contributions. Bill Clinton hit the lecture circuit, averaging almost a speech a day at upwards of $250,000 each. He received remuneration for only about 20 percent of those speeches, but those earned him almost $52 million in speaking fees. (Ronald Reagan was criticized for making $2 million lecturing in Japan after leaving office, and Jimmy Carter and George H.W. Bush also earned substantial sums on the lecture circuit.)

### TRUMAN

Harry Truman wrote about the fabulous salaries he was offered after leaving the White House in 1953:

> I turned down all of those offers. I knew that they were not interested in hiring Harry Truman, the person, but what they wanted to hire was the former President of the United States. I could never lend myself to any transaction, however respectable, that would commercialize on the prestige and the dignity of the office of the presidency.

> He turned speaking honorariums over to the Truman Library. This was a major sacrifice because Truman subsisted on his meager army pension. There was no federal pension for former President Truman or his predecessors until 1958. Visit the Truman Home in Independence, Missouri to see his modest lifestyle.

When Hillary Clinton wrote her first book, *It Takes a Village*, she dedicated all earnings to charity — over $1 million in total. Commentators suggested that she was given poor tax advice because she should have contributed the copyright to charity, thus excluding all the income from appearing on her tax return and maximizing the amount going to charity. But that would have hidden the charitable deductions. Perhaps she wanted that the public see the extent of her generosity.

Tens of thousands of dollars of self-employment tax were paid on the book royalties. Hillary has written four books. Bill has written two. The IRS exempts royalties from the first book a person writes as a sideline from self-employment tax. So perhaps their taxes were substantially overpaid by not claiming exemption from self-employment taxes on royalties from Hillary's *It Takes a Village* and Bill's *My Life*. (Jimmy Carter also paid unnecessary self-employment tax on his first book, *Why Not the Best?* So did First Lady Laura Bush on her first book, *Read All About It!*)

Dozens of articles have been written on whether their tax returns were properly prepared or planned. The Clintons established a defense fund for the impeachment proceedings. Some tax commentators suggested that they were required to report contributions to the legal defense fund as income, which they did not. Despite the publicity, there was no word on whether IRS examined their returns.

**Beyond Taxes**

Tax practitioners know that the tax returns we prepare and the tax controversies we win or lose will soon be forgotten. This book has reviewed our nation's many famous (and forgotten) tax heroes. Yet, their greatest legacy may be the humanitarian works they performed. Among the most accomplished tax practitioners were Treasury General Counsel Randolph Paul and Supreme Court Justice Robert Jackson. They pursued social justice with the same zeal that they applied to tax conflicts.

Henry Morgenthau enlisted his staff at the Treasury Department in an attempt to influence President Roosevelt to save the Jews of Europe. He had Randolph Paul prepare a report, "On the Acquiescence of This Government in the Murder of the Jews," which charged the State Department with procrastination and willful failure to act. Paul, a non-Jewish Wall Street lawyer, believed that U.S. inaction amounted to *para-delicto*, of equal guilt.

On January 16, 1944 Morgenthau, accompanied by Randolph Paul and John W. Pehle, presented this report with the toned-down title, "A Personal Report to the President." A few days later, Roosevelt issued Executive Order 9417, establishing the War Refugee Board, charged with rescuing "victims of enemy oppression" and establishing temporary sanctuaries.

Pehle was named executive director of the new agency. It brought 918 Jews from liberated Italy to Oswego, New York, 35 miles northwest of Syracuse. The July 1944 issue of *Jewish Frontier* called the action "impressive neither as a practical measure of alleviation nor even as a gesture." The camp was operated by the War Relocation Authority, the same agency that interred Japanese-Americans, and Jewish detainees were treated just as poorly, until released by President Truman in December 1945. Some argue that the War Refugee Board brought intangible benefits that played a crucial role in saving some 200,000 Jews in Europe. Others brand it a failure.

At the close of court in June 1945, Supreme Court Justice Robert Jackson began a one-year leave of absence to serve as chief U.S. prosecutor at the Nuremberg trials. Although history has validated international justice pioneered at the Nuremberg trials by its application against later perpetrators of genocide, Jackson's career detour was very controversial in 1945. Chief Justice Harlan Fiske Stone was his most bitter critic:

> Jackson is away conducting his high-grade lynching party in Nuremberg. I don't mind what he does to the Nazis, but I hate to see the pretense that he is running a court and proceeding according to common law. This is a little too sanctimonious a fraud to meet my old-fashioned ideas.

Jackson convinced former Third Circuit Court Judge Francis Biddle (who succeeded Jackson as attorney general in the Roosevelt administration) to serve as one of the Nuremberg judges. Their mission was successful, but Jackson paid a heavy price. Chief Justice Stone died while Jackson was away. His absence and involvement at Nuremberg were among the reasons that Jackson wasn't nominated for chief justice. Yet, shortly before he died, Jackson wrote that his service at Nuremberg was "the most important, enduring, and constructive work of my life."

Volunteering, doing what is right, and giving to charity have their own rewards, which are not predicated on tax benefits.

> We are under no illusions about the power of money, but it is silly to dismiss it as worthless. It is not. It means many good things. It represents dormitories, classrooms, hospitals. It represents research facilities and the priceless efforts of men of creative skill and genius. But money alone cannot build character or transform evil into good; it might as well stay in the vaults. It becomes palsied and impotent. It cries for full partnership with leaders of character and good will who value good tools in the creation and enlargement of life for Man, who is created in the Image of God.
>
> —Stanley S. Kresge

# Notes

The internet was an invaluable resource in piecing together common threads between stories, as well as biographical information such as provided at the website, Biographical Directory of the United States Congress. As this book progressed, many of the works that I traveled the country to read began appearing on the internet. Google Books has posted many of the old books that I spent days researching at the New York Public Library. California has posted its old statute books on the internet.

Many citations refer to court cases and law journals. All the Supreme Court cases (those with "US" in the middle) are accessible online. Many other publications are accessible online through the respective courts or through university libraries. Links to internet accessible materials are available at www.starkman.com.

Some abbreviations for publications and law books that appear in these notes:

| | |
|---|---|
| AC | Atlanta Constitution |
| AICPA | American Institute of Certified Public Accountants |
| AJC | Atlanta Journal-Constitution |
| AJ | Atlanta Journal |
| CPAJ | The CPA Journal |
| GAO | Government Accountability Office / General Accounting Office |
| IRC | Internal Revenue Code |
| JCT | Joint Committee on Taxation |
| JoA | Journal of Accountancy |
| JTax | Journal of Taxation |
| LAT | Los Angeles Times |
| NYT | New York Times |
| STT | State Tax Notes / State Tax Today |
| TNT | Tax Notes / Tax Notes Today |
| WP | Washington Post |
| WSJ | Wall Street Journal |

| | |
|---|---|
| CA-# | Court of Appeals - circuit # |
| CB | Cumulative Bulletin |
| EO | Executive Order |
| ET | AICPA Ethics Ruling |
| FR | Federal Register |
| PL | Public Law |
| TC | Tax Court Reports |
| TCM | Tax Court Memorandum Decision |
| TD | Treasury Decision |
| US | United States Supreme Court Reports |
| aff'd/aff'g | affirmed/affirming |
| cert den | certiorari denied (U.S. Supreme Court refused the appeal) |
| reh'g den | rehearing denied |
| rev'd\rev'g | reversed\reversing |

## CHAPTER 1: REMEMBER, YOU'RE AN ACCOUNTANT

3   Jane Mayer, "The Accountant's War," *The New Yorker*, 22 Apr 2002, 64.
3   **insomniac wife.** "The rage for complete solutions," *The Economist*, 5 Jul 2001.
4   **Charles Lamb.** R. Robert, "The Accountant in Literature," JoA, Mar 1957, 64; Charles Lamb, "The South-Sea House," *The Essays of Elia* (1823).
4   **Adding Machine.** Brooks Atkinson, *Broadway* (NY: The MacMillan Company, 1970), 123, 215; Ludwig Lewisohn, "Creative Irony," *The Nation*, 4 Apr 1923, 399. It ran for just nine weeks, 72 performances. "It has been revived a thousand times since, because its comments on an automated society now seem more relevant than ever." Edward G. Robinson, *All My Yesterdays* (NY: Hawthorn Books, 1973 (Signet Paperback edition, 1975)), 82-83, 346.
4   **new depths.** Tony Dimnik and Sandra Felton, "Accountant stereotypes in movies distributed in North America in the twentieth century," *Accounting, Organizations and Society*, Vol. 31, Iss. 2 (Oxford: Feb 2006), 129. They identified five accounting stereotypes: dreamer, plodder, eccentric, hero and villain.
4   **Zero Mostel.** "Zero Mostel Is Dead at 62," NYT, 9 Sep 1977; Arthur Sainer, *Zero Dances* (NY: Limelight Editions, 1988), 65; Phil Fink, "More on Mostel," *The Jewish Press*, 8 Jul 2005, 63. Fink was host of *Shalom America*, a Jewish radio program broadcast from Cleveland. He interviewed Mostel around 1975: "Mostel told me his [Hebrew] name was Yoel Simcha (Joel Sidney in English)."
5   **Death Wish.** Brian Garfield, *Death Wish*, (NY: Mysterious Press, 1985); Lee Burton, "Why You Never Saw Charles Bronson Cast as Hero Accountant," WSJ, 26 Apr 1984.
5   **Bob Newhart.** Alison L. Cowan, "CPA Rallying Cry: Dull No More!" NYT, 21 Dec 1989, D1.
6   **production accountant.** *Within A Minute*, a documentary about the filmmaking process explains the importance of production accountants and puts them *before* the caterers. Dreadful interviewees explain that they are the first to arrive and the last to leave so that the books balance. Available on Disc Two, Special Features, *Star Wars III: Revenge of the Sith*.
6   **Ritalin.** "Ritalin Controversy: A `Miracle Drug' Gets Closer Look," LAT, 28 Dec 1987, 1; "Sales Of Drug Are Soaring For Treatment Of Hyperactivity," NYT, 5 May 1987, C3.
6   **Funniest Accountant.** Mike Tierney, "The jokes add up — perfectly. Accountants make fun at own expense," AJC, 21 Oct 2005, A1.
6   Maureen Dowd, "Her Brute Strength," NYT, 17 Sep 2000, IV:19.
7   **same fate as dentists.** "Accountant Hopes To Sweeten Tax Season," *San Jose Mercury News*, 4 Feb 2001, 8F.
7   **washing windows.** "Which Spouse Wields The Power at Tax Time?" NYT, 11 Apr 1999, III:9.
7   **sex of a hippopotamus.** "Business Bookshelf," NYT, 29 Jun 1953, 31.
7   "Why I Became a CPA," JoA, Oct 2005, 79.

8   **Clark Kent.** Stephen T. Duffy, Letter to the Editor, WSJ, 9 May 1984.
8   **Michael G. Verner,** "Perception is Everything," *Current Accounts*, Jan-Feb 2003, Georgia Society of CPAs.
8   **Audit Brothers.** Lee Burton, "Why You Never Saw Charles Bronson Cast as Hero Accountant," WSJ, 26 Apr 1984.
8   **ingenious financial schemes.** Jack Bologna, Letter to the Editor, WSJ, 9 May 1984.
8   **Jeffrey Skilling.** "Cleaning Up the Boardroom," NYT, 8 Mar 2002, A20.
9   **David Duncan.** "Andersen Partner Says He Came to Accept Guilt," NYT, 16 May 2002, C1; *Andersen v U.S.*, 544 US 696 (2005).
9   **Harley-Davidson.** Dave Ulrich, Jack Zenger and Norm Smallwood, *Results-Based Leadership* (Boston: Harvard Business School Press, 1999), 38.
9   **Neville Chamberlain.** Keith Feiling, *The Life of Neville Chamberlain* (London: MacMillan & Co., 1947) 12; William R. Rock, *Neville Chamberlain* (NY: Twayne Publishers, 1969), 22. Howard Smith was founded in 1867 and merged into Price Waterhouse in 1963.
9   **John Grisham.** Eric Jensen, "The Heroic Nature of Tax Lawyers," 140 *Univ. of Penn. Law Review* 367 (Nov 1991), 371 FN22.
9   **style of Lewis Carroll.** Kurt H. Schaffir, "Random Sampling Is Useful When the Auditor Has No Prior Knowledge of Where Discrepancies Might Be Located," *The Michigan Certified Public Accountant*, Jan-Feb 1968, vol. 19, no. 4; reprinted by courtesy of the Michigan Association of CPAs.
10  **I Married an Accountant,** Joe Queenan, *Newsweek*, 14 Nov 1988, 12.

## CHAPTER 2: KAROSHI

11  **Caesar Augustus.** George S. Boutwell, *Excise and Internal Revenue Laws of the United States*, (Washington: Govt. Printing Office, 1863). The inscription was apparently handwritten on the fly-leaf of a copy owned by the author's friend, John Quincy Adams Griffin. See George S. Boutwell, *Reminiscences of Sixty Years in Public Affairs* (NY: Greenwood Press, 1968), vol. I, 312 (reprint of McClure, Phillips & Co. edition of 1902).
11  **25 karoshi deaths.** Peter Hartcher, *The Ministry: How Japan's Most Powerful Institution Endangers World Markets* (Boston: Harvard Business School Press, 1998), 22-23.
11  **Big Eight dad.** Beth Hurst, "A CPA: Seen through the eyes of his teenage daughter," JoA, Sep 1972, 106; Sylvia Ann Hewlett and Carolyn Buck Luce, "Extreme Jobs: The Dangerous Allure of the 70-Hour Workweek," *Harvard Business Review*, Dec 2006, 49, 54.
12  **Following mergers.** "Big accounting firms reap the rewards of Sarbanes-Oxley," *Financial Times*, 23 Aug 2007, 19; "Public Accounting Firms," GAO-03-864 (Jul 2003); "Accounting Firm Consolidation," GAO-03-1158 (Sep 2003).
13  **SEC reports.** SEC Regulation S-K, Item 402 (Executive Compensation), 17 C.F.R. §229.402.
13  **time management.** Bernard Isaacson, editor, *Guides to Successful Accounting Practice, A Selection of Material from The Journal of Accountancy's Practitioner's*

16 **Telex.** *Telex Corp. v IBM*, 376 FSupp 258, 347 (DC-N Okla, 1973), aff'd in part and rev'd in part, *510 F2d 894* (CA-10, 1975), *cert dismissed*, 423 US 802 (1975); *Floyd Walker v U.S.*, 202 F3d 1290 (CA-10, 2000), (DC-N Okla, No. CV-97-672-BU); "Control Data Settlement Seen as Setback By Others Suing IBM," WSJ, 22 January 1973; "IBM Discloses Plan for Separating Its Computer and Services Prices," WSJ, 24 Jun 1969, 38; "Telex Asks $877 Million In Damages From IBM for Alleged Monopoly," WSJ, 25 Jan 1972, 21; "Telex-IBM Trial Begins," WSJ, 13 Apr 1973, 9; "IBM Loses Antitrust Action for First Time," WSJ, 18 Sep 1973, 3.

17 **IBM History.** William Rodgers, *Think: A Biography of the Watsons and IBM* (NY: Stein and Day, 1969).

20 **Congregation Mount Sinai.** Telephone interview with Bennett Aaron, son of Rabbi Isadore Aaron who served Congregation Mount Sinai for 50 years. "Scrolls Are Saved in Synagogue Fire," NYT, 5 Jan 1948; "Stars to Aid Congregation," NYT, 21 Apr 1950.

21 **Lyndon Johnson.** Victor Lasky, *It Didn't Start With Watergate*, (NY: The Dial Press, 1977), 129-130; Bobby Baker, *Wheeling and Dealing* (NY: W.W. Norton & Co., 1978), 83, 185, 195-196; Suzanne Garment, *Scandal: The Culture of Mistrust in American Politics* (NY: Random House, 1991), 23-25; "Bobby's Busyness," *Time*, 31 Jan 1964; "Jenkins Denies Using Pressure," NYT, 25 Feb 1965, 1 (beneficiary was the LBJ Company).

25 **subway tokens.** "Discount Subway Token Sale Barred," NYT, 29 Jul 1976, 35:3; "2 States Seek Fraud Suspect's Funds," NYT, 4 Aug 1976, 37:4; "Order Given in Subway Token Case," NYT, 20 Aug 1976, II:22; "Cut-Rate Tokens — Lefky Throws Block," *New York Post*, 3 Aug 1976, 16.

26 **EFTPS.** Jay Starkman, "Are You Ready for EFTPS?" TTA, Apr 1997, 230.

27 **children on...welfare.** "Welfare Figures Cited in Report; Study Finds More Children Get Aid Than the Census Lists for Whole City," NYT, 27 May 1976, 36.

28 **Evelyn Davis** is still plaguing annual meetings. "Buzz off? Not this gadfly," AJC, 22 May 2005, F1. For a delightful comedy about a corporate gadfly, see *The Solid Gold Cadillac* with Judy Holliday (1956).

30 **scantily clad models.** "How to Dodge the IRS and Not Get Burned," *American Photographer*, May 1980. Articles like this always sell magazines in early April, as tax deadline approaches.

33 **J.K. Lasser merged.** "Why Lasser Found Touche Ross Taxing," *Fortune*, 18 May 1981. The article missed the root cause of the failure.

34 **eleven professionals.** Jay Starkman, "H.R. 10 plans: use of U.S. Retirement Plan Bonds after age 70½," TTA, Mar 1978, 141; WSJ, front page quote, 30 Apr 1997.

35 **fast-food chain.** *Cindy's Inc. v U.S.*, 740 F2d 851, 84-2 USTC ¶9763 (CA-11) (improperly paid the withholding taxes of a related company because of a mix-up in tax deposit forms); *Conklin Bros. of Santa Rosa, Inc.*, 986 F2d 315, 93-1 USTC ¶50,116 (CA-9) (bookkeeper improperly handled payroll tax deposits).

## CHAPTER 3: THE GLAMOROUS WORLD OF TAX ACCOUNTING

38  **The tax expert!** Louis Auchincloss, *The Partners* (Boston: Houghton Mifflin Company, 1974), 30.

40  **Treasury Inspector General.** "Opportunities Exist to Improve Tax Software Packages," Treasury Inspector General for Tax Administration, Jan 2005, Ref. No. 2005-40-025.

40  **offshore.** "The Truth About Tax Outsourcing," *CPA Computer Report*, Dec 2003; *San Francisco Chronicle* articles by David Lazarus: "A tough lesson on medical privacy. Pakistani transcriber threatens UCSF over back pay," 22 Oct 2003; "Bank of America to send tech work, data to India," 29 Oct 2003; "Pakistani threatened UCSF to get paid, she says," 12 Nov 2003; "Looking Offshore. Outsourced UCSF notes highlight privacy risk. How one offshore worker sent tremor through medical system," 28 Mar 2004; "Prognosis poor for privacy," 30 May 2004; also Liz Figueroa, "When private information goes abroad, security must follow," 4 Jun 2004.

44  **broker is not your friend.** C.C. Williams, "Do It Yourself!" *Sky*, Jan 2001, 96 (quoting investment advisor Al Bloomquist Jr.).

46  **IRS assessed Barrister.** *In re Tax Refund Litigation*, 698 FSupp 439 (EDNY, 1988), 766 FSupp 1248 (EDNY, 1991); *Barrister Associates*, 989 F2d 1290 (CA-2, 1993); *Irving Cohen*, 87-0265-CIV (SD Fla, 1994); *Paul F. Belloff*, TCM 1992-346; *Barrister Equipment Associates*, TC Memo 1994-205. Individuals continue to litigate: *Smith v U.S.*, 328 F3d 760 (CA-5, 2003), *Monahan*, 321 F3d 1063 (CA-11, 2003), aff'g TCM 2002-52; *Goettee*, 124 TC 17 (2005), aff'd 2006 TNT 146-17 (CA-4, No. 05-1975, 7/28/2006).

48  **upheld the windfall deduction.** *Gitlitz v Commissioner*, 531 US 206 (2001).

49  **conformity preference.** "Yes, ten million people can be wrong," *The Economist*, 19 Feb 1994: "[P]eople often have only limited knowledge; some things are unknown, or cost too much to find out. But everyone knows something. So, by watching what others do, each consumer can tap their information and so improve his own decision-making. Indeed, in many situations, it can make more sense to imitate other people than to try to work out the right thing to do for yourself. When it does, an informational cascade, in which the search for information leads a great mass of consumers to follow a few leaders, is likely."

52  **Falcons season tickets.** This is a rather commonplace issue. See "When couples split, who gets custody of Masters tickets?" AJC, 8 Apr 2004.

53  **Show World.** *303 West 42nd Street Enterprises, Inc. v IRS*, 916 FSupp 349 (SDNY 1996), 79 AFTR2d ¶97-338; reversed and remanded, 181 F3d 272, 274-76 (CA-2, 1999), 83 AFTR2d ¶99-939, 6/18/99; IRS upheld on remand, 86 AFTR2d ¶2000-5088.

54  **The Pagans.** "Pagans vs. Hells Angels: One Dead, 73 Arrested," Associated Press, 24 Feb 2002; "Long Island Biker Gangs Clash," WP, 2 Mar 2002.

56  **math homework.** Inspired by Jacqueline A. Hershey, "How Schools Sabotage A Creative Work Force," *Business Week*, 13 Jul 1987.

61  **Searchlight Nevada.** *Ralph Louis Vitael, Jr.*, TCM 1999-131.
61  **Roller Coaster.** "17 hours a day on the rails to nowhere," AJC, 16 Apr 1998, J1; "What a scream! 3 just won't quit," AJC, 30 Apr 1998, A1; "Coasting into the driver's seat. Three Scream Machine holdouts all win Jeeps after 12,456 rides," AJC, 12 May 1998, B1.
63  **prize Jeep.** In 2004, Oprah Winfrey gave all 276 audience members a new Pontiac 2005 G6 sedan, courtesy of Pontiac, which paid the sales tax. Then came the income tax bill, estimated at around $6,000 each. Sheldon I. Banoff and Richard M. Lipton, "Oprah's Car Giveaway: A Taxing Experience," JTax, Dec 2004, 382; "Oprah's Audience Gets Another Lesson In Taxes," JTax, Jan 2005, 63 (citing *Chicago Sun Times* "Car Winners Finding Out There is No Free Lunch," 20 Sep 2004, 11, and "Greene Back to Remind Us of the Good OP Days," *Chicago Sun-Times*, 24 Nov 2004, 11). But even smaller prizes come with a tax bill attached Should one accept that $495 leather duffel bag prize when it brings a $200 income tax? How about celebrity gift and goodie bags handed out at the Oscars, reportedly worth over $100,000? IRS "reminded" the 2006 recipients to make sure they report the goodies as taxable income. "IRS Statement on Oscar Goodie Bags," www.irs.gov/newsroom/article/0,,id=154941,00.html, 3 Mar 2006; Sheldon I. Banoff and Richard M. Lipton, "And The Losers Are...All The Oscar Nominees!" 104 JTax 250 (Apr 2006).

## CHAPTER 4: TURNING A PROFESSION INTO AN INDUSTRY

65  **I'm motivated by money.** Barbara Ley Toffler, *Final Accounting: Ambition, Greed, and the Fall of Arthur Andersen* (NY: Broadway Books, 2003), 115.
65  **KPMG.** "Narrow Escape. How a Chastened KPMG Got By Tax-Shelter Crisis," WSJ, 15 Feb 2007, 1.
65  **John Cook.** Letters, AJC, 3 Mar 2002, E9.
66  **Bookkeeper to Technician.** A.C. Littleton, *Accounting Evolution to 1900* (NY: American Institute Publishing Co., 1933); John L. Carey & William O. Doherty, *Ethical Standards of the Accounting Profession* (NY: AICPA, 1966); Robert L. Hagerman, "Accounting in the Bible," JoA, Jun 1982, 48-52, and *Accounting Historians Journal* (Fall 1980), 71-76.
66  **Roman numeral.** John W. Durham, "The Introduction of 'Arabic' Numerals in European Accounting," *Accounting Historians Journal*, Vol. 19, No. 2 (Dec 1992), 25; David W. Maher & John F. Makowski, "Literary evidence for Roman arithmetic with fractions," *Classical Philology*, Oct 2001, 376-399.
67  **mural slab** inscription is from a reference to chancel of St. Mary's Church, Chesham, Buckinghamshire, England by a correspondent in *The Accountant*, 1 Jan 1884, Littleton, 261.
68  **internal auditing.** Frank Lamperti & John Thurston, *Internal Auditing for Management* (NY: Prentice-Hall, 1953), 164-165.
68  **joint stock company,** predecessor of the modern corporation, was a popular form of doing business in the nineteenth century. It was a hybrid of corporation and

partnership characteristics. Like a corporation, the company was owned by shareholders who were free to sell their stock. Like a partnership, shareholders were liable for all debts of the company. Business was transacted by the organization using the "joint" capital invested by members who shared proportionately in the profits and losses.

69   **Frank Broaker.** JoA, May 1998, 109; "The First Century of the CPA," JoA, Oct 1996, 51-57.

69   **first black CPA.** JoA, May 2003, 78, reviewing Theresa A. Hammond, *A White-Collar Profession: African American Certified Public Accountants Since 1921* (Chapel Hill: "The University of North Carolina Press, 2002); Phaedra Brotherton, "A History of Determination," JoA, May 2003, 75; Bert N. Mitchell and Virginia L. Flintall, "The Status of the Black CPA: Twenty Year Update," JoA, Aug 1990, 59.

69   **Fortune.** "Certified Public Accountants," *Fortune*, Jun 1932, 62.

72   **Government Commercializes.** Kenneth J. Bialkin, "Government Antitrust Enforcement and the Rules of Conduct," JoA, May 1987, 105; old anti-contingent fee rule: ET §391.023-.024; Rule 302; consultants as principals, not partners: 1962 Rule 3.04; "AICPA Council approves non-CPA ownership," JoA, Oct 1994, 135.

72   **rejected...special status.** *Goldfarb v Virginia State Bar*, 421 US 773 (1975); *National Soc. of Professional Engineers v U.S.*, 435 US 679 (1978); *Virginia Pharmacy Board v Virginia Citizens Consumer Council*, 425 US 748 (1976); *Bates v State Bar of Arizona*, 433 US 350 (1977).

72   **AICPA's counsel.** "Report of the Special Committee on Solicitation," AICPA, 1981.

72   **Federal Trade Commission.** "FTC Order Concerning Restraints on CPAs," JoA, Oct 1990, 35-39; "AICPA Adopts Rules of Conduct Under FTC Final Order," JoA, Nov 1990, 31.

72   **contingent fees.** Rule 302 — Contingent Fees, effective May 20, 1991. JoA, Sep 1991, 167.

73   **admit non-CPA consultants.** "Revised Council Resolution Concerning Form of Organization and Name," JoA, Oct 1994, 135 (requiring 66-2/3 percent ownership by CPAs), reversing "Council Resolution Concerning Form of Organization and Name," JoA, Jun 1992, 143 (affirming that all owners must be CPAs); Anita Dennis, "The Case for Non-CPA Ownership," JoA, Dec 1994, 77.

73   **The Consulting Challenge.** Robert Mednick and Gary John Previts, "The Scope of CPA Services," JoA, May 1987, 220 at 224; Kenneth S. Axelson, "Are Consulting and Auditing Compatible?," JoA, Apr 1963, 54. "'Audit-Related Fees' to Ernst Were for Janitorial Inspections," WSJ, 11 Jun 2003; "Ernst & Young Gets SEC Penalty For Ties to Client," WSJ, 19 Apr 2004, A3; A.P. Richardson and George O. May, "The Accountant's True Sphere," JoA, Sep 1925, 190-191.

74   **like any other salesman.** "Before Enron, Greed Helped Sink The Respectability of Accounting," WSJ, 14 Mar 2002, 1 (also gives a brief history of accounting);

Cassell Bryan-Low, "Field's 'Wolf' Culture Drove BDO's Tax-Service Growth," WSJ, 12 Aug 2002, 1; Cassell Bryan-Low, "Accounting Firms Face Backlash Over the Tax Shelters They Sold," WSJ, 7 Feb 2003, A1.

74  **$2.69 in non-audit fees.** SEC Commissioner Harvey J. Goldschmid, "Post-Enron America: An SEC Perspective," Third Annual A.A. Sommer, Jr. Corporate Securities & Financial Law Lecture, Fordham University School of Law, 2 Dec 2002.

75  **extol their IT talents.** SEC Chairman Arthur Levitt, "A Profession at the Crossroads," speech before National Association of State Boards of Accountancy, Boston, 18 Sep 2000.

75  **Philip B. Chenok,** *Foundations for the Future: The AICPA From 1980 to 1995* (Stamford, CT: JAI Press, 2000), 85.

76  **naive soliloquy.** 1973 AICPA Code of Professional Ethics, ET §52.17.

77  **value billing.** "Thoughts on Value Billing," *The Practicing CPA*, Jan 1991, 1; "Value Billing," *The Practicing CPA*, Nov 1987, 1.

77  **Federal Reserve Bulletin.** John L. Carey, *The Rise of the Accounting Profession, From Technician to Professional, 1896 - 1936* (NY: AICPA, 1969), 133, 159-160; William D. Cooper and Ida B. Robinson, "Who Should Formulate Accounting Principles? The Debate Within the SEC," JoA, May 1987, 137.

78  **SEC delegated.** SEC Accounting Series Release No. 4.

78  **unfettered expression.** *Appalachian Power Company, Ohio Power Company and Indiana & Michigan Electric Company, Plaintiffs, v American Institute of Certified Public Accountants, L. H. Penney, William W. Werntz and Carman G. Blough, Defendants*, 177 FSupp 345 (USDC-SDNY, 5/20/1959); aff'd, 268 F2d 844 (CA-2, 6/17/1959), cert den 361 US 887 (11/9/1959).

78  **investment tax credit.** APB Opinion No. 2, "Accounting for the 'Investment Credit'," (Dec 1962); APB Opinion No. 4, "Accounting for the 'Investment Credit'," (Mar 1964). "[N]o taxpayer shall be required to use, for purposes of financial reports subject to the jurisdiction of any Federal agency or reports made to any Federal agency, any particular method of accounting for the credit," Revenue Act of 1971, PL 92-178, §101(c); "Accounting-Rules Board Backs Down on Change," 4 Dec 1967, 92; "Accounting Is Too Political," NYT, 5 Sep 1971, F12; "Tighter Accounting Urged on Tax Credit," NYT, 4 Nov 1971, 69; "Senate Bars Rule Change, Accounting Unit Favored," NYT, 19 Nov 1971, 63; "Debate Lingers on Accountants," 25 Jan 1973, 52.

78  **Wheat Commission.** "Objectives of Accounting Study Groups," JoA, Jul 1971, 70; "The Trueblood Committee Hearings," JoA, Jul 1972, 134.

79  **SEC concurred.** SEC Accounting Series Release No. 150 which recognized FASB pronouncements as GAAP.

79  **tough stance.** Arthur R. Wyatt and James C. Gaa, "Accounting Professional — A Fundamental Problem and the Quest for Fundamental Solutions," CPAJ, Mar 2004.

79  **rule checkers.** Shyam Sunder, "Rethinking the Structure of Accounting and Auditing," keynote address, Sixth International Accounting Conference, Indian

Accounting Association Research Foundation, Calcutta, 11 Jan 2003; Arthur Levitt, "Standards Deviation," WSJ, 9 Mar 2007, A15 (and rejoinder by Robert E. Denham, WSJ, 26 Mar 2007, A13).

79   **presented fairly.** John C. Burton, "Fair Presentation: Another View," Saxe Lectures in Accounting, Baruch College, 18 Feb 1975; "The Future of the Accounting Profession," The American Assembly (founded by Dwight D. Eisenhower and affiliated with Columbia University), 2003, 7 [www.americanassembly.org]; William T. Baxter, "Accounting Standards: Boon or Curse?" Saxe Lectures in Accounting, Baruch College, 13 Feb 1979.

80   **Continental Vending.** *U.S. v Simon*, 425 F.2d 796 (2d Cir. 1969); Ronald M. Mano, Matthew Mouritsen, and Ryan Pace, "Principles-Based Accounting, It's Not New, It's Not the Rule, It's the Law," CPAJ, Feb 2006; "On Principles-Based Accounting and *Continental Vending*," Letters to the Editor, CPAJ, Jun 2007.

80   **Congress investigated.** "Why Everybody's Jumping On The Accountants These Days," *Forbes*, 15 Mar 1977.

80   **stock options.** "Senators Lobby S.E.C. Chief To Delay New Options Rule," NYT, 8 Oct 2004; "Accounting for Stock-Based Compensation," FASB 123R; FASB Staff Position Nos. 123(R)-1, (R)-2, (R)-3; SEC Staff Accounting Bulletin 107 (Mar 2005); "SEC Chief Accountant Praises Options-Expensing Decision," WSJ, 16 Dec 2004; Nicholas G. Apostolou and D. Larry Crumbley, "Accounting for Stock Options: Update on the Continuing Conflict," CPAJ, Aug 2005.

80   **Lieberman.** "Accounting Board Yields on Stock Options," NYT, 15 Dec 1994, D1.

81   **Off-balance-sheet financing.** Arthur R. Wyatt, "Liabilities Belong in the Footnote — or do They?" *Georgia Journal of Accounting*, Spring 1983; "Accounting Hall of Fame, 1998 Induction: Arthur Ramer Wyatt," *Accounting Historians Journal*, vol. 26, no. 1, Jun 1999, 153 at 162.

82   **fair market value.** Eugene H. Flegm, "Accounting at a Crossroad," CPAJ, Dec 2005 (citing *Business Week*, 15 Feb 2002); "Blackstone Tests Fairness of Using 'Fair Value' Rule," WSJ, 18 Apr 2007, C1; "The Role of Fair Value Accounting in the Subprime Mortgage Meltdown," JoA, May 2008.

82   **answering critics.** L. Todd Johnson, "Relevance and Reliability," *The FASB Report*, 28 Feb 2005.

82   **earnings management.** "Arthur Levitt Addresses 'Illusions'," JoA, Dec 1998, 12; Paul Rosenfeld, "What Drives Earnings Management," JoA, Oct 2000, 106; SEC Chairman Arthur Levitt, "The 'Numbers Game'," Address at the NYU Center for Law and Business, 28 Sep 1998 (cookie jars); SEC Litigation Release No. 18403, 9 Oct 2003 (Enron).

83   **Sarbanes-Oxley Act.** Corporate and Auditing Accountability, Responsibility, and Transparency Act of 2002, PL 107-204, 116 Stat. 745 (2002).

83   **scoffed Senator Paul Sarbanes.** "Business Lobbyists for Audit Bill Find Doors Closed on Capitol Hill," WSJ, 19 Jul 2002, A3.

83   **standards for auditors.** "One on One: The PCAOB Chairman and the JofA," JoA, Dec 2003, 16-17.

84  PCAOB's first pronouncement. Auditing Standard No. 1, "References In Auditors' Reports To The Standards Of The Public Company Accounting Oversight Board," Public Company Accounting Oversight Board, 14 May 2004; "Reference to PCAOB Standards in an Audit Report on a Nonissuer," *U.S. Auditing Standards*, AU §9508.92, AICPA, Jun 2004.

84  **Gramm Leach Bliley Act,** PL 106-102, §503 (Disclosure of Institution Privacy Policy); *New York State Bar Association v Federal Trade Commission and American Bar Association v Federal Trade Commission*, 276 FSupp.2d 110 (DC-DC, 2003), aff'd 430 F3d 457 (CA-DC, 2005); "Financial Services Regulatory Relief Act of 2006," PL 109-351, §609.

84  **Defending CPA Tax Practice.** John L. Carey, "The Defense of Tax Practice," *The Rise of the Accounting Profession: To Responsibility and Authority, 1937 - 1969* (NY: AICPA, 1970), chapter 9; F. P. Byerly, "Relationship between the Practice of Law and of Accounting," JoA, Sep 1938, 155-160; Matthew A. Melone, "Income Tax Practice and Certified Public Accountants: The Case for a Status Based Exemption From State Unauthorized Practice of Law Rules," 11 *Akron Tax J* 47 (1995).

85  **worker's compensation claim.** *Chicago Bar Association v Albert Goodman*, 366 Ill. 346 at 350, 8 NE2d 941 at 944 (1937). The nonlawyer was fined $500 plus costs.

85  **Lowell (Massachusetts).** *Lowell Bar Association v Loeb*, 315 Mass. 176 at 183, 52 NE2d 27 (1943); *Matter of Louis G. Loeb*, 315 Mass. 191, 52 NE2d 37 (1943).

85  **Bernard Bercu.** *New York County Lawyers' Association v Bernard Bercu*, 273 AD 524, 78 NYS2d 209, 38 AFTR 958 (1948); aff'd without opinion, 299 NY 728, 87 NE2d 451 (NYCA, 1949); 188 Misc. 406, 69 NYS2d 730 (1947). Bercu cited I.T. 3441, 1941-1 CB 208 which was exactly the client's fact situation, right down to the years in the Treasury example.

86  **Congressman Gregory McMahon.** "Hearing on H.R. 3214, Before a Subcommittee of the Senate Committee on the Judiciary," 80th Cong., 2d Sess. (1948), 340.

86  **Ramsey County.** "Hearing on H.R. 3214," 87 (1944 Minnesota injunction), 125-132 (Bercu opinion); *Gardner et al. v Conway*, 234 Minn. 468 (1951), 40 AFTR 245, 48 NW2d 788, aff'g 42 AFTR 1112 (DC Mn, 1950).

87  **Rhode Island Supreme Court.** *Rhode Island Bar Association et al v Daniel R. Libutti*, 81 RI 182, 100 A2d 406 (1953). JoA, Jan 1954, 34. (Non-CPA barred from preparing income tax returns for anyone except wage-earners whose income is less than $5,000).

87  *Reuben Agran v Morris Shapiro*, 127 Cal.App. 2d Supp. 807, 46 AFTR 896 (1954).

87  **CPA committed a criminal act.** *Bancroft v Indemnity Insurance Co. of North America*, 203 FSupp. 49 (DC La, 1962); Reinhold Groh, "The responsibilities and legal liabilities of the CPA in tax practice," 25 JTax 296 (Nov 1966); "Tax advice is not 'unauthorized practice' under malpractice policy," 19 JTax 172 (Sep 1963).

87  **Supreme Court pointed to a solution.** *Sperry v Florida*, 373 US 379 (1963) (non-attorney admitted to practice before the United States Patent Office was not

engaged in unauthorized practice); "Lawyers and Certified Public Accountants: A study of interprofessional relations," American Bar Assn. & AICPA, Sep 1970.

88 **South Carolina Bar.** *In re Unauthorized Practice of Law Rules Proposed by the South Carolina Bar*, 422 SE2d 123 (SC, 1992).

88 **battleground shifted to Texas.** William D. Elliott, "The Unauthorized Practice Of Tax Law, The Unspeakable Subject," *Texas State Bar Section of Taxation*, vol. 28, no. 12 (Feb 1997), 97 TNT 73-51 (16 Apr 1997); William D. Elliott, "The Unauthorized Practice Of Tax Law: The Empire Strikes Back," 97 TNT 73-52 (16 Apr 1997); "Two CPA Firms Face Unauthorized Practice Complaints in Texas," 98 TNT 85-5 (4 May 1998); "Texas Probes Andersen, Deloitte on Charges of Practicing Law," WSJ, 28 May 1998; "Arthur Andersen Wins a closely watched Texas showdown," WSJ, 29 Jul 1998; Elijah D. Farrell, "Accounting Firms and the Unauthorized Practice of Law: Who Is the Bar Really Trying to Protect?" 33 *Indiana Law Review* 599 (2000).

89 **Couzens investigation.** B. Reams, Jr., ed., "Select Committee on Investigations of the Bureau of Internal Revenue," *U.S. Revenue Acts 1909 – 1950* (Buffalo, NY: William S. Hein & Co., 1979), 144 volumes. Vols. 3 - 6 are the Couzens Investigation, reproducing all the committee testimony and reports from 14 March 1924 to 2 February 1926 in over 5,000 pages. 26 Mar 1924, 249 & 269 (George May); 27 Mar 1924, 306 (A.C. Ernst); 6 May 1925, 3794 (Ernst & Ernst), 3808 (Seidman); Mike Brewster, *Unaccountable: How the Accounting Profession Forfeited a Public Trust* (Hoboken, NJ: John Wiley & Sons, 2003), 69 (George May); A.P. Richardson, "Tax Practice is Different," JoA, May 1925, 398 ("absolutely firm stand against all contingent fees"); "Report of the President," JoA, Oct 1919, 243 ("so-called 'tax experts,'…contingent fees [are] unprofessional and reprenhensible"). A.C. Ernst's resignation from the AIA is discussed by John L. Carey, *Rise of the Accounting Profession*, 233-234.

90 **Ernst & Whinney,** et. al. v U.S., 84-2 USTC ¶9618, 735 F2d 1296 (CA-11, 7/6/84), reversing and remanding 83-1 USTC ¶9237 (DC-NDGa, 1982), cert den 470 US 1050 (1985).

91 **registered U.S. patents.** "IRS Looking to Prevent Patents on Tax Advice," 2005 TNT 210-7 (1 Nov 2005); "Background and Issues Relating To The Patenting of Tax Advice," JCT, JCX-31-06, 12 Jul 2006; "The Patented Tax Shelter," WSJ, 24 Jun 2004, D1; Jeremy Kahn, "Taxes: Patent that loophole," *Fortune* 30 Aug 2006.

91 **BDO Seidman.** "Called to Account," WSJ, 12 Aug 2002, 1; "IRS Releases Names of People In Disputed KPMG Tax Shelters," WSJ, 17 Jul 2002; "Lawyer of Many Hats In Tax Shelter Case," NYT, 17 Mar 2006, C7 (KPMG); "Tax-Shelter Sellers Lie Low for Now," WSJ, 14 Feb 2003, C1; "Ernst & Young Partners Charged," WP, 31 May 2007, D1; "Tax Inquiry Is Moving Past KPMG," NYT, 16 Sep 2005; David Cay Johnston, *Perfectly Legal* (NY: Portfolio-Penguin, 2003) 267-273.

91 **American Jobs Creation Act.** PL 108-357, §§811 - 822.

91 **The Vision.** "The Vision Report: Taking Control of the Future," JoA, Dec 1998, 23-72.

| | | |
|---|---|---|
| 91 | **AICPA has a public responsibility.** "Barry C. Malancon to be New AICPA President," JoA, Apr 1995, 9. | |
| 92 | **Robert Elliot.** Peter D. Fleming, "Steering a Course for the Future," JoA, Nov 1999, 35-39. | |
| 92 | **ABV.** Neil J. Beaton and Michael J. Mard, "The ABV Credential: Leading the Way," JoA, Dec 2003, 41-43. | |
| 92 | **two percent.** Michael Chiasson, Catherine Gaharan, and Shawn Mauldin, "A History of the Development of the AICPA's Specialty Designation Program," CPAJ, Jan 2006. | |
| 92 | **tax specialty.** Certification of tax experts has been elusive because taxation is so broad. It encompasses individual, corporate, partnership, employee benefits, estate, nonprofit, international, state and local, IRS practice, and many other areas. Developing testing, experience, and membership criteria are virtually impossible. | |
| 93 | **WebTrust.** Glen L. Gray and Roger Debreceny, "The Electron Frontier," JoA, May 1998, 32; "AICPA Launches First Assurance Service: 'CPA WebTrust'," *The CPA Letter*, Nov 1997, 1; "CPA WebTrust Advertising Campaign Begins," *The CPA Letter*, Jan 1998, 1; Yves Gendron and Michael Barrett, "Professionalization in Action: Accountants' Attempt at Building a Network of Support for the WebTrust Seal of Assurance," *Contemporary Accounting Research* (Toronto), Fall 2004, 563; "Reporting on Systems Reliability," JoA, Nov 1999 (SysTrust). | |
| 93 | **XBRL** is an acronym for "eXtensible Business Reporting Language." "AICPA Establishes a Language for Electronic-Based Financial Reporting," JoA, Sep 1999, 15; "Attest Engagements on Financial Information Included in XBRL Instance Documents," JoA, Nov 2003, 112-113; Jeffrey W. Naumann, "Tap Into XBRL's Power the Easy Way," JoA, May 2004, 32-39 (lists prior XBRL articles); "XBRL: It's Unstoppable," JoA, Aug 2005; "Remarks of R. Corey Booth before the XBRL-US National Conference," San Jose, 18 Jan 2006; "SEC to Rebuild Public Disclosure System to Make It 'Interactive'," SEC Press Release 2006-158, 25 Sep 2006; "SEC Financial-Reports Database To Undergo $54 Million Upgrade," WSJ, 26 Sep 2006, C3; Speech by SEC Commissioner Kathleen L. Casey, 8 Feb 2008. | |
| 93 | **Cognitor.** "Members Vote Down Bylaw Amendment," *CPA Letter*, Jan 2002, 1. | |
| 94 | **crashing halt.** Timothy J. Fogarty, Vaughan S. Radcliffe and David R. Campbell, "Accountancy before the fall: The AICPA vision project and related professional enterprises," *Accounting, Organizations and Society*, Vol. 31, Iss. 1, Jan 2006, 1. | |
| 94 | **Cognitor II.** "A History of the Development of the AICPA's Specialty Designation Program," CPAJ, Jan 2006. | |
| 95 | **Brett Prager.** CPA2Biz press release, 17 Jan 2001. | |
| 95 | **bCentral.** "The Man With Nine Lives," *Forbes*, 25 Nov 2002, 60; "Microsoft's Small Biz Efforts," *Accounting Technology*, 1 Nov 2005. | |
| 95 | ***Journal of Business Ethics.*** William E. Shafer and Dwight Owsen, "Policy issues raised by for-profit spinoffs from professional associations: An Evaluation of a Recent AICPA Initiative," *Journal of Business Ethics*, Jan 2003, 181. | |

95 **secrecy surrounding CPA2Biz.** Letter from Nancy Newman-Limata, AICPA Member of Council and NYSSCPA President to AICPA Chair Kathy Eddy, 7 May 2002; *BDO Seidman, LLP v American Institute of Certified Public Accountants, CPA2Biz Inc., and Shared Services LLC* (DC-SDNY, Case No. BSL-VAACBI176480).

96 **Education Foundation.** "Audit Group's Chief to Donate Disputed Stock to Charity," NYT, 30 Mar 2002; Cassell Bryan-Low, "AICPA CEO's Pay Rises 22% Amid Reversals," WSJ, 20 Jun 2003, B2.

96 **AICPA Library.** John L. Carey, *The Rise of the Accounting Profession* (NY: AICPA, 1969), vol. I, 135-140; JoA, Dec 1994, 83-89; Karen Hegger Neloms, "History of the AICPA Library," JoA, May 1987, 388-392; Interviews with former AICPA directors of library services Karen Neloms and Pat Myer; Pledge Agreement between AICPA and University of Mississippi (signed but undated), obtained under Mississippi Open Records Act.

98 **Association of Certified Fraud Examiners.** Mary-Jo Kranacher, "The Battle Against Fraud: Seeking the Accounting Profession's Support" CPAJ, Sep 2006; Dick Carozza, "ACFE and AICPA utilize strengths to fight fraud: An interview with Barry C. Melancon," *Fraud Magazine*, Nov/Dec 2006.

98 **H&R Block.** "H&R Block Acquires McGladrey & Pullen," *Trusted Professional*, Jul 1999; "H&R Block To Acquire Finance Unit," NYT, 2 Aug 2005, C4. The CPA firm employees became employees of the parent corporation. Audits are accomplished by leasing those employees back to the shell CPA firm. "H&R Block Employee Accused in ID Scam," LAT, 3 Jan 2003. C12; "Former H&R Block Manager Accused in Identity-Theft Ring," NYT, 3 Jan 2003, B2; "Former Manager at H&R Block Is Named in Identity-Theft Case," WSJ, 3 Jan 2003, C7; "Identity thief to serve probation," *New York Journal News*, 13 Sep 2003; "ID thief gets home confinement," *New York Journal News*, 11 Oct 2003; "H&R Block Pulls Television Ad Promoting Its Tax Services," *CPA Letter*, Apr 2003, 2.

99 **Accounting Hall of Fame.** http://fisher.osu.edu/acctmis/hall/.

100 **Randolph Paul,** *Taxation in the United States* (Boston: Little, Brown & Company, 1954), 771-772.

101 **worst managers.** "The Best & Worst Managers," *Business Week*, 13 Jan 2003; "Bloodied and Bowed," *Business Week*, 20 Jan 2003.

101 **22 percent increase.** Cassell Bryan-Low, "AICPA CEO's Pay Rises 22% Amid Reversals," WSJ, 20 Jun 2003, B2.

101 **1990 study.** "A Special Committee on Governance and Structure," AICPA, 1990, 62-64.

102 **American Medical Association.** "AMA in Danger of Vanishing From Scene," *Boston Globe*, 10 May 1999; "Report of the Task Force on Membership," American Medical Association, Jun 1999, A-99.

102 **Charles Bowsher,** Interview, CPAJ, May 2003; "Accounting Hall of Fame Induction: Charles Arthur Bowsher," *Accounting Historians Journal*, vol. 24, no. 1, Jun 1997.

## CHAPTER 5: MALTOTIER

105  **Biblical census.** Exodus 38:26, Numbers 1:46, and Numbers 26:51; Rabbi Nosson Scherman, *The Chumash, The ArtScroll Series*, (Brooklyn: Mesorah Publications, 1993, 1994), 726 FN 1-19; Aryeh Kaplan, *The Living Torah*, (Brooklyn: Maznaim Publishing, 1981) 103 FN 23:15 (Hammurabi). The collections were for the upkeep and maintenance of the Tabernacle. Shekels in the Bible refers to a weight measure. A shekel was about 0.8 ounces of silver. Coins were not invented until around 500 BCE by the Lydians who lived on the west coast of Turkey.

105  **to pay the census tax.** Luke 2:1-7; *The Gospel of Luke*, Translated with an Introduction and Interpretation by William Barclay (Philadelphia: The Westminister Press, 1975), 20.

106  **England taxed Jews.** Max L. Margolis and Alexander Marx, "A History of the Jewish People (Philadelphia: Jewish Publication Society, 1927), 384-391, 398-400.

107  **Spanish tax collection.** Benzion Netanyahu, *The Origins of the Inquisition in Fifteenth Century Spain* (NY: Random House, 1995), 70-71, 1045, 1087-1092.

107  **Polish nobility.** Margolis/Marx, 551-557; Heinrich Graetz, *History of the Jews* (Philadelphia: Jewish Publication Society of America, 1895 (1956 reprint)), vol. V, 3-6; Paul Johnson, *A History of the Jews* (NY: Harper & Row, 1987), 250-260.

108  **Jewish councils.** Isaiah Trunk, *Judenrat: The Jewish Councils in Eastern Europe Under Nazi Occupation*, (NY: Macmillan Publishing Co., 1972; NY: Stein and Day, 1977), 236-243.

108  **Turkey.** Faik Ökte, *The Tragedy of the Turkish Capital Tax*, translated from the Turkish *Varlik Vergisi Faciasi* by Geoffrey Cox (London; Wolfboro, NH: Croom Helm, 1987). Ökte played a leading role in both the assessment and administration of the capital levy. David Joulfaian, "The Ultimate Death Tax," 108 TNT 951 (22 Aug 2005); C.L. Sulzberger, NYT: "Turkey is Uneasy Over Capital Levy" (9 Sept. 1943, 20), "Premier Defends New Turkish Tax" (10 Sep 1943, 8), "Turkish Tax Kills Foreign Business" (11 Sep 1943, 7), "Ankara Tax Raises Diplomatic Issues" (12 Sep 1943, 46).

109  **Koran**, 9:29, the *jizya* (retribution) tax in retribution for obstinacy in refusing to accept Islam. Hamas intends to implement a jizya tax should they ever establish Palestine. "Odd Allies, Bethlehem Mayor Courts Hamas," WSJ, 23 Dec 2005, A1.

110  **Salt Taxes.** Mark Kurlansky, *Salt: A World History* (NY: Walker and Company, 2002), 226, 233; James P. Collins, *Fiscal Limits of Absolutism: Direct Taxation in Early Seventh-Century France*, (University of California Press, 1988), 17 (France bankrupts); Michael Kwass, *Privilege and the Politics of Taxation in Eighteenth-Century France* (NY: Cambridge University Press, 2000), 1 (contributions publiques), 47, 208 (French debt and American Revolution); *A Compendious History of the Taxes of France, and the Oppressive Methods of Raising Them* (London: Richard Baldwin, 1694), 9-15; Barbara W. Tuchman, *Distant Mirror: The Calamitous Fourteenth Century*, (NY: Alfred A. Knopf, 1978), 15, 142 (inverted four, five and ten percent rates).

110 **"salary" derives from "salt."** Roman soldiers received payments in salt, called a salarium, hence the modern term salary. "Despite Big Health Concerns, Food Industry Can't Shake Salt," WSJ, 25 Feb 2005, A1; Claude Maneron, *Twilight of the Old Order* (NY: Alfred A. Knopf, 1977), (304, 1355 salt tax and origin of "salary": *sel*, salt; *saler*, to salt; *salairé*, salary), (227-230, Lavoisier); Will and Ariel Durant, *The Story of Civilization: Part IX, The Age of Voltaire* (NY: Simon & Schuster, 1965), 531-536.

110 **Confederate...death compensation.** *The Confederate Records of the State of Georgia, vol. II: State Papers of Governor Joseph E. Brown, 1860 to 1865* (Atlanta: Chas. P. Boyd, 1909). Over 100 pages of this 700-page book are devoted to the difficulty procuring salt. Prior to the Civil War, salt had been brought to the South by English vessels which used salt as ballast and sold it for one-fourth cent per pound. At that low rate, the South did not develop saline resources. Six months after the start of War, salt which had sold for 50 cents per 50 pound sack fetched $6 in Richmond and $8 in Raleigh — and it got much worse. Louise Biles Hill, *Joseph E. Brown and the Confederacy* (Chapel Hill: University of North Carolina Press, 1939), 112-116, referencing Ella Lonn, *Salt as a Factor in the Confederacy*, (NY: Walter Neale, 1933); Kurlansky, 257-275.

112 **a billion livres.** Will and Ariel Durant, *The Story of Civilization, Part X, Rousseau and Revolution* (NY: Simon & Shuster, 1967), 858-872, 872; Paul Kennedy, *The Rise and Fall of the Great Powers* (NY: Random House, 1987), 84. A billion livres appears to be at least $400 million today.

112 **Boston Tea Party.** Richard N. Rosenfeld, *American Aurora* (NY: St. Martin Press, 1997), 246-247; Samuel Eliot Morison and Henry Steele Commanger, *The Growth of the American Republic* (NY: Oxford University Press, 1962), vol. 1, 175-176; Andrew Preston Peabody, "Boston Mobs Before the Revolution," *The Atlantic Monthly*, Sep 1888, 321-333; Joseph Thorndike, "A Tax Revolt or Revolting Taxes?" 2005 TNT 243-2 (14 Dec 2005); Benson J. Lossing, "The Boston Tea Party," *Harper's*, Dec 1851.

112 **tariff on salt.** *Tariff Acts passed by the Congress of the United States From 1789 to 1895* (Washington: Govt. Printing Office, 1896), 12 (Tariff of 1790), 38 (Tariff of 1797), 47 (Tariff of 1813), 79 (Tariff of 1830); Dall W. Forsythe, *Taxation and Political Change in the Young Nation 1781 - 1833* (NY: Columbia Univ. Press, 1977) 68 ($500,000); Kurlansky, 245 (Erie Canal salt tax); Thomas Hart Benton, *Thirty Years' View* (NY: D. Appleton and Company, 1854), vol. 1, 142-148, 154-157, 714-717. Benton blamed U.S. tax for salt costing 300 percent extra. In 1829, the U.S. imported 6 million bushels worth $715,000. The tax was 20 cents per bushel, or $1.2 million. Merchants' profit at 50 percent increased the price another $600,000. The tax encouraged the false presumption that 56 lbs. of salt comprised a bushel, instead of the true weight of 84 lbs., thus adding another $450,000 to the cost. So, the total tax effect added $2.25 million to a $715,000 product.

113 **Gandhi's Salt March.** Mohinder Singh, "The Story of Salt," *Gandhi Marg*, Vol. 24, No. 3 (Oct-Dec 2002); Kurlansky, 343-353.

| | |
|---|---|
| 114 | **King Leopold.** Adam Hochschild, *King Leopold's Ghost* (NY: Houghton Mifflin Company, 1998), 158-159 (uses for rubber), 117 (interlocking directorates and taxes), 277 (profit); John de Courcy MacDonnell, *King Leopold II, His Rule in Belgium and the Congo* (NY: Negro Universities Press, 1969; reprinted from London: Cassell and Company, 1905). A satirical and factual account was written by Mark Twain, *King Leopold's Soliloquy: A Defense of His Congo Rule* (Boston: P.R. Warren Co., 1905); Arthur Conan Doyle wrote a comprehensive document, *The Crime of the Congo* (NY: Doubleday, Page & Company, 1909); C.C. Regier, *The Era of the Muckrakers* (Gloucester, MA: Peter Smith, 1957; reprinted from Univ. N. Carolina Press, 1932), 187; Robert E. Park wrote a three article series for *Everybody's*: "A King in Business" (Nov 1906, 624 - 633), "The Terrible Story of the Congo" (Dec 1906, 763 - 772), "The Blood-Money of the Congo" (Jan 1907, 60 - 70). "King Leopold Denies Charges Against Him," NYT, 11 Dec 1906, 5; Letter from Gov. Wahis, *Times* (London), 31 May 1897, 12 (Leopold's Congo Governor denied all accusations, except admitting one village "having refused to pay the tax, had to be repressed in October 1896. The inhabitants resisted and lost a certain number of men."); "Belgian Rule on the Congo," WSJ, 9 Feb 1907, 6. Joseph Conrad's novel, *Heart of Darkness* is based on the evils Leopold visited upon the "heart of Africa." |
| 115 | **taxing all commerce.** "The Congo Free State," *Times* (London), 20 Mar 1891, 13 (taxes on all commerce); *Times* (London), 5 Jul 1902, 7 (Leopold signs decree remitting 50 percent of taxes from religious, charitable, and scientific institutions in the Free State). |
| 115 | **U.S. participated.** "The Congo Free State," NYT, 26 May 1885, 5 (Sanford on conference); "The President's Message," NYT, 9 Dec 1885, 4; John A. Kasson, "The Congo Conference and the President's Message," *North American Review*, Feb 1886, 119 - 133; "Bank Scandal in France," NYT, 11 May 1890, 1 (repress slave trade, impose tariff). |
| 117 | **loudest exultation.** Charles Adams, "On Replacing the Federal Income Tax," *Hearings before the Committee on Ways and Means*, 6-8 Jun 1995, Serial 104-28, 172; Edwin R.A. Seligman, *The Income Tax* (NY: The Macmillan Company, 1911), 113. Britain's chancellor of the exchequer is equivalent to a minister of finance or secretary of the treasury. |
| 117 | **Italian ghetto income tax.** Exhibit in Museum of Taxation, Jerusalem, Israel. |
| 118 | **no Passover.** Seligman, 105 FN3, citing "A Letter Addressed by Col. John Grey to a Member of the House of Commons on the Subject of the Liability of the Pay of the Officers of the Navy and Army to the Tax upon Property," London, 1810, 28-29. Britain's early income tax was part of the property tax act. |
| 118 | **Biblical plagues.** "A Plague on 'Em Anyway," WSJ, 20 Nov 1957, 14. |
| 118 | **Whiskey Tax Rebellion.** Randolph Paul, *Taxation in the United States* (Boston: Little, Brown and Company, 1954), 6; "Duties on Distilled Spirits imported into, and distilled in the United States," 1 Stat. 199, Ch. XV, Secs. 14 - 15 (3 Mar 1791); William Hogeland, *The Whiskey Rebellion* (NY: Scribner, 2006); "George Washington, Whiskey Entrepreneur," WSJ, 21 Feb 2007, D8. |

119  Section 7421. *Cong. Globe*, 39th Cong., 2nd Sess., 1933 (1 Mar 1867), amendment to §10, of H.R. 1161. The word, "any [tax]" was added in 1874. J.S. Seidman, *Seidman's Legislative History of Federal Income Tax Laws, 1938 - 1861*, (NY: Prentice-Hall, 1938), 1053.

119  **summary and stringent.** *In re State Railroad Tax Cases*, 92 US 575, 614-615 (1875); §6214 gives the Tax Court the power to increase a deficiency above what IRS has assessed.

119  **hostile judiciary.** *Cheatham v U.S.*, 92 US 85 (1875).

119  **eulogizing him.** *Cong. Globe*, 41st Cong., 2nd Sess., 14 Dec 1869, 111-120 (Senate), 129-134 (House).

120  **place beside the great Generals.** Charles A. Jellison, *Fessenden of Maine, Civil War Senator* (Syracuse University Press, 1962), 191, citing *New York Tribune*, 4 Mar 1865.

120  **Fessenden believed...administrative matter.** *Cong. Globe*, 39th Cong., 2nd Sess., 1933 (1 Mar 1867); *South Carolina v Regan*, 465 US 367 (1984), discusses the legislative history.

121  **Grant and Sherman were stopped.** Francis Fessenden, *Life and Public Services of William Pitt Fessenden* (Houghton, Mifflin and Company, 1907; reprinted New York: Da Capo Press, 1970), vol. I, 313-374.

121  **supplies were "ample."** William Tecumseh Sherman, *Memoirs of General W.T. Sherman* (NY: Literary Classics of the United States, 1990), 570, 612.

121  **Clausewitz' advice.** "[I]n an area of average population density — say 2,000 to 3,000 per 25 square miles — a force of 150,000 combatants can live off the local inhabitants and communities within a very small area for a day or two, which will not preclude its fighting as a unit — in other words, it is possible to provision such a force without depots and other preparations on an uninterrupted march." Carl von Clausewitz, *On War* (pub. 1832), Book 5, Chapter 14, "Maintenance and Supply."

121  **drafted the Fourteenth Amendment.** Joseph Martin Hernon, *Profiles in Character*, (Armonk, NY: M.E. Sharpe, 1997), 58-96.

121  **Edmund G. Ross**, "Historic Moments: The Impeachment Trail," *Scribner's Magazine*, XI (Apr 1892), 519-524; Ralph J. Roshe, "The Seven Martyrs?" *American Historical Review*, LXIV (Jan 1959) 323-330.

121  **the law was the law.** Jellison, 47.

122  **Congressional mandate.** Senator Aaron A. Sargent, "Report of the Joint Special Committee to Investigate Chinese Immigration," Senate Reports v. 3 n. 689, 44th Cong., 2d Sess. (*Congressional Information Service*, Serial Set No. 1734, Fiches 1-14), iv, 38 (27 Feb 1877).

122  **Foreign Miners License Tax.** William C. Fankauser, *A Financial History of California: Public Revenues, Debts, and Expenditures* (Berkley: University of California Press, 1913), 135-137, 159-160, 199-200; Josiah Royce, *California from the Conquest in 1846 to the Second Vigilance Committee in San Francisco*, (Boston: 1886), 356-368, (reprinted Peregrine Publishers Inc, Santa Barbara,

1970, 281-290, "The Warfare Against the Foreigners"); Charles Howard Shinn, *Mining Camps: A Study in American Frontier Government* (NY: Alfred A. Knopf, 1948, reprint of 1884 work), 203, 264; *The People ex rel. Attorney General v Naglee*, 1 Cal 232, 253 (Dec 1850); *Ex Parte Ah Pong*, 19 Cal 106 (Oct 1861); *U.S. v Jackson*, 26 F.Cas. 563 (1874), citing 12 *Statutes of California* 449 (1861). Idaho Territory and other places influenced by California enacted similar anti-Chinese foreign miners taxes. "The Burlingame Treaty and Anti-Chinese Laws," NYT, 9 Nov 1869, 4; Liping Zhu, *A Chinaman's Chance: The Chinese on the Rocky Mountain Mining Frontier* (Niwot, CO: Univ. Press of Colorado, 1997), 47.

122 **only collected from the Chinese.** Sargent, 482, 1108.

123 **Chinese Police Tax.** 13 *Statutes of California* 462 (1862), Chapter 339.

123 **racist bills.** 6 *Statutes of California* 194 (1855), Chapter 153; 9 *Statutes of California* 295 (1858), Chapter 313, Chapter 316; "Passage of the Anti-Coolie Bills in the Senate," *San Francisco Chronicle*, 2 Mar 1870, 1; 18 *Statutes of California* 330 (1869-1870), Chapter 230, Chapter 231.

124 **Ogden Hoffman.** *U.S. v Jackson*, 26 Fed. Cas. 563 (No. 15,459), 1874 U.S. App. LEXIS 1541, 3 Sawyer 59 (C.C.D. Calif., 1874 — the date is likely a scrivener's error because the case was argued in January 1871; *San Francisco Chronicle*, 7 Jan 1871), Files 572, 583 (National Archives, San Francisco branch); Charles J. McClain, *In Search of Equality: The Chinese Struggle Against Discrimination in Nineteenth-Century America* (University of California Press, 1994), 30-41, also credits the 1868 Burlingame Treaty (which allowed free immigration from China), the 1870 Civil Rights Act, and *U.S. v Thomas W. Breeze* (C.C.D. Cal., 1871) File 709 (National Archives, San Francisco branch). There is misinformation over when the tax ceased. The *Los Angeles Times* (18 Nov 1896, p. 6) says it was "1869 when it was declared by Judge Hoffman to be unconstitutional under the fourteenth amendment." A display on the third floor of California's Capitol Building in Sacramento says "declared unconstitutional in 1870." It's not that Hoffman championed the Chinese cause, because he once declared, "unrestricted immigration of the Chinese to this country is a great and growing evil...it will be a menace to our peace and even to our civilization" (*Parrot*, 1 F. 481 at 498). Rather, despite his anti-Chinese orientation, he enforced economic rights and should not be seen an a defender of racial equality. Thomas Wuil Joo, "New 'Conspiracy Theory' of the Fourteenth Amendment: Nineteenth Century Chinese Civil Rights Cases and the Development of Substantive Due Process Jurisprudence," *University of San Francisco Law Review*, vol. 29, no. 2 (Winter 1995), 364 - 370.

124 **Coca-Cola.** War Revenue Act of 1898, §20; *Coca Cola Company v Henry A. Rucker, Collector of Internal Revenue*, USDC Atlanta, General Index Cases, Box 415, File No. 10042, 1902 (National Archives Southeast Region, Morrow, Georgia), aff'd per curiam, 117 F. 1006 (CA-5, 10/21/1902), 125 F. 1004 (CA-5, 10/17/1903). There's a list of juror names and alternates in the trial record, but no

indication of their race. "Say It Is Not Medicine," AC, 17 Apr 1900, 10; "Mistrial in Coca Cola Case," AC 15 Jun 1901, 11; Frederick Allen, *Secret Formula* (NY: Harper Collins, 1994), 41-46; Luke Dittrich, "Paper Trail," *Atlanta Magazine*, Jul 2005, 94-105, 95. Justice Oliver Wendell Holmes recounted the history of Coca-Cola's cocaine ingredient and that the cola nut (actually, the kola seed) was used to furnish caffeine. For many years, the drink was advertised as an "ideal nerve tonic and stimulant," *Coca-Cola Co. v Koke Co. of America*, 254 US 143 (1920). Coca-Cola also won a battle in 1916 with the Food and Drug Administration which argued that the 78 milligrams of caffeine in an 8-ounce glass was injurious to health, *U.S. v Forty Barrels and Twenty Kegs of Coca Cola*, 241 US 265 (1916). Today, an 8-ounce serving of Coca-Cola Classic contains 23 milligrams of caffeine.

125 **collector twice appealed.** There were actually three Coca-Cola trials. The first dealing with the $10,885.76 tax ended in a June 1901 mistrial as the jury deadlocked. Coca-Cola then raised the stakes by instituting a second suit for a refund of $29,502 tax paid from 7 August 1899 to 17 June 1901. In the second trial for $10,885.76 in February 1902, the jury ruled in Coca-Cola's favor. This was followed by a third trial in December 1902 on the $29,502 tax where the judge directed a verdict in favor of Coca-Cola, with a jury to determine the exact amount payable. Both verdicts were appealed and denied. "Mistrial in Coca Cola Case," AC, 15 Jun 1901, 11; "Coca Cola Jury Stood Nine to Three," AC, 16 Jun 1901, 5; "Government Again Sued," AC, 10 Sep 1901, 9; "Stamps Are Not Required," AC, 2 Feb 1902, 7; "Uncle Sam Loses in Lengthy Suit," AC, 22 Oct 1902, 9 (Gov't loses appeal of $10,858.76 case); "Coca-Cola Company Won," AC, 17 Dec 1902, 7; "Coca-Cola Case is Postponed," AC, 27 Jan 1903, 12; "Verdict Given Coca-Cola Co.," AC, 11 Feb. 1903, 7.

125 **Waleska.** Mark Bixler, "Ubiquitous Coke once contraband," AJC, 23 Aug 1998, D1.

125 **Henry Rucker.** Clarence A. Bacote, "Negro Officeholders in Georgia Under President McKinley," *Journal of Negro History*, vol. 44, no. 3 (Jul 1959), 217-239; "Pre-1925 newspaper clippings and official documents," Long-Rucker-Aiken Papers, Series II, Subseries I, Box 2, MSS 468, Kenan Research Center, Atlanta History Center Archives; "Black Georgians in History: Henry Rucker: Republican Leader, Federal Tax Collector," AC, 7 Feb 1989; "Black Georgians In History — Part 5: Henry A. Rucker," AJ, 7 Feb 1974, 1A; "Rucker Succumbs to Long Illness," *Atlanta Georgian*, 12 May 1924 (carried Georgia delegation in 1896); "Thrilling Story of the Hanging," AC, 21 Jul 1897, 1 (rumor of Rucker's appointment was printed on July 20, p. 7, and "The Forthcoming Triumph of Barber Rucker," on July 22, p. 5); "H.A. Rucker is Collector," AJ, 23 Jul 1897, 1 (Georgia delegation called upon the President [to] protest); "Atlanta Vexed Over Rucker," NYT, 31 Jul 1897, 7; "No Cause for Complaint," (editorial) AC, 24 Jul 1897, 4; "Georgia's Famous Negro Triumvirate," and "White Faction Angry At McKinley," AJ, 31 Jul 1897, 5; "Revenue Men Resign Jobs," *Atlanta Journal*,

5 Aug 1897. Owning a barber shop was apparently a path to affluence. Former slave Alonzo Herndon who founded Atlanta Life Insurance Company and became the South's first black millionaire, owned a five-chair shop in 1896. *Atlanta Magazine*, Dec 2005, 316.

126 **Loftin.** "Two Sides to the Loftin Shooting," AC, 18 Sept 1897.

128 **opium.** *Nigro v U.S.*, 276 US 332 (1928); A nominal excise tax on heroin began in 1899. Lillian Doris, *The American Way in Taxation: Internal Revenue 1862 - 1963* (NY: Prentice-Hall, 1963), 22.

128 **separate tax on marijuana.** IRC (1939) §2590; IRC (1954) §4711, §4712; repealed in 1970 by PL 91-513, §1101(b)(3)(A).

128 **manufacture of a certain beverage.** "Federal Legislation of 1930," 17 *ABA Journal* 95, 96 (Feb 1931); IRC (1939) §2551(b).

128 ***Timothy F. Leary v U.S.***, 395 US 6 (1969); "High Court Frees Leary; Voids 2 Marijuana Laws," NYT, 20 May 1969, 1.

128 **Jonathan Swift.** *Gulliver's Travels*, Book 3, Chapter VI; Billy Hamilton, "Of Vice and Men — Texas's Strip Club Tax," STT, 12 Feb 2008. A Travis County judge ruled the tax unconstitutional. The state promised to appeal. "Judge strikes down $5 strip club fee," *Houston Chronicle*, 28 Mar 2008.

128 **Arizona marijuana taxes.** *Daily Tax Report*, 28 Mar 1996, H1; "Meet Arizona's Happiest Taxpayers," NYT, 6 Oct 1996, 4; "America's Wackiest Taxes," CNN/Money, 22 Feb 2005 [http://money.cnn.com/2005/02/18/pf/taxes/strangetaxesupdate].

129 **alternative fuels.** "If You Paid Half Price For That New SUV, You Must Be in Arizona," WSJ, 26 Oct 2000, A1.

129 **bail bonds.** Tennessee Code Ann. §67-4-803 (bail bond tax), §67-4-602 (litigation tax), §16-18-605 (municipal litigation tax).

129 **Window Tax.** "Making History - Programme 3: Hearth tax and window tax," BBC Radio 4, 15 Apr 2003. [www.bbc.co.uk/education/beyond/factsheets/makhist/makhist7_prog3c.shtml (visited 12/2/2005)]; Richard N. Rosenfeld, *American Aurora* (NY: St. Martin Press, 1997), 186, 608-609; Randolph Paul, *Taxation in the United States* (Boston: Little, Brown and Company, 1954), 6; 1 Stat. 580, Ch. LXX, §9 (9 Jul 1798) and 1 Stat. 597, Ch. LXXV (14 Jul 1798).

130 **John Fries.** William Watts Hart Davis, *The Fries Rebellion 1798 – 1799* (Doylestown, PA: Doylestown Publishing Company, 1899); William H. Rehnquist, *Grand Inquests: The Historic Impeachments of Justice Samuel Chase and President Andrew Johnson* (NY: William Morrow and Company, 1992) 48-49, 95-62; William H. Rehnquist, "Remarks of the Chief Justice," Symposium on Judicial Independence, University of Richmond, T.C. Williams School of Law, 21 Mar 2003.

130 **Beard Tax.** Charles Mackay, *Extraordinary Popular Delusions and the Madness of Crowds* (NY: Farrar Straus and Giroux, 1932; reprint of 1841 and 1851 London editions), 351-353.

131 **Thomas Friedman**, "In Oversight We Trust," NYT, 28 Jul 2002, 4.13.

131 **French and Spanish laws.** Roberto Casas Alatristo, "Accounting in Mexico," JoA, Mar 1937, 197.

132 **Arab countries.** Gerald T. Ball and Frank J. Walsh, "Tax Consequences of U.S. Investments in Select Middle Eastern Countries," 37 *NYU Institute on Federal Income Taxation* (1979), chapter 8.

132 **Winston Churchill.** "How Winston Churchill fought Inland Revenue on wartime 'second front'," *Sunday Telegraph*, 4 Jan 2004.

132 **Rolling Stones.** "Rolling Stones Protest Taxes, Cancel Gigs," 89 JTax 64 (Jul 1998); "Stingy Stones avoid tax on £240m fortune," *Daily Mail*, 1 Aug 2006.

133 **national pastime.** "Italy Facing Tax-evasion Crisis," *Public Accounting Report*, 15 Aug 1990, 4; "Italy Goes After Tax Cheats (Again)", WSJ, 9 Nov 1992, A7; "Unhappy Returns: In Italian Crackdown, Tax Cheats Get the Boot," WSJ, 28 Jun 2007, A1.

133 **pandemic in New York.** Mayor Ed Koch, "Taxpayers' Obligations," *The Jewish Press*, 1 Dec 1989, 28A; "New York Battles Car License Fraud," NYT, 17 May 1987, 1.

134 **The Judicial Tax.** *Jenkins v Missouri*, 672 FSupp. 400 (W.D. Mo., 1987), 855 F.2d 1295 (CA-8, 1988), 495 US 33 (1990), 11 F3d 755 (CA-8, 1993), 515 US 70 (1995); Paul J. Collins, "Taxation by Judicial Decree: Missouri v. Jenkins," 44 *Tax Lawyer* 1141 (Summer 1991); Stephanie Simon, "High Cost for Low Grades; Kansas City's schools spent heavily some say frivolously in a futile attack on segregation and test failures," LAT, 18 May 2001, A1; Paul Ciotti, "Kansas City Proves Money Isn't the Answer; Schools: The $1.6 billion spent hasn't reversed the downward trend because good teachers were not the priority," LAT, 27 Mar 1996, 9; David G. Savage, "Ruling on Affirmative Action; Court Deals Blow to School Desegregation Rules," LAT, 13 Jun 1995, 15; Joan Biskupic, "Desegregation Remedies Rejected; Justices Say School Solutions Must Address Specific Discrimination," WP, 13 Jun 1995, A1; Edward Felsenthal, "Parts of School-Desegregation Plan Killed — High Court Decision Seeks To End Federal Judges' Supervision of Programs," WSJ, 13 Jun 1995, A2; "A costly quest for Racial Balance Kansas City's attempt to integrate schools poses test for court and urban education," *Christian Science Monitor*, 10 Jan 1995, 1.

135 **Robert Moses.** Robert A. Caro, *The Power Broker: Robert Moses and the Fall of New York* (NY: Alfred A. Knopf, 1974); Cleveland Rodgers, "Robert Moses, An Atlantic Portrait," *Atlantic Monthly*, Feb 1939; Robert Moses, "Slums and City Planning," *Atlantic Monthly*, Jan 1945, 63-68; "The World That Moses Built," *The American Experience*, WGBH-TV (Boston: PBS Video, 1988); "Shows Try to Renovate Moses' Reputation," WSJ, 14 Mar 2007.

139 **Port Authority...public transit.** Port Authority excused from funding public transit: *United States Trust Co. v New Jersey*, 431 US 1 (1977).

## CHAPTER 6: TAX 'EM, MY BOY, TAX 'EM

140 **"Tax 'em, my boy, tax 'em,"** is attributed to correspondence dated November 16, 1934 from Felix Frankfurter to William O. Douglas who five years later were both appointed associate justices on the U.S. Supreme Court. It reflected the New

Deal attitude of taxing away accumulations of wealth in order to redistribute income. Barbara D. Merino and Alan G. Mayper, "Prophets or Puppets of Profit: The Securities Legislation and the Accounting Profession in the 1930s," 1997 IPA Conference, Manchester, England.

140  **Second Bank of the United States.** For a list of the bank's 12 powers, including revenue powers, see Thomas Hart Benton, *Thirty Years' View* (NY: D. Appleton and Company, 1854), vol. I, 193-194. Benton was elected Missouri's first senator in 1820 and served until 1851. He died in 1858 after compiling an amazing 1600-page history of primary sources and commentary.

141  **Andrew Jackson.** Marquis James, *The Life of Andrew Jackson* (Indianapolis: Bobbs-Merrill Company, 1938), 633-657, (Webster $32,000 loan and letter, at 657, citing Biddle papers collection); Robert V. Remini, *Andrew Jackson and the Bank War* (NY: W.W. Norton & Company, 1967); Bray Hammond, "Jackson's Fight With The 'Money Power'," *American Heritage*, Jun 1956.

143  **Taney served...with distinction.** "Remarks by Chief Justice William A. Rehnquist on the Rededication of the Roger Brooke Taney House and Museum," 7 Apr 2004, www.supremecourtus.gov/publicinfo/speeches/sp_04-07-04.html.

143  *Okurasho.* Peter Hartcher, *The Ministry: How Japan's Most Powerful Institution Endangers World Markets* (Boston: Harvard Business School Press, 1998), 2-3.

144  **The Tariff.** William McKinley, *The Tariff in the Days of Henry Clay and Since: An Exhaustive Review of our Tariff Legislation from 1812 to 1896* (NY: Henry Clay Publishing Co., 1896; NY: Knickerbocker Press, 1904; New York: Krass Reprint Co., 1970). It's so forgotten, that at the New York Public Library, one must request the book several days in advance so that it can be pulled from an off-site warehouse.

144  **sole object.** *Cong. Globe*, 31 Mar 1824, 1978.

144  **Tariff of Abominations.** Benton, vol. I, 95.

145  **inimical...to enslaved labor.** McKinley, 8-9, citing Benton's *Thirty Years' View*.

145  **California gold.** McKinley, 22-23.

145  **party plank.** McKinley, 28-29.

145  **cause of the Civil War.** McKinley, 30; Francis Fessenden, *Life and Public Services of William Pitt Fessenden* (Houghton, Mifflin and Company, 1907; New York: Da Capo Press, 1970), vol. I, 115; Samuel Eliot Morison and Henry Steele Commanger, *The Growth of the American Republic* (NY: Oxford University Press, 1962), vol. 1, 667-668.

145  **Robert Augustus Toombs.** "[I]t is true that the present tariff was sustained by an almost unanimous vote of the South; but it was a reduction — a reduction necessary from the plethora of the revenue; but the policy of the North soon made it inadequate to meet the public expenditure, by an enormous and profligate increase of the public expenditure; and at the last session of Congress they brought in and passed through the House the most atrocious tariff bill that ever was enacted, raising the present duties from twenty to two hundred and fifty per cent above the existing rates of duty. That bill now lies on the table of the Senate." Toombs speaking before the Georgia Legislature, 13 November 1860.

146 **Robert Barnwell Rhett.** "Far worse than Great Britain ever did to our fathers, the Northern people...plunder our income, by unrighteous and unconstitutional tariffs," *Charleston Mercury*, 12 Jan 1860, 1. "We are in no new controversy. For more than 30 years, the struggle between the North and the South has been going on. That struggle, in the form of various measures, has been for power on the part of the North, and for protection against power, on the part of the South. It first arose onto the Tariff." Speech by Rhett, *Mercury*, 7 Jun 1860, 4. "In addition to the money collected by the customs-house, there is a vast amount taken from the consumers of the manufactures by the operation of our Tariff Laws. Whenever the duty on the foreign commodity excludes it from importation, and thereby the manufacturer in the United States is enabled to sell his manufactured articles in its stead, the consumer pays the tax to the manufacturer, in the increased price the manufacturer obtains, in consequence of the duty." Rhett speaking before the Charleston Ratification Meeting, 9 July 1860.

146 **omitted "general welfare."** The South might have required a constitutional amendment to institute social insurance programs. In 1937, the Supreme Court for the first time interpreted the general welfare clause of the Constitution, using it to uphold social security and unemployment insurance.

147 **Barack Obama** proposed S.3155-S.3163, S.3242-3245, S.3249-3251, 109th Congress. These were buried inside The Pension Protection Act of 2006 (PL 109-280, Title XIV, §§1401-1606). For example, S.3161 (sebacic acid, overturning an anti-dumping order) became §1555 (1,10-decanedioic acid). S. 3162 (bromoxynil octonoate, causes birth defects, possible carcinogen) became §1439 (2,6-di-bromo-4-cyanophenyl octanoate). S.3243 (metsulfuron-methyl, EPA category III toxic herbicide) became §1491 (4-methoxy-6-methyl-1,3,5-triazin-2-yl). S.3244 (dichlorprop-p acid, pesticide restricted in Denmark) became §1438 (2-ethylhexyl ester). S.3160 (triphenyltin hydroxide, causes birth defects and cancer) became part of The Tax Relief and Health Care Act of 2006 (PL 109-432, §1204). Justin Rood, "Despite Rhetoric, Obama Pushed Lobbyists' Interests," *ABC News, 16 Jul 2007* [http://blogs.abcnews.com/theblotter/2007/07/despite-rhetori.html]; "PACs and lobbyists aided Obama's rise," *Boston Globe*, 9 Aug 2007.

147 **better paid.** McKinley, 86-87.

147 **always ended in panics.** James G. Blaine, *North American Review*, Jan 1890, 37. The *North American Review* published a lively debate between protectionists and free-traders, around 20 pages each month from January 1890 through July 1890. Blaine (R-ME) was the former House speaker and senator who was the unsuccessful Republican candidate for president against Grover Cleveland in 1884. Other contributors included former British Prime Minister William Gladstone (January), Justin Morrill (R-VT, author of the Morrill Tariff Act of 1861, March), William McKinley (June) and Andrew Carnegie (July).

148 **remains controversial.** Douglas A. Irwin, "Tariffs and Growth in Late Nineteenth Century America," 24 *World Economy* 15-30 (Jan 2001); Douglas A. Irwin, "Tariff Incidence in America's Gilded Age" (Dartmouth College, Draft, Dec 2007).

148 **dump the surplus.** William Jennings Bryan and Mary Baird Bryan, *The Memoirs of William Jennings Bryan, by Himself and his wife Mary Baird Bryan* (Philadelphia: J.C. Winston Company, 1925), 254.

148 **Augustus Bacon.** David Graham Phillips, "The Treason of the Senate: Aldrich, The Head of It All," *Cosmopolitan*, Mar 1906 (masses of facts); "Blow TA Trusts Aimed by Bacon," AC, 12 Dec 1903; "Trust Iniquities Exposed by Bacon," AC, 26 Apr 1904; "Aldrich Forced to Tell Truth," AC, 27 Apr 1904, 1; "The Cost of Steel Rails, WSJ, 2 May 1904; "Favors for Foreigners," NYT, 3 May 1904, 8.

149 **Europe adopted the value-added tax.** Wilbur D. Mills, "Tax Legislation — A Look Into the Future," 38 *NYU Institute on Taxation* (1980), 31-6.

149 **trade fetish.** Edmund G. Brown Jr., "Free Trade Fetish," WP, 14 Sep 1992, A15.

150 **foreign-dominated tariff dispute panels.** GATT, the General Agreement on Tariffs and Trade, has been superseded by WTO, the World Trade Organization. Douglas A. Irwin, "Causing problems? The WTO review of causation and injury attribution in U.S. Section 201 cases," *World Trade Review* (2003), 2:3, 297-325; "Antigua claims the pot," *The Economist*, 14 Apr 2007, 19; Joseph J. Urgese, "Dolphin Protection and the Marine Mammal Protection Act Have Met Their Match: The General Agreements of Tariffs and Trade," 31 *Akron L. Rev.* 457 (1998).

151 **Digital Millennium Copyright Act.** Fred Von Lohmann and Wendy Seltzer, "Death by DMCA," *IEEE Spectrum*, Jun 2006, 24; email with Gwen Hinze, Electronic Frontier Foundation, 16 Oct 2006. In addition to copyright provisions, DMCA made it a crime to circumvent "technological protection measures" deployed on copyrighted works — like manufacturing a DVD player that bypasses commercials, workarounds to defeat encryption schemes, or even telling others how to circumvent protection. This can only work if all other countries have similar laws. Movie companies are using this law to enforce copy protection on DVDs and regulate the manufacture of certain machines. The DMCA provisions are usually buried in Model Treaty Article 16, "Intellectual Property Rights" in an untitled 1,000 word section which contains the phrase, "circumvention of effective technological measures." Free-trade treaties are around 250 pages long, plus 900 pages of tariff schedules, and multiple side-agreements.

151 **Civil War Income Tax.** Randolph E. Paul *Taxation in the United States* (Boston: Little, Brown and Company, 1954), 7-29; Joseph J. Thorndike, "An Army of Officials: The Civil War Bureau of Internal Revenue," 2001 TNT 249-39 (24 Dec 2001).

151 **Rent...was deductible.** Early income tax historian, Edwin Seligman says the 1864 statute limited the rental deduction to $200 and that the commissioner had recommended repeal. Edwin R.A. Seligman, *The Income Tax* (NY: The Macmillan Company, 1911), 439, 443. However, the legislative history shows that was the House version, which the Senate struck in favor of continuing the full rental deduction. J.S. Siedman, *Seidman's Legislative History of Federal Income Tax Laws, 1938 - 1861* (NY: Prentice-Hall, 1938), 1029. Paul, *Taxation in the United States* (p. 13) says, "the first 1864 bill extended the deduction for house rent to all persons; previously, only those paying rent had been allowed the deduction."

151 **tax complexity.** *Cong. Globe*, 37th Cong., 1st Sess., 315 (29 Jul 1861).
152 **George S. Boutwell**, *Reminiscences of Sixty Years in Public Affairs* (NY: Greenwood Press, 1968), vol. I, 303-315.
152 **export tariff...$39,000.** Steven R. Weisman, *The Great Tax Wars* (NY: Simon & Schuster, 2002), 56.
153 **South was fiscally ill-prepared.** Seligman, 406-407, 430-492, 482 (Jefferson Davis dispenses with apportionment provision), 468 (revenue not needed as reason for 1872 repeal).
153 **printing paper currency.** Henry D. Capers, *The Life and Times of C.G. Memminger* (Richmond, VA: Everett Waddy Co., 1893), 316-318. Some historians brand Memminger as "bewildered and incompetent." Morison and Commanger, vol. 1, 753.
153 **tithing was so hated.** *The Confederate Records of the State of Georgia, vol. II: State Papers of Governor Joseph E. Brown, 1860 to 1865* (Atlanta: Chas. P. Boyd, 1909), 541-544 (message to General Assembly, 20 November 1863).
154 **public women.** *Atlanta Daily Intelligencer*, 12 Sep 1863.
155 **deadline.** "What's a Deadline," *NPR Morning Edition*, 12 Aug 2002. One can see a layout and reconstruction of a physical deadline at the Andersonville National Historic Site, the infamous Georgia Civil War prison camp.
155 **Magazine articles.** David Wells, "The Communism of a Discriminating Income Tax," *North American Review*, CXXX, Mar 1880, 236-246.
155 **William Bourke Cockran.** 53-2 *Cong. Record* vol. 26, Appendix, 462-469 (30 Jan 1894) at 464-465.
155 **Bryan...retorted eloquently.** 53-2 *Cong. Record* 1655 at 1656 (vol. 26, 30 Jan 1894); Sir Walter Scott's *The Lay of the Last Minstrel* canto 6, stanza 1, is colloquially known as "My Native Land." It is not identified in the *Congressional Record*.
156 **Edward Everett Hale**, "The Man Without A Country," *Atlantic Monthly*, Dec 1863, 665-679.
156 **justices split 4-4.** *Pollock v Farmers' Loan & Trust Co.*, 157 US 429 (Argued March 7, 8, 11, 12, 13, 1895, Decided April 8, 1895, 226 pages), upon rehearing 158 US 601 (Argued May 6, 7, 8, 1895, Decided May 20, 1895, 115 pages).
157 **mystery.** "So was it Field, Gray, or Brewer? No one knows, but there is no lack of educated guesses," wrote Michael J. Brodhead, *David J. Brewer: The Life of a Supreme Court Justice, 1837 - 1910* (Southern Illinois University Press, 1994), 96.
157 **David Brewer.** McKinley, 234 in 1904 edition, 231 in Kraus Reprint of 1896 edition. "Wife of Justice Brewer Won't Let Her Husband Retire from the Bench," NYT, 22 Jul 1909, 1 (Brewer: "Under the hue and cry of to-day we must leave an income tax, which means a tax upon all income, and if that power is given the Government we will see the States taxed not out of their existence but out of their vitality. The idea leads up to the question of placing the entire power in the control of the Nation, and the State is left out of the matter."); Steven R. Weisman, *The*

*Great Tax Wars* (Simon & Schuster, 2002), 252-253. See David J. Brewer, "The Income Tax Cases, Address Delivered before the Graduating Class of the Law Department of the University of Iowa at the Annual Commencement," 8 June 1898 (n.p.,n.d.), cited in Brodhead, 119-120.

157 **uncle-nephew team.** David Ray Papke, *The Pullman Case* (University Press of Kansas, 1999), 74. Stephen Field was Brewer's maternal uncle. Papke calls this "an avuncular sibling rivalry run amuck."

157 **Charles Evans Hughes,** *The Supreme Court of the United States* (Garden City, NY: Garden City Publishing Co., 1936), 54. Though Justice George Shiras was identified as the turncoat in newspapers printed the day after the decision, Hughes wrote that he believed Shiras wasn't the one. Chief Justice Hughes had access to the Supreme Court case file.

157 **different tax rate to every state.** Seligman, 587, quoting William Henry Fleming (D-GA), 28 Apr 1898 speech on House floor, *Cong. Record*, vol. 31, Appendix, 381 *et seq.*

158 **Eugene V. Debs.** Gerald G. Eggert, "Richard Olney and the Income Tax Cases," *Mississippi Valley Historical Review*, vol. 48, no. 1 (Jun 1961), 24-41; *In re Debs*, 158 US 564 (1895) (Argued March 25, 26, 1895; Decided May 27, 1895); Papke, *The Pullman Case*. The specific issue was whether Debs could be imprisoned, without a jury trial, for violating a judge's labor strike injunction. The Supreme Court destroyed the American Railway Union by ruling against Debs. Such broad power granted to judges made the labor injunction a prime weapon against unions, until restricted by the Norris-LaGuardia Act of 1932. Debs went on to run five times as the Socialist Party's candidate for President. He garnered six percent of the national vote in 1912, and while serving time in the Atlanta Federal Penitentiary received 919,799 votes in 1920. A radio station, WEVD was named for him and broadcast in New York City from 1927 until 2001.

158 **Edwin Seligman,** 531-589 (history of "direct" vs "indirect" taxes), 552-554 (purpose of three-fifths compromise).

158 **Rufus King.** John Steele Gordon, "American Taxation," *American Heritage*, May/ Jun 1996, 63.

158 **tax on carriages.** *Hylton v U.S.*, 3 US 171 (1796).

159 **Theodore Roosevelt proposed.** "The Man with the Muck-rake," speech delivered 15 April 1906 at the laying of the corner stone of the Cannon Office Building in Washington, DC. "Annual Message to Congress," 3 Dec 1906.

159 **Nelson Aldrich.** Lincoln Steffens, "Rhode Island: A State For Sale," *McClure's Magazine*, Feb 1904, 337-353; David Graham Phillips, "The Treason of the Senate: Aldrich, The Head of It All," *Cosmopolitan*, Mar 1906; Jerome L. Sternstein, "Corruption in the Gilded Age Senate: Nelson W. Aldrich and the Sugar Trust," *Capitol Studies*, Spring 1978, 14-38; Ron Chernow, *Titan: The Life of John D. Rockefeller, Sr.* (NY: Random House, 1998), 352 (net worth); Cary Reich, *The Life of Nelson A. Rockefeller* (NY: Doubleday, 1996), 4 ("Deny nothing. Explain nothing.").

159  **Aldrich...King Leopold.** Jerome L. Sternstein, "King Leopold II, Senator Nelson W. Aldrich, and the Strange Beginnings of American Economic Penetration of the Congo," *African Historical Studies*, vol. 2, no. 2 (1969), 189-204; "Ryan's Congo Rubber Concession," WSJ, 13 Dec. 1907 (payments to Leopold), 4; "From the Papers," WSJ, 21 Nov 1906, 2 (rubber, railroad and mining concessions); "Congo Free State Concession," WSJ, 15 Nov 1906, 2 (8,400,000 acres ceded to French-American-British company); "Nelson W. Aldrich, Ex-Senator, Dead," NYT, 17 Apr 1915, 11; "Ryan Was A Partner of King Leopold II," NYT 24 Nov. 1928, 8.

160  **Suffrage in Rhode Island.** The U.S. Supreme Court declined to intervene when citizens challenged their disenfranchisement. *Luther v Borden*, 48 US 1, 43 (1841); Charles Evans Hughes, *The Supreme Court of the United States* (Garden City, NY: Garden City Publishing Co., 1936), 34-35.

160  **never be ratified.** 44 *Cong. Record* 4109, 4120, 4121 (5 Jul 1909, unanimous Senate vote), 4391 (Samuel McCall (R-MA) complains about prearranged program), 4440; Seligman, 595-596; Sidney Ratner, *American Taxation: It's History as a Social Force in Democracy* (NY: W.W. Norton Company, 1942), 215.

161  **Amendment was unnecessary.** Robert Stanley, *Origins of the Federal Income Tax, 1861 – 1913* (NY: Oxford Univ. Press, 1993), 176.

161  **municipal bond interest.** Bonds of "political subdivision" exempt from tax: *Commissioner v Shamberg's Estate*, 144 F2d 998 (CA-2, 1944), cert den 323 US 792 (1945); In *South Carolina v Baker*, 485 US 505 (1988), the Supreme Court rejected the argument that the tax exemption for state and local bonds is constitutionally protected. This removed most constitutional constraints against federal taxation and regulation of municipal finance.

161  **Dorsey W. Shackleford.** Randolph Paul, *Taxation for Prosperity* (Indianapolis, Bobs-Merrill Company, 1947), 22. In the events that led to passage of the 1909 corporate excise tax, Sen. Albert Cummins (R-IA) proposed a graduated rate on individual incomes over $5,000, ranging from two percent up to six percent on incomes over $100,000. Seligman, 592; Ratner, 282; John F. Witte, *The Politics and Development of the Federal Income Tax* (Madison, WI: University of Wisconsin Press, 1985), 74; 44 *Cong. Record* 1468 (1909).

162  **confiscate wealth.** Bascom Timmons, *Garner of Texas: A Personal History* (NY: Harper & Brother Publishers, 1948), 85.

162  **constitutionality.** *Springer v U.S.*, 102 US 586 (1880, on 1864 tax); *Pollock v Farmers' Loan & Trust Co.*, 157 US 429, upon rehearing 158 US 601 (1895, on 1894 Tax); *Flint v Stone-Tracy Co.*, 220 US 107 (1911, on 1909 Tax); *Brushaber v Union Pacific R. Co.*, 240 US 1 (1916, on 1913 Tax); *Dodge v Osborn*, 240 US 118 (1916, on 1913 Tax); *Dodge v Brady*, 240 US 122 (1916, on 1913 Tax); Recent cases challenging Sixteenth Amendment: *Coulter*, 82 TC 580 (1984); *Abrams*, 82 TC 403 (1984); Alan D. Egerdahl, TCM sur order Docket No. 6125-86 (15 May 1986), 1986 TNT 207-41, 87 TNT 99-9. Ratification procedure by states examined: *U.S. v Stahl*, 792 F2d 1438 (CA-9, 1986); *Mertens Law of Federal Income Taxation* (1991 ed.) §4.10.

## Notes 395

163 **withholding.** "Income Tax Law In Effect To-Day," NYT, 1 Nov 1913, 1; S. Rep. No. 1631, 77th Cong., 2d Sess., reprinted in 1942-2 CB 504, 514. All persons paying salaries or wages in excess of $3,000 were required to withhold "such sum as will be sufficient to pay the normal tax imposed thereon by this section." The early withholding tax ended in 1917, replaced by information reporting.

163 **first Form 1040.** Mary Duan, "The little 1040 form and how it grew," *San Jose Business Journal*, 25 Jan 2002.

163 **number 1000.** The set of early tax forms was published in the *Journal of Accountancy*, from November 1913 through February 1914, together with accompanying regulations.

163 **Sales Tax Rebellion.** Jordan A. Schwarz, "John Nance Garner and the Sales Tax Rebellion of 1932," *The Journal of Southern History*, May 1964, 162-180.

164 **Committee for Constitutional Government.** Paul, *Taxation in the United States*, 380; Norman Redlich, "Limit Whose Taxes," *The Nation*, 20 Oct 1951, 326;"Ceiling is Sought for Federal Taxes," NYT, 3 Oct 1943, 87; "Drive for 25% Limit on Taxes Revived," NYT, 2 Jan 1952, 18; "25% Tax Limit Held Aid to Big Incomes," NYT, 4 Jan 1952, 89.

165 **The FairTax.** H.R. 25 (108th Congress, introduced 17 Jan 2003). Tax Analysts awarded it the 2005 "Prize for Worst Idea in a Serious Public Policy Debate." Joseph J. Thorndike, "Fair Tax, Bad Tax: The National Sales Tax's Insidious Influence," 2005 TNT 105-3 (26 May 2005); *Simple, Fair, and Pro-Growth: Proposals to Fix America's Tax System*, The President's Advisory Panel on Federal Tax Reform, November 2005, Chapter 9; Neal Boortz and Congressman John Linder, *The FairTax Book: Saying Goodbye to the Income Tax and the IRS* (NY: Regan Books, 2005).

165 **Temporary Income Tax.** 1942-2 CB 624.

166 **Current Tax Payment Act.** Paul, *Taxation in the United States*, 326-349.

167 **Donald Duck.** "Donald Duck pays his income taxes," *Look*, 10 Mar 1942. *The New Spirit* and *The Spirit of '43* are available on the DVD, "Walt Disney Treasures — On the Front Lines: The War Years."

167 **Irving Berlin.** "Berlin Writes Song for Treasury," NYT, 26 Jan 1942, 17; "I paid my income tax today," Dick Robertson and His Orchestra; Vocal chorus by Dick Robertson and The American Four Fox Trot, Decca 4151; also Barry Wood and vocal quartet, Victor 27760; also The Charlie McCarthy Show, 15 Mar 1942; and there's a Danny Kaye recording floating around the internet. Lyrics shown are from the Decca recording. Irving Berlin Collection, Box 231, Folder 27, Recorded Sound Reference Center, Library of Congress. The New York Public Library has the Victor recording under their catalogue number "*LOP666" which the librarian called, "an appropriate number for that song."

167 **lack money.** John Morton Blum, *From the Morgenthau Diaries: Years of Urgency 1938-1941* (Boston: Houghton Mifflin Company, 1965), 303 (Berlin), 307 (tax anticipation certificates), 315 (Chester Barnard), 316 (November 5 meeting); John Morton Blum, *From the Morgenthau Diaries: Years of War 1941-1945* (Boston: Houghton Mifflin Company, 1967), 40 (lower exemption and withholding).

168 **Eisenhower.** John F. Witte, *The Politics and Development of the Federal Income Tax* (Madison, WI: University of Wisconsin Press, 1985), 147-148; Dwight D. Eisenhower, "Radio and Television Address to the American People on the Tax Program," 15 Mar 1954 at www.americanpresidency.org.

169 **John Kennedy reduced.** "Ronald Reagan's 1964 Cloud," WSJ, 25 May 1976, 20. Rates which had ranged from 20 percent to 91 percent range since 1954 were reduced to a 14 percent to 70 percent range by Kennedy (and enacted posthumously in February 1964).

169 **maximum 50 percent.** Tax Reform Act of 1969, §804, adding IRC §1348.

169 **weird plan.** Robert H. Jackson, *That Man: An Insider's Portrait of Franklin D. Roosevelt* (NY: Oxford University Press: 2003), 132-133; Paul, *Taxation in the United States*, 294-295; "Treasury Drafts Profits 'Ceiling'," NYT, 26 Sep 1941.

169 **dead-on-arrival.** "Text of President's Message to Congress," NYT, 28 Apr 1942, 12; Paul, *Taxation for Prosperity*, 100-101, 105; Paul, *Taxation in the United States*, 301-302. Revisionists claim that Roosevelt wasn't serious, but Randolph Paul, the Treasury official responsible for presenting the $25,000 plan to Congress, writes in earnest detail how he gained a hearing on Capitol Hill to present the 100 percent supertax proposal. Roosevelt repeated this proposal on Labor Day. The press called it the "C.I.O." proposal after the labor union.

169 **Public Debt Act of 1943,** PL 34 §4, *Statutes at Large*, 78th Congress, 1st Sess., vol. 57, Part I, Public Laws, 63-64 (11 Apr 1943), reads in part, "Executive Order Numbered 9250...which are in conflict with this section are hereby rescinded."

## CHAPTER 7: CULTURE BINGO

171 **Luntz Research.** Tax Report, WSJ, 31 May 2000.

171 **Holtsville Fire District.** *Fallica v Town of Brookhaven*, 69 AD2d 579, 419 NYS2d 102 (Suffolk County Supreme Court, 6 Aug 1979). This decision was reversed on appeal. 52 NY2d 794, 417 NE2d 1248, 436 NYS2d 707 (NY Court of Appeals, 22 Dec 1980)

172 **Kennedy.** "An Interview with Mortimer M. Caplin," 105 TNT 1701 (20 Dec 2004). The plaque is on the third floor in the corridor near 12th Street, outside the Commissioner's Conference Room.

172 **IRS...Conduct.** Rev. Proc. 64-22; 5 CFR 2635.

172 **Philadelphia IRS Service Center** was using Univac 1100/82 and Univac 1100/84 computers to process returns in 1985. They averaged 5 years old, rather new by IRS standards. "Information on IRS' Philadelphia Service Center," GAO/GGD-86-25FS (Nov 1985).

173 **Culture Bingo.** "Comments on IRS Economic Reality Training Modules," American Institute of Certified Public Accountants, 7 Feb 1996.

173 **lockboxes.** "IRS Lockbox Banks: More Effective Oversight, Stronger Controls, and Further Study of Costs and Benefits are Needed," GAO-03-299 (Jan 2003);

"DOJ Announces Mellon Bank Settlement Over Destruction of Returns," 2007 TNT 126-30 (28 Jun 2007).

174 **San Francisco.** "Tax Payments Lost Following Traffic Accident," 2005 TNT 185-7 (26 Sep 2005). "Problem Alert: IRS Reports Some Tax Payments From 13 States Lost," IRS Press Release, 23 Sep 2005.

174 **privatize collection.** "Hearing on Fiscal Year 2007 Appropriations for the Internal Revenue Service," House Committee On Appropriations: Subcommittee On Transportation, Treasury, Housing and Urban Development, and the District of Columbia, 29 Mar 2006, *CQ Transcriptions;* Tom Herman, "IRS Plans to Use Private Firms To Pursue Taxpayers This Year," WSJ, 21 Jun 2006; "Details Emerge Over IRS Contract Winner," *WebCPA.com*, 5 May 2006; "The Gifting of New Jersey Tax Officials," State of New Jersey Commission of Investigation, Dec 2005; "Workers for N.J. enjoyed freebies," *Bergen Record*, 21 Dec 2005; "City's debt collector gets hefty share," *Richmond Times-Dispatch*, 23 Apr 2006. A pilot program for private debt collection was attempted under the Clinton administration, but failed. PL 104-52 (1995).

174 **John Sanborn.** Joseph J. Thorndike, "Historical Perspective: The Unhappy History of Private Tax Collection," 2004 TNT 182-2 (20 Sep 2004); John Lewis, "Collecting Taxes Is Government's Responsibility," 2007 TNT 101-24 (23 May 2007), citing H.R. Report No. 559, 43d Cong., 1st Sess., 9 (1874).

175 **hate mail.** "At IRS, the check — and a lot of other stuff — is in the mail," AJC, 9 Apr 1997 (Associated Press).

176 **50 percent compliance.** *The New Republic*, 12 Aug 1916, 32-33.

176 **Virginia...repealed.** Steven R. Weisman, *The Great Tax Wars* (NY: Simon & Shuster, 2002), 253.

177 **class tax.** Carolyn C. Jones, "Class Tax To Mass Tax: The Role of propaganda In The Expansion of the Income Tax During World War II," 37 *Buffalo Law Review* 685 (1988-1989); Jay Starkman, "Simply Taxes: Just Get Rid of 89 Million Unnecessary Returns," 2005 TNT 157-26 (15 Aug 2005).

177 **farmers.** A.L.M. Wiggins, "They Can't Fool the Revenue Man," *Collier's*, 20 Sep 1947, 68-71. Wiggins was undersecretary of the treasury in 1947.

177 **accustomed to paying.** "The SET Tax: A Tax System for Our Future," CPAJ, Feb 2006 (Simple Exact Transparent Tax...Not everybody may pay, BUT EVERYBODY FILES!).

177 **Horse Act of 1884.** "Problems in Tax Compliance, A panel Discussion," *Georgia Journal of Accounting*, Spring 1981, 9; William R. Mathisen, "Enrolled Agents Since 1884?" *National Public Accountant*, Jun 2000.

177 **J.P. Morgan.** "Legal Tax-Dodging Upheld by Morgan," NYT, 8 Jun 1937, 27. In 1933, testimony before the Senate Banking and Currency Committee revealed that Morgan, the most powerful banker in the world, with liquid assets totaling $52 million, paid no income tax in 1931 and 1932. David Laro, "The Evolution of the Tax Court as an Independent Tribunal," 1995 *Univ. of Illinois. L. Rev.* 17.

177  **Leona Helmsley.** "Queen of Mean Hotelier Helmsley Dies," *Associated Press*, 20 Aug 07.
178  **Irwin Schiff.** *U.S. v Schiff*, 612 F2d 73 (CA-2, 1979), ("you're going to wind up in Leavenworth"); *United States v Schiff*, 647 F2d 163 (CA-2, 1981), cert den 454 US 835 (convicted of willfully failing to file tax returns for the years 1974 and 1975); *Schiff v Commissioner*, 751 F2d 116 (CA-2, 1984) (affirming criminal tax evasion conviction); *Schiff v Simon & Schuster, Inc.*, 766 F2d 61 (CA-2, 1985) (frivolous appeal, taxpayer must pay damages and double costs); *Schiff v Simon & Schuster, Inc.*, 780 F2d 210 (CA-2, 1985) ("has not filed tax returns since 1973"); *Schiff*, TC Memo 1984-223 ("respondent has clearly and convincingly demonstrated fraud for both 1974 and 1975"); *U.S. v Schiff*, 801 F2d 108 (CA-2, 1986) (self-proclaimed "professional tax resister" couldn't challenge jury instructions from his 14-day trial); *U.S. v Schiff*, 876 F2d 272 (CA-2, 1989) (criminal probation requirement to file tax returns doesn't violate his Fifth Amendment right against self-incrimination); *Schiff*, TC Memo 1992-183 (rejecting frivolous arguments that taxes are voluntary, "so many bites at the apple"); *Schiff v U.S.*, 919 F2d 830 (CA-2, 1990) ("Schiff had received federal reserve notes in 1976, which he distinguished from taxable dollars").
180  **delusional disorder.** "Schiff Owes Over $2 Million, Justice Says," 2004 TNT 120-16 (17 Jun 2004); "Casting a Web," WSJ, 10 Dec 2004, 1.
180  **flimflam.** "Pressing Recent Attack, Government Accuses Schiff of Encouraging Evasion," WP, 14 Mar 2003, E3; "Judge Tells Tax Adviser to Stop Selling Book," NYT, 17 Jun 2003; "Professional Tax Resister Sentenced To More Than 12 Years In Prison For Tax Fraud," U.S. Department of Justice Press Release, 24 Feb 2006; "Tax protester's friend sentenced to prison," *Las Vegas Review-Journal*, 24 Feb 2006; "Tax Protester Schiff Sentenced," *Las Vegas Review-Journal*, 25 Feb 2006.
180  **illegal tax protester.** PL 105-206, IRS Restructuring and Reform Act of 1998, §3707.
180  **Paul Petrino.** "Happy returns for acquitted tax accountant," *Newsday*, 4 May 2006; "In tax trouble? He's a good man to call," *Newsday*, 4 May 2006; "Long Island Tax Return Preparer Indicted For Tax Fraud," U.S. Department of Justice Press Release, 25 Mar 2005; "Private Practice Lawyer Profile for Robert S. Fink," Martindale.com.
180  **Wesley Snipes.** David Cay Johnston, "Wesley Snipes Cleared of Serious Tax Charges," NYT, 2 Feb 2008; *U.S. v Robert R. Raymond and Robert G. Bernhoft*, 228 F3d 804 (CA-7, 2000), cert den 533 US 902 (2001); "Wesley Snipes Gets 3 Years For Not Filing Tax Returns," NYT, 25 Apr 2008.
181  **Omar Burleson.** Obtained under the Freedom of Information Act, documents pertaining to issuance of Rev. Rul. 70-549 and Rev. Rul 71-7. Of particular interest are (1) Memorandum from Director-Interpretative Division to Chief Counsel, 17 Nov 1969, (2) Form M-1936, Record of Conference with Taxpayers and their Representatives, 6 May 1970, and (3) Letter from IRS Commissioner

Randolph W. Thrower to Mr. Burleson, 12 Jun 1970. The Tax Court has upheld the teacher-preacher tax, without mentioning the dubious history of the IRS ruling. *Lustig*, TC Summary 1995-6.

182 **repeal...housing allowance.** "Treasury Report on Tax Simplification and Reform: Treasury Department Report to the President, November 27, 1984," Commerce Clearing House Standard Federal Tax Reports, Extra Edition, Number 52, 29 Nov 1984, 73.

182 **Bobby Baker**, *Wheeling and Dealing* (NY: W.W. Norton & Co., 1978), 43-44.

182 **Dear Carolyn.** David Burnham, *A Law Unto Itself: Power, Politics and the IRS* (NY: Random House, 1989), 247. Abe Fortas' wife, Carolyn Agger was a top Washington tax attorney. She worked for Randolph Paul at Paul, Weiss, Rifkind, Wharton, and Garrison. Four years after Paul's death in 1956, she took its Washington tax department to her husband's firm, Arnold, Fortas and Porter. Bruce Allen Murphy, *Fortas, The Rise and Ruin of a Supreme Court Justice* (NY: William Morrow and Company, 1988), 79.

183 **30 percent of their assessments.** "A Vision for a New IRS," Report of the National Commission on Restructuring the Internal Revenue Service (Washington, DC), 25 Jun 1997, 47.

183 **3 cent notice.** "Peach Buzz," AJC, 5 Mar 1991, E2.

184 **locks and chains.** Letter from IRS District Director Paul Williams, 24 May 1993, in response to Jay Starkman letter, 30 Apr 1993.

186 **death of your CPA.** Rev. Rul. 79-417, obsoleted by Rev. Rul. 95-34.

186 **New York Sun.** Randolph Paul, *Taxation for Prosperity* (Indianapolis: Bobs-Merrill Company, 1947), 50.

186 **and tax purposes.** "Q&A," AJC, 18 Nov 2005, E2; "Use of Social Security Account Number," Internal Revenue Code §6109(d), 87th Cong., 1st Sess., S. Rep. No. 1102 (1961), accompanying H.R. 8876.

187 **H&R Block.** "Working Class Families Pay a Premium for Refund Loans," National Public Radio Morning Edition, 1 Feb 2005; "The Spitzer Savings Plan," WSJ, 3 Mar 2006, A10; "H&R Block Sued Over Fee Disclosure," 16 Mar 2006, D1; Eliot Spitzer, "How H&R Block Took Advantage of Clients," WSJ, 31 Mar 2006, A17; "Legal Proceedings," H&R Block 2006 Annual Report, 84.

188 **ITIN filers.** "Tax Returns Rise for Immigrants in U.S. Illegally," NYT, 16 Apr 2007; "Illegal immigrants filing taxes more than ever," Associated Press, 13 Apr 2007.

188 **Jackson Hewitt.** "U.S. Accuses Part of Tax Chain of Fraud," NYT, 4 Apr 2007, C3; "Fraud Suits Filed Against Tax Preparer in 4 States, U.S. Targets Jackson Hewitt Franchises," WP, 4 Apr 2007, D2.

189 **$2 per return.** "Taxpayer Service: State Experience Indicates IRS Would Face Challenges Developing an Internet Filing System with Net Benefits," GAO-07-570 (Apr 2007), 28-29; Chuck Lacijan, "Briefing for Use of Technology to Improve Returns," Briefing Materials for January 30-31 Meetings of National Commission on Restructuring the IRS, *Daily Tax Report*, 10 Jan 1997, L-19; *IRS e-Stategy for Growth*, IRS Pub. 3187 (Rev. 1-2005), 9.

190  **No return at all.** *Dixon*, 28 TC 338 (1957).
190  **Bruce Ungar.** Crystal Tandon, "IRS Seeing Overdisclosure of Reportable Transactions, Officials Say," 2006 TNT 197-2 (Oct. 12, 2006); "Description of Revenue Provisions Contained in the President's Fiscal Year 2009 Budget Proposal," JCT (JCS-1-08), Mar 08, 167 (prisoners), 176 (e-filing).
191  **Bankruptcy works.** *In re Covington*, 85 AFTR2d 2000-1706, (Bkrptcy DC-SC, 3/6/2000); *Torres*, 93 AFTR2d 2004-2428 (Bkrptcy App Panel, CA-1, 2004); *Matthews*, 75 AFTR2d 95-2445 (Bkrptcy DC Ala, 1995); Sheldon Banoff and Richard Lipton, "IRS Causes Emotional Stress, Must Pay Taxpayer," JTax, Sep 2004, 191.
192  **Face the Nation.** Charles O. Rossotti, *Many Unhappy Returns* (Boston: Harvard Business School Press, 2005), 7, citing interview with CBS' Bob Schieffer on 28 Sep 1997. Rossotti was IRS commissioner from 1997 to 2002. Jennifer Long later lost a suit against IRS claiming employment discrimination and retaliation resulting from her September 1997 testimony on IRS abuses before the Senate Finance Committee. "Court Dismisses Outspoken Agent's Complaint Against IRS," 2001 TNT 48-2 (12 Mar 2001).
192  **Employee Protection System Records.** *Federal Register*, volume 66, number 231 (30 Nov 2001), 59,839-59,841.
192  **Robert Cleveland.** *Cleveland v Rotman*, 297 F3d 569 (CA-7, 2002).
193  **Bruce Barron.** "Settling a Longtime Taxing Score, Woman is Victor in IRS War That Saw Her Husband's Suicide," *Boston Globe*, 15 May 1998, A1; "Death and Taxes: Blaming it for hounding her husband to suicide, a widow brings the IRS to its knees," *People*, 29 Jun 1998, 145; "Suicide Puts IRS on Trial; Salem Widow Seeking $1 Million in Landmark Wrongful Death Case," *Union Leader* (Manchester, NH), 31 Jul 1997; "IRS Denies Causing Derry Man's Suicide," *Union Leader*, 6 Aug 1997; "IRS Wipes Out Derry Widow's Debt 'After Five Years of Torture'," *Union Leader*, 6 May 1998;
193  **Judith Orlando.** "Delinquent taxpayers lose homes; Suffolk profits," *Newsday*, 9 Aug 2004.
194  **Ehsanolla Motaghed.** Christopher R. Brauchli, "From the Wool Sack," *The Colorado Lawyer* vol. 23, no. 8 (Aug 1994), 1741; *Omaha World-Herald*, 28 Apr 1990, 35; "Feds May Exhume Body of Delinquent Taxpayer," *Associated Press*, 3 Aug 1990; *Newsday*, 5 Aug 1990, 14 (Eternal Revenue Service). *Austin American-Statesman*, 9 Aug 1990, A18 (late taxpayer).
194  **Samuel Swartwout.** Billy Ray Brunson, *Adventures of Samuel Swartwout in the Age of Jefferson and Jackson* (Lewiston, NY: Edwin Mellen Press, 1989); Leonard D. White, *The Jacksonians: A Study in Administrative History 1829 - 1861* (NY: MacMillan Company, 1956) 332-343, 424-430; "Mr. Swartwout and Mr. Birdsall," NYT 2 Jun 1853; Paul Johnson, *A History of the American People* (NY: HarperCollins Publishers, 1997), 341.
194  **cipher letter.** *Ex parte Bollman & Swartwout*, 8 US 75 (1807); "Decisions of the Supreme Court," NYT, 3 Feb 1901; *United States v Burr*, 25 Fed. Cas. 187 (No. 14,694) (C.C.D.Va., 1807).

195 **investigation.** *House Report* 313, 25th Cong., 3rd Sess. (1839); House Report 669, 27th Cong, 2nd Sess. (1842, Tyler).

196 **two Supreme Court cases.** *U.S. v Irving*, 42 US 250 (1843); *Murray v Hoboken Land & Improvement Co.*, 59 US 272 (1856) ; Hannis Taylor, "Due Process of Law: Persistent and Harmful Influence of Murray v Hoboken Land & Improvement Co.," 24 *Yale Law Journal* 353, 369 (March 1915); "Letter from Samuel Swartwout, Esq.," NYT, 6 Apr 1853, 1.

196 *Jesse Hoyt v U.S.*, 51 US 109 (1850).

196 **James Couzens.** Fred F. Sully, "Those Refunded Millions," *Saturday Evening Post*, 21 Jun 1924, 36; "Shows Big Refunds in Oil Firms' Taxes," NYT, 11 Dec 1925, 10, (list of big corporate refunds); "Couzens Report Charges Tax Loss of $308,000,000," NYT, 13 Jan 1926, 1; Harry Barnard, "Granddaddy of the Tax Scandals," *The Nation*, 19 Jan 1952, 57; Harry Barnard, *Independent Man: The Life of Senator James Couzens*, (NY: Charles Scribner's Sons, 1958) 134-138, 158-167; "Investigation of Bureau of Internal Revenue, Pursuant to Senate Resolution 68," Senate Report 27, 69th Congress, 1st Sess. (1926), 3 parts. See also *Congressional Record*, 22 Mar 1929, 5149ff., for Couzens' comments on reports. "Select Committee on Investigations of the Bureau of Internal Revenue," *U.S. Revenue Acts 1909 - 1950*, edited by B. Reams, Jr. (Buffalo, NY: William S. Hein & Co., 1979), 144 volumes. Vols. 3 - 6 are the Couzens Investigation, reproducing all the committee testimony and reports from 14 March 1924 to 2 February 1926 in over 5,000 pages.

196 **Truman Newberry.** *Newberry v U.S.*, 256 US 232 (1921). The scandal concerned $100,000 he had spent on his election, which was in excess of the $10,000 limit set by the Michigan legislature.

197 **Francis J. Heney.** C.C. Regier, *The Era of the Muckrakers*, (Gloucester, MA: P. Smith, 1957, reprint of University of North Carolina Press, 1932), 72-75; "My Own Story by Fremont Older," www.sfgenealogy.com/sf/history/hbmos5.htm.

198 **tax fraud.** "796 Tax Officials Dropped for Graft," NYT, 20 Mar 1924, 1.

198 **geological experts.** Randolph Paul, *Taxation for Prosperity*, 304-307. He called depletion "sheer gifts [to] corporations." Percentage depletion for oil and gas was largely eliminated after 1974, following the 1973 oil crisis.

199 **refunds over $20,000.** Executive Order 5079, "Publication of Internal Revenue Tax Refund Decisions in Excess of $20,000," 14 Mar 1929.

200 **Truman Tax Scandal.** Andrew J. Dunar, *The Truman Scandals and the Politics of Morality* (Columbia, MD: University of Missouri Press, 1984); Jules Abels, *The Truman Scandals* (Chicago: Henry Regnery Company, 1956), 123-251; Robert J. Donovan, *Tumultous Years: The Presidency of Harry S. Truman, 1949-1953* (NY: W.W. Norton & Company, 1982), 372-375; "Mr. Truman and the Collectors," *The Nation*, 27 Oct 1951, 341; Lorraine Nelson, "The Trail of the Tax Thieves," *The New Republic*, 12 Nov 1951, 11-14; William Shannon, "The Tax Thieves of 1951: Business and Pleasure in New York," *The New Republic*, 3 Dec 1951, 14; "Internal Confusion in Internal Revenue," *The Nation*, 19 Jan 1952, 55.

200 **Daniel A. Bolich.** "Another High Aide Quits Tax Bureau," NYT, 20 Nov. 1951, 1; "Tax Inquiry Hears Bolich Killed Case," NYT, 2 Apr 1952; "Review for Grunewald," NYT, 16 Oct. 1956, 67; "2 Acquitted Here in Third Tax Trial," NYT, 18 Apr 1959, 16.

201 **Joseph Nunan...John Wenchel...waivers...Indianapolis Brewing.** "Treasury Granted Waivers To Nunan In Nine Tax Cases," NYT, 15 Feb 1952, 1; "Nunan Mentioned in Tax Cut Case," NYT, 15 Feb. 1952, 10; "Tax Bureau Ousts Official On Coast; J.A. Malone Faces Fraud Trial — Permits to Nunan Firm in 102 Cases Cited," NYT, 19 Feb 1952, 11.

201 **William Rhodes Davis.** "Williams Says 38 Million Tax Case Was Settled for 3% With Boyle Aid," NYT, 27 Jun 1952, 1.

201 **little tin box.** "Nunan is Indicted," NYT, 3 Dec 1952, 1; "Nunan Cash Cited in Taxation Case," NYT, 17 Jun 1954; "U.S. Agent Doubts Nunan Home Hoard," NYT, 24 Jun 1954; "Nunan is Guilty of Tax Evasion," NYT, 30 Jun 1954, 1; *Nunan v U.S*, 236 F2d 576 (CA-2, 1957), cert den 353 US 912 (1957), reh'g den 353 US 952; "[Sheriff Thomas] Farley deposited $360,660 in 7 Years; Most From Tin Box," NYT, 7 Oct 1931, 1; Tammany corruption was parodied by Frank Loesser in "A Little Tin Box," a comic relief song from his musical, *Fiorello*.

202 **Welburn Mayock**, 32 TC 966 (1959).

202 **Monroe Dowling...James Johnson.** "Dowling Ousted as Tax Head Here; Own Tax At Issue," NYT, 18 Mar 1952, 1.

203 **Joseph Marcelle.** "Ex-Tax Collector Accepts Subpoena," NYT, 25 Oct 1951, 1.

203 **James Smyth.** "Tax Collector Fired by Truman is Indicted," LAT, 12 Dec 1951, 1; "House Tax Inquiry Gets Smyth Data; Ex-Collector Appointed Despite Three Unfavorable Reports, Scandals Group Hears," NYT, 7 Feb 1952, 24.

203 **James P. Finnegan.** "Finnegan is Guilty on 2 of 5 Charges," NYT, 15 Mar 1952, 1.

203 **Robert Selden.** "2D Tax Aide Balks At House Inquiry; New York Official Refuses to Answer Bribery Question — Racing Enriched a Clerk," NYT 15 Mar 1952, 6.

203 **Adrian Ash.** "Former Film Aide Scored At Inquiry; Representative Says Business Men Should Be Jailed for Entertaining Tax Agents," NYT, 20 Mar 1952, 19.

204 **Hyman Harvey Klein.** "Perjury Inquiry Faced By Maloney; House Unit to Send Testimony of Grunewald's Attorney to Justice Department, Says He Sought Help," NYT, 22 Mar 1952, 1; *Klein*, 247 F2d 908 (1957), cert den 355 US 924.

205 **Eisenhower...campaign issue.** *Nation*, 19 Jan 1952; Dunar, 135-148.

205 **Willie Sutton.** "Sutton, Bank Thief Captured in Street by Brooklyn Police," NYT, 19 Feb 1952, 1, which appeared on the same front page with "200 Tax Aides Here Queried on Assets," about a House Ways and Means subcommittee investigation of New York's 2,300 BIR field employees and the dismissal of John Malone, assistant chief of the San Francisco BIR office following his indictment.

205 **IRS rigidity.** "Dobrovir Testimony Before IRS Restructuring Commission," 96 TNT 221-40 (8 Nov 1996), citing Marcus Farbenblum, *The I.R.S. and the Freedom of Information & Privacy Acts of 1974* (McFarland & Company, 1991), 7.

206   Tax Analysts. George Guttman, "Should IRS Chief Counsel Report To The Commissioner?" 79 TNT 1542 (22 Jun 1998).

**CHAPTER 8: THE POWER TO DESTROY**

209   wise exercise. Boris Bittker, *Federal Taxation of Incomes, Estates and Gifts* (Boston: Warren, Gorham & Lamont, 1981), ¶1.2.6.

209   Kennedy...audited Richard Nixon. Victor Lasky, *It Didn't Start With Watergate* (NY: Dial Press, 1977), 55; "Prepared Statement of David Burnham Before the Senate Finance Committee Oversight Hearing on the Internal Revenue Service, Tuesday, September 23, 1997," 97 TNT 185-54 (23 Sep 1997).

209   Senator James Couzens. *Couzens*, 11 BTA 1040 (1928); Robert Lacey, *Ford: The Men and the Machine* (Boston: Little Brown & Co., 1986), 165-179; *Dodge v Ford Motor Co.*, 204 Mich. 459, 170 NW 668 (1919).

210   William Boyce Thompson. "Charges Laxness in Income Audits: $597,000 Saving in Taxes by W.B. Thompson Cited in Couzens Revenue Inquiry," NYT, 7 Mar 1925, 1; "Calls Republicans Friends of the Rich," NYT, 15 Mar 1925, 16; "Report of Select Committee on Investigation of the Bureau of Internal Revenue," 69th Congress, 1st Sess., Report No. 27, Part I, 227 (12 Jan 1926).

213   Al Capone. Elmer L. Irey, *The Tax Dodgers* (NY: Greenberg Press, 1948); Dennis E. Hoffman, *Scarface Al and the Crime Crusaders, Chicago's Private War against Capone* (Carbondale: Southern Illinois University Press, 1993) cites *Chicago Tribune* (10 Oct 1931) as source for Coolidge, not Hoover, unleashing federal campaign against Capone; Francis X. Buxch, "The Trial of Alphonse Capone" from *Enemies of the State* (Indianapolis: Bobbs-Merrill Company, 1954) as reprinted in *Great Courtroom Battles*, Richard E. Rubenstein, editor (Chicago: Playboy Press, 1973) cites Elmer Irey's courtroom testimony that the Capone investigation began on October 18, 1928, during the Coolidge administration. John Kobler, *Capone: The Life and World of Al Capone* (NY: G.P. Putnam's Sons, 1971); David Burnham, *A Law Unto Itself: Power, Politics and the IRS* (NY: Random House, 1989), 89–95.

214   illicit business...income. *U.S. v Sullivan*, 274 US 259 (1927).

214   Elmer Irey was chief of the Enforcement Branch, United States Treasury Special Intelligence Unit. Irey, not the FBI, placed marked bills in the Lindbergh ransom that resulted in the arrest of Bruno Hauptman in 1934. Patrick O'Rourke was a pseudonym (Irey, 16). In some accounts, O'Rourke is referred to as Michael Malone. The IRS Criminal Investigation Division produced a promotional video in 2003, "The Elmer Irey – Frank Wilson Story." Exiting the Capone courtroom, Wilson says to Irey, "When history writes the Capone case, what do you want to bet, Ness takes the credit." "Nah, not a chance," replies Irey.

216   jury instructions. Kevin F. O'Malley, Jay E. Grenig, William C. Lee, *Federal Jury Practice and Instructions: Criminal, 5th ed.* (St. Paul, MN: West Group, 2000), §67.03. Improper jury instructions can result in overturning a tax protester's conviction. *Cheek v U.S.*, 498 US 192 (1991).

217 **Ronald Isley.** "Ron Isley Gets 3 Years for Tax Evasion," NYT, 5 Sep 2006 (citing AP).

217 **William Scholl.** *U.S v William L. Scholl*, 83 AFTR2d ¶99-437 (CA-9, 1999); Scott R. Fouch, "Recreational Gamblers: Gambling Once Too Often?" 2004 TNT 235-43 (7 Dec 2004); *Martin A. Sullivan*, "Gambling Taxes: The Fun Way to Raise Revenue?" 2004 TNT 144-4 (27 Jul 2004); "The Skinny Injustice," *Tucson Weekly*, 26 Apr 2001; *In the Matter of William L. Scholl*, Arizona Supreme Court, SB-00-0085-D (18 Apr 2001).

218 **Huey Long.** Irey, 88-117; Albert Fried, *FDR And His Enemies*, (NY: St. Martin's Press, 1999), 101-110; T. Harry Williams, *Huey Long*, (NY: Alfred A. Knopf, 1969), 794-798, 819-828, 876; *75 Years of IRS Criminal Investigation History*, Department of the Treasury, Internal Revenue Service, Document 7233 (Rev. 2-95), 31-33.

218 **Tax on Lying.** *Grosjean v. American Press Co.*, 297 US 233 (1936); Richard D White, *Kingfish: The Reign of Huey P. Long* (NY: Random House, 2006), 211-215.

218 **Joseph Fisher.** "Long Aide On Trial Says He Is Gambler," NYT, 2 Apr 1935, 8; "Long's Friend Paid Under False Name," NYT, 3 Apr 1935, 4; "Big Bank Deposits Made By Long Aide," NYT, 4 Apr 1935, 11; "Fisher, Long's Ally, Guilty of Tax Fraud, Is Sentenced to 18-Month Prison Term," NYT, 27 Apr 1935. Long's son, Russell B. Long, age 16 at the time of his father's assassination, became a U.S. Senator in 1948 and served as chairman of the Senate Finance Committee from 1965 to 1981.

219 **Charles Coughlin...Hamilton Fish.** Donald Warren, *Radio Priest: Charles Coughlin, the father of hate radio* (NY: Free Press, 1996) 161, 245, 249-251, 285-290; Ted Morgan, *FDR: A Biography* (NY: Simon and Shuster, 1985), 554; "Memorandum, Mr. Gaston to Secretary Morgenthau," 15 April 1942, Morgenthau Diaries, 516:386, Roosevelt Library (Irey is checking several years of Fish's returns).

219 **Bernard Gariepy** was convicted of tax evasion and filing fraudulent income tax returns and was sentenced to 30 months. *Bernard Gariepy v U.S.*, 189 F2d 459 (CA-6, 1951). His brother was also convicted of tax evasion. *Louis J. Gariepy v U.S.*, 220 F2d 252 (CA-6, 1955), cert den 350 US 825 (1955). Mary Gariepy divorced Bernard in 1943. She sued Drew Pearson and the American Broadcasting Company for libel for broadcasting the story about the $68,000 payment because "alienation of affection" implied that she was an unchaste woman. *Mary Gariepy v Drew Pearson*, 104 FSupp 681 (DC-DC, 1952), 207 F2d 15 (CA-DC, 1953), cert den 346 US 909 (1953), 120 FSupp 597 (DC-DC, 1954); "Pearson Case Jury Fails to Reach Verdict," LAT, 31 Oct 1954. On February 2, 1955, a second jury found Pearson innocent and required Mary Gariepy to pay his court costs. Warren, 289.

220 **Peter Bergson.** David S. Wyman and Rafael Medoff, *A Race Against Death: Peter Bergson, America, and the Holocaust* (NY: The New Press, 2002), 94-95, 110-112; Rafael Medoff, "When The U.S. Government Spied on American Jews," *The Jewish Press*, 30 Dec 2005, 7; Rafael Medoff, "Bob Hope and the Holocaust: No Laughing Matter," *The Jewish Press*, 27 Jun 2003, 7.

220 **National Gallery/Andrew Mellon.** *Mellon*, 36 BTA 977 (1937) (Mellon's estate owed a reduced $668,000); David Cannadine, *Mellon: An American Life* (NY: Alfred A. Knopf, 2006), 414-427 (painting acquisitions), 463-465 (Gulf Oil), 505-545, 583-585 (tax trial), 557-567 (National Gallery); David Edward Finley, *A Standard of Excellence* (Washington: Smithsonian Institution, 1973), 35.

221 **$20,000 apartment rent.** NYT, 20 Aug 1933, BR5, reviewing, *Mellon's Millions* by Harvey O'Connor.

221 **worked under Mellon.** Irey, xii - xiii.

222 **diplomatic pouch.** One of these Mellon paintings was "Pocahontas" which is on display at the National Portrait Gallery, www.npg.si.edu. It's portrait NPG.65.61.

223 **Robert Jackson,** *That Man: An Insider's Portrait of Franklin D. Roosevelt* (NY: Oxford Univ. Press: 2003), 124-126.

224 **credible evidence.** Paul Mellon, *Reflections in a Silver Spoon* (NY: William Morrow & Company, 1992), 137-141; David Burnham, "The Abuse of Power: Misuse of the IRS," *NYT Magazine*, 3 Sep 1989.

224 **Moses Annenberg.** Irey, 215-224; Christopher Ogden, *Legacy: A Biography of Moses and Walter Annenberg* (Boston: Little, Brown and Company, 1999); "Founder of 'TV Guide' dies," *USA Today*, 1 Oct 2002.

225 **privately told the prosecutor.** Ogden, 224, citing prosecutor's memorandum on conversation, 11/15/39.

226 **Landslide Lyndon.** Morgan, 556-559 (Corpus Christi Naval Air Station); **1941 election.** Robert A. Caro, *The Years of Lyndon Johnson: The Path to Power* (NY: Alfred A. Knopf, 1982), 459-468 (dam), 742-753 (IRS investigation). **1948 election.** Robert A. Caro, *The Years of Lyndon Johnson: Means of Assent* (NY: Alfred A. Knopf, 1990); Merle Miller, *Lyndon: An Oral Biography* (NY: G.P. Putman's Sons, 1980) 74-75; Irwin Unger and Debi Unger, *LBJ: A life* (NY: John Wiley & Sons, 1999) 86-87, 90-91, 101. **Brown & Root.** "Halliburton Deals Recall Vietnam-Era Controversy," *NPR All Things Considered*, 24 Dec 2003.

227 **John L. Lewis.** Morgan, 518.

227 **Board of Education.** Room H128 in south/southeast corner on the ground floor of the Capitol.

228 **Paul Johnson,** *A History of the American People* (NY: HarperCollins Publishers, 1997), 760-761.

229 **William Vare and Frank Smith.** "Senate Election, Expulsion and Censure Cases from 1789 to 1960," Senate Document No. 71, 87th Cong., 2nd Sess. (1962).

229 **Justice Hugo Black.** *Johnson v Stevenson*, 335 US 801 (1948); Anthony Lewis, "A Tough Lawyer Goes to Court," NYT, 8 Aug 1965, SM11; Victor Lasky, *It Didn't Start With Watergate* (NY: Dial Press, 1977), 119-121.

229 **old law.** Laura Kalman, *Abe Fortas: A Biography* (New Haven: Yale Univ. Press, 1990), 200-201.

229 **George Parr.** "U.S. Court Upholds Conviction of Parr," NYT, 26 Mar 1975, 17; "Texas Politician Dead; Ruled Suicide," NYT, 2 Apr 1975, 8; *U.S. v George*

B. *Parr*, 509 F2d 1381, 75-1 USTC ¶9349; *Parr v U.S.*, 363 US 370 (1960); "Parr Sentenced to 10-Year Term," NYT, 31 Jul 1957, 14.

230 **Tax Perjury Trial.** This story is rarely told. Even his biographers, when they mention it at all, devote but a few paragraphs to the story. Edgar Dyer, "A 'triumph of justice' in Alabama: the 1960 perjury trial of Martin Luther King, Jr.," *Journal of African American History*, 22 Jun 2003; Fred D. Gray, *Bus Ride to Justice*, (Montgomery: The Black Belt Press, 1995), 148-160 (King Trial), 161-172 (Times v Sullivan). Fred Gray was the attorney for Rosa Parks, M.L. King, and the four ministers. "Rev. King Arrested in Perjury Case," AC, 18 Feb 1960, 1 (Gov. Vandiver: "watch carefully"); "King Won't Fight Extradition," AC, 19 Feb 1960, 1 (Gov. Vandiver: "return criminals"); "Agent tells of King's Worth," AJ, 26 May 1960, 1 (King paid $1,722 in back taxes, never signed 1957 return, IRS agent present, Georgia revenue auditor testifies); "King to Take Stand in Own Defense," AJ, 27 May 1960, 1 (state hadn't cashed King's four month old check, backdated documents; threatened lien on bank account); "Auditor Says King Amended Tax-Error," NYT, 26 May 1960, 67; "Tax Agent's Praise Is Cited By Dr. King," NYT, 28 May 1960, 11; "Testimony Ended in Dr. King's Case," NYT, 28 May 1960, 13; "Dr. King Acquitted of Perjury on Tax," NYT, 29 May 1960, 1 (1400 exhibits); "Jury Acquits King in Perjury Trial," AJ, 29 May 1960, 1; "Dr. King's Church Greets His Return," NYT, 30 May 1960, 20; "Dr. King Is Cleared in 2d Perjury Case," NYT, 19 Jul 1960, 21; Jim Bishop, *The Days of Martin Luther King Jr.* (NY: G.P. Putnam's Sons, 1971), 224-225, 231-233; *The Papers of Martin Luther King, Jr., volume 5: Threshold of a New Decade, January 1959 - December 1960*, Clayborne Carson, ed. (Berkley: University of California Press, 2005); Martin Luther King Collection, Howard Gotlieb Archival Research Center at Boston University, #127, Box 4, File I-24, *Alabama v King*.

232 **Coretta Scott King,** *My Life with Martin Luther King, Jr.* (NY: Henry Holt & Company, 1993 revised edition), 169 (185 in 1969 edition).

233 **Committee to Defend MLK** was organized on March 7, 1960 with an impressive list of officers: A. Philip Randolph, Rev. Gardner C. Taylor, Hope Stevens, Rev. Thomas Kilgore, Harry Belafonte, Sidney Poitier, Baynard Rustin, and Stanley Levison. King's close association with Stanley Levison, a Jew with a communist background, would animate the FBI investigations which failed to prove that King was a communist.

234 **wiretap him.** "Intelligence Activities and the Rights of Americans," Book II, Final Report of the Select Committee to Study Governmental Operations, United States Senate, 26 April 1976.

234 **Ebenezer Baptist Church.** The author learned of this incident from his good friend, Lew Regenstein, son of the attorney. This was confirmed by Kilpatrick Stockton partner Miles Alexander who noted that "Daddy" King publicly thanked Louis Regenstein. The law firm destroyed its records years ago in accordance with its records retention policy for closed cases. 25 microfilm reels comprising the FBI's 1963-1968 MLK Files mention the 1960 Alabama trial and the 1968 SCLC IRS

audit handled by Chauncey Eskridge (Part II, Reel 8, Doc. 100-111180-9-1693, 6 June 1968). There appears to be no documentation linking a specific administration to the Ebenezer audit, but this author suspects the Nixon administration as the most likely culprit. The investigation was probably halted in the planning stage under a law passed in 1969 to protect churches from unwarranted audits (IRC §7605(c)). The Watergate SSS files are stored at the National Archives, so one day we may solve this puzzle. "Martin Luther King, Jr. FBI File," University Publications of America, Bethesda, MD, Part I: 16 Reels, Part II: 9 Reels.

234 **Seditious Libel.** Anthony Lewis, *Make No Law: The Sullivan Case and the First Amendment* (NY: Random House, 1991); "Times, 4 Clerics Lose Libel Case," NYT, 4 Nov. 1960, 67; "Alabama Justice," *Time*, 7 Apr 1961; *New York Times v Sullivan*, 376 US 254 (1964).

236 **Watergate.** "The Internal Revenue Service: An Intelligence Resource and Collector, Intelligence Activities and the Rights of Americans, Book II, Final Report of the Select Committee to Study Governmental Operations," 94th Cong., 2d Sess., Report No. 94-755 (Washington: U.S. Govt. Printing Office, 1976), 26 Apr 1976 (SSS, IGRS, Operation Leprechaun); Mortimer M. Caplin, "The Presidency and the Internal Revenue Service," 24 TNT 508 (30 Jul 1984); Randolph W. Thrower, "Internal Revenue Service: The Tumultuous 20," 57 TNT 951 (12 Nov 1992).

237 **Randolph Thrower.** Joe Renourd, *The Ties That Bind: The History of Sutherland Asbill & Brennan LLP* (Atlanta: Sutherland Asbill & Brennan, 2007), 119-120; "Federal Tax Chief Is Resigning; Cites Personal Considerations," NYT, 29 Jan 1971, 12.

238 **audits and repeat audits.** Transcript, Lawrence F. O'Brien Oral History Interview XXXI, 12/10/87, by Michael L. Gillette, Internet Copy, LBJ Library. www.lbjlib.utexas.edu/johnson/archives.hom/oralhistory.hom/obrienl/OBRIEN31.PDF.

238 **audit all members of Congress.** "Nixon Papers Detail Anger Over Leaks," WP, 18 Jul 1987, A5.

239 **courtesy storage.** Matthew G. Brown, "The First Nixon Papers Controversy: Richard Nixon's 1969 Prepresidential Papers Tax Deduction," 26 *Archival Issues* No. 1 (2001); James S. Byrne, "The Nixon Tax Caper: 10th Anniversary of a Team Effort," 23 TNT 14 (2 Apr 1984); "Is IRS treatment on back-dating documents inconsistent?" JTax, Aug 1974, 128.

240 **JCT found.** "Examination of President Nixon's Tax Returns for 1969 through 1972," JCT, JCS-9-74, 3 Apr 1974.

240 **Richard Nixon Library.** The original Watergate section was demolished in March 2007. Digital photographs of every line of text from the old exhibit are now displayed on a plasma screen. "Nixon library's changes start with Watergate," LAT, 8 July 2007. The old Watergate exhibit was an architectural inspiration. The exhibit was inside a long dark walk-through tunnel, with a bright light at the end.

241 **Hubert Humphrey donated.** William Safire, "Drugstore Liberal," NYT, 11 Mar 1976, 37.

241 **G. Gordon Liddy,** *Will: The Autobiography of G. Gordon Liddy* (NY: St. Martin's Press, 1980), 282-283, 285, 337, 359; "Liddy's Receipt of Most 'Watergate' Funds

Is Not Taxable; Wife Is Innocent Spouse," 26 TNT 1124 (18 Mar 1985); *George Gordon Liddy*, TC Memo 1985-107, aff'd 808 F2d 312, 87-1 USTC ¶9102 (CA-4, 1986).

242 **Conrad Black,** *Franklin Delano Roosevelt: Champion of Freedom* (NY: Public Affairs, 2003), 396.

243 **Clinton administration.** David M. Barrett, *Final Report of the Independent Counsel, In Re: Henry G. Cisneros*, (Washington, DC; Filed August 13, 2004, Published January 19, 2006); "Inquiry on Clinton Official Ends With Accusations of Cover-Up," NYT, 19 Jan 2006; Joseph Farah, "The White House Plays Politics With the IRS," WSJ, 22 Oct 1996; Carmen E. MacDougall, Letter, WSJ, 1 Nov 1996, A13 (refuting Farah's claim); Kip Dellinger, "Some Thoughts on Commissioner Richardson's Tenure at the IRS," 74 TNT 429 (21 Apr 1997); Joseph Farah, "How Clinton targeted me for audit," *WorldNetDaily*, 20 Jul 1999.

## CHAPTER 9: THE SEX OF A HIPPOPOTAMUS

244 **London Zoo.** "Hippopotamus Arrives in the Zoological Gardens," *Times* (London), 6 Jun 1850, 8; Nina J. Root, "Victorian England's Hippomania," *Natural History*, Feb 1993, 34-39; The hippo was named, Obaysch, after the island on the Nile where he was captured.

245 **sex of hippopotamus.** Thomas C. Atkeson, "Tax Simplification from the Viewpoint of a Professor of Taxation," *Essays in Taxation* (NY: The Tax Foundation, 1974), 95.

245 **legislative counsel.** Jeffrey H. Birnbaum, "Almost Nobody Knows Tax Scribe Ward Hussey, But With a Stroke of a Pen He Affects Everybody," WSJ, 22 Aug 1986, 1.

245 **Huxley.** His exact statement is elusive, and it may have been coined from an old *Punch* cartoon, or by his grandson, Julian, who was director of the London zoo. "Which raises Thomas Huxley's comment about the sex of a hippopotamus: is the question of interest to anyone but another hippopotamus?" Martin Meyer, *Whatever Happened to Madison Avenue? Advertising in the '90s* (Boston: Little Brown & Company, 1991), 10. "Julian Huxley tells a typical story. At the London Zoo a lady went up to the Keeper of the hippopotami. 'Tell me,' she said, 'is that hippopotamus a male or a female?' The Keeper looked at her in a shocked manner: 'That, ma'am,' he replied, 'is a question which should only interest another hippopotamus.' The Keeper of the hippopotami was also the keeper of Victorian prudery." Francesca M. Wilson, *Strange Island: Britain through Foreign Eyes 1395 – 1940* (London: Longmans, Green and Co., 1955), 261.

245 **a "which."** Middleton Beaman, "Bill Drafting," 7 *Law Library Journal* 64, 69 (1914).

245 **schoolmaster.** 50 *Cong. Record* 2375-80 (1913) (Bacon comment); 56 *Cong. Record* 701-2 (1918) (praise for Beaman's excess profits provision); Frederic P. Lee (Legislative Counsel to the Senate, 1923-1930), "The Office of the Legislative Counsel," 20 *Columbia Law Review* 381 (Apr 1929); Harry W. Jones,

"Bill-Drafting Services in Congress and the State Legislatures," 65 *Harvard Law Review* 441 (Jan 1952).

246 **three pages.** The final version was eight pages. Revenue Act of 1918, Title III, §§300-337, War Profits and Excess Profits Tax, *Statutes at Large*, vol. 40, part I, 65th Cong., Sess. III, 1088-1096. The Revenue Act of 1917 version was just 2 pages, *Statutes at Large*, vol. 39, part I, 64th Congress, 1000-1002.

246 **gentleman and a patriot.** *Cong. Record*, vol. 95, Part I, 81st Cong., 1st Sess. (2 Feb. 1949), 746-748.

247 **sexually explicit.** IRC §199(c)(6), added by the American Jobs Creation Act of 2004, PL 108-357.

247 **colloquy.** "Colloquies: What They Are and What They Do," 33 TNT 128 (13 Oct 1986).

248 **performance based compensation.** IRC §162(m), added by Revenue Reconciliation Act of 1993, PL 103-66; Reg. 1.162-27; "Outside Advice on Boss's Pay May Not Be So Independent," NYT, 10 Apr 2006; Rev. Rul. 2008-13.

248 **brick thick.** Jay Starkman, "Finding Real Spending Cuts is Easy," AJ, 2 Mar 1993.

249 **biggest attention getter.** "Panel hears citizens' gripes about taxes," AC, 21 Jun 1984, B-1; "Tax Reform: Citizens Call For Tax Code Simplification, Easing of Tax Burdens," *Daily Tax Report*, 21 Jun 1984, G-3.

251 **When he became president.** Robert Caro, *The Years of Lyndon Johnson: Means of Assent* (NY: Alfred A. Knopf, 1990), xxix; "President Johnson, as Well as His Wife, Appears to Hold Big Personal Fortune," WSJ, 23 Mar 1964, 12; "Johnson Fortune Put At $9 Million," NYT, 10 Jun 1964, 25; "Johnson, Virtually Penniless in 1937, Left a Fortune Valued at $20-Million," NYT, 28 Jan 1973. Caro says Johnson was worth $20 million when he became president. The *Times* noted that Kennedy was worth $10 million when he died and Herbert Hoover was worth more than that. KTBC was sold for $9 million in cash soon after Johnson's death in 1973 and had been valued at $7 million in 1963; "Johnson Interests Are Forced to Sell Austin TV Station," NYT, 2 Sep 1972, 25; "Times Mirror Buys TV Station," WSJ, 30 Oct 1973, 41.

251 **KTBC.** Caro, *Means of Ascent*, 86-87. Kingsbery's "Class of '45" graduated in 1944 due to the war, but Annapolis says he did not graduate. "How President's Wife Built $17,500 Into Big Fortune in Television," WSJ, 23 Mar 1964, 1.

251 **Johnson had friends.** Bobby Baker, *Wheeling and Dealing* (NY: W.W. Norton & Co., 1978), 82; "FCC's Disclosure of Stock-Option Terms Clears Way for Decision in Austin TV Case," WSJ, 27 Apr 1964, 4; "FCC Decision in Community Antenna Case in Austin, Texas, Is Appealed to Courts," WSJ, 1 Jun 1964, 20; "Johnson-Affiliated TV Firm Taking Over Rival Four Months After Purchase Pact," WSJ, 17 Nov 1964, 3; "Johnson TV Unit Gets Competitor," NYT, 13 Feb 1965, 8.

251 **no fingerprints.** "Remembering Former Senator Russell Long," 149 *Cong. Record* S6703 (20 May 2003).

252 **Sam Rayburn.** Caro, *Means of Assent*, 80.

252  **The Lobbyist.** For a "road map" on how to lobby, see Michael Waris, Jr., "Practical and Philosophical Observations on the Tax Legislative Process," 38 NYU *Institute on Federal Taxation* (1980), chapter 30.

252  **appear to come from Congress's mouth.** *Koons Buick Pontiac GMC, Inc. v Nigh*, 543 US 50 (2004), Justice Antonin Scalia, dissenting.

253  **Representative Sam.** Richard L. Doernberg and Fred S. McChesney, "On the Accelerating Rate and Decreasing Durability of Tax Reform", 71 *Minnesota Law Review* 913 (Apr 1987), at 933, FN 102.

253  **18 super-wealthy.** "Spending Millions to Save Billions: The Campaign of the Super Wealthy to Kill the Estate Tax," Public Citizen's Congress Watch (Washington, DC) and United for a Fair Economy (Boston), Apr 2006.

253  **Tom DeLay.** "Golfing with Tom DeLay," *Salon.com*, 2 May 2005; "DeLay and Company," *Time*, 13 Mar 2005; "Gambling Interests Funded DeLay Trip," WP, 12 Mar 2005, A1; Jack B. Siegel, "The Wild, the Innocent, and the K Street Shuffle: The Tax System's Role in Policing Interactions Between Charities and Politicians," *The Exempt Organization Tax Review*, Nov 2006, 117-160, 2006 TNT 220-46 (10 Oct 2006).

254  **David Barry.** Donald A. Ritchie, *Press Gallery: Congress and the Washington Correspondents* (Cambridge, MA: Harvard University Press, 1991), 194.

254  **Forrest C. Donnell.** "Hearing on H.R. 3214 Before a Subcommittee of the Senate Committee on the Judiciary," 80th Cong., 2d Sess., 339 pages (22 Apr 1948) at 133-134.

255  **suggestion was enacted.** PL 100-203 §10702(a), adding IRC §6104(e). Internet postings are at www.guidestar.org.

255  **Moynihan.** "Unofficial Transcript of Finance Committee Hearing on IRS Oversight Board Nominations," 2000 TNT 29-27 (3 Feb 2000).

255  **1936 Tax Act.** Randolph E. Paul, *Taxation in the United States* (Boston: Little, Brown and Company, 1954), 195.

255  **three days.** Brian Baird (D-WA), "We Need to Read the Bills," WP, 27 Nov 2004, A31.

256  **Nobody complains.** "Unofficial Transcript of Tax Simplification Conference: Invitational Conference on Tax Law Simplification," 2002 TNT 17-37 (4 Dec 2001); Donald Morris, "Education-Friendly States: The Tuition Deduction," 45 STT 113 (July 9, 2007).

256  **disabled veterans.** Birnbaum, Jeffrey H., and Allen S. Murray, *Showdown at Gucci Gulch: Lawmakers, Lobbyists, and the Unlikely Triumph of Tax Reform* (NY: Random House, 1987), 80.

257  **airline taxation.** Georgia Tax Code, OCGA §48-7-31(d)(3.1)(B).

258  **charge his clients $200.** The newspaper actually wrote, "If the state doesn't conform, Starkman said, it will cost his clients almost $200 more for him to compute their 1987 Georgia taxes…He said the average taxpayer would see probably a $50 increase…." "State tax filing will cost more, accountant says," AJC, 14 Nov 1986, A20.

260  **Crosby was defeated.** "7-term Crosby losing timber vote to foe," AJC, 7 Jul 1990, B3. Years later, the foe's husband, a superior court judge, was at the center of a

federal corruption investigation and accused of seven counts of violating the Georgia Code of Judicial Conduct. Federal agents raided his chambers. The county court clerk pleaded guilty to federal charges of felony mail fraud and resigned. "Ethics charges may force Clinch judge from bench," AJC, 3 Nov 2007.

260 **Charitable deduction.** "Urge Many Changes in War Tax Measure," NYT, 8 Jun 1917, 12 (Jacob H. Schiff); "Except Gifts from Income," NYT, 18 Jun 1917, 3 (Sen. Hollis amendment); "Objects to Tax on Gifts," NYT, 18 Jun 1917, 8 (Untermyer on Red Cross deduction); "Nation Aroused for Red Cross Week," NYT, 18 Jun 1917, 8 (fundraising dinners); "Would Exempt Charities," NYT, 23 Jun 1917, 12 (Samuel Untermyer); "The Tax on Philanthropy," NYT, 24 Jun 1917, 22; adopted *Cong. Record*, 7 Sep 1917. A charitable deduction proposal was rejected for the 1913 Act, 50 *Cong. Record* 1259. A corporation charitable deduction wasn't enacted until 1935.

262 **best anecdotal evidence.** Carol Adelman, "America's Helping Hand", WSJ, 21 Aug 2002; "Charitable giving in U.S. hits record," *Financial Times*, 25 Jun 2007, 7.

262 **rather easy.** Jay Starkman, "Simplify Taxes: Just Get Rid of 89 Million Unnecessary Returns," 2005 TNT 157-26 (15 Aug 2005); Michael J. Graetz, "100 Million Unnecessary Returns: A Fresh Start for the U.S. Tax System," 112 *Yale Law Journal* 261 (2002); Jay Starkman, "Prelude to Tax Simplification," JoA, May 1990, 78.

263 **George H.W. Bush.** *Cong. Record* — Extensions of Remarks, 16 Jul 1970, E6715.

264 **V for Vendetta.** Allen Kenney, "Protesters Launch Antitax 'Vendetta' in Washington," 2006 TNT 220-7 (15 Nov 2006).

265 **black art.** "Caution: Tax Cuts Are Bigger Than They Appear in Budget," WSJ, 19 May 2003, 1.

265 **small revenue raiser.** John A. Szilagyi, "Where Have All the Dependents Gone?" IRS Research Conference, Washington, DC, 16-17 Nov 1989, 1.

266 **Ken Kies.** April 13, 2000 letter to Treasury Secretary Lawrence Summers, reproduced in 2000 TNT 87-36 (4 May 2000).

266 **credit card receipts.** "Republicans Challenge Everson on President's Tax Gap Proposals," 2007 TNT 34-2 (20 Feb 2007).

267 **Virgin Islands.** Tax Reform Act of 1986, Title XXII - Foreign Tax Provisions, Subtitle G - Tax Treatment of Possessions, Part II - Treatment of the Virgin Islands, PL 99-514, §1277(c)(2); "Disguising Those Who Get Tax Breaks," *Philadelphia Inquirer*, 13 Apr 1988, A1; "A Millionaire Business and His Island Tax Shelter," *Philadelphia Inquirer*, 11 Apr 1988.

267 **professional sports.** American Jobs Creation Act of 2004, PL 108-357, §886(a), deleting IRC §197(e)(6); "Estimated Revenue Effects of H.R. 4520," JCT, JCX-38-04, 8 Jun 2004.

267 **NASCAR.** PL 108-357, §704, amending IRC §168(e)(3)(C) and adding §168(i)(15). Aggressive preparers had treated NASCAR racetracks as amusement parks (ADR Asset Class 80.0) which are depreciated over seven years. PL 107-16, §803(e)(2), "any inference."

267  finance stadiums. "Stop Tax-Exempt Arena Debt Issuance Act," introduced by Sen. Moynihan, S.1880 (104th Congress, 1996), S.122 and S.434 (105th Congress, 1997), S.224 (106th Congress, 1999); Andrew Gasper, "Senator Moynihan's Field of Dreams; If You Build It, They Will Come...But Not At the Federal Taxpayer's Expense: A Proposal to Curb Tax-Exempt Bond Financing of Sports Stadiums," 17 *Va. Tax Rev.* 341, 362 n.116 (1997); "Stadium Construction For Professional Sports: Reversing The Inequities Through Tax Incentives," 18 *St. John's Journal of Legal Commentary* 981 (Summer 2004); "Sports Writer Testifies on 'Sports Industry's Dirty Little Secret'," Testimony of Neil deMause, Subcommittee on Domestic Policy, Committee on Oversight and Government Reform, 2007 TNT 62-57 (29 Mar 2007).

268  **George W. Bush.** Charles Lewis and the Center for Public Integrity, *The Buying of the President 2000* (NY: Avon Books, 2000), 194-220.

269  **Mr. Taxes.** "Wilbur Mills...'Mr. Taxes' in the Congress," *Newsweek*, 14 Jan 1963, 14-18; C.B. Seib "Steering Wheel of the House," *NYT Magazine*, 18 Mar 1962, 30; Rep. Ray Thornton, "Wilbur Mills: A Chairman's Chairman," *Tax Foundation Tax Features*, Jun/Jul 1992. Donald R. Kennon and Rebecca M. Rogers, *The Committee on Ways and Means: A Bicentennial History, 1789-1989* (Washington, DC: Supt. of Doc., 1989), 329-356.

269  **recite without falter.** "The Wooing of Wilbur Mills," *Life*, 16 Jul 1971, 52.

269  **Mills as treasury secretary.** Julian E. Zelizer, *Taxing America: Wilbur D. Mills, Congress, and the State, 1945-1975* (NY: Cambridge University Press, 1998), 332-337.

270  **addicted to prescription drugs.** Zelizer, 336. *Congressional Quarterly Almanac*, Vol. XXX (1974), 36.

270  **where are you.** "The Struggle Over Mortgage Bonds," NYT, 19 Jun 1979, D2.

## CHAPTER 10: THE LAWGIVERS

271  **bends over backwards.** "A Crippling Backlog Has the Tax Court in Chaos," *Business Week*, 16 Apr 1984, 87.

272  **spoke frankly.** Woods, 92 TC 776, 790 (1989), Judge Chabot dissenting. The Tax Court decided that it had equitable power to correct an erroneous taxpayer consent, thereby granting a victory to the IRS.

272  **equity authority.** "Tax Court...lacks general equitable powers." *Commissioner v McCoy*, 484 US 3, 7 (1987) citing *Commissioner v Gooch Milling & Elevator Co.*, 320 US 418 (1943). This limits Tax Court (and remedies available in appeals courts) to situations the statutes empower it to rule on. Woods, 92 TC 776 (1989). There should no longer be any doubt that Tax Court has, and Congress intended it to have, equitable powers. In 2006, Congress amended IRC §6214(b) to specifically allow the equitable power that the Supreme Court ruled was lacking in its predecessor, IRC(1939) §272(g); PL 109-280, §858(a); *Branson*, 113 TC No. 2 (1999), aff'd 264 F3d 904 (CA-9, 2001), cert den 535 US 927 (2002).

272  **principles of equity.** Nina J. Crimm, *Tax Court Litigation: Practice and Procedure* (Boston: Little Brown and Company, 1996), ¶11.4[2]: "The court has applied...

equitable estoppel, abuse of discretion, waiver, duty of consistency, tax benefit rule, laches, substantial compliance, equitable reformation, and equitable recoupment."

272 **one academic study.** James Edward Maule, "Instant Replay, Weak Teams, And Disputed Calls: An Empirical Study of Alleged Tax Court Judge Bias," 66 *Tenn. L. Rev.* 351 (Winter 1999); "National Taxpayer Advocate 2006 Annual Report to Congress," Taxpayer Advocate Service Division of Internal Revenue Service, 555; David Laro, "The Evolution of the Tax Court as an Independent Tribunal," 1995 *Univ. of Illinois. L. Rev.* 17.

272 **most litigated issues.** "National Taxpayer Advocate 2007 Annual Report to Congress," Taxpayer Advocate Service Division of Internal Revenue Service, volume I, 561, 678-716.

273 **penal in nature.** *Globe Life and Accident Insurance Company v Oklahoma Tax Commission*, 913 P2d 1322, 1996 OK 39 (1996).

274 **Oracle or Lawmaker.** James Eustice, "Tax Complexity and The Tax Practitioner," 45 *Tax Law Review* 7 (Fall 1989); G. Edward White, *The American Judicial Tradition: Profiles of Leading American Judges* (NY: Oxford University Press, 1988), 461.

274 **Judge Learned Hand.** Gerald Gunther, *Learned Hand: The Man and the Judge* (NY: Alfred A. Knopf, 1994), 4 (Colonel Courageous Stanton); *Commissioner v Newman*, 159 F2d 848, 850-51 (CA2, 1947) (L. Hand, J., dissenting) (nothing sinister); *Helvering v Gregory*, 69 F2d 809, 810 (CA-2, 1934), aff'd 293 US 465 (1935) (not even a patriotic duty); "Learned Hand tribute to Thomas Swan," 57 *Yale Law J.* 167, 169 (1947) (cross-reference to cross-reference).

275 **among the record-holders.** Walter Jones (former Congressman around the turn of the nineteenth century) argued 317 cases before the Supreme Court. Daniel Webster is second with nearly 200. Lawrence Wallace argued 157 cases by serving 34 years in the solicitor general's office until his retirement in 2003. John W. Davis (former congressman, solicitor general, and 1924 Democratic presidential candidate, who argued the losing side in *Brown v Board of Education*) is fourth with 140 cases. Erwin N. Griswold argued 118. William O. Douglas, *The Court Years 1939 - 1975* (NY: Random House, 1980), 27, 178; "The Cal Ripken of Lawyers; U.S. Supreme Court Honors Ex-Syracusan For His Service," *Post-Standard* (Syracuse, NY), 6 Dec 2002; "Lawyer to make his 130th argument before the Supreme Court," *Knight Ridder/Tribune News Service*, 12 Apr 1995. In the first contest where Davis and Griswold faced each other, Davis passed a note to another lawyer, "Who is this lad?" Griswold, *Ould Fields*, 93-94.

275 **student...not prepared.** Robert F. Bradney '50, "Lessons from a Cold January Day," *Harvard Law Bulletin*, Summer 2002.

275 **as low as possible.** *Gregory v Helvering*, 69 F2d 809 (CA-2, 1934), aff'd 293 US 465 (1935). Learned Hand expanded this most quoted aphorism a dozen years later in *Brooklyn National Corp. v Commr.*, 157 F2d 450 (CA-2, 1946), cert den 329 US 733 (1946):

> Over and over again courts have said that there is nothing sinister in so arranging one's affairs as to keep taxes as low as possible. Everybody does

so, rich or poor; and all do right, for nobody owes any public duty to pay more than the law demands: taxes are enforced exactions, not voluntary contributions. To demand more in the name of morals is mere cant.

Forgotten is that both of these cases pontificating on taxpayer rights ruled against the taxpayer.

276 **no use in thinking.** Erwin N. Griswold, *Cases and Materials on Federal Taxation* (Brooklyn: Foundation Press, 6th ed. 1966), 14. Griswold became strict despite having served in 1942 as an aide to Treasury General Counsel Randolph Paul, who believed, "The guiding influence should be what may be called, for lack of a better term, the spirit of the statute." Randolph E. Paul, *Taxation in the United States* (Boston: Little, Brown and Company, 1954), 662; Erwin N. Griswold, *Ould Fields, New Corne* (St. Paul, MN: West Publishing Co., 1992), 139.

276 **fair and adequate...remedy.** *Anniston Manufacturing Co. v Davis*, 301 US 337 (1937), citing cases since 1918.

276 **no jurisdiction to review.** Paul, *Taxation in the United States*, 631-633; *Texas Pacific Coal and Oil Company*, 59 CtCls 984 (1924); *Sara L. Meyer v U.S.*, 60 CtCls 485 (1925); Roger John Traynor, "Administrative and Judicial Procedure for Federal Income, Estate, and Gift Taxes — A Criticism and a Proposal," *Columbia Law Review*, Dec 1938, 1393 - 1435.

276 **To rid itself...of the need to hear tax cases.** *Dobson v Commissioner*, 320 US 489 (1943), reh'g den 321 US 231 (1944); Randolph Paul, "Dobson v Commissioner: The Strange Ways of Law and Fact," 57 Harv. L. Rev. 753 (1944).

276 **I know no lawyers.** "Hearing on H.R. 3214 Before a Subcommittee of the Senate Committee on the Judiciary," 80th Cong., 2d Sess. (1948), 168.

277 **upholding the Social Security Act.** *Steward Machine Co. v Davis*, 301 US 548 (1937) (upholding the unemployment compensation provisions of the Social Security Act of 1935); *Helvering v Davis*, 301 US 619 (1937) (upholding the law's old-age benefit provisions). In terms of general welfare, Randolph Paul explained that these acts protect the average citizen and his family against the loss of a job and poverty-ridden old age. The Confederate Constitution omitted general welfare.

277 *Korematsu v U.S.*, 323 US 214 (1944), Jackson was one of three dissenters; reh'g den 324 US 885 (1945).

277 *John Kelley Co. v Commissioner*, 326 US 521 (1946), rev'g 146 F2d 466 (CA-7), aff'g 146 F2d 809 (CA-1), 1 TC 457 (Kelley), 3 TC 95 (Talbot). The Tax Court continued to insist that *Kelley* and *Talbot* were dissimilar, despite being ruled similar by the appeals courts and a dissenting Supreme Court justice who complained that they were "substantially identical." *Universal Castings Corporation*, 37 TC 107, 116 (1961).

278 **Tax Court decisions...appealed.** IRC §7482.

278 **distaste for tax cases.** Paul L. Caron, "Mamas Don't Let Your Babies Grow Up To Be Tax Lawyers," 94 TNT 141-59 (18 Jul 1994), FN 26 & 28 (excerpt from his article, "Tax Myopia, Or Mamas Don't Let Your Babies Grow Up To Be Tax Lawyers," 13 *Virginia Tax Review* 517 (1994)).

278 **Thurgood Marshall.** Stephen B. Cohen, "Thurgood Marshall: Tax Lawyer," 80 *Georgetown Law Journal* 2011, 2039 (Aug 1992).

278 **dread tax cases.** "As Clerk for Rehnquist, Nominee Stood Out for Conservative Rigor," NYT, 31 Jul 2005, I:1.

278 **William O. Douglas.** Bernard Wolfman, Jonathan L.F. Silver, Marjorie A. Silver, *Dissent Without Opinion, The Behavior of Justice William O. Douglas in Federal Tax Cases* (Philadelphia: Univ. of Pennsylvania Press, 1975), xii (forward by Erwin N. Griswold), 125-126 (citing review of L. Eisenstein, *The Ideologies of Taxation* (1961)), 128; *Herald Tribune*, 24 Sep 1961, §6 (Books), 13.

279 **turn square corners.** *Commissioner of Internal Revenue v Lester*, 366 US 299 (1961, J. Douglas concurring), citing *Rock Island, A. & L. R. Co. v U.S.*, 254 US 141 (1920), 143; Wolfman, 67.

279 **Cour de Cassation.** Robert H. Jackson, *The Supreme Court in the American System of Government* (NY: Harper Torchbooks, 1955), 21; Hannis Taylor, "Due Process of Law: Persistent and Harmful Influence of Murray v Hoboken Land & Improvement Co.," 24 *Yale Law Journal* 353, 369 (March 1915).

280 **Board of Tax Appeals.** Harold Dubroff, *The United States Tax Court, An Historical Analysis* (Chicago: Commerce Clearing House, 1979).

280 **summary opinions secret.** Leandra Lederman, "Tax Court S Cases: Docs the 'S' Stand for Secret?" 98 TNT 70-76 (13 Apr 1998); David Lupi-Sher, "Small Tax Court Cases — Has Their Time Come?" 1999 TNT 83-1 (30 Apr 1999); Sheryl Stratton, "S Cases Available, but not Necessarily Accessible," 2001 TNT 12-6 (17 Jan 2001).

280 **3,000 taxpayers.** "At 87, Erwin N. Griswold Is the Dean of Supreme Court Observers," WP, 15 Jul 1991, F5; *Freytag v Commissioner*, 501 US 868 (1991); "Obituaries: Erwin Griswold of Harvard, Ex-Solicitor General, 90," NYT, 20 Nov 1994; Lawrence M. Stratton Jr., "Special Trial Judges, The Tax Court and the Appointments Clause: Freytag v Commissioner," 45 *Tax Lawyer* 497 (Winter 1992). The appointments clause provides: "[T]he Congress may by Law vest the Appointment of such inferior Officers, as they think proper, in the President alone, in the Courts of Law, or in the Heads of Departments." Art. II, Sec. 2, cl. 2.

281 **special trial judge reports.** *Ballard v Commissioner*, 544 US 40 (2005); *Estate of Kanter*, TC Memo 2007-21 (457-page remand opinion); rev'd, vacated, and remanded, *Ballard v Commissioner*, 2008 TNT 68-16 (CA-11, 7 Apr 2008); *Investment Research Associates Ltd.*, TC Memo 1999-407; Crystal Tandon and Karla L. Miller, "Judges' Statements on Kanter, Ballard Provoke Dismay," 2005 TNT 140-3 (22 Jul 2005); Sheryl Stratton and Crystal Tandon, "Initial Ballard Special Trial Judge Report Has No Effect, According to IRS Tax Court Filing," 2005 TNT 150-1 (5 Aug 2005); "Tax Court findings secretly changed in at least 5 cases," *Chicago Tribune*, 1 Sep 2005; *Snow*, TCM 1996-457; "Practitioners Praise Ballard Decision," 2008 TNT 70-6 (10 Apr 2008).

282 **J. Edgar Murdock.** In Memoriam, 68 TC ix (1977).

283 **fattening himself.** *Marlor*, 27 TC 624, 626 (1956), rev'd 251 F2d 615 (CA-2, 1958).

283 **Theodore Tannenwald.** Martin D. Ginsburg, "In Memoriam: Theodore Tannenwald, Jr. (Lawyer and Tax Court Judge)," 52 *Tax Lawyer* 231 (Winter 1999). Tannenwald's former clerk tells a similar story about his fairness toward a no-show prisoner residing at the federal penitentiary in Englewood, Colorado. Howard E. Abrams, "In Memoriam: Judge Tannenwald on the Tax Court: An Enduring Legacy of Fundamental Fairness," 48 *Emory Law Journal* 863 (Summer 1999).

284 **lottery.** *Alfonso Diaz*, 58 TC 560, 564-65 (1972).

285 **presumption of correctness.** *United States v Rindskopf*, 105 US 418 (1882); *Wickwire v Reineche*, 275 US 101 (1927); *Jones v Commissioner*, 38 F2d 550 (CA-7, 1930); *Welch v Helvering*, 290 US 111 (1933).

285 **burden of proof.** IRC §7491; TC Rule 142(a); *Alegria*, TC Summary 2005-147; *Sarni*, TC Summary 2005-189; *Bond*, TC Memo 2005-251; Sheldon I. Banoff and Richard M. Lipton, "The Eighth Circuit Resolves Its Burden Of Proof Conflict," JTax, Mar 2005, 192. There's also a little known IRC §6201(d) which requires IRS to prove that an information return (Form 1099 or W-2) is correct, but the courts have never ruled in favor of the taxpayer on this issue. *Cathy Miller Hardy*, TCM 1997-97, aff'd 84 AFTR2d ¶99-5003 (CA-9, 1999); *Christensen*, TCM 2006-62. For a history of "burden of proof" in tax cases see Harold Dubroff, *The United States Tax Court, An Historical Analysis* (Chicago: Commerce Clearing House, 1979), 319-334.

286 **explain its 2002 conclusion.** Philip N. Jones, "The Eighth Circuit weighs in on the burden of proof — Will it change the outcome after all?" JTax, Apr 2003, 226; *Griffin*, TCM 2004-64, 315 F3d 1017 (CA-8, 2003), rev'g and rem'g, TCM 2002-6.

286 **taxes are the life-blood.** *Bull v U.S.*, 295 US 247 (1935).

286 **home equity.** *Pau*, TCM 1997-43 (home acquisition limited to $1 million of debt).

286 ***Marshall Hugo Martin***, TCM 1993-399 (tax year 1988), TCM 1992-331 (tax year 1987), aff'd 73 AFTR 2d 94-1722 (CA-5, 3/30/1994, unpublished *per curiam* opinion).

287 **refused to swear.** *Ferguson v Commissioner*, 91-1 USTC ¶50,052 (CA-5); *Stanton v Fought*, 486 So2d 745 (La., 1986). These cases cite numerous other cases supporting religious rights.

287 ***Zarin***, 92 TC 1084 (1989), rev'd, 916 F2d 110 (CA-3, 1990); Daniel Shaviro, "The Man Who Lost Too Much: Zarin v Commissioner and the Measurement of Taxable Consumption," 54 *Tax Law Review* 215 (1990).

288 *Spina v Forest Preserve District of Cook County, Ill.*, 207 FSupp2d 764 (N.D. Ill., 2002); Adam Liptak, "Tax Bill Exceeds Award to Officer in Sex Bias Suit," NYT, 11 Aug 2002, 1.18; Stephen Cohen and Laura Sager, "Kafka at the Tax Court: The Attorney's Fee in Employment Litigation," 2002 TNT 175-24 (6 September 2002); *Alexander v IRS*, 72 F3d 938 (CA-1, 1986) ("smacks of injustice" at 946), aff'g TCM 1995-51; *Commissioner v Banks*, 543 US 426 (2005); Robert W. Wood, "Will the IRS Pursue Attorney Fees Post-Banks?" 2005 TNT 133-36,

(13 Jul 2005); This unfair result was partially mitigated by the American Jobs Creation Act of 2004 (PL 108-357, §703(b), adding IRC §62(a)(19)).

288  **arbitrary and capricious.** *Frew v Bowers*, 12 F2d 625 (CA-2, 1926), L. Hand concurring.

288  **Harmless Error.** *Dixon*, TCM 2006-97, TCM 2006-90, 316 F3d 1041 (CA-9, 1/17/2003), reversing and remanding TCM 2000-16, TCM 1999-101, TCM 1991-614, 90 TC 237 (1988); *DuFresne v Commissioner*, 26 F3d 105 (CA-9, 1994); "Dixon Update-IRS Attorneys Sanctioned For 'Fraud On The Court'," JTax, Aug 2004, 127; Young, TCM 2006-189; *Hartman*, TCM 2008-124.

290  **Spencer Tracy.** *William Lee (Spencer) Tracy*, 39 BTA 578 (1939). There were three issues, and his CPA won two of them.

290  **Dingell amendment.** IRC §7452.

290  **Board of Patent Appeals.** 37 C.F.R. §§10.5, 10.6 and 10.7.

290  **7,300 CPAs.** "Hearing on H.R. 3214 Before a Subcommittee of the Senate Committee on the Judiciary," 80th Cong., 2d Sess. (1948), 106.

290  **in that age category.** Maurice Austin on CPAs in Tax Court practice, "Hearing on H.R. 3214," 212, 217, 224.

291  **Project Notes.** 1988 Tax Court Admission Exam, Question S-29; Jay Starkman, "The Tax Court Exam," TTA, Jun 1996, 373; *Haffner v U.S.*, 585 FSupp 354 (ND Ill, 1984); *U.S. v Wells Fargo*, 485 US 351 (1988). I mentioned this ridiculous question to AICPA Tax Division Vice President Gerald Padwe. He responded instantly, "Isn't that the *Haffner* case?" I was flabbergasted.

291  **unresolved issue.** An IRS deficiency notice is required to state the last day for filing a petition with the Tax Court. Suppose IRS fails to mention that date? 2000 Exam, Question P-3. *James A. Rochelle*, 116 TC No. 26 (24 May 2001), reviewed by the court with five dissents, holding that the standard 90-day rule applies, and imposing no sanction upon IRS for failure to follow the statute.

291  **Sidney Goldin.** *Reed v Tax Court of the United States*, 157 F2d 79 (CA-DC, 1946); *Sidney H. Goldin v U.S.*, Civil Action No. 96-0658 (USDC-DC, 10 Mar 1997 and 4 Apr 1997), aff'd per curiam, 1998 U.S. App. LEXIS 7893 (No. 97-5148) (CA-DC, 17 Mar 1998), 1997 U.S. App. LEXIS 35904 (No. 97-5271) (CA-DC, 5 Nov 1997).

292  **pro se.** "National Taxpayer Advocate 2006 Annual Report to Congress," Taxpayer Advocate Service Division of Internal Revenue Service, 275 - 276 (93%/83%); Brett Barenholtz, "Fees for the Taxpaying Fool: I.R.C. Section 7430 Fee Awards to Pro Se Attorneys," 38 *Case Western Reserve* 408 (1987-1988); *Frisch*, 87 TC 838 (denying pro se awards); *Cowie*, TCM 2007-108 (fee shifting); *In re: Hudson*, No. 00-11683, (Bankr. NDNY, 4/27/2007), 2007 TNT 104-9; IRC §7475 (registration fee).

294  **ABA inadvertently approved.** Richard A. Zitrin and Carol M. Langord, *Legal Ethics in the Practice of Law* (Charlottesville, Virginia: The Michie Company, 1995), 4-16 ("character" at 11); Richard A. Zitrin and Carol M. Langord, *The Moral Compass of American Lawyers: Truth, Justice Power and Greed* (NY: Random

House, 1999), 125-126; David Ray Papke, "Very Quiet, Very Powerful: The American Bar Association," *The Nation*, 30 Jul 1973, 75.

295 **Russian Jew boys.** ABA Proceedings, 1929, 622-23, reprinted in Robert Stevens, *Law School: Legal Education in America from the 1850s to the 1980s* (Chapel Hill: University of North Carolina Press, 1983), 184. Henry Drinker's partner was Charles J. Biddle, great-grandson of Nicholas Biddle president of the Second Bank of the United States.

295 **act as a preceptor.** Deborah L. Rhode, "Moral Character as a Professional Credential," *Yale Law Journal*, Jan 1985, 491-603, at 501; Tax Court Rule 200(c).

295 **judicial deference.** *Chevron USA Inc. v Natural Resources Defense Council, Inc., et al.*, 467 US 837 (1984); *U.S. v Mead*, 533 US 218 (2001); *National Cable & Telecommunications Association v Brand X Internet Services*, 545 US 967 (2005); Kirstin E. Hickman, "The Need for Mead: Rejecting Tax Exceptionalism in Judicial Deference," 90 *Minnesota Law Review* 1537 (2006).

296 **Regulatory Flexibility Act.** "A Guide to the Regulatory Flexibility Act," Office of Advocacy, U.S. Small Business Administration, May 1996, at 11; *Thompson v Clark*, 741 F2d 401 (CA-DC, 1984, opinion by Judge Antonin Scalia); *Associated Fisheries of Maine, Inc. v Daley*, 127 F3d 104 (CA-1, 1997), 954 FSupp 383 (DC-Maine, 1997); *Small Refiner Lead Phase-Down Task Force v EPA*, 705 F2d 506, 539 (CA-DC, 1983); *Rep. Mike Synar, et. al., v U.S.*, 626 FSupp 1374 (DC-DC, 1986, Judge Scalia participating).

296 **additional safeguards.** Executive Order 12866 issued by President Clinton in 1993 requires 12 principles be addressed before issuing regulations which are likely to result in "an annual effect on the economy of $100 million or more." Section 553(b) of the Administrative Procedures Act requires a public hearing for new regulations, unless "impracticable, unnecessary, or contrary to the public interest." These rules require the agency to prepare a Regulatory Flexibility Analysis. IRC §7805(f) requires Treasury to submit proposed or temporary regulations to the Chief Counsel for Advocacy of the Small Business Administration who is required to submit comments within four weeks. President Bush issued EO 13272 in 2002, "Proper Consideration of Small Entities in Agency Rulemaking," which requires SBA to monitor compliance with the Regulatory Flexibility Act of 1980.

296 **less than rigorous.** William Buzbee, "The 'Legislative Mirage' of Single Statute Regulatory Reform," Symposium on Statutory Interpretation and Environmental Law, Regulatory Reform or Statutory Muddle, *NYU Environmental Law Journal*, 1996.

296 **APA and RFA simply do not apply.** Kristin E. Hickman, "Coloring Outside the Lines: Examining Treasury's (Lack of) Compliance with Administrative Procedure Act Rulemaking Requirements," 82 *Notre Dame L. Rev.* 1727 (2007); Jasper L. Cummings Jr., "Treasury Violates the APA?" 2007 TNT 200-28 (24 Sep 2007).

296 **non-complying agencies.** *N.C. Fisheries Ass'n v Daley*, 16 FSupp2d 647, 652 (ED-Va., 1997) (remanded back to agency to consider RFA); *Northwest Mining Ass'n v Babbitt*, 5 FSupp2d 9 (DC-DC, 1998) (remanded back to Bureau of Land

Management for writing "small business" instead of "small mines"). The courts concluded that a mere statement that a rule will not have a significant effect on a substantial number of small entities is insufficient. Agencies must provide an analytical basis for certification.

297 **SBA has warned Treasury.** "Re: Notice of Proposed Rulemaking: Income Attributable to Domestic Production Activities (70 Fed. Reg. 67220, 4 Nov 2005)," SBA Office of Advocacy, 3 Jan 2006; TD 9263, IRB 2006-25, 1063, 1079 (17-page triple-column preamble followed by 54 pages of triple-column regulations on the extraordinarily complex "Income Attributable to Domestic Production Activities" (IRC §199)).

297 **Crude Oil Windfall Profits Tax Act of 1980.** *U.S. v Ptasynski*, 462 US 74, 81 (1983).

297 **origination clause.** *History of the Committee on Finance, United States Senate* (Washington: U.S. Govt. Printing Office, 1981), 39-40; *Flint v Stone Tracy Co.*, 220 US 107, 158 (1911) (upheld 1909 corporate excise tax).

297 **rebuked by Senator Daniel Webster.** Thomas Hart Benton, *Thirty Years' View* (NY: D. Appleton and Company, 1861) vol. 1, 321.

298 **Rostenkowski.** Michael W. Evans, "'A Source of Frequent and Obstinate Altercations': The History and Application of the Origination Clause," 2004 TNT 230-19 (29 Nov 2004).

299 **Individuals sued.** *Armstrong v U.S.*, 759 F2d 1378, 85-1 USTC ¶16,433 (CA-9, 1985); *Texas Association of Concerned Taxpayers v U.S.*, 772 F2d 163, 85-2 USTC ¶16,441 (CA-5, 1985), cert den 476 US 1151.

299 **ex post facto...not an impediment.** *Stockdale v Atlantic Ins. Co.*, 87 US 323, 331 (1874) (1864 retroactivity); *Brushaber v Union Pacific R. Co.*, 240 US 1 (1916) at 20 (1913 retroactivity).

300 **retroactive tax increase.** *U.S. Bank N.A. v U.S.*, 74 FSupp2d 934 (DC-Neb, 9/15/99) (Dinsmore); *NationsBank of Texas v U.S.*, 269 F3d 1332 (CA-FC, 2001), aff'g 44 Fed Cl 661 (1999), cert den 537 US 813 (2002) (Garwood); *Kane v U.S.*, 942 FSupp 233 (ED PA, 1996), aff'd without op., 118 F3d 1576 (CA-3, 1997); *Quarty v U.S.*, 170 F3d 961 (CA-9, 1999).

301 **manifest injustice.** *Oberhand v Director*, 22 NJ Tax 55, 2005 STT 68-45 (Tax Ct Dkt No 004-150-2003, 2/23/05), 23 NJ Tax 431, 907 A2d 428, 2006 STT 196-17 (App Ct Dkt Nos A-3886-04T2 & A-4243-04T2, 9/26/06, 2008 NJ Lexis 110, 2008 STT 41-14 (NJ Sup Ct, Dkt. A-106 (Sep Term 2006), 2/27/08). Oberhand was based strictly on equity relief because the same NJ Tax Court Judge Harold A. Kuskin ruled three months later that this retroactive law *was not manifest injustice* under slightly different facts where the tax resulted from a disclaimer by the beneficiary. That retroactive tax was not triggered by the decedent. *Rappeport v Director*, 2005 STT 152-15 (Tax Ct Dkt No 003893-2003, 6/27/05). When the 1894 income tax was before the U.S. Supreme Court the second time, it considered whether the tax was unconstitutional or manifest injustice. It opted for unconstitutional.

301 **Tomato is a vegetable.** *Nix v Hedden*, 149 US 304 (1893).

301 **bill of attainder** is a legislative act that declares the guilt of an individual and doles out punishment without a judicial trial. It is forbidden by Article 1, sections 9 and 10 of the Constitution. IRC §6707A(b)(2)(B) assesses a $200,000 penalty for undisclosed "listed transactions." *David B. Barr*, 51 TC 693 (1969), holds "bill of attainder" inapplicable to civil tax cases.

302 **taxed...in his state of residence.** *Mobilia sequunter personam*, (income from) mobile (property) follows the person" and is taxed in his state of residence is the multistate taxation principle violated by the Georgia courts. The taxpayer's lawyers were politically connected, so the following year, they prevailed upon the Georgia legislature to amend the "doing business" statute, thereby reversing this decision. OCGA §48-7-24(c) (added 1997). *Scherer Trust v Georgia Department of Revenue*, Fulton County (Georgia) Superior Court, Case No. 895D0805, Civil Actions No. E-25101, E-25102, E-25103, E-25104 (13 Jan 1995).

302 **hiring a Texas law firm.** Texas Comptroller of Public Accounts, Hearing No. 40,927 (21 Oct 2002). "Not even the most aggressive state tax administrator would take such a position," wrote multistate tax expert Walter Hellerstein before this decision was released. Walter Hellerstein, "Federal statutory restraints on state tax nexus generate continuing controversy," 97 JTax 290 (Nov 2002).

302 **Texas tax ALJs.** Texas administrative law judge Anne K. Perez (Hearing 40,927) was a revenue department prosecutor, as were Alvin Stoll, Roy Scudday, and Elizabeth Wilson Davis, while Thomas L. Poole was a tax auditor.

302 ***Shell Oil Company v St. Charles Parish School Board***, 848 So2d 129 (2003), writ denied 2004 La. LEXIS 544 (La., 13 Feb. 2004), writ granted by, reversed by, judgment entered 2004 La. LEXIS 499 (La., 13 Feb. 2004); *Anthony Crane Rental v Fruge*, 859 So2d 631 (La. Sup. Ct., 2003).

303 ***Michael D. Hamilton** v Royal International Petroleum Corporation and Elmer B. Litchfield, Sheriff and Tax Collector*, 934 So2d 25 (2006), rev'g La. App. 2003CA2660 (1st Cir, 3/2/2005), cert den __ US __ (No. 06-455, 1/8/2007), 127 S.Ct. 937.

303 **Great Neck.** *Temple Bnai Shalom of Great Neck v Village of Great Neck Estates*, 32 AD3d 391, 820 NYS2d 104 (2d Dept, 2006), lv denied 8 NY3d 813, 868 NE2d 235, 836 NYS2d 552, reargument denied 9 NY3d 899, 874 NE2d 745, 842 NYS2d 778 (2007), 2008 TNT 18-45 (5 Dec 2007) (cert petition), cert den __ US __ (No. 07-760, 2/19/2008), 2008 STT 34-1 (20 Feb 2008); *Jones v Flowers*, 547 US 220 (2006); *In re: Temple Bnai Shalom* (Bkrptcy ED NY, case no. 04-80707, filed 2/5/2004); discussion with foreclosed property owner, Alan Guthartz.

304 **To Pay or Not to Pay.** *Evans v Gore*, 253 US 245 (1920) holding judges salaries exempt (Holms and Brandeis dissenting); *O'Malley v Woodrough*, 307 US 277 (1939) followed Holmes dissent in overruling *Miles v Graham*, 268 US 501 (1925) and held federal judges salaries taxable. Footnotes in *O'Malley* give citations to the origin and history of the salary tax exemption for president and judges, citing *Federalist 78*'s purse and sword argument, contrary construction of this provision

by other English-speaking courts, and a long list of dissenting legal treatises regarding the U.S. Supreme Court's position.

304 **Taney wrote...Chase.** Taney's 1863 letter was published in 157 US 701 (1894).
304 **Chase had not issued.** George S. Boutwell, *Reminiscences of Sixty Years in Public Affairs* (NY: Greenwood Press, 1968), vol. I, 312 (reprint of McClure, Phillips & Co. edition of 1902, vol I, 304). Boutwell doesn't mention taxation of judges. But he discusses the ruling process he developed and adds, "[Chase] never gave an opinion or tendered any advice in relation to the business of the Internal Revenue Office while I was at the head of it."
304 **tax of three per cent.** George S. Boutwell, *Excise and Internal Revenue Laws of the United States* (Washington: Govt. Printing Office, 1863), 195.
305 **old friends.** Boutwell, vol II, 210. (suggested Hoar) vol II, 204.
305 **refund was probably granted.** David Burnham, *A Law Unto Itself* (NY: Random House, 1989), 13 (IRS granted the Lincoln refund, but no sources are cited). Shelley L. Davis, *Unbridled Power* (NY: HarperCollins, 1997), 200-201.
307 **after June 6, 1932.** Revenue Act of 1932, 47 Stat. 169 (6 Jun 1932), §22(a); Economy Act of 1932, 47 Stat. 403, (30 Jun 1932), §109.
307 **Port Authority employees.** *Helvering v Gerhardt*, 304 US 405 (1938); *Graves v New York ex rel O'Keefe*, 306 US 466 (1939) (states may tax salaries paid by the Federal Government).
307 **prospectively taxing.** Roosevelt's April 25, 1938 message to Congress, 83 *Cong. Record* 5683. The Public Salary Tax Act of 1939 (4 USC §111 (1939)) codified repeal of *Collector v Day*, 78 US 113 (1870); Lucien W. Shaw, "The Public Salary Act of 1939," 27 *Calif. Law Review* 705 (1939); Boris Bittker, *Federal Taxation of Income, Estates and Gifts* (Boston: Warren, Gorham & Lamont, 1981), ¶1.2.8. It's still occasionally litigated. Michigan Circuit Court Judge William Beer unsuccessfully raised the old arguments that his state salary was not subject to Federal income tax. *Beer*, 64 TC 879 (1975), appeal dism'd 77-2 USTC ¶9491 (CA-6, 1976), cert den 431 US 938 (1977).
307 **remitted...to their estates.** F.J. Dundon, "Illogical Ruling Exempted Official Salaries from Tax," NYT, 3 Jan 1932, E2.
307 **Calvin Coolidge.** "Coolidge Paid $14,091 Income Tax for 1924; Will Recommend Repeal of Publicity Clause," NYT, 2 September 1925, 2.
308 **Herbert Hoover.** Correspondence, Herbert Hoover Presidential Library, White House Precedents, Permanent File, 25 May 1929; Economy Act of 1932, 47 Stat. 403 (30 Jun 1932), §107 (Special Salary Reductions), §109 (Remittances from Constitutional Officers); Receipts, Herbert Hoover Presidential Library, RG130, Gen. Acc. 597, Miscellaneous Records, Salary as President. The 1932 and 1939 amendments each simply added a single sentence to the definition of gross income. These additional sentences were eliminated in 1954 as unnecessary.
308 **IRS still possesses.** Davis, 199-201.
308 **Taxation of judges.** *U.S. v Hatter*, 532 US 557 (2001); Jonathan L. Entin and Erik M. Jensen, "Hatter v. United States and the Taxation of Federal Judges," 2001

TNT 146-98 (30 Jul 2001); Jonathan L. Entin and Erik M. Jensen, "Taxation, Compensation, and Judicial Independence: Hatter v. United States," 2001 TNT 48-103 (12 Mar 2001); "Supreme Court Roundup; Court to Review Benefits Tax on U.S. Judges Voting Rights Petty Offenses," NYT, 17 Oct 2000, A29.

308 **booster for...West.** "Hearing on H.R. 3214 Before a Subcommittee of the Senate Committee on the Judiciary," 80th Cong., 2d Sess. (1948), 16. Congressman Devitt testified, "I am very well acquainted with many of the editors and experts of the West Publishing Co., and especially with Mr. Harvey T. Reid, editor in chief... I have the highest possible regard for the legal ability, the technical competence, and unquestioned integrity of these gentlemen."

308 **favorite judge.** Ron Meshbesher and Joe Friedberg, "Minnesota Criminals We Have Known," *Minnesota Law and Politics*, Aug/Sep 2005.

309 **detail phobia.** *U.S. v Barta*, 888 F2d 1220 (1989); *Grosshandler*, 75 TC 1 (1980).

309 ***Stelten***, TC Memo 1982-512; *U.S. v Stelten*, Cr. 6-87-19 and 6-87-20 (DC-MN, 1987).

309 **Distinguished Service to Justice Award.** Lee A. Sheppard, "The Tax Treatment Of The Brethren's Fun In The Sun," 95 TNT 71-4 (12 Apr 1995), 21, citing *Minneapolis Star Tribune*, 5 Mar 1995, 1A, and 6 Mar 1995, 1A.

310 **Mead Data Central.** *West Publishing Co. v Mead Data Central*, 616 FSupp 1571 (D.Minn., 1985), aff'd, 799 F2d 1219 (CA-8, 1986), cert den 479 US 1070 (1987); "Mead, West Publishing Are Expected To Settle 3 Suits Over Legal Databases," WSJ, 19 Jul 1988, 1;

310 **Texas sued.** *State of Texas v West Publishing Company*, 882 F2d 171 (CA-5, 1989), 681 FSupp 1228 (DC-W Texas, 1988). In 1995, West attempted to add a provision to the Paperwork Reduction Act that would allow the company to claim copyright interest in government information when the firm added value to it, and prohibit public information from being copied. The provision was deleted prior to passage. "House Panel Strikes West Publishing Provision," 95 TNT 29-4 (13 Feb 1995).

311 ***Matthew Bender & Co. v West Publishing Co.***, 158 F3d 693 (CA-2, 1998), 158 F3d 674 (CA-2, 1998), cert den 526 US 1154 (1999); *Matthew Bender & Co. v West Publishing Co.*, 240 F3d 116 (CA-2, 2001) (a/k/a Hyperlaw III).

311 **Abe Fortas.** Sen. Richard Russell (D-GA) told Sen. Robert Griffin (R-MI) that his senators would silently support the Republican effort to deny Fortas the nomination. The October 1, 1968 vote for cloture was only 45 in favor out of the 88 senators present, far short of the two-thirds majority needed, and indicating weak Democrat support for Fortas. That night, Fortas asked Johnson to withdraw his nomination for chief justice. Laura Kalman, *Abe Fortas: A Biography* (New Haven: Yale University Press, 1990), 332, 355; "Fortas Refuses to Appear Again," NYT, 14 September 1968, 1; "Griffin Rebukes Nixon for Stand Opposing a Filibuster on Fortas," NYT, 15 September 1968, 76; "Fortas Approved by Senate Panel; Filibuster Looms," NYT, 18 September 1968, 1 (One contributor's son had

a pending Appeals case which might have reached the Supreme Court.); "Critics of Fortas Begin Filibuster, Citing Propriety," NYT, 26 September 1968.

312 **his own conscience.** Robert H. Jackson, *The Supreme Court in the American System of Government* (NY: Harper & Row, 1955), 16.

312 **David Brewer.** *Clement v Field*, 147 US 467 (1893) was argued by Aaron P. Jetmore, husband of Brewer's daughter Harriet. Michael J. Brodhead, *David J. Brewer: The Life of a Supreme Court Justice, 1837 - 1910* (Southern Illinois University Press, 1994), 114.

312 **Ruth Bader Ginsburg.** Richard A. Serrano and David G. Savage, "Ginsburg Has Ties to Activist Group; "The justice lends her name to a legal fund's event on women's rights. Critics see a conflict," LAT, 11 Mar 2004, A1. Speaking before the National Press Club on 9 March 2004, Anthony D. Romero, Executive Director of the American Civil Liberties Union, justified this: "As I understand, there are many judges who hear and determine cases on behalf of colleagues or for colleagues with whom either they worked or had relationships with. The Code of Judicial Ethics is rather clear, that if there is a time when a judge or justice believes that they have a conflict of interest then they are to recuse themselves from those deliberations. And I'm sure that the finest judges who serve this country are able to make that determination..."

312 **Antonin Scalia.** Memorandum of Justice Scalia, *in re Richard B. Cheney, Vice President of the United States*, 541 US 913 (2004); *Cheney, Vice President of the United States, et al. v United States District Court For the District of Columbia et al.*, 542 US 367 (2004); "Judges as Cheerleaders," (Editorial) LAT, 12 Mar 2004, B16; David G. Savage and Richard A. Serrano, "Clashing Opinions on Justices' Recusals; Supreme Court jurists have different views on how they define a conflict of interest," LAT, 21 Mar 2004. A1; Monroe H. Freedman, "Duck-Blind Justice: Justice Scalia's Memorandum in the Cheney Case," *Georgetown Journal of Legal Ethics*, Fall 2004, Vol. 18, Iss. 1, p. 229.

312 **Joel Gerber.** *Nobles v Commissioner*, 105 F3d 436 (CA-9, 1997).

313 **Ogden Hoffman.** "Judge Hoffman Dead," *San Francisco Chronicle*, 10 Aug 1891, 10; Christian G. Fritz, *Federal Justice in California: The Court of Ogden Hoffman, 1851 - 1891*, 48, (dinner); *Los Angeles Tribune*, 9 Jul 1887, 1 (already longest serving judge in 1887); "Judicial Conduct Guidelines Blurred," NYT, 15 May 1969, 28 (Brandeis).

## CHAPTER 11: A PRURIENT INTEREST

317 **public record.** Richard D. Pomp, "The Disclosure of State Corporate Income Tax Data: Turning The Clock Back to the Future," 22 *Cap. U. L. Rev.* 373, 379-384 (1993).

318 **1865 song.** Walter Howard, "That's Where The Laugh Comes In," H. De Marsan, publisher.

318 **1909 corporation income tax.** Pomp, 388; Harold P. Roth, "The Payne-Aldrich Tariff Act of 1909," JoA, May 1987, 181.

318 **Publicity was resurrected.** "Publicity Limited on Income Taxes," NYT, 3 Jun 1934, N9 (brief history of publicity); "Income Tax Books Here Now Guarded," NYT, 26 Oct 1924, 1 (women seeking what husbands and fiancés were earning); "Policy of Publicity Assailed," NYT, 24 Jun 1934 (purchase and sale of lists); "Income Tax in Brooklyn; Returns of Incomes Over $10,000," NYT, 2 May 1869, 5 (tax list publicity); "Recapitulation of Income Tax Payments Through Country Previously Published," NYT, 26 Oct 1924, 2 (earnings of movie stars and moguls); "Coolidge Paid $14,091 Income Tax for 1924; Will Recommend Repeal of Publicity Clause" NYT, 2 Sep 1925; "More Income Tax Payments Made in 1925 by Residents of New York City," NYT, 3 Sep 1925, 12; "Cost of Publicity Scored in Treasury," NYT, 3 Sep 1925, 1 (Coolidge and Mellon opposed); "Tax Payments of $500 and More Made on Last Year's Income by Individuals," NYT, 3 Sep 1925, 9; "Chicago Tax Sets Record," NYT, 18 Mar 1925, 33; "Some Pay High Tax to Gratify Vanity," NYT, 20 Jan 1925, 14 (fool creditors, not alarm creditors).

319 **published in the newspapers.** "Rockefeller Jr paid $7,435,169; Ford Family and Company Pay $19 million," NYT, 24 Oct 1924; "Rockefeller Jr leads with $6,277,699; Ford Payments Total $21,260,023," NYT 2 Sep 1925.

319 **Lawsuits.** *U.S. v Dickey*, 268 US 378 (1925); *U.S. v Baltimore Post*, 268 US 388 (1925); "Income Tax List Publication Upheld By Supreme Court," NYT, 26 May 1925, 1.

320 **Congress granted...access.** IRC(1939), §55(a); IRC 1954, §6103(a)(1).

320 **Executive Order 11697,** 17 Jan 1973, 38 FR 1723 (No. 12, 18 Jan 1973), 1973-1 CB 592; EO 11709, 27 Mar 1973, 38 FR 8131, 1973-1 CB 595; TD 7255, 1973-1 CB 595 (adding Reg. 301-6103(a)-108, Inspection by Department of Agriculture); EO 11773, 24 Mar 1974, 39 FR 10881 (revoking EO 11697 and 11773), 1974-1 CB 334; "Farm Tax Returns Are Made Available," NYT, 11 Feb 1973, 46; "Agriculture Agency Limits Nixon Tax Return Orders," NYT, 18 Feb 1973, 37; "Nixon To Limit Data On Farmers' Taxes," NYT, 28 Mar 1973, 41; PL 105-277, §4006(a)(1), adding IRC §6103(j)(5) (1998 farm amendment); Homeland Security Act of 2002, PL 107-134, §201, adding IRC §6103(i)(7) (terrorist amendment).

321 **National Archives.** Shelley L. Davis, *Unbridled Power* (NY: HarperCollins, 1997), 33-37.

321 **Agriculture Department access.** "Disclosure Report For Public Inspection Pursuant To Internal Revenue Code Section 6103(p)(3)(C) For Calendar Year 2004," JCT, JCX-63-05, 19 Aug 2005; "FSA Notifies Producers of Inadvertent Release of Personal Information," Farm Services Agency, Release No. 1414.06, 15 Feb 2006.

321 **perfidious attempt.** H.R. 4818, Division H - Transportation, Treasury, Independent Agencies, and General Government Appropriations Act of 2005, Title II, §222; 2004 TNT 226-11 (20 Nov 2004):

> SEC. 222. Hereafter, notwithstanding any other provision of law governing the disclosure of income tax returns or return information, upon written request of the Chairman of the House or Senate Committee on

Appropriations, the Commissioner of the Internal Revenue Service shall allow agents designated by such Chairman access to Internal Revenue Service facilities and any tax returns or return information contained therein.

321 **dumbfounded.** "Aide Takes Blame for Tax Return Provision," WP, 3 Dec 2004, A1.

321 **lists of shame.** Internal Revenue Code §6039G(d), effective 6 Feb 1995; Health Insurance Portability and Accountability Act of 1996, PL 104-191, §512; Sheldon I. Banoff, Richard M. Lipton, "Tax Delinquents Exposed!" JTax, Mar 2006, 190.

322 **Fidelity & Deposit.** Ted Morgan, *FDR: A Biography* (NY: Simon & Schuster, 1985), 246, 263.

323 **so widespread and so amazing.** "President's Message Asking Action to Halt Tax Evasions," NYT, 2 Jun 1937, 17; 81 *Cong. Rec.* 6704 (1937).

323 **Merrill-Lynch.** *Morgenthau Diaries*, 67:173, 179, Franklin D. Roosevelt Library. Treasury Secretary Henry Morgenthau had all his telephone conversations recorded and transcribed. His secretary toiled untold years indexing all his papers, correspondence and transcriptions. The result is a detailed record that is loosely called, "The Morgenthau Diaries."

323 **173-0.** "House Unanimous in Voting Tax Bill," NYT, 17 Aug 1937, 9.

323 **two minutes.** "Congress Clears Way for Last Lap," NYT, 20 Aug 1937.

323 **foundations of society.** Randolph Paul, *Taxation in the United States* (Boston: Little, Brown and Company, 1954), 207.

324 **Eleanor...radio broadcasts.** "Fish Lays Evasion to Mrs. Roosevelt," NYT, 10 Jul 1937, 4; Boris I. Bittker, "Refusal to Accept Compensation," *Federal Taxation of Income, Estates and Gifts* (Boston: Warren, Gorham & Lamont, 1981), ¶75.2.4 (vol. 3); "Hearings, Joint Committee on Tax Evasion and Avoidance, 75th Cong., 1st Sess., Part 4, 426-431 (28 Jul 1937). Notwithstanding Robert Jackson's opinion, there was an existing ruling, Mimeograph 3040 (21 Dec. 1922) by Commissioner Blair, holding that such arrangements would be taxable to the donor. Lest there be any lingering doubts, a 1957 revision to Treasury regulations made the taxability crystal clear. Treas. Reg. 1.61-2(c), added by T.D. 6272, 1957-2 CB 18, 21; See *Mertens Law of Federal Income Taxation* (1991 ed.) §31.91 FN68, citing Treas. Reg. 118 (1939), §39.22(a)-2; *George C. Johnson*, 11 TCM 31 (1952).

325 **contradicted.** Transcript, telephone conversation between Morgenthau and Helvering, 6 Jul 1937, *Morgenthau Diaries*, 77:157-159, Franklin D. Roosevelt Library.

325 **Fish alleged.** "Hearings, Joint Committee on Tax Evasion and Avoidance," 75th Cong., 1st Sess., Part 3, July 9 and 13, 1937, 329 - 324.

326 **press conference.** "The Roosevelt Week," *Time*, 19 Jul 1937, 9; *Cong. Rec.*, vol. 81, 75th Cong., 1st Sess., 5590, Appendix 1610, App. 1823-1824, App. 1875-1876, App. 2128-2129, citing *Chicago Tribune*, 14 Feb 1934 ("The President once admitted to deducting farm losses").

326 **two...misdemeanors.** *Spies v U.S.*, 317 US 492 (1943), opinion written by Justice Robert Jackson. The Bush administration made a similar proposal in 2007. Jay Starkman, "CPA Seeks Reconsideration of Proposals in 2008 Budget Plan," 2007 TNT 149-27 (23 Jul 2007).

326 **Hitler.** "Hitler Was a Tax Dodger, Researcher Finds," *Reuters*, 17 Dec 2004.

326 **Rockefeller.** *Estate of Rockefeller*, 83 TC 368 (1984).

327 **Ronald Reagan.** Steven R. Weisman, *The Great Tax Wars* (NY: Simon & Schuster, 2002), 360. Weisman claims that once he reached the 90 percent tax bracket, Reagan stopped making movies and relaxed for the rest of the year, refusing to work when whatever he made would be transferred to the government. In his autobiography, *An American Life* (NY: Simon & Schuster, 1990, p. 117), Reagan complained about reaching the 94 percent bracket, but didn't mention stopping work on account of tax rates. He didn't mention his own personal taxes in his 1965 autobiography, *Where's the Rest of Me?* (NY: Duell, Sloan and Pearce, 1965) though he wrote that after he got out of the army, his studio contract paid him $3,500 per week (p. 140) which would not put him at the very top rate. I doubt whether Reagan had enough high income years that he became independently wealthy so he could refuse work, and there were widespread techniques prior to 1969 that sheltered income from taxes. Reagan had a penchant for exaggeration, as described by Carl M. Cannon, "Untruth and Consequences," *The Atlantic*, Jan/Feb 2007, 56 at 59-60.

327 **embarrass Reagan.** "Ford Says U.S. Taxes Totaled Nearly 38% of His Gross Income," WSJ, 21 April 1976, 14; "Data on Reagan Indicate He Paid No U.S. Tax in '70," NYT, 16 May 1976, 1; "Reagan Refuses Tax Inspection," WP, 17 May 1976, A3; "Aide Denies Report That Reagan Paid No '70 Income Tax," NYT, 18 May 1976, 19; "Reagan Insists He Paid Some 1970 U.S. Tax," WP, 18 May 1976, A5; email to author from Michael Deaver, Reagan's Deputy Chief of Staff (27 Feb 2007).

327 **476 delegates.** "Reagan Gets 46 Delegates in Five States," NYT, 17 May 1976, 21.

328 **favored to win.** "Ford's Hurrah," NYT, 20 May 1976, 35. Reagan expected to lose the May 25 Oregon primary, but unexpectedly, he lost in Kentucky and Tennessee too.

328 **Jack Anderson,** "Ronnie's taxes: what's the whole story?" *New York Daily News*, 20 Jul 1976, 28.

328 **only slightly ahead.** "Nomination of Ford Remains Uncertain Despite Clear Lead as Convention Opens," WSJ, 16 Aug 1976, 2.

328 **Jimmy Carter's 1976 taxes.** "Carter Owes No U.S. Tax for '76 But He Volunteers to Pay $6,000," NYT, 25 Jun 1977, 1.

328 **Arnold Schwarzenegger.** "Few details on tax return. Governor reports how much he paid and gave to charity," *Sacramento Bee*, 9 Dec 2004.

329 **Clarence Thomas.** "Thomas cries, tells of battling to get by," AJC, 12 May 2001 (Associated Press).

329 **Charlie Chaplin.** *75 Years of IRS Criminal Investigation History*, Department of the Treasury, Internal Revenue Service, Document 7233 (Rev. 2-95), 46-48.

329 *Charles Laughton,* 40 BTA 101 (1939), 113 F2d 103 (CA-9, 1940).

330 *Charles Johnson*, 78 TC 882 (1982).

330 *Gary Sargent*, 93 TC 572 (1989), rev'd 929 F2d 1252 (CA-8, 1991).

330  *Allen Leavell*, 104 TC 140 (1995).
330  **collapsible corporations...456 words.** IRC §341(e)(1), repealed in 2003 (PL 108-27); *Fox*, 37 BTA 271 (1938).
330  **combustible corporation.** *Ivey v U.S.*, 60-1 USTC ¶9322.
331  **NFL players.** "SEC Shuts Down Firm That Had NFL Clients," *Associated Press*, 27 Jan 2004; "NFL Warns Players About Florida Investment Program," WSJ, 16 Jan 2004.
331  *Irving Berlin*, 42 BTA 668 (1940).
332  **Will Rogers.** *U.S. v Rogers*, 120 F2d 244 (CA-9, 1941).
332  *Jose Ferrer*, 304 F2d 124 (CA-2, 1962), reversing in part, 35 TC 617 (1961); 50 TC 177 (1968).
332  *Jack Benny*, 25 TC 197 (1955), appeal dismissed (CA-9).
332  *Julius H. (Groucho) Marx*, 29 TC 88 (1957). Groucho was represented by Thomas Tarleau (Henry Morgenthau's Tax Legislative Counsel).
333  **Liberace.** *International Artists, Ltd.*, 55 TC 94 (1970).
334  **Willie Nelson.** "Mamma, Don't Let Your Babies Grow Up to Work for the Tax Boys," WSJ, 29 Jan 1991, C1; "Willie After the IRS and on the road to 60: a time to look back and ahead," LAT, 30 Aug 1992, 5; "Willie Nelson Settles With IRS," WSJ, 2 Feb 1993, A3; "Willie Nelson's Paid the Bill," WP, 9 Apr 1993, N11; Lee A. Sheppard, "Individual Bankruptcy: The Tax Shelter of the '90s," 92 TNT 208-7 (12 Oct 1992), 166; "If the Tax Man Says, I'll Be Seeing You," NYT, 26 Feb 1995, F11.
334  **Conway Twitty.** *Harold Lloyd Jenkins*, TCM 1983-667, nonacq. AOD 1984-022, 23 TNT 175 (9 Apr 1984).
335  **Bud Selig.** *Allan H. Selig*, 740 F2d 572, 84-2 USTC ¶9696 (CA-7, 1984), aff'g 565 FSupp 524, 83-2 USTC ¶9442 (1983). The 1983 district court case tells a little-known history about Bud Selig and the Brewers.
335  **Dennis Rodman.** *Eugene Amos, Jr.*, TC Memo 2003-329; "Dennis Rodman's On-the-Court Antics and Out-of-Court Settlement Lead to In-the-(Tax)-Court Litigation," 100 JTax 62 (Jan 2004).
335  **Madonna.** Sheldon I. Banoff, Richard M. Lipton, "What do Madonna, young NBA hopeful have in common?" 91 JTax 191 (Sep 1999).
335  **Martha Stewart.** *In the Matter of the Petition of Martha Stewart*, DTA No. 816263, 2000 STT 27-37, 13 Jan 2000; "Martha Stewart Living (in New York)?" 2000 STT 24-12 (4 Feb 2000); "Tax Inquiries Can Combine Guesswork and Digging," NYT, 17 Nov 2007.
335  **Sammy Sosa.** "Sosa loses lawsuit over income taxes," *Chicago Tribune*, 27 Jun 2003, 6; *Chicago Tribune*, 4 Mar 2003, 9; J. Fred Giertz, "Illinois Circuit Denies Baseball Star Credit for Taxes Paid Other States," 2003 STT 126-7 (1 Jul 2003); David Schmutter and Ari Lazaar, "State Taxation of Professional Athletes and Entertainers," TTA, Feb 2004, 85-86; *Samuel and Sonya Sosa v Glenn L. Bower as Director of the Illinois Department of Revenue* (Cook County Cir. Ct., Docket 02 L 50670, 6/26/2003). In 2005, the Chicago Cubs traded Sosa to the Baltimore

Orioles. As a result of the Sosa publicity, Illinois modified its tax law in 2005 to reduce athletes' double tax exposure. Garland Allen, "With Ballplayers' Help, Illinois Employee Compensation Bill Advances," 2005 STT 89-3 (10 May 2005); J. Fred Giertz, "Illinois Legislature OKs Modifying Taxation of Pro Athletes," 2005 STT 102-11 (27 May 2005).

336   **David Bar-Illan**, "Taxation Without Due Deliberation," *Newsweek*, 21 Jul 1986, 7.

336   **Louisiana has a special law.** Louisiana RS 47:1602.1, 47:1604.1; Tax Form IT-540B-NRA.

336   **Derek Jeter.** "State Tax Officials Dispute Claim of Florida Residency by Jeter," NYT, 16 Nov 2007; "Pro Baseball Player Disputes Liability for Back Taxes in New York," 2007 STT 225-4 (21 Nov 2007).

336   *Sugar Ray Robinson*, 44 TC 20 (1965).

337   *Sammy Davis Jr.*, TCM 1989-607.

337   **Judy Garland.** Lorna Luft, *Me and My Shadows*, (NY: Pocket Books, 1998), 155-156, 191, 201-202; David Shipman, *Garland, The Secret Life of An American Legend* (NY: Hyperion, 1992), 508-509.

337   **O.J. Simpson.** *Chamales*, TCM 2000-33.

337   **Alan Jay Lerner.** "4th Ex-Wife Sues for Sixth Time," NYT, 26 Oct 1979, B4:1; "Alan Jay Lerner Sued by U.S. for $1.4 Million," NYT, 20 Feb 1986, C13; obituary, NYT, 15 Jun 1986, A1; obituary, *Time*, 21 Jul 1986.

338   **sue his accountants.** Edward Jablonsky, *Alan Jay Lerner: A Biography* (NY: Henry Holt & Company, 1986), 307, citing *New York Post*.

338   **Charles Strouse.** "Snapshots of Alan Jay Lerner," NYT, 11 Jun 2000, 2.28.

338   **very day he died.** *Micheline Lerner v U.S. et al*, No. 85 Civ 6091 (SDNY, 14 Jun 1986), 87-1 USTC ¶9339.

338   **settle with the IRS.** "The Informer," *Forbes*, 31 Mar 2003.

339   **Sergeant York.** David D. Lee, *Sergeant York: An American Hero* (Univ. Press of Kentucky, 1985), 101-115, 128-130.

339   **Lasky made over $1 million.** Warner paid Lasky $40,000 for his contract with York, plus a $1,500 weekly salary for one year, an advance royalty of $85,000 and a percentage of the film's gross. He sold the percentage contract for $805,000. John Perry, *Sgt. York: His Life, Legend and Legacy* (Nashville: Broadman & Holman Publishers, 1997), 281-282. Lasky treated the $805,000 as capital gain rather than ordinary income, was challenged by IRS, and lost in court. *Lasky*, 22 TC 13 (1954), aff'd 235 F2d 97 (CA-9, 1956), aff'd 352 US 1027 (1957).

339   **Reagan tested four scenes.** Perry, 253.

339   **capital gains.** Rev. Rul. 54-409 states the IRS position that sale for a percentage of receipts should be treated as royalty income, not capital gains. A letter from Acting Commissioner Charles I. Fox to Rep. Joe Evins on April 21, 1959 indicated that the dispute was whether capital gain could be claimed when it was stretched out over several years, rather than being earned in a lump sum. Perry, 306.

339   **Truman and Eisenhower.** Section 210 of the Revenue Act of 1950, amending IRC(1939) added §117(a)(1)(C) which treats income from the sale of writing

books as ordinary income. It's called the "Eisenhower amendment" because it changed the law after General Eisenhower, as an amateur author, treated the sale of his 1948 book, *Crusade in Europe*, as capital gain; "Eisenhower to Pay Tax As an 'Amateur' Writer," NYT, 2 Jun 1948, 31:5; "Eisenhower Taxes on Memoirs Cited," NYT, 28 Sep 1952, 64. Capital gain treatment was afforded Harry Truman's memoirs sold on the installment basis; Rev. Rul. 234, 1953-2 CB 29, *Mertens Law of Federal Income Taxation* (1991 ed.) §22.23 FN 78. A further restrictive amendment of this Code section in 1969 would result in tax assessments against Richard Nixon and Hubert Humphrey. The 1950 Act also added self-employment tax, making the total tax even more onerous.

339 **IRS settled.** "10,000 Give to End Hero's Tax Debt," NYT, 9 Apr 1961, 76; "Sgt. York's Financial Burden Is Detailed by Revenue Service," NYT, 22 Apr 1961, 15; "Sergeant York, War Hero, Dies," NYT, 3 Sep 1964, 1.

340 **pending in Tax Court.** York contested the IRS assessment in Tax Court in 1950 (Dkt. No. 30527), but the case was still pending in 1960, never came to trial, and appears to have settled without decision after the $25,000 payment which IRS accepted. IRS modified its position in Rev. Rul. 60-226 holding that capital gains was applicable regardless of the form of consideration paid. Properly represented, York should have won.

340 **Joe Louis.** Richard Bak, *Joe Louis, The Great Black Hope* (Dallas: Taylor Publishing Company, 1996), 204, 248, 259, 274; "How Joe Louis Lost Two Million Dollars," *Ebony*, May 1946, 10; Joe Louis, *Joe Louis: My Life* (NY: Harcourt Brace Jovanovich, 1978), 169, 205, 217 (Getting on your nerves), 239 (I just tried my best), 243; Joe Louis Barrow, Jr. and Barbara Munder, *Joe Louis, 50 Years An American Hero* (McGraw-Hill Book Company, 1988), 150; Harry V. Jaffa, "Terminator IRS Hounded Joe Louis Into Poverty," WSJ, 27 Dec 2002, A11; "Boxing Pay Is Featherweight Class," WSJ, 12 Dec 2002, D10; Burton W. Folsom, "Joe Louis vs. the IRS," Mackinac Center for Public Policy, 7 Jul 1997, www.mackinac.org/article.asp?ID=22.

## CHAPTER 12: AFFLUENZA

342 **Affluenza,** KCTS-TV (Seattle: Bullfrog Films, 1997).

343 **Hotel del Coronado.** www.hoteldel.com.

345 **Advertising helps.** This was the first advertisement to feature a large picture with so few words. Walt Disney's Herbie "Love Bug" comedies also helped. The twin images of post-college freedom and cuddly personification still linger.

345 **really was a lemon.** Bruce McCall, "Ad Campaign," *American Heritage*, May/Jun 1998, 45; James J. Childs, "The Rating Game," *American Heritage*, Jul/Aug 1998, 8. The prize for lemon car goes to the great Broadway producer, David Merrick. He ran a front page advertisement in the *New York Times* on 24 December 1971 which read, "My Chrysler Imperial is a pile of junk." This resulted in an uproarious *Wall Street Journal* front page story about Mr. Merrick's troubles with his $14,000 made-to-order 1967 Chrysler limousine, a lot of money for a car back

then. "Wherein a Consumer Attacks a Big Firm — & Attacks, & Attacks," WSJ, 9 Jun 1972, 1.

346 **Bismarck.** Edward Crankshaw, *Bismarck* (NY: Viking Press, 1981), 359-60, 378; I.M. Rubnow, *Social Insurance: With Special Reference to American Conditions* (NY: Amo Press, [1913] 1969), 13-16.

346 **Legacy tax.** "History, Present Law, and Analysis of the Federal Wealth Transfer Tax System," JCT, JCX-108-07, 13 Nov 2007; *Knowlton v Moore*, 178 US 41 (1900), includes a brief international history of the tax; Bascom Timmons, *Garner of Texas: A Personal History* (NY: Harper, 1948), 114; Andrew Carnegie, "Wealth," *North American Review*, Jun 1889, 659.

346 **Squander it!** Richard B. Stephens, Guy B. Maxfield, Stephen A. Lind, *Federal Estate and Gift Taxation* (NY: Warren Gorham & Lamont, all editions), ¶1.01.

348 **Henry Clay Frick.** M. Susan Murnane, "Andrew Mellon's Unsuccessful Attempt to Repeal Estate Taxes," 2005 Tax History Conference, UCLA School of Law, 18-19 Jul 2005, reprinted www.taxhistory.org (Readings in Tax History, 22 Aug 2005); *Frick et al v Pennsylvania*, 288 US 473 (1925).

348 **John Dorrance.** *Dorrance's Estate*, 309 Pa 151, 163 Atl 303 (1932), cert den 287 US 660 (1932); *New Jersey v Pennsylvania*, 288 US 618 (1933); *In re Dorrance's Estate*, 115 NJ Eq 268, 170 Atl 601 (1934), aff'd 116 NJL 362, 184 Atl 743 (1932), cert den 298 US 678 (1936), reh'g den 298 US 692 (1936); *Dorrance v Martin*, 12 FSupp 746 (DC-NJ, 1935), aff'd *Hill v Martin*, 296 US 393 (1935); Note, 37 Mich. Law Rev. 1279, 1280 (1939).

349 **John Dorrance III...Kenneth Dart.** "And don't come back," *Forbes*, 18 Nov 1996; "The new refugees," *Forbes*, 21 Nov 1994; *Cecil Furstenberg*, 83 TC 755 (1984).

349 **Hetty Green.** John Steele Gordon, "The Dogs They Loved," *Barron's*, 1 Oct 2007, 55; 53-2 Cong. Record 1656 (vol. 26, 30 Jan 1894); "Now For Delinquents," NYT, 17 Apr 1895, 8; "Not a Resident of New York," NTY, 26 Apr 1895, 3; "Hard Times and Income Taxes," NYT, 1 May 1895, 3; "Mrs. Hetty Green, Menaced, Arms Herself," 9 May 1902, 16; "Hetty Green At The Plaza," NYT, 5 May 1908; "Hetty Green Moves Back to Hoboken," 11 May 1915, 11.

349 **Three biographies.** Boyden Sparks and Samuel Taylor Moore, *Hetty Green: A Woman Who Loved Money* (London: William Heinemann, 1930; reprinted in the U.S. in 1935 as *The Witch of Wall Street*); Arthur H. Lewis, *The Day They Shook The Plum Tree* (NY: Hartcourt, Brace & World, 1963); Charles Slack, *Hetty: The Genius and Madness of America's First Female Tycoon* (NY: Harper Collins Publishers, 2004).

349 **song.** Slack, 191: "If I Were As Rich As Hetty Green," by Sidney S. Toler (1905): *Each day I'd give the poor a thousand dollars / A diamond ring to every little queen — / O you bet your life that I would go to the limit / If I were just as rich as Hetty Green.*

350 **swearing off a tax.** Sparkes, 219 (citing Gustavus Myers, *The History of Great American Fortunes*).

350 **New York Tribune.** Lewis, 49 (citing article published 27 May 1886).

350  **Frankenstein.** Sparkes, 319, 337.
350  **amputated.** Peter Wyckoff, "Queen Midas: Hetty Robinson Green," *New England Quarterly*, June 1950, 147, 156.
350  **no grandchildren.** "Sylvia Green to Wed," NYT, 12 Feb 1909, 1; "Silvie Green Weds Matthew A. Wilks," NYT, 24 Feb 1909, 9; "1,000 Would Wed Col. Green," NYT, 17 Apr 1912, 16; "5,000 Would Wed Green," NYT, 23 Apr 1913, 4; "Col. Green Marries; Gives Bride $625,000," NYT, 11 Jul 1917, 8.
351  **tenderloin steaks.** Sparkes, 318.
351  **Hetty died.** "Hetty Green Dies, Worth $100,000,000," NYT, 4 Jul 1916, 1; "Hetty Green's Will Is Read In Court," NYT, 23 Jul 1916, 1; "State Loses $6,000,000 Tax," NYT, 30 Jun 1917, 16; "Tax Hetty Green's $38,000,000 Estate," NYT, 15 May 1920, 7; "Hetty Green Had No 'Business' Here," NYT, 1 Jun 1921, 7.
351  **Thomas R. Marshall,** "Memories of the Senate," NYT, 3 Oct 1925, 17 (excerpt from his book, *Recollections of Thomas R. Marshall* (Indianapolis: Bobbs-Merrill Company, 1925), 325.
351  **Ned lived in Texas.** "A Reed-McKinley Fight in Texas," NYT, 12 Jan 1896; "Mrs. Hetty Green in Politics," NYT, 21 Jun 1896, 23; "E.H.R. Green for Vice President," NYT, 17 Mar 1900, 1; "Convention Odds and Ends," NYT, 18 Jun 1900, 2; "Hetty Green's Son Named," NYT, 15 Aug 1906, 1.
351  **Ned died in 1936.** *Texas v Florida*, 306 US 398 (1939); "Green Left Will; Nothing to Widow," 6 Aug 1936, 5; "Bulk of Green's Millions Goes to a Sister; "Green Grist," *Time*, 19 Apr 1937; Widow Gets $500,000 as Will Fight Ends," NYT, 5 Nov 1937, 1.
353  **Anna Nicole Smith.** "Anna Nicole Smith Goes To Supreme Court," *Forbes*, 28 Feb 2006; "Supreme Court Looks at History of Conflicting Rulings in Anna Nicole Smith Case," WP, 1 Mar 2006; "Former Playmate Wins Procedural Round in Fight Over Estate," NYT, 2 May 2006; *Marshall v Marshall*, 126 S.Ct. 1735 (No. 04-1544, 5/1/2006); "Andersen faces fire in court this week," *Houston Chronicle*, 6 May 2002; "Smith, stepson have no share of estate, Jury rules billionaire's son sole heir," *Houston Chronicle*, 8 Mar 2001; "Star-maker tales: Would you invest in Anna Nicole Smith?" 89 JTax 127 (Aug 1998) (New York jeweler); *Estate of J. Howard Marshall, II, Deceased, Donor*, TC Docket No. 543-98 (filed 1/9/98 - Anna Nicole Smith case), U.S. Tax Court Records, Washington, D.C.; *Succession of J. Howard Marshall, II, Deceased*, TC Docket Nos. 23891-94, 9467-95 (filed 12/27/94; stipulated decision 7/21/99 - "Lady" Walker case), Files I - IV, U.S. Tax Court Records, Washington, D.C.; *Marshall v Marshall*, DC-Central Dist Calif, No. SA CV 01-97 DOC (3/7/2002); "College Finally Got Alumnus To Pledge; Next Job: Collecting," WSJ, 24 Jul 2003; *In re: Howard Marshall Charitable Remainder Annuity Trust*, 709 So2d 662 (La. Sup. Ct., 1998) (left $2.9 million in tax-advantaged trust, but pledges exceeded funding).
356  **Doris Mercer.** *Doris Farid-Es-Sultaneh*, 160 F2d 812, 47-1 USTC ¶9218 (CA-2, 1947), 6 TC 652 (1946).

357 **Howard Hughes.** James R. Phelan and Lewis Chester, *The Money: The Battle for Howard Hughes's Billions* (NY: Random House, 1997); "Texas rules Hughes was Texan," NYT, 16 Feb 1978; *California v Texas*, 437 US 601 (1978); *Cory v White*, 452 US 904 (1981); *California v Texas*, 457 US 164 (1982). An Oscar-winning 1980 movie was made about one of the fake wills, *Howard and Melvin*, a dispute which continues. "Mr. Dummar Is Back, Taking Another Shot At the Hughes Estate," WSJ, 13 Jun 2006, A1.

358 **Hughes Medical Institute.** Fred J. Cook, "Foundations as a Tax Dodge," *The Nation*, 20 Apr 1963, 324; "Hughes Institute Settles Tax Case," NYT, 3 Mar 1987, A17; "Howard Hughes's rich legacy," *U.S. News & World Report*, 28 Mar 1988, 54.

359 **guise of charity.** Randolph Paul, *Taxation in the United States* (Boston: Little, Brown and Company, 1954), 549.

359 **New York University.** *C.F. Mueller Co.*, 55 TC 275 (1970); 190 F2d 120 (CA-3, 1951), rev'g 14 TC 922 (1950); "Foremost-McKesson to Purchase Mueller Stock," NYT, 29 Sep 1976, 86; *U.S. v Knapp Shoe Manufacturing Corp.*, 384 F2d 692 (CA-1, 1967), cert den 390 US 989.

360 **Turner...Avalon.** "Ted Turner, Gone With the Wind," *Fortune*, 26 May 2003; "Turner's Florida Tax Path Familiar," AJC, 5 Feb 2003, D1. Florida's intangible tax rate was 0.2 percent through 1998, 0.15 percent in 1999, 0.1 percent from 2000 to 2005, 0.05 percent in 2006, and repealed thereafter.

361 **pledged...$1 billion.** "Q&A," AJC, 26 Dec 2004, D2; "Turner's foundation wants others to give," AJC, 31 May 2001.

362 **charity tightwads.** "A wealth of cheapskates," LAT, 18 Mar 2007, M1; "The power of philanthropy," *Fortune*, 7 Sep 2006; "Gates After Microsoft," *Fortune*, 7 Jul 2008.

362 **Clinton's tax returns.** Lisa Schiffren, "Bill and Hillary at the trough," *American Spectator*, Aug 1993, 20; "Tax Notes Audits the Clintons," 63 TNT 18 (4 Apr 1994), 18-23; "Tax Experts Believe Clintons Likely Took Improper Deductions," WSJ, 7 Feb 1994, A3; David Cay Johnston, "It Takes a President To Overpay the I.R.S.," NYT, 19 Apr 1998, 9; Barbara Olson, *Hell To Pay* (Washington, DC: Regency Publishing, 1999), 135-144.

363 **Whitewater.** "Clintons Pay $14,615 in '80 Back Taxes," WP, 12 Apr 1994; "Clintons Pay $15,000 In Taxes And Interest To Cover 1980 Liability," 94 TNT 70-1 (12 Apr 1994); "The Clintons' Financial Dealings," NYT, 13 Apr 1994, B9; "For Clinton, New Wealth In Speeches," WP, 23 Feb 2007, A1; "Clintons Made $109 Million in Last 8 Years," NYT, 5 Apr 2008.

363 **Harry Truman,** *Mr. Citizen* (NY: Bernard Geis Associates, 1960).

364 **IRS exempts royalties.** IRS' longstanding position is that "if an individual writes only one book as a sideline and never revises it, he would not be considered to be 'regularly engaged' in an occupation or profession and his royalties therefrom would not be considered net earnings from self-employment." Rev. Rul. 55-385; Rev. Rul. 68-498; *W.R. Langford*, 55 TCM 1267, TC Memo 1988-300, affd without published opinion 881 F2d 1076 (CA-6, 1989).

365 **War Refugee Board.** Rafael Medoff, *The Deafening Silence: American Jewish Leaders and the Holocaust* (NY: Shapolsky Publishers, 1987), 140-145; David S. Wyman, *The Abandonment of the Jews, America and the Holocaust 1941-1945* (NY: Pantheon Books, 1984), 184, 203-204, 268-269, 285-287, 405-406; Ted Morgan, *FDR: A Biography* (NY: Simon & Schuster, 1985), 715.

365 **high-grade lynching.** Harlan Fiske Stone letter to former classmate Sterling Carr, 4 Dec 1945, Alpheus T. Mason, *Harlan Fiske Stone: Pillar of the Law* (NY: Viking Press, 1956); Telford Taylor, "The Nuremberg Trials," 55 *Columbia Law Review* 488 (Apr 1955). Francis Biddle was another descendant of Nicholas Biddle, president of the Second Bank of the United States.

366 **Stanley S. Kresge,** *S.S. Kresge Company and its builder, Sebastian Spering Kresge* (NY: Newcomen Society in North America, 1957).

# Index

## A

Abernathy, Ralph D. · 234, 235
Abilene Christian College · 181
Abramoff, Jack · 253, 267
Accounting Hall of Fame · 81, 99, 100, 102, 376
Accounting Principles Board · 78–81
accounting profession · 65–102, See American Institute of CPAs, enrolled agent.
    accounting standards · 77–84
    Big Eight · 11–12, 33, 73, 78, 80
    British origin · 68
    consulting · 73–77, 91–94
    continuing prof. education · 35–37
    disputes, FTC · 72, 80, 84, 90
    disputes, Justice Dept. · 72, 80
    Financial Accounting Standards Board · 79–82
    Gramm Leach Bliley Act · 84
    Metcalf Report · 80
    minority CPAs · 69
    practice of tax law · 84–88
    Public Company Acctg Oversight Board · 83–84
    *ro'eh cheshbon* · 66
    Sarbanes-Oxley Act · 83, 94
    tax season, origin · 162
    value billing · 77
    venture accounting · 67
Adams, John · 130
*Adding Machine, The* · 4, 369
Administrative Procedures Act · 296, 418
affluenza · 342
Agger, Carolyn · 182, 399
Aldrich, Nelson · 140, 148, 159–61, 254, 266
American Association of Public Accountants · 68, 162
American Bar Association · 72, 276
    accountants practicing tax law · 84–88
    Gramm Leach Bliley Act · 84
    Pennsylvania Preceptor Plan · 294–95
American Civil Liberties Union · 312, 423
American Institute of Accountants · 77, 89, 185
American Institute of CPAs · 77, 207, 264, 292, See accounting profession, ethics.
    Cognitor · 93–94, 98, 100, 101
    CPA2Biz · 94–96, 101
    Durham, N.C. relocation · 101
    Education Foundation · 96
    ethics code · 69–73
    library · 96–97
    specialty certifications · 92, 379
    *Tax Adviser, The* · 96, 98
    Tax Division parties · 10
    Tax Executive Committee · 92, 98
    The Vision · 98
    Trueblood Committee · 78
    Vision, The · 91–94
    WebTrust · 93, 100
    Wheat Commission · 78
    XBRL · 93, 97, 379
American Judicature Society · 309, 311
American Medical Association · 102
American Society of Certified Public Accountants · 77
Anderson, Jack · 237, 328
Annenberg, Moses · 218, 224–26
Annenberg, Walter · 225–26
Arthur Andersen & Company · 12, 16, 37, 39, 65, 73, 76, 88
    Enron · 9, 353
Arthur Young & Company · 14, 34, 38
Arthur, Chester · 115
Ash, Adrian · 203
Association of Certified Fraud Examiners · 98
Astaire, Fred · 331
Atlanta Olympics · 36, 48
automobiles · 213, 344-45, 429-30

## B

Bacon, Augustus · 148, 245
Baker, Bobby · 21, 182, 251
Bank of the United States, Second · 140–44, 389
Bankman, Joseph · 266
bankruptcy · 27, 67, 75, 191, 255, 274
Bar-Illan, David · 336
Barnes, Roy · 260
Barron, Bruce · 193
Barry, David S. · 254
BDO Siedman · 91, 95
Beaman, Middleton · 244–46
Benny, Jack · 332
Benton, Thomas Hart · 110, 144, 382, 389
Bercu, Bernard · 85, 377
Bergson, Peter · 220
Berlin, Irving · 167, 331–32
Berlusconi, Silvio · 133
Bible · 118, 381
    auditing · 66
    Stanton statement · 287
    taxes · 106, 117
Biddle, Francis · 365, 433
Biddle, Nicholas · 142, 144, 418, 433
Bismarck, Otto von · 346
Black, Hugo · 229
Blackmun, Harry · 278
Blaine, James G. · 390
Boortz, Neal · 6, 165
Boston Tea Party · 112
Boutwell, George S. · 11, 152, 159, 163, 171, 370
    John Sanborn scandal · 174
    salary exemption ruling · 304–5, 421
Bowsher, Charles · 102
Brandeis, Louis · 294, 306, 313
Braverman, Saul · 99
Brennan, William · 310
Brewer, David · 157, 312, 392, 393, 423
Broaker, Frank · 69
Brown & Root, Inc. · 226–30
Brown, Edmund G. · 149
Brown, Joseph E. · 153
Bryan, Mary Baird · 148
Bryan, William Jennings · 155–56, 263, 349
Buchanan, James · 145
Buffett, Warren · 347
Burger, Warren · 278
Burleson, Omar · 181–82
Burr, Aaron · 194
Bush, George H.W. · 6, 263, 363
Bush, George W. · 207, 263, 296
    Texas Rangers · 268
Bush, Laura · 364

## C

Calhoun, John C. · 140, 144, 146
California gold rush · 122–24, 145, 385
Campbell Soup Company · 348–49
Candler, Asa · 125
Capone, Al · 8, 213–16
Carey, John L. · 69–70, 76, 96, 99
Carnegie, Andrew · 347, 362, 390
Carter, Jimmy · 242, 328, 363, 364
Caudle, Theron Lamar · 202
Chamberlain, Neville · 9
Chaplin, Charlie · 329
charity · 362
    Annenberg Foundation · 226
    Clinton, Bill and Hillary · 362–64
    deduction, origin of · 260–62, 411
    foundations · 96, 202, 222, 253, 311, 327, 356, 359
    Hetty Green Hall, Wellesley College · 353
    Howard Hughes Medical Institute · 358
    New York University · 359–60
    United Nations Foundation · 361
Chase, Salmon · 120, 304, 421
Chase, Samuel · 130
Chenok, Philip · 75
Cherecwich, Paul · 207
Chinese immigration · 122–24
Chistoff, Steve · 330
Churchill, Winston · 109, 132
Cisneros, Henry · 243
Civil War · 120–21, 126, 160, 163, 175, 177, 178, 392
    Confederate Constitution · 414
    income tax on judges · 304–5
    salt scarcity · 110, 382
    tariff as a cause of · 145–46, 389–90
    tax return publicity · 317–18
    taxation during · 151–55, 299
Clausewitz, Carl von · 121, 384
Clay, Henry
    Second Bank of the U.S. · 140–44
    tariff · 144, 297
Cleveland, Grover · 115, 156, 390
Cleveland, Robert · 192–93
Clinton, Bill · 52, 124, 207, 243, 296, 300, 418 & Hillary · 362–64
Coca-Cola · 124–25, 257, 386

Cockran, William Bourke · 155
Colley, Chad · 256–57
colloquies · 247–48, 250
Commercial Trading Co. · 23–28, 29, 31–32
Committee for Constitutional Government · 164
Congo · See Leopold II.
Congregation Mount Sinai · 20
Conn, Billy · 340, 341
Cook, John · 65
Cook, Michael · 100
Cooke, Jay · 121
Coolidge, Calvin · 197, 220, 308, 347
   Capone investigation · 214, 216, 403
   income tax paid · 307, 322
   tax return publicity · 319
Corrupt Practices Act · 197, 226, 228
Coughlin, Charles E. · 218, 219
Couzens, James · 222, 229
   investigation of BIR · 89–90, 196–200
   tax trial · 209–13
Crosby, Tom · 258–60, 410

# D

Darrow, Clarence · 158
Davies, Marion · 329
Davis, Evelyn · 28
Davis, Jefferson · 154
Davis, Sammy, Jr. · 337
Davis, Shelly · 305, 308
Dawes, Charles G. · 214
deadline · 155, 185, 392
death/suicide · 190–94
   death of CPA · 186
Debs, Eugene V. · 158, 393
Declaration of Independence · 55, 112, 146
DeLay, Tom · 253
Deloitte & Touche · 12, 88, 91, 100
   J.K. Lasser merger · 33–34
Delta Air Lines · 257
Devitt, Edwin J. · 308–11, 422
Digital Millennium Copyright Act · 151, 391
Dingell, John, Sr. · 290
Dirksen, Everett · 257
Disney, Walt · 167
*Dobson v. Commissioner* · 276–78
Dodge, John and Horace · 211
Donnell, Forrest C. · 254
Dorrance, John · 348–49

Doughton, Robert · 164, 168, 323–24
Douglas, William O. · 140, 278, 388
Drinker, Henry · 295, 418
*droit administratif* · 280, 302

# E

East India Company · 4, 67, 112, 113
Ebenezer Baptist Church · 233, 234, 406
Edison, Thomas A. · 261, 319
e-filing · See tax returns.
Ehrlichman, John · 238
Eisenhower, Dwight D. · 165, 168, 205, 239, 339, 376, 429
Empire State Building · 12
enrolled agent · 205
   National Association of Enrolled Agents · 292
   origin of · 177
Enron Corporation · 8, 81, 82, 83, 353
Enzi, Mike · 81
Erie Canal · 113
Ernst & Ernst · 89, 378
Ernst & Whinney · 90
Ernst & Young · 12, 74, 76, 91
Eskridge, Chauncey · 407
ethics · 45, 76, 89, 94
   ABA Canons of · 294
   AICPA Code of · 69–73, 83, 117
   Code of Judicial · 311–13, 423
   Georgia Code of Judicial · 411
   House Ethics Committee · 254
   Internal Revenue Service · 172
   IRS Office of Professional Responsibility · 177
   Pennsylvania Preceptor Plan · 294–95
   tax obligations · 117
   Treasury Circular 230 · 205
Eustice, James · 274
Exxon Corporation · 14–15, 349

# F

Fairbanks, Douglas, Sr. · 319
FairTax · 165, 395
Farah, Joseph · 243
Fawkes, Guy · 244, 264
Ferme Général · 111
Ferrer, Jose · 332
Fessenden, William Pitt · 118–21
Field, Stephen J. · 157, 393
Financial Accounting Standards Board · 79–82
Fink, Robert · 180

Fish, Hamilton · 218, 219
    FDR's tax returns · 324–26
Ford, Gerald · 326
    1976 primary · 327–28
    Nixon pardon · 240
Ford, Henry · 196, 210–11, 213, 220
foreign countries · 40, 93, 131–33, 156, 349
    Belgium · 22, See Leopold II.
    France · 279-80
        French Revolution · 110–12
    Germany, Holocaust taxes · 108
    Great Britain · 65, 68, 106, 112–14, 116–17, 132, 135, 200, 244, 246, 298, 383
    India · 113, 131, 251
    Israel · 15, 110, 131, 305
    Italy · 117, 133
    Turkey · 108-10, 381
foreign miners license tax · 122–24, 385
Fortas, Abe · 182, 229-30, 311, 399, 422
Frankfurter, Felix · 140, 388
fraud · 24–27, 98, 123, 189–90
Frick, Henry Clay · 148, 348
Fries Rebellion · 130

G

Gandhi, Mahatma · 113
Gannett, Frank · 164
Gariepy, Bernard and Mary · 219, 404
Garland, Judy · 337
Garner, John Nance · 222, 246
    presidential bid · 227
    Sales Tax Rebellion · 163–65
    tax rates · 161
Gates, Bill · 347
Gen'l Acct'g/Gov't Accountability Office
    accounting firm merger · 12
    lockboxes · 174
    penalty abatement · 183
Gilbert, John & Lewis · 28
Gingrich, Newt · 52, 254
Ginsburg, Martin D. · 31–32, 273, 283–85
Ginsburg, Ruth Bader · 32
    ACLU · 312, 423
Gladstone, William · 390
Goldin, Sidney · 291, 313
Gould, Jay · 350
Grant Thornton LLP · 12, 99
Grant, Ulysses S. · 121, 174, 305
Grassley, Charles · 207
Gray, Fred D. · 233, 406

Green, Hetty · 349–53
    *If I Were As Rich As* · 430
Griffith, D.W. · 319
Griswold, Erwin N. · 99, 275, 278, 414
    before Supreme Court · 275, 281, 313, 413
    diffuses AICPA-ABA conflict · 87
Gulf Oil Company · 89, 198, 200, 220
Guthartz, Alan · 303

H

H&R Block · 98–99, 186, 187–88, 380
Haldeman, H.R. · 237, 240
Halliburton Inc. · 230
Hamilton, Michael D. · 303
Hand, Learned · 274–75, 288, 413
Hardin, Rusty · 353
Harding, Warren G. · 220, 307, 308
Harrison, Benjamin · 115
Hayes, Rutherford B. · 146
HealthSouth Corporation · 76
Hearst, William Randolph · 164, 323
Helmsley, Leona · 177
Heney, Francis J. · 197
Hermitage Museum · 221–24
Hirsch, Jack · 13, 79
Hitler · 219, 326
Hoar, Ebenezer Rockwood · 304–5
Hoffman, Ogden · 124, 313, 385
Holmes, Oliver Wendell · 279, 306
Hoover, Herbert · 199, 220, 222, 282, 403, 409
    Capone investigation · 214, 216
    remittances to Treasury · 308, 322
    return publicity · 322
    salary exemption · 306–7
Hoover, J. Edgar · 318
Hotel del Coronado · 343
Howard Smith, Slocombe & Co. · 9, 370
Hoyt, Jesse · 195, 196
Hughes, Charles Evans · 157, 393
Hughes, Howard · 238, 357–59
    *Howard and Melvin* · 432
Humphrey, Hubert · 241, 429
Hussey, Ward · 245
Huxley, Thomas Henry · 245, 408

I

*I Paid My Income Tax Today* · 332, 395
Iacocca, Lee · 149
IBM · 16–19
Ickes, Harold · 225, 354

income tax · 165–69, 394
  100% rate · 169, 396
  1894 individual · 155–59, 279, 349
  1909 corporate · 160, 162, 298, 318, 394
  capital gain · 45, 86, 202, 204, 212, 213, 258, 330, 332, 333, 339–40, 361, 363, 428–29
  Civil War · 151–55
  earned income credit · 187, 266, 293
  illegal immigrants · 188
  judges and presidents, exemption from · 304–8, 420–21
  municipal bond · 157, 394
  origin · 116–18, 383
  Port Authority employees · 307
  residence rent deduction · 151, 391
  Sixteenth Amendment · 159–62, See U.S. Constitution.
  withholding at source · 101, 163, 166, 168, 176, 181, 187, 305, 395
Internal Revenue Commissioners · See Boutwell, George.
  Alexander, Donald · 171, 238
  Blair, David · 210, 212, 425
  Bolich, Daniel (assistant) · 200
  Cohen, Sheldon · 182
  Everson, Mark W. · 174, 189
  Gibbs, Larry · 172, 206
  Helvering, Guy · 228, 323, 324
  Lewis, Joseph J. · 304
  Nunan, Joseph · 201
  Roper, Daniel C. · 212
  Rossotti, Charles · 193, 400
  Schoeneman, George J. · 200
  Thrower, Randolph · 237, 399, 407
  Ungar, Bruce (deputy) · 190
  Walters, Johnnie · 237-38
Internal Revenue Service/Bureau · 38, 143, 326, See Watergate.
  collection, privatize · 174, 397
  Culture Bingo · 170, 173
  economic reality audits · 173
  hate mail · 175
  Holtsville Service Center · 171
  Kennedy visit · 172, 396
  litigation misconduct · 288–89
  lockboxes · 173
  National Commission to Restructure · 205–8
  origin of · 152, 196
  Oversight Board · 189, 207
  Philadelphia Service Center · 172
  Reorganization Plan No. 1 · 204
  Rules of Conduct · 172
  scandal, 1920s · 89, 196–200
  scandal, 1950s · 200–205, 402
  tax compliance · 176
  tax protesters · 180
  Taxpayer Advocate Service · 191, 272, 292
Irey, Elmer · 403
  conviction of
    Al Capone · 214
    Moses Annenberg · 225
  investigation of
    Andrew Mellon · 221
    Franklin Roosevelt · 324
    Hamilton Fish · 220
    Huey Long · 218
    Lyndon Johnson · 228
Isley, Ronald · 217

J

Jackson Hewitt Tax Services, Inc. · 188
Jackson, Andrew · 113, 263
  appoints Samuel Swartwout · 194
  Second Bank of the U.S. · 140–44
  tariff and nullification · 144–51, 297
Jackson, Howell E. · 156
Jackson, Robert · 169, 223, 312, 425
  biography · 277
  Eleanor Roosevelt's taxes · 324–25
  Nuremberg trials · 277, 364–66
Jeter, Derek · 336
Jewish National Fund · 361
Jews · 106–10
  charitable tax deduction · 260
  Congregation Mount Sinai · 20, 371
  Holocaust · 108, 220, 365
  Italian ghetto income tax · 117
Johnson, Andrew · 121
Johnson, Charles · 330
Johnson, Lyndon · 202, 218, 239, 257
  1960 Democratic convention · 182
  and Russell Long · 251–52
  campaigns for Senate · 226–30
  KTBC · 21, 251, 409
  life insurance · 21
  wealth · 409
Joint Committee on Taxation · 207, 240, 247, 249–50, 256, 269
  origin of · 199
joint stock company · 68, 373
judicial deference · 295–97

## K

Kansas City School District · *See* tax, judicial.
*karoshi* · 11
Kempson, Ken · 264
Kennedy, John F. · 121, 169, 172, 209, 239, 269, 283, 396, 409
Kennedy, Robert · 234
Key, Francis Scott · 194
Kies, Ken · 266
King, Coretta Scott · 232
King, Martin Luther, Jr. · 230–34
   Committee to Defend · 233, 234, 406
KPMG · 12, 65, 91
Kresge, Sebastian S. · 356–57
Kresge, Stanley S. · 366

## L

LaGuardia, Fiorello · 138, 164, 347
Las Vegas · 10, 58–61, 336, 357
Lasky, Jesse · 339, 428
Lasser, J.K. & Company · 32–34
Laughton, Charles · 329
Lavoisier, Antoine-Laurent · 112
Leary, Timothy F. · 128
Leavell, Allen · 330
Leno, Jay · 344
Leopold II, King · 114–16, 159–60, 383
Lerner, Alan Jay · 337–39
Levison, Stanley · 406
Levitt, Arthur · 75, 80, 82
Lewis, John L. · 227
Liberace, Walter V. · 333
Liddy, G. Gordon · 236, 237, 241–42
Lieberman, Joseph · 80
Lincoln, Abraham · 63, 120, 121, 239, 304–5
Linder, John · 165
Lloyd, Harold · 319
Loftin, Isaiah H. · 126
Long, Huey · 218–19
Long, Jennifer · 192, 400
Long, Russell · 251–52, 404, 409
Louis, Joe · 340–41
Lowery, Joseph E. · 234
Luft, Lorna · 337
Lummis, William Rice · 358

## M

Madison, James · 158
Madonna · 317, 335
Magill, Roswell · 276, 324
Magna Carta · 297
*maltotier* · 110
*Man Without A Country, The* · 156
Marshall, J. Howard II · 353–56
Marshall, John · 143
Marshall, Thomas R. · 351
Marshall, Thurgood · 135, 278
Marx, Groucho · 332
May, George O. · 73, 78, 90, 96
Mayer, Louis B. · 319
Mayock, Welburn · 202
McGovern, George · 269
McKinley, William · 126, 144–47, 157, 351, 389, 390
McMahon, Gregory · 86
Melancon, Barry · 91, 95–96, 99, 100–101
Mellon Bank · 174, 220
Mellon, Andrew W. · 164, 210, 213, 218, 277, 325
   Couzens investigation · 196–200
   National Gallery of Art · 220–24
   tax return publicity · 319
Mellon, Paul · 224
Memminger, Christopher G. · 153, 392
Mercer, Doris · 356–57
Merrick, David · 429–30
Merrill Lynch · 33, 323, 325
Metcalf Report · 80
Microsoft · 93, 95, 362
Mills, Wilbur · 149, 240, 269–70, 330
*Missouri v. Jenkins* · 135
*Money* tax preparer contest · 240
Montgomery, Robert H. · 77, 99, 162
Morgan, Jack P. · 177, 220, 261, 397
Morgenthau, Henry · 169, 218, 221–22, 225, 228
   Diaries · 425
   FDR's tax returns · 323–26
   saving Jews · 365
Morrill Tariff of 1861 · 145–46, 390
Moses, Robert · 135–39, 352
Mostel, Zero · 4, 369
Motaghed, Ehsanolla · 194
Moyers, Bill · 251
Moynihan, Daniel Patrick · 255, 268
Murdoch, Rupert · 226
Museum of Taxation · 305
Myers, Robert · 346

## N

NASCAR · 267, 411

National Archives · 239, 240, 305, 321, 407
National Gallery of Art · 220–24
National Press Club · 149, 345, 423
Nelson, Willie · 330, 334
Ness, Eliot · 216, 403
New Deal · 186, 218, 222, 224–25, 227, 275, 324, 388
New York · See state tax.
*New York Times v. Sullivan* · 234–36
New York University · 359–60
Newberry, Truman · 196, 210, 229
Nixon, Edward · 241
Nixon, Richard · 169, 209, 238, 320, 429
   Library · 240, 407
   Watergate · 236–42
nullification movement · 144–45, 297
Nuremberg trials · 277, 365–66

## O

O'Brien, Lawrence, Jr. · 236–38
O'Connor, Sandra Day · 310
Obama, Barack · 147, 390
Office of Legislative Counsel · 246
Oliphant, Charles · 201
Olney, Richard · 158
Opperman, Dwight · 309–11
Orlando, Judith · 193

## P

Pacioli, Luca · 66, 97
Packwood, Robert · 270
Padwe, Gerald · 417
Parr, George · 229
Patman, Wright · 327
Paul, Randolph · 99, 162, 255, 276, 359, 396, 399, 414
   biography · 165–66
   saving Jews · 364–65
   social security numbers · 186
Pearson, Drew · 219, 404
Pennsylvania Preceptor Plan · 294–95
Perot, H. Ross · 345
Peter the Great · 130–31, 221
Petrino, Paul · 180
Phillips, David Graham · 159
Port of New York · 136, 138–39
   Swartwout, Samuel · 194–96
Prager, Brett · 95
Price Waterhouse & Co. · 13–16, 71, 73, 78

Howard Smith, Slocombe & Co. merger · 370
   Willie Nelson · 334
PricewaterhouseCoopers · 12, 91, 93
Public Authority · 135–39
Public Company Accounting Oversight Board · 83–84

## R

Rayburn, Sam · 252, 339
Reagan, Ronald · 169, 267, 282, 339, 363, 426
1976 primary · 327–28
Regenstein, Louis, Jr. · 234, 406
Regulatory Flexibility Act · 296, 418–19
Rehnquist, William · 130, 278
Rhett, Robert Barnwell · 146, 390
Robinson, Sugar Ray · 336
Rockefeller, David · 138
Rockefeller, John D. · 220, 319, 326
Rockefeller, John D., Jr. · 148, 159, 261
Rockefeller, Nelson A. · 138, 326
Rodman, Dennis · 335
Rogers, Will · 332
roller coaster contest · 61–63
Rolling Stones · 132
Roosevelt, Eleanor · 235, 323–25, 425
Roosevelt, Franklin D. · 109, 203, 217–20, 223, 227, 236, 242, 307
   and Lyndon Johnson · 226–30
   personal tax returns · 322–26
   Sales Tax Rebellion · 163–65
   social security · 346
   tax policy · 169, 323, 396
Roosevelt, Theodore · 159, 261, 275, 350, 351
   estate tax · 347
Rostenkowski, Dan · 270, 298
Rucker, Henry · 125–27
Ruml, Beardsley · 166

## S

Sales Tax Rebellion · 163–64
Sanborn, John · 174
Sarbanes-Oxley Act · 83, 94
Sargent, Gary · 330
Savage, Michael · 6
Scalia, Antonin · 252, 308, 312
Schiff, Irwin · 178–80, 398
Schwarzenegger, Arnold · 328
Seay, Solomon S., Jr. · 234
Securities and Exchange Commission ·

46, 77, 79, 81, 331
XBRL · 93
seditious libel · 234–36
Seidman & Seidman · 90
Selig, Allen H. (Bud) · 335
Seligman, Edwin · 158, 391
September 11th · 63, 321
sex of a hippopotamus · 7, 249, 286, 408
   London Zoo · 244, 245
Shapiro, Les · 177
Shay's Rebellion · 130
Shell Oil Company · 302
Sherman, William T. · 120–21, 154, 305
Shiras, George, Jr. · 393
Shumway, Leslie · 8, 215
Shuttlesworth, Fred L. · 234
Simpson, O.J. · 337
Sixteenth Amendment · *See* U.S. Constitution.
Small Business Administration · 296–97, 418
Smith, Anna Nicole · 342, 353–56
Snipes, Wesley · 180–81
Social Security Administration · 182, 189
   origin of · 246, 345–46, 414
   social security numbers · 186, 188, 265
   W-2 information · 187
songs
   *A Lopsided Bus* · 4
   *Ballad to Barry* · 100
   Beatles, The · 132
   *I Paid My Income Tax Today* · 167, 332, 395
   *I Wanna Be a Producer* · 4
   *If I Were As Rich As Hetty Green* · 430
   Irving Berlin's RKO musicals · 331
   *Ode to Conway Twitty* · 334
   Porter, Cole · 132
   *Sarbanes-Oxley Blues* · 83
   *That's Where the Laugh Comes In* · 318
   *Voilà le maltotier* · 105
Sosa, Sammy · 335, 427–28
South Sea Bubble · 65
Southern Christian Leadership Conference · 232, 234, 406
Spanish-American War · 124, 347
Spina, Cynthia · 288
Stanley, Henry Morton · 114, 115
Starkman, Jay · 183, 258, 410
   articles authored · 34, 371, 397, 409, 411, 417, 425
   letters from clients · 55–56
state tax · 302–3
   Arizona · 128–29
   California · 336, 357
      foreign miners · 122–24, 385
   Florida · 336, 352, 360, 432
   Georgia · 57, 257–60, 265–66, 360–61, 420
   Illinois · 335, 428
   Louisiana · 302–3, 336
   Massachusetts · 352
   multistate · 420
   Nevada · 357
   New Jersey · 174, 348–49
   New York · 31–32, 113, 193, 303, 335, 352
   New York City · 27, 133, 350
      Moses, Robert · 135–39
      World Trade Center · 64, 138–39
      World's Fair · 22, 135
   Pennsylvania · 347, 348–49
   Tennessee · 129
   Texas · 128, 268, 302, 313, 352, 357, 420
   Virginia · 174, 176
Steffens, Lincoln · 159
Stewart, Martha · 335
stock options · 28, 80
Stone, Harlan Fiske · 365–66
Strouse, Charles · 338
Sullivan, Lester B. · 234–36
Sutherland, William A. · 276
Sutton, Willie · 205, 402
Swanson, Gloria · 319
Swartwout, Samuel · 194–96

# T

Taft, William Howard · 127, 160, 275, 294
Taney, Roger B. · 141–43, 304
tariff · 144–51, 263, 297–98, 301, 389–91
Tarleau, Thomas · 324, 427
tax · *See* income tax, state tax, tariff.
   beard · 130–31
   book royalties · 179, 326, 364, 428–29, 432
   charitable deduction · 222, 239, 260–62, 411
   cheating · 39, 133, 177
   death/suicide · 190–94

depletion · 89–90, 198, 401
estate and gift · 159, 250, 253, 261, 300, 327, 346–49, 351, 352, 355, 357
FairTax · 165, 395
gambling · 150, 217, 287–88, 293
investment credit · 78, 90, 328, 375
Islamic · 109, 132, 381
jock · 336
judicial · 134–35
litigation · 129, 303
lottery/prizes · 217, 284, 373
lying (newspaper) · 218
multistate · 302, 420
narcotics · 128–29, 386
sales · 163–65, 166
salt · 110–14, 382
SET Tax · 397
sex · 61, 128, 154–55, 237, 247, 387
teacher-preacher · 181–82, 399
telephone · 124, 299
value-added · 149, 151
window · 129–30
*Tax Adviser, The* · 34, 96, 98, 102
Tax Court · 119, 162, 190, 280–82, *See* tax litigation.
   abusive tax shelters · 47, 288–89
   *Dobson v Commissioner* · 277, 414
   equity · 272, 301, 412–13
   exam for non-attorneys · 290–91, 295, 313, 417
   IRS misconduct · 288–89
   judges · 282–85
      Chabot, Herbert · 272
      Couvillion, D. Irvin · 281–82
      Dawson, Howard A. · 271, 281–82, 287, 309
      Gerber, Joel · 312
      Goldberg, Stanley A. · 282
      Haines, Harry A. · 282
      Hall, Cynthia Holcomb · 282
      Kuskin, Harold A. (N.J.) · 419
      Littleton, Benjamin H. · 282
      Murdock, J. Edgar · 282–83, 290, 415
      Sterrett, Samuel · 281
      Tannenwald, Theodore · 283–85, 288, 330, 416
      Wells, Thomas B. · 292
tax farming · 106, 115, 174
tax legislation
   colloquies · 247–48, 250
   how a tax bill becomes law · 246–47

lobbyists · 252
milker bill · 253
revenue estimates · 129, 265–66
tax litigation · *See* Tax Court.
   administrative law judges · 57, 302
   Anti-Injunction Act · 119
   burden of proof · 271, 285, 313, 416
   choice of tribunals · 273
   *Dobson v Commissioner* · 276–78
   judge appointments · 280, 302
   judge recusal · 312–13
   judicial deference · 295–97
   jury instructions · 216, 308, 403
   last known address · 184, 282, 284
   manifest injustice · 301, 419
   oath before testifying · 287
   presumption of correctness · 285
   *pro se* · 289, 292, 309
   property foreclosure · 303
   tax clinics · 292, 294
tax protesters · 112, 114, 118, 130, 162, 175, 180, 264, 272
tax returns
   e-filing · 187, 189–90
   extensions · 185–86
   forms, origin of · 163
   misdemeanors as felonies · 425
   offshore preparation · 40
   prisoners · 190
   publicity · 242, 317–21, 424
      charities · 255
   refund anticipation loan · 187
   signatures · 190
   software · 40, 256
tax shelters · 45–49, *See* charity–foundations.
   abusive · 47, 288–89
   annuities · 44
   Barrister Associates · 46–47
   BDO Siedman · 91
   Couzens investigation · 89
   Ernst & Whinney · 90
   Joint Congressional Committee on Tax Evasion · 323, 326
   sports · 267–68
tax simplification · 248–51, 262–65
   complexity · 151, 256
Teapot Dome · 199
Telex Corporation · 16–19
Texas Rangers · 268
Thomas, Clarence · 135, 308, 329
Thompson, William Boyce · 210
Thomson Publishing · 95, 311

Toombs, Robert Augustus · 145, 389
Tracy, Spencer · 290, 417
Treasury Inspector General for Tax Administration · 26, 40
Truman, Harry · 165, 168, 229, 239, 339, 363, 365, 429
   tax scandal · 200–205
Tucker, Sophie · 20
Turner, Ted · 360–62
Twitty, Conway · 334
Tyler, John · 195

## U

U.S. Constitution
   amendments
      first · 236
      fifth · 214, 300
      fourteenth · 121, 152, 236, 303
      sixteenth · 157, 159–62, 279, 300, 305
      seventeenth · 160
   appointments clause · 415
   bill of attainder · 301, 420
   contract clause · 136
   direct tax · 130, 154, 156–58
   *ex post facto*/retroactivity · 299–301
   general welfare · 146, 277, 390, 414
   how a tax bill becomes law · 246–47
   origination clause · 297
   three-fifths compromise · 158
   uniformity clause · 157, 297
U.S. Supreme Court · 194, 214, 218, 236, 286, 296, 297, 300, 303, 353
   1894 income tax · 156–59, 419
   accounting profession, commercialization · 72
   *Dobson v Commissioner* · 276–78
   ethics conflicts · 311–13
   judicial tax · 134–35
   recordholders · 413
   Sixteenth Amendment · 161

unauthorized practice of law · 84–88
Ungerman, Josh · 282
Untermyer, Samuel · 261

## V

Van Buren, Martin · 143, 195
*Varlik Vergisi* · 108–10

## W

Walker, Jewell Dianne ("Lady") · 354–56
War Refugee Board · 365
Washington, George · 119
Watergate · 236–42, 320
   Special Services Staff · 234, 236, 407
Watson, Thomas · 17–18
Webster, Daniel · 140, 142, 297, 413
Wells, Joseph · 98
West Publishing Company · 308–11, 422
Whiskey Rebellion · 118, 130
White, Byron · 310
Wilkerson, James · 215, 225
Williams, Paul · 184
Wilson, Woodrow · 294, 307, 308, 351
Winfrey, Oprah · 373
World Trade Center · 64, 138–39
World Trade Organization · 151
Worldcom Inc. · 83
Wyatt, Arthur R. · 81

## X

XBRL · 93, 97, 379

## Y

York, Sergeant Alvin · 339–40, 429

## Z

Zarin, David · 287–88